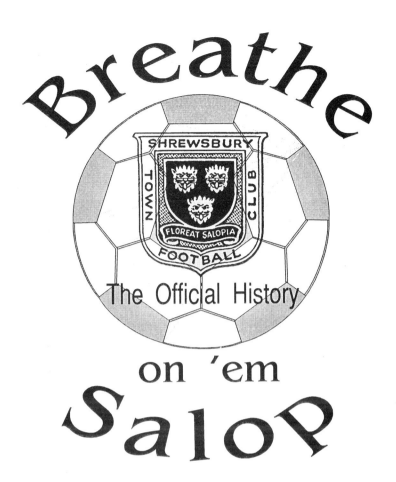

Breathe

The Official History

on 'em
Salop

Mike Jones

(Statistics by Kevin Davies)

Published by

YORE PUBLICATIONS

12 The Furrows,
Harefield, Middx,
UB9 6AT

Printed by:
THE BATH PRESS

ISBN 1 874427 06 2

Published by:
Yore Publications
12 The Furrows, Harefield,
Middx. UB9 6AT.

© Mike Jones 1995

....

British Library Cataloguing-in-Publication Data.
A catalogue record for this book
is available from the British Library.

ISBN 1 874427 06 2

(Every effort has been made to acknowledge the source of illustrations
and to ensure that copyright has not been infringed)

Introduction and Acknowledgements

I was asked what were my qualifications to write this book, and on consideration - apart from being slightly mad - the main one is that I was never good enough to play for the club. So over the years I have become involved in other ways. Having been carried into a Midland League game aged two, my first real memories are of the second League season. My late Grandfather, Fred Jones, stands accused of introducing me to the game, and club. The bug bit deep and in 1968-9 Bob Wilson and I made the Guinness Book of Records for doing all 93 grounds in a season.

For the early recollections I am indebted to the Library Staff and Library copies of 'The Chronicle' and 'Wellington Journal' and meetings with former players - Bill Haycock (20's) Den Hopley (30's) and Mervyn Molyneux (40's) plus valuable information from Les Smith and Horace Statham, whose family looked after many pre-War players. Also to Ken Roberts for a treasure trove of facts and programmes. The staff at The Meadow, particularly Joan Fox, who can now come out of hiding, Malcolm Starkey, Mike Thomas, Chris Jarrett, Margaret Starkey, Jo Kelly and Graham Pearse, who put up with my witterings, also to Graham for organising the subscribers applications. Ruth Williams for all her recollections of the players who lodged at The Abbey Gardens, the press box for the odd snippets, John Bray, Neil Sambrook, Brian Binnersly, Russell Mulford, Bob Davies and Gordon Riley. The 'Shropshire Star' and 'Shropshire Weekly' newspapers for waiving copyright on their pictures. To the late Ray Davies (Midlight) and most especially to Stan Hall, who should have written the History, but was probably to sensible. Also to Keith Carswell and Geoff Croft. Thanks to Dave Twydell and Yore Publications for all their work. Matthew Ashton and Chris Smith for access to their comprehensive picture and programme libraries, but most of all to Kevin Davies. Without Kevin's years of research this tome would not have appeared before the millennium.

Shrewsbury born statistician Kevin Davies, is a life-long Town supporter, and began compiling detailed records on the club at all levels in 1978. He has since researched and built up a comprehensive wealth of information from the club's earliest days to date. A regular contributor to the club programme he has recently been appointed the club's official statistician.

Anyone spotting mistakes kindly address the information to the club with either my name or Kevin's on the envelope. There will be errors, but every effort has been made, and I mean every effort, to make this the most comprehensive and accurate synopsis ever produced.

Back to qualifications I have followed Town literally all my life, been Chairman of the Junior Supporters Club, written for the programme, compiled records for the Bob Wardle Brochure, and have been fortunate enough to know several club dignitaries. These include Tim Yates, and the subsequent Chairmen, Walter Rowley and all subsequent Managers since Arthur Rowley, with the exception of Alan Durban. Alan was in charge when I lived in Hertfordshire for two years. Since 1988, I have reported extensively on all Town's matches (and a number of other local sports) for Beacon WABC, which has given me another excuse to 'live' at the ground.

I also had a less than illustrious playing career, but did manage one competitive appearance on the Meadow (see overleaf - young Jones was no.8 for Wenlock Juniors). I founded Shrewsbury Cricket Club F.C., which became Brick Sports, and thanks to Dave Roberts' influence and many subsequent Managers, they became the Counties best known Sunday League side.

I just hope the readers find the book as interesting as I found compiling it.

Mike Jones

Chairman: J. W. A. Jones

President: Sydney Yates

SHREWSBURY TOWN FOOTBALL CLUB
LIMITED

Secretary:
L. E. Rimmer

Player-Manager:
G. A. Rowley

THE GAY MEADOW, SHREWSBURY
Telephone: SHREWSBURY 6068

OFFICIAL PROGRAMME PRICE 2D.

SHREWSBURY MINOR LEAGUE

KENWOOD JUNIORS versus WENLOCK JUNIORS

Saturday, 15th February, 1964 Kick off 3.p.m.

TEAMS

Right   Red Shirts.   WENLOCK JUNIORS   White shorts.   **Left**

Goal
J. Sibbell.

     2   3
   B. Fry.   D. Campion.

4   5   6
T. Barrow.   B. Williams.   P. Heath.

7   8   9   10   11
C. Davenport.   M. Jones   F. Thomas.   R. Barlow.   G. Bowers.

Referee: Mr. B. Harper
(Shrewsbury)

11   10   9   8   7
Derek Hinton.   Dave Beer.   Terry Bullock.   Terry Gray.   Mike Bridges.

6   5   4
  Peter Holloway.   Peter Herbert.   Bobby Rimmer.

3   2
   Keith Carswell   Jimmy Evans.

Robin Launchbury
Goal

Left   White shirts.   KENWOOD JUNIORS   Black shorts.   **Right**

HALF-TIME SCOREBOARD

A	Luton Town. Shrewsbury Town.	J	Bristol Rovers. Millwall.	S	Wrexham. Hull City.
B	Arsenal. Liverpool.	K	Coventry City. Brentford.	T	Notts Forest Blackpool.
C	Barnsley. Man Utd.	L	Crewe Alex. Southend Utd.	U	Sheff Wed. West Brom.
D	Burnley. Huddersfield Town.	M	Crystal Palace. Notts County.	V	Tottenham. Sheff Utd.
E	Oxford Utd. Blackburn Rovs.	N	Mansfield Town. Bournemouth.	W	Leeds Utd. Scunthorpe Utd.
F	Preston N.E. Carlisle Utd.	O	Oldham Ath. Colchester Utd.	X	Southampton. Middlesbrough.
G	Sunderland Everton.	P	Peterborough Utd Watford.	Y	Chesterfield. York City.
H	Swindon Town. West Ham Utd.	Q	Reading. Bristol City.	Z	Doncaster Rovers. Chester.
I	Stoke City. Swansea Town.	R	Walsall. Port Vale.		

NEXT MATCHES AT THE GAY MEADOW Sat, 22nd Feb, 1964. PETERBOROUGH RES,
Kick off 3.p.m. Sat, 29th Feb, 1964. 1st v. BRISTOL ROVERS, 3.15.p.m.
Today keen Supporters have the opportunity to see our Nursery Side
Kenwood Juniors in action. They are having a very good initial season
and play today against the very sporting Wenlock Juniors who are one of
the three teams ably fostered by Mr. T.L. Williams. A good game to all.

Contents

Chapter:		Page:
1	Before The Dawn	6
2	In A League Of Their Own	10
3	Keeping Score - Up To The War	16
4	The Early Thirties - Becalmed In Mid-Table	22
5	Picking Up The Threads	32
6	Promotion	38
7	Older Manager, Younger Team	47
8	A Ton Of Goals, Arthur Lightens The Darkness	54
9	Enter The Sixties, And Frank Clarke	59
10	World Cup, Cricket, And Almost Promotion	69
11	End Of An Era, Followed by The Great Escape	74
12	Goals Without Strikers?	82
13	Into The Eighties, In The Second Division	95
14	The Dream Ends - Relegation	109
15	Another Dream Realised - Promotion	122
16	Managers 1950 - 1994	128
	Who's Who	130
	Things You Still Don't Know & Statistical Notes	136

APPENDIX:

	Page
Seasonal Statistics And Team Groups 1886 - 1994	137
Teams For All Seasons	254
Advanced Subscribers	255
Yore Publications	256

CHAPTER 1 - BEFORE THE DAWN

A match at the Racecourse - the lack of goal nets suggest a date of pre-1882

The Godfather of Shropshire football, John Hawley Edwards, was a constant source of innovation in the early days of the sport, having a hand in forming several sides and, most notably, the Shropshire Football Association in 1877 which led to the Shropshire F.A. Cup in 1877-8.

Those initial sides were built on the Grammar school teams, or public schools as we would now refer to them. The first side to carry the name of the County town were to win the initial County Cup final with a 1-0 victory over Wellington Parish Church Institute. However, despite the fact that the team had been seeing off 'Local Raiders' for at least 3 years, their demise was at hand.

The team who regularly played Newport at the Racecourse over Christmas and had entertained a large crowd at that ground on Xmas Eve 1875 with a 1-0 victory, were to stumble into oblivion after a Shropshire Challenge Cup game staged on Thursday 27 November 1879. Shrewsbury F.C. could raise

only eight players so they withdrew from the competition, although they borrowed three players - C.Crump of Stafford Road, Wolverhampton, Ellsmore of Stafford F.C. and W.H. Southern of Meole Brace - and played a friendly which ended in a 7-3 defeat.

Shrewsbury had many sides who were not pretentious enough to take over the name of their town, with the Swifts, Trinity, Crusaders, Engineers, Blues, St. George, and even a team called Scarlet Runners who sprouted forth in 1879. It was the Castle Blues who came forward as the main force, but their undoubted ability was backed up by an over zealous approach to the game, which ultimately led to their demise, after a particularly unsavoury battle with Wellington at the Comet Bridge ground over Christmas 1885.

Three of the Blues team were suspended for their part in the game and Wellington failed to complete their next fixture against Birmingham Excelsior, due, according to their Secretary, "... *to The Blues, leaving their well known Blue mark on several of our players"*. That season Wellington reached the final of the Shropshire Challenge Cup before losing after a replay to St. Georges 3-0, the local rivalry attracting a crowd in excess of 2,000, and proving the popularity of the emerging sport.

THE BIRTH OF THE BLUES

The two main sporting hostelries of the time were the Lion at the top of Wyle Cop, and the Turf in Claremont Hill. The Shropshire F.A. meetings were held at the Lion, while several sides used the Turf as a base. This may explain why the reports in the local press about the formation of the club differ. The Eddowes Shropshire Journal of 26 May 1886, reports that the club was formed at the Lion Hotel, whilst two days later the Shrewsbury Chronicle reported the club's birth on Thursday 20 May 1886 was at the Turf Hotel.

It is eminently possible that both reports are based on fact, and that an early get together at the Lion moved on to the Turf to finalise details with the potential playing strength. Either that or the club was initiated on a pub crawl.

The first honorary secretary was Mr A.W. Lloyd of, 102 Frankwell, who told the papers the newly created side... *"hoped to make at least as good a show in cup-ties and friendlies as the Blues, without gaining the unbelievable notoriety which the old club revelled in"*!

Despite these noble sentiments the local press were not about to give the fledgling club an unqualified welcome, with the Shropshire Journal its major sceptic. Having questioned what right these people had to take the name of the town as their own, this august journal went on to have a further dig at the new side and the defunct Castle Blues on 11 August 1886.

The article ran as such *"It is to be hoped that the name of Shrewsbury as a football town will be purged of the evil repute it acquired during the last season - a repute which was well deserved, and earned by some of the most blackguardly exhibitions ever presented to the public"*.

Town's first competitive match was perhaps fittingly in the Ditherington Flower Show six-a-side on 28 August, "from little acorns mighty oaks doth grow".

The competition attracted ten teams, John Street Blues, Shrewsbury Wanderers, Castle Rovers, Bayston Hill, Shrewsbury St. Georges, Working Mens Club, Mr Davies' Team, two sides from Church Stretton and Shrewsbury Town. The six-a-side competitions were quite popular in these times and were played with flags placed six yards outside the goal posts, each time the ball passed between post and flag or over the tape at a certain height (i.e. crossbar) two points were awarded. However, no number of points equalled a goal, and for wilful kicking two points were deducted.

The Town team beat Working Mens Club in round one, John Street Blues followed and then St. Georges, before meeting Shrewsbury Wanderers in the final. The Wanderers team consisted of some signed Town players, and though Town scored 8 points to Wanderers 4, the solitary goal scored by Wanderers secured the trophy.

Things were now beginning to move apace with the draw for Town's first ever competitive match taking place on the 15 September and pitting them with Stafford Rangers in the Birmingham Challenge Cup. The local papers support continuing with an article which said, *"if they are worth anything, ought easily, playing on their own ground, to win their way into round two"*, this they duly did with 'Alty' Davies netting two, Watkins another brace, and France and Pearson providing the goals in a 6-1 victory on 9 October.

It was Alty Davies who scored in Town's first eleven-a-side fixture, a 1-1 draw at Shrewsbury Road Wellington on 18 September He was a leading light in the early days and as a well known crowd-pleaser was generally referred to as just 'Alty' in the match reports of the day. Success eluded the Town in several competitions that season, Darlaston All Stars beat them 1-0 in a third round replay in the Birmingham Challenge Cup, Newtown scored the solitary goal in the Welsh Cup second round, and even in another 6-a-six at Ditherington and St. Michaels Athletic Society, they lost 2 goals and 4 points to 1 goal and 4 points to the Barracks 'A' team. In the latter event six gold medals should have been presented to the winners and six silver to the runners-up, but due to a small entry the gold medals were withheld and Town had to wait for their first trophy.

Their patience was rewarded on 21 May when they won the Shropshire Football Association Cup 3-2 after a replay, following a goalless draw at Amblers Field a fortnight earlier. 'General' George Blazier scored Town's first goal in that victory, he later became secretary of the horticultural society and organised the Flower Show. Town's first competitive hat-trick was scored by H.A. Rhodes who moved on to be Headmaster of a public school. Whilst another notable forward was J.C.H. Bowdler, destined for international honours and founder of the well known local solicitors.

These gentlemen would probably have been at the meeting at the Lion before joining up with their future team-mates at the Turf, these would have included local chimney sweep John Edwards and of course Alty Davies who sadly ended his days in Shrewsbury Asylum.

By winning the County Cup competition Shrewsbury Town had displayed their right to carry the name of the county town and started to honour the name of Shrewsbury, and major strides were to be made in a short time in order to back up the early promise.

INTERNATIONAL HONOURS

The second season saw Town enter the Welsh Cup for the first time losing 2-0 to Oswestry, they also departed the Birmingham Senior Cup by the same score, both games being first round matches. Whilst a Pearson goal was insufficient to stop an exit at St. Georges from the Shropshire Mayor's Charity Cup.

St. Georges again came out on top in 1889, when, after a 6-1 victory at Wem, Town overcame the loss of full-back J.Jones with a broken jaw, after just 10 minutes, to score a solitary goal win over Oswestry. Only for the Dragons to repeat their 2-1 victory over Town.

However, it was the Birmingham Senior Cup which saw the high, and low, spot of the season. A bye in the first qualifying round was followed by a 9-0 drubbing of Asbury and after a replay with Aston Shakespeare, which Town won 4-1, they met their first ever Football League opponents.

The oldest known Town programme - 30 March 1889
(Shrewsbury won 1-0 in this Shropshire Mayor's Charity Cup match)

A home match with the - even then - mighty 'Wolves' was their reward. A crowd of 2,000 turned up to witness the spectacle on Christmas Eve 1888, despite the admission charges being doubled. There the dream ended for Town who had warmed up for the game by beating Crewe Steam Sheds 3-1, as they were outplayed, and five goals in each half sent the crowd home chastened.

It did prove, again, that Town could attract big crowds, and probably helped attract the Welsh F.A. to add Shrewsbury to their list of possible international venues. On February 8th 1890 Town, staged the Wales v Ireland match at the Racecourse ground.

The night before the game the Irish were entertained at an invitation smoking concert held at the Crown hotel (by St. Mary's Church). Shrewsbury Gymnasium Club gave displays of dumbells and boxing, and new caps, J.C.H. Bowdler and goalkeeper S.G. Gillam, sang ditties as part of the frivolity (the original karaoke!).

The Welsh team lined up as follows S.G. Gillam (Shrewsbury), R. Roberts (Chester), W.P. Jones (Wynnstay), P. Griffiths (Chirk), A. Hayes (Wrexham), Humphrey Jones (Corinthians), D. Lewis (Bangor), W.E. Pryce Jones (Newtown), W.Owen (Chirk), A.R. Wilcocks (Oswestry), J.C.H. Bowdler (Shrewsbury).

Ireland took an early lead through Dalton, an inside right from Linfield Athletic, but Wilcocks, in his only appearance, equalised with a free kick. Then Bowdler set up Owen to put Wales in front, only for Torrens the inside-left (and also from Linfield), to level before half-time. Wales were gradually exerting their authority, and after Lewis put them ahead again ten minutes into the second half, a Lewis header and a Pryce Jones shot wrapped up a 5-2 victory.

The game attracted a crowd 'computed' as (how?) 4,000 and both the Irish and Welsh parties were fulsome in their praise. Mr H.J. Hearn the Chairman of the organising committee, and president of the Town club, saying that this was the first international match to be played at Shrewsbury or in Shropshire, and that he hoped it would not be the last! Sadly despite everyone's assurances this remains the only full international to be staged in the county thus far.

The tide of support still survived though with 500 travelling on a Great Western Railway special to see a Town team, containing both their internationals, lose 4-1 to Ironbridge in the Shropshire Challenge Cup semi-final. The Chronicle reported: *"that no unbiased person, who was privileged to witness the match could deny but that Town ought to have won"*. But luck was dead against them, and the article then went on to record that Ironbridge's first goal was clearly offside.

Ironbridge went on to beat Oswestry in the final, but in the Mayors Charity Cup on April 19th, Town reversed the scoreline in the semi-final of that competition, in front of a crowd of 3,000. They then took the trophy thrashing Newport 5-1 in the final.

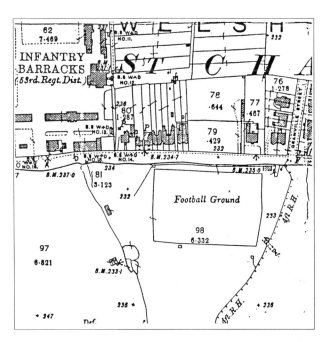

(Top) Programme from the 1889-90 season, when Nantwich were beaten 3-2 in this 1st qualifying round match. The game was played at Ambler's Field.
(Below) In 1895 the club moved to the basic Barracks Ground, in the Copthorne District, as located on this Ordnance survey map of 1902

CHAPTER 2 - IN A LEAGUE OF THEIR OWN

own moved to Amblers Field, opposite the Racecourse ground, in 1889, and the following year were founder-members of the Shropshire League. The League was set up thanks to the foresight of Arthur Baxter, the Town secretary, who later became chief constable of Shropshire.

The first season saw a league of Shropshire based clubs, with Town travelling to Wellington for their opening game. They lost 2-1 in front of just 400 people. However, they were unbeaten at home that season, and despite clubs from outside the county joining the following campaign, Town continued to boast an excellent home record. In fact they lost just 3 home League games in their five year stay in the League, losing to Wolves Reserves in 1891-92 and St. Georges in each of the next two seasons. The League itself was made up of eight teams during its first season, and was formed just two years after the Football League, making it one of the oldest competitions. That first season Town finished runners up to Ironbridge, but the high spot was victory in the Welsh Cup final.

Town in fact had an excellent season in the cups, which produced its own problems, for they also reached the final of the Shropshire County Cup, and both matches were scheduled for Easter Monday. Much correspondence went back and forth between the Shropshire F.A. and the Welsh F.A., before, very reluctantly, the Shropshire final was advanced 48 hours.

The Shropshire final saw Town defeat Oswestry 3-1, and on the Monday a crowd of 4,500 gathered at Oswestry to see Wrexham try to repel the English challenge. Late arrivals missed most of the action as the game started in breath-taking fashion. Oswald Davies, the Wrexham right-wing, opened the scoring on two minutes, but Town - who had opened the season losing 3-1 at Wrexham in a Friendly - hit back in style. Holloway equalised and Alf Ellis made it two, before good work by Ellis and 'Alty' Davies set up G. Green for the third. W. Turner reduced the arrears only for 'Alty' Davies to crack in a fourth for Town - and all this in the first twenty minutes. Town made it five in the second half with Alty Davies hitting his second; 5-2, a memorable victory regally celebrated.

Town returned to Shrewsbury Station where, *"a brake was on hand to transport the jublilant team to*

the Unicorn Hotel headed by a band playing 'Hail the conquering hero comes' and flourishing the Shropshire Cup, as they were unable to bring the Welsh Cup home".

The matches took their toll on the players, however. Centre-half Jack Davies, who twisted his knee on the Saturday, sat under a cold tap for two hours and played through the pain on the Monday, *"but went home lame as a cat after the match had finished"*.

A disappointing sixth position was Shrewsbury's fate in 1891/2, despite A. Ellis' goals - he hit five against Whitchurch - and was a constant marksman. Town did beat Oswestry 10-0 in one friendly but lost to Brierley Hill by the same score. They also played away against North Meole, but not somewhere near the cemetry, this team came from Southport and ran out 6-3 victors. One game which failed to reach a completion was against the charmingly named Willenhall Pickwick; it sank in a deluge after 30 minutes.

The following season the Mayor's Charity Cup semifinal at Ironbridge was left in some disarray, when Town's opponents Wrockwardine Wood went to Wrexham to play in the Welsh Junior Cup final, instead of the Charity competition. In the event Wrockwardine lost both games 1-0, the final against Wrexham Gymnasiums, and the semi-final because, *"Shrewsbury kicked a goal and claimed the match"*. In order to raise revenue for the Charity, Shrewsbury played Ironbridge in a friendly.

Town went on to beat Wellington 2-1 in the Charity final, the second goal awarded because, the *"keeper stepped over the line to punch the ball out"*. Fortunately the referee was ideally placed so no need for the Russian linesman! There are no reports of problems resulting from this decision, but the Shropshire and District League season ended in some disarray. An away game at Stafford Rangers in late March drew the following report from the Chronicle, *"At the conclusion of the game a scene of utmost disorder ensued. As the visitors left the field, they were subject to gross treatment by a portion of the spectators, principally rough youths and lads. They surrounded the team and as the players proceeded towards the clubhouse, threw mud, clods of dirt and stones at the Shropshire men; several of the players were struck - one with a bottle - but fortunately no one was seriously hurt. It is only fair to state that Rangers themselves had nothing to do with this rowdyism, and did all they could, to prevent it, but were powerless to do so against such odds".*

Meanwhile, in the final League game, at home to St. Georges, play came to an end 15 minutes early due to a pitch invasion after Fowler the visitors right-back kicked out at Earnest Bowdler, and Bowdler's father went on to remonstrate with the errant defender.

Both of Town's final two seasons in the Shropshire and District League saw them finish third. 1893-94 started disastrously for the club who had now moved to Sutton Lane. They began with a 9-0 thrashing at Newtown, and ended with an 11-1 victory at Hereford, and featured a day of real tragedy on Saturday November 11th. Town played Madeley in the first round of the Wednesbury Charity Cup and reports of the day record that Town full-back Jack Morris (Senior), known as Sticky, collided with Evans of Madeley and was carried off badly hurt. *"Morris was conveyed to the Salop Infirmary in a cab, and we regret to say, died in that institution from the effects of the injury received at about noon on Sunday".* He was just 23.

Shrewsbury's last season in the local League left one thing outstanding. They never played their last scheduled match, away against champions St. Georges, both sides final positions being already decided. The outstanding performance of the season came early on with the total demolition of Mold Alyn Stars in the first round of the Welsh Cup on Saturday 27th October. Alf Ellis hit seven, still a club record, E.H. Bowdler and Horley hit hat-tricks, R.C. Jones, Rogers and Morris weighed in with a brace and G. Ellis and an own goal made it 21-0. Goalkeeper Rufus had so little to do, he left his goal and joined the forward line but failed to score. It was perhaps as well that the eccentric goalkeeper did not hit the net as he often marked a Town goal by turning somersaults or running up the goalpost and swinging on the bar, but he was nevertheless a fine custodian.

Three weeks after this all-time club record score, Town travelled to Druids, and although fielding an unchanged eleven crashed 4-0, and left the Welsh Cup until 1905.

BIRMINGHAM AND FURTHER AFIELD

Town, whose first clash with a League club was against Wolves six years earlier, started their Birmingham League career against Wolves Reserves and crashed 14-0, four goals worse than the original

clash. It took Town 12 games to record their first victory, a healthy 5-2 win over Albion Reserves, but the season improved from that point. In fact 8 wins and 2 draws in their last 19 games was an ideal springboard for an assault on the F.A. Amateur Cup.

The campaign started away to Casuals on February 1st, which saw a frantic period of extra time after a 1-1, 90 minute score. Town eventually ran out 4-2 victors, and a fortnight later entertained Old Brightonians who succumbed 6-2. Another fortnight gap and off to Marlow, (the Buckinghamshire side are one of only two sides - Maidenhead United are the other - to enter every F.A. Cup competition since its inception) and a battling 2-1 victory. Cup fever built until the semi-final, a trip to Reading to play the Royal Artillery. Dreams of the club lifting their second major trophy were sadly dashed by two first half goals and some dubious refereeing, which saw Town have three second half goals disallowed, but Town were now an established force well outside the county borders.

After an indifferent second season in the Birmingham League, highlighted only by Lenny Benbow hitting all six goals against Halesowen, and missing a penalty in the final League game. Town bounced back and they were still picking up silverware back home in 1898. They won the Mayor Charity Cup, after throwing away a two goal half-time lead in the first round, they progressed to round two because St. Georges scratched rather than travel to Shrewsbury for a replay. A 5-2 semi-final victory over Newport, and a single goal success at Wellington against Ironbridge in the final clinched the trophy. It was an up tempo end to a season which started with six scoreless performances out of seven, just a 4-1 victory over Hereford Thistle in the second game breaking the run.

The last full season of the century had few high spots. It featured two heavy away defeats in successive matches - 9-1 at Bristol Eastville Rovers and 8-2 against Villa Reserves. The fourth, fifth and sixth goals in the latter game came within 4½ minutes early in the second half, during which period Morris was kicked on the knee and carried off, Town finishing with nine men.

Goalscoring was again a problem in 1899-1900, despite the arrival of Town's first all professional team. The decision to pay players had been taken after a heated meeting at the Unicorn, in August 1896, and initially only affected a few key players. At this time Town had five internationals. Charlie and Ernie Bowdler, Matthias, Oakley and Sam Jones, but it was not until the fourth game of 1899, away at West Brom. Reserves, that all the players received recompense.

The indifferent League season, not helped by the withdrawal of Worcester Rovers and Wolverhampton St. Georges - both of whom Town had defeated - brought a cutting comment from the Shrewsbury Chronicle of April 13 1900. The report on Town's 2-0 home defeat by Kidderminster Harriers, their fifth game without a goal, stated: *"Spectators grumble sadly at having to pay 6d and 9d to see the team cut such a sorry figure"*.

It was that sort of season. In the F.A. Cup on October 14th 1899, Town left-winger Tracey opened the scoring against local rivals Wellington in just 15 seconds, but Town lost 2-1. While in the Mayor Charity Cup, they missed the chance of revenge over Druids but felt aggrieved. The game, played at Raubon, saw Mr R. Davies of Wrexham replace the unavailable Mr R.T. Gough of Oswestry as referee, and the substitute official disallowed a goal in each half as the Welsh side won 3-2.

NEW CENTURY - OLD PROBLEMS

The start of the Twentieth Century did little to improve Town's performances, in the League they finished bottom. They lost their opening game at Berwick Rangers 4-0 - not the Scottish League team but Worcester City before their name change - and had only a 2-1 victory over Dudley Town to show after ten games. They did manage seven home victories, but suffered 8-1 defeats at Ironbridge and Stoke Reserves, plus 6-0 thrashings at West Brom. and Kidderminster Harriers.

Cup competitions provided little respite, having been somewhat surprisingly exempted to the third qualifying round of the F.A. Cup. Town lost to Walsall 1-0 after a 1-1 home draw. Meanwhile in the Shropshire Mayor's Cup they reached the semi-final solely due to Wem being thrown out over a fixture disagreement, and after another 1-1 home draw lost 2-0 to Wellington.

Improvement was hard to find in 1901-2, although the 1-1 draw at Kidderminster did end a run of 25 consecutive away defeats, and the end of season 3-1 victory at Brierley Hill Alliance was the first away win of the century, in fact the first for 40 games - if one ignores the 2-0 win at Wolverhampton St. Georges, who, withdrew from the League soon after

and whose record was expunged. The F.A. Cup saw a first qualifying round exit at Oswestry after a home draw, and the Walsall Senior Cup produced a home draw 2-2 with Druids, followed by withdrawal, rather than run the gauntlet of the local referees perhaps! The one bright spot was the Shropshire Mayor's Charity Cup, two midweek victories in April 1902, 1-0 over Wellington and 4-1 against Wrexham, saw a light appear at the end of the very dark tunnel.

A 4-2 away win at Kidderminster started the next campaign, and a solid season saw Town finish sixth, easily their highest position. It may have been better had the Stourbridge home game not been abandoned after half an hour because of a Waterlogged pitch, for when it was replayed - on March 30th - Town players Rhodden and Poole missed their connection at Wolverhampton, and Town started with nine men, in a game which ended 1-1.

Three wins and a draw promised much in the opening games of 1903-04, but it ended with a respectable mid-table finish, and the cup competitions also promised, but failed to deliver. The Mayor's Charity Cup saw Town lose a semi-final replay 2-0 at Wrexham, and the F.A. Cup sortie, following a first qualifying round bye, proved an exciting campaign. It started against local rivals Wellington at Copthorne Barracks, and a hat-trick by left-winger Tom Jones saw Town sneak home in a seven goal thriller. The trip to Stourbridge in round three looked daunting, after a 4-0 League defeat, but they ran out 2-1 winners.

A single goal victory over Oswestry United set up another home tie, this time against Second Division Walsall, but again Town scored the solitary goal. This put them in the intermediate round, prior to the first round proper, and meant an epic away trip to Stockton, the F.A. Amateur Cup holders. Town put up a tremendous fight, but Wharton's second half goal was not enough, and the heroic battlers returned home defeated 2-1. Surprisingly Town did not enter again until 1908, although they did return to the Welsh Cup in 1905.

One of the main problems at this time was finance, and despite several players moving on to higher things, Town rarely received big transfer fees. H.Clements moved to St. Mirren for £50, but although Lenny Benbow went to Notts Forest and won an F.A. Cup medal, Town did not receive a notable fee until 'Hetty' Morris went to Small Heath for *"substantial sum"*.

The club were helped by donations, particularly by M.P. Henry Greene who made a gift of £60 when he was president of the club, and Charlie Bowdler who once kept the club going for a month out of his own pocket whilst chairman.

TRAVEL SICKNESS RETURNS

Town's early seasons in the Birmingham League had seen a weakness which was easy to pinpoint - they did not travel well. Their awayday record proved the train was not taking the strain; in their first seven seasons they won 6 drew 10 and lost a mammoth 95 games away from home. The battling spirit which saw them sustain their excellent cup run saw a marked improvement for the following two seasons with 9 wins and 9 draws in 34 games, but by 1904-5 they had come off the tracks again with just a single victory and 16 defeats. A minor recovery saw four successes the season after, but 1906-7 saw Town pick up a single point on their travels and finish bottom , and in so doing having to apply for re-election for the third time.

The combined away record for the three desperate seasons of 1900-1, 1904-5 and 1906-7 was one win and one draw in 51 excursions. However, the tactic of donating a home victory to every team ensured a solid vote in favour of retaining the League's most North-westerly outfit.

The eight consecutive defeats which ended the third dismal season obviously led to significant changes, and much better performances ensued until the First World War, except for 1911-12. Town also returned to cup action, given a bye in the Welsh Cup of 1905-6 until round 3, they drew Whitchurch Town and after 300 minutes of battling finally lost 1-0 away in a second replay, their only appearance in the competition between 1895 and 1922.

The Mayor's Charity Cup of that season did, however, afford them the opportunity for revenge, and three weeks later a 2-1 victory set Town on their way. A semi-final win over Oswestry, 1-0, led to a final tie against St. Georges Victoria at Wellington where two second half goals overturned Town's half-time lead.

As previously stated 1906-7 was another poor season apart that is, from a couple of six-hits, against Stourbridge - when a Riddell hat-trick, two from Billy Scarrett and a goal for Evans set up a 6-0 win - and a 6-2 victory over Crewe Alexandra with Scarrett again hitting a brace and Price, Clements,

Evans and skipper Bob Morris on target. Morris was the beneficiary in March when First Division Derby County threw off their unsuccessful relegation battle, and thanks to a Long hat-trick, beat Town 3-0, raising £22 for Shrewsbury's long serving captain.

The need to strengthen the team for 1907-8 saw the arrival of a new keeper, Harry Jones, who was to be a regular for around four seasons. A new full-back was Arthur Hemmings who struck up a fine partnership with Bill Home, whilst centre-half was taken over by Colley who had previously appeared at left-back and centre-forward. The forward line was boosted by Welsh international winger Gordon Jones and 1907-8 was an altogether better season. It resulted in a new highest spot in the Birmingham League as Town finished fifth, and success in the Mayor's Charity Cup. A thumping 7-0 victory over Ironbridge set up a semi-final with Chirk which Town won with an emphatic 5-1 home victory, but not until the second replay. The final, staged at Wellington, saw Town lead Whitchurch 2-0 at the interval, and share the two second half goals to lift the trophy.

Town re-entered the F.A.Cup after a five year absence, in 1908-9, and disposed of Witton Albion 4-1 in the preliminary qualifying round before losing away at Nantwich 2-1. In the League, an indifferent opening victory and three defeats was followed by a record equalling nine match unbeaten run, including five successive draws, a rare event for a team who had only drawn more than six games in a season once before in the Birmingham League. Ironically on that occasion (1902-3 with eleven draws) the team also finished in sixth place.

Boxing day 1908 was an important day as the regular local derby with Wellington ended in a 1-1 draw, in front of the record crowd for Copthorne Barracks of 5,000. In a season of draws the return on Good Friday ended with the same scoreline. Although Town were soon to move to a new ground, work on improving Copthorne was continuing with the press box moved from the unreserved side to beside the dressing rooms, and a new entrance was built for reserved ticket holders. Whilst the removal of the large tree, *"will not be regretted except in wet days"* reported the Chronicle.

The paper also ran a series of articles on the state of football from 10 January 1908, topics including the desirability of a professional footballers union, the need for a residential qualification to curb spiralling transfers, and an article by a cleric warning young

The oldest traced team group - the 1907-08 season (at the Barracks Ground)

men that dubious play could lead to an embarrassing moral dilemma when facing their maker!

Junior teams in the Town included Shrewsbury Rovers, Shrewsbury Athletic and Shrewsbury Ivanhoe and a wide range of Saturday Leagues was complimented by a strong Thursday League.

FAREWELL COPTHORNE

The Barracks had served Shrewsbury well and it was fitting that the final season there should feature a major highlight in the club's history. The League season was to prove slightly disappointing, a slump to eleventh, a lack of goals, and little of note apart from a double over Burton United. Formed in 1901, by the amalgamation of Burton Swifts and Burton Wanderers, they had been relegated from the Football League. They joined the Birmingham League in 1907, and were the only team to do the double over the Town. The season after, they drew both games with Shrewsbury but continued their trip to oblivion when relegated in 1910, and were the only team Town beat twice.

The centre of interest was to be the F.A. Cup. It started in promising style with a 3-0 home victory over neighbours Wellington Town in the preliminary qualifying round on September 13th. That set up a home tie against Druids three weeks later, with Town winning 2-1. It then became a series of two week gaps and lengthening away journeys, with Town confining their trauma of travelling to history. A 2-1 victory at Connah's Quay, and Town's Nomads moved on to a 2-0 victory at Tranmere Rovers, before a solitary goal success at Kings Lynn.

The most remarkable fact about these three victories was that Billy Scarratt played in goal. The ever dependable Scarratt had first come to prominence as leading goalscorer in 1907, and whilst largely performing at inside-forward was versatile enough to appear in all eleven positions for the club, crowning it with conceding only one goal in the second half at Connah's Quay in his 270 minutes of cup goalkeeping. Town and Billy's reward in the fifth qualifying round was a daunting away challenge against Isthmian League Clapton. They had been exempted until round four of the qualifying tournament due to their fine cup record which included successes in the London Charity Cup, London Amateur Cup, Middlesex Senior Cup, Essex Senior Cup, and West Ham Charity Cup, not to mention the F.A. Amateur Cup, which they won in 1906-7 and regained in 1908-9.

So for the second time in six years Town had fought their way through the preliminary rounds only to see their way to the first round proper barred by the current Amateur Cup holders. Undaunted they set off for London, with Harry Jones back in goal and Billy Scarratt auditioning for the number six shirt, to face a home side containing two amateur internationals in goalkeeper H.M.Lemoine and left-half J.E.Olley. After a scoreless first half, a goal from left-winger Paddock set up a replay at Shrewsbury on Thursday December 9th. Town made one change, bringing back Grady at inside-right in place of Sambrook, who had scored the winner at Druids. It proved to be an inspired move, for Grady scored Town's first goal as they romped to a 4-1 victory, and for the first time ever made it to the first round proper.

Dreams of a major League club visiting the Barracks and shattering the ground record were dashed, for the fifth round running Town were second out of the hat and faced a long trek to Portsmouth. 'Pompey' were a Southern League side at the time but proved too strong for Town's valiant fighters, scoring two first half and one second half goal, to ruin their visitors hopes on Saturday 15th January 1910.

Three months later Town left their erstwhile home, with Bert Dobson's goal in the 2-0 victory over Walsall the final epitaph, as they took up the council's offer to lease part of the Gay Meadow Fields which the council had recently purchased. The club committee was delighted to accept, although the Salop Infirmary raised objections on the grounds that their patient's would be upset by the crowd's cheering.

MEADOW - LARK

Life at the Meadow started with two public trial matches, which the effective first team won 1-0 and 5-1, over arguably the reserves. Both teams in both games had H.Jones in goal, but Harry was not working overtime, for his opposite number was corporal Jones from the local Army depot. Billy Scarratt, no doubt upset at this development, played centre-half for the first team in the opener, and left-half for the reserves in the follow-up. The opening League game of the season was away at West Bromwich Albion Reserves, and new left-winger Dilley scored Town's goal in a 3-1 defeat. So it was September 10th when Wolverhampton Wanderers Reserves arrived to change in the clubs palatial new dressing rooms (an old railway carriage), trotted out past the stand - a diminutive building not of elaborate character - and

literally started the ball rolling. Sadly Wolves failed to enter into the spirit of the occasion, with Shinton scoring the opening goal in their 2-1 victory. Town's first ever scorer at the Meadow was, who else, but Mr 'versatility', Billy Scarratt. Town were pleased with their facilities and Charlie Bowdler said, *"When the team went away, it was nothing out of the ordinary for them to be called on to change in a cow shed"* (sounds like the first season of the Sunday League 57 years later!).

Town's first victory at the Meadow was 2-1 over Halesowen in their next home game, and that started a run of six consecutive League victories. So expectations were high when Town drew strong opposition in Merthyr Town, but Tarplin's second half goal put Town into the final qualifying round of the F.A.Cup. They had been exempt until round four after their epic run the previous season. They again faced a difficult away tie, this time at Gainsborough, (it should be remembered that Trinity and Merthyr played almost 1,000 League games between them around this time) and sadly succumbed 4-0.

The new ground did, however, throw up some new problems. On December 17th, Town took a first minute lead through Dilly and were sailing to victory, 3-1 up after 70 minutes, when the match was abandoned, the Shrewsbury Chronicle reported: *"This match was part played at Shrewsbury on Saturday. The Severn being in flood, the ground adjoining was nearly surrounded by water at the start, and the water was actually encroaching on the playing pitch while the game was in progress. Presently it occupied so much of the ground and threatened so much more mischief that the game was abandoned."*

The first time First Division opponents arrived at the Meadow was Thursday April 6th, when Everton (about to finish fourth in the Football League) came for a benefit match for Bill Home and Billy Jones. Freeman did manage to net a first half goal for Town, but Everton - not surprisingly - ran in six. A defeat which took fifty years to avenge!

Town finished eleventh in their league, and incidentally beat Birmingham 4-3 in the re-arranged game. It was not a mammoth season but Town had arrived, and many many memories were about to be forged.

CHAPTER 3 - KEEPING SCORE UP TO THE WAR

Things did not start smoothly in 1911-12. A rail strike meant several players were unable to make the public trial match, setting the season off badly, and it never improved. True, Town won their first match 2-1 at home to Wrexham and then managed a goalless draw with West Brom. reserves, but they then lost thirteen consecutive League games and crashed out of the F.A. Cup 6-1 at Chester. Billy Scarratt played right-back in that game although his notable career with Town was drawing to a close, but in his own indomitable way he provided one final highlight.

The home game with Stourbridge on 13th April 1912 was designated as his benefit match, a crowd of 1,500 turned out, and Town recorded their biggest win of the season running in five unanswered goals. Billy, who the week earlier had missed the train to Stoke, turned up in the right place at the right time, scoring the second just before half-time.

Town ended the season in 17th place, and their only away point came in the Easter derby game with Wellington, a 2-2 draw. However, while Town struggled, football in the county was still expanding. The Jackfield F.A. founded a league with ten teams:- Jackfield Amateurs and Excelsior, Broseley Town and United, Madeley Colliers and Amateurs, Ironbridge Victoria, Lawley United, Hinkshay and Beveley - with president Captain George Forester reporting a sound financial position and announcing several cups would be put up for competition.

Town again looked to strengthen the squad and signed a new goalkeeper, Fred Boxley who was soon joined by his brother Harry, a forward. The team improved and held a healthy mid-table position when the F.A. Cup came round. Still exempt to the fourth qualifying round, Town negotiated a tricky away tie at Northwich and drew a daunting home tie against London Caledonians. All square at one-all at half-time, Town slipped behind in the second period so Fred Boxley came out of goal to add weight to the side. He was replaced in goal by Crump, with Home moving to full-back and Fred playing centre-half, the tactic allowed Town to level through Williams. Fred returned to his custodial duties and five days later Town travelled to the Capital for the replay. The game played at Turnell Park was settled by a goal from Melhuish who, the Chronicle reported, *"was undoubtably three or four yards offside"*, on a pitch *"mainly composed of bare clay"*.

Town finished the season in tenth position and used their improvement as a springboard to push for the Birmingham League title the following season. They lost their way around the turn of the year losing 6-0 at West Brom., 1-0 at home to Stoke and 5-1 at Worcester, but after the later setback they suddenly galvanised themselves into championship material. They won eleven, drew two (the away derbies at Walsall and Wellington) and lost only one (3-2 at home to Aston Villa Res.) in their last fourteen fixtures. But Worcester City's last game victory at Coventry denied Town the title by a solitary point.

Two first half goals at Stoke had curtailed their Cup ambitions, and a friendly with Aston Villa on April 2nd resulted in a 3-0 defeat, but 48 hours later they avenged their Cup defeat of the previous season, with a goal from Parsonage enough to beat London Caledonians.

The practice match of 1914 promised an exciting season as it ended in a four-all draw, and a friendly with Shrewsbury School a fortnight later saw E.F.Haycock hit five as Town won 7-1, in a game which raised £20 for the war relief fund, but the Great War was to disrupt matters.

The F.A. Cup paired Town with League champions Worcester City, and a second half penalty from goalkeeper Fred Boxley put Town through. His brother Harry was already in the trenches and sent home for a football which was duly provided. Town then disposed of Walsall 2-1 to set up a sixth qualifying round game with Nottingham Forest. Forest had been one of the game's big innovators, Sam Weller Widdowson had introduced shinguards in 1874, the first use of a referee's whistle was at Forest's Racecourse ground in 1878, and they also replaced the string with a crossbar. They also proved too inventive for Town, who on Saturday 19th December 19th crashed out of the competition 6-1 at the City ground. The proximity to the river proving no advantage to the visitors, in this the only first team game between the two clubs, apart from two friendlies in 1939.

The Great War of course then created a void in the football world in fact for the cup-tie with Walsall it was noted that in a crowd of 2,000 no less than 748 were uniformed soldiers. Early news of the battles recorded the death of former Town skipper F.M. Aston who led the side to their Welsh Cup win in 1891.

RESUMING AND REBUILDING

Of the twenty-six players who turned out in the two public trial matches in August 1919 only five had played in the four-all draw five years previously, and all were defenders, namely Lucas, Fletcher, Bowser Nicholls and Jones. Town's League campaign began in fine style with three victories - a double over Walsall and a home victory over champions Worcester. True, Worcester gained revenge in the return, but nine victories in the first eleven matches put Town top of the League and seemed like champion's form. However, four consecutive League defeats and an 8-0 F.A. Cup defeat by Hednesford spelled out problems were back. Injuries to both full-backs early in the Cup exit gave some excuse, but just one win in their final eleven games, in which they conceded 42 goals, left them languishing in fourteenth place. All this despite the supporters providing a new black and white strip, with thirteen games remaining - unlucky for some!

Local junior players had their chance to stake a claim when Town played the Shrewsbury and District League on December 13th, but Town won 5-1 and a week earlier a Parker hat-trick including two penalties helped defeat Northern Nomads 5-0. But at the end of the season it was obvious major changes were required and the club gratefully welcomed back their goalkeeping penalty taker Fred Boxley.

Just one point from four opening games was not encouraging, but gradually things improved. Five

The first Town programme - so it states. Certainly the first after the War.

wins out of seven games ended with a 7-1 win against Nuneaton, and a crushing 6-0 defeat at Worcester, that was avenged 5-0 at home two games later. Apart from a 5-0 defeat, ironically at Nuneaton, a consistent season ensued.

The Cup thrashing by Hednesford meant Town were back to the preliminary qualifying round, but a 2-1 away win at St. Georges and a 1-0 win over Walsall set up a revenge clash against the Pitmen. The first half saw four goals shared, but Hednesford snatched a second half winner, and repeated the 3-2 victory late in the League season. When Town ended the season with a 7-2 drubbing of Hednesford it must have been all the sweeter. Winger Roberts hit four, Williams scored a brace and Parker, who had registered Town three previous postwar hat-tricks, completed the rout.

The major changes in the Birmingham League during the close season should have given Town an excellent chance to press for the honours. Wrexham and Walsall had joined the Football League Third Division, whilst the Central League annexed the reserve sides of Birmingham, Stoke, West Brom. and Wolves. The pre-season saw five players promoted from the reserves (the Reds), to the first team - the Stripes. After the Reds won the first trial 6-1, the Stripes duly triumphed 3-0 a week later. One change saw the new pairing of full-backs 'Happy' Sheldon and 'Chucky' Edwards split, but they would soon be re-united.

The season started well, three wins and two draws, and only once did the club lose two League games running. The Cup battles were less productive, with a first game exit in the F.A. Cup to Third Division North, Walsall (1-0), and in a return to the Welsh Cup, Wrexham's trip over the border eliminated the interlopers 3-1. The Walsall Senior Cup campaign saw Town use 28 players, including 4 goalkeepers, in just five matches, until they lost 2-1 at Stafford. While in the Walsall challenge cup four more players, including a fifth different 'keeper, failed to see them overcome Bilston who ran out 4-1 winners.

Their League performances continued to impress, and four end of season victories pushed the club into fifth place, but despite three hat-tricks during the season, one each from Roberts, Pearce and Parker - who netted 19 League goals - a new strike force was about to arrive.

On the national scene twelve months earlier, Thomas 'Tansy' Lea, played right-wing for Wolves in their 1-0 defeat by Spurs, this was later claimed to be the only occasion of a Shrewsbury born player in an F.A. Cup final.

THE BEST SO FAR

The rebuilding, both on and off the field, was gathering momentum at the start of 1922-23. Town made an inspired capture when they signed Chris Elvidge the ex-Wrexham centre-forward. In his first game, away at Cradley Heath, he cracked a hat-trick, and formed notable partnerships with inside-forwards Taylor, Whatmore and Williams, who were all served by Jack Evans, a winger from Walsall, who ended up second highest goalscorer.

On October 8th Town opened their new grandstand, the ceremony being performed by the Mayor, Alderman W.Toye, and the structure which cost £5,000 was to see Town through well into their Football League days. (In fact part of the structure was rediscovered under the main stand during the work carried out in 1994).

Town spent most of the season chasing Bilston for the title, but received a setback at Stourbridge on January 6th when goalkeeper Causer was injured, Harry Sheldon went in goal and Town won 1-0. It was ironic that the Stourbridge 'keeper that day, Hauser, was destined to replace Causer the following season. Leslie Tudor Owen stepped into the Town side but he was already destined to move away for a time. He played against Oswestry in the Welsh Cup

on January 18th having delayed signing professional forms for Derby County, a deal completed 4 hours later (Oswestry, Shrewsbury and the Welsh Cup would return to the Tudor Owen story). Town included C.Jones in goal, until Causer - an ex-Preston man - recovered, but Causer came back after the 5-4 victory over Bilston at the Meadow, having kept a clean sheet as Town reserves beat Bilston 1-0.

Town were scoring goals but only Elvidge and Evans achieved real consistency. J.Williams was brought in when Elvidge missed the Welsh Cup tie with Oakengates, and made the second and scored the third as Town won 3-1. He then played centre-forward against Hednesford with Elvidge at inside left, and was in inspired form cracking in five goals as Town's 8-1 victory finally avenged their F.A. Cup thrashing a couple of years earlier. This triggered a run of nine consecutive victories, including a 2-0 win over leaders Redditch, who then began to slip away.

Williams, after a six match barren spell, was replaced by Whatmore, who had scored twice in the reserves 9-2 demolition of Stafford. He scored five goals in the next ten games, but after the 2-1 defeat by Wellington on Good Friday - in front of 10,000 - goalkeeper Causer was axed. He was replaced by Gamble who had been signed on amateur forms from Welshpool, and was to play in Town's remaining games without ever keeping a clean sheet.

Two home victories over Darlaston and Cannock took Town top, but defeat at Willenhall meant Bilston moved back above the Shropshire side. Williams hit four for the reserves at Tamworth and was recalled, scoring the winner at Redditch. So Town travelled to Bilston with their destiny in their hands. The League table was as follows:-

	P	F	A	Pts
Town	32	78	35	48
Bilston	31	95	40	45

Victory would clinch the title, defeat would make Bilston strong favourites as they had the superior goal average - 2.375 compared to Town's 2.229. The tension built among the 1,000 travelling fans through a goalless first half, and Town were under pressure when Williams' clearance off his own goal-line found Evans, whose centre picked out Elvidge, who in turn netted with a brilliant overhead kick. Williams was also to play a part in Town's second, for he sent a pass to Reg Jones who, *"scored a grand goal with a first-timer"*. Bilston hit back, Toy scored a penalty, and in the very last minute Gamble denied Newman with a fine one-handed save.

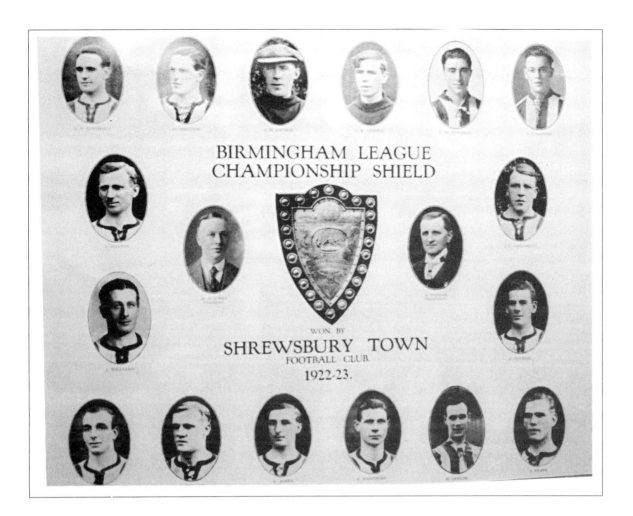

BIRMINGHAM LEAGUE
CHAMPIONSHIP SHIELD

WON BY

SHREWSBURY TOWN
FOOTBALL CLUB.
1922-23.

Town had won their first ever League title! The rest of the season was an anti-climax, as they crashed 5-2 at home to Stourbridge in the final League game and were again lethargic in the Shropshire Charity Cup Final which St. Georges won 4-2. The local charities benefitted to the tune of £13.15.6d as a large crowd turned out to see Mr S.Dallard present the League shield to Mr Sam Hatton, Town's captain and left-half.

The committee tried to strengthen the squad by bringing in two wingers, Ernie Cull (Nuneaton) and Len Rhodes (Wolves), as Jack Evans had gone to Sheffield United for a record fee of £300. They also signed inside left Vaughan from Stafford and 'keeper Hauser from Stourbridge. They never looked like retaining the league however, as Stourbridge raced to the title (was the wrong keeper signed?), but they did produce one of the club's best Cup performances.

They had threatened to make an impact in the F.A. Cup beating Darlaston, Worcester, Willenhall (who were undefeated in the League), and Bloxwich Strollers (all at home), before losing at Birmingham

Combination Hinckley, 3-1. But it was the Welsh Cup which created the excitement. They drew Cardiff City, giants of the First Division, who were locked in a battle with Herbert Chapman's Huddersfield for the title. (Huddersfield won on goal average, but Cardiff's achievement produced the only time a non-English club has made the top three). Cardiff boasted seven current full internationals with full-back Nelson later capped for Scotland, and had also made the quarter finals of the F.A. Cup. It looked like being a St. Valentines Day massacre on paper, but a crowd of 7,462 saw the game kick off at 3.50 p.m. on Thursday February 14th, and they were about to see an heroic performance. In the first half, Town lost former Cardiff forward Cashmore, who limped off with a knee injury, and Crutchley received a cut over the eye, so Town were down to nine men. They started the second half still two men short - but eventually returned to eleven - and held on to a goalless draw. Receipts for the game totalled £434.1.0d.

The replay on the 7th was watched by only 2,000, but again Town put up a stirring display before left-half Hardy and inside left Joe Clennell, with two, finally subdued their battling opponents. It is somewhat ironic that these two, and inside-right Hagen, were the only players not to attain international recognition. Cardiff centre-half Keenor became player-manager at Oswestry in 1934-5.

Obviously spurred on by these exploits, Town ended the League season with a flourish, and on the final day faced second placed Willenhall in the game which would settle the runners-up spot. Salop stormed to a half-time lead of 4-0, and despite Lovibond seeing his penalty saved, they cruised to a 6-1 victory which clinched the Keys Cup; the trophy originally provided for the top non-reserve side now went to the runners-up. Where to from these dizzy heights? Well sadly it was largely downwards.

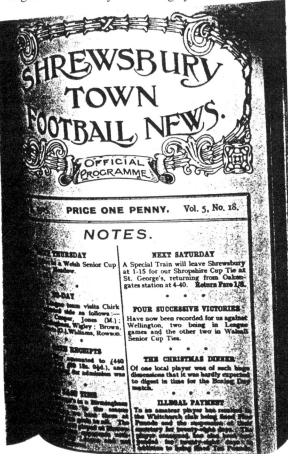

A programme cover from a bound volume.
Of the 1924-25 season.

RUGBY CLUB AND RUGBY SCORES

First Division opposition visited the Meadow again on 25th October 1924, when Town - with two goals from Elvidge and one from Cashmore - drew 3-3 with Aston Villa in a Friendly. It was to be a season of feast and famine. Town hit four or more goals ten times and failed to score on eleven occasions in 34 League games. Chris Elvidges' 23 goals included six against Cannock at home and hat-tricks against Brierley Hill and Darlaston, but after two at Redditch in the first game he only hit two more away all season. In the F.A. Cup Chirk were hammered 8-0 and Stafford Rangers beaten 2-1, after a replay, but with Elvidge and Sheldon both sick Town lost 2-1 at Willenhall. The Welsh Cup followed similar lines, Rhos 3-2 and Rhyl 2-0 were eliminated, but Merthyr Town (they did not become Tydfil until 1945) in front of 1,500, ran out 3-1 winners.

Other ups and downs at the time saw Yeaton Rovers withdraw from the Shrewsbury and District League Division Two because of foot and mouth disease (presumably not among the players), this happened in the January of 1924, but in October Shrewsbury Rugby Club was reformed.

For 1925-26 Town welcomed back Jack Evans and he took over from Chris Elvidge as leading marksman, in fact Elvidge's chances were few and his only goal came in the 4-4 draw at Oswestry. Leslie Tudor Owen back in the county was Oswestry's regular goalkeeper at the time whilst Town's search for goalscorers had seen three ex-Stourbridge players having trials in the pre-season matches. But Messrs Davies, Etheridge and Yarwood obviously did not make the right impression. Local player George Savage, hit five, in the second game and became the team's regular centre-forward, scoring in each of the first 3 rounds of the F.A. Cup, as did inside left Jackson. They beat Oswestry 3-2, Stourbridge 3-1, and Stafford 6-0 after a replay, but at Wellington, Town only managed a Biddulph own goal and lost 5-1. A more even season saw Town finish fifth, an improvement of four places on the previous term.

Leslie Tudor Owen returned to home base for 1926-27, but in a disappointing League season Salop slumped to 13th, went out of the Walsall Senior Cup 3-1 at Walsall, and after a 2-0 victory at Worcester crashed 6-0 at Cradley Heath, following a 1-1 draw at the Meadow.

The two public trial matches in 1927-28 pointed the way for the season. Four goals for Castle in the first, and a hat-trick for Morgan in the second were instrumental in building a potent attack, with these two either side an inside left called Rowley. With Harry, who later went to Manchester United, and the right-wing pairing of Roberts and Rice, the club achieved a ton of League goals for the first time.

Harry Rowley hit 35 in Town's total of 119 (31 years later Arthur Rowley promised a ton, achieved it, and contributed 38), including four hat-tricks, Castle hit four once plus a hat-trick, and Rice also hit a threesome. On April 7th at the Meadow, Rowley hit a hat-trick whilst Happy Sheldon (still going strong) recorded the 99th with a penalty, and Roberts headed number 100 as Town beat Bilston United 7-0. They also hit seven against Cannock, eight versus Hednesford, and double figures when Darlaston visited. Forty-two goals in seventeen away games was impressive, but seventy-seven - at an average of 4½ per game - at home was devastating.

Perhaps it had something to do with their new kit supplied by Mr W.J.Browning, Councillor J.Lewis and an anonymous donor, which was first used against Oakengates at the Meadow on September 3rd in the 2-0 F.A. Cup extra preliminary qualifying round game. Progress past Wolverhampton Amateurs 6-1 and Cradley Heath 1-0 came to a sudden halt when Oswestry, 2-1 down at half-time, hit back to win 4-3 at the Meadow.

Despite all the goals, Town only finished fourth with local rivals Wellington missing out on the title by goal average from Burton Town. Town lost Harry Rowley and came up with a rotten replacement, not Johnny Rotten, but a centre-forward called Billy Rotten. The trial matches, 4-4 and 5-3, set the tone for another high scoring season, and featured a forward called Shakeshaft. He was to play a part over the next few seasons, not always with Salop teams but also with Oakengates, so it was ironic that his first hat trick was against that same team, as Town won 6-0. Hat-tricks were again common place, in fact Billy Rotten twice went nap, and Rice did likewise against local rivals St. Georges who were blown away 11-2, with Rotten weighing in with a hat-trick, one from Morgan, and a brace from Wood completing the massacre, a new Birmingham League best for the club.

The F.A.Cup was disappointing, for Town drew 1-1 away at Leamington but lost the replay 4-2, to two second half goals. The club re-entered the Welsh Cup and beat Druids 6-0 and Llandudno 2-1 before a third home match saw Town draw 1-1 with Bangor. Despite a goal from their aptly named left-half 'Scorer', they lost 3-1. (In a season when Town scored 110 competitive goals it was his only strike). So despite a run of six victories mid-season, Town finished fifth, with Oswestry - who did the double over Salop - in their highest spot, third with 126 goals netted.

Town were achieving consistency, and finished fourth again in 1929-30 without quite hitting the goal standard. True centre-forward 'Sacker' Mound topped 20 goals, twice hitting four - remarkable, as he did not score in the first six or last nine games. 'Sacker' was a versatile player, not quite emulating Billy Scarratt but playing most half-back and forward positions. It is not clear where the nickname originated but he did not have a job outside football, save for collecting golf balls out of the brook in a sack. However, it was an average season, only notable for an unusual February.

In the F.A. Cup Town won 12-0 against Cannock and 5-2 over Bloxwich Strollers, before slipping to a 1-0 home defeat by Wellington in the Welsh Cup. Town also hit 12, routing Holt United 12-1, and on February 22nd they beat Oswestry 3-2. Former Oswestry goalkeeper Leslie Tudor Owen was recalled to play in goal for Town due to a work injury to Bishop - the regular custodian. Town having transferred the reserve 'keeper to St. Georges, Owen, who was signed was their only registered goal minder. Oswestry protested Town had played an unsigned player, which they amended to, 'not registered 14 days prior to playing', at the hearing. The Welsh F.A. upheld their protest, which Oswestry offered to withdraw if Shrewsbury would replay at Oswestry. Town declined and Oswestry went through to play New Brighton (59 years later the goalies name was Green the team Caernafon).

Town had again built a good mid-season run this time, winning 10 games and losing only one in a twelve match run which ended after the 2-1 home victory over Worcester City on February 15th. As previously stated, February was a notable month; on the Thursday prior to playing Worcester, *a little before one o'clock a fire was discovered at 35 Mardol Quay, a house occupied by Mr John Thomas Palmer, groundsman of the Shrewsbury Town Football Club*, the fire was quickly brought under control but *Shrewsbury Town team jerseys and knickers were kept in the house and are a total loss*.

It is to be hoped the replacement kit was of a sturdy nature as the Worcester game featured a second half snowstorm. Another note in the local press complimented three Frankwell supporters unable to attend the game who sent along their money.

Footnote to season:- Worcester City won the League scoring 153 goals, just 3 short off double Town's total, however this was not a League record, for Birmingham Reserves scored 160 in 1914-15.

CHAPTER 4 - THE EARLY THIRTIES - BECALMED IN MID-TABLE

Town secretary Albert Weston stepped down in May 1930 after a lengthy spell with the club, during which he was also a referee of some standing. He had been with the club during a time of much building work, financed thanks to backing from certain key members of local society, and the fund raising supporters club. A leading figure in all this, was chairman Henry Jones whose nickname became 'Money', for his unstinting efforts.

The improving surroundings were not however reflected on the pitch, as Town somewhat stagnated finishing ninth, tenth, eighth and tenth in successive seasons. In 1930-31, Town also suffered an early exit from the F.A. Cup away at local rivals St. Georges, by 4-0. This was a big setback as the Dragons had achieved unwanted consistency finishing bottom of the Birmingham League in each of the previous two seasons. Town did avenge their Cup exit with an 8-1 home League win, with Frank Taylor scoring five, but in the final fixture St. Georges again triumphed, 4-2. This result meant Town took only one point out of their last six games, but was not sufficient to stop St. Georges completing a hat-trick of wooden spoons and dropping out of the competition. The one area of real success was the Welsh Cup. Double hat-tricks by Jack Buckingham, versus Gwersylt in round three and Frank Taylor against Welshpool Town in round four, helped Town win 10-2 and 11-2 respectively.

In round five, Newport County were sent packing 5-2, but another Newport side proved a tougher nut. Lovell's Athletic held Salop to a goalless draw on March 19th, but a week later Frank Taylor's goal was enough to extend the Cup run. The contrast in gate receipts was quite startling, for at the Meadow £125 was the total, while the away match realised just £14. No matter it set up a chance to avenge the memorable defeat by Cardiff City seven years previous. The game, played on Monday April 13th, drew a crowd of 5,900 to the Meadow, and the home fans who contributed to a gate of £331 certainly had their money's worth. Cardiff had slipped into the Second Division by now but still presented strong opposition, however a second half goal in off a post from right-winger Roberts on 63 minutes put Town into the final. That match was played two weeks later at the Racecourse, but Town were never at the races. Wrexham, three up at half-time, won 7-0 in front of a crowd of 9,000; the end of the season saw them finish third in the Third Division North.

The following season saw some heavy defeats early in the season, notably 7-0 at Stafford, 9-0 at Burton and 10-2 at Worcester, but after the return of Billy Rotten their fortunes picked up. Left-winger J.Williams and inside-forward George Sambrook had been their main goalscorers, with both on target in the 6-1 F.A. Cup win over Bournville. Sambrook hit a hat-trick as Walsall LMS fell 4-1, before Oakengates - despite another Sambrook goal - won 2-1, a result soon to be overturned as Town won the home League game 3-0, with Williams on the mark.

Billy Rotten was not the only new face in the side, for there was also goalkeeper Prince, who saved a penalty on his debut. But one name missing was promising young forward Lenny Tranter, who was killed in a motorcycle accident.

The 5-1 Welsh Cup victory over Colwyn Bay set up another clash with Wrexham, in the quarter-final. It was a much closer affair, but the Welsh team again won this time 4-2. The return of Rotten - 16 goals in 20 games - and the career of Prince, who played 21 times in the League, were to be shortlived experiences, as both left at the end of the season. Prince was sold to Derby County, after having failed to emulate Frank Boxley when he missed a penalty, with Town 8-1 up against Stourbridge. Town filled their goalkeeping vacancy by signing Ben Olney, the former Aston Villa 'keeper, who appeared twice for England four years earlier in a 5-1 victory in Paris and a 3-1 win in Antwerp. Ernie Cull returned to the club and a centre-forward called Taylor led the attack, but by now it was Joe Taylor.

The F.A. Cup started at Nuneaton with a 3-1 victory, continued with a 5-1 home win over Kidderminster, and, after a 3-3 draw at Whitchurch a 1-0 replay win set up a trip to Hereford. All square at half-time, Town lost to two second half goals, so it was left to the Welsh competition to keep interest going. Once again Town made the last eight, but after scoring three against both Llanidloes and Machynlleth, they hit three more against Bangor but were forced into a replay by their North Wales rivals, and full-back Wigley's own goal sent Bangor through. This was somewhat ironic as Salop humbled City 6-1 in the League a few weeks earlier.

The high spot of 1933-34 was a new record goalscoring performance by Joe Taylor, he hit 55 League goals including double hat-tricks at Oswestry and at home to Colwyn Bay; he hit four against Port Vale Reserves, and hat-tricks when Brierley Hill, Stafford and Cradley Heath visited the Meadow. He also scored three goals in the F.A. Cup, as Town beat Oswestry 1-0, Hereford 3-1, Wellington 4-1 (after a replay), and Brierley Hill 2-1, before forcing a goalless draw at Gainsborough Trinity, but sadly losing 3-1 in the replay at the Meadow in front of 4,000. In fact the Cup run saw receipts totalling over £1,000 paid, including £201 for the final game. (Oswestry must have fancied their chances as they had beaten Badsey 19-0 in their first game).

A record 11,836 pack Wellington's Buck's Head Ground for the Birmingham League match v. Town in April 1935. Goals from Lloyd and Hopley gave Town a 2-1 win.

CHALLENGING AGAIN

Luton Town snapped up goal machine Joe Taylor, but Town were not to suffer unduly making an excellent start to the season. In the first nine weeks they played nineteen times losing only once, 3-1 at Oswestry. The high number of matches was due to frantic activity in the F.A. Cup. In the first qualifying round Town played Cannock twice at the Gay Meadow winning 5-2 after a 2-2 draw, round two saw a draw again, two-all at Brierley Hill, followed by a 3-1 replay victory, while the 1-0 home win over Stafford Rangers in round three was straightforward.

Round four however, saw Town draw 1-1 with Dudley on no less than three occasions - at home, at Dudley, and then at Molineux. The third replay, also on Wolves' ground, saw Town win 3-1 and put them through to meet Birmingham Trams just 48 hours later. It looked like a certain victory, particularly as the Trams - who were drawn at home - asked for the game to be played at the Meadow, but sadly Town's leg weary troops, 2-1 down at half-time, collapsed in the second half and lost 4-1, in front of 3,534 who paid £185. The match report stated: *"Trams with a hard kicking defence and fast forward line were a good side"*, and to add insult to

injury Wellington beat Cradley Heath 7-0 to knock Town off the top of the League.

Wellington were to go on and win the League, although Town's Cup commitments helped their rivals cause, as they were involved in further Cup action in the Welsh competition. Exempt until round four they beat Kidderminster Harriers 2-0, Llanidloes 3-1 and Troedyrhiw 5-3, before meeting New Brighton. This quarter final tie became another serial as the teams meet on three successive Thursdays, all at the Gay Meadow, in front of a total of 12,500 people who paid £635 to see a goalless draw followed, by an eight goal extra time thriller, which in turn led to a 2-0 victory for Town.

In the semi-final Town were again at home with the runners-up of the previous year, Tranmere Rovers, as their opponents. A crowd of 8,000 paid £391, but saw Town no match for their Birkenhead opponents and Rovers won 3-0 to reach the final. In fact Tranmere went on to win the trophy for the only time in their history. Town meanwhile had played seventeen cup-ties in one season, it was just as well that Port Vale Reserves, after just one season, pulled out of the Birmingham League leaving two extra dates free.

Points of interest during this season included the fact that on October 20th, Shakeshaft, of Oakengates, signed in the morning and played against his old club in the afternoon, while in the 3-1 defeat by Oswestry, Town's goal was scored by Meaney, it was his only goal for Town but despite being transferred to Halesowen he later returned to run the off-licence in Crowmoor Road. While Jack Roscamp, who twice hit four goals during the season, had been the star of the 1928 Cup final, netting twice in Blackburn Rovers 3-1 victory over Huddersfield Town, and had cost Town £350 from Bradford City. But despite early promise he lost the goal touch and left in the close season. Roscamp's departure was seemingly speeded up by interference from the committee, alluded to by 'Rocket' in the Chronicle but denied by secretary Hicks. Another to depart was Jack Driscoll who netted five against Bangor City, including a penalty, but was soon transferred to West Bromwich for £250, and when Quayle was injured Town lacked goalpower.

This lead to an end of season run of just seven points from eight games and Town finished fourth. It was not an ideal springboard for an application to join the Football League but Town did apply, although a dispute centring on three committee members held up the printing of a booklet to promote the bid. On the credit side, literally, Town made a profit of £652.16.2d which wiped out a previous debt of £202.4.2d. The supporters club A.G.M. on Friday June 8th announced they had raised £200. Meanwhile the Football League A.G.M. saw Southport and Carlisle re-elected with 46 votes, compared to the 6 mustered by Salop.

Town's desire to join the League was despite an appraisal by 'Rocket' in the Chronicle that it would cost around £200 a week to run a successful League side. His breakdown was as follows: 14 players - £96, trainer/referees - £6, rail fees - £14, entertainment tax and insurance - £40, rent/trainer/groundsman - £6.10s, sundries - £5. This totalled £167.10s and left little room for manoeuvre.

There was also talk of Town joining the Northern League but Llanelli despite crowds of 20,000 and financial guarantees failed to gain admission. What was needed was a Midland League - why are the Midlands always lagging? The same situation still existed when the Northern Premier and the Southern League played pass the parcel with sides like Kings Lynn and Burton Albion 50 years later.

Roscamp, who took over the Boot Inn at Welshpool, had originally been brought in as coach, so the gap in that area was filled by appointing Sam Ramsey as player-manager. It was to be a hugely entertaining season with 194 goals scored in Town's 38 League games, due in no small way to a 22 year old centre-forward from Oldham Athletic, W.J.Hewitson. One of six centre-forwards tried in the two practice matches he showed some promise scoring once. (There was a third practice match held but solely for local amateurs). However, once the season was underway, Salop found they had discovered a veritable goal machine. Two at Hereford, followed by two more - including a penalty at home to Colwyn Bay - preceded a rare blank away to Oswestry. The response was emphatic, six, including another penalty at home to Cannock in a 10-1 thrashing. In total he was to hit 58 League goals, despite missing another 10-1 victory, against Cradley Heath, through injury. He hit five more hat-tricks and four goals on three other occasions. It could have been more, 4-0 ahead in eight minutes at home to Rhyl, Town declared, and won 5-1.

But the season was not without its setbacks, for having pasted Brierley Hill 9-2 on January 25th, with Hewitson missing a penalty, Town played the return game on March 14th and amazingly crashed 11-2. It was, and still is, the most goals conceded by Town in a League game this century. They had dropped Hewitson and wingers Lucas and Jeavons due to poor finishing in the 3-1 Welsh Cup defeat at Aberdare. While Town's first team were being thrashed, Jeavons hit a hat-trick and Hewitson also scored in the reserves 5-2 victory over Walsall. Hewitson was recalled, but Town lost 5-2 at Hednesford before - with Jeavons also playing - they beat Dudley 6-0 with four from Hewitson. Despite the goal-feast Town finished third in both the League and goal-scoring charts. Brierley Hill came second with 128 goals while neighbours Wellington retained their title with 129 goals scored.

The F.A.Cup was another happy hunting ground for Hewitson, he scored twice in the 3-0 victory over Boldmore St. Michael, and once against Oakengates as Town won 3-1, Wyness netted the other two. Wyness had signed for Spennymoor after playing for Wrexham, but Town offered him better terms, Spennymoor sportingly released him and he had signed on August 30th.

Worcester City away was a two-all draw, Salop winning the replay 1-0 with Sharp's goal ensuring it was the only game in which Hewitson failed to score. Kidderminster away was another 2-2 draw, but Town lost the replay 2-1. Hewitson scored all the goals in the last tie and a total of seven in the run.

In the Welsh Cup, Town were exempt to round six, and hammered New Brighton 8-1 before losing to Aberdare 3-1. But after appeal the Welsh F.A. declared Aberdare's ground, *"did not comply with the rules of Welsh football",* and the game was replayed at the Meadow. Salop won 4-1 and met Crewe at Bangor in the semi-final. This ended goalless so 48 hours later, on Friday April 4th, they met again at Rhyl when Crewe won 4-0, and then beat Chester 2-0 in the Final. Town had lost to the winners two years running, and for the only time in Welsh Cup history the final featured two English teams for the third year running. It had been a tremendous season, but not all the action was on the pitch, for a major upheaval had happened in the boardroom.

RESIGNATIONS UNLIMITED

After failing to secure a Third Division North place in June 1935, Town Chairman Mr Harry A. Jones had said they would not be deterred and would keep applying until successful. The committee did much soul-searching in the following months which would eventually lead to blood-letting. The majority of the committee decided that moving into the Football League could be financially disastrous, no doubt looking at teams like Leeds City, Thames and Wigan Borough, and also taking into account the believed financial problems of other lower divisions sides.

So despite a mini-referendum and their previous assertions the announcement was made in January that there would be no application to join the Football League. This sparked an immediate and strong reaction from three board members, and an extraordinary general meeting was called for February 3rd.

Mr A.E. Anderson a committee member led the attack saying 96% of the average fans were in favour, and disputing that any financial hardship would follow Town's admission to the Football League. He was seconded by another committee man, Arthur Jones, and supported by Jimmy Fulwood. Mr Fulwood stated that Town should aim for the day when they could play Wolverhampton Wanderers on equal terms, it was met with some hilarity, but he was to see Town's standing surpass Wolves before he died.

In reply Chairman Harry Jones said *"in two years time, they* (the committee) *feel the club would meet disaster and the possibility of the club going out of existence"*!

Mr Bernard Hayes proposed making the club a limited company with 6,000 10/- shares, directors having to take a £10 shareholding. 2/6 per share would become payable immediately, with the balance due on admission to the League. Mr L.Edwards, the third 'rebel' committeeman, seconded this motion which was carried unanimously.

Twenty-four hours later Chairman Harry Jones, Treasurer Herbert Jones, and Secretary W.R.Hinks, plus all but three others resigned from the committee. They had all been stung by a resolution asking for resignations which though withdrawn and replaced by a vote of confidence at the end of the E.G.M. had undermined their authority; was this the first fatal vote of confidence!

The three remaining members - A.E.Anderson, Arthur Jones and L.Edwards co-opted Bernard Hayes, Jimmy Fulwood and A.H.Allen onto the committee, with Mr Allen taking over as Chairman. When the previous members offered to withdraw their resignations, this was not accepted, although Harry Jones was encouraged to return as a committeeman due to his experience of running the club, and offer which led him to becoming president.

Town's Board of Directors in 1936-37.
(Back): C.L.Edwards, A.H.Jones, E.A.Bousted, V.Greenhous, J.Fulwood.
(Front): A.H.Jones, B.Hayes, A.H.Allen, E.P.Tucker, J.B.Smart.

On Valentine's day, the Chronicle suggested that a combined Shrewsbury and Wellington team would be strong enough for Division Two, it was not a notion likely to draw much support then, or even now. But while Town survived their upheaval, sadly, on March 13th, St. George's demise was reported.

Town's new committee should have celebrated one trophy at the end of the season, but the reserves Mid Wales League title was snatched from them by a dispute involving non-fulfilment of a fixture between Aberystwyth Town and Llanidloes. It led to Aberystwyth's record being deleted and Town lost two points more than Llanidloes; from being champions by one point, they became runners-up by the same margin.

The application for Football League status was duly presented, with the voting resulting in Southport 47, New Brighton 38, Shrewsbury 7, and Wigan 6. But on July 3rd, the Chairman Mr Allen said it was possible one team may be unable to continue and Shrewsbury as next in line (albeit at some distance), were willing to step into Division Three.

Meanwhile on June 12th, Town signed the previous season's Oldham Captain, Tommy Seymour, he had been an ever-present in the previous two seasons, despite being leading goalscorer for Plymouth over one Christmas, due sadly to three own goals. When reminded of this in the 1970's he said *"I'd rather hoped everyone had forgotten that by now"!* Tommy was, like several 1930's personalities, to have a long connection with Shrewsbury Town, in his case probably the longest.

All the boardroom troubles had masked the fact that this was Town's Golden Jubilee, and no real celebration was held.

EVEN MORE GOALS...
... AND WHAT A SEND-OFF

Not surprisingly Salop could not hold on to Hewitson, he was snapped up by Third Division North side York City, but Town were not about to suffer a goal famine. Although the first trial match ended goalless, a week later the probables beat the possibles 8-0 with Liggins hitting five. Three straight wins opened the season with left-winger Dennard Hopley netting in each game, Alec Brown also notched three, Liggins two and Ernie Breeze's penalty saw Town travel to Kidderminster with six points and a 9-2 goal tally; Harriers proved the masters, 4-1, Liggins again on target.

In fact Town only failed to score once in their first 17 League matches, ironically against Cannock Town. The previous season Town's 6-1 victory was Cannock's biggest ever defeat, but this time their victory was expunged as they later resigned from the League. Around the turn of the year, after a minor slump, the Town hit a rich seam of form. Three home victories 3-0 over Kidderminster, 11-1 against Bangor and 4-2 over Dudley were followed by a bizarre 9-5 away success at Nuneaton. Ernie Breeze hit six, including one of his seven successful penalties versus Bangor, while Danny Williams cracked in four at Nuneaton, who Town had earlier beaten 8-0. Goals were flowing from all areas, no less than seven players hit double figures with the main honours going to Welshman Danny Williams with 27 successes, all scored in the second half of the season.

Town's biggest victory came in a remarkable game on April 3rd which saw a half-time score of: Shrewsbury Town 9 - Oakengates T 1. Added to this, Ernie Breeze and Ron Pearce were sent off for an incident in the goalmouth. Ron Pearce was also dismissed for a foul on Tommy Seymour in the County Cup replay on the Meadow on 30th December 1936, an eye witness tells that after persistent fouling Breeze took exception, threw one punch which toppled Pearce, and walked from the pitch before the Referee's decision. He was to be the last Shrewsbury player to be sent off for 23 years and 16 days. The next one was ever more unlikely!

Bristol Rovers Reserves had looked like champions all season, but when they lost 1-0 at Brierley Hill on April 10th, Salop - who had five games left - were five points adrift with three games in hand. Williams with a double hat-trick, led the way as they thrashed, a demoralised Colwyn Bay 10-3, (Colwyn Bay had already announced they were not entering the League again), but Town managed just one point in their final four games, all away from home. So in what was to be their final season they won the Keyes Cup as runners-up, with 133 goals for and 64 against, making 197 goals the most ever seen in a Town League season.

While the League was exciting the cups were disappointing. The F.A.Cup saw a 5-1 victory over Brierley Hill set up a local derby with Wellington which Town lost 3-2 in a replay, after a 2-2 draw. Two second half goals saw Kidderminster Harriers come from behind to win 2-1 in the only Welsh Cup tie, this of course meant the only team Town played, who they did not score against, was Cannock - who folded. As the man said, 'funny old game'.

Before the season finished Nuneaton, Colwyn Bay and Dudley had announced they would not re-apply and the Birmingham League looked likely to be much depleted. Therefore after Town, once more, failed to join the 'Big Boys' they successfully applied to the Midland Counties League, which, despite the presence of 12 Reserve sides, was claimed to be on a par with the Third Division North.

The income for 1936-37 was £5,284 which included a supporters donation of £162.10.0d and showed a profit of £227.16.4d. A new manager, Ted Boustead was appointed and a new left-wing pairing from Merseyside was recruited; inside-left Sidney Roberts from Liverpool and left-winger Jack Almond from Tranmere Rovers. It was to be a whole new adventure, at least until war broke out.

THE BIG TREBLE?

Town opened their Midland League career at home to Nottingham Forest Reserves, a game which attracted a crowd of 4,814 and saw Town record a 2-1 victory with goals from Jack Almond and Danny Williams. A 1-0 defeat at Rotherham was avenged in fine style when Town thrashed the Millers 11-0 in the next League game. This was the only time in their seven Midland League seasons they hit double figures. Danny Williams cracked home four, Monty Wilson hit a hat-trick, Dennard Hopley a brace, Sydney Roberts one and Ernie Breeze a penalty.

Although not hitting double figures again in the League, Town had already smashed ten past Evesham in the F.A. Cup. This was on September 4th and in front of 2,558, hat tricks from Hopley and Wilson and two each from Roberts and Williams made it a 10-2 stroll.

After the eleven against Rotherham, Town played their only goalless draw in the League, at the City ground Nottingham. But progress was made in the Cup with a 2-1 win at Hereford, a 6-0 win over Denaby followed (which included the first of four own goals in Town's League season), and a 5-2 Cup win over Shirley Town kept the goals flowing. Town's inside-right Race scored in the latter two games but it was not Roy, of the Rovers, but Harry, an experienced inside-forward who was more of a provider than scorer. Successive 1-0 League defeats at Scarborough and Burton and a goalless Cup draw with Stourbridge meant a sudden lack of goals, and the 3-2 replay defeat saw Town out of the F.A. competition.

A win at Gainsborough and seven points from four home games improved matters, but only one victory - 7-0 over Notts County Reserves - in the next six fixtures saw the worst spell of the season. True, one match against Peterborough at home was abandoned due to snow, but despite ending the year with a 2-1 victory over Grimsby Reserves, Town were ninth as 1938 dawned. Hull Reserves headed the table with 28 points from 26 games Town had 22 from 18, but Grantham with one point more and Boston with four extra both had a game in hand on Salop.

The backlog of fixtures was caused by Cup competitions, with Town having beaten Oswestry 6-3 after a 1-1 draw in round three of the Welsh Cup, then seeing off Macclesfield 7-0 in round four. Round five saw just two ties played with all other clubs, including Shrewsbury, given byes, and in round six a Danny Williams hat-trick - taking his tally in the competition to ten - saw Town win 3-1 at the Racecourse.

The success over Grimsby also rekindled the League season, the win being the first of seven consecutive victories, featuring four away from home, and highlighted by a 9-1 win at Denaby United - Town's biggest ever away League victory. Suddenly the League looked like a two horse race, Boston beaten 3-0 at the Meadow had slipped, but Grantham who Town had not yet played were the title favourites.

Ted Boustead had overcome the loss of Sydney Roberts, he had joined Chester in a move which upset a number of fans. Roberts had been listed by Liverpool at £750 but appealed to the Football League on January 24th, and was granted a free transfer. The next day he joined Chester and received a substantial amount of the £500 fee, with Town not dissatisfied at their cut. However, the fans felt that with Shrewsbury receiving similar support to Chester, more effort to retain the popular player should have been made. There were also complaints of the lack of local players in the team, whilst in another part of the county, Oakengates Town were enjoying improved form thanks to a diminutive local winger, a youngster named Johnny Hancocks.

Town's good run - unbeaten in nine games - ended at Grimsby where they lost 4-0 to a side containing seven players with First Division experience, including all the forward line, but they bounced back and won six and drew two of their next eight, making 31 points in 18 games. Manager Boustead was still having to shuffle the pack as he lost goalkeeper Rigby to Stockport County, *"for a fee larger than*

An group of players, officials and directors, before a match during the 1937-38 season

Aston Villa had paid two years earlier" (Villa paid £350), and took County's reserve keeper Ashley in exchange. His debut at Grimsby started in the worst possible way with centre-half Smith conceding a second minute penalty for a handball.

One of Rigby's final games was the goalless draw at Chester in the Welsh Cup, and with Ashley ineligible Goodchild took over for the replay. He performed well, as Alec Brown gave Town a first half lead, but Chester levelled to force extra time. The crowd of 6,728 made it a heady atmosphere and Danny Williams extra-time winner put Salop into the semi-final.

(Below) 1937. Sam Powell (standing on left) - the Shrewsbury Town physio, who was renowned for turning out the fittest team in the League

Goodchild retained his place until a 4-1 defeat at Boston ended Town's good run, and a young amateur from Cannock - F.Halston - was given his debut at, of all places, Grantham. Town had been strengthened by the return of Horace Baker, whose 28 goals the previous season had helped win the Keyes Cup - from Southport - and he scored on his comeback at Bradford Park Avenue. He did not repeat the feat at Grantham, and Town, for only the second time lost successive matches despite a fine performance from their debutante goalkeeper. In fact Town should have shared the spoils as Ernie Breeze hit the crossbar with a penalty.

Halston was retained for the Welsh Cup semi-final with Newport County. This was another nail biting affair, and despite a Breeze penalty, Town trailed 2-1 at half-time, and after Alec Brown equalised, another thirty minutes was required during which right-winger Davies hit the winner. This match was watched by 7,642.

A thumping 6-2 home win over Grantham, Town's first home League game for some time (they had played six successive away games), saw Dennard Hopley notch the 100th League goal. Town faced two away games and the re-arranged League encounter with Peterborough, but were not about to throw away their opportunity, in fact it was Grantham who faltered. Town drew the matches at Hull and Bradford City and went into their final game one point ahead of Grantham - victory would clinch it.

It was the re-arranged game and reports showed that Town were rather nervous. Skipper Ernie Breeze again hit the crossbar with a penalty in the first half, but made no mistake when a second chance arrived in the second half. Danny Williams hit two with Harry Race, and Alec Brown making it 5-1. Danny Williams was the League's leading scorer with 49, just one short of the League record, and the Chronicle felt he should have taken the two penalties to break the record. Town had scored 111 goals, and lifted the championship at the first time of asking, with the Shropshire Senior Cup also in safe keeping, they had eyes on a magical treble.

On Wednesday May 4th they staged the Welsh Cup final against Swansea Town in front of a record crowd of 14,500, who paid record receipts of £786. Town playing their 13th game in 25 days were trailing 2-1 at half-time but Harry Race equalised. Once more Town finished more strongly than their opponents, and they would surely win in extra-time. The large crowd eagerly awaited, the final whistle

went, and Swansea pointed out that the extra half-hour could only be played if both sides agreed - they declined. So the final was held over until the following September. Halston, Miller, Race and Hopley had left the club, but the spirit remained and although Fred Swift, brother of England keeper Frank, was beaten in the first half, Town again showed their fight and fitness. Second half goals from Alec Brown and N.Roberts, a winger from Carlisle, sent the crowd of 8,000 home convinced justice had been done.

A big crowd had also attended on May 7th when champions Shrewsbury drew 2-2 with runners-up Grantham, before which the championship trophy was presented. Some of the celebrating which had been passed over two years earlier was now unleashed. After 52 years Shrewsbury Town were a force to be respected.

The last full season before the war had started in fine style with the Welsh Cup win, but sadly the players, including Den Hopley who had left the club, did not receive any recognition.

It was not to take Hopley long to extract some revenge as he returned with Wellington Town on November 12th and a goal from Charlie Ballantyne, with another ex-Town man, Jack Driscoll, hitting the bar, was enough to knock Salop out of the F.A.Cup.

In 1994, and indecently fit, Dennard Hopley remembered his time at Shrewsbury with great affection and agreed that Town's secret weapon was trainer Sam Powell. *"We always came on strong in the last ten minutes"*, he said and added, *"the training at Wellington was easy in comparison"*, but at least his stay with our local rivals did one thing, it provided that missing Welsh Cup medal, when Wellington beat Swansea 4-0 in 1940. He also won a Welsh Amateur Cup runners-up medal with Llanidloes after the war, and having been a keen Bowler for over 50 years has a stand at Sir John Bayley No.2 Green bearing his name, a club to which Jack Driscoll introduced him in the late thirties.

Wellington also came back in April and won 5-1 in the revived Shropshire Mayor's Charity Cup, but nevertheless it was a good League season. Whilst not quite reaching the heights, Salop started with five wins and a draw, and then they scored a remarkable 7-0 away victory against Nottingham Forest Reserves - ruining their unbeaten home record - on the opening day of October. This was followed by three home victories, with Danny Williams, who hit five at Nottingham, scoring a hat-trick against both Hull and Gainsborough. His absence against Lincoln had little effect - Town won 8-0 - and the four game goal column read, for 26 against 2.

All this had come after a defeat at Newark on Thursday October 29th, which led to 'stern disciplinary measures' and several changes. Sam Powell, who was to retire at the end of the season, earned praise from winger Gordon Priestley who travelled down from the North-east with a bad knee injury, but was soon cured by the Meadow marvel.

April 1938. Groundsman Jack Palmer (with the club since 1903), prepares the pitch.

Mr A.H.Allen the Town Chairman caused outrage in some areas by suggesting no-one over 65 should hold office on the Football Association. The Shropshire F.A. disassociated themselves from his views which they called, *"unjustified and irresponsible"*, and also, *"undiplomatic with regard to the club's application to join the Third Division"*. The remarks made in the close season were amongst Mr Allen's last major contributions to Shropshire soccer, as a work promotion meant he moved to Southport, and he handed over the reins to Bernard Hayes.

The Supporters Club were extending their involvement, with Mr C.Duffill having announced at the celebration supper-dance, they had accepted a quote to build three bays on the Popular Side. This was extended to four at the A.G.M., and the pressure to join the League was mounting, but received a setback on January 18th when Welsh Cup holders Town

were beaten 2-1 by South Liverpool. The team who would launch several top careers had been Town's nearest opponents in the 1938 vote; Town being third with 15, South Liverpool fourth with 5 ahead of Scunthorpe and Wigan with one each. In the South, Ipswich with 36 deposed Gillingham who only managed 28. (sadly South Liverpool folded in 1991, although they reformed soon after).

In the League, Town avenged their defeat at Newark with a 7-0 home win, and after a 1-1 drawn at Denaby - Cyril Lello's only pre-war goal - they hammered their luckless rivals 9-1, again. Danny Williams hit 33 goals and the team managed 125, with Ernie Breeze still on penalties hitting four, including two as Nottingham Forest won 4-2 at the Meadow. Town keeper Fred Smith saved penalties at Grimsby and Peterborough, but having led 2-0 at Doncaster, Town lost 4-2 and had to settle for third place.

The end of season highlight on the Meadow was a battling three part Welsh Cup semi-final between Oswestry and Cardiff, which first saw a penalty earn Cardiff a 1-1 draw. A fortnight later it was 2-2 before Cardiff finally won 2-1 at the third attempt. One of Oswestry's heroes was veteran centre-half Matthews who had left Town two seasons earlier.

On June 9th, Town moved closer to League status, when the voting was: Hartlepool 38, Accrington 29, Shrewsbury 22, South Liverpool 5, Scunthorpe 4 and Wigan and Burton Town nil. M.P. Arthur Duckworth was elected President and immediately joined up in an anti-aircraft unit, as if he was not receiving enough flak! A.H.Allen came back, but only to resign from the Presidency of the Shrewsbury and District League, and Tommy Seymour took over as trainer. While Town right-half Joe Dalton returned to training bristling with fitness after playing baseball all summer. But although the season kicked off on August 26th full of optimism, with a victory over Mansfield and the superfit Dalton scoring the first goal, it was not to last. Two 4-2 defeats, away at Scunthorpe and home to Peterborough, were the only games played before the war ended League action.

The only other competitive match was the 4-2 fourth round Welsh Cup defeat away against Chester on January 13th 1940, Town's last external competitive match for over five years. The Shropshire Senior Cup Final was played with Danny Williams making his first appearance since outbreak of the war, but Wellington won 4-0, and ex-Town men featured prominently - Jack Driscoll scored the first, Den

Hopley made the second - scored by Heinemann - Price added a third, and Hopley in the last minute wrapped up the victory.

The Crown Hotel, scene of the entertainment before Town's staging of the 1890 International match, was sold to Pearl Assurance in November 1940. While with football taking a back seat, the Co-op Childrens Gala was held on the Gay Meadow; 2,500 kids turned up, Little Bo Peep (Joy Nicholls) and Little Boy Blue (John Davies) won the fancy dress.

Town played a series of friendlies against League opposition, 21 in total, 19 at home. The team was boosted by several guest players, including Grosvenor - Bolton Wanderers and England International - Johnny Hancocks, Jack Rowley and Neil Franklin among others. On 6th April 1940, Manchester United made their only ever appearance at the Meadow in a 2-2 draw. All goals came in the first half, with Powell and Armstrong (Aberdeen) scoring for Town and Morris and Jack Rowley for United. For all friendlies all uniformed members of his majesty's forces were admitted to the ground for half price.

BRIDGING THE GREAT DIVIDE

The war caused an unfortunate break, in every form of normal life, but various challenges and charity matches continued to grace the Meadow. These games usually featured a Shropshire Select XI, under various names, playing a top side. However, despite this interruption, several established figures would continue illustrious careers after the war.

Sam Powell, well known the length and breath of the land, as a physiotherapist ahead of his time, would be on hand to guide his replacement, Tommy Seymour. Sam had been a trainer, who had always turned out a team, whose fitness would outlast the opposition. The number of last gasp victories were legendary. He was also a keen boxing trainer, publican, and handyman of unbounded versatility. It was he who lightened Town's darkness by installing the first electric light at the Gay Meadow, and Tommy Seymour was aware it was a hard act to follow.

Tommy would handle the responsibility with aplomb. He emulated Sam, by painting anything which did not move, and training anything that did. He was, according to Arthur Rowley, *"the most knowledgable man, I have ever met, on the subject of football"*. He had time for everyone, but lacked Sam's knowl-

edge of the human anatomy - a cold sponge, and 'run it off son' being his most likely diagnosis. He stayed for many post war seasons and also saw his son-in-law and grandson make the first team.

Leslie Tudor Owen had already featured as a goalkeeper who was twice able to join the League ranks. He also, subsequently, joined the board of directors and rose to vice-chairman, a position he held at the time of Town's memorable promotion to the old Division Two. Alongside him on that board was another former stalwart of defence, 'Chucky' Edwards, a pork butcher by trade. 'Chucky' would have made a fortune, as an after-dinner speaker in the modern era. His old full-back partner, 'Happy' Sheldon, was another to cross the great divide of the Second World War, as a prominent member of the supporters club and the Third Division fund. The club were indeed fortunate to be so well served by such an illustrious group.

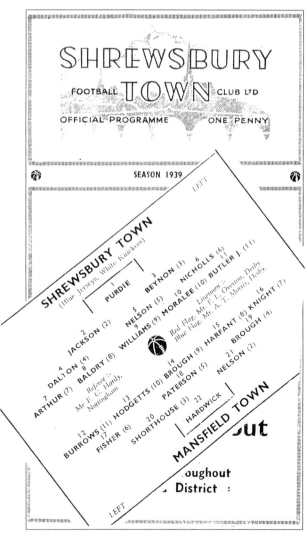

The season soon came to an abrupt end

The interruption caused by the war probably cost Town an early entry into League football, but they tried to make up for lost time, by appointing former Arsenal and Chelsea Manager Leslie Knighton to steer the club through the early post-war seasons. With the Football League resumption still a year away the Midland League was awash with League stars, Town's practice match line ups reflected this:-

BLUES:

Sorrell (West Ham), Sykes (20th I.T.C.), Gennoe (Stockport), Downing (RAF), Wheatley (Port Vale), Riding (Army), Dunns (Sunderland), Buchanan (Army), Acquoroff (Norwich), Rogers (Chester), Aldred (Sentinel).

REDS:

Whitelaw (Wrexham), Pitts (Fulham), Tabbener (Nottm. Forest), Nicholls (Shrewsbury), Hughes (New Brighton), Lane (Plymouth), Maund (Nottm. Forest), Bailey (Oldham), Richardson (W.B.A.), Jones (RAF), Mulraney (Ipswich),

Second half changes:

BLUES:

Wild (RAF), Reeves (RAF), Birch (Shrewsbury), Howard (Army), Armstrong (Aberdeen), Rhodes (Hull City).

REDS:

Lloyd (RAF), Taylor (Bradford), Dowling (Rotherham), Stringer (Hednesford), Rogers (Hanwood).

The Reserves application for the Birmingham Combination was turned down so they went in the Shrewsbury and District League. Town's opening selection was Sambrook Tabbener, Birch, Soo, Hughes, Nicholls, Maund, Lane, Armstrong, Bailey, Rogers; but Armstrong's absence led to a last minute change with Billy Richardson stepping in, it was to be the start of a wonderful season.

Local Derby - but hardly a local player in sight!

Shropshire Senior Cup

FINAL TIE

GAY MEADOW

EASTER MONDAY, APRIL 10th, 1944

KICK-OFF 3-30 P.M.

Right   Left

SHREWSBURY TOWN
Colours : Blue and White.

WILLIAMS
(Walsall)

TURNER   OWENS
(Birmingham)   (Tranmere)

WATT   TOPHAM   CLANCY
(Cheltenham)   (Wolves)   (Celtic)

BUCHANAN   CROOKS   VAUSE   DOHERTY   McCORMICK
(Wolves)   (Wolves)   (Chelsea)   (Man. City)   (Tottenham)

Referee : R.S.M. BAKER.

HOPLEY   MULLIGAN   PEACOCK   WATTS   A N OTHER
(Wellington)   (Sheff. Wed.)   (Notts. Forest)   (Walsall)

JONES   COLEMAN   BATES
(Grimsby)   (Partick Thistle)   (Chelmsford)

CHILDS   LEA
(Wellington)   (Millwall)

ROBERTS
(Wellington)

WELLINGTON TOWN
Colours : White Shirts, Black Knicks.

Left   Right

PROGRAMMES 2d. EACH.

Lane and Richardson, in open play, and a Frank Soo penalty wrapped up the points while Tom Sambrook in his only game kept a clean sheet - in the opening 3-0 win over Barnsley. It was to be the club's best ever start - fourteen wins and five draws, during which Bernard Streten added seven more clean sheets and 'Billy' Richardson hit 35 goals including five hat-tricks, a four, and a club record equalling seven against Notts County Reserves. Town averaged four goals a game, despite two goalless draws at Ransome and Marles (Newark) and Scunthorpe and Lindsey United.

Apart from Richardson's seven (which equalled Alf Ellis' record in 1894), the high spot was the second half against Boston United. Town led 1-0 at half-time, through a Johnny Hancocks goal, but ran out 8-0 victors. Hancocks added another and completed his hat-trick from the spot while Maund, two, and Bailey made it six, before Richardson on 86 and 89 minutes completed the rout. Town continued their run with a 3-1 win at Notts County before travelling to Boston on February 16th 1946. The home side stung by their thrashing fielded five guest players including Lincoln City 'keeper Skelton. It was an exciting game with Town trailing 4-3 in the dying minutes when they were awarded a penalty. In the absence of Frank Soo or Johnny Hancocks it fell to left-winger White to take the kick. He had scored Town's first goal, but was destined never to score two in a game, his spot-kick was punched out by Skelton and he drove the second chance over the bar. The 20th game, the record had gone, Town lost 4-3.

The next game at the Meadow on the following Saturday was played on a surface of river silt. The Severn had been in full flood and a fortnight earlier an estimated **ten million** gallons of water lay on the ground. The National Fire Service had pumped off the last one million gallons but at its peak the water almost reached the crossbars. On this tricky surface Town went 2-0 ahead in 2 minutes through Jackie Butler and Richardson, Leverton pulled one back for Ollerton Colliery, and in fact completed a first half hat-trick, but by then Town led 5-3. Four more second half goals helped Bailey to a hat-trick, Maund from a hard-to-find penalty spot, and Joe Wheatley made it 9-3.

Despite surprising defeats at Denaby 2-1 and by 5-1 earlier at Barnsley, Town stayed on course for the title, but did not hit top spot again until winning over Denaby 6-0 and dismissing Frickley 7-2, before the crunch game. Town had dropped only one point all season at home, but Ransome and Marles, their big rivals ruined their record and won 1-0 at the Meadow on April 27th. Town only failed to score three times, on two occasions against Ransomes. An end of season double header, with Doncaster Rovers saw two victories. Town pipped their Newark opponents by one point to lift their second Midland League Championship. On both occasions - in 1938 and 1946, the decisive victory was on May 2nd.

Town's F.A.Cup run saw Bourneville beaten 6-2, and Walsall in the first round proper hammered 5-0 at the Meadow, but in the two leg tie they lost 4-1 at Fellows Park - it made Salop sweat! Wrexham then won 1-0 at the Meadow in front of 8,000, and although Town hit back at the Racecourse, a 1-1 draw saw Wrexham through. This was the season of the Burnden Park tragedy, with 33 killed and around 500 injured in the sixth round tie between Bolton and Stoke. A collection raised £58.11.0d to which Town Directors and staff added 70 guineas (over £73).

A charity match organised by the Hospital Charity Jazz Band Committee saw Town beat Aston Villa 2-1. Jackie Butler and Johnny Hancocks were on target in front of a crowd of 7,000 who paid £597.18.6d.

Town's young star Cyril Lello had been stationed at R.A.F. Coningsby and played for Lincoln City, in 1943-44 he hit 21 goals in 14 games, including matching Billy Richardson's seven against Notts County. Lincoln tried to buy him but Town refused.

The supporters club improvements to the ground continued, with Station End concreted in August, but on the field - without Billy Richardson - the chance of following the previous season's magnificent goal tally seemed fairly remote, despite the arrival of a centre-forward of international pedigree in Maxwell. Town also had Cyril Lello ready to claim a place, so even with a downpour the practice match attracted 3,000, with Lello and Girdham scoring for the Blues, and Maxwell and W.H.Rogers each hitting a brace for the Reds.

In fact in the first three games Town were unstoppable. Maxwell five, Jackie Butler and Cyril Lello (with three each), helped secure three convincing home victories. Town had made a successful start, but not quite as successful as Mr William Breeze of Waters Upton who won £8,073 on Littlewoods Penny Points with his forecasts for September 9th. A defeat at Peterborough was followed by three more victories, Maxwell scoring in all the first five games, but Jackie Butler hitting eleven in the first seven.

In fact after 26 games, Town had pulled in 39 points but then lost their way a little. Their biggest win was again against dear old Denaby, 8-1 at the Meadow. Town went ahead with a Jackie Butler penalty on 3 minutes - his third in successive games - Cyril Lello hit the second, Black added a third, and Butler and Philips made it 5-0 at half-time.

Roy Philips added a sixth, and then Town were awarded another penalty. Philips, keen to complete his hat-trick took it and scored, but Jackie Butler not to be outdone scored in the dying minutes as Town won 8-1; two hat-tricks each containing a penalty, a little unusual. Philips hit two more hat tricks in his 21 goals, while Jackie hit 35 goals including 7 penalties and 3 hat-tricks.

1945-46 season: Proud captain - Steve Hughes - with his twin daughters display the Midland League Championship trophy.

of Loughborough thrash Town 5-1, the Welsh Cup was more rewarding. A Jackie Butler penalty brought Bala back to the Meadow for a 9-1 thrashing, Lello and Philips hit hat-tricks. Oswestry fared little better in round five beaten, 8-2; Philips 3, Lello 2, Butler 2 and A.Hughes scoring Town's last goals in the competition. Round six saw Newport County visit the Meadow twice, first a goalless draw then a first half winner from County took the replay.

Not all was sweetness and light however, in January pleas for the lifting of the Iron Curtain round the Boardroom went unheeded as Bernard Streten's departing proved. His non-appearance was glossed over, but after being selected for England Amateurs verus Wales at Dulwich Hamlet it was admitted he had signed for Luton. Ostensibly due to his wife being, *"ordered South for health reasons"*.

In November Scunthorpe installed floodlights, so part-timers could train at night, while in May, Notts County played several first-teamers, but the Shrewsbury press were upset by the 5-1 defeat. They bemoaned the lack of the Meadow mud to slow down the game and help control, and accused Town of too much 'pretty-pretty-you-to-me-stuff' - good entertainment which doesn't get goals.

The harsh winter snow, ice and floods meant an unusually long season, with Town beating Wellington 3-1 in the Senior Cup Final on June 7th, while Rotherham United still had two League games to play by this date. Town finished sixth in the League, their hopes of retaining their title finally evaporated on April 30th at Gainsborough, when they lost 1-0 with ex-Town favourite Jimmy Harkin on the mark. The F.A. Cup had seen Brush Sports

The next season, 1947-48, started with a low key practice match, Greehalgh scored Blues goal in their 1-0 victory but the left-winger had little chance of dislodging Jackie Butler. Jackie's brothers, Billy - before the war - and Joe, after, also made appearances for Town teams.

The Iron curtain still existed with Town not informing the press of the capture of Ambrose Mulraney from Birmingham until half-time in the practice match. Another who did not play pre-season was Jack Davie, although he scored the first League goal as Town beat Bradford Park Avenue Reserves 3-1, but of all people Denaby United beat them 1-0 on the Meadow in the second match.

Town then won eight and drew one of their next nine games. That draw was to be significant, a home game with Scunthorpe, with whom Town seem almost twinned, and who were to be their rivals all season. Defeat at Ransome and Marles, a dropped home point in a 3-3 draw with York reserves, and Denaby completing the double were rare blemishes. Town set up an unbeaten home run of nineteen, including eleven consecutive victories, the second of which saw Town beat Boston 4-0, Roland Depear soon to move to Leeds was the opposition centre-half.

The F.A.Cup was to feature an epic fight, it started at Wellington, with a crowd of 10,500 at The Bucks Head, and a single Jock Sheen goal settled the tie. A 4-1 away win at Great Yarmouth then put Town up against Stockport County at Edgeley Park. Town had 3,500 fans in a crowd of 17,800, and it was a memorable performance. Jock Sheen limped off and was out of action for 20 minutes with an ankle injury. Jack Davie gave Town the lead, Tom Barkas missed a penalty but then later equalised. The game was played in gathering fog, but went into extra time. Town keeper, Harry Rowley, was knocked unconscious making a brave save and Eddie Hapgood went in goal. The former Arsenal international produced some good saves and with eight minutes of extra time remaining the fog caused an early end. One Town follower covered her eyes every time Stockport attacked in the first half, saying: *"Oh no, here they come again"*, but not realising the change round continued the action when Town threatened in the second half! Town came from behind in the replay, watched by 13,489, with Sheen and Argue scoring, and again extra time was needed, but the deadlock remained.

The second replay at Maine Road was another close run thing. Again Stockport scored first, but Philips and Butler made it 2-2 by full time so 12,812 people again witnessed extra time and this time County found the vital goal. Over 44,000 had witnessed the epic trilogy, and it no doubt helped advance Town's League ambitions. Winning trophies would add to their claims. The League season was continuing well and an attack on the Welsh Cup was launched.

Exempt to round five, Town beat Troedrhiw 6-3 before receiving a bye in round six. A trip to Bangor City went to extra time but was settled by Jackie Butler's second goal. The semi-final, against Barry Town, was played at Merthyr Tydfil and two second half goals put Town through 3-1. The final, at Wrexham, was a keenly contested affair with Town taken to extra time for the fifth time in the season. Their opponents, Lovells Athletic, broke Salop's resilience with three unanswered overtime goals in front of 12,000.

So it was all eyes on the championship. Early April was a bad time, with successive away defeats at Scunthorpe, Hull and Peterborough, and all without Town scoring. A 2-2 draw at Boston steadied the

ship, and back to back 3-0 wins over Gainsborough Trinity and Frickley Colliery, all three games featuring Jackie Butler penalties, put Town back in the driving seat. Victory over Notts County Reserves on April 24th would clinch the title. It was achieved in controversial style, with the Notts 'keeper Mowl fumbling a Jock Sheen shot, and the linesman flagging for a goal which County hotly disputed, it stood, and proved to be the winner. Town beat Grimsby 2-1 and Ollerton Colliery 4-2 on the Monday and Tuesday, and finished seven points clear of Scunthorpe, their biggest ever margin of supremacy.

The champions versus runners-up game was surprisingly held at Scunthorpe, on May 1st, because the Midland League executive decided Scunthorpe was more central to the spread of clubs. Domestically, Town failed to add to their success, losing the Senior Cup final to Oswestry 4-2, and the Mayor's Charity Cup to Wellington 4-3, thanks to a Hopley inspired winner.

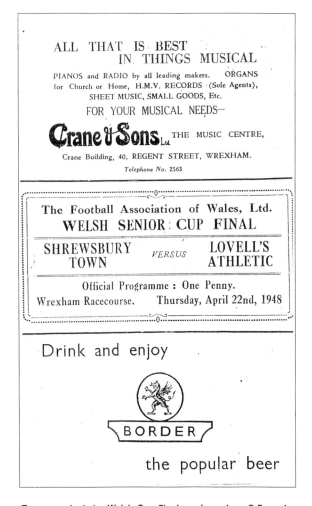

Town reached the Welsh Cup Final - only to lose 0-3 to the strong war-time works team from Newport, Monmouth.

THE AFTERMATH

Champions three times in five Midland League seasons, Town fans were used to success, but 1948-49 was not about to add to it. Things even went wrong in the practice match, the probables crashed 3-0 to the possibles. Jackie Butler, two, and Jock Sheen scored, and forced their way back into the team. Centre-forward Jones and Jock Sheen hit a brace each in the 4-4 draw with York City Reserves at the Meadow. Harry Rowley returned in goal for the trip to Denaby, but Town were 3-0 down at half-time, fortunately a more even second half meant no further damage. Steve Hughes missed his only game of the season at home to Rotherham Reserves, Town winning 3-2 with Jones and Sheen (two) again the scorers. Another 3-0 defeat at Scunthorpe was followed by two home victories - 4-2 over Frickley (Sheen hat-trick), and 5-0 - but the season was a real 'win-some-lose-some' affair.

For the fans, used to their side winning, it was upsetting and when on October 9th Town lost to Nottingham Forest 3-0 on the Meadow it was their first home defeat in 25 games and 2,000 fans walked out in disgust in the second half. Things were obviously not too happy in the corridors of power, George Oakley had resigned in August due to *"business and other calls"*, and in October Jimmy Fulwood and Frank Palmer both resigned with P.S.Tucker being co-opted. In the close season Town had signed V.Robinson (W.B.A.), Dennis Kirby (Leeds), John McCall (Bradford Park Avenue), and John Johnson (Grimsby), but all were missing when the F.A.Cup trip to Witton Albion arrived in November. Witton, a Cheshire League side, should not have been an impossible task but the Chronicle reflected the lack of confidence, *"for the first time in many years, Shrewsbury Town approached this first hurdle in the English F.A. Cup competition, with little hope of clearing it. Indeed 90% of the supporters who travelled to Northwich to see the Town meet Witton Albion, did so with the thought that some Cup-tie freak might give Shrewsbury a lead they could keep!'* No such luck, result:- Witton Albion 4 - Shrewsbury Town 0.

There was an outbreak of chanting caused by unrest at Witton. With the threat of an Extraordinary General Meeting, concern was at sufficient level for the supporters club to send a letter to the Directors enquiring about the problems. One small glimmer of hope came on Thursday November 18th, Western Command beating Scottish Command 6-4 after extra time, with Ivor Allchurch scoring for the winners.

Town stepped in, and two days later Allchurch made his debut in the 2-1 victory over Denaby.

Results did not improve dramatically so the frustration kept simmering, and in the programme for the home game with Grantham on January 8th, manager Leslie Knighton hit back at his critics. Town drew 3-3, with Ivor Allchurch scoring his first League goal (he had scored in the 5-1 friendly defeat at Carlisle for whom Ivor Broadis scored one). The Welsh Cup gave no respite, losing 1-0 at holders Lovells Athletic.

Manager Knighton signed Ken Holland from Bournemouth, but also announced his retirement at the end of the season. The club had around 30 applications for the position of secretary-manager but many fans preferred a player-manager. Two months later the appointment of Harry Chapman (Nephew of Herbert) - the chief scout of Hull - was announced, and the crowd started hoping for a player-coach. The away game at Bradford City was abandoned due to a half-time snowstorm on March 5th.

The frustration of the season spilled over on March 19th, at the end of the 2-2 home draw with Lincoln. Referee Walker of Sheffield, who had earned much displeasure during the game, and had cautioned Roy Philips, took out his notebook to skipper Steve Hughes. An unruly element seeing this, surrounded the referee, and as police rescued the official, blows were struck.

The first weekend in April, saw Town play Grimsby away on the Saturday, and Goole on the Monday. The team - accompanied by both Leslie Knighton and Harry Chapman - led 1-0 at half-time in both games, but lost both 2-1. A fortnight later Town did win the Senior Cup, 2-1 over Oswestry, but even this was a poor game. Mr Chapman was obviously unimpressed, for he signed David Robinson from Manchester United, Harry Potter from Winsford United, Kenneth Harper from Hindsford, Frank Griffin from Manchester junior side St. Augustines and Charles McNeil. Only McNeil failed to survive to the League season. Trials were also offered to the Herrick brothers, but Steve Hughes - skipper for four years - went to Worksop as player-manager.

The annual trip to the League vote was again disappointing, Town polled five votes as did Gillingham and Worcester, while Scunthorpe managed four, Merthyr three and Yeovil, who had beaten Bury and Sunderland in the Cup, two. There was talk of a third Division being formed from the combination of the top half of the North and South Divisions and a Fourth Division North and South. It did not happen, but one League extended, the Shrewsbury and District added a third division.

In July the Royal Show was held at Sundorne Castle Estate, on a site covering 115 acres. It was its fourth and final visit to Shrewsbury (the first in 1845 was the last to a town lacking rail communications). The Duke and Duchess of Gloucester, along with the Princess Royal opened the first day, but the highlight was Princess Elizabeth and the Duke of Edinburgh the following day.

FROM HULL AND BACK

Harry Chapman was obviously an excellent chief scout, for he brought several players to the Gay Meadow who would prove beneficial to their League career, most notably Frank Griffin and Arnold Jackson. Jackson came on as substitute for the Maroons in the second half of the pre-season practice match, they won 7-2 over Blues, with Glyn Vaughan hitting a hat-trick; Arnold scored one.

The team started promisingly enough, four wins, and a draw at Scunthorpe, in the first five matches. Ron Hood and Arnold Bonell along with Dudley Kernick, had signed just prior to the season and all scored in the opening games. With the board looking more settled, after a 6 from 6 vote on St. Swithan's Day, which recruited T.Harold Davies of Berriew, and Frank Weston of Bishop Street, the problems of the previous season seemed a long way off.

In fact they were just round the corner, just one win in eight games, and Town were back in mid-table. Jimmy Veacock was signed from Ellesmere Port Town in mid-September, but Town lost at Scarborough on his debut to slip off top spot, and despite the opening goal of the victory 3-0 over Frickley Colliery, he never really established himself. The manager sold his son, Reg, to Hereford and Leonard Robertson joined Kidderminster, but things did not improve. The Council were also discussing the burning issue of the day, whether to site a crematorium on Berwick Road, the objections were lead by Leslie Tudor Owen.

The heat was definitely on at Bromsgrove in the F.A. Cup, two Arnold Jackson goals put Town 2-1 ahead at half-time, but Rovers hit four unanswered second half strikes, and Town were out of the Cup. The Chronicle reported: *"Bromsgrove's long passes, first time shooting and sudden forward rushes, that never looked like good football but were often effective"*. Town signed the experienced Stanley Scrimshaw from Halifax, but after eight games he picked up an injury, a shame as Town had won five and drawn two since his inclusion.

In late January Town signed Freddie Pye, but not for long, he made his debut in the Reserves 3-1 defeat at Halesowen, Harry Rowley injured a shoulder in this game, went off, but came back as an outfield player, and converted a penalty. February started with a 6-1 (Arnold Jackson hat-trick) thrashing of Goole, but two weeks later Town lost the return 4-0. March featured four defeats, three by four goals (6-2 twice and 4-0), and manager Harry Chapman - amidst rumours of interference - announced he was not willing to renew his contract. It needed something exceptional to make March 1950 memorable for the right reasons, on March 27th it happened.

The Football League met in London and arranged to extend the Third Division by four clubs, although the meeting was in secret. However, at the time few Town players were not showing anything approaching League form, even so one fan was heard to remark, *"the Gay Meadow does not look dressed unless Joe Wheatley and Jackie Butler are on the ground"*. On April 26th they certainly were, as a Football League XI played Shrewsbury Town as a benefit to these two stalwarts.

The League XI consisted:
Bernard Streten (Luton), Joe Wade (Arsenal), Doug Farquahar (Arsenal), Billy Wright (Wolves), Reg Foulkes (Walsall), George Antonio (Mansfield), Johnny Hancocks (Wolves), Noel Kelly (Arsenal), Billy Richardson (WBA), Alec James (Arsenal), Bob Barker (WBA),
Town's line-up was:
H.Rowley, Hornby (Crewe), Lewis, Kernick, Hodson (Crewe), Robinson, Griffin, Hood, Jackson, McCall, Butler.

Joe Wheatley, who was suffering from Tonsillitis, kicked off but was unable to play, the game ended 2-1 to the League select. Bob Barker earning himself a contract with Town, by scoring both goals, one direct from a corner, Ron Hood in his last appearance scored Town's goal, in front of 9,000.

Harry Chapman ended as he began, on a good run - three wins and a draw, before returning to Hull City as chief scout.

_____

CHAPTER 6 - PROMOTION

The feeling, that, after their worst ever Midland League season - they finished tenth - Town were on the verge of their greatest moment, was gaining impetus. On April 21st, well known local newsagent, and long-time Town fan, Edwin Gregory, offered to donate £100 to launch a fund. The money was to be payable if matched by 24 others and if Town were elected to the League, this led to the setting up of the fund for Division Three. Mr E.Bate was appointed Chairman, Mr W.Corfield, Treasurer, while A.C.Sykes and A.C.Williams represented the Chamber of Commerce, W.A.Reade and 'Happy' Sheldon the L.V.A plus Sam Powell, E.G.Lambert, E.Duffill, E.S.Cooper, S.H.Jenks and F.W.G.Morris from the supporters club with power to co-opt.

On May 22nd, Sammy Crooks who had started his League career with Durham City in 1926, was appointed Town secretary-manager. He started work the next day in the full expectation of guiding a fledgling Football League club, something which

would be decided in only eleven days. The League had to select two sides from: Ashington, Bangor City, Nelson, North Shields, Northwich Victoria, Scunthorpe and Lindsey United, Shrewsbury Town, South Liverpool, Wigan Athletic and Workington.

Shrewsbury sailed through with 30 votes but Wigan and Workington tied for second on 19, with Scunthorpe in fourth having polled 17. Nelson managed 11 and South Liverpool and Northwich Victoria 1 each. However, after a further ballot it was, as expected, Scunthorpe who joined Town in the Third Division North.

Town had retained Edwin Rowley, Harry Potter, Norman Lewis, Joe Wheatley, Ken Harper, David Robinson, Gordon Herrick, Harry Hewitt, Frank Griffin, Eric Dale, Arnold Jackson, Roy Herrick, and Jackie Butler. While Sammy Crooks made Roland Depear his first professional signing in early July, with Harry Smale and Bobby Brown following a week later.

SOUVENIR PROGRAMME

3d.

The Benefit match for two Town Stalwarts - Joe Wheatley and Jack Butler.

The football club was not the only centre of sporting excellence at this time, for at London Road, Shropshire played Warwickshire and a crowd of 6,000 turned up. Former Town manager, Ted Boustead, recorded figures of 11 overs, 2 Maidens, 39 runs, and no wickets, and when the counties ninth wicket fell in the last over, he defied Eric Hollies, without breaking his duck, to save the game.

Meanwhile the current Town manager, despite a 500 Guineas contribution from the Directors, was struggling to sign a goalkeeper. Manchester United's Ignatius Feehan, better known as Sonny, joined Northampton instead of Town, and it was not until the week before the season, that he secured Pat Egglestone from Halifax. The press felt Town would need a Gluckstein or a Needler, in retrospect Charlton and Hull fans may not agree.

The popular (River) side entrance fee was priced at 1/6d (7½p). The practice match ended 7-0 while

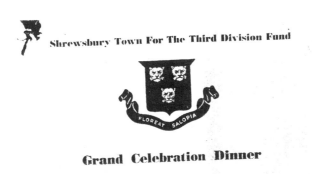

Shrewsbury Town For The Third Division Fund

FLOREAT SALOPIA

Grand Celebration Dinner

Morris's Cafe
Pride Hill
Shrewsbury

Monday
July 24th
1950

No. 2.

MONDAY, AUGUST 21st, 1966

SHREWSBURY TOWN F.C. LTD.

Official Programme

THE GAY MEADOW, SHREWSBURY. Tel. 5027

President: HARRY A. JONES, Esq
Chairman: Mr. B. D. J. Hayes   Vice-Chairman: Mr. C. L. Rawside
Directors:
Messrs. W. C. Allen, T. Davies, L. W. Drew, J. W. A. Jones, L. T. Owen, B. Russell, R. Tucker, G. F. G. Tudor, J.P., F. Weston, J.P., A. E. Williams.
Secretary-Manager: S. D. CROOKS.
Finance Secretary: W. NORMAN BRADFORD.
Hon. Medical Officer: Dr. J. Millard Bryson, M.A., M.B., B.Ch.

WELCOME TO THE LEAGUE

We are more than pleased to have as our visitors for Shrewsbury Town's first home match in the Third Division our old friends and rivals from Wrexham. When Wrexham gained admission to the League many years ago they soon showed that a club from the Welsh border could hold its own in English League football. Now Shrewsbury has come along to reinforce the Western contingent, and we have every confidence that the Town will acquit itself with credit.

It is no exaggeration to say that football supporters all over England and Wales will be looking out to see how Shrewsbury Town fares against the experienced side from over the border. Team building in a limited time has not been an easy task, but Sammy Crooks has done his best, with the support of the directors, and the result you see before you today.

It remains for supporters to give the necessary encouragement to the team. They will have ninety minutes of good football and must not be backward in showing their appreciation. Let the players who appear for the first time before you know that they are welcome. We want to develop the team spirit, and in this the crowd can help as much as the players.

And when you go away, after seeing a hard, clean game, make up your minds to come and bring your friends to see the Town play Lincoln City next Saturday.

PRICE 2d.

PRICE 2d.

among the multitude of amateurs signed was 19 year-old Ronald Harold Boxley, son of Harry Boxley our 1913 forward.

Finally the big day arrived, Saturday August 19th, and it was fitting that the 'new boys' should meet, but Town set off without too much expectancy behind them according to the local press. It was pointed out that Scunthorpe had not only finished 15 points clear of Town the previous season, but had also invested a five figure sum in the transfer market.

Therefore the goalless draw achieved in front of 11,847, by - Egglestone, Fisher, Lewis, Wheatley, Depear, Robinson, Griffin, Hope, Jackson, Brown and Barker - was hailed as a notable victory. So when on the Monday night, the Gay Meadow witnessed Wrexham succumb 2-1, goals from Arnold Jackson and Frank Griffin, to the League newcomers, expectations were suddenly sky high. *"No better than the Midland League"*, was an early judgement.

Shrewsbury Town had arrived, well not quite, for seven consecutive defeats followed, producing just 3 goals and seeing 17 conceded, what had gone wrong?

The euphoria caused by the Wrexham match, which at the time was only tempered by the chaos of trying to gain entrance to the ground, had soon disappeared (the official attendance was 16,070 of which 15,298 actually went through the turnstiles - but local legend says over 20,000 attended). The problem with the team was identified as the half-backs. Right-half Joe Wheatley was dropped after game seven, left-half Dave Robinson two games later, and apart from a single appearance by Robinson, on the left-wing, in the final League game, neither appeared again. This was a particularly sad end for Joe Wheatley, a favourite with the crowd, whose skilful play just seems to have lacked that extra pace demanded by League football.

Having identified the problem, Sammy Croocks set about putting matters right. His solution - Ron Crutchley, a craggy left-half from Walsall, and Jimmy Bullions, signed from Leeds, but a former teammate of the manager at Derby. They were to prove vital cogs in Town establishing themselves in the Football League, between them playing over 270 League games. The effect was immediate, Town thrashed Hartlepools United 1-0, while neither missed another game that season.

The nucleus of the side was emerging, goalkeeper Pat Egglestone, centre-half and captain Roland Depear plus inside-left Bobby Brown were ever-presents. Frank Griffin and Arnold Jackson, along with Crutchley and Bullions managed 37 appearances. The full-backs revolved around Peter Fisher, Norman Lewis and Harry Potter, although Harry Smale also made nine appearances. Smale's first appearance was as centre-forward at Darlington where, he notched Town's first away goal. The night before that game the players went to the Darlington Hippodrome and bumped into the New Brighton Team; one trusts the performance was better than their own the following day, for both teams lost.

The following Tuesday, Town, *"looking like a lot of Robin Redbreasts"*, lost 5-0 at Rochdale. The conjecture was that, having been forced to play in red, Town still passed to the players in blue (Rochdale), and were confused. The theory evaporated six days later as Town, in blue, lost 2-0 to Rochdale at the Meadow.

The club's new found prominence led to a feature on BBC radio, 'Town topic', featuring the team which was recorded on September 20th, and three days later 'the big one' - Town v Hartlepools United, was reported on, for 'Sport in the Midlands'. In spite of these developments supporters were restless at the Board's complacency, however, a fine draw at Carlisle raised spirits. It was Cyril Treherne's debut, where he not only scored - ironically his only League goal - but 'stiffened the front line'. Victory was denied when Roly Depear was harshly adjudged to have handled, a penalty decision which left.... *"the sporting Carlisle fans dismayed"*.

A fortnight later, Town recorded their first away win, 2-1 at Southport, albeit slightly fortunately. Southport's former Wellington Town right-half, Trevor Hitchen, crashed in a shot, which swerved over Pat Egglestone's hands and hit him in the face. The force knocked him out, but the play was at the other end when he 'came to'. Town skipper, Depear, claims Pat said, *"look Roly no hands"*, but in fact it was nearly 'look Roly no teeth'. Treherne again impressed and after the game signed part-time, however, the next Saturday's draw with Oldham was his final first team match.

The other aspiring young striker was Billy Dodd. He had made one appearances, at home to Rochdale, before returning on Armistice Day, at Bradford Park Avenue. Arnold Jackson was ill, so Dodd took over at inside-right with Eric Hope replacing Treherne at centre-forward. It was a potent mixture and Bobby Brown scored the Town's first League hat-trick, with Eric Hope adding another goal, as Salop won 4-2. A week later another victory, this time over York, lifted Town off the bottom rung. A 1-0 success over Gateshead, completed a hat-trick of wins, something Sammy Crooks had to wait until April 1954 to repeat - two games before he left the club.

On December 9th, Town met Walsall as a League club for the first time. It was only a friendly, but Town, 3-1 down at half-time, staged a rousing comeback to draw 3-3. A week later a 3-1 victory over Scunthorpe lifted the team to 15th. It was to be their zenith, for two Christmas defeats put them back in the bottom six. A new spark was needed, especially after the New Year started with an abortive trip to Valley Parade, Bradford, where 'no match' signs, and a pitch covered in ice greeted the team. The spark arrived in the form of Ted Gorin, who made his debut, just a fortnight before his 27th birthday, against Halifax. Goals from Bobby Brown and Jackie Butler, plus a clean sheet by Pat

Egglestone against his old club, set up a victory repeated against Bradford City seven days later. Gorin with 12 goals in 26 appearances for Scunthorpe cost a club record fee of around £3,000. Much was expected, sadly for all, little happened.

Mid-February saw one possible solution to the club's problems. Sammy Crooks, just passed his 43rd Birthday, played in a 3-1 victory over Western Command; Jackson 2 and Brown scored in front of 5,000. However, on the same day, one player who slipped through the net, earned rave reports - Keith Thomas, who played in trial matches for Town, starred for Sheffield Wednesday against Wolves. The Four Crosses winger had been sold to Wednesday by Oswestry for £3,000, and went on to play for Cardiff, Plymouth and Exeter.

On March 16th, 'Midlight', in the Chronicle wrote under a headline of *"Form suggests win for Town tomorrow"*; result Shrewsbury Town 1 - Southport 5. It could have been worse, for half-back Hitchen was again thwarted, having a goal ruled out for offside. The only memorable moment for home supporters was Ron Crutchley's late consolation goal, his only strike in 146 League games. Town bounced back to win at Crewe on Good Friday, but lost to Oldham and Crewe in the return over Easter. One player who had lost form, was Billy Dodd. The youngster had made his debut against Rochdale in the September aged just 17 years and 17 days, but dropped to the reserves in early April. He was described as playing *"with the vivacity of a super annuated Civil Servant"*. At this time Grimsby and Chesterfield were nose diving out of Division Two, so Town looked likely to become the new shuttlecock and be bounced into the Southern Section.

On April 14th, Ted Gorin scored a brilliant goal to beat Barrow at the Gay Meadow. It was his first strike and was also Frank Griffin's final game before his transfer to West Bromwich for a substantial fee. Incidentally, Barrow's club masseur was former Town defender Alf Miller. Town's penultimate home game saw Mansfield awarded two penalties both against Peter Fisher, first for a tackle - Pat Egglestone saved - then for a harsh handball when the ball was driven at him, and he tried to protect himself. The second was converted and the game ended 1-1.

The final game of the season looked uninteresting, when Walter Galbraith brought New Brighton to the Meadow. Ted Gorin scored two - his other Town strikes - and Town won 4-2. It was to be New Brighton's final ever League game, and Town's last in the Third Division North. Town did pick up one new trophy, the Herefordshire Senior Cup, beating Hereford 3-1 at Edgar Street, with a goal each for Ted Gorin, Bobby Brown and Arnold Jackson. In the absence of a trophy cabinet, it was displayed in Tommy Seymour's hostelry, the Royal Vaults, at the top of the Cop.

Fourteen players were retained, Jackie Butler was added to the groundstaff, Bobby Barker transfer-listed and Edwin Rowley, Joe Wheatley, Ken Harper, Dave Robinson, Cyril Treherne, Eric Dale and the Herrick brothers given free transfers.

Town played a Festival of Britain game against Dundalk losing 2-1 after Sammy Crooks equalised. Two interesting amateur signings were brothers Eric and Derek Price, but controversy reigned in May as Town director W.C.Allen walked out of a Shropshire F.A. meeting in a dispute over whether the senior club representatives were full members of the council. Town pointed out that on page 4 of the F.A. handbook, Mr Allen was listed as a full member, and rule six stated each senior club was allowed one full member on the council, but the dispute continued.

The absence of any mention of the F.A.Cup, was due to Town not entering, as they felt they could not afford the financial implications. Having not won a F.A.Cup tie since 1947, they would have faced four Saturday qualifying games in order to reach Round one. Already faced with four extra League games, they decided it would be impractical, and costly, as teams who were forced to have Saturday League fixtures rearranged were entitled to compensation - for subsequent smaller midweek gates - from the side causing the postponement.

Surprisingly Town received a cheque off the F.A. from the Cup pool even though they did not enter!

BY HOOK OR BY CROOKS

No-one could doubt that Sammy Crooks faced a difficult job when he accepted the task of guiding Town's first steps in League football. His main method of making the transition was to bank on experience, and his only visible youth policy was to subtract three or four years off the age of several of his new signings. Typical of this was the arrival in June 1951 of Birmingham City left-winger Harold Roberts, he left 'Brum' aged 31½ and arrived at the Meadow aged 27! He cost Town a new record

£4,000, as did Jimmy Ayton an inside-right from Leicester, and soon after Town secured full-back Joe Thompson from Luton.

Financially Town's first season had been a big success, they reported a profit of £2,287 and paid a dividend of 7½%, also the Third Division fighting fund, of £3,150, remained untouched, due to the excellent support; the average home gate was 9,096. Several of the Town squad were useful cricketers, as they displayed when beating Kenwood C.C. easily. Pat Egglestone hit 40 not out and took 3-10, Tommy Seymour hit 27, Roly Depear 19 not out (including 4 fours), Harry Potter took 4 for 7, Arnold Jackson 2-14, and Billy Dodd 1-21.

Just before the season started Town recruited Tommy Halpin from Bury and Albert Collins from Bournemouth, but neither featured in the early games. The club also announced, they were not going to participate in the Senior Cup, and were sending the Shropshire F.A. £25, in lieu of not playing, but the F.A. queried the 'right of withdrawal'.

Town again made a poor start, with just one win and one draw in seven opening games. This time the spotlight fell on the full-backs, Joe Thompson and Peter Fisher, and after six games both were dropped, with Harry Potter and Norman Lewis taking over. Also replaced after just five games was Martin Reagan, but he was unavailable due to a 'Z' (military) call-up. Albert Collins took over the right-wing slot, at home to Walsall - Town lost 2-1. Lewis and Potter started at Norwich where a 3-2 defeat continued the slump. Town then faced the return with Walsall, where they recorded their best away win over their local rivals. Collins twice, Bobby Brown, and a rare Jimmy Bullions goal made it a 4-0 scoreline. It was to start a run of five unbeaten games including four victories, ended by a home defeat against Southend. The week after Albert Collins was made captain for the trip to his old club, Bournemouth. Town lost 2-0, Collins was disappointing and never played for Town again in a League game.

On October 18th, Eric Hope, who had made just one appearance, and Peter Fisher, went to Wrexham in exchange for Robert Williams and Eddie Beynon, and the following month Fred Ashworth arrived from Blackburn.

Town went to Leytonstone in the Cup, but a side containing 6 amateur internationals proved too strong for them, with a giant centre-half called Hockaday outstanding as the Londoners won 2-0. A fortnight later Town travelled to Northampton, who had just signed Coventry 'keeper Alf Wood. He had an easy day, Town lost 6-0 with centre-forward Adam McCulloch scoring two. It was Town's biggest defeat in the League, at that time. The three ever-presents of the first season had still not missed a game, but that record was soon to change.

Bobby Brown missed the Boxing Day game with Newport County, Pat Egglestone was dropped after the 6-1 defeat at Plymouth. Brown had made 69 consecutive appearances, Egglestone 71 but Roland Depear had the longest run and the quickest demise.

Due to a shortage of power at centre-forward, Sammy Crooks asked his obliging skipper to lead the line. At Exeter on January 19th 1952, Roland Depear made his 74th consecutive appearances, scored Town's opening goal in six minutes, and never played League football again. He was still slightly bemused by his manager's actions 40 years later, when he recalled that he knew he was not the long-term answer up front, but felt he could still have continued as a defender. He was not bitter, in fact as player-manager of Bangor City, he recommended players to his former club. Pat Egglestone, after a two game break, returned and went on to be the first Town player to make 100 appearances.

Stan Hall's New Year plea in the Wellington Journal was, *"let us have a more direct policy with one object in view - the quickest and easiest way to goal - and that is best achieved by making the ball do the work, with the players moving into the open spaces"*.

Town manager Sammy Crooks was travelling the country looking to pep up his attack. He almost signed Millwall striker Jimmy Constantine in time for Town's trip to Watford on January 12th. The move was put on hold and while Town lost 4-1 at Vicarage Road, Constantine - 100 goals in 191 League games - broke his collar bone in Millwall Reserves. Another forward causing concern was Jimmy Ayton who displayed a, *"tendency for temperamental demonstrations towards his teammates"*. So it was with some relief, that Salop completed the signing of Adam McCulloch, for a club record fee, in time for their game with Swindon on Thursday January 24th. It was not a dream debut, for Town lost 1-0. Eddie Beynon returned to the attack for the next match, a 1-0 home win over Colchester, and it started a memorable run of ten matches unbeaten.

True, Town drew seven of the fixtures, but Sammy Crooks who had travelled 5,000 miles looking at forwards must have been relatively pleased. However, the slump in attendances due to the previous poor run meant concern at Town's bank balance, and this with a squad of 23 professionals. It was slightly alleviated when Ted Gorin, now a reserve team regular, joined Lovell's Athletic to be near his widowed mother.

On February 27th, Oswestry became the first Shropshire side to play under floodlights, losing 5-1 at Kidderminster. While on March 8th, the Gay Meadow hosted an amateur international, which England won 8-3 over Eire. J.Fitzgerald, Hennessey and D.Fitzgerald scored for the Irish; Noble 4, Lewis 2, Fullam and George Robb netted for England, in front of 9,174.

Meanwhile in London, Town played Millwall, and Stan Hall wrote: *"If and when the history of Shrewsbury Town FC is ever written a thrilling chapter should be devoted to their glorious feat at the Den, Millwall, on Saturday, when they confounded the critics and wrecked the football pools by forcing a goalless draw!"* Town, facing one of the Division's top promotion contenders in hostile surroundings, lost hard man Ron Crutchley with a knee ligament injury on 23 minutes but held out. (Sorry, it was not a chapter Stan!).

The injury ended the Bullions Crutchley partnership after 73 games, and Jackie Butler wore the No.6 shirt for the rest of the season. It was to be a relatively promising end to the season, apart from a 4-1 loss at Leyton Orient and a 3-0 reverse at Bristol City, the only defeats by more than one goal in the last eighteen games, although it could have been worse; Pat Egglestone saved two penalties at Ashton Gate.

Town again won the Senior Cup, beating Wellington 2-1 at the Bucks Head in front of 9,599. Reagan and Jackson scored, Fletcher replied. While the final saw Reagan - twice - and McCulloch set up a 3-1 victory over Oswestry, with Kelly their marksman, watched by 10,256. All this occurred after the Football Association made Town participate.

Town's reserves, playing in the Birmingham League, used no less than 53 players. Harry Smale and Albert Leach - the 'keeper who dented Egglestone's record - made most appearances but both departed, Smale going to Aldershot. Promising young striker Michael Picken, defender Ron Manders and the Price brothers all played, Derek Price only once as he was stationed in the South of Scotland in the Army, while Eric missed a lot of the season with a cartlidge operation.

1952-53 pre-season photo call

CUP GLORY

As usual there was much activity pre-season. A new goalkeeper, Wilf Birkett, defenders Jimmy Bannister, Ken Booker, Pat Comerford, wingers Freddy Fisher and Jimmy Bradley and striker John Clowes all arrived. While Roly Depear moved to Bangor, Albert Collins to Accrington, and Jimmy Ayton, who turned down a League club, went to Bedford. The most significant amateur recruited was Stan Keery from Wilmorton. Martin Reagan, who refused his new contract but signed a week later, had spent the summer playing cricket for Cathedral.

The supporters club continued to expand with branches formed in Ludlow, Ironbridge, Madeley and Church Stretton. They faced higher admission charges though; ground up 3d (1¼p), enclosure 6d (2½p), stand 1/- (5p). Main stand, stand A, season tickets rose from £4.15.0 (£4.75) to £6.10.0 (£6.50).

The annual meeting heard that Shrewsbury had their biggest ever professional staff, 29, and having spent £13,000 on players in the previous year, they reported a loss of £9,708. A shareholders association had been formed, and club chairman Bernard Hayes was concerned it would damage the supporters club, *"one of the finest bodies of men possible to find"*, who had raised £10-12,000 for the club. A.C.Williams twice challenged the Chair, and Frank Leath the share-holders secretary deprecated what the chairman had said.

On the field, Blues with goals from Beynon and Jackson beat Whites 2-0 in front of only 4,674. The first League game, at Bristol Rovers, with Michael Picken as 12th Man, saw Town lose 2-1 after leading at the half-time. The Reserves played Boldmere St. Michael with Graham Gaut, aged just 15, as 12th man in front of 3,163. Unusually the first team were identical to the Blues line-up in the practice match, and the Reserves to the Whites.

Fred Ashworth was injured at Bristol, and Ken Booker made his debut in the next game - at home versus Brighton - but two games later it was almost all change. Ashworth returned for the injured Booker, and so did Bobby Brown, while Pat Comerford, young Stan Keery and Jimmy Bradley all made their debuts, for Bradley it was also his last appearance. The diminutive Keery had made great strides and after two games on the right-wing switched to inside-right, and scored in the 3-1 victory over Watford. Freddy Fisher, on his debut, also scored in Town's first win of the season.

Two days later, disaster! Shrewsbury Town 1 - Norwich City 8, still the club's record League defeat at home, Tom Johnston, of the withered arm, hit four, and Pat Egglestone was close to tears.

The chopping and changing continued, as Town gave trials to two defenders. Wally Quinton played three matches but declined an extension to his month's trial, while Frank Wood left halfway through his allotted stay. Stan Keery continued his meteoric rise, and despite Town losing nine of his fifteen games, was snapped up by Newcastle for a record five figure fee. Keery's last game was the 3-1 defeat at Northampton which was also Wilf Birkett's debut. Birkett, a reliable 'keeper, was hard of hearing but was to play an important role in Town's memorable cup run. Having not won a F.A.Cup-tie for five years, Town set off to Loftus Road more in hope than expectation, especially as Q.P.R. had already won 3-0 at the Meadow. Two first half goals from Cameron seemed to quantify their doubts, but Bobby Brown's header from Martin Reagan's corner, 10 minutes after the re-start, and a Jackie Butler penalty four minutes later for handball after a flowing move, forced a replay.

In the replay, a route one goal - Birkett's kick, flicked on by McCulloch, and finished by Arnold Jackson - put Town into an early lead, but they again trailed at the interval. Never say die, Martin Reagan levelled after a Bobby Brown shot was parried. Villa Park was the venue of the second replay, and this time Town stormed to victory. Lewis' lovely pass to Reagan, on to Brown, a 1-2 with McCulloch - 1-0 on 7 minutes. Fisher on left centres Jackson's header - 2-0. Reagan felled when about to shoot, Butler penalty - 3-0 all before half-time. Midway through the second half Fisher closed in to make it four, and although Smith hit a consolation, Town were through.

Jimmy Banister's old team, Chesterfield, were next, and a goalless draw at home meant a trip to Saltergate. Two fine goals put Town ahead. First McCulloch passed to Reagan, who centred for Jackson to set-up Bobby Brown. Then Reagan to McCulloch, centre to Brown, a neat backheel, and Fisher netted. Chesterfield hit back, levelling before half-time, and dominated until midway through the second half. Lewis cleared to Brown who, *"danced past three men before selling a dummy and with a Brown drive of old hit a delightful shot into the corner of the net"*. It was a goal worthy of winning a game, but Martin Reagan using pace and power made it 4-2 near the end.

Three days later, on an obvious high, town hit their record League score hammering Southend 7-1 with Fred Ashworth's only goal starting the rout. Pat Egglestone, recalled for the Christmas double header with Millwall, sadly conceded four in each game. They were to be his final appearances and brought his League total to 109, before, on January 30th he joined Wrexham. Another leaving was Martin Reagan who on New Years Eve was sold to Portsmouth for £13-15,000. He possessed blistering pace, and some said unkindly he was more danger-ous without the ball, but he was to stay in the game until the 1990's, as the England women's team manager.

The third round of the Cup on January 10th saw Town pitted against Finchley. A ground record 16,277 turned up to see the tie and all eyes were on Finchley winger George Robb - destined for Spurs - who had scored in the amateur international on the Meadow the previous March. But it was Town winger Harold Roberts who stole the glory, with a header and a penalty. It was Town's first home F.A. Cup victory since 1945. On the following Thursday, Salop visited Walsall and although behind four times earned a 4-4 draw, with Adam McCulloch completing his hat trick in injury time. The next day John McBride was signed from Reading and Jimmy Bradley went back to Scotland. The glamour of a home draw with Southampton on January 31st meant Town's first ever all-ticket match. All tickets were sold in one hour, with 5,000 written applications and claims that 30,000 tickets could have been sold. On the day 17,249 packed the ground and Town did well. Goalless at half-time, but Wilf Birkett had picked up a back injury, which would keep him out for 3 weeks. He continued, but despite Arnold Jackson equalising within a minute of Southampton's opener, the visitors ran out 4-1 winners.

Birkett's injury meant a debut for John McBride the following Thursday, when a Bobby Brown goal beat Walsall, and another clean sheet set up a 3-0 win over Colchester, but in his third game at Aldershot he broke his right arm. Norman Lewis went in goal and McBride came back to play well on the right-wing but Town lost 4-2. Town had played a Hun, (not a German) - an amateur goalkeeper, Philip Hun, from Windsor & Eton - in the reserves against Brush Sports, but secured former Villa custodian Alan Wakeman from Bloxwich Strollers in time for the home game with Swindon, which they won 2-1.

Adam McCulloch was dropped for the trip to Crystal Palace, having not scored for five games. . John

Clowes, who had scored 17 goals in 21 Reserve games, was recalled but only for one game, as Town signed Eric Marsden. McCulloch played for the Reserves in the 7-5 defeat by Brierley Hill, netting one, but six days later he was sold to Aldershot. His replacement, Eric Marsden from Southend was 22 years old, weighed 12 stone, and stood at 6 foot. He had scored 6 goals in 14 games for the Essex team, and came with a reputation as a good shot and excellent with his head, but sadly he never produced the goods at Shrewsbury. Another addition to the front line was George Stewart, who was signed from Q.P.R. He made his debut against Northampton and played in the final 10 games, but when Town lost 1-0 to his former team they dropped into the bottom two.

Three Town stalwarts, Jimmy Bullions, Ron Crutchley and Bobby Brown all passed 100 appear-ances in April, but Town finished in their lowest ever position, 23rd, albeit 12 points clear of Walsall. Home attendances had slumped to 8,532, and in an effort to improve matters former manager Harry Chapman was recruited as Northern scout.

The retained list saw 15 players retained, although two - Michael Picken and Billy Dodd - were in the forces. Two more, John McBride and Freddie Fisher, were by now qualified F.A. coaches. Pat Comerford was given a free transfer, and offers were invited for Wilf Birkett (who returned to Southport) and John Halpin. Norman Lewis went to Hereford, then Gravesend, followed by Newport and on to Merthyr before an ankle injury ended his career in 1961. Fred Ashworth, who had played Lancashire league cricket, went to Tonbridge, Ken Booker left, and Harold Roberts joined Scunthorpe.

PROFIT AND LOSS

The club balance sheet improved thanks to the Cup run and transfers receipts were up almost 60% at £40,088; a profit of £10,486 meant a bank balance of £3,594. So Town went out to strengthen the squad, and Maurice Candlin, the Northampton captain, his teammate James Davie plus Brian Loughnane from Leeds arrived in late June. While amongst the amateurs, Ron Manders and Brian 'Curly' Edgley's names stand out. There was also Ron Rafferty, who went on to a distinguished League career, particular-ly with Grimsby Town.

On July 11th, Town accepted a bid of £7,000 from Barnsley for Bobby Brown, who had been signed from Southend for £450 three years earlier. He scored 41 goals in 104 League games and was to give the Tykes similar excellent service. Three days later experienced full-backs Billy Cooke and Jackie Parr arrived, and then Les Johnston came from Stoke to fill Brown's position. He had a seven handicap at golf and entered the P.F.A. golf competition with the threat of a cold bath if he did not qualify for the final. John McBride, Maurice Candlin, Jacky Parr, Arnold Jackson and Freddie Fisher also competed, but only David Walsh (Villa) off 10 and Geoff Thomas (Forest) off 8 could match Johnston who netted a 74, so the chilly reception was avoided.

Alex McCue arrived at the end of July from Grimsby, and the practice match saw Whites - with goals from Loughnane, Clowes and amateurs Edward Darlington and John Brown - beat Blues 4-1. The Blues' goal was scored by Eric Marsden, it was his only Town goal. Another Town amateur stepping up was Bernard McGuire, who signed professional just before the season began.

The campaign started at home to Watford in sensational style; a ten goal thriller, with a 6-4 victory, and an Arnold Jackson hat-trick after Jimmy Bannister's penalty had started the fun. Les Johnston scored on his debut and must have wondered what he had joined. A draw against Palace and a win at Exeter - an Alec McCue goal on his debut - built expectations. However, just two wins in the next ten games led to changes, and by the eighth match, Ron Dickinson, John Brown plus Derek Price were included. Town invested £2,500 in Jack Hudson from Chesterfield, who had been on loan at Bangor City, with Roland Depear having a hand in the move. A brace of goals each for Brown and Hudson saw off Walsall 4-1, but Johnston, after five goals in five games, lost his goal touch. Despite Hudson's goals - including a hat trick against Leyton Orient - the form remained indifferent. Ten winless games, including six successive defeats, ended on Boxing Day when a rare Maurice Candlin goal beat Swindon Town. By now Jimmy Davie had been released, but Town had signed Harry Brennan from Gresley Rovers (manager Crooks would in time lead Gresley), and midway though December the manager returned to Derby to sign Jackie Stamps.

The changing structure of the team was causing unrest with Harry Cooke first on the list, soon followed in the first week of the New Year by Eric Marsden, Les Johnston, and Freddy Fisher, the latter due to his wife's ill-health. A fortnight later the 'blue-eyed boy' Arnold Jackson and Alec McCue made it six malcontents, with McCue almost moving to Barrow. The season was heading nowhere. Queens Park Rangers had extracted revenge for the previous season's defeat by winning 2-0 in the first

round of the F.A.Cup, but the signing of Stamps gave the campaign a real boost. Just one defeat in an eight game run took Town into February, a month although not obvious at the time, which was to be crucial in the club's development. On February 1st the board co-opted a youngster to join their number - Tim Yates would later become the club's best chairman, to date (sorry Mr Bailey, there's still time), and on the 26th Joe Wallace was demobbed. Wallace had made his debut in the Birmingham League on October 11th 1952 and was a reserve team regular in a strong side. He was the only player without first team experience when they thrashed Wolves 8-1, and signed professional immediately on his release from Donnington.

Town's revival was being noticed, and the BBC decided to do live commentary of the Shrewsbury versus Gillingham match on March 20th. Town celebrated by losing four consecutive games, and then managing a goalless draw for the radio broadcast. The goals had dried up, until a late burst from Alec McCue of seven in eight games, which helped Town to three Easter victories over Brighton twice and Torquay, to equal their longest League run.

Even so the rumblings of discontent were growing, which led to a vote of no confidence carried by 110 votes to 68 at the shareholders meeting on June 3rd. Although overturned on a proxy vote after an objection by 'Chucky' Edwards, this may have hastened Sammy Crooks' departure. On June 21st he resigned but the board insisted he stay on until a new man was appointed, and they also appointed Les Rimmer as secretary.

The retained list had seen Freddy Fisher move to Leyton Orient, Harry Cooke to Watford, and Eric Marsden to Bath. Also to leave were Arnold Jackson, in an exchange deal with Ray Weigh from Stockport, Jackie Stamps who refused terms, and Ron Dickinson who was offered a professional contract but joined his home team Coventry, and never played League football again.

Arnold Jackson was the first player, in Town's League career, to have a love-hate relationship with the fans. Some loved him, some loved to hate him, but he was a fine servant, distinctive in appearance and a regular scorer, as he was to be in four seasons at Stockport. Jackie Stamps had but a short stay with the club, and was past his best, but was a big man, who, although no longer with us, is remembered with great affection. Freddy Fisher was a tricky diminutive winger, who must have been good because he was the writer's first idol!

CHAPTER 7 - OLDER MANAGER, YOUNGER TEAM

The major irony of Sammy Crooks departure was that arguably his best signings were made in the month before his departure. Certainly 'Gentleman' Joe Maloney should be included in any Shrewsbury Town select eleven, and his Liverpool team mate Russell Crossley would also bear consideration. Forwards Willie O'Donnell, the Town leading scorer pre-Arthur Rowley and part-time professional Ray Russell along with Ray Weigh, would all provide goals for the time to come. He also signed Arthur Atkins - born in Tokyo - from Aston Villa, a centre half, who sadly died in 1988.

The accounts showed a loss of £7,087, so when Town appointed a new manager, he was, like many after him, not suffering illusions about spending large sums. The new incumbent appointed on July 21st was Walter J. Rowley, former manager of Middlesbrough and previously secretary-manager of Bolton, but with local roots for his parents came from Oakengates. His opening comments hit many chords as he was quoted thus *"I am sure we shall go places in Shrewsbury. I know you have not got money to throw around. That plays into my hands very nicely because I believe in bringing on the young player"*. Sammy Crooks left ten days later to run his business in Derby.

The practice match, for which Jimmy Bullions had recovered from a slipped disc, saw seven goals, Blues 5 - Whites 2. New boys Willie O'Donnell, who scored four for the Blues and Ray Weigh, one for the Whites, were joined on the score-sheet by Harry Brennan who changed sides at half-time and scored for both teams. Even so Brennan did not make Town's opening line-up and neither O'Donnell or Weigh scored in the first ten games. The early goals came mainly from the flanks, three each for Derek Price and Brian Loughnane, two for Alec McCue, one on his debut for Ray Russell and the final goal at Gillingham was Joe Maloney's only League goal in 276 appearances.

Another brace from Price set up the first victory over Brighton, on October 2nd. Willie O'Donnell demanded a first-team recall by hitting a double hat-trick as Salop beat Wellington Reserves 9-0, and later that month Norman Hobson signed professional, the first Shrewsbury born player to do so since Town entered the League. Norman was beaten by Ray Manders, as the first Shrewsbury born player to play a League game, he made his debut on September 11th against Leyton Orient, but did not sign professional papers until December 6th.

Shrewsbury Town Chairman Bernard Hayes, although only 64, had been in poor health for around a year, and on October 24th passed away whilst staying with his daughter in Nairobi. He had joined the Town board as Vice Chairman, in 1936, and took over as Chairman two years later. He was an Independent Councillor from 1921-27 and 1936-46, a brilliant advocate, tenacious in an argument, and a life member of Pengwern Boat Club. He was succeeded by C. Lewis Edwards, with J.W.A.Jones becoming Vice-Chairman.

Manager Rowley backed up his policy of giving youth a chance by signing Gordon Skeech from Runcorn and Alex McNab, a Scottish schoolboy international. The move towards youth obviously made life difficult for some senior players and the end of the year was marked by the trusty stalwarts being granted transfers. Jimmy Bullions, 131 appearances and Ron Crutchley with 146 - a record at that time - had both given yeoman service, but neither had been selected since Sammy Crooks departure. Also listed at this time were Billy Dodd and Alec McCue (again), Arthur Atkins and Eddie Beynon dropped early in the new year joined them in February.

Stan Hall launched operation revival in January, but efforts to attract two crowds of 12,000 in order to encourage the board to give Mr Rowley sufficient money to buy two players failed miserably. Bad weather and apathy saw gates of 5,864 and 7,331 for Aldershot and Millwall respectively. The search for talent continued through the club's junior ranks, and on February 5th, Town fielded 5 teams and none lost; the first team beat Millwall 3-2, the Reserves won 2-1 at Gresley, whilst the Colts drew 3-3 with Church Stretton, the 'A' Team also drew (1-1 at Bayston Hill), and the 'B' Team beat Hopesgate 4-3.

The only good thing about Town's F.A. Cup exploits was the crowd of 18,311 at Fellows Park as Town crashed 5-2 to Walsall. The other five goal defeat came at Leyton Orient on January 22nd, with Johnny Hartburn netting a hat trick in 2½ minutes. That game was Joe Maloney's first at centre-half. With Arthur Atkins and Maurice Candlin both injured, Walter Rowley asked Joe to play at number five, *"I'm not big enough"*, Joe protested.

"Son if you're good enough you're big enough', was the reply.

His first opponent was Ken FACEY of Leyton Orient, then on successive Saturdays Bill LACEY of Aldershot and Dennis PACEY of Millwall. Town won the last two, and Joe played the next 108 consecutive games at centre-half, and 223 in total at No.5.

In the mid-1950's, the trees come down in the Gay Meadow approach road.

11th; and President Harry A. Jones 79, passed away on June 4th. Jones was a season ticket holder when the club joined the Birmingham League sixty years earlier. He joined the committee in 1906, had 2 years as Vice-Chairman and 18 as Chairman, before resigning over the Third Division controversy in 1936.

The season needed a boost, and as it happened it received more than one. A mid-April run of three consecutive victories all at home set off a run of one defeat in seven games, which ended with a 7-0 home victory over Swindon Town. This result created nine club (Football League) records:-
1. Highest League finish (16th).
2. Most points (42).
3. Most goals (70).
4. Biggest win.
5. Equal highest score.
6. Highest score of season.
7. Undefeated at home in 1955.
8. Highest individual League scorer (Ray Weigh 18).
9. Most individual goals in a game (Weigh 4).

What could they do for an encore? Easy, beat Oswestry 7-1 in the Senior Cup semi-final, when Ray Russell hit four - the only time successive scores of seven have been achieved since League status. Then what? Crack six past Wellington in the final; 20 goals in just three games, in eight days, with only two against.

Sadly, off the field Town were losing some of their guiding lights. Bill Hinks 51, the clubs former Secretary, died on March 8th; Director Ernest Tucker 58, a former club Treasurer died on May

The charges for 1955-56 went up to 2/- (10p) for ground, 3/- enclosure, 4/- 'C' stand, 5/- 'A' and 'B' stand, with season tickets from 50/- (£2.50) to 115/- (£5.75). The increases were levied in an effort to balance the books, after another loss, this time £7.849. On August 13th, Sydney Yates was appointed President and A.C. 'Freddy' Williams and H.J.Harrison joined the board.

The season started without Maurice Candlin who decided to retire, while Eddie Beynon and Ron Crutchley moved to Wellington, Harry Brennan and Jack Hudson to Buxton, Bernard McGuire to Winsford. Jimmy Bullions, Arthur Atkins and Michael Picken were also released and Ashworth, Ayton, Depear, Johnston and Stewart whose registrations Town still held were not renewed. New signings brought in were, Alec Simpson from Southampton, Arthur Tyrer from Leeds, John Arnott ex-West Ham, and Ralph Oliver who turned professional.

The practice match went to Blues 4-3 with another rare successful shot from Maloney, this time an own goal for the Whites! The League season also started with goals, a 5-0 defeat of Newport County, Town's best ever Football League start (and only bettered by the opening 7-1 drubbing of Oswestry in 1926-7). Two away defeats followed, but the 3-1 reverse at Norwich was soon overturned as Town won 6-0 just

48

five days later, with Ray Russell hitting the season's only hat-trick.

Town were not renown travellers, but had solid home form, until Torquay ended a 14 match unbeaten run, and Town won at Crystal Palace 1-0 after 6 consecutive away defeats. The team used to kick-off at 3.15 p.m. in those days, and the Reserves played home games on Saturdays, so it was a happy bunch of supporters who left the Gay Meadow after the tannoy announced the victory at Selhurst Park. It started a run of seven successive wins; away at Palace, Millwall and Watford, plus home to Southampton, Brighton, Gillingham and Reading - riches indeed. Russell Crossley was recalled at the start of the run and kept three clean sheets, the goals tally being 17-6.

Some interesting signings at the time included goalkeeper Eric Skeech, brother of Gordon, plus Brian Edgley, and Ron Walker on part-time terms. While Arkle, a North Eastern lad stationed at Donnington and R.Muir an inside-forward from the Orkney Islands, played for Town's junior teams. Famous faces also appeared on October 6th, when Town beat Western Command 4-0 - 2 goals each for Ray Weigh and Willie O'Donnell. The visitors included Don Howe and, five days after his 19th birthday, Duncan Edwards. While on February 18th an under 18 youth international saw England beat Wales 5-1. Malcolm Lucas beat Joe Dean to score the Welsh goal but David Bennett, John Barnwell, Bert Llewellyn, John 'Budgie' Byrne, and Jimmy Greaves - with a 45 yard free-kick - scored the English goals. Town had two players, centre-half Melwyn Cross and right-half Dave Elias in the Welsh side.

The season lost its way due to long term injuries to Derek Price and Ray Weigh, and like John Arnott it failed to live up to early promise. On February 4th, Joe Maloney was married in Liverpool, he was to drive to the Meadow afterwards to take his place against Crystal Palace. But the game was called off because of a waterlogged pitch. A fortnight later, the Football League Management Committee produced a five point plan:-
1. League matches to take total preference.
2. Formation of four divisions of 22 clubs for 1957-8 relegation of 2 or 3 clubs.
3. Installation of floodlighting for League games.
4. Other floodlight games to be limited to floodlit competition under League control.
5. Reduction in number of representative games.

Any reduction of numbers could easily have affected Town in any of their first four seasons, but now, in their sixth season they reached the dizzy heights of 13th. The F.A. Cup had produced some revenue from four games. A 1-1 draw at Priestfield brought Gillingham to the Meadow, for a 4-1 defeat - thanks to three extra time goals. Then Torquay attracted 11,490 for a goalless second round tie, but four first half goals at Plainmoor set up the Gulls 5-1 win. Willie O'Donnell scored 19 League and 1 Cup goal, so becoming the first Salop player to score 20 goals in a season since joining the League.

During the season Norman Hobson made his debut at Exeter on November 26th, 'Curly' Edgley broke through at Colchester on January 28th, Ralph Oliver at Brentford on St. Patricks Day, while Ron Walker made his only start at Reading on March 3rd. The only home debut, apart from Alec Simpson and Arthur Tyrer, in the opening two home games, fell to Keith Webb at home to Southend in April, when the diminutive seventeen year-old made his mark with Town's only goal.

LOCALS, YOUNGSTERS AND KILTS

Town's close season activity saw Jimmy Shields join from Hibernian in late May, Arnold Rogers arrive - he had hit 25 goals in 26 games for Bristol City but was overshadowed by John Atyeo - and Colin Whitaker come for a small fee from Bradford Park Avenue. Arthur Tyrer left for Aldershot, complete with his favourite step-over trick, and John Arnott plus Brian Loughnane - after the League granted Brian a free - both joined Bournemouth. John Mcbride was released, as he was not prepared to take a drop in salary, to become just a coach. Honest John asked to be dropped because of poor form in January 1953 and was never recalled.

The proposed Third and Fourth Division set-up was rejected by just three votes, while the club balance sheet showed a loss of £3,098. Amongst many amateur signings were goalkeeper Alan Humphreys, wingers Albert Harley and Michael Henry Jones, and also two ill-fated centre-halves, John Draycott and Fred Campbell.

Also at this time former Town inside-forward Arthur 'Hetty' Morris was assisting groundsman Jack Jones. Hetty played for Town in 1905, and was transferred to Birmingham two seasons later, when his wages rocketed from 17/6 (87½p) to £4 per week during the season and £3 in summer. He was the last Shrewsbury born player to be transferred by Shrewsbury Town to a First Division club, until 'Curly' Edgley joined Cardiff in July 1960. However, before World War I, Morris returned to Town, had a spell at Wellington, and a further six seasons at the Meadow in the post-war period.

The Supporters Club agreed a £3,000 interest free loan to the football club and announced a record membership of 3,951. They had already donated £14,200 for ground improvements and the purchase of a house, but the shareholders meeting on August 9th heard that the bill for floodlighting would be £8,000. It was also announced that the club had turned down bids for Derek Price and hoped to give Jimmy Bannister the maximum benefit allowed of £750.

The Blues won the practice match 3-2, Jimmy Shields scored for both teams, and along with Colin Whitaker made his debut in the opening game at Brighton. Norman Hobson, Willie O'Donnell and Whitaker all scored in an exciting second half but Town, 2-0 down at the interval, lost 4-3. On the Monday Arnold Rodgers made his debut and scored a terrific volley in the second half to add to a Whitaker penalty, as Salop beat Millwall 2-0. The following day John Curran, a goalkeeper from East Fife and a qualified S.F.A. coach, joined Town, who beat Gillingham 1-0 thanks to fit again Ray Weigh. They then drew 0-0 at the Den, to record three consecutive clean sheets for the first time in the Football League.

John Curran made his debut in the reserves along with Albert Harley, and Fred Campbell, against Halesowen. Of the eleven, only Campbell did not play League football, he had played representative matches for the Army in Kenya, and had been recommended to Walter Rowley. Young Albert obviously impressed, and on September 10th became Town's first groundstaff player, he was 16. Town drew 0-0 with Bournemouth that day to start a remarkable sequence of nine draws in eleven matches; three were goalless, but six were 1-1 - pools fans eat your heart out - and Town managed 10 jackpot draws that season. The first against Aldershot on September 15th saw three local players appear in a Town team for the first time in the League - Brian Edgley, Norman Hobson and Ron Manders.

The Watford game was Town's one victory during the sequence, and also featured a collection for Jimmy Bannister - which amounted to £117.3.0d - and was more than double any previous amount to hit

the blankets during a benefit. The one defeat was 6-0 at Colchester on September 29th, Russell Crossley broke his arm and Joe Wallace deputised. This meant serious problems for Mr Rowley as John Curran had a septic arm and his two youngsters were injured, Alan Humphreys - a shoulder injury - and Eric Skeech, a cut forehead. Skeech looked the likelier choice, but in the end the manager selected young Humphreys, who became Town's first ever 16 year-old to make a senior appearance; he was 12 days short of his 17th birthday and 29 days younger than Billy Dodd when he appeared against Rochdale in 1950. Ray Weigh gave Town a first half lead and young Alan had a quiet day, until an underhit (Alec Simpson) backpass set up the Reading equaliser. It was his only appearance that season as John Curran recovered for the next fixture, a fact which meant Eric Skeech never quite emulated his brother Gordon.

October 11th saw Town's League debut under lights, at Selhurst Park, and they enjoyed the experience, Arnold Rodgers hitting the only goal. A week later Alan Humphries signed professional terms and was called up as reserve for the England youth team, but a dubious penalty against Joe Wallace sent Town crashing out of the Cup at Weymouth. They were the last team not currently in the League to knock Town out of the competition. Town had another bad experience on the South coast the following week losing 4-0 at Southampton with Derek Owen becoming the fourth Shrewsbury born player to make the League side. Another local lad, Tony Reece, signed for Port Vale in December, during which month C.A.D. Nesscliffe beat Longtown C.A.D. Carlisle 7-1 on the Meadow not surprising really as apart from a goal from Ronnie Gryba, Nesscliffe's other strikes came from hat-tricks for Duncan Edwards and Bobby Charlton.

Town's Reserves beat Rugby 5-1 on December 22nd with Jackie Butler coming out of retirement due to a late withdrawal. However, he soon hung up his boots as 1957 started with Town fielding a reserve side all aged under 21, and every player had progressed from the Colts. The Colts meanwhile contained Humphreys, Harley and Michael Henry Jones who would all play League football.

The first team meanwhile had played three home games in December and hit 16 goals, even more remarkable because it was in a season in which they scored no hat-tricks. Colin Whitaker hit two in each game as Coventry 5-0, Brighton 4-0, and Swindon 7-3 all left soundly beaten.

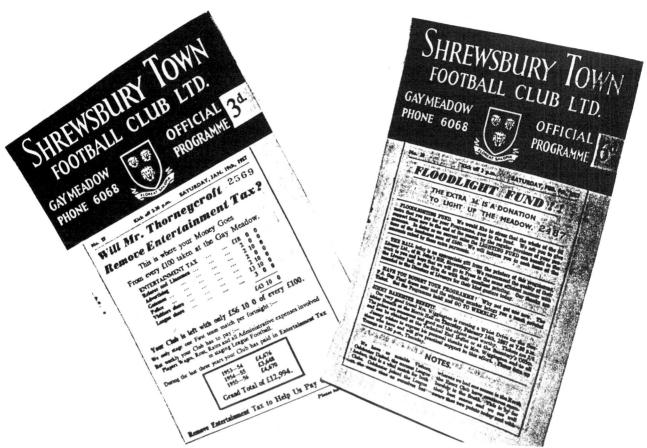

The supporters club launched a floodlight fund committee on January 22nd. Dennis Bellingham was chairman and it consisted of club directors, manager, secretary and supporters club members. Their first decision was to add 3d (1¼p) to the price of the programme, effectively doubling its price, in order to raise £500 towards the new estimate of £12,000 for installation; reserve issues went up 1d (and like petrol after Suez, it never came down).

Town's problem position this season was right-wing. Derek Price had an injury ridden time and news of a cartilage operation led to the signing of Archie Kerr from Motherwell. He, and the dearer programme, made their debuts against Colchester, and Kerr should have felt at home, for the team included six Scotsmen all from the Glasgow area - Wallace, Simpson, O'Donnell, Shields, Curran and Kerr (he replaced Alex McNab, who although a Scottish schoolboy international was born in Birmingham). Ironically while Colchester visited the Meadow, Russell Crossley who broke an arm at Layer Road, hurt his back in a reserve team 4-1 defeat at Bromsgrove, this game was Ron Manders 100th reserve team match.

In late February, George Walters, having completed his apprenticeship and national service, signed part-time and Arnold Rodgers joined Chippenham Town (he later managed Welton Rovers on their best ever F.A. Cup run). March saw a remarkable game, when Town, 4-1 up with 15 minutes left, lost 5-4 to Norwich.

Sammy Chung hit two, and John Gavin and Ralph Hunt added to Billy Coxon's goal. Coxon had a trial with Town in 1952 after leaving Derby but joined Norwich instead the week after. On March 16th, Mr W.C.Allen resigned from the board, Town youngster Elfyn Williams played for Wales U-18, and Norman Hobson developed 'flu on the bus to Southend. The final item may have passed unnoticed save for the fact that it meant a debut for 12th man Albert Harley. At 16 years 333 days he became Town's youngest ever player, beating Alan Humphreys by 20 days. The two youngsters joined Town at the same time from Lache F.C. of Chester. Albert was also the seventh player to play right-wing that season.

At the turn of the year a possible promotion opportunity threatened, but a small squad and injuries were a big factor in their slump. The defence, which had conceded 13 goals more than the previous season, was praised, while the attack who hit a new record total of goals, was labelled the worst in League history. On April 9th entertainment tax was abolished. It was costing Town 18% of their home gates, and in the previous three years they had paid £12,994 - enough to provide floodlights. A day later Town played Bangor City in a benefit match for Roland Depear, which Town won 3-2 with Freddie Morris guesting and scoring.

George Walters made his debut against

A Colts line-up around 1957: (Back): Draycott, Tristham, E.Skeech, Manders, Stephan, Davies, A.Mann. (Front): A.Harley, Griffiths, Cherrington, Martin, Jones. (Harley and Manders made it to the League)

Ludlam had been outstanding in Roland Depear's benefit match at Bangor and Jimmy Bannister's testimonial at the Meadow. Jimmy scored a late penalty in that game, after a sporting Sam Rogers decision. This saw Jimmy run from penalty box to penalty box before striking the ball.

Newport County on Good Friday, reportedly as a nineteen year old, two months earlier he was correctly said to be 22. Town lost 2-0 but reversed the scoreline on Easter Monday. The reserves beat Whitwick Colliery 5-1 that day and 24 hours later won the return 10-1; Bobby Mayle (18) hit five goals in the two games, Dave Pountney (17) hit three, in his first two reserve matches, and Derek Price on the mend also hit three. While goalkeeper John Curran received awful stick from the watching first team, for Whitwick's break-away consolation. It was one of his final games as he joined Watford in the close season, Jimmy Shields went to Cowdenbeath, Archie Kerr returned to Motherwell and Ray Weigh - who was going into business with his father-in-law in Bournemouth - joined Aldershot. Billy Dodd who had been at Banbury Spencer joined Southport as did Tommy Dunne. Two players in the forces were retained, Brian Edgley and Harry Philips; Bobby Mayle, John Draycott and Dai Rees signed part-time.

Town finished ninth (in fact only six sides managed more points), despite the bottom club, Norwich, completing a double in the last game. Norwich for the fourth and last occasion successfully applied for re-election. Bobby Mayle scored on his debut for the first team in the Senior Cup final victory over Wellington. The floodlight fund was boosted by a £220 cheque from Shrewsbury and District Master Butchers, and in late May Town signed goalkeeper Ron Ludlam from Bangor, and Johnny McAlinden from Celtic.

His cheque was for £703, just short of the maximum allowed.

DEPARTURE AND FAILURE

Walter Rowley, aged 66, having made consistent progress during his time at the club announced his retirement on June 27th, and Town were forced to look for a new manager. He said, *"it has been the hardest, but happiest job I have taken on"*. It was important the directors made the right decision, as the top halves of the Third North and South were set to combine to form the new national Division Three, and the bottom halves a Division Four. The club settled on Wolves chief coach, Harry Potts, a former inside-forward with Burnley and Everton, and as a native of Hetton-le-Hole, the third consecutive appointment with North-Eastern overtones.

Potts first signing was left-winger James Hill and he soon followed up with inside-forward Bernard Jones. Both were 5 feet 8 inches and 10 stone 12 pounds when signed, on July 24th. On the same day the supporters club waived loans of £8,250 to the parent club, and a fortnight later handed over a cheque for £2,500. The season started well, and after two home wins Town headed the table. Two away draws followed then a third consecutive home win, then tragedy.

On Monday September 9th, Town entertained Norwich City at the Meadow. Town were unchanged

52

for the sixth consecutive game, but a sickening crack saw Colin Whitaker stretchered off with a broken right leg, despite this, and Alec Simpson sustaining an ankle injury they drew 0-0. Five days later reserve centre-half Fred Campbell also broke a leg, in a 1-0 home defeat by Brierley Hill, and it was to end his career.

Bernard Jones had scored on his debut, Ray Russell and Johnny McAlinden along with Derek Owen and Whitaker had also netted eight early season goals, but now Town went five games without scoring, culminating in a 4-0 home defeat by Bournemouth. Two days later Dave Pountney signed professional and Harold Taylor joined the groundstaff. On the following Saturday, just before his 18th birthday, young Pountney made his debut at Torquay and Town won 2-0. Manager Potts was prepared to risk his youngsters, having given Bobby Mayle a four game run due to an injury to John McAlinden. Equally his experienced men played their part Jimmy Bannister made his 200th appearance at Reading, and was selected for the final Division Three South versus North game, the club's first representative honour.

Joe Wallace received a set back, tonsillitis ending a run of 123 consecutive League games, all - bar the first - at right-half. His record ended at Newport County, where Ken Smith, described as a wing-half come centre-forward, made his debut at No.9, the day after signing from Blackpool. In November Tony Ingham of Queens Park Rangers was sent off by Dennis Howell at the Meadow, a week before Port Vale ended Town's Cup dream by 2-1 at Vale Park, in the first round.

After a promising start Salop were finding consist-ency a problem, but a 5-1 defeat at Southend (Dave Pountneys first goal) stung them into life. Three successive victories started a run of just one defeat in eight League games, culminating in their happiest Christmas yet with maximum points, due to a double over Walsall; their first 100% Christmas treat (shame about the opposition). The New Year started with Alec Simpson appointed player-coach-captain of the reserves, and Harold Taylor signing professional. January ended with the recruitment of winger Ken Tucker from Cardiff, a Welsh amateur international. Later, Ken was for many years, the secretary of Merthyr Tydfil.

It proved to be Harry Potts' final signing, for on February 25th he resigned and joined Burnley, who he was to guide to League honours and a Cup Final. Town again turned to the North-East. Johnnie Spuhler - manager-coach of Stockton, friend of Harry Potts, former player under Walter Rowley at Middlesbrough - came well recommended. He was the first Town manager granted a contract, but it was not destined to be a golden era.

Town had 33 points from 33 games and stood 14th when Mr Potts departed, they had lost their last two games, and proceeded to lose their next two. A draw with Southend, and victories over Gillingham 3-1 and Aldershot 5-1, including a Ken Smith hat trick (Town's first for exactly 31 months) promised a false dawn. A wretched Easter - losing 3-1 at home and 5-0 away against Coventry - steered Town towards Division Four.

Alec Simpson received a surprise recall, some say from out of the crowd, at Highfield Road. The season ended with seven defeats (albeit five away), out of the last eight games, and only three goals. Even the 1-0 victory over Exeter was delayed, the visitors late arrival meant a 3.50 pm kick-off, in front of 3,338.

Colin Whitaker was making steady progress, and his first game back was against Nesscliffe on March 25th. Ten days earlier Johnny Gryba signed pro-fessional, but in early April, Johnny Draycott con-tracted tuberculosis, and it ended his very promising career. His last game was on April 7th at Rugby, a 3-0 victory. Manager Spuhler, after 13 games and 7 points was sacked on Wednesday May 14th. He complained he had been promised 15 months, and, *"thought he had suffered raw treatment"*. The club gave him an ex-gratia payment of £300.

In the Senior Cup final, Bobby Mayle scored for the second year running in his final first team game. While Ludlam, Rees, Philips and Derek Owen, who joined Kidderminster were given free transfers. Derek Price went to Aldershot, Jimmy Bannister joined Northampton, and Ron Manders linked up with Wellington. Town were in Division Four without a manager, and after the steady progress under Walter Rowley needed a really big boost.

CHAPTER 8 - A TON OF GOALS, ARTHUR, LIGHTENS OUR DARKNESS

O n June 5th 1958 it arrived, or rather he arrived, Leicester City's goal machine. George Arthur Rowley joined Shrewsbury Town at 2.30pm, it was to prove a moment to savour, an historic signing. His opening riposte was, *"I believe in going all out for goals, that is what the fans want to see, and that is what wins matches"*. He also promised 100 goals for the coming season, for a team who managed 49 the previous term it looked optimistic. Arthur's first two signings, full-back John Price from Walsall and young forward Lenny Copp from Leeds did more to strengthen the reserves than the first team, but the season started well enough.

Having not gone to the North-East for the manager, Town set off to open their season there instead. Two Ken Smith goals at Hartlepool and two from the manager at Gateshead, followed by a 4-1 home win over Coventry had Salop riding high. Just one defeat in the first ten, including successive goalless draws at Aldershot, Carlisle and Millwall, kept up the momentum.

Then bump! Home defeats to Barrow and Millwall had the sages nodding knowingly, and after 12 matches led to the first changes. Defeat at Oldham increased the pressure, but victories at Walsall - always sweet - and Torquay steadied the ship.

November saw Arthur miss two League games, returning for the 'boat trip'. Town drew Newport, Isle of Wight, in the Cup. The trip to the picturesque isle ended 0-0, Arthur still unsure why his 'goal' was disallowed. So it was back to Shrewsbury on Thursday November 20th, Arthur again failed to score but Town, including a rare George Walters goal, won 5-0; a little under two miles away Shrewsbury Crematorium was officially opened. The second round saw Town travel to Selhurst Park where they came from behind thanks to a Ray Russell goal in each half. The replay, the following Thursday, was the last half day closing Cup match played on the Meadow, and again it finished 2-2, Town coming from behind once more.

A typical line-up during the 1958-59 season. These eleven players between them went on to make over 2,300 League appearances for the Town. Jackie Butler (Asst.Trainer) totalled over 200 games, Tommy Seymour (Trainer) played over 200 pre-war games. Humphries made his first team debut aged 16 and was transferred to Leeds 6 years later. (League appearances in brackets):
(Back): Butler (58), Wallace (337), Hobson (212), Crossley (173), Maloney (237), Skeech (223), Walters (246), Humphreys (32)
(Front): Seymour, Whitaker (152), Edgley (113), Rowley (236), Russell (168), Pountney (229 + 4 sub.)

Arthur Rowley scored the first, but surprisingly when Town were awarded a penalty Gordon Skeech converted it. The second replay at Molineux on the Monday attracted 50% more spectators, because of the evening kick off, but despite a first half Ray Russell goal, Town lost 4-1. To their credit they bounced back, winning all four League games in the month.

Right back in contention going into the New Year, Town went back to the North-East on New Years Day, but lost 2-1 at Darlington, then two days later, Jack Mycock - in only his sixth League game - sustained a pox fracture in a tackle with Bob Harvey, and it ended the promising amateur's League career. Another young player, John Gryba, joined Bangor City, while Ray Ambler was signed from Leeds. He made his debut a day later, and pulled a thigh muscle, as Town lost 1-0. It was their third consecutive defeat, but again they bounced back; 2-0 down at half-time at Sealand Road, they scored five times in just fourteen minutes and ran out 5-3 winners. The final goal was Arthur Rowley's 300th League strike.

Town's problem position was again right-wing, for they fielded six different No.7's in the League, plus Len Copp in the Cup. They also gave trials to John Gillingham, Brian Adlam and Ivan Marks, but within 23 days Gillingham also broke a leg. The upturn came from the start of February, with 12 wins and 3 draws in the final 17 games, when 50 goals were scored. Another second half blitz saw Town hit 3 in 7 minutes and 4 in 13 minutes against Torquay. While at Crewe Colin Whitaker missed out, as referee Hickson blew, with the ball about to cross the line for Town's fifth.

It was significant that Arthur - 20 goals in the last 16 games - missed just one match, the defeat at Bradford Park Avenue, with a thigh injury. In the other loss Town, 3-0 down at Crystal Palace, recovered but still went down 4-3. Town's 2-0 win over Walsall put them a point behind Exeter with three games remaining, and the final fixture was Exeter at home. The manager's guidance continued to grow, and against Chester he set up Ray Russell for one and netted two himself.

The following Tuesday Exeter beat Southport 1-0 while Town were cruising to victory at Vicarage Road. 5-2 up with 12 minutes to go when 'the sky fell in', or at least the lights went out. Mysteriously, several fuses - in order before the kick-off - were reported missing. Watford were fined £100, while

Exeter manager, Frank Broome, not suprisinigly demanded the match be replayed. Two days later the match Town were determined to win - versus Exeter on the Meadow - saw a crowd of 15,318. A tense atmosphere was relieved on 36 minutes, with a telling 15 yard drive from - of course - Arthur Rowley. A minute before half-time, a hand ball stopped Brian Edgley, and up stepped the manager - 2-0. On 52 minutes the big man robbed wing-half James Thompson, held off several challenges and beat 'keeper John Lobbett to complete the victory and his hat trick. A week later justice was done. Arthur again set the ball rolling from 25 yards, as Town - despite conceding a late penalty - romped home 4-1. In the crowd was proud brother, Jack Rowley, who had guided Plymouth to promotion to Division Two, a unique family double. The Town youth team also triumphed, beating Donnington Swifts 7-0 in the County Youth Final, with Mickey Pragg's 4 goals making his season total 58.

The manager ended on 38 goals, double the club League record, and the 101 total was another record unchallenged since. The supporters club completed the Technical College Terrace (Wakeman end), and named it the Duffill Terrace in memory of their late secretary. The only sad note was the sudden death of Billy Richardson who collapsed and died on March 29th while playing for Midland All Stars v. T.V. All Stars at Birmingham; he was just 49.

At the beginning of the 1959-60 season, Town gave a two month trial to Gibson Makatelele, a black South African left-winger - the club's first coloured player - but he was released after some reserve team appearances.

The busy round of presentations, including a reception arranged by the Mayor Councillor Mrs C.E.Thickpenny, kept the spotlight on the team in the close season. The floodlight committee announced on June 3rd that the purchase of the ground, and planning permission for the lights had both been finalised, and that the task should be completed in the Autumn. Four days earlier Colchester United and Shrewsbury Town were elected to the Football Combination.

Players departing included Ralph Oliver to Hereford, Alex McNab to Rugby, Bobby Mayle to rivals Walsall, Lawrence Devine to Headington United, and Alan Grundy on trial to Aldershot. New signings brought Allen Cornfield from Lower Gornal, Malcolm Starkey - who had partnered Stan Matthews - from Blackpool, and the versatile Norman Smith from Barnsley, along with Spurs winger Geoff Ireland. Youngsters Michael Henry Jones and Paul Miller, both 19, signed professional forms. However, the funeral of Leslie Knighton, which took place on June 2nd in Bournemouth, overshadowed the close season.

Expenditure of £35,631 meant a loss on the promotion season of £8,427, but the supporters club produced a donation of £19,250 to create a profit in excess of £10,000. The manager told the annual meeting: *"When I arrived the ability was there, but for some reason the spirit had died"*. The transition to the higher division started well, two draws and a win - 3-0 at Vale Park - meant Town's 5-0 victory over Accrington Stanley on the last day of August put them top, until Grimsby won 24 hours later.

Defeat at home to Norwich led to the first changes of the campaign and a debut for Malcolm Starkey at Elm Park. Receiving an uncommonly good press he was reported, *"to have scored twice and upset the home defence with his speed, determination and clever positional play"*. Five days later in the return a Geoff Ireland cross headed down by Colin Whitaker was cheekily back-heeled home for the winner by the club's current secretary-director. A Whitaker hat-trick destroyed Colchester, but Southampton hit Town for six, 6-3. A scoreline which was reversed ten days later when Town beat Mansfield. That win included a Rowley hat-trick, as did the 6-2 victory over Newport County in the following home game. Goals kept coming but at Christmas the team was 'buried' twice.

The F.A. Cup was also a goal bonanza, but unfortunately, Salop one up at half-time, lost 4-3 at non-

League Peterborough. Another body-blow, a month earlier, happened at Halifax, when Town - wearing their red change strip for the first time - beat the League leaders 2-1, despite losing Joe Maloney with a knee injury, from which he never fully recovered. On a brighter note 'keeper Alan Humphreys played for the F.A. XI at Norwich as they beat the R.A.F. 9-2, and his absence meant Paul Miller made his debut in Town's demolition of Newport. A week later Town reputedly turned down a bid of £11,000 from Leicester for Malcolm Starkey, such decisions alter lives.

With Humphreys and Miller now blocking his way, Russell Crossley joined Kettering, while young 'keeper Jeff Newell and winger Allen Cornfield went to the Hawthorns for an England youth trial. Another ex-Town keeper in the news was John McBride who played 3 reserve and 7 first team games for Aberdeen. The Pittodrie side amazingly won all ten matches, but John had to fly off to Cairo to take up a coaching job with the English F.A.

The Town's floodlights were opened with a game against Stoke City on November 25th. Allen Cornfield made his debut and opened the scoring, whilst Arthur Rowley, Colin Whitaker (with two), and Geoff Ireland made it a 5-0 victory. Ireland running England left-back Tony Allen ragged. Only 5,448 turned up for the official opening, but over 10,000 had a foretaste on the previous Saturday against Q.P.R. when a 3.15pm kick off, was finished under lights.

January saw David Humphries and Michael Howard Jones join the staff, while on February 17th Peter Dolby was signed from Heanor Town, a deal done with their manager - one Samuel Crooks. Another ex-Town man, John Clowes, was also a player in the Heanor squad. Reserve centre-half Dave Martin left the R.A.F. and returned to Scotland for a trial with Cowdenbeath. On the 22nd, Alan Humphreys was snapped up by Leeds United for £5,000. He had originally been recommended, along with Albert Harley, to Walter Rowley by Joe Wheatley. It was a hectic time. Joe Wallace asked for a move in March, a day before Ray Russell moved to Crewe, and four days later Mike Gibson arrived from Nuneaton as Humphreys' replacement. Two days later, the 10th, Wallace was listed, and six days later Ken Tucker joined Northampton and Terry Davies joined the groundstaff.

Next it was discipline in the spotlight. 'Curly' Edgley missed the bus to Coventry so Michael Henry

Jones played in the 1-1 draw. Then on April 18th Arthur started a seven day suspension (Town's first in the League), which saw him miss three games. The following day - the Easter Tuesday - Town played their second fixture in two days with Barnsley, and Roy Ambler on 52 minutes became the first Town player sent off since Ernie Breeze in 1937.

Salop rose above all these problems, and the following Monday a Rowley penalty secured a home draw with Halifax, which established a new unbeaten run of 11 games, beating the draw-laden fun in 1951-52; it was also their sixth consecutive draw in this sequence. The penalty was Arthur's 353rd League goal, beating Steve Bloomer's record and moving him to second in the English League goalscoring chart. Town also won their final match at York, extending their run to 12 games unbeaten. This excellent record pushed Town up to third, behind Southampton and Norwich, but above Coventry and Grimsby on goal average.

The team scored exactly 100 goals, including the F.A. Cup match, while another vital goal at Maine Road sealed the First Division championship. Burnley, managed by Harry Potts, lifted the title, thanks to winger Trevor Meredith's strike. Born at Stottesdon into a farming family, Trevor was deputising for England star John Connelly. He would soon return to Shropshire, but the Town players were concentrating on the big share-out, for third place brought £330 of 'talent money'.

SWINDON - BAD START, SWINDON - CUP GLORY AND, SWINDON

Talent money or not the search for new talent continued. Welsh under 23 international George Baker arrived from Plymouth, Tony Corbett a part-time professional from Wolves, and James Christopher McLaughlin an Irish winger from Birmingham - for £2,500 - all joined the club and all made opening day debuts at Torquay. Ex-Town man Ray Russell joined Wellington, but the big departure from the Meadow was 'Curly' Edgley to Cardiff City for £5,000. Les Rimmer had signed Edgley and Tommy Talbot in April 1953, Talbot was sadly later to be killed in a road accident.

Town's third match was a 1-1 home draw with Swindon who included three seventeen year olds, John Trollope, Mike Summerbee and 'Ernie' Hunt, it was an early foretaste of events to come. With just two points from five games, it was a poor start to the season, improved slightly by an own goal by

a young John McGrath and a penalty from Arthur as Town beat Bury 2-1. It would be their only victory in the first fourteen League games - after a 12 match unbeaten run ending the previous term.

The season needed a boost - enter Lenny Copp. Town had drawn Swindon away in the newly launched League Cup, and a second half equaliser from Copp earned a replay. On the Saturday, Town beat Grimsby in the League and having lost 3-1 at Hull (scorer Copp) they again played Swindon on the following Monday. A first half goal from Copp, his only home success, and a Rowley penalty, cancelled out a brace from 'Bronco Layne', requiring another replay which was staged 48 hours later at Swindon. Apart from a cup-tie at Selhurst Park two years earlier, these four games and three goals, represented unfortunate Lenny's first class career. The trip to Swindon was played on an absolute quagmire. It was 0-0 after 90 minutes and the officials consulted about calling a halt to the match. They decided to play extra time, and ten minutes into it Jimmy McLaughlin converted a George Baker centre. A minute later Mike Gibson saved an 'Ernie' Hunt penalty. Five minutes into the second period, the wingers combined, McLaughlin setting up Norman 'I'm a full-back really' Hobson. This wrapped up the victory, with debut boy Dave Humphries earning much praise for shackling 'Bronco' Layne.

Round three came out of the hat thus:- 'Shrewsbury Town will play Bradford City or Manchester United'. The deciding game saw United ahead at half-time but Bradford ruined the dream with two second half goals. In the next round, Town made them pay after City opened the scoring. Arthur equalised before the break and Jimmy 'Mac' popped up with the winner two minutes from time.

Eleven days earlier Jimmy had notched his first hat trick as Town thumped a Newport County side containing Trevor Ford, 4-1, in the F.A. Cup. The second round draw was almost predictable:- 'Swindon Town will play Shrewsbury Town'. So exactly a month after putting the Robins out of one cup competition, Town recalled Dave Humphries and set off to Wiltshire once more. Mike Gibson was outstanding and Arthur hit the only goal 20 minutes from time. The League Cup run continued, thanks to Jimmy Mac converting a defence splitting pass from Malcolm Starkey in the 18th minute against Norwich City, on December 14th. The following day the Midland P.F.A. voted 180-12 in favour of strike action, and on the Saturday Town met in-form team Torquay United.

Two Malcolm Starkey goals ended Torquay's 15 match unbeaten run, and stretched Town's unbeaten record to eleven matches, six cup and five League. Three days before Christmas Len Copp and Roy Ambler asked for transfers, while a holiday double over Chesterfield just left one game outstanding, a New Years Eve trip - to Swindon. The teams met for the sixth time in 126 days, and the 2-2 draw saw Town keep an unusual unbeaten record, but 48 hours later Bury curtailed the 14 match run by a 3-1 margin at Gigg Lane.

Cup action returned on January 7th, Malcolm Starkey's goal earning a replay at Aldershot. The return, (the only game the Author's father ever attended), saw Arthur Tyrer cancel out Jimmy Mac's opener and then Malcolm Starkey secure a second replay, which was staged at Molineux. It ended in a 2-0 defeat, which took 18 years to avenge, and came two days after Peter Dolby's League debut.

An unbeaten run of eleven home games ended in a sea of mud against Tranmere. The visitors 'keeper Gordon Glayton was brilliant and defied Town until a late own goal cancelled out Keith Williams' successful effort. Just when Town thought they had rescued a point Joe Wallace steered a back pass wide of Mike Gibson, and as the pair slid into one another, Williams bounded through the mud to score. Amazingly Gordon Clayton, who died in 1991, joined Sankey's F.C. seven weeks later, a week after Harold Taylor also moved, to Hadley Castle.

Despite the Aldershot defeat, the Town was still Cup daft, the reason being the visit of Everton on February 15th. A crowd of 15,399 turned out, paying in excess of £2,000, to see a team which had cost over £250,000 to assemble. The Toffees had signed Alex Young from Hearts three months earlier, and when on 12 minutes the 'Golden Vision' headed in a Brian Harris corner, all hope appeared to evaporate. Until a gangly inside-right, making his Cup debut, latched onto a Rowley pass from Mick Jones' centre and fired Salop level on 35 minutes. Nine minutes after the break dreams became reality, a Jones corner, a Rowley knockdown and Pete Dolby's place in Town folklore was secure, as he hit the winner.

One man not playing was Colin Whitaker, sold to Queens Park Rangers for £2,000, 24 hours earlier. The two leg semi-final saw Town paired with Rotherham with the away leg first. The local fire brigade watered the pitch and Town 2-0 down in 18 minutes were sliding to defeat, but Jimmy Mac's brace reduced a two goal deficit, and hopes remained high.

In the second leg, a slip by giant defender Peter Madden let Malcolm Starkey - preferred somewhat surprisingly to Peter Dolby - level matters, on 15 minutes. With no addition to the score the tie went into extra time, and home hearts, among the 16,722 crowd sank when the Millers grabbed the winner. 84,466 had watched Town's best ever cup run, with another 54,307 turning out for the F.A. Cup; a total of 138,773, was almost double the 77,071 who saw their best previous effort in 1952-3.

Back in the League, Arthur was closing on 'Dixie' Dean's English record, although fog cost him a goal when Town led Newport County 2-0 on Easter Tuesday. But he hit a hat-trick in the rearranged game a fortnight later, as Town won 5-0. His last goal of the season, at Valley Parade, put him on 380, one ahead of Dixie's record. George Baker, meanwhile, finally broke his duck at home to Queens Park Rangers in his 38th appearance at No.9. Town played him as a deep-lying centre-forward, still having got the taste, he hit four in five games. The final home game on April 26th was against Walsall, who were striving for promotion to Division Two for the first time. Town's record gate of 18,917 crammed into the Meadow, with many on the Station End roof and hoards on the grass. Colin Taylor's 32nd of the season on four minutes was cancelled out by a Rowley penalty on the stroke of half-time. Colin Askey hit a second half winner which with Q.P.R. losing 3-1 clinched promotion for the Saddlers. Celebrations went on into the night, and the following day local landlords went down the A5 collecting glasses, hardly any were broken and all along the road as far as Atcham, where some fans had parked, they were neatly stacked.

Ted Hemsley and Terry Morrall made their debuts at Bradford City, while in the rearranged Newport game, Roger Walker made his only appearance, in so doing he became the **ninth** player to wear the No.7 shirt in a League game that season. Dave Humphries, whose five appearances were all away, was given a free, as were Billy Jeffrey, trialist Mervyn Rooke and 'Gentlemen' Joe Maloney. Joe's parting gesture was to blaze a Mick Jones corner into the roof of the net as Town reserves beat Crystal Palace 2-0 at the Meadow on April 29th, Allen Cornfield scored the other goal. Also Bernard Jones, Norman Smith and Geoff Ireland were freed from Town's register. Including Cup games Town had, for the third consecutive season, topped a hundred goals - 83 in the League and 21 in the two Cups.

ARTHUR ROWLEY: At Valley Parade, 29 April 1961.
Town's most famous 'son' breaks the 23 year-old Football League goalscoring record

A season which had started unimpressively had ended as 'a hard act to follow'. Early efforts were made to, at least start, the next campaign on the right note, with a two match pre-season challenge with Wrexham, instead of the usual practice match. So bolstered, by new signings Mike 'Chippy' Kenning, England schoolboy cricketer Ted Hemsley and apprentice professional Graham French and honed by the two Derby clashes, Town started in positive mood.

An opening day 4-2 victory over Port Vale, saw Mike Kenning score on his debut, Arthur Rowley hit a hat trick - his second goal completing his 100 for Shrewsbury - and Joe Maloney return to oppose his old club. An opening six match unbeaten run, ended with a 2-1 reverse at Grimsby. Centre-half Terry Morrall had needed a knee operation before the opening game while club stalwart Jack Allport, a right-winger in 1922, former reserve and 'A' team trainer and still involved with training duties, was presented with a cheque for his 39 years service. The club was also searching for, *"young attractive usherettes"* to operate in the stand on match days.

The League season was beginning to go wrong, but the arrival of the League Cup rekindled interest and form, a goalless draw with Newport, led to a replay on Thursday 28th September. Jimmy McLaughlin

had just been selected to replace Peter McParland in the Northern Ireland team to meet Scotland. On the Monday evening he hit a memorable hat trick at Peterborough. Then, appointed Captain on the Thursday to recognise his international selection, he led his side to a 3-1 victory and round two.

The cup match featured the debut of Graham French, who at the age of 16 years 175 days, was Town's youngest player, he retained his place for the League game with Reading two days later, and the talented young winger set-up all four goals as Town won 4-1. French then scored his first goal, in Town's 3-1 defeat by Bournemouth, in the League Cup, for whom Johnny Arnott returned to the Meadow as Captain. Meanwhile Jimmy 'Mac' was an instant hit for his country, scoring on his debut - an equaliser on 17 minutes - as Scotland ran out 6-1 winners. He kept his place, and had even better fortune against Greece scoring both his side's goals in a 2-0 victory.

One man still suffering was Terry Morrall, injured on his debut, he was injured again in the reserves at Crystal Palace and broke down on his comeback in the intermediates at Walsall, leaving his young team-mates to lose 12-0. The away match at Hull was nearly postponed twice due to a Polio outbreak, still a sensitive disease just two years after England full-back Jeff Hall's sad demise.

Peter Dolby, had finished his apprenticeship, and signed full-time, but Arthur felt his young squad needed another 'wise old head', and he signed Derek Hines from Leicester. A day later Norman Hobson, Mick Jones and George Baker went on the list. Town had signed an amateur centre-forward in August 1960 from St. Giles Willenhall. He had written for a trial, and went on to score 53 goals in junior games. On November 13th, he signed professional and started a dynasty, his name was Frank Clarke. A centre-half from Earlstown Lancashire, Vic Dalton, also signed full-time, and early in the New Year Tony Everall joined the professional ranks, and 'Razzer' Harris signed apprentice forms.

Gordon Skeech was described in the Journal, as: *"The Jimmy Armfield of Division Three'*, in the end of year round-up. Ten days into 1962 Norman Hobson moved to Sankey's, and six weeks later Mick Jones moved to Wellington. Frank Clarke made his debut at Lincoln, but it was his only appearance of the season, as Town signed Harry Middleton from Portsmouth the same week. They also recruited Lenny Beel as apprentice professional, and a month later Billy Nixon from Norwich.

The F.A. Cup run had been a focal point. Banbury Spencer, wore a dazzling kit but were thrashed 7-1, Town's top score in the F.A. Cup as a League side. Brierley Hill did better losing to three second half goals, and the third round saw a trip to the seaside with Southport swept aside 3-1. Round four brought Middlesbrough to the Meadow, where a rare missed penalty - by Arthur - left the Town trailing 2-0 at half-time. A tremendous second half fight-back with Rowley and Kenning cancelling out Alan Peacock's first half goals set up a replay. The receipts were good £6,300, but the score was disappointing 5-1 to Boro', ironically a Rowley penalty was Town's solitary score.

A former Town player on the mark was Roy Ambler who hit one of three hat tricks as Wrexham hammered Hartlepool 10-1 on March 3rd. Three weeks later, a twenty-yard free kick, from Town's 'goal machine' flew into the Notts County net, and George Arthur Rowley became the first Englishman to crack home 400 League goals. A week later, an extremely young Town reserve side, held Spurs to a goalless draw. On duty were Miller (21), Everall (18), Morrall (25), Dawes (17), Dalton (19), Hemsley (18), Pragg (20), Pountney (22), Hines (30), Starkey (26), French (16). Two weeks later, the first team trip to Newport resulted in a 3-2 defeat, and Town's George Walters and Jimmy McLaughlin, along with

George Harris of the home side, were all sent off. In the return a week later Derek Dawes made his debut in a convincing 4-1 victory.

An anti-climax to the season saw Town finish just two points above the relegation zone, but they retained 19 professionals, releasing Vic Dalton, Trevor Hancke, Tony Everall and Tony Corbett - the only one with League experience. In the May, 15 year old Tony Gregory signed up as an apprentice, making seven, of whom only Beverley Mitchell failed to make a first team appearance. Among many amateurs signed up was David Rowley, nephew of the manager, Alf Pountney and Les Harley, brothers of first team players.

Joe Wallace spent the summer as groundsman at Shrewsbury Cricket Club, Mike Pragg played for England Amateurs - in Zwholle against Holland - and at Rheydt against the BAOR. Elsewhere Jimmy Bullions dropped the 'player' from his player-manager tag at Alfreton, and Norman Smith returned to Barnsley after 2 years as player-manager at Sankey's.

Despite the money from the Cup matches, a loss of £17,485 was recorded in late July, and Town appointed a commercial manager, Ivor Hookway, who started one month later. Pre-season, Town played Oldham, home and away, and Birmingham at home, winning 3-2, with goals from Derek Dawes, Mike Kenning, and Harry Middleton. Early season transfers saw, Alan Humphries join Gravesend and Northfleet on a big contract, Ron Manders on his way to Kidderminster, and Town signed 16 year-old Robin Scott.

Everything was set-up for a good season, until it started that is; the 5-0 defeat at Reading was the biggest opening day margin of defeat, beating the 6-2 loss on the same ground ten years earlier. It was also to be Joe Wallace's last game, his 337th, before his move to Southport, a disappointing end to an invaluable career with Salop. George Walters and Jimmy McLaughlin, were suspended for the opener, but returned for the home game with Crystal Palace. Wingers Jimmy 'Mac' and 'Chippy' Kenning hit a goal each, as Town led 2-0 at the interval, while Arthur's penalty, with the last kick of the match, cancelled out Palace's reply.

A thrilling 3-3 draw with Bristol City saw Harry Middleton and Arthur - twice - net Town's goals, this took the Rowley record to 406 just four short of Jimmy McGrory's all-time British record.

July 1962 · Shrewsbury Town Colts. (Back): Gregory, Clarke, Beel, Wall, Harris, Hemsley.
(Front): French, Goodall, Pragg, Dawes, Mitchell. Of the 11, only Beverley Mitchell failed to make the first team.

They could have been Arthur's last goals, for the following night, on the way to Wolverhampton and in windy conditions, a large branch fell across the bonnet of the manager's car, as he took his father back to Wolverhampton. Also in the car was Arthur's wife, nephew and niece, fortunately all escaped injury. Two of the manager's nephews, David and John, were now playing for Town's junior sides, although neither were destined for stardom.

Peter Dolby had an interesting start of the season, in successive Football Combination games, he played at left-back, inside-left, centre-forward, left-half, right-half and centre-half. Mike Pragg played on the right-wing and scored for England Amateurs v. Eire in a 2-2 draw, but was dropped for the next game with Northern Ireland. While Peter Wall made the step up from apprentice to professional, with Alan Taylor supplementing the apprentice ranks.

On September 17th a right foot Rowley volley, on 46 minutes, equalled the goalscoring record, and helped Town beat Millwall 2-1. He received a round of applause from the, *"generous East London crowd"*. Nine days later, just before the interval - in the return match - another right foot shot saw the 411th and record-breaking goal recorded. They say nothing is forever but this record looks a shade permanent.

Town's next game was at Meadow Lane, a game remembered well by the Author. Town, unbeaten in five games fell behind to a Barry Jones goal in the third minute. Sitting in the Notts County directors box, the writer took a deal of stick, and bravely said, *"there is 87 minutes left yet"*, rarely have I managed a more succinct comment. Arthur hit a brace, as Town moved into a 2-1 half-time lead, Mike Kenning hit another pair before Arthur completed his hat trick, as Town won 5-1 -at this time a club record away League win. Harry Middleton was denied on several occasions, by home 'keeper George Smith, or Town could have emulated Spurs, who that day hit nine past Forest. Nottingham was a very quiet City when we left.

Ex-players in the news included Colin Whitaker, who moved from Rochdale to Oldham, and Arnold Jackson sent off in an F.A. Cup game between Stalybridge Celtic and Hyde - a week after being dismissed in a Celtic Reserves match.

Ironically Colin Whitaker would go on to be player-manager of Stalybridge.

October 13th saw Town hit seven for the fourth time in a League game. It was Pat Wright's debut, and Jimmy McLaughlin and Frank Clarke both hit hat-tricks - the only time Town have managed two in one match. Also Frank's hat trick, in this his second game, was only the fifth for the club; Andy McCulloch January '53, Jack Hudson October '53, Ray Weigh May '55 and Ken Smith March '58, were the others, by a Town No.9. The crowd obviously ecstatic kept shouting, *"breathe on 'em Salop"*, along with, *"windy"*, for unnecessary back passes - both long forgotten chants.

Eleven days later, another hat trick, this one by Albert Harley, helped Town beat Oswestry 5-0 in the first Shropshire Senior Cup-tie under lights. While on November 3rd, Jimmy Mac hit four as Town crushed Chelmsford 6-2 in the F.A. Cup, and a week later Town won an epic battle with Peterborough 5-4, after trailing 4-3 at half-time. Also in Cup action Wellington lost 4-2 to Bristol City, where John Atyeo scored twice after Ray Russell - on his 100th appearance - put the Lilywhites ahead.

One man missing out on Cup action was Mike Kenning, sold to Charlton for £10,000. Roy Ambler, after 13 goals in 21 games for Wrexham, moved to York, while Town recruited Bobby Walters from Winsford and added Dave Isherwood to the apprentices. Other youngsters - Len Beel and Robin Scott - went on a special England youth squad coaching course at Lilleshall. Beel was made travelling reserve for England youth versus Switzerland, ironically at Coventry. For the following youth international Graham French joined Beel on the bench. Another ex-Town man on the move was 'Curly' Edgley from Brentford to Barnsley, with Norman Smith, a member of the magic circle, helping produce the deal.

Town had, in the draw made on November 26th, been paired at home to Sheffield Wednesday in the F.A.Cup. The tie was made all ticket, but Wednesday sent back all but 1,200 of their 5,000 allocation, and Town sold only 11 of their 15 thousand tickets. So the dream of a 20,000 crowd evaporated, and the game itself - postponed a record number of times - did not take place until Thursday February 21st. When it was finally played, 'Bronco' Layne, (in the absence of Dave Humphries) scored on 19 minutes for Wednesday, but in the first minute of the second half Albert Harley equalised, in front of just 11,428.

The replay a fortnight later, before 24,407, saw Town reportedly outplay their lofty opponents. A neat 'one-two' with Jimmy Mac from a free kick allowed Arthur room to crack in a first half goal.

However, six minutes into extra-time, Johnny Fantham hit the winner, and Town - despite a foul on Jimmy 'Mac' - saw their penalty claims, and Cup ambitions, swept aside.

Two days after the first game, Town returned to League action, their first game since Boxing Day in that competition, against Halifax. The score, 4-2, was the same as their previous League match with Wrexham, and featured a Rowley penalty - his 20th goal of the campaign - this the 13th consecutive season he had achieved that total.

The transfer merry-go-round continued; Malcolm Starkey joined Chester, Mike Gibson went to Bristol City, and Roger Walker signed on Welsh F.A. forms for Welshpool, with Town retaining his English registrations. George Walters was listed, and John Gregson, as part of the Starkey deal, arrived from Chester. The apprentice pool was kept up to strength when Ruabon youngster Trevor Jones signed up.

On the international front Jimmy McLaughlin scored for Northern Ireland under 23's at Swansea, but Wales won 5-1, and Graham French made two goals against the Irish Youth team at Wembley, and also played in victories over Scotland and Russia.

Town travelled to Burslem on Good Friday, and played a revolutionary 4-2-4 system, with Peter Dolby and Arthur, at the heart of the defence. It was described as a *"somewhat negative style"*. On April 20th, Town - without their player-manager - lost 3-0 at home to Q.P.R. and missed two penalties. Dave Pountney and Derek Dawes were the culprits. This game also featured Bobby Walters' only appearance, and while the last game of the season saw young Len Beel concede a penalty on his debut against Coventry, but Town won 2-1. John Gregson, hit the winner with 15 minutes left, but Sky Blues manager, Jimmy Hill - to much derision - went onto the pitch to examine a 'hole' in the side-netting.

The long period of wintry weather, meant the Midland Intermediate League fixtures were not completed, the title being decided on a percentage basis, with Town having abandoned 4 fixtures. Meanwhile Bobby Mayle emigrated to Australia leaving his brother Tony and Johnny Draycott at Knighton. The records show the season ended with free transfers for

Gordon Skeech - who returned to Runcorn - Terry Morrell off to Wrexham and Dave Goodall, who moved to Wellington. Lenny Beel and Tony 'Razzer' Harris moved up from apprentice to full professional status.

Town had finished 15th but the steady improvement was to be given a major overhaul. Jimmy McLaughlin was sold to Swansea for a fee described as a record, but less than £16,000. A fee was agreed with Reading for full-back David High, but the deal fell through. Then the month of June saw Town 'taking the high road', on the first, Eric Brodie - a Scottish junior international - arrived from Dundee United. A fortnight later, George Broadman - a Scottish amateur international - came South from Queens Park, and seven days on Hearts winger Bobby Ross completed the hat trick.

Harry Middleton, Billy Nixon and George Walters all refused terms, with Middleton also turning down an approach by Aldershot. Nixon re-signed on 1st August 1963, but Walters and Middleton went on month to month contracts. Ex-players on the move included, Roy Ambler joining Southport, and Norman Hobson who became player-manager at Holywell Town. Brian 'Snowy' Harris became an apprentice, with Lewis Richardson signing professional.

Troublesome talent, Graham French signed for Swindon for £12,000, with ex-Walsall winger Brian Taylor signed from Rotherham as replacement, just days after his brother Colin went from Walsall to Newcastle. Another signing from Yorkshire was full-back Ken Turner, Ray Wilson's understudy at Huddersfield.

July 20th saw the staging of international freestyle wrestling at the Gay Meadow, like the introduction of half-time bingo, seven months earlier, it was the brainchild of Ivor Hookway. The wrestling failed to take off, partly due to the fact that standing in the enclosure, one could hear the next move being discussed in the ring, which had been erected just in front of the tunnel.

The changing personnel had heightened interest, but just six days before the kick-off, the whole Town, - not only the club - was rocked by the news of the tragic death of young goalkeeper Paul Miller. He joined Town in July 1959 after a spell as an amateur with Walsall, and represented England Boys clubs in the match with the Scottish Boys clubs in 1958-9. He had been the County javelin champion, a keen tennis player, a good bowler at cricket, and a strong swimmer. He had travelled to Trentham Gardens, to enjoy an afternoon in the open air swimming pool, unaware that he suffered from a condition which slowed down his digestion. An inquest recorded an accidental death verdict, and the funeral at Meole Parish Church, with Messrs Middleton, Nixon, Walters, Pountney, Wright and Dolby as bearers, was followed by interment at Gnossall.

The club moved quickly to sign Alan Boswell from Walsall for a substantial fee, and a single Frank Clarke goal saw Town to victory over Port Vale in the opener. Town lost 2-1 to Q.P.R. and beat Notts County 1-0, with Clarke again their only marksman. Harry Middleton re-signed, and after a 3-0 victory against Crewe, returned for the return with Q.P.R. He hit a hat trick in the No.9 shirt, as Town won 4-3, Albert Harley scored the other goal. A three goal defeat at Crystal Palace meant a debut for George Boardman in place of Bobby Ross. Boardman's father had played for Partick and Bradford Park Avenue while Bobby Ross won a Scottish League Cup Winners Medal despite missing the final. Boardman took his chance scoring on his debut, as Town won 2-0, and then hit two as Town overcame Walsall 2-1, in spite of losing Alan Boswell with a shoulder injury.

The injury to 'Bozzy' left Town searching for a keeper, and signing John McLaughlin from Third Lanark on a month's trial, filled that gap. During his stay Town won 2, lost 2 and drew 1; Ken Turner scored his only goal from the penalty spot, Eric Brodie made his League debut, and Arthur did not play. Town had crashed out of the League Cup 6-2 at Bristol Rovers, three days after the Walsall game, with Lenny Beel on duty and Eric Brodie also included. Town welcomed Alan Boswell back for a couple of games, but when he was taken ill Len Beel deputised at Coventry on October 30th. It was a disastrous night, for it produced Town's biggest ever away defeat, by 8-1. Another player missing from the debacle was Dave Pountney who was sold to Aston Villa for £20,000 two days before. Two months earlier Dave and Arthur Rowley had received benefit cheques bringing the number paid out to eleven. The team it formed would read as follows:- Crossley, Bannister, Skeech, Wallace, Maloney, Walters, Price, Harley, Rowley, Pountney, Hobson.

Foreign opposition took centre stage a week after bonfire night, when Spartak - a Czechoslovakian side over here to play Partick Thistle in the Inter-City Fairs Cup - lost 3-1 to Town in front of 7,763; Frank Clarke 2 and Harry Middleton scored.

A month later Town reserves had three penalties in the same game against Notts County - they missed two. Derek Hines and Tony Harris were at fault, with Harris scoring the middle one of the trio, but the 'stiffs' still won 4-1.

Young 'Razzer' Harris had featured in a youth international trial, while Alan Taylor had signed professional and Harold Williams joined as an apprentice, old boys John Price and Roger Charlesworth (both ex-Town and Sankey's), had teamed up again at Hednesford, while Ron Manders moved from Halesowen to Machynellyth as player-manager, and Fred Ashworth joined Mossley. The scouting continued, with Tommy Seymour and Arthur Rowley going to Chesterfield, to watch a youth game featuring a 14 year old Luigi Macari. He impressed but sadly joined Celtic.

Just before Christmas Harry Middleton hit a hat trick against Notts County, to make up for the previous season's frustrations. However, this and his third trio of the season against Bournemouth were both in the No.10 shirt. Christmas saw Town win at Wrexham 3-2, then lose the return 2-1. While the New Year started badly, Billy Nixon broke his leg, a pox fracture, in a training accident, and Town lost to both Watford and Crewe. The Crewe Match was Albert Harley's 200th League game - and he was still 3 months short of his 24th birthday, whilst among Crewe's goalscorers was Billy Haydock later physio' under Asa Hartford. Meanwhile at Sankey's on the same day, Joe Maloney playing for Winsford marked Derek Price and went back to Derek's for a cup of tea afterwards!

Other milestones in January 1964 saw Alan Humphreys, Albert's contemporary, join Mansfield, and hospital radio hit the airways for the 1-1 home draw with Palace on the 18th. Ironically the first Town score on air was an own goal by Alan Stephenson. Town's reserves lost 7-0 at Highbury, Mick Richards was in goal but Town were decimated by injury. Arthur was concussed in a clash of heads with Terry Neill; Harry Middleton limped off and Lewis Richardson was also hurt.

On February 11th, Chairman Arthur Jones 71 died. He had followed Town since their Copthorne days, apart from his playing for Upton Magna, and joined the committee in the early 1930's. He became a director of the Limited Company in 1936.

Also in February, 15 year-old Trevor Jones became Town's second youngest football combination player - just five weeks before the youngest-ever, Derek Dawes, left the club to join Wellington; he wanted to combine part-time football with a job. Another 15 year-old to sign on was Howard Wright. This youngster was not 16 until October, but made his combination debut on Easter Monday and scored against Spurs the following Saturday.

On March 31st, Town recalled Len Beel and gave a debut to Robin Scott (whose dad Gerald played just after the war), in a home game with Brentford which ended in a 1-1 draw. On the Saturday, with Alan Boswell and John Gregson back, Town crashed 7-1 at Southend. It could have been different, for Harry Middleton robbed 'keeper Peter Goy just 90 seconds into the game, but then lifted the ball over the empty net. Town's only consolation was a late goal from Pat Wright. The day before the final game Derek Hines left, and Town - after five games without a win, finished on a high note beating Hull 5-1.

The action continued, however, with a three match tour of Czechoslovakia on May 20th. Brian Taylor's goal helped Town draw 1-1 with Karlovey Vary, while two days later Trevor Meredith - on his debut - scored as Salop again drew 1-1, this time with Spartak Hradec. The third game, with Spartak Brno ended in a 3-1 defeat, with Bobby Ross being Town's marksmen. The tour party consisted:- G.E.G.Tudor (Chairman), Harold Davies (Director), Les Rimmer (Secretary), Tommy Seymour (Trainer), Dr H.Foy, G.A.Rowley, G.Boardman, A.Boswell, E.Brodie, F.Clarke, P.Dolby, J.Gregson, A.Harley, T.Harris, T.Meredith, H.Middleton, R.Ross, B.Taylor, P.Wall, P.Wright.

Apart from Meredith from Burnley, Town also signed a goalkeeper and a wicketkeeper. Mike Walker from Watford was the custodian and Bobby Stephenson an inside-forward from Derby was the glove expert. He was Bob Taylor's understudy at Derbyshire but later moved to, and captained, Hampshire. After their continental holiday, which for three included a night in the cells for being out after Police curfew, the players returned to a wide selection of summertime employment. Peter Dolby worked at Shropshire Produce, Peter Wall in a garage and Brian Taylor, John Gregson and Albert Harley for Murrell's nurseries.

Old boys moving again were Ray Russell to Halesowen, Roger Charlesworth to Lower Gornal, and - in slightly more exotic climes - Ken Smith moved to Port Elizabeth in South Africa.

Without the fear of a dividend being declared, Town did at least announce a trading profit (of £2,081), for the first time in ten years, thanks to a transfer surplus of £22,625, due to the sales of Pountney, French and Walters, outweighing the incomings of Meredith for £4,000, Boardman, Boswell, Brodie, Richards, Ross, Taylor and Turner. Town also signed several amateurs amongst whom John Ray and Geoff Croft made most progress. The released players included Mike Richards to Wellington, Bobby Walters to Sankey's, Alan Taylor joining Brierley Hill, and Len Beel snapped up by Birmingham City, while Derek Hines had joined Rugby.

Season 1964-5 kicked off with two difficult looking away games at Southend and Reading. Two defeats proved just how difficult. A home draw with Barnsley, 3-3, and a 4-0 victory over Reading in the return steadied the ship, and despite a narrow loss at Scunthorpe the team was beginning to take shape. Missing were Albert Harley who after the first three games moved to Swansea, and Arthur Rowley who made only another nine appearances after the opening two.

A single Brian Taylor goal beat Exeter, and Walsall succumbed to a Bobby Ross hat trick which included a penalty. Victory at Exeter completed the double, and a draw at Watford preceded another epic League Cup battle. Town drew Stoke City away, and a Ted Hemsley equaliser on 39 minutes, set up a replay, aided by Gerry Bridgwood missing a sitter. Town thrashed Workington 6-1 on the Saturday but on the Tuesday failed to register. It was the first season of regular Tuesday games and 15,304 fans paid record receipts of £2,345 (£4 more than the Middlesbrough F.A. Cup game in January 1962), to see Stoke win 1-0.

It was the final games of a month which saw the first Sunday League formed in the County, the 'Shropshire Youth Sunday League' which consisted of eight teams in the Ludlow area. Other events saw Joe Maloney join Colwyn Bay, wing-half Mike Jones join Haverfordwest, and his namesake, winger Mickey, arrive at Halesowen.

On October 10th, Mike Walker and new signing John Regan made their debuts as Town beat Bristol Rovers 2-1, with goals from Boardman and Regan, and three days later Boardman again scored as Town beat Gillingham 2-0. The other goal was a Bobby Ross penalty, despite Arthur playing at centre-half. Bobby always credits Arthur with teaching him how to take penalties, the secret being in the run-up, and

he only ever missed two, ironically one was for Cambridge against Shrewsbury. This game was the end of a run of one defeat in nine games, and was followed by a spell of one win in eleven. The eleventh was a 3-1 home defeat by Oldham on Boxing Day, but two days later a 3-1 away win at Boundary Park, one of Town's happiest away grounds, started an improved run.

The poor run had started in October, a month in which nine League games were played, commencing at Brentford in a game which saw Eric Brodie and Tommy Higginson of the home side sent off. Also during the month, Watford tried - unsuccessfully - to secure Arthur Rowley as manager, and John Gregson went on the transfer list. The reserves played in a remarkable 5-5 draw at Portsmouth, Bobby Stephenson 2, Frank Clarke, Robin Scott and Harry Middleton scored, but Middleton also had a goal disallowed and missed a penalty against his old club. They followed this up with a 3-1 victory at Highbury. Stephenson's opener cancelled out by John Radford, but Scott and Regan secured the points.

The F.A.Cup first round draw sent Town to the far East, well Kings Lynn, actually. It also provided the opportunity to honour Roland Depear. He travelled on the team coach from Spalding (where he still currently lives), to the Walks Stadium, where Town won, thanks to John Regan's eleventh minute goal. They drew Exeter away in round two, and Regan was again the hero, scoring both goals in a 2-1 victory. A victory tinged with good fortune, as John Regan, with Bobby Stephenson and Pat Wright - as passengers - crashed on the way back from a P.F.A. meeting, the previous Monday. However, Town had no luck with the draw, away again, this time at Maine Road. Another having little luck was Norman Smith, who became the first person to have five cartilage operations.

A home win over Scunthorpe was a prelude to another Cup day to relish. A Bobby Ross header on the quarter hour saw Town lead their illustrious opponents for 73 minutes until Derek Kevan snatched a dramatic late equaliser. The replay set a new receipts record (£6 more than the Stoke game), but Town looked to be slipping out of contention when Matt Gray headed City into a 16th minute lead, and Bobby Ross missed a penalty. Then a man for big occasions, Peter Dolby, playing centre-half, put Town level on the hour. Trevor Meredith pushed Town ahead on 77 minutes and five minutes later Bobby Ross redeemed himself to seal the victory. City's disappointed young centre-half was Alf Wood.

Using the theory of strengthening when playing well, Arthur went out and provided Town fans with a real treat. He signed Peter Broadbent from Wolves for a reported *"record five figure fee"*, a more up to date estimate put this at £7,000! He replaced Bobby Ross at Walsall as Town drew 1-1, and George Boardman in the 2-2 home draw with Watford.

However, for the trip to the Den, Arthur re-united the Manchester City line-up recalling Boardman and Peter Wall. It was Saturday 30th January 1965, the day of the state funeral of Winston Spencer Churchill, but Town - with their full allocation of tickets - took a detour to avoid the funeral, and with over 3,000 fans entered the Lions Den. The East London side were in the middle of a record run of 59 consecutive League games without defeat. So a half-time score of Millwall 1 - Shrewsbury 0, was not unexpected. But two minutes after the interval George Boardman levelled, and 30 minutes on Trevor Meredith hit a shot with his left foot - yes left - to cement the victory (only Norwich in the League Cup emulated Town's feat until Plymouth won in the League in 1967).

Leeds United, the Football League leaders, away was the Town's fifth round draw. The last sixteen for the first time, and the Cup bug had bitten deeply as 6,000 travelled to Elland Road. Peter Broadbent replaced John Regan in an otherwise unchanged Cup side. Town had lost 4-0 at home to Hull seven days earlier, and although the fairytale was to end, they put up a tremendous fight, losing just 2-0, in front of 47,740.

Back in League action Town drew at Bristol Rovers, before a Ross penalty beat Brentford, in front of 5,564 at the Meadow. The next game was away to Luton, Razzer Harris and Robin Scott were brought into the team, as Town went on the rampage winning 7-2. Still their record away win, George Boardman hitting four, Robin Scott's brace were his only League goals, and Bobby Ross completed the rout. The reaction of the Town faithful, apart from disbelief, was for eighteen fewer to turn up for the following home game - a goalless draw with Port Vale. The next four games were all lost, including the return with Luton, 2-0, so David Pleat who played in both matches earned some revenge.

The season stuttered to a close with the exception of a 3-2 victory over Q.P.R., which included Peter Broadbent's first goal, a 25 yard drive. Over Easter, Bristol City rescued their season, winning 5-1 at the Meadow and 3-0 at Ashton Gate - John Atyeo hitting

five goals - which helped them to promotion on goal average over Mansfield. Town also lost the final game, 2-1 at home to Bournemouth, to end with just five points out of 22.

The one notable event was Arthur Rowley's final Football League appearance, at centre-half, and he signed off, in expected style, scoring his 434th League goal in 619 games.

The two highspots at the end of the campaign were the reserves 3-1 victory at West Ham which pre-served their status in the Football Combination Division One. While at the Meadow Tony Gregory made his debut against Bournemouth. Peter Wall and Bobby Stephenson were listed and Billy Nixon freed, Stephenson joined Rochdale and Nixon returned home to Ireland. Brian Taylor moved to Port Vale and Geoff Fellows was signed from Aston Villa. New apprentices recruited included Alan Jones and Terry Matthias, and Town tried to sign a winger - Lewis Thom - and a centre-half Jim Moore, from Dundee United.

Mike Walker started the 1965-66 season as Town's goalkeeper. Geoff Fellows made his debut and Town won 4-1 over York. The away trip to Bristol Rovers was notable, as Tony Gregory replaced John Regan for the last 19 minutes. Regan was carried off with a leg injury, and Gregory, the unused substitute in Town's first game, wrote his place in the club history. The other major personnel alteration was Eric Brodie, wearing the No.5 shirt for the first half of the season.

Against Swansea Town, 'Bozzy' returned to League action, and Frank Clarke became the first player to hit a second hat trick in the No.9 shirt, in this, the Town's fifteenth League season. Defeats at Walsall 3-0, and Brentford 4-0, pushed Town into the transfer market. Lewis Thom finally arrived, and two days later made his debut in the 1-1 draw with Workington. Two weeks later he scored his first goal against Southend as Town won 3-0.

Progress in the League Cup, with victories over Torquay 3-0 and Bristol City 1-0, set up the chance of revenge against Rotherham. It was not to be, for Town were outplayed and lost 5-2. A fortnight later 7,743 saw Arthur's first testimonial night when an international XI beat ex-Wolves 3-2, and Town beat Wolves 3-0, with Thom (two) and Meredith their marksmen. Bonfire day saw Peter Wall join Wrexham, before Town put Torquay out of the F.A. Cup, 2-1. John Regan was not involved and the following Thursday was listed. After their run of away ties the previous season, Town managed to come out first again in round two and were paired with Peterborough United. Trevor Meredith scored twice and Frank Clarke helped clinch a 3-2 victory to avenge the 4-3 defeat of six seasons earlier. Round three threw up a trip to Shepherds Bush, never a happy hunting ground, but a battling goalless draw with Q.P.R. kept hopes alive.

A nervous-looking 'Razzer' Harris in the replay, came in for Peter Dolby who had a leg injury. An early pass, straight to Les Allen, looked fatal but Alan Boswell saved, and 'Razzer' settled down to snuff out his illustrious opponent. It was a tense battle settled by Trevor Meredith's strike with twelve minutes remaining. In the League, Town were doing well apart from the occasional blip. Amazingly they conceded four on six occasions - including once at home over Christmas against Scunthorpe, losing 4-1. For the second year running they reversed the losing scoreline immediately in the return, also surprisingly both games were 1-1 at half-time. The week before the trip to Q.P.R., Town had lost 4-2 at Millwall, with George Boardman scoring a brilliant goal. He flicked it over his shoulder and over the defender before spinning to volley home from 20 yards.

Reserve skipper Ken Turner was listed shortly after the club announced they would leave the Fooball Combination and join the West Midland League. Derek Lokier was in the England Amateur XI to play the Southern Counties at Wycombe, and the club announced the inclusion of the Football League review in the programme. However, the Ford branch of the supporters club was annoyed at the news that the fourth round match with Carlisle, would see no concessions for children and old age pensioners, and prices would be up 1/- (5p) to 5/- (25p) for the ground and to 8/6 (42½p) for Stand A.

To add insult to injury the game was a drab goalless draw. Carlisle included a former England schools 'keeper - Joe Dean - who had made his international debut at the Meadow, along with Willie Carlin - later to star for Brian Clough at Derby - and Chris Balderstone who went on to play first class cricket and League football on the same day. When Bobby Ross scored in the replay, with eight minutes left, hopes rose, but as a centre came over Peter Dolby somehow managed to thrust out a telescopic leg, and score his finest ever goal; tragically it flew past Alan Boswell, whose bemused look is etched in the Author's memory. The best thing about this unfortunate equaliser was that it set up Town's most memorable match.

Not everybody saw all the drama of the second replay, because both ends of the game were packed with incident. A first minute Chris Balderstone free-kick was juggled by Alan Boswell, but adjudged to have crossed the line. It took Town 64 minutes to reply, Eric Brodie slamming in the equaliser. It looked all over when Dave Wilson put Carlisle ahead again on 85 minutes, and many fans left the ground before the astonishing finale. Four minutes into injury time Town were awarded a free-kick on the right edge of the penalty area. Trevor Meredith stood over the ball, Peter Broadbent - for some unknown reason patted his head. Trevor chipped the ball accurately towards Peter, who nonchantly headed Town level, with a goal which rates - with Trevor Brooking's 1980 Cup Final winner - as the game's unlikeliest headed goal.

The nail biting had only just begun, for 13 minutes into extra-time, George Boardman picked out Frank Clarke to blast Town ahead, but a mistake two minutes later and Willie Carlin cashed in to level. A third replay seemed probable, but with just four minutes remaining, a beautifully struck George Boardman shot clinched the fifth round trip to Stamford Bridge.

Memories of the 1965-66 F.A.Cup run. Franke Clarke gives Chelsea a fright in the fifth round with this goal. Town eventually narrowly lost 2-3 before a packed Stamford Bridge.

A crowd of 51,144 assembled, as Salop made the last sixteen for the second successive season. An early offside goal could have destroyed many sides, but with Peter Broadbent showing a young Peter Osgood the meaning of the word class, Town threatened to reach new heights. Goals from Frank Clarke and Peter Broadbent rocked the pensioners, who spent the last ten minutes time wasting by the corner flags. The 15,000, yes fifteen thousand, Town fans, although slightly disappointed, proudly sang all the way home. Sadly memories were shortlived, for the next home game a fortnight later attracted just 5,333. They saw Town lose 2-0 to Bournemouth.

Town bounced back in the following game at Mansfield Town, with goals from Clarke, Brodie and Hemsley, who set up a 3-0 victory. This was cemented by Alan Boswell saving two penalties and racing off his line to head clear on another occasion. At Watford on Good Friday, John Ray made his debut and only one fan travelled down from Shrewsbury - Town lost 1-0. All the extra games meant Town had picked up several niggling injuries, and for the trip to Hull, Arthur saw Ted Hemsley and George Boardman fail fitness tests. Boardman played, despite his groin injury, and was outstanding.

Frank Clarke gave Town the lead, but a recurrence saw Broadman limp off. Hemsley limped on, and Town lost 2-1. Frank Clarke stated: *"That's promotion luck"*. It was, for Hull won the title. The Cup run had been accompanied by a lucky mascot, a 'Gonk', but before the Grimsby game on May 4th another 'lucky charm' - a Koala bear called 'High Score' backfired. Tony Gregory challenged Matt Tees and the referee gave a penalty, which was converted by Ron Cockerill, and timed at ten seconds. A week later, Town 4-0 up against Wellington in the Senior Cup semi-final drew 4-4. They won the replay 2-1, but in the final on May 23rd, Ted Hemsley and Billy Birch were sent off, as Town beat Oswestry 5-4.

Mike Walker - seven games and five wins - plus John Ray, despite appearing in all the last four games, were listed, while Robin Scott and Ken Turner were freed. A month later Ray was given a free and Gordon Lee was signed as player-coach. Attempts to sign Eddie Monan from Ayr United failed, so Arthur paid a big fee for Alf Wood. Alan Turner arrived from Coventry and Pat Wright's transfer request was granted. A new apprentice signing was Colin Hemsley, younger brother of Ted.

CHAPTER 10 - WORLD CUP, CRICKET, AND ALMOST PROMOTION

A nation proudly boasting the best side in the World looked forward to the new season with no little anticipation. For Shrewsbury it opened on a glorious sunny day in West London. Whilst Ken Higgs and John Snow were caning the Australian attack - for a record last wicket partnership - across Town, Salop ran out to face Queens Park Rangers. A goal down at half-time, a Trevor Meredith penalty and a header - yes a header - from twelve yards saw the Town ahead with just minutes remaining. Then a ball in from the right-wing hit Rodney Marsh, who was on all fours, on the head for an unfortunate leveller.

The following Wednesday, Town entertained Wrexham in the League Cup, or rather blew them away, for it was 5-1 at half-time, and though Town added only one in the second half the 7,003 crowd should have left contented. However, the Saturday game with Colchester was the first time an opening home League game drew less than 5,000 spectators. After two away defeats only 4,286 turned up for the 1-0 victory over Oxford, but on the Wednesday, 10,320 thought the League Cup visit of First Division Burnley worth a look. Again the Cup crowd saw an inspired Cup performance. A Board-man goal set up a replay at Turf Moor

October 1965:
Work commences on new offices and boardroom at Gay Meadow.

It was a disastrous night, Ted Hemsley and Alf Wood both scored own goals as Town, 4-0 down at half-time, lost 5-0. The Burnley fans not content with this set on a young Town fan, chopped his scarf into little pieces and burnt it. That youngster - Chris Smith - now runs buses to Town's away games.

In the Author's role, then as Chairman of the junior supporters and travel organiser, a letter was written to Bob Lord to complain, but sadly he never replied. Action taken then, from such an incident, could have helped stop the malaise which was to tarnish the game for the next quarter of a century.

The next game played saw more problems, as Alan Boswell was injured in the first half at Swindon, and Tony Gregory came off the bench to take over. In an heroic second half, Town, a goal down at the break rescued a point thanks to goals from Frank Clarke and Peter Dolby twice equalising new signing Willie Penman's goals. Despite this a crowd of under 4,000 watched Town beat Reading 1-0, so in a bold move Town went into the transfer market, lashing out £11,000 for big John Manning. The money came from Peter Broad-bent's departure to join Villa, as a replacement for Phil Woosnam, who went to the United States to launch a Football League.

Although not scoring on his debut, Manning had a hand in three of Town's goals in their 4-1 victory over Bourne-mouth, Frank Clarke, in the No.8 shirt, hit a hat-trick. The next home game - Mansfield on October 29th - saw a rare Geoff Fellows goal settle the on the field business. While off it, Minister of Sport Dennis Howell, opened the new office block.

Three days later, despite John Manning's first two goals for the club, Bristol Rovers ended Town's unbeaten home record with a 4-3 scoreline. Out of favour Peter Dolby had asked for a transfer but this result led to a recall. Meanwhile Town showed interest in Graham Carr from Northampton and Tommy Knox from Mansfield. Interest in Knox probably waned when Alan Turner - recalled on the left-wing - hit a brace, as Town won 3-0 at Bournemouth to complete an emphatic double. A 2-0 victory at Peterborough was a battle of offside traps before a crushing 5-2 victory over Hartlepools United started the F.A. Cup glory trail.

December was a mixed month, typified by the Boxing Day game at Swansea. George Boardman was taken ill on the way to the game, near Brecon. At the stop-off point he looked horrendous, suffering with sympathetic pregancy pains. 'Tiger' Brodie was recalled and thirteenth man Tony Gregory became substitute. Undeterred, Town raced into a 2-0 lead in 15 minutes, only to collapse like poor George, and lose 5-2. The following day player-coach Gordon Lee made his debut in the return match, and Tony Gregory started, replacing injured full-backs Pat Wright and Geoff Fellows, as Town drew 2-2 with the Welsh side. After a 3-1 defeat at Colchester, Wright returned for the Cup tie with Wrexham.

Having been beaten 6-1 in the other Cup, Wrexham must have hoped for better things, but despite just one goal in the first half Town again ran out easy winners. A hat-trick from the fit again Boardman and one each from Trevor Meredith and John Manning sent the English section of the 13,430 crowd home happy as Town won 5-1. Second Division Ipswich away was a memorable trip, for our bus at least, but when a John Manning header hit the woodwork seconds after Gerry Baker had seen a goal disallowed Shrewsbury's luck ran out. Following up Boardman, Meredith and Clarke all saw efforts cleared, four minutes later Trevor Meredith missed a 'golden chance' and John Manning saw another header hacked off the line; it was not to be, Salop lost 4-1.

Injuries had played their part in the reserves losing their unbeaten home record, in style, 6-1 to Halesowen and also defeat for the first team, losing to Oxford for the first time. While crowd barracking had lead to Arthur resting Alf Wood, and 'Razzer' Harris, frustrations led to a transfer request. Mike Walker, after moving to York, was called up by Wales U-23 side and Town tried to sign Ayr United winger John Grant. In the 1966 close season Town wrote to all other Third Division clubs requesting the opportunity to try Saturday night kick-offs, two - Swindon and Doncaster - agreed.

So after 3,491 turned up to see Town beat Workington 3-1, the Swindon game gave the club a chance to experiment. Incidentally Wellington had a home gate of 2,994 for their previous home game, and the local press reported the crowd cheered Alf during the Workington victory. The Swindon crowd of 5,057 was judged a success, but despite a big victory in between, the Doncaster crowd of 4,875 was a disappointment to the club.

Early in March 1967, Lew Thom joined Pat Wright, Peter Dolby and 'Razzer' on the list but a week later John Manning was in the spotlight. The local manager of Littlewoods, Austin Stephens, offered to give a food hamper to an old folks club for every Manning goal. The following day Manning recorded his only League hat trick for the club in the 6-1 victory over Leyton Orient. Tony Gregory's season was brought to an untimely end, when he broke his leg in training, landing awkwardly and sustaining a hairline fracture of the shin.

Queens Park Rangers were walking away with the title, but Town still had an outside chance of promotion as did Middlesbrough, who were staging a late charge, and the clubs met at Easter. It was not a pretty sight for the 23,452 gathered at Ayresome Park; 3 players booked, 1 helped off, and John Hickton in the last minute piled into a ruck and put Geoff Fellows and the ball over the line. A George Boardman goal won the return, which featured 11 free kicks, in the first 13 minutes, but Middlesbrough, literally, powered their way to promotion. Trevor Meredith missed the return, John Manning limped off and Dolby, Wood, Wright and Brodie were all carrying injuries by the end. Not surprisingly Town lost the next home game, 1-0 to Grimsby, their first home defeat for five months.

On April 5th, West Ham United came to the Meadow for a friendly in aid of the Shropshire World Cup appeal fund, their line-up consisted:- Mackleworth, Burnett, Bowkett, Peters, Heffer, Moore, Redknapp, Boyce, Bennett, Dawkins and Eadie, and they won 4-1. Town played Les Aston in goal in the first half, while George Boardman hit the consolation goal. The only surprise was in the West Ham scorers, with Bobby Moore hitting two; Martin Peters and Peter Bennett netted the others.

John Manning having missed this and two League games, returned against Gillingham to net two more hampers, and on April 22nd Town ended Torquay's unbeaten home record 2-0 at Plainmoor.

The season ended with a run of eight games unbeaten, culminating with a 3-2 victory at Workington in front of 1,175. In fact there were more people at the fair on the football club car park than at the match. The only Town fans were two car loads transported by Harold Wright and Alan Roberts in a deal struck in the 'Brick'. In these early days of arranging transport, several unusual trips were undertaken including a taxi journey to Torquay. One man who remembers the trip to Workington is Pat Wright, whose brave header saw him clash with a post. He spent the next week doing a fair impression of a panda, with his two lovely black eyes!

On May 12th Lewis Thom moved to Lincoln while Colin Hemsley and Terry Matthias signed professional. Soon after Alan Turner joined Jack Rowley - who had moved from Wrexham - at Bradford City, and Town signed apprentices Pat Douglas and Trevor Boucher. Aston Villa were rumoured to want Arthur Rowley as manager, and Town turned down a substantial bid from a leading London club. The Football League threatened to deduct £100 off the pool money allocation to clubs playing on Friday nights, so causing a fixture re-think for Town. David Pleat was signed from Luton on a free and Tony Gregory trained throughout the summer to regain fitness. While Alan Boswell refused terms with Cardiff after an exchange deal featuring Welsh U-23 winger Bernard Lewis was proposed. The 1967 close season ended on a sad note when Chairman G. Emery Tudor died in late July.

NEW CHAIRMAN, CUP GLORY AND LEAGUE HOPES

Tim Yates was appointed as the new Chairman and Leslie Tudor Owen as Vice-Chairman, although the new regime started with mixed blessings. The supporters club boosted affairs with a cheque for £19,500 but Frank Clarke asked for a transfer. A licence for a new bar under the Stand was granted in August, but it did not open until the Darlington game in December.

Graham Clapham was signed from Newcastle, and arrived at the ground with goalkeeper David Lawson, who was on a two month trial, in time for the pre-season match, and 'Tiger' Brodie rejected Southend United. David Pleat made his debut in the opening game against Oxford United, who relied on two brothers - Ron and Graham Atkinson. Second half goals from Frank Clarke and Ted Hemsley gave little hint of the drama to follow for these clubs.

A flurry of transfer activity at the end of September came after Eric Brodie went on the list, and Alan Boswell turned down Aston Villa because he preferred Town's training facilities. After five League games without a goal John Manning scored on his final appearance against Orient. He moved to Norwich for £20,000 on the following Thursday, having heard Town's fickle fans start to moan in the opening three home games. His other goals had been a brace at Walsall as Town lost 4-2 in the League Cup. The day after, Jimmy McLaughlin became the first player to be re-signed by Town since they joined the Football League, when he returned from Peterborough for £7,000. Arthur tried to make it a double by negotiating with Aston Villa for Dave Pountney. As if all that was not enough, a week later Brian Clough paid £8,000 for Pat Wright.

Just one goal in four games saw Town plunge around £12,000 for Barry Stobart from Villa. They immediately won four straight games, including a 5-0 victory over Torquay, during which both Stobart and McLaughlin scored their first goals since their transfers. Three players not featuring were David Pleat - diligently attending motor maintenance and financial management courses - while fellow injury victim 'Razzer' Harris had broken a bone in his left foot after previously recovering from a dislocated shoulders on three occasions, and a fractured cheek bone. David Lawson, meanwhile, after a trial spell disrupted by lack of fixtures, joined Jack Rowley at Bradford Park Avenue, so keeping the brotherly assistance going. He went on to become the British record goalkeeping signing when moving from Huddersfield to Everton for £65,000.

After a first round victory over Darlington, Town drew Tow Law Town away in the F.A.Cup - they had hammered Mansfield in round one - when according to their fans the Stags suffered frost bite in the second half. Having left Town at 5 a.m. on the first supporters coach, we arrived at Tow Law at 11.20, just after the referee - thanks to the odd prompt from Arthur - had called the game off. Locals were saying a Northern League game would have been played on the surface, but there again so could ice-hockey! The match finally took place eight days later, but few Town fans made it to see an heroic performance by Alan Boswell and a Frank Clarke goal earn Town a replay. The slanting pitch was a problem, the dressing room door let in a stream of water, and Ted Hemsley looked bemused - until a gap in the crowd was cleared, by the author, for the team to take the pitch!

16 January 1968: Gay Meadow under two feet of water from the flooded River Severn.
Town's F.A.Cup replay with Durham Amateurs Tow Law Town, was postponed one day.

For all that Town were lucky to survive, particularly as Arsenal at home was the prize third round draw. The Tow Law people were superb, and when the author rang the secretary a dozen years later, he was pleased to relate they had a young gangly left-winger who could play a bit; the information was passed on, but Chris Waddle went to Newcastle United.

The Gay Meadow was under water 48 hours before the return, but, amazingly with a little help, recovered. The game saw a crowd of 14,508, with many of the visiting fans arriving late due to traffic problems. Eric Brodie hit his only Town hat-trick, and Town were easy 6-2 winners, but the battling part-timers received a standing ovation at the final whistle. On the Saturday, Town visited Orient and drew 1-1 thanks to a remarkable 25 yard volley off the shin, by Jimmy 'Mac', but all talk revolved around the London opponents due to arrive in Shrewsbury a week later. The mighty Arsenal drew a crowd of 18,280.

Town battled like trojans, but just before half-time, John Radford - although clearly offside - collected a George Graham back-heel to put the Gunners ahead. Town laid seige to the Arsenal goal in the second half, and time was running out when Peter Dolby, rose to grab a late equaliser. For the replay the team travelled by train, and the supporters - thanks to Dave the normal team driver - travelled by plane, doing the last 89 miles to Highbury in one hour. Almost 42,000 watched the game, and Town lost 2-0, a goal in each half. Jon Sammels and David Jenkins scored, with Geordie Armstrong (who was impressed with our performance at the Meadow) outstanding - more on Jenkins a little later. Young 'Ged' Garbett had come on as 'sub' against Tow Law in the replay and did so again at Highbury, but with respect he looked strangely out of place. In fact the young man failed to break through in his own back-yard, but went on to play nearly 200 League games with Barrow and Stockport, scoring 40 League goals, mainly with his cannonball left foot.

The dust had hardly settled on the Cup run when transfer activity restarted on February 9th. Dave Pountney finally returned, but within a fortnight Frank Clarke moved to Queens Park Rangers. When asked if he regretted selling any players, Boss Arthur Rowley said - in 1994 - that this was the deal which cost us promotion. The hard working Clarke, who was sold for £35,000, should have been replaced by Oxford United striker Graham Atkinson, but the deal fell through. Despite the loss of Clarke, Town won their next two games before a needle game with Tranmere saw 7,836 witness a memorable match. Sadly memorable for largely the wrong reasons; Alf Wood, former Telford boss Stan Storton, and Gerry Casey were all booked, and George Yardley finished the night in the R.S.I., the seemingly unimportant scoreline was 1-1.

Aston Villa winger Dave Roberts was signed 2 days later and made his debut in the 1-0 loss to Swindon. Town bounced back to go five games undefeated until, on Good Friday, they travelled to Bury and lost a hard fought contest 2-0 in front of 13,400. In the absence of Clarke or a replacement, Barry Stobart took over at centre-forward and he hit two in the 4-0 victory over Scunthorpe the following day. 'Ged' Garbett also hit his first goal in that game, and on the Easter Monday, Stobart hit the first half winner against Bury in front of 13,517. Efforts to sign another striker failed but John Macey came in as a cover goalkeeper, but sadly it was cover in the wrong area.

Stobart had been looking really lively, but at Oldham on the Saturday, a sickening clash saw him stretchered off and taken straight to the nearby hospital; it was the end of his season and it left Town woefully short of firepower. They responded well, when Eric Brodie pulled on the No.9 shirt and scored the winner against Barrow. The League table read:-
Top - Bury 43 games 52 points, Second - Shrewsbury (43 and 52), Oxford (3rd - 43 51), and 4th placed Torquay - 42 50. A five match spell of clean sheets ended in a 3-0 defeat in a gale at Barrow.

One game left, away at Gillingham, but Town were out of the promotion spots. Oxford, who with Graham Atkinson's goals had sneaked up on the blind side led, Bury (who played Watford at Gigg Lane with a 3.15 p.m. kick-off), were second. Town recalled Dave Roberts, and Jimmy McLaughlin took over at No.9. In a ding-dong battle Town snatched an 88th minute winner with a Jimmy McLaughlin header. Back to the bus for the Bury result, and the knives were literally out, for the Gills fans not amused at the result. *Sports Report* confirmed our fears, Bury's 3-1 victory promoted them at Town's expense. At Burnley, as well as at Gillingham, the home fans had produced knives, the malaise, which was to haunt the game was building, unchecked by any authority.

Harry Gregg
He was to take over as Manager in the Summer of 1968 after Arthur Rowley's successful ten years.

CHAPTER 11 - END OF AN ERA, FOLLOWED BY THE GREAT ESCAPE

own finally landed a goalscorer in the last week of May with Eddie Loyden being signed from Chester for around £10,000. Coach Gordon Lee joined Port Vale, a move he was to regret soon after, and David Pleat, Colin Hemsley and Tony Harris were freed. In June Alf Wood had a cartilage operation and Maurice Parkin signed from Leeds United, not quite 19, he was about as laid back as Victor Kasule. Meanwhile Brian Taylor - by then with Barnsley - turned down a move to join Inglewood of Los Angeles, to move instead to Aggborough; it must have been the soup. David Pleat signed for Exeter after a close season as a settler in a bookmakers, and Tony Harris signed for Bradford Park Avenue in the July. Few people were surprised at this latter transfer, for just like winning promotion together and a seemingly endless list of moves, it was just another link-up between Arthur and his brother Jack, but none realised it would - as far as Town were concerned - be the last.

On 3rd July 1968, Arthur resigned. In ten years he had broken all scoring records, taken Town to the edge of the Second Division, seen the side almost reach a League Cup final, and battle through 43 F.A. Cup-ties, twice reaching the last sixteen. By any criteria it was a remarkable stewardship and his last decision was - by his own later admission - his worst, he joined Sheffield United. Even then he stayed on in Salop to take pre-season training.

The job attracted a hefty mailbag of applications, and on July 22nd a successor was chosen. It is rumoured that a pipe brought from the paper-shop on the corner gave the board reassurance in the man whose relaxed appearance won the day. Harry Gregg was the new man, a giant in the game, a hero at Munich, intensely proud, but relaxed is not an epithet which readily described the man as a football manager.

Harry's first games in charge were in Scotland, against East Fife, Arbroath and Queen of the South. Maurice Evans arrived as Coach but travelled up on the train to join the party. The low spot of the trip was Alf Wood's sending off in the 2-0 defeat at East Fife, but he scored the winner in the 1-0 victory over Arbroath. Harry's disbelief that Town could have supporters at this match probably said something about the sanity of, Ron Barrett, Paul Gibbons and the author!

The final game, at Palmerston Park, was a 2-0 victory with Ted Hemsley and Jimmy McLaughlin on target. It was to be the club skipper's final goal, for on the 21st August he joined Arthur at Sheffield United, for £20,000. The Scottish trip was not without its problems, with Jimmy McLaughlin, Eddie Loyden, George Boardman and the manager returning under the weather due to a stomach bug. However, Dave Pountney was alright, and on August 9th he opened *Salopian Sports* in the old Sidoli shop on the Cop, in partnership with Malcolm Starkey.

Town had a new groundsman, for Tommy Seymour allowed Jim Morgan to take over, leaving Tommy as only the physiotherapist - having been everything from chief scout, trainer, chief painter, physio and general factotum. It must have seemed strange, but Tommy soon had a new interest. After six games Alan Boswell joined Wolves for £15,000, leaving just two goalkeepers on Town's books - an amateur trailist Peter Wright, and Tommy's grandson John Philips, who was just 17.

The next game was a trip to Hartlepool on a Friday night. The Town fans gathered behind the goal, where the directors box is now sited, and tried to encourage the nervous looking debutante. It was arguably the only time John looked nervous, for at the end of the goalless draw John Philips - all 17 years and 68 days of him - was a man. These were difficult times, injuries meant first starts for Maurice Parkin and Alan Jones - against Stockport - whose centre-forward Jim Fryatt was in devastating form. The youngsters battled brilliantly but Town lost 4-3. George Boardman, Jimmy Mac and 'Ged' Garbett's goals keeping Town in the fight. It was 'Ged's' last goal for the club, but George followed up with a hat-trick against Reading in the 3-3 draw, ironically his last strikes for Shrewsbury. The following 3-0 defeat at Swindon was the final match for Alan Jones while Maurice Parkin would manage just one more. It had been a traumatic start to a season, launched by a home League defeat, an away League Cup defeat - by Walsall - and with just seven points in nine games, the future looked difficult. Add to this a cartilage operation for Peter Dolby and a new impetus was required.

Manchester City sent Joe Corrigan out on loan for Harry to coach, and his debut (in the reserves) a 4-1 defeat at Southport on October 1st, was not too promising. Within a week Dennis Hawkins arrived from Leeds for £10,000 and a fortnight later Malcolm Starkey left his counter to join the coaching staff. The club moved its training ground from Sundorne to the West Midland Showground, but despite the good form of their young goalkeeper, points were hard to find. Just eight goals in fourteen League games was a paltry return. Dennis Hawkins with three, was the only player to hit the net more than once, apart from Alf Wood's two F.A. Cup goals which forced a replay with Port Vale, before the 3-1 defeat in Burslem.

John Philips had attracted some notice, and along with Orient's Stephen Bowtell, he was in line for England Youth honours after a trial at Lilleshall. The young influence continued as Gregg signed 16 year-old Kenny Howells as his first apprentice. Eddie Loyden had struggled to fulfil his potential, and after his appearance at Gillingham, which saw him prone at the final whistle, failed to regain his first team place. In fact within a few days, he and George Boardman were on the list; Loyden within weeks and George in the June would both join Barnsley. In order to strengthen his squad, Harry Gregg bid for Alex Ingram from Ayr United and Jimmy Conde from Bangor City. Ayr wanted twice Town's valuation for Ingram, who a year later joined Nottingham Forest, and Bangor manager Mick McGrath would not release Conde because of an approaching Welsh Cup-tie with Wrexham.

Manchester City recalled Joe Corrigan in mid-January, before he had made his League debut, but after he met his wife. On February 5th Gerry Bridgewood was secured from Stoke City for £12,000, and later that month Barry Stobart was released to join Adlington in Durban, South Africa. To counteract this, Irish international Terry Harkin was signed for £10,000 from Southport. However, despite his debut goal at Luton it ended in a 2-1 defeat, Town reached 31 games with just 21 points and were bottom. One last signing before the deadline saw Ricky Moir join Town from Cumnock Juniors - not 'Rovers' as reported; he had been recommended by Jock Fulton, but Cumnock wanted him to play in a Scottish Junior Cup-tie against Rob Roy. He started the game, but did not finish, being one of four players sent off in a hard fought match.

Town were again in a goal famine run, this time just 7 in 10 games, although a 1-0 win at Crewe gave hope, which was soon dashed. The visit to Southport saw John Philips injured diving at Colin Alty's

feet. After treatment the young 'keeper continued, and at half-time bravely offered to continue. However, in the second half, after Pat Douglas replaced Trevor Meredith, young John collapsed with concussion and was stretchered off to the hospital. Town crashed 5-0, and some harsh words particularly from John Moore awaited the manager at the final whistle.

Whether this was the catalyst for the following events, we may never know, but rarely can such a transformation have occurred. Town were bottom, dead and buried, elsewhere Northampton in eighth place had outside hopes of promotion. With Philips injured Bob Tooze who had been released by Bristol City, and was on trial, made his League debut at home to Bournemouth. He started, just like Philips with a clean sheet, and Terry Harkin's second half goal made it a winning debut. A week later at Plymouth a fine full length penalty save secured a point, and another 1-1 draw - this time with Swindon - kept the pot boiling. An ankle injury ruled Bob out of the Easter Monday visit of Stockport, so John returned as Town won 2-1.

Twenty-four hours later the game that changed the season took place at Northampton. Despite an own goal Town trailed 3-1 at half-time, and it was not until the 63rd minute, that Alf Wood reduced the arrears; another own goal soon after levelled matters, and unbelievably Peter Dolby hit the winner. On the Friday, Town went to Elm Park, Reading. Dave Roberts was outstanding, and Colin Meldrum was never the same again after Town ripped the Royals to shreds, winning 4-2. Alf Wood hit two, including a penalty, and having been released from defensive duties was on his way to becoming the leading scorer. Terry Harkin was also proving his worth and his goal completed the double over beleagured Northampton. A draw with Hartlepool and another single goal victory over Torquay extended the run to 15 points out of 18 in a nine game unbeaten sequence, and lifted the team above Hartlepool, Mansfield, Crewe and Oldham - safety!

Then crunch, a 4-0 reverse at Orient. It takes character to bounce back, but by then that was available in abundance. Southport, 5-0 victors just six weeks earlier, were spanked, when old boy Terry Harkin hit his only League hat trick for Town and Alf Wood weighed in with a brace as Salop won 5-1.

Bob Tooze had finally signed professional forms on April 26th, but would not play any further part as the drama built. The final home game was against Gillingham.

With five minutes remaining, Northampton manager Ron Flowers left, confident Gillingham would hang on to their 1-0 advantage. It was a tragic error, albeit with a hidden benefit, for 'Charlie' Clapham hit an equaliser two minutes into injury time, which condemned Northampton to join Hartlepool, Crewe and Oldham to Relegation.

It completed a crazy sequence of Division Four to Division One and back between 1960-1 and 1968-9 for Northampton Town, however, it did allow Ron Flowers - who was sacked by the Cobblers - to return to Wembley with Telford. It also meant Town had gleaned 20 points, in their last 13 games - from a maximum of 26 - or at least victory at Mansfield in the final game did, as this created the final grand finale to a remarkable season.

The players dedication to this recovery led to Terry Harkin who was promoted to the full Northern Ireland team, Dennis Hawkins - Welsh under-23 - and John Philips England Youth, foregoing caps. Although Philips was due to go to Leipzig with the England Youth squad for a tournament, along with Malcolm Webster of Arsenal.

Youngsters Maurice Parkin, Alan Jones, and 'Ged' Garbett were given 'frees', and Trevor Meredith - who went into teacher training - became a part-timer. Terms were offered to Pat Douglas and Joe Healey, but George Boardman for £10,000 joined Eddie Loyden at Barnsley. Also in the close season Les Rimmer received a 21 year long service medal from the Football League, and young 'keeper Phil Hoyle went with Nottingham Forest on a youth trip to Amsterdam. Town signed Terry Hughes on June 9th, and soon after a local BBC radio station was being discussed.

Pre-season of the 1969-70 campaign still causes shudders to many of the former players. Harry discovered Haughmond Hill, the players redefined the word pain, and fitness reached a new 'pique'.

A DAE-RTY TEAM

The August of 1969 saw two Town old boys facing different seasons. In Ireland, Billy Nixon - now with Ards - was anticipating a tilt at the European Cup-Winners Cup. Whilst Arthur Rowley, after seeing Sheffield United finish ninth the previous season, was dismissed a week before the restart. The Town's own campaign, after an opening defeat at Halifax, looked brighter, when a second half Jimmy McLaughlin goal put Walsall out of the League Cup

at the Meadow. It was fitting that things looked brighter, for in the close season the floodlights were cleaned, then re-assembled and re-focused.

Town's cup run came to an end in early September, Southend United becoming the first side to score at the Meadow - after four clean sheets - and earned a 2-2 draw. The following Monday, a goal in each half at Roots Hall put Southend through, but Gerry Bridgwood was lucky to escape injury, when, not satisfied with the win, someone threw a bottle through the team coach window. The month ended in gloom, the accounts showed a loss of £13,987, gates were below 4,000, and there was a lack of goals. In fact Dave Roberts was the leading scorer with four, after not scoring in his first 28 games, (he only managed one more, in February), thanks to his two successes at Luton. In this game Town drew 2-2 with Geoff Fellows taking over as captain, but Alec Stock was unimpressed, for he said somewhat disparagingly afterwards, *we knew they'd be a dae-rty team*. However, they were being loyal to the manager, Dennis Hawkins withdrawing from the Welsh U-23 game, to score the winner against Torquay.

Rumours were growing that Aston Villa were chasing young John Philips, but at Rotherham, former Aberdeen and Leeds man Jim Storrie said, *he makes good angles but if he's any sense he won't join the 'Doc'*. Tommy Docherty having recently moved from Rotherham to Villa. Town won that game 2-1 - despite Rotherham having future England man Dave Watson in their team. It was the season's first away win, the first double, the first win at Millmoor, and featured Ricky Moir's first goal. After a home draw with Brighton, Villa duly signed John Philips for £30,000 plus £5,000 if he played for England under-23 and £10,000 for a full cap; ironically he went on to pick up four Welsh caps at U-23 and full level! His first game for Villa, who were bottom of Division Two, saw him keep a clean sheet against Birmingham in front of 54,000, (roughly double the total attendance at Town's seven home League games before his move).

Town moved quickly to buy cover for Bob Tooze, paying Oswestry Town £2,000 for Derek Williams, but his debut was delayed by a two week suspension for being sent off against Skelmersdale in the Cheshire League. Another goalie in the news was Alan Boswell who had his contract at Wolves cancelled at his own request. More goalkeeping news surrounded Terry Gennoe, who along with Pat Douglas, Paul Bevan, and Terry Hughes, was in the youth team who twice held Derby before losing 5-0 at the Baseball Ground. The result came back to Terry some years later when he made his First Division debut at Derby, but this time kept a clean sheet.

The F.A. Cup threw up a difficult looking away tie at Yeovil, Alec Stock no doubt sent them a report, but the visitors, thanks to a fine all round perform-ance, won 3-2. The only problem was a perimeter wall collapsing, fortunately without causing serious injury. A home draw with Torquay followed and Stan Hall, ever the optimist, pointed out that with 19 points from 19 games, we were on a par with two seasons earlier, when we almost won promotion.

In November, much to the disappointment of many, economics decreed that advertising boards started to arrive around the ground. The team may have been having a few disciplinary problems but the supporters were named the Third Division's most gentlemanly crowd, winning an award named after the late Spurs star John White.

Terry Hughes attended a Welsh Youth trial, and was chosen with Dennis Hawkins' brother Peter to go on a close season tour. Not so good was the home defeat by Mansfield in the F.A. Cup, it was Town's first home F.A. Cup reverse for seventeen years, and only their second since joining the League, this in their 27th home F.A. Cup tie.

January saw three home games all of special interest. For the match with Luton, it was decided to exploit a perceived weakness. Dave Roberts would be fed the ball, then hit a first time pass towards the heart of the penalty area. Steve Nichol was the Hatters centre-half, strong in the air, but his headers at this time of his career lacked power. So Town apart from George Andrews would hang back and 'steam in' on the knockdowns. It worked, Town 4-0 up at half-time against the League leaders won 5-1, and Alf Wood also saw a shot on an empty net, stick in the mud - another dae-rty game. The second match saw George Boardman and Eddie Loyden return with Barnsley, the game ended 1-1 and honours even. The final game of the trio, with Rochdale, was the first with the Riverside Terrace cover completed.

Elsewhere, ex-Town goalkeeper Mike Walker played a major part in Watford's quarter final F.A. Cup victory over Peter Wall and Liverpool. On the South-east coast, Arthur Rowley took over at South-end United.

The club had more than its fair share of bookings and dismissals, so perhaps it was fitting that in the final home game with Plymouth, Ricky Moir was sent off prior to being awarded the Player of the Year award. Town won that game 3-0 but lost by the same score at Torquay four days later, the game being played on a wet windy night was Derek Williams' only Football League appearance. The end of season list saw Pat Douglas and Joe Healey both freed, Dave Pountney - who had been restricted after a cartilage operation - was open to transfer, with Dennis Hawkins and 'Charlie' Clapham told the club would listen to offers; soon after Clapham turned down a move to Darlington. One man staying was manager Harry Gregg, he signed a new three year contract on June 1st, that was effective from July 1st.

LOCAL BOYS AND A LOUD NOISE

The sceptre of Haughmond Hill again cast its shadow over pre-1969/70 season training, as the club's professionals returned to action. Kenny Howells joined their number, and local schoolboys Michael Jones, Russ Johnson, and Tommy Knight had a month's trial with a view to being offered apprentices. They were joined by Robert Caves and Trevor Buchanan from Belfast and Glaswegians Tommy Aiken, Bobby Dickson, Neil Keirs, Gregor Stevens and 15 year old Jackie King. The club agreed a fee with Stockport for winger John Price but could not agree terms with the player.

In the close season ground improvements costing £40,000 had been completed including extending the centre stand and putting in new seating and installing a new press box in place of the old 'pigeon box'.

A private practice match saw Town recover to draw 3-3 with Wolves. A 4-3 victory over Crewe and a 2-0 win over Fairs Cup entrants Coventry ensured a big crowd for Stoke City's visit in the final practice match. The record practice match crowd of 5,304 were not treated to Gordon Banks presence, but saw Town in their new blue and gold strip, earn a 2-2 draw.

Central defenders Alf Wood with a hat trick and John Moore scored all the goals as Town beat Rotherham 4-2 in the opening game, but another Town defender, Dave Pountney, then at Chester, scored the goal which put Town out of the League Cup. The goal inside the last two minutes made up for an Alan Tarbuck effort disallowed earlier.

Town's four goals gave them a good start in the Watney's Goals Competition, while no bookings or sending-off gave their standing in the Ford 'Fair Play' League a boost. A 2-2 draw at Bristol Rovers was followed by a 5-2 revenge victory over Mansfield, but late in the game Dave Roberts picked up a back injury from which he still receives pain. He was probably thankful to miss the subsequent 5-0 thrashing at Swansea.

The September 12th derby with Port Vale was an explosive affair; crowd trouble, five booked, and the visitors 'keeper sent off late in the game, which also featured ten goals. Town won 7-3 with Terry Hughes scoring one and winning two penalties. Town's away form was, however, poor and anchored them in mid-table, and when Alan Ball senior's Preston side won 1-0 at the Meadow, the League's last 100% home record also disappeared. The goals had dried up but the bookings had not, and at the end of October John Moore and Terry Hughes were hauled before the F.A. in London. Both received suspended suspensions but Hughes was instructed to take a course on the laws of the game.

Local youngster Paul Bevan, who was set to be released, won a professional contract and a full debut in the 2-0 victory at Gillingham, Town's first away win for 23 matches covering ten months. This was followed by a remarkable visit to Plymouth. Town were 3-0 down at half-time, including own goals from Wood and Moore, but rallied in wonderful fashion. They scored three goals in nine minutes before George Andrews put them in front, but Plymouth eventually managed to rescue a point. Each Town goal was greeted by a blast on a euphonium, with Tony Gregory saying he thought it must be foggy in Plymouth sound.

The euphonium failed to make it to Minehead for the Cup, just as well, for one blast and the temporary stand could have collapsed. Despite Minehead managing a first half equaliser, Town's 2-1 victory was never in real doubt. At the end of November, Malcolm Starkey took over as secretary in succession to Les Rimmer, and Jimmy McLaughlin succeeded Starkey as Assistant Trainer. It failed to change Town's fortunes, for having outplayed Reading in the F.A. Cup, Town threw away a victory by sloppy defending. They then crashed 4-1 at home to Bristol Rovers and had two goals disallowed at Elm Park as Reading won the Cup replay 1-0 with an 87th minute winner. Christmas arrived with the outlook decidedly gloomy.

However, on Boxing Day, a spirited performance at Villa Park saw Town hold out until the introduction of £100,000 substitute Bruce Rioch led to two Villa goals. They had to wait until January 15th, when a Terry Harkin goal ensured a 1-0 victory over Wrexham, to end a winless run of five games.

Town youngster Mickey Ward was called up by England Youth but Bernard Fagan who had been on trial was released in late January. Meanwhile ex-Town man John Regan left Doncaster Rovers to join Cape Town City, and Town took Alan Groves on a month's loan from Chester, and then signed him for a moderate fee.

The Riverside covering was extended in January 1970.

There was some respite for Town fans on March 10th, when Terry Hughes scored in the 18th minute on his 18th birthday, as Town beat Reading 3-1, only their second victory in just over four months. Town paid £5,000 for Ken Mulhearn, a Manchester City goalkeeper, just prior to the transfer deadline, but he had to wait to make his debut. Seven teams were within one point of the final relegation place as the season entered its last phase..

Mulhearn's chance arrived when Bob Tooze dislocated a thumb in training, and Dennis Hawkins who had earlier in the season spent three months at Chester, was sidelined with a muscle injury having recovered from two broken legs in a three month period. Mulhearn and Groves were both earning praise as Town hovered just above the relegation positions. After several abysmally poor games, the Easter clash with Aston Villa drew 13,636. It was a cracking match which was won by an excellent goal from Dave Roberts, it was his first of the season, an angled half volley of real power against his old team.

Suddenly life did not seem so bad, and an Alf Wood 40-yarder sent Torquay packing, thanks to a fumble by 'keeper Donnelly, before a 2-0 victory over Bury extended the run to eight games unbeaten and confirmed safety for another year. A third successive home victory, this one over Swansea, produced a points total of 45, but there it stayed thanks to away defeats at Tranmere and Torquay - where Kevin Morris made his debut. Town won the Senior Cup final beating Telford's Wembley winners 2-1, it was Tony Loska's last game as he was then released. Terry Gennoe held the Scots at bay in an under-18 international at Airdrie, while Terry Hughes was off to Czechoslovakia with Wales Youth. A Town youth side minus Gennoe went to represent England in a youth international tournament in Holland. Jimmy McLaughlin was in charge of the following party:- Kevin Morris, Tommy Knight, Mike Jones, Kevin Adams, Steve Kemp, Peter Bradley, Geoff Murphy, Tony Dawson, Stephen Kelly, Kevin Tudor, Russ Smith, Geoff Forrester and John King (representing England?).

George Andrews had a cartilage operation, as did John Moore who also had a cist on his knee removed, but both were expected to be fit for the new season as was Town's new signing, Alex 'Sandy' Brown from Everton. He was a late substitute for the Merseysiders so often, the crowd used to chant at night games *its five to nine it's Sandy time'*.

In June, a new competition, the Associate Members Cup, was introduced. The club announced a scheme to lease a pitch at the Rugby Club, and also that nine of the following season's fixtures would be on Friday nights. Despite the late rally steering the side to thirteenth - Harry Gregg's highest finish - the manager gave free transfers to Derek Williams and Kenny Howells but demanded fees for Terry Harkin, Dennis Hawkins, Gerry Bridgwood and Graham Clapham.

WOOD HE DO IT?

Early July 1971 saw new signing Jim Holton look in at the ground, released by West Brom on a free, he had appeared as substitute for the Baggies without actually playing. His first team opportunities were limited due to the form of John Wile, who amazingly never won an England cap. Enquiries were being fielded for all three transfer listed players while Tony Loska moved to Port Vale, Dave Pleat, then manager at Nuneaton, was talking to Kenny Howells, and Derek Williams made the return trip to Oswestry.

The season opened at promoted Bournemouth who scored two early goals in their 3-1 victory. Alf Wood scored Town's goal, and followed up with two in the League Cup victory over Port Vale, it set the tone for the season. Another brace at Barnsley, in Town's first ever win at Oakwell, could have been a hat-trick, as he had another effort disallowed. Gerry Bridgwood was showing improved form but Terry Harkin had been transferred to Finn Harps and Dennis Hawkins had gone on loan to Waterford. A thumping 4-1 victory over Walsall, was highlighted by a Dave Roberts goal of 'George Best' quality according to the reports. But not all was serene, the closure of three-sides of the ground for floodlit and junior games upset some fans.

A mini-slump saw four defeats and a goalless draw, which included an exit from the League Cup at Grimsby. John Moore was starting the long road back and two new apprentices joined the club - Alan Cochrane and Ian Roberts.

The main concern was a lack of goals but after Ricky Moir and George Andrews struck in the 2-1 victory over Wrexham, Alf Wood after just one goal in four games, bounced back to form. He netted five times as Town hit Blackburn Rovers for seven. True Roger Jones their keeper injured his ribs in a collision with Jim Holton, but Wood's ariel power - four goals were headers - and a penalty, took Alf to the top of the League goalscoring charts.

The Town directors vowed to keep Wood, Roberts, Moir and Holton, in the build-up to the arrival of Bournemouth. John Bond's side were top of the table thanks to the ability of Ted MacDougall and Phil Boyer, and only Town had scored more goals. It was billed as a classic and for once lived up to expectations. A goal in each half from MacDougall twice rescued his side from a two goal deficit, albeit the second in the final minute was a consolation. A typical driving run from the late Alan Groves set up

George Andrews to open the scoring, Alf Wood added a second and Jim Holton's first goal, a header from a corner wrapped up the points. Fred Davies was in goal for the visitors and other subsequent managerial material included Mel Machin, John Benson, and John Sainty. As with the Walsall victory a slump followed, with no goals for three matches, until at least some fireworks on November 5th with a 3-0 win over Swansea. The week before at Brighton, Alf was taken to Hospital with a suspected broken arm, fortunately it was only severe bruising.

The F.A. Cup trip to Layer Road looked fraught with difficulties. Colchester, redoubtable cup fighters - ask Leeds - were also Watney Cup Holders and possessed a near perfect home record. Town have often achieved the impossible whilst making the simple difficult, and this was a classic case. A George Andrews hat trick, his first for Town and an Alf Wood goal set up a 4-1 victory which ended a 27 match unbeaten home run for the Essex side. The only real blemish was Peter Dolby's first booking by Ray Toseland. The next round - Guildford City at home - was preceded by Bolton Wanderers' first visit to the Meadow and a trip to Plymouth. Town won all three by an odd goal. The victory at Home Park was their first at that venue, whilst Guildford's single goal was scored by former Spurs winger Terry Dyson.

Before the Guildford tie Town had turned down an approach from Reading for the services of Harry Gregg. For his first third round tie, Harry was rewarded with a trip to Brian Clough's high flying Derby County. The team celebrated by dumping Oldham 4-1; Alf Wood scoring in his seventh consecutive game, sharing the goals with Dave Roberts. Roberts, now first team skipper, was in such fine form he won the Stan Hall player of the year accolade, ahead of Alf Wood.

Sadly though the season's best crowd, on Boxing Day, saw a lacklustre goalless draw. The six match unbeaten run ended on New Year's day at Port Vale, while a day later another record went. The recently formed Shrewsbury Junior League had its first ever draw, Belle Vue and Lythwood United ending 3-3 in the competition's 38th fixture.

A victory over Barnsley boosted morale for the daunting trip to the Baseball Ground. Derby sported six full internationals including their 1994 management team of Roy McFarland and Alan Durban. Town lost 2-0 in front of 33,463 who must have enjoyed it more than Hugh Johns, whose commentary seemed to revolve around the phrase, *"Holton kicks it the way he's facing"*, being as that was away from his own goal, it seemed like a good idea to the writer!

Four days later, in front of 27,239, Town lost 3-0 at Villa Park. It was the second season in which Town's Cup exit preceded a trip to play in front of a large crowd at Villa Park. Town were to play seven more games before returning to winning ways, including two remarkable home defeats - 4-3 to Chesterfield and 5-3 to Brighton. In both games the drama was reserved for the second half, half-time bringing 1-1 and no goal scorelines respectively. The Chesterfield game also contained a piece of history. 'Coracle' Fred ran the line, after referee Matthewson, suffering from 'flu, left the field with ten minutes left. Harry Gregg sent Fred out with strict instructions to flag for offside if Chesterfield scored. Three minutes later, Alan Groves equalised, but two minutes after David Wilson hit the winner. Fred ran onto the muddy pitch, in his patent leather shoes, but stand-in referee Lewis quite rightly overruled his deputy linesman's vigorously waving flag! Town were not alone, stumbling about in the dark, for at Rotherham the power dispute meant the teams changed by candlelight, and the midweek home game with Halifax was switched to May 3rd.

Doncaster Rovers' manager Maurice Setters sent his teenage keeper Glen Johnson to the Meadow to pick up some hints - he had hair then. Bob Tooze was listed on February 23rd, two days after Peter Dolby's booking at Doncaster was rescinded, so keeping his excellent - and among Town player's of the time almost unique - record of no cautions. Dennis Hawkins was off on his travels again, joining Workington on loan.

Another near departure was Alf Wood to Fulham for £40,000, but the deal collapsed. However, Town signed Ian Moir from Wrexham for £10,000, while Graham Clapham on loan at Chester joined the Sealand Road outfit permanently for £2,000 and Bob Tooze went on loan to Gillingham. Aston Villa, unsurprisingly drew the biggest home gate, 16,335 and also drew the game 1-1. Alf played centre-half, because of Jim Holton's flu, but retained the No.9 shirt. He had a real battle with Andy Lockhead and left the field sporting an impression of the Scotsman's teeth on his shoulder. Town's poor run had left them with an outside chance of relegation, but Alf's ding-dong battle with Ted MacDougall for the goalscoring accolades would dispel any fears.

After a battling performance at Blackburn, Town lost 1-0 but Wood and Groves had 'goals' disallowed, Dave Roberts celebrated his recall with a brace against Bradford City. Town had been having a problematic season but in the Junior League Cup semi-final, Hanwood failed to convert any penalties in a shoot-out with Annscroft (two saved, two wide, one hit woodwork).

The season now revolved around whether Alf could beat Arthur Rowley's record of 39 Cup and League goals in a season, for he had seven games in which to score eight goals. One against Rochdale, two versus Mansfield but then just a penalty in the 4-1 defeat at Walsall plus three blanks made it look improbable. Against Halifax (a game which saw Ian Roberts make

Fred Davies · The Coracle Man.
(Sadly Fred died in 1994)

his home debut four days after playing at the Shay aged 16 years 214 days), Alf scored on 33 minutes, and it stayed that way until the last five minutes. Halifax looked set to level but Alf hit a shot in off a post and then converted a penalty to complete his hat-trick.

One game left, Tranmere away. After the Yardley incident the last team in the League to do Alf a favour, on a ground where Shrewsbury had never won. A drab goalless first half was followed by a lively second period. Alf fired in a George Andrews centre eight minutes after the restart, after a further eight minutes, Tranmere's Crossley missed a penalty. A minute later, Jimmy 'Mac' 35 yards out, made it two. It was on 68 minutes that Alan Groves found Woody who 20 yards from goal held off a challenge and cracked a record breaking drive past Tommy

Lawrence. George Andrews completed the scoring with his 20th goal of the season for a memorable 4-0 win. Referee Bob Matthewson must have been expecting second half fireworks, for he was in charge for the 4-3 home defeat by Chesterfield, but on that occasion, as related, left the field with 'flu. The retained list saw Tony Gregory, Terry Matthias and Bob Tooze up for offers, while Sandy Brown, Dennis Hawkins and Kevin Morris were freed. Peter Dolby moving into teaching went part-time while Gerry Bridgwood came off the list. The Gregg regime continued its careful progress up a place to twelfth.

What the team needed was strengthening, but Alf's understandable desire to try life higher up saw him join Millwall in May for £45,000. This move came after Spurs dropped out of the chase. Elsewhere Mike Gibson at Bristol City and Eric Brodie at Tranmere were given frees. Peter Loughnane, 14, the son of former Town player Brian was signed on associate schoolboy forms by Manchester United.

At the Football League meeting minimum charges of admission went up from 30p to 40p with stand seats up £2 for a season ticket to £10 or £12 for the 50p or 60p seats. The club's accounts highlighted the need for a regular big money sale, for there was little change, with the £30,816 record loss of the previous season surpassed by just over £3,000, although this took no account of Alf Wood's transfer.

CHAPTER 12 - GOALS WITHOUT STRIKERS ?

Harry Gregg promised 83 goals for 1972-73, an increase of ten on the previous season, but few shared his belief. However, after an opening goalless draw with Notts County, Town did hit 3 at Chester in the League Cup, unfortunately Chester - 2-0 down at the interval - hit four second half goals. A 2-1 victory at the Valley came courtesy of a late own goal after Town had equalised through a Ricky Moir right foot volley (yes, right foot).

Supporters were almost as hard to find as goals. Three consecutive goalless draws took the lowest ever opening home game gate - of 3,775 - down to 2,772 by the time Blackburn Rovers arrived in early September. Blackburn, even with Jack Walker's millions, still find Town a problem. True it took 82 minutes for Town to conjure up a goal against Rovers, but like busses, then two came along. Terry Hughes raced to the top of Town's scoring charts with his second of the season, but in injury time Alan Groves joined forces with the youngster.

Manager Gregg's assertion that: *"I desperately want a striker to score goals"*, was like preaching to the converted. It seemed the only goalscorer in the area was young Peter Loughnane who in four under 15 games, had hit 32 of his side's (Belle Vue Boys), 38 goals.

Still on the bright side two narrow home wins lifted morale before defeats at Bournemouth and Southend, the latter coming the day Town sold ill-fated Alan Groves to John Bond's Bournemouth for £45,000. Town bounced back beating Grimsby 3-2 in front of just 1,763, but the following day the club issued a statement.

"Mr Harry Gregg today resigned his post as manager of Shrewsbury Town Football Club". The manager said, *"I am leaving as a matter of pride and two issues of principle"*. It appeared obvious that the two principles were namely Wood and Groves.

The usual rumour factory had Dennis Law taking over at the Meadow, but Town already had two fine managers on their books, in Maurice Evans and Jimmy McLaughlin. Evans' first match as caretaker saw a 5-1 reverse at Bristol Rovers, Rick Moir scoring Town's first away goal for 7 weeks. A 1-1 draw at Port Vale recorded Town's 1,000th Football League point. Terry Hughes kept scoring; he hit his sixth in Town's sixth consecutive home win, but only

2,694 attended despite having Roger Kirkpatrick in the role of redcoat.

The future looked brighter when the youth team hammered Port Vale 4-0, away travellers ask why Clive Podd was one of only five of this side not to make a first team appearance. Stan Harland was the man who was expected to manage Town but when the announcement came Maurice Evans' promotion was put on a permanent footing. Promotion from within had started!

Town lost at York 2-1 in Maurice's first game in full charge and had drawn Spennymoor United in the F.A. Cup. It was a time before Mickey Heathcote joined them, Spennymoor that is. A 1-1 draw with Rotherham made it 19 points in 19 games, consistency or what, but nobody promised promotion.

Peter Dolby produced another important Cup goal as Town drew 1-1 in the North-east. The timely recovery of George Andrews boosted the 3-1 replay victory, he came on as sub with 15 minutes left. Scoring with his first touch, a back-heel, and two minutes later grabbing a second.

Harry Gregg had taken over at Swansea and the first of many to follow was Jimmy McLaughlin, so Maurice Evans promoted Norman Hobson to take over training duties. Another new face was Mike Kearney whose second child arrived the day before he came down to play in a friendly match at Keele, scoring twice as Town drew 2-2 with Crewe. Next it was Laurie Calloway, signed for £6,000 from York. Changes of manager often point to a change of emphasis, so it was again, with Tony Gregory and Terry Matthias both coming back into favour.

The unbeaten home record miraculously survived until the final game of the year. Charlton Athletic avenged the opening away win, on a day when Ian Moir failed to arrive due to a car breakdown. The upheaval's continued in the New Year, when Jim Holton and John Moore asked for transfers on January 4th.

Five days later Jim Holton was sold, six clubs including four from the First Division had made offers with Tommy Docherty winning the auction at £90,000. Having bought John Philips for Villa he was now in charge at Manchester United, while Philips was at Chelsea.

Graham Turner

Six days later, without playing another fixture, Town secured Graham Turner from Chester for £30,000. It was a case of Graham who at the time, but before he left everybody was full aware. He made his debut in the 2-2 draw with Oldham, George Andrews scored one on his last appearance. He was swapped for Geoff Morris, with Walsall also receiving £6,000. West Ham and West Brom enquired about Ken Mulhearn, and John Moore went to Swansea for £4,000. Maurice Evans had been told by Tommy 'Doc' he would do anything to help Shrewsbury; so Maurice asked if Dennis Law or Bobby Charlton were available!

Plymouth scrambled a draw, Jim Furnell denying Ian Moir a winner, before Mike Kearney replacing Moir hit two on his full debut at Grimsby. Tony Gregory came off the list and Ipswich wanted around £40,000 for Frank Clarke, now 30, so Town took Terry Smith on loan from Stoke for a month. He played just twice before the search for an experienced striker settled on Alan Tarbuck, bought from Preston for £17,000. He made his debut against Rochdale, as did young full-back, John King ('Jake' came later).

The 4-2 home victory over Bristol Rovers was a triumph for the new signings, as Tarbuck and Morris hit their first goals, Kearney added another and Dave Roberts converted a penalty. Another youngster pushing for recognition was Sammy Irvine but after a substitute appearance in a friendly match with Exeter on February 2nd his debut was put back because of a sending off against Leicester in the intermediate League 29 days later. The day before Town went to Burnden Park to play League leaders Bolton they had a disastrous practice match, which saw Ricky Moir, Dave Roberts and Tony Gregory all pick up injuries. Bolton won 2-0 and repeated the score three weeks later in the return. The final home game with Bournemouth was goalless, Town's eighth 0-0 of the season and the nineteenth time they failed to score in a League game. They did however, keep sixteen clean sheets, Alan Tarbuck's goal at Watford ended another four game barren patch.

Ian Moir, Gerry Bridgwood and Bob Tooze were not retained and three weeks later were given frees. Ricky Moir had a cardiology operation, while Ken Mulhearn requested a move, after refusing improved terms. The club was unable to further improve the offer because of government wage restrictions.

MONEY BAGS - TALENTLESS?

It was a time for travel, and the youth team went to Holland for an international tournament. Pete Oliver deputising for Jimmy Jackson who had examinations. The first team travelled to Scotland, and although a fixture with Raith Rovers fell through, they played Stirling Albion and East Stirling. Laurie Calloway scored in the 1-1 draw at Annfield, whilst the match at Firs Park was scoreless. Town had signed David Butler from West Brom on a free (shades of Jim Holton) and given trials to Ian Ward, David Cunningham, Jim Greenhorn and Jim McLuskey. They were all Glaswegians, and McCluskey - who had been released by Rangers - had been a goal machine in juvenile football. He had scored over 1,000 goals as a youngster including an incredible 250 in one season. However, his contract was terminated for disciplinary reasons in early August. Dave Roberts, at his own request, was listed for £7,000, but despite interest from Swansea, Southend, Oldham and Halifax he did not move.

The club had made £110,420 profit on transfers, reporting a record trading profit of £69,504 on July 17th. On August 10th, Malcolm Starkey had a cartilage operation, was it caused by carrying all that money to the bank? However, the money raised had left a squad short on experience and goals, as was soon to be discovered. An opening 3-0 defeat at Port Vale was followed by a 6-1 thrashing at Walsall in the League Cup. It was the club's biggest defeat for nine years. Maurice Evans was faced with an awesome task, he did though continue to lay the grounds for the future. He signed Sammy Irvine and Alan Cochrane as professionals, gave Ian Atkins and Steve Peate apprenticeships, and trials to Peter Dolby's brother Stephen plus David Collier.

Alan Durban

Town badly needed a boost and it came in the middle of September with the signing of Alan Durban from Derby County for £12,000. He made his debut against Rochdale scoring in Town's first victory of the season, and was quickly made captain and assistant-manager. This win was, however, only a small respite in a run of ten games without a victory, which left the record reading - P 15 W 1 D 4 L 10 F 11 A 26 Pts 6, these were desperate times. Ricky Marlowe was signed on loan, like Durban he came from Derby and scored on his debut in a 2-0 victory, he also scored in the F.A. Cup against Wrexham. That goal forced a replay but it was the only one scored in six games, the other five were lost and after the 1-0 defeat by Chesterfield in front of just 1,397, Maurice Evans was sacked.

The pressure had obviously been building, and three weeks earlier he had collapsed with a poisoned leg, however, it was the job - something of a poisoned chalice - which Maurice hardly deserved. He was, and is, a thoroughly decent, upstanding, loyal, hard-working man who may very well be too nice to be a football manager. He deserved better, and has since achieved better. He had an influence on several youngsters who would blossom, Jake King, Sammy Irvine, Ian Atkins, Alan Cochrane and Ian Roberts - who was called up for Scottish Youth trials, amongst others. However, one youngster to appear at the Meadow at this time was not with Town, Martin Wallace made his Northern floodlit debut for Crewe on the ground his dad Joe had graced a dozen years earlier.

Alan Durban took over as caretaker manager and after a defeat at Walsall, Town enjoyed three successive victories. Christmas week produced, the first 100% holiday record for 13 years, but sadly it was

another false dawn. In the next eleven games Town failed to score eight times and managed just 3 points. Gordon Lee had moved to Blackburn and Town played them in their first ever Sunday League game, losing 2-0, and then drawing 0-0 with Aldershot in the first home Sunday fixture, all this of course because of the power dispute.

The speculation on the new manager was naturally far reaching, but the strongest contender appeared to be Tom Johnson, the successful manager of York, who over 20 years earlier had hit four goals in Town's worst ever home defeat.

Yet on 13th February 1974, Alan Durban was confirmed as Town manager after exactly five months at the club. Within two hours of the announcement he secured Peter Cruse on loan from Luton, but it was not destined to be a memorable move, for after two appearances the young striker went back. Shortly after Town coach Norman Hobson announced he was joining Mooroolbark of Melbourne as coach on a 2 year contract, having been talked into the joys of Australia by their manager 'Curly' Edgley. Durban meanwhile had lined up a 'straight man' - his ex-team-mate Richie Barker - who was ideal for the part, (ask John Barnwell, Ron Atkinson and Trevor Francis) - he arrived on February 26th.

Winger David Butler was the first departure, joining Workington on loan on March 12th. Four days later Brian Clough's first visit as a manager saw Brighton lose 1-0. Ex-Nottingham Forest goalkeeper Peter Grummitt was carried off, central defender Steve Piper was sent off, and referee Baker, blew for time five minutes early, before bringing the teams back onto the field. Young striker Lee Roberts was knocking at the door, having made an appearance as sub versus Southend 15 days before his 17th birthday, and his full debut, against Halifax, three days after his party. In April Terry Hughes' ankle injury caused his retirement, aged just 21. He never quite convinced Town fans of his ability but 22 goals in 66 first team starts was a respectable return, particularly for one so young.

Town were, naturally, relegated. Any team who fails to score in 23 League games has obvious problems, but the goals against column of 62 had only been bettered twice during the previous season, and the club's highest-ever finish at that time, in 1968. The answer was obvious, sign some proven strikers, and from early April two players had been top of the hit list.

Stourbridge pair Ray Haywood and Phil 'Chic' Bates were the targets and the prolific duo finally signed for around £10,000.

The retained list gave 'frees' to goalkeeper Mike Jones, along with Terry Matthias, Steve Kemp, Peter Bradley, Dave Butler and Ricky Moir. Only Ricky could consider himself unlucky, having been asked to play up front for the last seven games, he scored three goals in an unbeaten run which won Alan Durban the manager of the month award.

It was missionary time for Town players past and present. Tony Gregory and Terry Matthias joined a Southend XI for a tour of Rhodesia. Laurie Calloway went to America to link up with San Jose Earthquakes. While Matthias on his return from Africa set off for another continent, he and Steve Kemp journeying to Australia. Sadly another Town stalwart called it a day, Geoff Fellows who had broken his leg against Wrexham in a reserve game accepted medical advice and retired. Another departure was Dave Roberts, who a fortnight after the season ended moved to Swansea for £4,000.

Chic Bates had a small cyst removed in early June, Manchester United signed Peter Loughnane and Bob Wardle came from Bristol City on a free, a week before Maurice Evans rejoined Reading as Chief coach. The merry-go-round continued with Ricky Marlowe sold to Brighton for £6,000, Kevin Moore and David Fowler signing apprentice forms, and John Malam arriving as trainer/assistant coach.

With the departure of Dave Roberts, Town were on the lookout for a winger. Paul Adams from Ipswich came for a trial which did not work out, and then David Jenkins, the ex-Arsenal player, appeared in a pre-season game at Worcester. The Town won 1-0, Chic Bates played his first 20 minutes after his operation and scored.

The 1974-75 season started with Town in indifferent form, a home draw with Rochdale 1-1, was matched by a similar scoreline at Hereford in the League Cup, a game in which Tony Gregory was sent off for two very harsh bookings. An excellent 3-0 victory at Stockport, in which first 'Chic' Bates then Ray Haywood scored their first goals, soon faded in the memory, as Town lost two home local derbies. First Hereford in the League Cup, then Crewe in the League notched 1-0 victories. The Club needed a boost, and Alan Durban, returning to South Wales, provided it. He hit his first hat-trick for the club, the sixth of his career as Town won 4-2 at Somerton

Park. The Manager picked up a knock in the 2-0 win over Swansea, which followed, so David Jenkins made his debut against Chester and scored as Town again won 2-0. The following game at Northampton Town - 2-0 down at half-time - saw Town hit back to draw 3-3, Jenkins was substituted and never played again. He had a spell at Workington before going to South Africa.

A seven match unbeaten run ended in a third 1-0 home defeat, this time by Hartlepool. Away form was keeping the ship afloat and a 2-0 victory at Cambridge was set up by a first half Durban header. A left wing corner came over, the ball bounced two yards out, and Durban stooped to head home. Having received a boot in the face, he ran straight off the field for stitches. Cambridge tried valiantly to level, but a fine solo Ray Haywood goal, running from halfway and hitting an unstoppable cross shot, sealed the victory.

The next setback was caused by Lincoln City, who had made an excellent start to the season, and on November the 2nd destroyed Town 4-0 at the Meadow. It was the heaviest home defeat for 10 years. However, it was a month later before Town lost an away League game, with fellow promotion candidates Mansfield winning 3-1, and ending a run of 13 away matches without defeat.

This defeat came quickly on the heels of the F.A. Cup exit, non-Leaguers Wigan Athletic - managed by Ian McNeil - beat Town 2-1 at Springfield Park in a first round replay. Twenty years on this was Town's last defeat by a non-League club in the competition - mind you the club have only played two - Rossendale United and Chorley - since. Nigel O'Loughlin who had made his full debut at the end of November was recalled for the Christmas games and scored in all three, his first League goals.

David Collier was called up for a Welsh Youth trial, while another youngster Shaun Westray joined the club. Terry Matthias was back in the country but managed just four games for Oswestry before returning to Australia, but Steve Kemp enjoyed a return to the club, on a trial which was extended to three months before his release. Despite their successes Salop were accused of being 'Wingless Wonders' something the signing of Alex McGregor from Hibernian was no doubt intended to remedy. Alex already knew Mike Kearney and soon settled in with fellow Glaswegians Jake King, Sammy Irvine, Ian Roberts and apprentice Walter Cameron.

Town having lost to Mansfield and Barnsley 1-0, bounced back in McGregor's first game beating Darlington 2-1, and then on his home debut set a new League aggregate record for the club. Entrance prices had been held for three years but an increase from 40p to 45p was announced in late January. However, they did at least come up with value for money. Town were 2-0 ahead at half-time against Doncaster, but in the second half a 4-1 lead shrank to 5-4 before they moved on to win 7-4. Seven goals came in one 25 minute spell and Ray Haywood - in the No.9 shirt - hit his only hat-trick with 'Chic' Bates and Alex McGregor sharing the other four. It set up an abortive revenge mission to Sincil Bank but Graham Taylor's men again won easily, this time 3-0.

Four clean sheets followed setting up a run of just 2 goals conceded in nine outings, culminating in a 6-0 thrashing of Northampton Town. Fourteen year-old Jimmy Steele, nephew of Freddie, came for a one week trial and Les Lawrence joined on loan from Stourbridge, before signing 'Pro' on March 10th. Another local celebrity in the news was 'Coracle Fred', for Fred Davies was featured on Nationwide TV. (Sadly during the writing of this book Fred passed on, a true character, he will be greatly missed).

The P.F.A. Divisional team contained Alan Durban, who, having made the Fourth Division side a season earlier, now had, with his First and Second Division Championship Medals, a complete set of honours at all levels. At Easter the club, who had given out 50 bottles of Sherry at Xmas, gave out 50 Easter Eggs to lucky programme holders. Graham Turner was voted Player of the Year and the first congratulations telegram on clinching promotion was from John Bond. He had led Bournemouth straight back four years earlier, the last occasion on which it had been achieved.

Just one player was freed, Geoff Morris who went to Bangor City, while Les Lawrence hade his first team debut in a challenge against Blackburn on May the 6th, and scored the winner. This came after Lawrence had hit 17 goals in 18 competitive games, and Alan Durban remarked, *"he could become the first coloured England International."* Another youngster enjoying life was David Collier who was off to Switzerland with Wales for the finals of the UEFA Youth Cup. The squad for the next season was strengthened on May 16th with the signing of skilful winger Chris Duffey from Bury for £5,000, but he was not to fulfil his potential. Young winger Alan Cochrane who had asked for his contract to be cancelled joined Telford United, who were then a Southern League club.

Other items of interest were the appointment of Alan Brett as Shropshire's representative to the F.A. ... an entrance price increase to 65p. ... and the Football League Cup First Round consisting of two legs. Laurie Calloway despite his groin injury flew off to rejoin San Jose Earthquakes, and Steve Hickenbottom, just 18, was advised to give up full time football because of a knee injury.

The club announced a trading loss of £51,681 only £7,000 down on the previous season record deficit of £58,570. Was selling Wood, Holton and Groves such a good idea after all, or to look at it another way, would the club have survived if not?

The pre-season build-up saw Manager Alan Durban emphasising he had a 'squad' of players and not a team. Ironically the Shareholders meeting was a happy affair, unlike the furore two years earlier when a record profit was made, but two seasons of large deficits brought praise! The loss was tempered by donations of £35,000 from the Supporters Club, and the radical step to put up the car park charge from 5p. to 20p. was approved, although the price would now include a programme.

The season started on a high note for Graham Turner, for the club skipper won £100 in the 'Grand Slam'. The season opened with business as usual, and Bates and Haywood scored in the 2-1 victory against fellow Fourth Division promotion winners Mansfield at Field Mill. A 3-1 home win over Peterborough featured David Collier's first goal from the spot, the seventeen-year-old had made his debut against Stockport the previous season. This match also featured one of the finest own goals ever witnessed at the Meadow. Peterborough full back Keith Bradley, positioned by the touchline in front of the site of the Pigeon Box, lofted the ball over his keeper Eric Steele from fully 25 yards.

Either side of this game Town drew 0-0 at Fellows Park, before recovering from a half-time deficit to beat Walsall 2-1 thanks to substitute Chris Duffey's penalty and an Alex McGregor goal. It set up a home tie with Queens Park Rangers, led by England captain Gerry Francis. Town lost at Grimsby before two more penalties from Collier helped dispatch Swindon 3-0. But after 'Chic' Bates gave Town a half time cup lead, Q.P.R. stamped their authority winning 4-1. Collier's remarkable sequence continued, as he scored another penalty in the home match with Crystal Palace to become joint leading scorer with Ray Haywood, on four. He had scored in three successive home League games, with a League career record of played 5, goals 4 - not bad for a full-back.

Unfortunately it was downhill from then on, for apart from a Welsh Cup semi-final penalty shoot-out he never scored again.

On September the 4th, another youngster - Carleton Leonard - signed professional and the same week 'Hannibal' Hayes went on loan to Torquay. Town also signed Kevin Hewson as an apprentice and gave a trial to Sammy Irvine's brother Lloyd, Sammy although only 19 had just completed 100 appearances.

A very young Town side lost 4-0 to Telford United without calling on the experience of Secretary Malcolm Starkey who was acting as substitute. The 4-2 defeat by Palace had featured on ATV Sunday Sport and the cameras were blamed for increased violence and 1½ streakers; the semi-streaker was fined £100. Palace Manager Malcolm Allison was fulsome in his praise of both sides, his team included Peter Wall.

Dave Collier turned down the chance to turn professional and missed the trip to Brighton, but a week later, along with Kevin Moore, completed the step-up. Ken Mulhearn passed 200 League appearances for Town and Jake King returned to action after a thigh muscle injury picked up at Grimsby. Chris Duffey made his final appearance as sub against Rotherham, having scored his only League goal on his full debut at Southend. Elsewhere Graham Clapham hit Grantham's winner against Telford and at the end of October 'Jos' Wynn retired from the County Ground. Lee Roberts went out on loan to Telford and made his Southern League debut against Wimbledon. Carleton Leonard made his debut in the No. 12 shirt at Ninian Park; fitting as he would join Cardiff much later.

A 1-0 F.A. Cup win at Rossendale brought Chester to the Meadow and Town progressed with an easy 3-1 victory. That win set up a home tie with Bradford City, with club president Sidney Yates - father of the Chairman - donating the ball to commemorate his 95th birthday. City were spoilsports, winning 2-1 to upset the celebrations. Meanwhile the enigmatic Chris Duffey returned from a loan spell at Rochdale. Kevin Moore made his debut at home to Grimsby, allthough he was a little way behind the manager, as Alan Durban's appearance against Halifax a fortnight later was his 500th League game.

Another debut, to start what would become a record-breaking Town career, was made by Colin Griffin who came on loan from Derby, and who also began in that Grimsby game. It took Griffin just five games to prove his worth, Town won three and drew two, before he signed for £10,000 on February 4th.

A young man leaving was the likeable Glaswegian Walter Cameron to take up an apprenticeship outside football.

In fact Town built up an eleven game unbeaten run, including a 3-2 win over Wrexham, where in Collier's absence, 19 year-old Ian Atkins secured the points from the spot. Town were now fourth and had hopes of a second straight promotion. Alan Durban was expected to make the 3rd Division select side, and his own selections had quite a bit of character, for they contained Brian Williams, then with Bury, and four men destined to become managers - 'Dixie' McNeil plus (at the time of writing still employed), Alan Buckley (then Walsall, currently West Brom.), Brian Horton (Port Vale and Manchester City) and Peter Taylor (Crystal Palace and Southend).

Durban failed to make it a hat-trick, but his team ended February with 5 wins and a draw. Chester earned some revenge for their Cup exit by ending Town's run, and Ray Haywood was recalled for the trip to Brighton where he scored as Town drew after leading 2-0.

Just four points from eight games virtually strangled hopes of a second promotion and earned Steve Hayes an end of season run in Graham Turner's No.6 shirt. The one victory, in March, was 3-1 over Cardiff, complete with the usual display of mindless violence on the terraces. The Club's problems were not helped by the 'flu virus which saw Town try to re-arrange the away game at Bury, but the 'Shakers' would not budge. To say Alan Durban was upset would be an understatement!

However, a 3-0 defeat at Swindon extinguished any lingering hopes, and losing the final three games saw the team slump, to finish ninth. The announcement of Peter Dolby's retirement after a record number of appearances, 390, was soon followed by five free transfers. Alex McGregor, Alan Tarbuck, Nigel O'Loughlin, Tony Gregory plus Ian Roberts were the players released, and all must have caused some careful thought, but in order to move upwards changes were necessary.

One major success in the area was the victory of Shrewsbury under 13's, managed by Eric Morgan, in the Welsh Schools Shield Final, the first time an area team from Shropshire had won a national title.

Most of the threat was created by, *"one of the smallest, but probably the most skilful players on the field"*, Stan Hall's words used to describe a cherubic Bernard McNally.

The Old Station Stand - had only 600 seats.
The new Stand (built in the early 80's), cost over £¼m.

The need to strengthen the squad was filled by the signing of Brian Hornsby from Arsenal for £20,000. Chairman Tim Yates was not often given to moments of self-congratulation but his delight at this capture was obvious. Town also tried to sign Everton's John Hurst on a free but Oldham stepped in and opened a career path out of Goodison that is still extensively used.

A five figure bid for Rochdale's Keith Hanvey failed, but two players arriving for trials were 19 year old Paul Maguire and 16 year old Steve Cross. Of those who had left, Tarbuck and O'Loughlin joined Rochdale, McGregor went to Aldershot (after a trial at West Ham), Harry Gregg took Ian Roberts to Crewe and Tony Gregory joined Telford.

The pre-season was interrupted by Alan Durban and Jake King seeing a specialist about troublesome knees, but Paul Maguire signed on as a professional. The pre-season games made up a competition called the Lilleshall Trophy, and featured Shrewsbury, Crewe, Wrexham and Plymouth, while Town also met the Saudi Arabian National XI. Town beat Crewe 3-1 (Irvine, Kearney and Bates scored from Maguire passes), whilst Stan Bowles netted Alex-

andra's consolation. Steve Cross was signed as an apprentice with Bill Trench a goalkeeper also having a trial after picking up a hand injury the previous season, but Tony Riley from Bolton was released.

Town were also set to play an Indonesian XI but that fell through, however, on August 6th 1976, Shrewsbury Town beat one of the 1994 World Cup finalists. Bill McGarry was the Saudi manager, and after a goalless first half, Sammy Irvine opened Town's account on 52 minutes, but the Saudi's equalised within a minute, through Dennaseih. Mike Kearney restored the Town lead, and after 16 year-old Jimmy Steele, on for Paul Maguire, almost scored with his first touch, Sammy Irvine wrapped up the victory, in the last minute.

The League season started with a debut goal for Brian Hornsby at Lincoln, while Paul Maguire on as sub. netted in the home victory over Gillingham. The follow-up victory over Reading went some way to obliterating the memory of the earlier League Cup exit - two 1-0 defeats by Walsall, before the League action had started. The happiest man at the Meadow was Steve Hickenbottom, who, 18 months after being told to retire was cleared to resume training.

Town were playing Steve Hammond in the reserves as a non-contract player and Richie Barker was considering the odd outing at that level.

Having lost their unbeaten League record at Wrexham, Town fought out a 3-3 draw at Walsall and then strung three victories together. The third success, 4-1 over Portsmouth, put Town top of the Division on goal difference from Brighton. It only lasted three days, before Brighton beat Walsall 7-0 and the following Saturday Town lost 1-0 at Swindon.

Jimmy Steele made his debut in the Senior Cup Semi-final with Oswestry, and Shaun Westray - despite being troubled by a knee injury - signed professional at the end of the season. After six consecutive home wins Town were the last team with a 100% record in the League and it was built on a settled team. Up to the 14th game, a goalless draw with Mansfield which ended the record, numbers 1-10 had remained unchanged and 11 and 12 had been shared between Alan Durban, Paul Maguire and Ray Haywood.

The Supporters Club paid tribute to Fred Pyatt's 25 years as secretary on November 9th - when he handed over to current Chairman Peter Sandford - and took over as Treasurer.

Crowds had been disappointing, with only 6,161 against Mansfield breaking five thousand, until the F.A.Cup came round. Doncaster away were the first round opponents, and after a hard fought 2-2 draw 6,234 turned out for the replay. Paul Maguire had scored at Belle Vue (his F.A. Cup debut), and he was to star in the second match. Rovers scored first and later twice equalised but Chic Bates hit the winner. It all evoked memories of Deepdale, but Paul Maguire's hat-trick was a reminder of another match with Doncaster, as it was the first since Ray Haywood's in the 7-4 epic almost two years earlier.

A 3-0 win at York followed and then a top of the table crunch match - Brighton at home. The visitors brought over 1,000 but the gate of 9,121 was exceptional. Mike Kearney set up Brian Hornsby for a simple goal and he almost had a second when Sammy Irvine flicked up a free-kick and Brian Hornsby volleyed from 20 yards, but Peter Grummitt miraculously tipped over. No matter Town were back on top of the table.

The F.A.Cup draw gave Town the chance to right a wrong - going to Bury with a full team. A battling goalless draw set up another replay with a re-match versus Q.P.R. as the prize draw.

A League game at Preston intervened with a Irvine-Hornsby free-kick seemingly snatching a late point, only for North End to nick it with a David Sadler header. The Cup glory was not allowed to slip though, as two excellent second half goals by Irvine and Turner secured the victory despite a late reply from Philips.

Town should have started the year with a home game versus Rotherham, but it was postponed, focusing ever more attention on the trip to Loftus Road. After much debate Paul Maguire's youthful flair just edged out the manager's hardened experience. Rangers were without skipper Gerry Francis but had already reached the last eight of the UEFA Cup and the Semi-finals of the League Cup. A goalless first half in which Town had ten efforts to Rangers' four, gave way to a second half in which 'Chic' Bates' goal was just not quite enough. Paul Maguire, twice, and Bates went close but Phil Parkes rescued his side and a Mike Kearney effort stuck in the mud on the line. Dave Sexton was full of praise, but Bury were unimpressed, for they gained their revenge three days, later ending Town's unbeaten home record 1-0.

Town's worldwide esteem, after the Saudi Arabia and Indonesia involvements, led to a request for a trial by Trinidad's Leading goalkeeper Earl Carter. On February 10th, Peter Louchnane joined Town on loan, and two days later the first sponsored match took place. It turned out to be a cracker, as 10,487 people watched Wrexham being beaten 3-2. Mike Kearney gave Town a half-time lead but Graham Whittle equalised. The famous free kick made it 2-1 but Bobby Shinton levelled on 82 minutes, only for Kearney with his tenth goal of the season to net the winner two minutes later.

Richie Barker made a Reserve team debut two days later hitting the bar from 20 yards when Wrexham Reserves took revenge with a 3-1 victory on the Meadow. The first team also came unstuck losing 2-1 to Gillingham and Walsall before losing a crazy game at Northampton 5-3. It was their 40th game of the season and their first defeat by more than one goal.

The Town goalscorers were an unlikely trio - for Colin Griffin gave them a way back from 2-0 down, Lee Roberts equalised and Kevin Moore cancelled out the Cobblers third - but all to no avail. 16 year-old Jason Seacole helped Oxford repeat the dose 4-2 at the Manor, with Les Lawrence hitting his first League goal. Suddenly nothing was going right, and an eleven game run without a win toppled promotion ambitions.

Lee Roberts went out on loan to Exeter, Ray Haywood was sold to Northampton and Peter Loughnane's loan was extended. He hit his first goal at Saltergate on March 26th in his second full game. Earl Carter finally arrived in mid-March, just as Steve Hickenbottom lost his unequalled struggle to overcome his knee problems. Carter made his debut in a Midland Intermediate Cup game which Town won 3-1 over Aston Villa. Peter Loughnane was signed on a free transfer, and Mike Kearney joined Chester for £8,000 making his debut against Town who won (finally), 2-0.

The Senior Cup final in the Shropshire F.A. Centenary year drew a crowd of just 842, and Telford won 3-2. Ken Draycott hit the winner and 'Ged' Garbett was only denied by a brilliant Bob Wardle save; David Arch made his senior debut for Town. Ian Loughnane accepted an apprenticeship to follow his dad and brother in joining the club. With four players having gone during the season, only youngsters Dave Collier, Shaun Westray and Steve Hinckenbottom were given 'frees' as the season ended with a brief glory - a 3-0 victory over Cardiff lifting the Welsh Cup. The first leg's 2-1 defeat saw Robin Friday's late winner rob Town - who had led through Hornsby's first half strike - but Colin Griffin after 3 minutes cancelled the deficit, and a Keith Pontin own goal plus Lee Roberts effort brought the Welsh silverware to the Meadow for the first time since 1938.

The need to bring in a midfield general occupied the manager's mind during the close season. Two players with Everton backgrounds and destined for managerial fame were targets. Howard Kendall, in late May, and Bryan Hamilton - in July - then with Birmingham and Everton respectively, were the players for whom Town put in offers. But Kendall joined Stoke and Hamilton moved to Millwall. The one signing completed was Jon Nixon from Peterborough, who said he was joining, *"a club going places"*. Apprentices joining included Michael Roberts plus Trevor Jones, and from Scotland, Jackie Keay.

The trading loss for 1976-7 was announced as £29,286 but a donation of £39,500 helped improve the club's bank balance to £12,934. Teenager Derek Hood played in a practice match with Watford - Elton John, Graham Taylor and all - which Town won 1-0, thanks to a Sammy Irvine header, but young Hood went to Hull City instead of joining Salop. Chester lodged a bid for Graham Turner, but Town rejected their efforts to buy him back. Jon Nixon scored his first goal in the Senior Cup Semi-final - a 2-1 victory over Oswestry ('Chic' Bates hit

the other goal), before Town captured Jimmy Lindsay from Hereford for £12,500. His debut came at Oxford as Town crashed 3-0 in the League Cup, a result which resulted in only 2,253 watching the return game, when Town came from behind for an inadequate 2-2 draw.

Lee Roberts opened the League season at left-back, and after victories over Wrexham and Lincoln he was in the unusual situation of knowing where he would play in the third game, but uncertain as to for which team. Exeter City had an £8,000 bid accepted, but the deal was not completed until after the game - which they won 2-0 - with Lee making his ninth and final full appearance for Shrewsbury. Steve Cross, in his only start of the season, replaced Roberts for the trip to Chesterfield, but was substituted and young Jackie Keay made his debut. In so doing he equalled Alan Humphries record of appearing in the first team six weeks after joining as an apprentice.

Young Scottish goalkeeper Bill Trench was injured in an intermediate match against Notts County and the team centre-forward took over in goal. Town were short on numbers and the 'substitute' was Bob Wardle, but despite such goalkeeping prowess Town lost 4-0. The game also saw Nigel Morgan, son of schools liaison officer Eric, make his debut as sub.

On September 27th, Town hammered Rotherham 4-1, the win putting them clear at the head of the table - three days earlier a 3-0 win at Bury put them joint top - but the glory was short-lived. The next fixture at Swindon saw Town suffer their biggest defeat for seven years, by a 5-0 scoreline. A two-all draw at Plymouth followed, watched by Dave Sexton and Matt Busby, plus the St. Etienne team who were due to play a European match at Home Park due to a UEFA ban on Old Trafford for crowd trouble.

'J and B' whisky had set up a sponsorship deal with the Football League to provide a crate of whisky for every League hat-trick, Town's last League triple had been back on February 1st 1975, when Ray Haywood hit three. Amazing what a little encouragement can do, for on October 8th, 'Chic' Bates hit his first trio in the 3-0 win over Port Vale, a fortnight later Town hammered Portsmouth 6-1 with three from Ian Atkins, and in the following home game Sammy Irvine scored all three against Hereford. This is believed to be the only time three different players have scored hat-tricks in successive home fixtures for a Football League side.

As if that was not enough the Portsmouth game, which started with an Atkins penalty, also featured a

Hornsby free kick which bounced off a stanchion and back into play without ever going between the posts, but was give as a goal. The third goal was another penalty, after a Hornsby dive, then Ian completed his hat-trick with a thunderous volley in a 6-1 win which put Town back on top. They then travelled to former leaders Gillingham, recording a creditable 1-1 draw, before Sammy Irvine's treble, which was completed with yet another penalty, this one for an off the ball incident with Ian Atkins. Sammy was acting skipper so there was no chance of him not taking the spot-kick, but he admitted after - with a dozen bottles of whisky on it - it was a pressure kick.

Young custodian Bill Trench left by mutual consent and joined Morton, but Town's efforts to sign Blackburn's Graham Hawkins failed. A Memorial game for Dave Thompson, who had collapsed and died playing junior football, saw Town beat a Henry Quinn Select XI by approximately 14-0.

Meanwhile, the F.A.Cup little bag of balls had obviously not been shaken up because for the second season running it was Doncaster Rovers away, in the first round. John Nixon came up with a second half winner and Town drew Stockport County at home in the next round. It was exactly thirty years since the epic second round battle with County, and again it would take more than one game to settle. Paul Maguire scored in the 1-1 draw at the Meadow, and also gave Town a first half lead at Edgley Park, but it took a Jimmy Lindsay goal to wrap up the victory; it was his only ever Town goal.

In fact, after all the hat-tricks, goalscoring became a problem. Only two goals came in the subsequent six League matches, which included an Irvine header and made him top scorer, until the Christmas home game with Bradford City. An injury to Ken Mulhearn ended his record 236 consecutive appearances, and provided a debut for Bob Wardle; he kept his goal intact and Town hit four. Another clean sheet against Colchester set up a 1-0 win, and a debut goal from new signing Steve Biggins gave Town a first half lead at Hereford, who spoilt Wardle's record with an equaliser.

Biggins scored in all his first three appearances for Town, all at different levels, but needed a hernia operation so his Hereford appearance was his only senior outing until April. Town had also signed Steve Cross as a professional but had failed in a £30,000 bid for Doncaster's Brendan O'Callaghan (Alan Durban would sign him for more than twice that for Stoke in the March).

It was all change time again, with 'Chic' Bates playing his 200th match against Wrexham before joining Swindon for £30,000. It was Alan Durban's last deal as Town manager as he moved to Stoke shortly after and offered Richie Barker his No.2 spot, but Barker stayed and he took charge at home to Swindon in a game Town lost 3-2. Town then drew 0-0 with Sheffield Wednesday in front of just 2,901, it was Jon Nixon's last game, for he moved to Barnsley for a small fee. Victory at Port Vale was Brian Hornsby's last match, he moved to Sheffield Wednesday for £45,000. The fans were disappointed at this latter transfer, but the manager said it was his decision. Richie was quoted as saying he was, *"more of an Alan Durban type player"*.

It did, however, leave Town short of players. Jock Fulton, who was continuing the good work of Bill Dennis, as Scottish scout, recommended Tommy Graham, but he joined Aston Villa for £5,000 and went on to make around 350 League appearances, mainly for Yorkshire sides. A deal was set up to bring striker Alan Guy from Newcastle on loan, but Town also secured 'Danny' Bowers in a similar deal from Stoke. The League would only sanction one of the moves so the unfortunate Guy was sent back, and Town went six League matches without scoring. They did score two at Bangor in the Welsh Cup, but in wild conditions referee Kevin McNally blew up after 84 minutes, Town trailing 4-2 thought he had abandoned the game, but despite an appeal the result stood.

Town President Sidney Yates had passed on, aged 96, and Leslie Tudor Owen took over the post with Patrick Newbrook being co-opted onto the board, the first new Director for ten years. A bid of £40,000 for Trevor Storton of Chester was rejected, but Town were convinced they had solved their goal-scoring problems with Steve Biggins scoring six in the final eight games. Kevin Moore, Jimmy Steele and Paul Hampson were unlucky to be released but they were not the only departures.

After an initial bid of £25,000, Stoke matched a Blackpool offer and paid £60,000 for Sammy Irvine. The deal finally completed at the start of July came six weeks after Graham Turner's promotion to player-coach. Tony Larkin was recruited from Wrexham, Jock Fulton sent Tom McKay and 15 year old Don Cameron for trials, but a £25,000 bid for Walsall's Miah Dennehy was rejected. Dean Edwards and Steve Perks were both young trialists but senior players were not forthcoming. Les Bradd from Notts County and Dave Gregory from Stoke failing to materialise.

Bradd a former teammate of Richie's went to Stockport and Gregory after a loan at Blackburn signed for Bury for £35,000.

Everyone knew this was the season Town would return to the lowest League level. The Club were kicking off with a side, nine of whom had been unable to improve their lot for two seasons, and three with similar credentials after one season - and there were also no new faces. In the previous two seasons, Sammy Irvine £60,000, Brian Hornsby £45,000, 'Chic' Bates £30,000, Lee Roberts £8,000, Jon Nixon £5,000 not to mention Mike Kearney, Ray Haywood, Lew Lawrence, Dave Collier, Kevin Moore, 'Danny' Bowers and Alan Durban had left the club.

In the Senior Cup Semi-final played pre-season, Steve Cross scored, but Town lost 2-1 to Oswestry, who included Tony Gregory, Paul Hampson, Steve Norris, Steve Blakemore and Patsalides Panicos, the latter better known locally as 'Barry the Greek'. It was proof, if proof was needed, that the months ahead would prove taxing.

Richie Barker set about organising his side so that like Alan Ball Senior's Preston eight years earlier, if they scored, they won. An Atkins penalty beat Brentford in front of 2,346, ninety-nine fewer than the League Cup crowd against Stockport. A Steve Biggins goal won that game but Les Bradd led County to a 3-1 victory in the return. It would be over six months before anyone had the audacity to score three against us again.

Victory over Oxford 1-0 was followed by a goalless draw with Swindon. Walsall scored the first League goal against us in a game which saw Sammy Chapman's debut, as substitute for Jimmy Linsday. Chapman was signed from Notts County for £5,000, having spent most of his career just across the Trent. The first manager of the month prizes featured Alan Durban and Maurice Evans taking Division Two and Four, with no mention of the miracle worker in Division Three. Dave Tong, initially on loan, arrived from Blackpool and did enough for Town to lash out £25,000 to make the move permanent.

By the end of September 'no-hopers United' had played ten League games, scored ten goals, conceded just two and secured seven wins and two draws; it was not miraculous it was impossible. Although unbeaten in October, the team won just once - at Rotherham - and three times leaked two goals. These five games were our longest run without a clean sheet. People were taking notice, Town drew two home games and then lost at Swindon; it was

their seventh defeat in thirty four League games under Richie, it was also his last game in charge.

Ironically he started and finished with a defeat by Swindon, but 14 wins and 13 defeats testify to his organisational ability. He had seen Town go top on September 26th, when a last minute free kick from 'Squire' (Paul Maguire) hit a backside in the wall and sent Jeff Wealands the wrong way. Having donated the ball, the writer was chuffed, having played brilliantly Wealands was not, as the dressing-room door discovered!

On October 9th, Town beat Zambia 4-0 in front of 2,791. Atkins, Biggins and Maguire scored before the break, with 'Biggles' from a precision pass from a guest player making it four. The guest was Bobby Charlton, so what else, but a precision pass, would one expect.

Youngsters in the news were Trevor Jones, who signed professional, Ian Loughnane, who was released, and Bert Williams' son Nigel, who played in the intermediates. Another goalkeeper in the limelight was Ken Mulhearn. Recovering from a wrist injury, he came on as substitute at Bromsgrove in midfield, replacing Bernard McNally, on his way to another cartilage operation.

Town were watching Jimmy Williams, Worcester City's centre-forward, but he did not join the Club, neither did young Don Cameron who went to Clyde. Ritchie's departure to be John Barnwell's No.2 at Wolves was a body-blow, his team had been built around three words, determination, organisation and defence, but Graham Turner - who took over as caretaker on November 20th - carried on the good work.

By the time he was confirmed as manager Town had reached round three of the F.A. Cup, winning at both Mansfield and dear old Doncaster, and secured a victory at Peterborough and drew with Gillingham. The third round cup-tie was Cambridge United at home. It was a bitterly cold day, only four games survived, and the Match of the Day cameras, having not previewed the game, turned up at the last minute to cover the action. The platitudes offered to the player-manager were initially accepted, before he lambasted the crew for the way Shrewsbury, like so many smaller teams, were ignored.

If Graham Turner was ever to win over the people of Shropshire this was it. Three early season gates were under 3,000, none after this fell below 5,600, while the five subsequent Cup matches were watched by 97,000.

The playing of the The Manchester City match was possible through the help of supporters who helped clear the pitch.

The bunch of no-hopers who started the season had made that amazing transformation around the Town, from being the sole possession of a few die-hards to being common property. The disparaging, *"how are your team doing"*, was replaced by, *"our boys will give Manchester City a hard time"*.

Tony Book was officially the City manager, but Malcolm Allison was the focal point. He tried to have the game postponed and several of his players obviously did not relish the task. Town cheered on by most of the 14,215 crowd were revelling in the atmosphere. Paul Maguire was outstanding and he literally skated through the City defence, to give Town a deserved half-time lead. Sammy Chapman's second half header from Maguire's corner was the icing on the cake. He had, before the kick-off, brought forth a large cheer from the City fans. Wearing, Martin - the writer's brother's - fedora, he came out of the tunnel and strode towards the City fans.

The station end erupted at the sight of their hero, but when he doffed his hat they lapsed into stunned silence, as it was Chapman's cheeky grin not Malcolm Allison who they saw! Both they and Allison remained silent for the rest of the day. Some old and future friends were involved in this game, for Joe Corrigan and Asa Hartford played and Ray Toseland, something of a lucky charm for Town, was referee.

The fifth round draw sent Town to Aldershot, but the game was postponed until the Tuesday. Town now had a tremendous following, for apart from seemingly dozens of coaches, British Rail laid on a train. It turned out to be a tortuous journey (was that a sign for Gretna or Great Yarmouth we just passed) but an epic match. To be fair, Aldershot battered Shrewsbury, and the corner count ended 19-2 in their favour.

John Dungworth, who had scored in every round, put his side ahead on 65 minutes, but Paul Maguire levelled four minutes later. However, when Sammy Chapman conceded a free kick two minutes from time, Alex McGregor's centre was knocked down by Joe Jopling and Dungworth seemingly won the tie. As at Preston several fans had already left and only the prospect of a bleak journey home remained, until David Tong struck and hit a shot over a now bald Glen Johnson into the top right hand corner of his net.

The build-up to the Wolves game saw Town using their new multi-gym donated by the supporters club, and not officially handed over until August 10th in a ceremony featuring their chairman Fred Brown and treasurer Jim Leighton. Town upheld their Cup pedigree with a fighting 1-1 draw at Molineux in front of 40,946. Steve Biggins was outstanding, but with ten minutes left Billy Rafferty converted a Steve Daley free kick.

But Town would still not lie down, and with five minutes remaining Peter Daniel fouled Paul Maguire in the area. Ian Atkins stepped up and secured a replay, to the delight of 12,000 Town fans.

The queue for tickets had to be seen to be believed - out of the ground, past the school, over the English Bridge, up the Cop, past the R.S.I. and down towards the station. The ticket office opened, and the writer's favourite memory is of a tall figure on a bike, riding past the queuing fans, putting his trusty steed against the wall, walking to the ticket office buying his ticket and with a cheery wave setting off home. The cyclist was Tony Crump, a Town fan through and through, and known as Scooby, but on this occasion everyone wished they could do like Scooby Doo. Wolves were simply too good in the replay. Steve Daley made Steve Hayes' life difficult, and had a hand in the first two goals - a half cleared corner converted by Willie Carr and a cross for Billy Rafferty. The third was a penalty given by Clive Thomas, and executed by Peter Daniel. Jackie Keay scored Town's consolation in front of 16,279.

Four days later Terry Gennoe played at Wembley for Southampton, but Forest won 3-1. Town enquired about 'Chic' Bates but Swindon wanted £50,000, so Town signed young Liverpool reserve Trevor Birch for £40,000. With 15 games left Town were second, 2 points behind Watford, but with a game in hand. A week after the Cup exit Town went to Blackpool and lost 5-0, and Blackpool looked poor. That result and a 3-0 defeat at Bury brought the team back to earth. A victory over Peterborough and two 1-1 draws with promotion rivals Swansea and Watford steadied the ship.

Shrewsbury were now 4th but with games in hand, however, after they lost 2-0 at Gillingham in front of 14,902, the home supporters celebrated clinching their first ever promotion, a bit prematurely. Shrewsbury had five games left in May. The first, at Sincil Bank, attracted just 1,677 to see Salop beat relegation bound City 2-1; a home win over Bury, was followed by a nervous 2-2 draw at Mansfield. 8,450 watched Rotherham lose 3-1 at the Meadow, leaving one game left - why is it always Exeter? It was the West Midland show on Thursday, and victory meant the championship, but defeat would mean fourth place and no promotion. A magic start, Jake King and the 'Shrewsbury' corner after 2 minutes made it 1-0, but Exeter had not read the script, for John Delve equalised three minutes later. No matter, two minutes on and back to the trusted formula Maguire corner - Keay flicked on, and King with a brave header made it 2-1. The third was an Ian Atkins penalty on the half hour after Maguire was tripped, and a Biggins effort off the post relaxed the 14,441 crowd. With 12 minutes left a Steve Cross header, was parried to David Tong, and the top came off the writer's bottle of champagne, as the player made it 4-1.

A memorable season, which - remember - started with a load of no-hopers losing at Oswestry. Jackie Keay was voted player of the year but the happiest people were probably Leslie Tudor Owen - emergency goalie to President over a 60 year span, Tommy Seymour - 43 years with the club, all he failed to do was make the board, he painted enough, and Ron Manders - intermediates trainer and occasional sub, with 30 years of service. Only one player, Steve Hayley, was released.

The Third Division Championship Trophy on display at Gay Meadow. The players include, Steve Cross, Bob Wardle, Steve Biggins, Jake King, Paul Maguire and Ian Atkins.

CHAPTER 13 - INTO THE EIGHTIES, IN THE SECOND DIVISION

Did Town deserve to be in Division Two? Jack Charlton did not think so, and many thought it would be a short flirtation, but memories like Thursday May 17th 1979 are for savouring not fretting. The first congratulations came in a 'phone call to chairman Tim Yates from Watford chairman Elton John, despite seeing the championship snatched from his grasp. Mr Yates was moved to say, *"I don't know if I could have done that"*. He probably would have, but it does not diminish the gesture.

Admission prices went up 25% on average, but no-one complained and season tickets were being snapped up - Newcastle, Sunderland, West Ham, Chelsea, Fulham, apart from one cup-tie and a friendly, the nearest we had been to clubs like this was five lines away on the coupon. Town signed Arthur Mann for £30,000 from Notts County and then discovered they would be the first opponents at the Meadow. Trevor Jones signed professional and Brian Coyne arrived, Mark Adams joined Dean Edwards as apprentice, Steve Perks had a trial and Bernard McNally - with an apprentice form beckoning - went to Oswestry for an explanatory operation on his right knee.

Graham Turner tried to recruit Ken Roberts - his ex-boss - as his number two, while Tommy Seymour and his number one, Ethel, celebrated their Golden Wedding. Robinson - The Jewellers - presented the players with gold plated Excalibur watches worth £65 each, a nice gesture, and Ivor Hookway launched 'the Shrew', happily no longer preferred to 'the loggerheads'. The first open day attracted 500 people and young Dean Edwards went for an England Youth trial.

There was no real noticeable close season, for the buzz about the place was like an on-going Cup run building up to the final. Town gave John Whiteford from Rutherglen Glencairn a trial game against Stoke Reserves, but it was Paul Maguire who was causing most concern. He went for X-Rays and blood tests, and missed the first dozen games.

An opening defeat at Swansea encouraged an air of realism, but a 1-1 draw with Notts County, thanks to Colin Griffin scoring Town's first ever Second Division goal, was slightly encouraging. Defeats by Bristol Rovers, Cambridge and Cardiff meant Chelsea came in mid-September as long odds on favourites.

It is still hard to believe that Shrewsbury beat them 3-0, including Arthur Mann's only ever Town goal. Despite it being all ticket their fans reeked revenge, painting the Town and causing damage at the station.

A brief League Cup interest had seen us scramble past Halifax before falling to Chesterfield. The arrival, first of Reg Matthewson a former team-mate of Graham Turner's at Chester, and then the return of Sammy Chapman from Tulsa gave everyone a boost, except perhaps Arthur Mann. He moved to Mansfield for £36,000 and speculation about a bid for Billy Rafferty or John Dungworth grew, but Wolves and Aldershot both wanted £200,000. A win over Orient, a draw with Leicester and then a thrashing at Meadow Lane - when Gordon Mair was rampant as Town crashed 5-2 - followed. A battling 1-0 defeat at St. James Park, no not Exeter, but Town's first visit to Newcastle, came next.

Two days later John Malam joined Wolves and missed Steve Biggins only League hat-trick in the 3-1 victory over Wrexham. It was an impressive trio which left Dai Davies helpless. Then a visit to St. Andrews, where an Alan Ainscow goal from a Willie Johnston pass would be Birmingham's only goal against Shrewsbury for years. Meanwhile a £70,000 bid from Town, and an appeal by John Dungworth, led to his arrival at the Meadow for £100,000, which is still a club record fee. Aldershot manager Tommy McAnearney said it was ill-advised, perhaps he was right. Initially he was not, a neat header on his debut augured well as Town drew 2-2 with Swansea, but it would be ten weeks before he scored again. Jackie Keay, on penalties, netted four times, and his goal at Fulham was his fifth of the season - the leading scorer with Steve Biggins, who after the hat-trick went ten games without a goal.

Other hat-trick scorers were Tim Cook - as the youth team beat Wolves 5-3 in a Youth Cup second replay (Dean Edwards and Mark Taylor scored the others), and Trevor Birch who hit three in a Reserves match which was also against Wolves.

Sammy Chapman, for whom Town had paid Tulsa £5,000, went down with 'flu and never reproduced the fairy-tale spark of the previous campaign. Town's new physiotherapist arrived on New Year's Eve, Wayne Jones from Bristol Rovers, whose career had been curtailed by injury.

However, five days later Town equalled their worst F.A. Cup defeat since 1926, going down 5-1 at the Den to Third Division Millwall. The East-London crowd, upset at a linesman, vented their displeasure - despite the scoreline - and the errant official collapsed after running into a passing lump of concrete. Bernard McNally finally signed on that weekend, and Jock Fulton sent Town three new apprentices, namely John McGrath, John Munro and Mike O'Neill.

John Dungworth's goal drought ended with an overhead kick against Cardiff and was followed up with two at Stamford Bridge, as Town won 4-2 to complete a memorable double. Another - against Charlton - and wins at Orient, and over Newcastle, won Graham Turner manager of the month, despite an outbreak of Chicken Pox.

Then the club was rocked. Ron Manders, undergoing heart surgery, died, he was just 48 and had appeared as substitute for the intermediates earlier that season. A reliable, pleasant man, he just went quietly about his job and had encouraged many aspiring youngsters. The same day Sammy Irvine - half Ron's age - nearly lost his life in an horrific car crash on his way back from Stoke, but despite initial fears he made a slow steady recovery.

Transfer interest revolved around strikers, both in an out, but without real action. Trevor Birch was listed at his own request, Aldershot showed interest, but then bought Colin Garwood from Portsmouth for £45,000. Town wanted Alan Gowling but Bolton started utilising him as a defender and Greenock Morton, who wanted £50,000 for Roddy Hitchinson, would not let their man out on loan. The club did hang on to Ian Atkins, despite an initial bid of £80,000 - raised to £125,000 - by Chesterfield.

Young Martin Sankey, just 15, hit a hat trick in a match against Bristol Rovers' under 16's, and followed it up with successive three goal hauls in two Shropshire County League games. Even more amazingly it was a feat he would repeat. At the other end of the age scale, Leslie Tudor Owen, then 80, stepped down as vice chairman, his replacement was Ken Woodhouse.

On the field, Trevor Birch scored, on what was to be his final appearance, against Sunderland, but Chris Turner put in a brilliant performance and the Wearsiders won 2-1. Bob Wardle emulated Turner, at Luton, where Tony Larkin for the first time played as a central defender in the goalless draw.

A trip to West Ham saw Town complete another Metropolitan double, beating the 'Bubble-blowers' 3-1. The season ended with Fulham 'congo-ing' their way into Division Three, as Town won 5-2, not quite so impressive from Fulham's point of view, as their seven goal exit from Division One twelve years earlier at Goodison.

Steve Hayes, Sammy Chapman, Mike Roberts, Trevor Jones and Mike Neil were released. Birmingham bid for Paul Maguire, and David Tong was elected player of the year. Jock Fulton recommended Gordon Boyd, but he rejected a trial, Glen Chambers from Mansfield did accept a trial and Tim Cook signed as an apprentice, as did Wayne Williams. The club announced plans to spend £100,000 on safety and ground improvements, and Joe Wheatley sent 17 year old Mick Hardman for a trial. It all seemed like a regular close season until Reg Matthewson resigned to return to the security of an industrial career.

Graham Hawkins was appointed as his successor on July 8th, 48 hours before Trevor Birch moved to Chester for £10,000. Ken Mulhearn went to Crewe Alexandra and Town signed Glyn Jones as cover goalkeeper. Ross Maclaren, 18, released by Rangers signed as Stoke and Everton bid for Paul Maguire. It would turn into a saga with Everton withdrawing due to a back problem, and Stoke trying to win a reduction in the agreed fee. Eventually the deal went to a tribunal and Stoke were told to pay the agreed amount, but as a deposit and three further staged payments. The total amount was set at £262,000. Town then went to another tribunal to sign Paul Petts, with £15,000 plus £20,000 after 30 games and half the sell-on profit being the outcome on this occasion.

The seventies finished with a financial loss of £151,575, £109,708 of which was a deficit on transfers and the rest boosted by a rise of £90,000 in the wage bill. All this despite a season's average home League gate of 7,782 - definitely a case of where are they now? It was not as if the Club were greatly overstaffed, for instance early in the new season five players played for the intermediate team against Stoke in the morning and then fulfilled a County League fixture in the afternoon.

Home draws with Grimsby, Chelsea and Norwich in the League Cup and away defeats at Swansea, Blackburn plus Norwich in the second leg started the season. The first victory came thanks to two John Dungworth goals at home to Watford, but West

Ham, despite a fine performance from Paul Petts, revenged their previous two defeats with a 3-0 victory.

Away form improved, with two goalless draws at Preston and Oldham, before two 2-1 home defeats by Bolton and Orient. Tony Larkin asked for a move which was granted, ironically just before his first team recall. Glen Chambers, after two months, was released and young goal-keeper Steve Perks went for an England Youth trial. Graham Turner lined up a bid for Tommy Hutchinson from Coventry but John Bond stepped in and paid £50,000 to take him to Manchester City.

A battling performance at Newcastle

In the early 1980's, the current Station Stand was built

whilst another target was Port Vale winger Mark Chamberlain. Boxing Day saw Town playing in front of 22,863 at Hillsborough, it looked a daunting task but Ian Atkins' goal saw Town to a 1-1 draw, with Wednesday throwing on young giant John Pearson, 17, for the last 20 minutes.

The F.A. Cup third round brought Town face to face with Terry Austin's Huddersfield at Leeds Road, it would be an unusual game even for the long established competition. The visitors took a first half lead, when David Tong's corner was turned past Andy Rankin by Chris Topping, but shortly after Chic Bates and Rankin clashed, and though Chic recovered after

came to nothing, for in a late goalmouth scramble, Jake King was kicked on the bridge of his nose, as he bent to head clear, and Bobby Shinton stabbed the ball home. Town gave a trial to cosmopolitan, Manuel De Costa, a South African who had emigrated to Australia, but was living in Birmingham, and he scored on his debut as Town drew 1-1 with Walsall in the Intermediate League.

David Tong suffered from an unusual double at Loftus Road, the previous season he was booked by mistake - Jake King the offender on that occasion - and this time he again received a caution after Jackie Keay erred. Town signed young Mark Adams on professional forms at the start of December, and on the twelfth, 'Chic' Bates finally returned for £20,000 from Bristol Rovers.

Shrewsbury enquired about Mansfield striker Terry Austin but he joined Huddersfield for £120,000,

treatment, Rankin, with a cut left eye and concussion, left the field. Steve Kindon took over in goal, but Steve Cross fired Town two up, and Huddersfield decided they needed Kindon's firepower, so Mark Lillis donned the jersey instead. His hopes of a clean sheet evaporated when, from Paul Petts' corner, 'Chic' Bates headed home. Three-nil to Shrewsbury, all scored against different keepers. Ian Atkins played in this game despite losing two teeth and having two more loosened against Wrexham a week earlier, this led to the suggestion that gum shields should be worn.

Another player in the wars was ex-Town man Paul Bevan who on January 10th broke his leg playing for Worcester against Minehead in the F.A. Trophy. Town's Youth team were also enjoying a good cup run, in the F.A.Youth Cup. They had beaten holders Aston Villa, thanks to a brilliant Bernard McNally goal.

He picked the ball up in the centre circle, beat two men, and hit a stunning chip-drive home from 20 yards into the Wakeman goal. It sealed a victory which put the youngsters into the last sixteen, against Leeds at the Meadow. A crowd of 1,683 turned up but Leeds had a player Town could not handle, a young strong mobile striker called Terry Connor and they won 3-0.

Dutch midfielder Theo Worbts had a trial in January but Graham only managed to see him play one full game, and although useful he was released. The F.A. Cup draw started the Ipswich trilogy with Town in front of 18,000 battling out a goalless draw at the Meadow, before a trip to Portman Road. Ipswich were much the better side but the first goal - a Gates header - Bob Wardle claimed did not cross the line, while the third was scored by John Wark, who was yards offside.

The search for new talent continued with first Steve Brown from Hibernian and then Charlie Gibson having trials, while young full-back John McGrath went for a Scottish U-17 trial. The youth team's form had brought an invitation to attend a youth tournament in Mons, Belgium, in June, which would feature both Eastern and Western European sides. Another Scotsman, Brian Coyne, had featured in Welsh Cup victories over Llanidloes 5-0 and Abercynon Athletic 6-1 (which included a Steve Biggins hat-trick). But he left to join Motherwell before the low point of the season, when Fourth Division Hereford thumped Town 5-0 in a Welsh Cup replay on March 4th.

Trips to London had been traumatic, with no wins, and West Ham and Orient completing doubles, but the Hereford defeat seemed to rekindle the fighting spirit. The season ending with a ten match unbeaten run, which dispelled relegation fears and achieved mid-table respectability.

Jake King became the fifth Town player to pass 300 appearances after Graham Turner earlier that season, plus Ken Mulhearn, Joe Wallace and Peter Dolby. Tim Cook went to an England coaching session at Lilleshall, meanwhile Steve Perks signed professional.

Jimmy Lindsay, Tony Larkin, Glyn Jones and youngsters Graham Lewis and Michael O'Neill were all released, but Paul Johnson for £20,000 was signed from Stoke. Jones whose only Town starts were the four Welsh Cup games left League football but returned two years later to play three times for Newport County. Tony Larkin won a two year contract at Carlisle shortly after Alan Durban left Stoke for Sunderland, but recommended Richie Barker as his successor at the Victoria Ground. Steve Biggins and 'Chic' Bates achieved their full coaching badges in July, and Peter Blundell signed as an apprentice.

The 1981 close season transfer talk revolved around Ian Atkins, with Chesterfield and Wrexham bidding, while Newcastle also showed an interest, and Town enquired about 'Dixie' McNeil from Wrexham, but eventually neither player moved. Jack Keay and David Tong put in written transfer requests, and Frank Clarke returned to the area, when he was appointed to the staff at Wem's Adams Sports and Leisure Centre.

Bernard McNally after all his problems signed professional, Richard Pike joined as an apprentice, Andy Foote - an eighteen year-old centre-half from Luton - came on trial, and he was soon followed by midfielder Peter Farrell from Port Vale. Steve Biggins had talks about a move to Walsall and Ron Jukes arrived as part-time chief scout.

The ten match unbeaten run was ended in style on the opening day with Barnsley hitting four. A home defeat by Blackburn followed, but Town bounced back to hit four themselves against Derby. For the second season running a first round bye meant entry straight into round two of the League Cup, which was now called 'The Milk Cup'. Town drew West Bromwich Albion for their first meeting as League clubs. Led by Cyrille Regis, they looked a formidable outfit, and few were surprised by the way they raced into a 3-0 first half lead. Half-time however, saw a transformation. Ian Atkins' penalty reduced the arrears, Steve Biggins made it interesting and a couple of minutes from time Ross Maclaren blasted home a free-kick for an unlikely draw. It was three weeks before the return and Town were again adrift at the interval, this time 2-0, but again Ian Atkins scored - this time a crashing 25 yard drive - and on 88 minutes he hit a fine shot to equalise, only for it to be ruled out for offside. This was not the only disappointment, as the local constabulary - obviously used to a higher class of hooligan - gave Town's fans behind the goal a hard time.

John Dungworth missed all this excitement, for he was out on loan at Hereford but returned to make another 22 appearances. In between the West Brom matches Town went to Norwich where Steve Biggins caused havoc but could not score, Paul Petts hit

Town's goal, and City - inspired by teenage debutant substitute John Fashanu - grabbed a late winner. Scoring goals was a real problem, only Ian Atkins who was revelling in his striker's role stopped a complete drought. Peter Farrell, like Andy Foote before him, was released on November 9th just as Nigel Pearson was arriving from Heanor Town. Wayne 'Bomber' Williams signed professional a week later, and was joined on their respective 18th birthdays by John McGrath and Tim Cook.

Town's two home games in November saw an own goal and an Atkins penalty beat Bolton, and a week later another penalty - after 'Budgie' Burridge brought down Dungworth - and an excellent five man move give Atkins the two goals which beat Queens Park Rangers. The Londoners £1 million man Clive Allen being overshadowed by Atkins and Bernard McNally.

The New Year started with Cup action. Mark and Neville Chamberlain ran Town ragged, but a late 'Chic' Bates goal put Port Vale out of the competition. Eight days later Town played their first ever Sunday Welsh Cup-tie, at Caernafon, and he - much to Ian Atkins' delight - hit five in an 8-1 romp. Another undistinguished performance rescued by a second half Chic Bates goal disposed of Burnley in the F.A. Cup, and Ipswich were drawn in round five. It would be the fourteenth meeting between the club, with Town yet to win. Jake King, who had missed most of the season with a stomach problem caused by scar tissue, had returned to action a week earlier, and would play a vital role.

The opening goal came when King, in the absence of Paul Petts, lifted the ball over the wall and Steve Cross volleyed home. Then from a David Tong corner Jackie Keay flicked on and King dived in to make it two. Mitch D'avray reduced the arrears with 15 minutes left, but Town recorded a first-ever win against the Suffolk team.

February 23rd 1982 saw the first-ever, and so far biggest, reunion of former Town players. It was a wonderful night with over 100 former stars attending. It was the brainchild of Pam Ravenscroft who had been connected with the Club for years, and she enrolled the help of Peter Dolby and Diane Clewlow amongst others to set up the evening. Of the first ever League eleven, Norman Lewis, Joe Wheatley and Frank Griffin were present, and all subsequent teams were well represented. It was a night for nostalgia which rates alongside any of the famous games.

That evening was a difficult act to follow, but eleven days later the quarter final of the F.A. Cup gave the club their best chance ever of reaching the last four of that competition.

Town's opponents were Leicester City, the sides had yet to meet in the League, and a close battle was expected. Larry May gave City the lead but Mark Wallington was injured in a tangle with 'Chic' Bates and soon after Chic equalised, before Jackie Keay put Town ahead. Town needed to hold that lead, but with everyone transfixed a Colin Griffin back pass trickled over the line and it was 2-2 at half-time. Alan Young had replaced Wallington in goal, but he was injured. This time Bernard McNally was the Town man involved, and Steve Lynex took over.

Town's chance passed them by with Jim Melrose, Gary Lineker and Melrose again setting up a semi-final with Tottenham Hotspur. A crowd of 29,117 paid a record £71,000 to watch this match. John Dungworth came on as substitute in the game, but a week later started his best scoring run, netting equalisers against Cardiff and Wrexham, and then making it a three game run by hitting the Town's only goal at Watford. The following match, a 1-0 win over Cambridge, marked Noel Blake's first game on loan from Aston Villa. In fact Town tried to bring in more help but were refused the following star studded list:- Mickey Thomas (Brighton), John Richards (Wolves), Ashley Grimes (Man Utd), Terry Donovan (Villa) - all internationals - plus Alan Biley, Mick Ferguson, Joe McBride, Alan Ainscow, Mick Lyons and Peter Eastoe all Everton.

It was building to a nail-biting end to the season, as defeats of 5-1 at Grimsby, and 4-1 at Luton, increased the problems, although a rare Paul Johnson' goal at Grimsby ended a run of 16 games during which the team's only goals came from Atkins (6) and Dungworth (4). Successive home wins over Crystal Palace and Grimsby meant a draw at Leicester would be sufficient to stave off relegation, and Town achieved just that in a goalless match.

Declan Edge and Gerrardo Nardiello - successfully - plus Scottish winger Bobby Dickson had trials. While the end of season list released John Dungworth, Charlie Gibson (who is still currently banging in goals in Scotland), Tim Cook, full-backs Jake King (after 304 games), and Carleton Leonard (after 224), plus Steve Biggins, and David Tong. Also leaving was John McGrath a young full-back who had captained the reserves to win their Cup completion and narrowly missed out due to Martin Sankey hitting another very timely three consecutive hat tricks. All these departures were inspired by the need to further cut overheads. Ian Atkins and Jackie Keay joined the exodus by asking for moves. Chairman Tim Yates also moved, selling Boreton Farm to ex-Champion jockey Bob Davies for £700,000. The reserves were staying put however, an application to join the Central League failing because it appeared, of a lack of motorway links.

The biggest departure, was not employed by the club. Journalist Stan Hall, to whom Mr Yates had made a special presentation at the reunion, retired after 47 years of reporting on the club. His column was to all Town fans, obligatory reading.

The search for new talent continued with Town having Martin Myers, Karl Foster, Richard Pike, Gerrardo Nardiello and Andy Kerr newly signed apprentices. Junior professionals numbered four - Steve Perks, Wayne Williams, Martin Sankey and Nigel Pearson. The quartet would make over 600 appearances for Town, and Nigel may yet push their League total past the 1,000 mark. The usual pre-season tour to Scotland became a casualty of the cost-cutting.

At the end of July, Town were involved in two significant exchange deals. Ian Atkins went to join Alan Durban at Sunderland, with Alan Brown moving to the Meadow in a six-figure deal. Then Steve Ogrizovic arrived from Liverpool with Bob Wardle going to understudy Bruce Grobbelaar. Town netted around £130,000 in these deals. Steve Ogrizovic had started his goalkeeping career in a youth club team run by former Town man Alan Humphreys.

The season started with a major shock, when Graham Hawkins left to become manager of Wolves. Graham Turner's name had been linked with the move but few expected his No.2 to land the plum job. Young Karl Foster made an immediate impression, scoring the goal as Llanidloes were beaten 1-0, and adding another in a 2-0 win over Stafford, Paul Johnson netting the second. Jackie Keay was on trial at Birmingham, while Cardiff City striker Gary Stevens was training with the Town. A tribunal decided on a £20,000 fee for Stevens but Jackie Keay went to Wrexham and joined up with Jake King.

Bernard McNally had a problem which looked like setting up a third cartilage operation, and he missed the first few games of the season. The supporters club were upset at the lack of any directors at their annual meeting. Although Tim Yates did make a statement soon afterwards admitting the manager had been forced to cut his small squad even further because of the escalating overheads.

The season started with Ross Maclaren playing in a new sweeper role which worked fairly well at Oldham, apart from a left-wing centre turned past the new goalkeeper by the new sweeper. Gary Stevens made his debut in the second match at home to Fulham - another 1-0 defeat - and including a 1-0 first leg defeat at Wrexham, Town had lost all their first five matches, scoring just once. Only 2,850 turned up for the Cup second leg, and after a scoreless first half, they were convinced a miracle was **not** about to happen. It took a sending off to kick-start Town's season. Eddie Niedzwiecki handled outside his area and was dismissed, Town scored two goals - Alan Brown's first and Steve Cross. On the Saturday it was Newcastle, Kevin Keegan et al. Town were the only League side without a point but they won 2-1, the Magpies were so upset they went out and bought two more internationals, Terry McDermott and David McCreery. A trip to Burnley and a home game with Cambridge also resulted in 2-1 victories. Just one point from the following three matches, ending with a 4-0 defeat on the plastic - in the wet at Loftus Road - gave way to a nine match unbeaten League run, which carried them into the New Year.

November was an eventful month, for Colin Robinson was signed from Mile Oak Rovers, Alan Brown scored the winner against Sheffield Wednesday in a game which saw Nigel Pearson need five stitches in his mouth, and two goals in the last five minutes beat Chelsea at Stamford Bridge. One man missing all this action was Paul Johnson who had suffered a broken toe. He made a comeback in the Welsh Cup tie at Rhyl which saw Steve Perks make his senior debut. A Mickey Brown penalty set up a replay few wanted, and only 513 turned up for a game which Town won 3-0, despite having Ross Maclaren sent off. A 2-0 Boxing Day defeat by Wolves, was followed two days later by an excellent 3-2 victory at Derby, both games being witnessed by crowds of over 13,000.

Ross McLaren missed the 2-1 defeat at Fulham and the 3rd round Cup-tie with Rotherham. Two Pauls' - Johnson and Petts - had scored the second half goals against the Millers in the League game, so Emlyn Hughes' side came to destroy. A crowd of 6,027 watched in disbelief and dismay as Rotherham played one of the most outrageous offside plans of all time.

A goalless first half became even worse when a long range John Seasman effort put the visitors ahead on the hour. For once justice was seen to be done, for after a further seven minutes, a brace of goals from Alan Brown - separated by just sixty seconds - clinched a deserved victory.

It set up a trip to Goodison, and Steve Cross at full-back in place of Wayne Williams and Paul Petts should have given Town a third minute lead. They did not, and the sweetest left foot in football (Alan Walsh apart), was sufficient to win the tie. A Kevin Sheedy free-kick just before half-time and an 'Inchy' Heath goal on 62 minutes put the Toffees through, despite a Steve Cross goal.

Town had signed Darren Hunting, Ian Smith and Lee Payton, on schoolboy forms and in early February granted Graham Turner a testimonial, after 10 years service. A week later, in front of Leicester's smallest home crowd of the season, Wayne Williams a League ever-present and Colin Robinson on for just 14 minutes, scored as Town lost 3-2. Internationals Gary Lineker 2 and Ian Wilson netted the Leicester's goals. A home goalless draw with Q.P.R. followed, it was Martin Sankey's last League appearance.

A week later, Wayne Williams - for the second away game running - scored as Town proved Emlyn Hughes right, by winning 3-0 at Millmoor. On the same day, Willie Carr made his only appearance for Town, albeit in the intermediates 5-2 victory over Notts County. The mid-March victory over Barnsley saw Gary Stevens' first game in defence and started another sequence of nine unbeaten games. The eighth game of the sequence saw Wales manager Mike England at the Meadow watching Carlisle midfielder Russell Coughlin. A Welsh Cap escaped him, but a spell at Town would happen and, if Jack Charlton had been in charge earlier he may have qualified for Eire.

Gerry Nardiello came on as substitute in the final game at Blackburn a week after Karl Foster replaced Paul Petts at home to Leeds. Nardiello at 17 years 9 days was not - as Rothmans claim - Town's youngest debutant. Nigel Pearson won the 'Player of Year' award. Meanwhile, on the day Nardiello made his debut, England played Wales on the Meadow, in the Centenary Shield, with England manager Bobby Robson in attendance. A day later it was Russia versus Spain and with due respect to Bobby, an even bigger world great attended - 'the man in black' - Lev Yashin, to many eyes the finest goalkeeper ever. He was in charge of the Russian

youngsters. Later that week Town splashed out £10,000 on Cheltenham Town winger Paul Tester, who had scored 25 goals the previous season. Steve Cross needed a cartilage operation, but physiotherapist Wayne Jones did not wait for his recovery, he went back to Bristol Rovers. Having lost his physio, Graham Turner appointed Derek Mann to that position, and 'Chic' Bates became player-coach in the July. Early pre-season saw Paul Johnson break his toe again, in the 5-1 win over Llanidloes. Off to Scotland, and Paul Tester opened August with a goal, backed up by 'Chic' Bates, as Town beat Meadowbank 2-0.

However, pre-season 1983 was soon to rebound on Tester, for he suffered knee trouble and would not make his full League debut until March. More problems arose, with local magistrates refusing to renew the license for the ground, even striking out the Directors "G. and T.'s" - was nothing sacred?

The season opened with a 1-1 draw at Grimsby, but most of the County were more interested with events at Lord's, particularly, goalkeeper Steve Ogrizovic. Whereas almost twenty years earlier, Higgs and Snow had made cricket headlines on the opening football Saturday, now it was Shrewsbury C.C., thanks in no small way, to 'Oggy's' prowess as a quick bowler, for the local cricket team were gracing the hallowed turf. A former member of the goalies union, Ken Mulhearn, was on wicket-keeping duty, although his daughter as scorer, was not allowed into the pavilion. Shrewsbury's opponents - Hastings and St. Leonard's - were cruising to victory, until in the sensational finale, Richard Tudor and the local men secured the unlikeliest victory by two runs.

Continuing the cricket theme, sometime Shropshire captain Brian Perry took over as groundsman from Harold Bowen, on October 17th, Harold, after six years in the job, having reached retiring aged.

The football season had started (unusually) well, apart from a 4-1 defeat at Portsmouth - Town always lose there - the only other reverse was a late Don O'Riordan blockbuster at Brunton Park. Undoubtably the highspot was a hat-trick in eight minutes, late in the game, by Paul Petts against Leeds. The visitors had led at half-time, but goals from Colin Robinson and Alan Brown had left their fans considering serious damage. However Petts' three goals, all struck from the edge of the area, left them little option but to skulk off home; 2-1 you can argue about, but 5-1 is an open-and-shut case.

Another Yorkshire side, Sheffield United, were next into the fray, in round two of the Milk Cup. Trailing at half-time, again Town managed a first leg lead through goals from Gary Stevens and Alan Brown. A one goal lead did not seem sufficient, but trips to Sheffield hold little fear for Shrewsbury sides, and second half goals from Gary Hackett and 'Chic' Bates secured a draw and a place in round three.

The youth team sampled cup success under the guidance of Derek Mann and Clem McBride when they beat Stoke 2-1. The goalkeeper was Lee Goodall, son of Dave, and the substitute was Mickey Brown, who was kept out of the team by Salem Ahmed (a youngster born in South Yemen), who like Tony Spray, Richard Southall, Nick Richards and Steve Philips would fail to make the ultimate breakthrough. Two youngsters on the upgrade were Gerry Nardiello and Karl Foster, who were both called into the England youth squad. Not enjoying such happy times was Paul Johnson who fell over a step and broke the some bone for a third time.

Town signed Mark Bowater from Rushall Olympic but failed to secure Geoff Palmer from Wolves. They also hit a slump losing four consecutive matches including the Milk Cup exit at Walsall, but then drew three, including another trip to Sheffield, this time against Wednesday. Defeat on St. Stephens Day, 4-2 by Chelsea, meant a run of 12 games without a victory, but this ended the following day at Swansea where Gary Hackett scored his first League goal. Hackett suddenly became a potent threat and was to score in three home games during January. His first came in the 2-0 win over Portsmouth - which preceded the 3-0 F.A. Cup victory over Oldham, in which Gary did not score. However, he did net one in the defeat by Grimsby, before Ipswich - once more in the Cup - arrived at the Meadow. Town would win, thanks to two second half goals, from Colin Robinson and a fine shot from Gary

Hackett, the latter gracing the 'Match of the Day' introduction for many months. The unfortunate goalkeeper was Paul Cooper, who several years earlier hit a couple of goals against Leicester for Town's youth team, when he was an aspiring forward.

The well trodden path from non-League football to the Meadow was once more in use, when Boldmere St. Michael's left-back Kevin Collins signed in January. He made his debut against Colwyn Bay in the Welsh Cup, and was one of five scorers as Town won 5-2 in front of just 489.

Andy Kerr and Andrew O'Connor also made first appearances and Paul Tester and Paul Johnson made comebacks after injury.

Town had drawn Everton in round four of the F.A. Cup, or to be more precise Gillingham or Everton, for the Kent side, were twice unlucky not be beat the Merseysiders, before the Toffees finally went through. Wayne Williams managed to make the starting line-up against the Merseysiders, but Town lost 3-0. In fact Town achieved nil seven times in nine starts, with Alan Brown and Paul Petts scoring the only goals. It would be Brown's last goal for Shrewsbury, for he moved to Doncaster on transfer deadline day for £40,000.

Derek Mann resigned as Shropshire F.A.'s director of coaching in March 1984, and was replaced by John Malam. The youngsters kept arriving, with Jason Mason, Neil Meredith, Richard Green and Tim Steele becoming apprentices. Gerry Nardiello was called into the England youth squad to play in a tournament in Russia, but Karl Foster had his contract cancelled at the end of April. He must have thought it was a blessing in disguise when Ron Saunders took him to Aston Villa, but there was to be a sting in the tail.

(Right) Gary Hackett, who scored the 'Match of the Day' goal.

(Left) Colin Robinson, the other scorer at Ipswich.

The season ended with a not unusual flourish, two excellent strikes from Steve Cross started it in the home draw with Newcastle. Three victories, a defeat at Chelsea, three victories and defeat at Cambridge (which did not rescue United) were followed by a final victory over Derby County who also finished in the relegation trio. Town's first close season signing was Mark Bates from Walsall, but Bobby Gould wanted Steve Ogrizovic. The Coventry manager took the deal to a tribunal and a fee of £72,500 was set. Town immediately went out and signed - for the first time - Ron Green for £10,000 from Walsall.

A pre-season tour to Partick and Falkirk was lined up but Graham Turner would not be going. He joined Aston Villa in mid-July, and Doug Ellis paid Town £27,500 compensation with Graham signing a five year contract - deadly Doug had never had it so easy. Groundsman Brian Perry was enjoying his summer, Shropshire beat Yorkshire with the scorecard reading G.Boycott c + b, Perry 27.

'Chic' Bates was appointed the Town manager on July 23rd, and took the team to Scotland with mixed results before suffering a major setback. On the eve of the season it was announced that Nigel Pearson was to have a knee operation. It was a big blow, but not one which 'Chic' allowed to deflect him from his desire to play a more positive brand of football. Gary Stevens, who was signed as a striker, had spent most of the previous eighteen months in defence, but despite Pearson's injury was back in the front line.

He scored in both the opening victories, missed out at Carlisle, but hit his first hat-trick in the remarkable 5-1 victory at Huddersfield. Colin Robinson and Gary Hackett also hit the goal standard, but then Town lost at home to Wimbledon, whose chairman Stanley Reed played for Salop in 1927. They arrived at a time when Town were giving a trial to Dave Villa Lobes, from Chile.

Gary Stevens hit another hat-trick, against Notts County, with the team substitute sitting in the stands; Manager Bates was in the number 12 shirt and admitted: *"I became aware of gaps left in the defence by the attacking play, but thought at times the side looked good"*.

The club announced a loss of £17,203, but the retained profit was still £79,968, and of course did not include the £100,000 from the Ogrizovic and Turner moves. Ron Green turned in his best per-formance of his first spell at Shrewsbury, in the goalless draw at Birmingham, and four days later Paul Tester went to Hereford on loan. Meanwhile party time became suspension time, with Richard Green, John Dale, Martin Hudson and Mickey Brown each suspended for 2 games, for breaking curfew.

The early promise gave way to a Milk Cup exit against Bolton, and after a 1-0 victory over Manchester City, a run of five successive draws became ten games without a victory up to Christmas. Graham Turner let Leigh Palin join Town on loan in mid-December, and he made his League debut at Middlesbrough alongside Steve Perks. It is ironic that both Town's locally born goalkeepers - John Philips and Steve Perks - made their debut on a Friday night in the North-east, and in drawn matches. Their second game together would be Palin's last for Town - he was injured in the victory over Wolves - which was also Mark Bates' last League match. Colin Robinson put Town ahead on the stroke of half-time, but Alan Ainscow equalised, before Bernard McNally sent the locals in the 9,183 crowd home happy. It ended Town's winless sequence, but extended Wolves run of defeats to five.

Gary Stevens had been sent off a week earlier in the Senior Cup defeat at Oswestry and missed two Cup ties - the 2-0 F.A.Cup exit against Oxford and the easy 6-0 Welsh Cup success over Cardiff AFC. His sixteen League goals inspired a £40,000 bid from Brentford, which Town rejected.

Chairman Tim Yates invited Ray Bailey to join the club board early in 1985. Paul Tester, after his knee problems, was about to string together his longest unbroken and most productive run. Although in the Notts County game an innocuous looking tackle ended Martin O'Neill's League career. He hit his only hat-trick at Rhyl in a remarkable 7-1 victory in the Welsh Cup quarter final, during which Town scored their last five goals in a five minute spell. Birmingham City, boasting the best away record in the League, were defeated by a Paul Tester goal, and keeping up his good spell he hit two more as Town repeated their 5-1 victory over Huddersfield.

Steve Perks good form saw Ron Green going to Bristol Rovers on loan at the end of January, while Ron Jukes left to join Derby at the end of February. Ross Maclaren was being tracked by Oldham, Derby, Portsmouth and Crystal Palace.

Full-back Kevin Collins left the club on March 20th, while young Andy Kerr was in trouble, having been sent off at Swansea in the Welsh Cup semi-final, just five days before his 19th birthday. The club fined Kerr for his indiscretion, but he was not the only defender with problems, as Colin Griffin missed out on an ever-present season by being suspended for the Oldham game.

Oxford's victory over Town clinched their promotion, so they shared their champagne with their opponents. One man absent on another champagne occasion was Bernard McNally. The Welsh Cup final second leg was on a Sunday, so when Town beat Bangor 5-1 on aggregate Bernard was missing, but he was back for a hastily arranged friendly in Malta. Town travelled to play Hibernians of Malta on May 27th and won 3-2, goals from Steve Cross (2) and Bernard clinching the victory.

Close season activity was brisk, and the arrival from Everton of Daren Hughes set the mood. Ron Green, who said: *"I did not get a fair crack of the whip"*, was signed by Bobby Gould for Bristol Rovers for £12,000. Ross Maclaren went to Derby for £67,500, after a tribunal, with Town picking up Paul Malcolm from Rochdale and Gary Leonard from West Brom. Nigel Pearson was given the all clear - the first player to recover from a carbon fibre implant on his medial ligament - but Paul Petts was told he faced the same operation. Nigel made his comeback in a friendly with Evesham in July.

The whole football world had been devastated by the successive tragedies at Bradford, Birmingham and Brussels, and the Popplewell report called for a drinks ban at football grounds, twelve years after the Meadow went dry. Sepp Blatter was in charge of UEFA, and their decision to ban English clubs playing 'abroad' meant the pre-season tour to Scotland and defence of the Welsh Cup would not be allowed. The County Council sent Blatter a letter to plead Town's case.

Town were linked with Ian Atkins, Paul Maguire and Joey Jones - that would have been a culture shock all round! Bernard McNally was on World Cup duty, called up by Northern Ireland for their qualifier against Turkey. On the domestic front, the Club introduced passes for under 16's for the coming season.

The 1985-86 campaign started badly, with defeat at home to Crystal Palace, and in the away game at Oldham Paul Johnson broke his leg.

The balance sheet showed things were healthy off the pitch - a profit of £46,000 left a retained profit of £126,000 - while Sainsbury's had declared an interest in building on the Meadow site. The only early success on the Park was a 2-0 victory over Preston by the youth team, with goals from Jon Narbett and Mickey Brown.

A ten match winless run, which included four successive 1-1 draws, ended at Carlisle, just before 'Chic' Bates' first big signing arrived. Salop signed Gerry Daly from Birmingham City and he scored on his debut, a convincing 3-0 victory of luckless Huddersfield. This win came four days after a 2-0 win at Leeds Road, which overturned a first leg deficit from Paul Malcolm's debut game. The defence would still be a problem, and after conceding seven goals in two away games, Bryn Gunn came in on loan.

He arrived just after Town's Milk Cup exit, a 4-1 home defeat by Everton - with Darren Hughes against his old side scoring in the wrong net. Gunn's debut saw a victory over Brighton and Town won six of his nine League games. However, they crashed 3-1 at Kiddermister in the Welsh Cup, with Bryn playing. Mickey Brown wore the substitute's shirt against Bradford on November 23rd, but would have to wait until late August to actually make the pitch.

Crowd trouble continued to be a problem and close circuit television cameras were to be employed to catch the miscreants. Mark Kelly arrived from Blackpool around the start of December. The year ended with a 4-0 defeat at Portsmouth again, and New Year's Day was little better, with a 3-1 defeat at Grimsby - seven goals in the two games after Gunn's departure. These matches were a prelude for another battle with Chelsea in the F.A. Cup, round three. Town went close, through Pearson, McNally and Nardiello, but eight minutes from time, on a snow covered pitch, David Speedie hit the only goal.

Paul Tester was out with a knee injury before Paul Johnson returned from his broken leg, and Ken McKenna of Telford was attracting Town's interest. A three month goal drought ended at Hull, but despite scoring three, Town lost to an 88th minute winner. Gerry Nardiello went to Cardiff on loan in March, and around this time Tim Steele made a couple of appearances (his first) as substitute. Tony Rees came on loan from Birmingham but made little impact, his one start was against Stoke City. This game saw Paul Johnson's return to the potteries for the first time in his five year spell with Salop.

Steve Perks was the fans Player of the Year, with Nigel Pearson winning the Players Player of the Year, a new shield presented by the late Chris Pilkington. These awards were given out at the last match at home to Middlesbrough. If Town had lost they could have been relegated, but the Boro also needed to win to stay up. Town's 2-1 victory was clinched by Darren Hughes' only goal for the club. Crowd violence reached new depths and dozens of Teesiders had to make return trips to Shrewsbury for Court appearances.

Town captain Colin Griffin congratulates the scorer, Darren Hughes, after the youngster's match-winning goal.

Paul Malcolm was released and looked set to join Bournemouth for £5,000, but on July 9th - just three days before his wedding - Harry Redknapp pulled out of the deal. He married without telling his wife of the setback. Gerry Nardiello joined Torquay, and Steve Cross was being tracked by Watford, Oxford, Palace, Sunderland and Port Vale, but eventually (after a tribunal) joined Derby for £70,000. Andy Kerr went to Cardiff and Town signed Dave Waller from Crewe for £20,000 and Ken Hughes on trial from Crystal Palace. Shrewsbury also signed up new shirt sponsors, when after six years 'Link 51' were replaced by 'Wem Ales'. Secretary Malcolm Starkey became a board member on July 20th 1986.

A Hands-On Experience

The trip, 'up the road', was back on and saw a 2-0 defeat at Falkirk and a 1-1 draw at Stirling, with Tim Steele's penalty, providing the goal. Falkirk, newly promoted, were improving their ground, and the game kicked off early since the floodlights were not completed, but was still only 40 minutes each way. All this happened just two hours after an unknown Liz Long won a gold medal in the Commonwealth Games in nearby Edinburgh.

Dave Waller scored on his debut in another draw in Sheffield, and the Milk Cup tie with Crewe, three days later, drew just 1,819. It was a goalless draw and then a 1-0 defeat, by Blackburn, also at home, followed. Late in the cup second leg, Dave Waller gave Town the lead and Colin Robinson hit a hat trick in five minutes, it was the fastest ever - at that time - by a Town man.

Paul Petts was released from his contract on September 8th, just before Town played Barnsley. Paul Malcolm, now with the Yorkshire side, missed the game with an ankle injury. Another player who nearly played in this game was David Geddis, who Alan Clarke was trying to secure on loan. Town had already suffered a blow against Ipswich with Colin Griffin in his 400th League game snapping his Achilles tendon.

Darren Hughes had started to play regularly, but left to join Brighton for £30,000 in late September. A bid to secure Kevin Steggles from Ipswich fell through, but Paul Franklin arrived from Watford, on loan, in time for the home game with Derby. This match was played two days after Town's scheduled match with Huddersfield. The latter game was called-off since Gerry Daly was in the Eire party - for their game with Scotland - and Bernard McNally was in the Northern Ireland squad, Town being entitled to the postponement because of the two international calls.

The Council announced they wanted to create a 640 space surface car park on the ground, something which would be encouraged by Cardiff fans! Having beaten Crewe, Town then removed Stoke and Hull from the Milk Cup competition before meeting the Welshman. Bernard McNally's winner sent the Welsh 'supporters' on the rampage. Six policemen injured, twenty-one arrests, ten windows were kicked in, five cars turned over, a bus window smashed and a van attacked, in a carnage of destruction.

It was of course the clubs Centenary season and a game with Nottingham Forest was arranged for April 26th, but it would never take place. One game which did was the Bob Wardle Testimonial, much delayed it was finally played on December 16th. Over 7,000 attended and saw the double winners trophies, they arrived in the skips along with the kit. It was a magic night, with Steve Perks keeping a clean sheet and Steve Nichol scoring twice, past Bob, in the second half. Liverpool's recent signing, Alan Irvine showed up well in this match.

The club announced a loss of £86,518 and set about doing something about it. They launched 'Safe', 'Soccer as family entertainment', with Mike Thomas as its guiding light. For the Ipswich game on January 3rd, adults £2 and children £1, was the offer which 475 people took up. It was another in and out season, with the Littlewoods Cup run providing a high spot, the quarter-final paired Town with Southampton away.

The winners would meet Liverpool in a two leg semi-final, but a momentary aberration by Gary Hackett led to a penalty for handball, just as a replay was seeming inevitable. The dream was gone, but one dream achieved that night was wheelchair-bound Town fan Peter Rodway, meeting up with his hero, Peter Shilton. The late Tony Barton showed his mettle, by arranging the trip into the home dressing-room, despite the late arrival of the Town supporter's coaches, due to traffic jams.

It would be a major turning point in the season, four days later a home defeat by Hull ended interest in the F.A. Cup. A week after, a loss to Blackburn started a run of eight League games without a win, and a 1-0 defeat by Newport County cut short Welsh Cup ambitions. The latter game was most notable for an injury to Steve Perks, it ended his 91 match unbroken League run. Ken Hughes made his debut against Huddersfield, a game which also saw Tim Steele's first full League appearance, while David Geddis scored his first goal. Geddis had arrived on loan, just over a week earlier, from Birmingham and completed his move for £25,000 on March 4th.

Gary Hackett requested a transfer, Gerry Daly moved to Stoke, and attempts to sign Chris Maskery, on a months loan, failed. Town ended their win drought at Grimsby, thanks to Colin Robinson's first goal since November. Robinson scored again a week later at Plymouth - Salop led twice but lost - Tommy Tynan twice and Garry Nelson, were the Pilgrims scorers.

Leeds United came to the Meadow with Town seeking their first home win in 11 weeks. But Steve Perks was sent off after a tackle on Andy Ritchie,

which looked suspiciously like a dive. Paul Tester went in goal and made a brilliant save from the free kick, but Town lost 2-0. The overdue home win arrived four days later, when Town, now in the bottom three, beat Stoke 4-1. Another victory followed at the Hawthorns, but defeats at home by fellow strugglers Sunderland and away at Hull, left relegation a distinct possibility.

A vital 2-0 home success over Oldham meant victory at St. Andrews would clinch survival. A goalless first half was followed by two second half strikes by Gary Hackett and Colin Robinson, and safety. Town, who had given a trial to David Aggar (who scored on his debut in the reserves against Bristol City), and signed Mark Jones from Walsall, also overcame a goalkeeping crisis. Steve Perks was suspended, for April 25th, and Ken Hughes went to hospital after a kick to the kidneys, against Cardiff Reserves on April 20th. Two days later Lee Webb picked up an arm injury in the intermediates' team which ended his season. Fortunately Ken recovered sufficiently to play at Hull.

A mini clear-out saw Mark Kelly, Neil Meredith, Brian Carmichael, Duane Mellors, Mark Jones and Paul Johnson all released. Bernard McNally and Gary Hackett were on the transfer list, and after three requests, Nigel Pearson joined them on July 9th.

Town introduced a £1 membership scheme and welcomed the new two substitutes role, before capturing Andy Crane - a 20 year-old full-back from Ipswich - on a free transfer. Crane was a former England youth international, as was Phil Priest, the next signing, when Town beat five clubs - including one from Belgium - on chief scout Harry Maney's recommendation. He was a midfielder from Chelsea, and also aged 20. Another signing, was Brian Williams, a former team-mate of Chic's at Swindon, who had been Bristol City's skipper the previous season, and he arrived for a small fee.

RELEGATION SCOTCHED

Gary Hackett went to Aberdeen for £75,000 - just beating the rest of the clubs trip for the pre-season games with Morton and Alloa. Town also beat fourth Division opposition, 4-1, in another pre-season match, Wolves were two Divisions below Shrewsbury at that time.

The 1987-88 season started with a tough looking trip to Leicester, but a late David Geddis goal secured the points and an 'assault' from Steve Walsh, which fractured the Town man's jaw in three places. It was three excellent points but at a high price, Geddis would not start a game again until February, while Town would not score a League goal in their next three and a half games, or win a League game in their next nine.

The defence was looking solid with Nigel Pearson and David Linighan outstanding. The one early defensive hiccup was a 3-3 draw at Crewe in the Littlewoods Cup. Nigel Pearson missed this game but returned for the 4-1 second leg victory, in which Colin Robinson scored twice, his only goals until the turn of the year. Town drew Sheffield Wednesday in round two - a 1-1 draw at the Meadow was part of a sequence of six consecutive draws, which ended with a 2-0 victory over Crystal Palace.

The trip to Hillsborough held few fears as Town were unbeaten there in seven outings. Also their away form was good, the win at Leicester being followed by a draw at Huddersfield, whose £100,000 winger Mark Barham missed the game with an Achilles injury. Then, the only away defeat, from Ron Atkinson's first game in charge at West Brom. during his second spell, preceding draws at Hull, Birmingham and Swindon.

However, for once Town's hoodoo over Wednesday failed in a 2-1 defeat. Nigel Pearson was outstanding and Wednesday bid £200,000 for his services. 'Chic' battled to keep his man, particularly as David Linighan had been injured in the Senior cup-tie with Telford and the manager wanted to wait for him to recover before closing the deal. Mr Yates and the board decided to accept the offer and a major upheaval would follow.

Mark Cooper had been on loan from Spurs, playing six times and netting twice, with both goals coming in a minute at the Wakeman end against Cambridge. At £80,000, Town were interested in making the move permanent, but Gillingham - of all people - bid £105,000 to sign the big striker. He was replaced by David Leworthy from Oxford who scored three times in his six games, all of which Salop lost. David Moyes was signed from Bristol City for £30,000 and made his debut at Middlesbrough, but after the seventh consecutive defeat, against Blackburn, the crowd were becoming uneasy and the Board was about to respond.

Patrick Newbrook called an infamous meeting, at the Quarry Lodge, at 4 p.m. on Tuesday November 17th, to cement support from his fellow directors for the removal of 'Chic' Bates. The Town won 2-0 against Sheffield United that evening, but the board wanted a new manager. Chairman, Tim Yates refused to sack 'Chic' and on Wednesday November 18th, Mr Yates resigned. The writer spoke to Chic that day and he already realised his fate, saying: " *My best friend at this club has just left*". I replied, *"In five years time they will rue the day Tim Yates went'*, neither of us were wrong.

Malcolm Starkey was in charge for the home game with Stoke and selected the same side to play against Plymouth. Ken Brown, just three weeks after his surprise sacking from Norwich, was appointed acting manager. Ken Woodhouse had taken over as Chairman, with Patrick Newbrook as Vice-Chairman. Mr Newbrook, in an ill-advised moment of triumphalism, announced *"The start of a new era"*. Even in Lady Jane Grey's time, eras lasted longer than eight days.

Mr Brown, still traumatised by the Norwich situation which included his possible re-instatement was not prepared to move to Shrewsbury and recommended Town appoint Ian McNeil, which they did on December 9th. He was an instant hit, taking off Gary Leonard and sending on Paul Tester, who scored the equaliser, as Town drew 2-2 with Hull.

For the trip to Ipswich, the following Friday, Town took 14 players, including young 'Carel' (the richness of the manager's Scottish accent meant young 'Griff' became young 'Carel') Griffiths, already the manager had taken a shine to the lad. If he had played, he would have been Town's youngest ever player, but he was the odd one out on this occasion. McNeil's first signing, on Christmas Eve, started a trend which would continue. 'Douggie' Bell came on as substitute against Birmingham on December 28th, and immediately produced a dazzling dribble which took him past four bemused Blues players before laying an excellent pass.

What was a player of this quality doing playing for Shrewsbury? Two 3-1 victories followed, at home to Huddersfield and away at Maine Road. Bell scored in both, the only time he scored in successive games in his whole career. Mickey Brown, whose only other goals came in 'Chic's' last three games in charge, scored against Huddersfield and hit a tremendous effort - which led to a corner and one of David Moyes' brace - in Manchester. Moyes, again, and a Brian Williams free-kick accounted for Bristol Rovers in the Cup. Brian really enjoyed this goal against his former club. A young side lost at Caernafon in the Welsh Cup, and then the goals dried up.

Three League games and a Cup exit at Plymouth followed without Town netting. The club needed a boost. David Geddis returned to action, Bernard McNally turned down West Brom and signed an 18 month contract. Then on January 14th it happened, Victor signed, he cost £35,000 from Meadowbank Thistle. I'm not sure the area has yet recovered; he passed his medical, and they probably never thought to examine his mental state. Jim Melrose came on loan from Leeds, Dick Pratley for £60,000 from Derby, Alan Irvine for £40,000 from Dundee United, and the interest created saw gates doubling from the 2,000 present against Sheffield United.

Colin Robinson moved to Birmingham for £35,000 on January 21st and Derek Mann went to Watford on February 5th. Richard Green was sent off for elbowing Keith Curle, of Reading, with Stuart Beavon scoring their winner. Plymouth's Cup victory came courtesy of a Stewart Evans header, despite Tommy Tynan missing a penalty and Victor seeing a last minute header scrambled off the line by Leigh Cooper, with Town claiming it was over.

Dick Pratley's arrival had been speeded up by David Moyes breaking his leg, in a training accident, with Andy Crane. Dick's arrival also coincided, with a three match winning run. Phil Priest's first goal completed the double over Sheffield United, a McNally penalty and Victor's first strike - a cracker - beat Swindon Town, (where Chic was now coach), and Alan Irvine's only goal of the season saw off Crystal Palace.

Two home blanks followed, goalless with Millwall, and a 1-0 loss to Middlesbrough. A two-all draw at Oldham on the plastic included a Victor goal - and a 2-0 lead - but the one we all remember, was his 71st minute conversion of Tim Steele's cross against Leeds. The subsequent somersault causing a dislocated toe.

Les Helm, had taken over as Physiotherapist, but Bernard McNally nearly missed the Swindon match, due to a plane strike, after he played for Northern Ireland in their 3-2 defeat in Athens (on his 25th Birthday).

That Swindon game had finished with much acrimony when Chris Kamara hit Jim Melrose after the final whistle. At the subsequent court case, Kamara was fined £1,200 with £250 compensation and £15 costs. He claimed racist jibes, directed at his children, caused the assault. Lou Macari called Victor a cheat, but Ian McNeil said he was his 'black diamond'.

John Narbett and Victor scored in a 2-1 Friendly victory over St. Mirren at Love Street. However, Brian Williams had picked up a suspension, while skipper Wayne asked for a move. Jim Melrose's move was completed, for £25,000 plus bits and pieces, but Leeds said they received £40 - £50,000.

The president of the supporters club, Wilf Richards, joined the board, and Ian McNeil said he had turned down strong offers for Linighan, McNally, Brown and Wayne Williams. Paul Petts' hopes of a comeback finally ended with the news that Town felt unable to offer him a contract, after he had resumed training.

Town won the Macbar League Cup final, 1-0, with Carl Griffith's goal beating Bristol City, but they then resigned from the League. They wanted to join the Central League, but nobody wanted to leave so there were no vacancies. The last 22 games had produced 33 League points, and Dave Geddis' two goals clinched the final victory over Plymouth. He had scored the first and last goal of the season. Town flew to Marbella to celebrate staying-up, but Gary Leonard, Andy Crane, Andy Hodgetts, David Mulcahy and Lee Webb were released.

Leonard, who had been on loan at Hereford, signed a two year contract there, and was joined by Andy Crane, who after five years as a professional finally made his League debut at Scunthorpe in the first game at Glanford Park. Bernard McNally was voted Player of the Year, with David Linighan runner-up. Manchester City's Mel Machin admitted watching Linighan, but Ipswich moved in to sign him, just ahead of Spurs, although Dave did not fancy the move to London. Ipswich offered £100,000, Town wanted £½ million, and on July 12th a tribunal settled on £300,000, of which Derby received £137,500; Town still await a third of any sell-on fee.

CHAPTER 14 - THE DREAM ENDS - RELEGATION

At the start of the next season (1988-89), Secretary-director Malcolm Starkey was quoted as saying he wanted football hooligans flogged, at this time he appeared to be referring to the fans. Town made a big signing, 6-4" defender Alan Finley, from Marine. He had played for Everton and Wigan reserves and numbered 'page 3' girl Kathy Lloyd among previous girlfriends.

Not surprisingly Town's pre-season tour was to Scotland, this time more Northerly than normal. An opening 3-0 win over East Fife, with goals from Geddis, an own goal, and Bell, was followed by winning the A.C.Yuill Trophy, by beating Cove 5-1. A home fan refused to believe that Victor was a Scotsman, his Ugandan parentage, colouring the issue. Irvine, Geddis, Tester and Victor twice scored. Vic's second was an excellent chip from the edge of the area, the local fan turned to the writer and said, *"Aye laddie perhaps he is Scottish after all"*. A 4-1 victory over Forres Mechanics on a virtual 'ploughed field', featured goals by Tester, Steele and a brace from Melrose. The final two games were against the (1994) new League clubs. Against Inverness Caledonians, Priest, Finley, Geddis, Griffin and Tester scored, in the 5-0 victory, and a 4-1 win over Ross County completed their tour. This last match was an emotional return for Town's manager. He had, as player-coach, led County to their first Highland League Championship and also a Scottish Cup-tie, with Glasgow Rangers. Alan Irvine hit two, an own goal and Jim Melrose completing the scoring on a tour which had seen Town based at Aberdeen University.

The players had not been extended, and they were without Dick Pratley, who had needed a serious knee operation, and Dave Moyes who was still recovering from his broken leg. Three youngsters had returned with the team, John Hay, David Baxter and Scott Thompson, having impressed the manager. Newtown 1-0, Steele, and a 1-1 draw with Wrexham (Narbett), preceded a 14-0 victory over a Sunday League XI, when hat-tricks from Melrose and Irvine, two each from Geddis and McNally, Green, Finley, Steele and a first Town goal from Mickey Thomas, were the providers. Thomas had been signed, on his return to these shores, after playing 6-a-side soccer in America, for Wichita.

Peter Dolby had resigned, and Paul Tester joined Hereford for £10,000, but efforts to sign Doug Rougvie were not completed in time for the opener. A first game home defeat, by Portsmouth, and a League cup draw with Walsall, preceded Rougvie's arrival from Brighton for £50,000. It was a move causing aggravation in the corridors of power. A 3-0 defeat, in the second leg, ended the early season cup ambitions, it was a poor start once more. The second League game, at Bradford, saw Victor manage another first, when he came on in place of Doug Rougvie, but was later replaced by Dave Geddis. Rougvie scored, in the draw at Palace, and in the 5-1 home defeat by Ipswich. The manager said the first half hour was the best he had played, but it was the worst home defeat for 23 years (since Easter 1965 against Bristol City), thanks mainly to a hat-trick from Simon Milton, all struck from the edge of the box.

A draw with Sunderland was followed by the resignation of Patrick Newbrook, on September 28th. He claimed the club was on the road to financial ruin, with Doug Rougvie on £800 per week and Mickey Thomas on £600 per week. If this was true, had not his meeting at Quarry Lodge, help create the situation?

Billy Whitehurst had clashed with Steve Perks, in the draw with Sunderland, and Gavin Ward (18), a free transfer from Aston Villa, was on standby until Ron Green returned - on loan - from Wimbledon. Green made his comeback, against Oxford United, in a game when Carl Griffiths made his debut, as substitute, for Victor. But Town were unable to handle Dean Saunders, and lost 4-1. The Welsh youngster signed professional, but David Geddis joined Swindon for £40,000 and Clem McBride resigned. The longest wait for a first victory, ended thanks to Alan Irvine's goal at Bournemouth, the 13th game of the season.

Meanwhile, Phil Priest had returned to action, in the reserves, scoring in the 4-3 victory over Walsall, and after Gavin Ward was injured, keeping a clean sheet in goal. Bernard McNally's testimonial, against Arsenal on December 14th, saw Town field a side without a Scotsman.

The line-up consisted:
Ron Green, Mal Donaghy, Nigel Worthington, Nigel Pearson, Dave Linighan, Mickey Thomas, Mickey Brown, Bernard McNally, Frank Worthington, Richard Green and Gary Hackett.

Arsenal fielded:
Lukic, Dixon, Sansom, Richardson, Bould, O'Leary, Rocastle, Davis, Quinn, Groves and Marwood.

A crowd of 3,612 saw Paul Davis give Arsenal a first half lead and after eight youngsters came on at half-time, Kwame Ampudu scored a stunning second. Town's consolation was scored by Frank Worthington, who was at least five yards offside. A penalty shoot-out competition, was won by young Jason Evans, who was destined to join the club.

Wayne Williams had joined Northampton on loan, and Gary Osbourne had made his debut in the Simod Cup at Elland Road, where Town lost 3-1, Phil Priest's penalty coming after Carl Griffiths was tripped. Griffiths' first senior goal was in the 2-0 victory over Caernafon - Town's last Welsh cup-tie - which was later overturned because Ron Green was deemed ineligible.

A run of four home games unbeaten ended against Swindon. Chic would have been pleased, and ironically the single goal was scored on 40 minutes by David Geddis, from Dave Hockaday's free kick. Another Swindon victory came in the F.A. Youth Cup. Town, 3-0 down, were awarded three penalties. Carl scored the first, missed the second and Dale Jones missed the third, as Salop lost 3-2.

An upturn in fortunes led Ian McNeil to say that over the last eleven games Town had shown top six form, and he turned down £110,000 from Hull for Douggie Bell. Young Gary Osbourne's first two full first team games saw him mark Vince Hilaire and David White. He did well, as Town beat Leeds 3-2 and drew 2-2 with Manchester City, both away. Carl scored twice, on both occasions, and the Daily Mail labelled him the first £1 million teenager, which ruined him for four years.

The worst ever Boxing Day game, saw Town and Birmingham both defend for ninety minutes, in a goalless draw with the only excitement coming from six 'bookings', Pratley, Moyes and Richard Green, balanced out by Ian Atkins, Overson and Bird. The year ended with Town trying to retain Ron Green, but Bobby Gould wanted £50,000. His last game was against Barnsley, Town lost 3-2, and David Moyes scored his first ever own goal. Amazingly he repeated the feat in both Town's next two games. A 4-0 defeat by West Brom, came after a goalless first half, but Town were odds-on favourites to make progress in the F.A.Cup.

They faced a home time with Colchester United, who were 92nd in the Football League. It was a memorable match for two people. Tony Kelly, on loan from West Brom, controlled the game from midfield, whilst up in the press box, a nervous reporter made his debut. Instructed to script my report, I did so, and awaited the call. The 'phone rang - standby - the programme continued then around the grounds. It transpired I was fourth in line, during the third report, Colchester scored. Looking at the worthless piece of paper in front of me, I heard, *"and now over to Mike Jones at the Gay Meadow'*. I still have a recording of the next half-minute, it seemed like an eternity. I replaced the 'phone and said, *"things can only get better"*, I trust that has been the case!

Wayne Williams joined Northampton for £25,000, Gavin Ward went to Telford to cover for injured Mike Harrison, currently manager at Stafford, and Douggie Bell would 'never play for the club again', as a disciplinary measure after gesturing to the crowd when substituted against Colchester. The manager bemoaned the fact that, largely due to injury, his dream midfield of McNally and Bell, had played just one full game together.

The Blackburn game was typical of Town's season. Town, through the eccentric Kasule, took an 80th minute lead, but Blackburn equalised two minutes later. Tony Kelly signed initially on loan, and later for £30,000, on January 25th, while Carl Griffiths was voted Young Eagle of the Month. Doug Rougvie, made an assisted passage to Fulham for £40,000 (on February 8th), but Tim Steele's £80,000 move to Reading fell through due to the cost of houses in Royal Berkshire. Victor's turbulent career saw him sent off, for two bookable offenses against Stoke, a game which marked Tony Kelly's debut.

Darren Ryan, signed apprentice, and scored in the 2-1 intermediates team win over Leicester, Wayne Maclean netted the second. Bernard McNally went to Middlesbrough, to see a specialist, which led one radio station to report his £250,000 transfer, while a national newspaper made the fee £400,000 the following morning! A month later, the visit 'paid off', for he returned to first team action with Shrewsbury.

Something else that paid off was the signing of an unknown striker from Elgin City, for £25,000 on February 18th. Ian McNeil's son recommended John McGinlay, and he made his debut alongside a trialist full-back, Graeme Worsley - a Tony Kelly reccommendation - against Chester reserves at Sealand Road, which Town won 2-1. A brief spell as substitute, at Fellows Park, was prelude to a goalscoring full debut, against Plymouth for Johnny 'Mac'. Brian Williams' cross being headed in for Town's second goal, and the first victory in ten games.

David Moyes was listed, at his own request, but another Scotsman arrived in Steve Pittman for £30,000, from East Fife on March 21st. He made his first appearance, as substitute, against Bradford City and made his first impact in the opening minute of his full debut, at Birmingham. Straight from the kick-off he put Robert Hopkins into orbit. Town, 1-0 down at half-time, with just two points from five games, bounced back to win 2-1. The goals were from Mickey Thomas - his only Town strike - and Tony Kelly. The same day Crystal Palace missed 3 penalties, against Brighton, but still won 2-1.

Five days later, Steve Coppell's men lost 2-1 at the Meadow, John McGinlay backing up an outrageous Tony Kelly free-kick. His third successive strike and fifth in eight games. Coppell's assessment was that he must maintain that consistency, and was in a way harsh, but explains why he never quite managed to match his skill to his achievements. Jim Melrose returned to partner John McGinlay and they produced five goals between them, in a four game spell. Tony Kelly spent 13 minutes in goal, as Ken Hughes had stitches in a knee injury at Oakwell. Carl Griffiths went to play for the English League Under-18's against the Soviet Youth side, in Moscow, under Lawrie McMenemy on April 22nd, but these plus points were being overshadowed by off the field 'incidents'.

Douggie Bell had gone to Hull, on loan, but Alan Irvine's absence was partly due to a breach of club discipline, which led to a two week deduction of wages, transfer listing, censuring and warned as to his future conduct. Unfortunately the ability to distinguish curfew nights (Thursday and Friday), was becoming increasingly difficult to several players, particularly those with Scottish accents! On Thursday April 20th, Steve Pittman was charged with assaulting a taxi-driver outside 'Pews'. Alan Irvine, who was also present, was questioned. Victor, who was not present, tried to clear up the argument as to whether a bottle was involved, with the classic line: *"It was a vodka bottle he didn't hit him with"* !

The players were letting down the club, the Town, and most of all the manager, whose loyalty would have been admirable if it had not been so misinformed.

For the final game of the season, Carl was recalled and hit another brace against Leeds - his first home goals - to end the season as top scorer, with six. Neil Smith, Gary Osbourne and Gavin Ward were released, and Mickey Thomas - voted Player of the Year -joined Leeds for £10,000 a fortnight later.

It all had to be somebody's fault, and on June 15th an embittered Colin Griffin was sacked. It was a sad end to one of the finest servants the club had ever seen.

Alan Irvine, joined Mazda of Hiroshima for £70,000, and Bernard McNally, after talks with Sunderland and Stoke, went to West Brom - for a tribunal fee of £385,000, which was roughly ten times their first offer the previous season. Andy Gray, released by Rangers, was linked with the player-coach vacancy, but Asa Hartford was the man appointed in mid-July. Town also signed Jon Purdie, on a free from Oxford.

BLACK DIAMOND TO FLAWED DIAMOND

Victor Kasule

The 1989-90 pre-season open day saw Dunfermline striker John Watson at the ground, but with a £30,000 move being mooted, the player joined Fulham on a free. Pre-season, Town hammered St. Johnstone 5-1, Melrose and McGinlay both hit two and Kasule made it five. A tougher task - with West Brom - ended 1-1, with Melrose as Town's scorer. A 3-0 win over Wrexham saw Willie Naughton's debut after his £35,000 move.

John McGinlay was injured in training and missed the opening game, a three-all draw at Reading, but returned with a brace against Leyton Orient in a 4-2 victory. A 3-0 home win over Notts County set up a League Cup aggregate win, just, by 4-3. Further League victories, over Blackpool and Birmingham, fuelled dreams of an instant return to higher things.

Steve Pittman scored at Northampton, but Town lost 2-1, and Jon Purdie's debut meant an exit for Victor Kasule. The 'black diamond' was substituted, and his eccentricities would mean he would never play for Salop again. Initially, he joined Brian Little's high-riding conference side Darlington, on loan. He failed to settle, was sent back, and chairman Ken Woodhouse said he would not play for Town again. John Lambie was prepared to take him to Hamilton Academicals, but Victor 'lost' the train fare and a courier was sent down from Scotland to drive him North. One final problem remained, in his own indomitable way, Victor, had left his boots in Darlington (not to mention a pair of crutches in the White Horse, and the odd outstanding account).

Town won only one of eight games in a four week spell. Swindon led by Ross Maclaren, scored two convincing victories in the League Cup and the only win was a 3-1 victory over Bury. The match featured a goal which picked John McGinlay out as an outstanding striker. Mickey Brown's right-wing centre hit the referee on the heel, sat up, and was rifled into the corner of the net from 20 yards by super 'Mac'. He had turned and was heading for the restart, before the ball had passed the static keeper, pure class!

Asa Hartford came on as substitute at Wigan, his first appearance since Reading, and a five match unbeaten run followed. One man missing was Dick Pratley, who had teamed up well with David Moyes and conceded just five goals in five League games, until an injury at Bristol City, which coupled with an infection was destined to wreck the big man's career. Headlines claiming 'Bell to stay' in mid-September had the inevitable effect - he joined Birmingham four

weeks later for a tribunal fee of £57,500. Town had Eddie Gormley on loan from Spurs, but he failed to breakthrough.

The home game with Brentford featured a double sending-off, with Jon Purdie feeling hard done-to, after Keith Jones' assault; perhaps something to do with a spell they had as 'team-mates' the previous season. After a rare eight game barren spell, John McGinlay hit two against Tranmere Rovers. The second one was an outstanding strike overshadowing a fine goal by Mark Hughes for Rovers.

Willie Naughton's goal, from a 'Worzel' centre, against his old club, did not improve Town's record on the plastic. November was a poor month, with three defeats in the League and another embarrassing home Cup loss, this time 3-2 to Chesterfield - despite two McGinlay penalties. Kim Wassall was taken on trial on November 2nd, a deal to sign Derek McWilliams from Falkirk collapsed, but John Cornforth arrived on loan on 23rd and he made his debut, along with Paul Gorman, at Rotherham.

Ian McNeil agreed a fee with Sunderland, to make it a full time move, but personal terms saw the deal fall through during Christmas week. A spineless display, at Notts County, on Boxing Day, featured a Phil Stant goal as Town crashed 4-0. A much more spirited performance at Craven Cottage produced a wonder goal from Clive Walker to ruin Town's hopes. Ian McNeil was pleased to start his sixth decade in professional football as Town drew 1-1 with Swansea (he had signed professional for Aberdeen in 1949), but his career was about to be interrupted. Talks with Cornforth, had resumed on January 4th, but a day later, the axe fell.

Mr Woodhouse said, *"our disciplinary record is the worst it's ever been, and at the moment the club's name stinks"*. Asa Hartford was appointed caretaker-manager and took over for the game at Leyton Orient. Town lost 1-0, and Steve Pittman was on his way to train with the U.S.A. International team. It was his first ever trip to London and little did we realise when I put him on the train, for the airport, he would never play for Shrewsbury again.

Asa listed both Pittman and Purdie, before signing three players. Tommy Lynch on loan - on January 16th - plus Brendan Ormsby (also on loan) and Paul Wimbleton for £60,000 from Bristol City 48 hours later. They all made their debuts against Reading but only Tommy was fit by the end. 'Wimbs' picked up a hamstring injury and was out for five weeks, and Brendan's calf injury made this his only Town appearance.

A victory over Birmingham at St. Andrews saw Town go to Bury with some confidence. David Moyes had a torrid time, with Dean Spink on loan from Villa, but Town held out for a goalless draw. In fact only seven goals were leaked in Asa's first eleven games in charge, but Town scored only six.

So on March 15th, Town paid £75,000 to sign Dean Spink from Villa, and he scored on his debut at Mansfield, but Town lost 2-1. Two games later, Mark Blake arrived on loan from Southampton, on deadline day. Willie Weir had come from Baillieston Juniors, on trial, but Jon Purdie had moved to Cheltenham on a free. Steve Pittman had a month at Dunfermline but failed to clinch a move and his contract was cancelled, so he could go back to the States. John Bond watched Town against Wigan, a painful experience and joined to take training, twice a week.

Ian McNeil became assistant at Millwall (on April 18th), while Douggie Bell and Victor Kasule turned up at Portadown. Willie Weir signed a two year contract, Mark Blake looked unlikely to join Town and Hibernians wanted John McGinlay, who - including a hat-trick against Huddersfield - hit Town's third best individual total in a League season. Chairman Ken Woodhouse said the club had twice improved offers to John McGinlay, and privately the board were not sure they could really afford the contract. However, equally they knew the fans would be upset if the ace marksman left.

Steve Perks and Mickey Brown also declined the clubs offers and the chairman stated that all three were available, but at a price - £½ million for John McGinlay, £300,000 for Mickey Brown and £¼ million for Steve Perks were the club's calculations. Richard Green, Willie Naughton, Jim Melrose and Phil Priest were also listed. Asa Hartford was given a two year contract, and amongst his first dealings he gave Dick Pratley and Brian Williams free transfers.

Millwall wanted McGinlay for £100,000, but he was having talks with Bury and eventually joined them for a tribunal fee of £175,000. It was an exceptional deal for the player, funded by the Bury chairman, who had made a - then - shrewd investment in the company 'Polypeck'. Central defenders were also an active close season transfer area. Town had talks with George Berry, before signing Mickey Heathcote for £55,000.

John McGinlay. The ex-Elgin player, later a Scottish International

David Moyes moved to Dunfermline for £30,000 and Mark Blake was eventually signed for £70,000 plus V.A.T. Alan Finley went to Stockport - on loan - after refusing terms and not joining in pre-season training, he would eventually sign for County for £25,000.

Graham Baker had a trial at the Meadow and played in a 2-2 pre-season draw with Wolves. A Willie Naughton penalty and Baker scored Town's goals, but the former Southampton man, joined Fulham. Physiotherapist Les Helm joined Everton, in late July 1990, while striker John Moore arrived a week later on trial.

A NICE LYNE, IN CHOCS

Steve Perks re-signed, the Monday before the season started, and ironically he and Mickey Brown were the only two from the previous season's line-up to start the opening game. It was not a great start, for defeat at home by Bolton and a Cup reverse at Gillingham saw Town travel to Rotherham still looking for a first goal. Willie Naughton managed to score in the second half, and Town rescued a late point when Paul Wimbleton's shot - which was flying wide - hit a defender and deflected home.

The second leg cup-tie with Gillingham saw John Moore and Tony Kelly turn the tie around and (for a change) Town drew Ipswich, in round two.

Moore scored his only League goal against Fulham and Willie Weir, on as a late substitute, scored his solitary League goal at Tranmere. Town drew both fixture, before two defeats in the League were the prelude to the first leg game with Ipswich. Carl Griffiths' only Cup goal of the season, in his only Cup appearance, set up the 1-1 draw. On the Saturday, the first and only League victory in twelve opening games followed at Stoke. Dean Spink opened the Town's account, and Tony Kelly - 'Zico' to the Stoke fans - beat three men and played a ball into the net off a defender's leg. Graeme Worsley, with a splendid second half goal, wrapped up a memorable victory, despite John Moore being sent-off in an incident with Noel Blake.

Gary Shaw scored on his debut at Bury, but Russell Coughlin, who was on loan from Blackpool, fouled Tony Cunningham, and John McGinlay converted the penalty. Town wanted to make Coughlin's move permanent, but Swansea - his home Town club - made him a better offer. Billy Haycock had arrived from Norway as Physiotherapist in late September, and Wayne Clarke came on loan from Manchester City in mid-October. Clarke scored a penalty on his debut against Chester, at Macclesfield, but Town lost 3-2 - it was the fourth successive game they had conceded three goals and lost.

Mark Blake and Mickey Heathcote, had lost confidence. Both players were inexperienced and probably needed some guidance, and it arrived on Bonfire Day. Kenny Clements, who had been player-manager at Limerick, signed to steady the ship. Wayne Clarke had been sent off - on his last game at the Meadow before his loan when a Birmingham player - and nine years earlier, Kenny had suffered a similar fate, as an Oldham player, at Boundary Park. Town had won one game in the interim, with Clarke scoring a hat-trick as Town beat Birmingham 4-1. Wayne stayed two months, scoring 6 goals in 7 appearances, but was not allowed to appear in the F.A. Cup. Town faced a tough trip to Valley Parade and decided to play Mark Blake just in front of the back four, marshalled by Kenny Clements.

It worked admirably and two second half goals, from Gary Shaw won the replay. Gary scored ten goals in his stay with Town, and Bradford City and the F.A. Cup both played a significant part in the total.

Town drew non-League Chorley in round two, but defeats - 3-1 at Cambridge and 4-3 at Preston - meant goals and points were still escaping in League games. A trip to Chorley to run the rule over the Cup opposition appeared to give Town an excellent chance of progress. A goal by Dean Spink, on the quarter-hour should have been the ideal launch pad, but Chorley were unlucky to be defeated 1-0.

After a draw with Wigan, Town were back at Bradford and trailing 2-1 at half-time, for a team with just three League victories in 18 outings it was not a promising situation. A long range Mark Blake goal was Town's strike, it was his first for the club, but the second half started in sensational fashion. From three Tony Kelly passes, Gary Shaw scored a hat-trick in a two minute forty-seven second period - within five minutes of the restart.

The New Year opened badly, with a 3-0 defeat at Brentford. But the F.A. Cup run continued, with a 4-1 thrashing of Watford. Mickey Brown was 20-1 to score the first goal, and he did just that. A Tony Kelly penalty and a brace from Gary Shaw completed the scoring. It was arguably the highspot of Asa Hartford's stewardship, sadly the low spot was only 11 days away. After a goalless draw with Rotherham, Town faced Torquay in the Leyland Daf competition.

Town had played Torquay and Swansea in this competition and as the three games in the group resulted in similar scores the whole section had to be replayed. The game scheduled for Tuesday January 15th was put back 24 hours due to the inclement weather. Tommy Tynan led a Torquay goal feast, which ended with a 6-2 hammering, and a day later Asa Hartford was sacked.

Town could not score goals in the League, but when First Division Wimbledon arrived, a moment's intuitive adjustment, allowed Gary Shaw to hit his final goal for the club. It set up a fifth round home draw with Leeds or Arsenal, and came from Billy Askew's pass. It was Askew's debut - his previous game at the Meadow saw him sent off, whilst a Hull City player. The other arrival that week would last a little longer. Fred Davies was appointed first team coach, on January 23rd, but Willie Naughton joined Walsall a day later.

The League goal drought ended, at Crewe, on February 22nd and was a tragedy for Paul Edwards. The - then - Crewe goalkeeper dived bravely at the feet of Dean Spink and Darren Carr.

It was the big defender who reached the ball first and also collided with his keeper, breaking 'Eddies' leg. 'Viv' Taylor, in his second game on loan, scored his first Shrewsbury goal, when he curled the winner past stand-in Dave McEarney.

Town's big tie, with Arsenal or Leeds, was put on hold until the Gunners won the third replay. The high-flying Londoners found Town in determined mood, but one moment of class allowed Michael Thomas to score the only goal on 64 minutes.

The month had started with Manchester City refusing to renew Wayne Clarke's loan, but Scott Cooksey arrived on trial from Derby and Malcolm Musgrove came from Plymouth. The Loyalty of Town fans was once more exposed with 12,356 at the Arsenal match, but the two League games either side attracting less than 3,000 each.

Darren Ryan had been on the bench four times before finally coming on at Bury in place of Mark Taylor. Although only on for the second half, he was so exhausted by the end he had to be carried off the pitch. That's what comes of living in the Las Vegas of the Borders - Paul Evans take note! John Bond's role, as the 'loan arranger', continued with Neil Lyne from Forest, who arrived on March 14th. His first game, against Stoke at home, saw Town complete the double over the Potters, with Neil scoring both goals in the first half. His League debut had been on the Meadow - for Walsall - against Salop. Leyton Orient were the next visitors, and they were looking to extend a run of six consecutive defeats, Town obliged by winning 3-0.

Winger Mike Burton - who had been at Birmingham with Fred - started a trial in late March, just before Pat O'Toole signed from Leicester. Pat had been on loan at Exeter earlier in the season and his third appearance in a Town shirt was back at St. James' Park. John Bond said before the trip, *"I've never won an argument, never mind a game at Exeter"*. Well, this time he won a reprieve. Town were being swamped, and so was the pitch, the game being abandoned at half-time with Exeter 1-0 ahead. Three days later, four second half goals from Fulham had Craven Cottage celebrating staying up, but putting Town in deep trouble. Jimmy Hill, for once, was right when he said that the season was not yet over.

On the Saturday, Town played Brentford and drew, 1-1. Tony Kelly was sent off in an incident with Wilf Rostron - Tony still has a scar on his cheek and Wilf had a squint for a time.

Stoke's Wayne Clarke and Kenny Clements go up for the ball, during the League match at Gay Meadow on 16 March

The writer only missed two matches that season - the manager was sacked after one and Tony sent off in the other. To date I have not dared miss another one. Mickey Heathcote was scoring some vital goals, a winner against Bradford, one against Cambridge and another three-pointer to dispose of Chester. Carl Griffiths was in the squad for the latter two games and claimed both Town's goals in the win at Elm Park. He limped off with a hamstring injury on 54 minutes - was it in order to lobby support for the 'goal' he never touched? An own goal at Swansea yielded another important victory, before the return to Exeter. To be fair justice was done, as Town lost 3-0. Carl was substituted by Mickey Brown, and it was his ninth consecutive game, stretching back to October, in which he was either replaced or went on as substitute.

Three fixture left. Town needed a victory at Birmingham, and again, within a minute, they scored the winner. They kicked off and the ball reached Mark Blake in the old left-half position, he chipped a 50 yard pass down the line, and Carl outpaced the defence, cut in and scored in 54 seconds. Carl's reward, was to play all 90 minutes. Tony Kelly returned - having missed three matches through suspension - against Reading, believing he owed Town fans an apology. It was also his 100th game, so as a double celebration he turned in a virtuoso performance and hit a hat-trick. His only previous triple was for the Liverpool Youth team, when he hit a first half hat-trick; his team won 10-1 without Kelly in the second half. He was substituted, by coach John Bennison, for bragging in the interval, *"son that's not the way we do things here, have a shower"*! A final victory, with two more Heathcote goals, over Bournemouth, meant safety and respectability. The end of season clear-out saw Mickey Burton and Scott Cooksey's trials ended, Gary Shaw released, and Paul Wimbleton and Willie Weir listed.

Neil Lyne's six goals in sixteen games meant Town were keen on his signature, but on June 6th he signed a new 12 month contract at Forest. Another deal put on hold was Mark Taylor, for whom Wednesday wanted over £50,000.

Plans were laid to travel to the West Country for the pre-season tour, with games against Ellmore, Ilfracombe and Crediton. Robert Hopkins signed on July 26th - the day of departure - and joined the squad which surprisingly included Neil Lyne. It was a deal thrashed out between Bondy and Brian Clough, and revolved around Forest receiving the Lion share of any sell-on fee.

Bondy also left with an unlikely bonus, a box of chocolates for his wife, from Cloughie; I hope the tax man was informed.

TRANSFERS, INJURIES AND CONTRACTS

After their three match introduction, in the West, Town returned to face Derby County in Dick Pratley's testimonial. The build-up continued, with Tony Henry's first appearance against Wolves. He scored the winner after Tony Kelly had converted a penalty. The pair were destined never to be in the same side again, for within a week Bolton Wanderers snapped up Kelly and Micky Brown in a deal reported to be worth £200,000. Bondy's plans were dealt a major blow by the Board's need to appease the Bank.

The Football League could not manage to tell its computer that the Shrewsbury Flower Show was being held on the opening Saturday, so Town kicked off 24 hours later, at home to Wigan. A late goal from trialist Cliff Carr secured a solitary goal victory, in his only full game for Salop. Carr was on the bench as Town drew with Plymouth in the first leg Cup-tie, and at Bury for the League match which preceded the return.

Obviously acclimatised to the Devon air by the tour, Town came from behind, thanks to Kevin Summerfield against his old side, but despite Robbie Turner being sent off for demolishing Carl Griffiths with his elbow, Town still trailed 2-1 in the dying stages. Carr had been summoned off the bench and was to take a free-kick on the edge of the Pilgrims penalty area. The usual wall was lined up, and one wonders if the home 'keeper knew Carr was advancing, certainly he never moved, as the diminutive defender floated the kick over the home defence and into the net. Town went through on away goals, secured a lucrative tie with Wolves, and it was Carr's last kick, as he was released.

Alan Ball's Exeter were next at the Meadow, and Robert Hopkins first goal started an onslaught as Town won 6-1. A second half Stoke winner dented the unbeaten run, but Neil Lyne's goal disposed of Brentford, and things looked rosy. Something had to go wrong, and it did; Cambridge United bid £125,000 for Mickey Heathcote. The directors, still under some pressure from the Bank and worried about the defender's supposed suspect back, took the money. Mickey was a virtual ever-present at Town and his current problems are connected with a pelvic problem - not his back- but his departure eventually gave Town a bad back.

Tommy Lynch moved to central defence for the game at Torquay, where John Bond - a former United player - received a standing ovation, and saw his side win 2-1, with Stuart Cash making his debut. He was on loan from that nice Mr Clough! Whilst the other, not so new face, was 'Viv' Taylor, who was back for keeps - for £70,000 officially.

Trialist keeper, Scott Cooksey, had joined Bromsgrove in the close season and was involved in an unusual Beazer Homes game with, now defunct, Dartford. He and his opposite number, were both sent off, for professional fouls, and the subsequent penalties were the only goals. I doubt if Scott was laughing, and Tommy Lynch certainly wasn't, he was demoted to the bench for the trip to Bournemouth, a move which prompted a transfer request. Jimmy Case's elbow flattened 'Viv' Taylor and both left the field. 'Hoppy' came on to replace 'Viv', and with Bournemouth leading, Carl was replaced by Tommy. He took over the central striker role, and his first shot was a real hit - it removed a policeman's helmet some ten yards wide of goal. A goalless draw, with Swansea followed before Town started leaking goals.

Mark Smith had signed on loan, to replace Mickey Brown just before the season started, and the move became permanent on September 19th. He missed the Swansea game, with another loan player - Tim Parkin - wearing the number 7 shirt, but was back for the trip to Wolves. After a bright opening which saw Kevin Summerfield equalise and Dean almost grab the lead, things went wrong. Steve Bull's goal just before half-time saw him show an awful lot of studs, but it counted and made the score 4-1. Despite several promising moves, Town finished the night, 6-1 behind. They then went to Bradford, played all the football, and lost 3-0 before a hat-trick of local derbies.

A draw with Birmingham, a spirited victory over Wolves - which but for a Tim Steele header might have been even more interesting - and a 2-0 defeat by Albion. Carl Griffiths after 5 goals in 3 reserve games was recalled for the trip to Darlington, who had Howard Clark on loan from Coventry at fullback. 'Darlo' were awful, Town led 2-0 at half-time and some plank on the radio said Darlington could never score three. Of course they did, but Carl's second goal did at least mean a point.

Steve Perks replaced Ken Hughes for the home game with Reading, but Town lost 2-1, and only 1,866 turned up for the 2-0 win over Peterborough. Carl,

with his fourth in three games, and Stuart Cash with his only goal, scored for Town. Cash's last game was the next one. A firework display before the match, some strong running from Leigh Jenkinson, and an inept Town performance led to a 4-0 defeat. It was a bad Bonfire night, although the press box seemed more concerned with the news of Robert Maxwell's fatal swimming excursion.

The Darlington game was Tim Parkins last, Port Vale's fee of £50,000 for a 33 year old was not to Town's liking. After Hull, a slight respite was caused by a flu epidemic, with 11 players suffering Town postponed the trip to Stockport. The F.A.Cup saw a trip to Hartlepool, where 'Smudger' scored his first goal, but a dubious penalty saw Town lose 3-2. A week later, there was a revenge match in the League, when 'Tufty' Donaldson scored on his debut. Hartlepool had four shots, all cleanly hit, and left the Meadow 4-1 winners.

Dave Bennett also made his debut in that game and showed promise, but it was the defence which was most worrying. In the opening eight League games, just four goals were conceded, in the next eight, nineteen had been scored - not to mention ten in the three Cup games. For the re-arranged trip to Stockport, Dean Spink was drafted in to mark the giant Kevin Francis. Deano did an excellent job and Dave Bennett was brilliant. Pat O'Toole played a 1-2 for Bennett's first goal and after Steve Perks saved Andy Kilner's penalty, 50 seconds after the restart, it looked like Town's night. It was, but at a price, for after having scored a marvellous second goal, Dave Bennett was carried off with what he correctly diagnosed as a broken leg. 'Tufty' replaced him and set up Neil Lyne for a fourth, and young 'Evo' made his debut in the dying minutes. He replaced Mark Smith, and immediately hit a 'miracle ball', neatly weighted with the outside of his foot.

Town's search for a defender was solved, by Dean Spink. They had previously failed to convince Rob Hindmarch and Gary Bellamy to leave Wolves, but 'Bondy' wanted to replace the 'class' Bennett had shown. After a 3-1 home defeat by Bolton, Paul Gorman was effectively sacked, his week-to-week contract not being renewed by the club, largely due to the misplaced throw-in which led to a goal.

On December 12th, Steve Mackenzie arrived, on loan from Wednesday, and scored on his debut at Moss Rose against Chester. Just 1,016 watched the game, with Carl Griffiths hitting two second half goals as Town won 4-1. Howard Clark arrived from

Carl Griffiths, became a Town record transfer sale.

He moved to Manchester City for £450,000.

Coventry, in time to make his debut against Bury, with Worsley hitting Town's goal in a 1-1 draw. Clark, Graeme Worsley and Tommy Lynch would rotate the full-back shirts throughout the rest of the season. Defeat at Exeter on Boxing Day maintained the Bond record, but the New Year started brightly.

Stoke City on New Year's day provided the biggest post Second Division League crowd, 8,557, and started a three match winning run. Things seemed to have been sorted out and promotion was a distinct possibility. Steve Mackenzie's seven match run had seen Town win four and draw two, but an ankle ligament injury in training with Wednesday cut short his run, and he would never play as many consecutive games again.

This promotion form, was set to be replaced by an unbelievable run. A week after Mackenzie's injury, Alan Walsh 'the best left foot in football' arrived after a spell in Turkey. He would make his debut against a former side, Darlington, but Town lost 2-0. After being substituted at Reading, he joined Southampton on February 18th.

Carl Griffiths had scored just once in nine games and John Paskin was recruited on loan. His would be the shortest ever stay, for he arrived on Friday, played

on Saturday and signed for Wrexham the following Monday. Town drew 2-2 with Chester, in his only game and repeated the scoreline in unusual circumstances at Preston the following week. Darren Harmon came on as a late substitute and scored with two headers to rescue a point. A week later, he made his only full appearance, but Town lost to Leyton Orient.

Sean Parrish, who had been on loan at Telford, since September, completed the move while a month earlier, Pete Dolby made his debut for Corinthian Casual Veterans, against Shrewsbury School 'A' XI. The club were allowed an extra loan, because they suffered two injuries and Paskin's quick departure.

They tried to sign Tony Ellis (Stoke), Dave Puckett (Aldershot), Jim Steele and Steve Cooper (Tranmere) but failed, however, Lee Power (Norwich) was due to arrive - until a hamstring injury in training spoilt that move.

Gary McKeown arrived, on loan from Arsenal, and made his debut at Huddersfield - it was Town's tenth League game without a win. Defeat by Hull made it eleven, but on the Monday, the management team signed three year contracts. With the untimely sales of Kelly, Brown and Heathcote, plus injuries to Bennett, Mackenzie and Blake, there was some sympathy with the off the field problems, but it was a remarkable piece of backing, from the board.

Peterborough were Town's next opponents, and a crowd of 7,377 saw the Posh scramble a ninth consecutive victory. Stockport gained revenge at the Meadow, Hartlepool made it a hat trick of wins, and Torquay 2-0 down hit back to level. Defeat at Griffin Park and at home to Bournemouth, made it five draws and twelve defeats.

Behind at half-time at Swansea, the run looked set to continue, but second-half goals from 'Viv' Taylor and 'Hoppy' made it a really Good Friday. The Hartlepool defeat saw Mark 'Bomber' Williams and Kevin Bremner make their debuts, with Kevin scoring. He hit his other goal in the 3-2 victory over Bradford City, when Tony Henry scored the other two. Bremner's final appearance was at Birmingham, Tony Henry came on as substitute, and 'Hoppy' plus Ken Hughes also signed off with this game.

Neil Lyne and Kevin Summerfield had reason to be happy, as Town beat Stoke City at home on New Year' day - but by the end of the season there was not so much to smile about!

The rumours proved correct. Steve Perks, Ken Hughes, Tony Henry, Darren Ryan and Sean Parrish were released. Robert Hopkins, Mark Blake and Tommy Lynch were on the list, Hoppy was released on May 20th - a month after his sending off against Bradford City. John Brough had signed six days earlier on a free from Notts County, while Jon Narbett's move from Hereford to Luton netted Town £18,750.

TRIALS, TRIBULATIONS AND DEPARTURES

The 1992-93 season started as a trying time. Darren Ryan had trials at Forest and Ipswich, Sean Parrish went to Oldham, but Town had a host of hopefuls. Maurice Evans recommended Matthew McDonnell and Stuart Fisher, from Oxford, but Fisher picked up a hamstring injury. Goalkeepers, there were many; Mark Grew and Peter Fox had talks, Mark Deegan and Gary Penhaligon had trials, as did Paul Edwards - who also appeared for West Brom against Stoke. Dave Hodges, an experienced striker with Mansfield and Torquay, did enough to make the opening line-up, alongside John Brough.

York City had finished in the bottom four the previous season, but they played a neat passing game and Town lost 2-0, then a 2-1 home Cup defeat by Wigan, did little to improve matters. Carl Griffiths scored his first goal in that defeat, and hit the winner as Doncaster were beaten 2-1 in the opening home League game. Nigel Smith made his debut in that game and scored the only goal at Wigan in the second leg, but his stay would be short. A draw at Scunthorpe and a win at Colchester promised much. The writer told John Bond, *"if we beat Rochdale we had a chance of promotion"*, we lost 2-1; Mark Barham and Paul Haylock came on as substitutes and Haylock scored.

Almost all the trialists had stayed, as players for nearly 30 years had, at the Abbey Gardens Hotel, where owner Ruth Williams was considering installing a revolving door, to keep up with the turnover. After five League games, Town had paraded twenty different players, amazingly ten of these had appeared for at least part of all the games. Two of them played a big part at Colchester. 'Bomber' Williams sampled Roy McDonough's elbow, the player-manager being dismissed, and John Brough scored his first goal. Carl Griffiths also scored in that game, but two goals in the opening six matches gave little hint of the season to come.

Rumours that Steve Perks and Ken Hughes were to be released, led to Ken walking out and the club's youth 'keeper, Michael Barton, who had already been told he was not retained, made his debut in the final fixture. Mark 'Evesy' Williams came on as substitute for his debut and Paul Evans made his first start. 'Tufty', in what he believed for a long time was his last game, scored a consolation goal, young Barton did well, but the Baggies fans celebrated a 3-1 victory by pulling a crossbar down. It was a sad end to the season, although Bobby Gould said Albion would buy a new set of posts, which they did.

Darren Harmon became the next player used, but only as substitute against Scarborough. Just 1,527 saw Town take an early lead, with a move rehearsed all week, when Mark Smith's centre was whipped in by Carl. Two Griffiths goals, one a penalty, beat Bury in a game which saw 'Evesy' Williams' last appearance. Darren Harmon moved to Northampton, and young Paul Evans made his international debut for Wales Youth at Cardiff against Israel, alongside Luton youngster John Hartson.

Carl 'scored' at Lincoln, but it did not count; it was an overhead kick, a brilliant goal, but disallowed for dangerous play. A minute later Mark Barham cracked home his only Town goal, to secure the points.

A breathtaking first half display at Barnet saw Town lead 2-0, but Barry Fry's team hit back down the slope. Darlington again caused an upset, before another brilliant 45 minutes - this time the second half - destroyed Chesterfield, who had frightened Liverpool, in the League Cup. It would be Mark Barham's last game, due to an achilles injury. The board was extended, with the appointment of three associate directors, Mike Ashton, Harry Wilson and Roland Wycherley.

The Chesterfield game was the eighth time Carl hit a brace, but never three, until Town entertained Cardiff, on October 24th. Eddie May's young team played really well, but Carl scored an opportunist hat-trick, which included a late winner and made it 10 goals in seven games. All good things come to an end, however. A goalless draw at Northampton, and a Pat O'Toole winner beat Halifax, but a Kevin McDonald inspired Walsall, won 3-0 - including a Wayne Clarke penalty - at the Meadow.

Paul Haylock was given a contract for the season, and Lee Williams on loan from Villa made his debut against Mansfield in the Cup, scoring Town's third goal. Burnley were drawn in the next round, which created all sorts of problems, not least of which surrounded the manager. John Bond was a folk hero in the Lancashire Town, his period of management was revered - no sorry - reviled by the locals, to such an extent that after discussions with the Police he 'decided' not to attend!

Fred Davies and Malcolm Musgrove appeared in tin hats, to some amusement from the spectators, but Town had more problems when Roger Eli collapsed and Dean Spink was sent off for elbows. However, a fine battling performance brought a replay.

Carl Griffiths scored, to seemingly set-up a victory, before a disgraceful tackle by 'Inchy' Heath saw Carl carried off. To add to the trauma two goals in the final two minutes put Burnley through. Spink's sending off, effectively finished his first team career as a defender, and when Mark Blake was dismissed against Cardiff in the Autoglass for a foul on his namesake, Nathan, it created a hole in the defence.

Joe Wallace, Dave Goodall, Alf Wood and several others who could, in earlier years, have filled the void, attended a reunion, which was organised by Pete Dolby in aid of Albert Harley. Always such a bundle of energy, Albert was suffering from motor neuron disease and was confined to a wheelchair. However, on November 26th at the Shrewsbury Hotel, he clearly enjoyed a night of nostalgia and fun. Danny Dalton's assertion, that... *"he was pleased to be asked to perform, as not many people know, but Albert and I had the same probation officer"*, saw Albert almost topple from his wheelchair with laughter. It displayed what a family club Shrewsbury Town has always been.

The search for defensive cover saw Ian Knight give a trial, but sadly he had not recovered sufficiently from Gary Bennett's horrendous tackle to resurrect his career. So the spotlight moved to another Wednesday man, Julian Watts, although he could hardly have travelled further for a debut, starting on a swamp at Torquay. Dean missed that game and the icy draw at Hereford, but 'Bomber' and Julian were doing so well he had to await his return. Mickey Brown returned from Bolton for £25,000 without making much impact for the Hereford game. Dean came on as substitute for Neil Lyne in the 4-1 victory over Crewe, which featured Lyne's last goal, and after defeat at Wrexham, was recalled as a forward, against Lincoln.

Town sold Neil Lyne to Cambridge for £75,000 but Nottingham Forest netted most of the fee. Dean scored against Lincoln, but picked up a dead leg, and limped off late in the game, for Jason Evans to make his only appearance. That night at a restaurant, Dean was taken ill and was rushed to hospital, his dead-leg had formed a blood clot and an operation was required. He would be out of first team action for ten games.

John Bond lined-up David Johnson from Sheffield Wednesday on loan, but having had two previous loans, from Premier Division sides, was not allowed a third. He tried for Kevin Bartlett, Phil Gee and Ian Ormondroyd, but failed to clinch a deal, so

Tommy Lynch was pushed forward against Scunthorpe. The visitors led at half-time, but Tommy and Carl with second half goals, won the points. A 1-0 away win at Doncaster, thanks to a fine rearguard action, and a home draw versus York, with Graeme Worsley on the right-wing and Howard Clark in midfield kept the promotion dreams on course.

Striker Chris Brooks from Luton and winger Paul Kinnaird had both arrived, and played in the 7-3 reserves win over Northampton. They both made debuts at Rochdale, and the home 'keeper - Tim Clarke - on loan from Huddersfield, had an easy day; Julian Watts did not, for he limped away after the game and has yet to play again for Town. Nigel Pearson's broken leg meant a recall for Watts, whose second month loan had been arranged after much pleading by 'Bondy', and won Mrs Trevor Francis a bouquet of flowers in gratitude.

Carl Griffiths scored twice, in each of the victories over Colchester and Darlington, with Smudger's annual goal important in the former. The big promotion clash with Barnet saw Paul Kinnaird's only goal - a header in his final match - separate the teams. It was, Carl's goals apart, just about the final highlight of the season.

Steve Mackenzie, after three substitute appearances, made his first start at Carlisle in place of Gary Piggott, who had made a promising debut against Barnet. This was the start of a run of four away games, after a defeat at Brunton Park, draws at Halifax, Walsall and Bury, kept the promotion hopes alive. The Halifax game (apart from a rare Mark Blake goal), was notable for an unusual spectacle, a daylight firework display in March. A run was developing, particularly with defeats by Carlisle and Gillingham. A Notts County bid for Carl of around £400,000, after one from Oxford for £300,000, was knocked back, and after failing to secure Kevin Bartlett or Kevin Wilson on loan, the arrival of Robbie Turner, should have helped clinch a play-off place.

Town had also needed a cover goalkeeper, they had given an unsuccessful trial to David Adams, but on St. Patrick's Day, Ron Green became the first player to sign for the club on three separate occasions; Dave Pountney, Jimmy McLaughlin, 'Chic' Bates, Mickey Brown and Alan Boswell, as cover, had been signed twice. Mark Blake picked up a calf strain at Walsall, so Dean returned to the defence, but the nine games, up to the trip to Scarborough, produced just five draws. That game attracted, the smallest Division Three gate of the season, just 1,325, being 202 fewer than at the Meadow, but Town did at least win 2-1. A draw with Chesterfield, and an unlucky defeat, at Cardiff followed. The Cardiff game finished with around half the 17,253 crowd ringing the playing area, it was fortunate Town did not equalise. Dean Spink and 'Bomber' Williams were both suspended for this match and Robbie Turner deputised well in defence.

Unfortunately Turner kept his defensive role for the visit of Northampton, and it was a vital game to both sides. Defeat would mean possible relegation to the Conference for the visitors, and the probability of missing the play-offs for Town. Northampton displayed their frailty, with an inept first half display, which left the homesters 2-0 ahead - and included Carl's 30th first team goal of the season. Robbie Turner's second half nightmare had to be witnessed to be believed, suffice to say he was involved in all three goals, most notably hitting a back pass to the 'Eagle', which Eddy saw bounce past him off Pat Gavin as he tried to clear upfield. It was all too much, for Town fans, and seemingly three days later for the Board as well.

Chairman Ken Woodhouse and Manager John Bond resigned. Mr. Woodhouse should not have been Chairman, he is too nice a man. John Bond was not an obvious Shrewsbury Manager, a high profile character, in a low profile club.

John Bond in pensive mood.

New Chairman, Ray Bailey, appointed Fred Davies as Caretaker-manager, and it was he who produced the retained list. Pat O'Toole, Paul Haylock, Gary Piggott, Jason Evans, and most interestingly, both Graeme Worsley and Howard Clark were given frees. Robbie Turner returned to Notts County, but 'Tufty' Donaldson and Nick Brookman were each offered three month contracts. Brookman had played several reserve games and possessed obvious ability, scoring two of the finest goals ever seen on the ground, but was lacking fitness. 'Tufty' had suffered a virus and several injuries.

The First thing Fred organised was a trial match for free transfer players, on Tuesday May the 18th. Amongst several players on view one stood out, and the following Wednesday week, Gary Patterson was signed. Others who did well were invited to come to pre-season training; Justin Philips and Chris Withe did so, but Craig Boardman, son of George, joined Peterborough. Fred was still concerned about the size of his squad, and tried to sign Martin Hicks, but he went as Player-manager, to Newbury Town. Trialists included Allan Lewis from Cardiff, and Paul Fitzpatrick and Matthew Fox formerly at Birmingham.

The main action was reserved, for the last few days before the season. Dave Hockaday and Chris Withe (for three months) on the Wednesday, plus Wayne Clarke on the Friday, were all signed in time to take their places on the trip to Mansfield. Irish under-21 International Joe Gallen was the other close season signing, from Watford, but he was not included.

Steve Mackenzie was appointed Captain after extensive pre-season training at Shawbury, but Mansfield are always a bit of a 'Bogey' side, and Town lost 1-0. A Cocoa Cola Cup victory over Scunthorpe, by the same score, was thanks to a brilliant Paul Evans goal, but only 3,681 turned up for the derby with Walsall. Mickey Brown scored for Town, however Michele Cecere's late effort took a deflection, and looped into the net, to give Walsall an unlikely victory. The return at Scunthorpe saw Carl score, but limp off with a calf injury, and despite Tommy Lynch being sent off and Scunthorpe hitting a late goal, Town went through.

For the visit to Preston's plastic pitch, Fred decided on a sweeper system. To say it did not work, would be kinder than naming the guilty. Suffice to say 5-0 is a big deficit in the first quarter. Mickey Brown's goal was just a consolation, and privately, some of the Board were worried by the experiment. A 3-1 half-time deficit at Colchester was unpromising, but two late goals - from Brown centres - registered the first point. It was a turning point, well John Bray said so, and this remark was to be proved correct.

'Tufty' Donaldson always fancied a place in history, and from Mark Blake's through ball against Bury he achieved it. His strike, the winning goal, was timed at 14 seconds, an all-time Club record. He also set up a goal for Wayne Clarke in 54 seconds a week later, at Darlington, but broke a bone in his foot later in the game. A home draw with Gilingham was the build up game before the Cup clash at the Dell. Mark Blake scored his last Town goal against the Gills, before pitting his wits against his training partners, at Southampton. Town's other strike from Carl Griffiths was inside the first minute, surely a unique hat-trick.

Only Kevin Moore, currently a team-mate of Mark's at Fulham, found a way through Town's resolute defence, with the forwards providing enough problems to give hope for the second leg. Carl scored his second hat-trick, at Scarborough in front of only 1,137, before Town lost 3-1 at Wrexham in the Autoglass Trophy match. Tommy Lynch was injured during the game, and Kevin Seabury made his full debut. Wayne Clarke played in the 3-2 win over Torquay, but then had a hernia operation, and like Matthew Le Tissier missed both legs of the 2nd round Coca Cola tie.

'Viv' Taylor set up Kevin Summerfield to level the cup-tie on 36 minutes, and four minutes later Ken Monkau was sent off for a foul on Dean Spink. Southampton were a poor Premier side, but Town deserved to progress, and when Paul Evans' corner was headed out on 69 minutes it fell to Mickey Brown, who cracked home a 20 yard volley. Round three saw Town given a daunting trip to Blackburn.

Carl scored what turned out to be his last goal to defeat Carlisle, but a poor 'Eddy' clearance at Chester, and an outrageous offside decision against Doncaster, saw Town lose two games running, for the last time during the season. The day Town travelled to Ewood Park, Kenny Dalglish signed David Batty for £2.7million, Town made it look as if Rovers needed his ability. Mickey Brown was outstanding and Carl Griffiths, did enough to convince Manchester City to make this his final match for Town. They stepped in with an offer, which depending on appearances, was valued at £450,000, easily a club record.

On a high, Town travelled to Wycombe. Steve Mackenzie, who had played an important midfield role in the Cup, cried off ill two hours before kick-off. The re-organised side out-passed the home team and somehow only drew, they were also unlucky at home to Crewe, in a game which saw Mark Blake dislocate his shoulder. Blake had been in outstanding form, particularly when controlling his former team-mate Alan Shearer at Blackburn, so Town moved quickly to find a replacement.

On November the 3rd, David Walton, came on loan from Sheffield United. In an interview, that day, the writer asked him about his strengths, *"I'm good in the air"* he said, and his weakness, *"passings not me strongest point."* Jokingly I said, *"you and Bomber should get on well then"*. Rarely have I been so accurate. His debut at Northamapton started badly, for eager to impress he attacked the ball in the air on the centre-line, and missed. Tommy Lynch tidied up, after a powerful downward header from a Chris Withe free kick, which set up Dean for the first goal, Dave settled.

Steve Mackenzie returned for the cup replay with Blackburn, and Wayne Clarke made the bench. Paul Evans who missed the first leg again missed out, and made only one more appearance all season.

Mike Newell was man of the match; he opened the scoring after six minutes. However, Town bounced back. Kevin Summerfield levelled, and when Newell tripped Smudger, Steve Mackenzie made it 2-1. A Tommy Lynch header, touched over the line by Kevin Summerfield stretched the lead, but David Batty conned Keith 'Tommy' Cooper, for a penalty straight from the kick-off. (Not that I'm biased!) David May levelled from an Andy Pearce knock-back, and in extra-time Pearce finally put Jack Walker's side through.

A mistake in packing the skip, meant Pearce had no name or number on his shirt. Kenny Dalglish explained to the referee, but Fred said, *"are you trying to slip another £3million signing past me"*, to which Kenny replied (according to the translation), *"you should be worried, its another 'keeper"*, . Kenny was most helpful after both games, unlike his national press image, and was genuinely impressed with Town's efforts to play a passing game, two factors which led to Paul Harford's loan 13 months later. The signing of David Batty was reputed to have pushed Blackburn's spending on their squad to £25million.

Chairman, and keen fisherman · Ray Bailey · casts his line, over Christmas 1993 · in Gay Meadow!

So the V.A.T. on their outlay, would be approximately five times Town's total outlay on players, in 43 seasons of League football!

The following Saturday it was F.A. Cup action, and Joe Gallen came off the bench to score a late equaliser against Doncaster. A draw with Scunthorpe saw John Brough's only start of the season, in midfield. But Wayne Clarke's return saw Town hammer Wigan at Springfield Park. Clarke hit two, and Dean Spink hit his first hat-trick, as Town romped home 5-2. Deano scored again in the Cup replay at Doncaster, and Dave Walton powered in his first goal, the winner. The good run lasted just another three days, until Preston - the one time they passed the ball - scored and won 1-0.

The Tuesday before the Scunthorpe game, Dave Walton complained during training, Tuesday is running day, and the big defender tried to pull out, with 'the stitch' - the nickname has stuck. Efforts to sign a left-winger, seemed to have succeeded when Louie Donowa arrived, interviews were arranged, when suddenly the deal was off. Terry Cooper and Birmingham City, were about to divorce.

On December the 8th, Brian Croft arrived on loan from Queens Park Rangers. His debut was at Walsall where a quick counter-attack saw Dean Spink's goal grab the points. A home draw with Mansfield, the Friday before Christmas, was a prelude to another Boxing Day trip to Hereford. Dave Walton scored against Mansfield, his first League goal, and was signed, on a pay as you play deal, on the following Wednesday.

Wayne Clarke also scored against Mansfield, but his goal at Hereford was a little special. Brian Croft sent a through ball to Dean Spink, but Alan Judge raced off his line, and fly-hacked the ball straight to Clarke, 30 yards out. Clarke in turn chipped the ball back into the net and over the despairing keeper. This win started a run of five consecutive victories for the first time in 18 years. Brian Croft went back to London after the victory at Chesterfield, whose 'keeper - Chris Marples - dislocated his shoulder diving backwards trying to rescue a mistake, which led to Town's opening goal.

Three home victories, over Colchester, Chester and Wycombe, meant Town had beaten two of their main rivals for promotion. Louie Donowa had finally arrived, albeit on loan, and made his debut against Wycombe. The run of wins ended in a goalless draw with Doncaster, who were managed by Ian

Atkins. A last minute penalty against Rochdale came after Wayne Clarke was replaced by John Brough, so Gary Patterson took the kick and pushed it wide of the 'keepers left hand post. Preston, and their loathsome style, were next, and thankfully Tommy Lynch's goal sent them home, with the number of points they deserved - none! The fifteen match unbeaten run, looked to be about to end at Bury. Despite playing well, Town trailed 2-0, at half-time, but three second half goals made it an exhilarating victory.

'Bomber' Williams and 'Stitch' Walton, who had become closer than brothers, had been split only once, when Mark Blake - although not fully fit - deputised for 'Stitch' against Rochdale. Their record was impressive, but they admitted faults, as Town finally lost at home to Lincoln. Although 'Stitch' scored, they tried to be too classy and came unstuck. It was a lesson well learnt. After a 1-1 draw with Darlington, who led at half-time, Town went over 600 minutes without conceding a goal. The Lincoln game marked the full debut for Mark Rutherford, who had signed on loan from Shelbourne, and he proved an honest hardworking winger. The final player to join the championship bandwagon was Ray Woods, on loan from Coventry; he and Rutherford would share the left-wing duties.

The home win over Northampton featured Ray Woods first goal, and a classic Clarke finish which clinched promotion. The trip to Scunthorpe will be committed to the Town Hall of Fame, for well over a thousand Town fans travelled to Glanford Park. Gary Patterson had appeared in all but three games during the season, without scoring. He wanted five tickets for his family for the final game, with Wigan, and had been told he could have them if he scored.

The unbounded joy of the whole squad was obvious when he hammered Town ahead. In his delight, he pulled his shirt over his head and ran-towards the wrong set of fans! Mickey Brown, whose brilliant form all season had been such a factor in Town's success, hit the second. Wayne Clarke made it three, and after Ian Juryeff scored an excellent consolation goal, 'Viv' Taylor crowned his consistent season with the final goal. John Bond said 'Viv' would win the crowd over, during this season he did. The scenes at the final whistle, were a tribute to all present.

Shrewsbury Town and Scunthorpe joined the League together, and after the game their fans congratulated one another in a manner which restored many peoples faith in football supporters. The year before, Cardiff clinched promotion with a win over Shrewsbury, and the title at Scunthorpe. It is fair to say that the same 'bonhomie' never existed on those two occasions. This was Town's sixteenth away game without defeat, but despite a Mickey Brown goal, they finally lost, at Carlisle. The final game was also an anti-climax, a goalless draw with Wigan. However, by then nobody cared, for the Championship Trophy was at the ground to be presented, and a team, who lost their opening three league games were about to collect it.

Fred Davies, Dean Spink and Malcolm Musgrove look satisfied, after a job well done.......

........and the rest of the players seem to be happy!

Carl Griffiths proudly shows his 'golden boot', his reward for being the top goalscorer in Division 3 in 1992-93

A memorable day spilled into a memorable night, and Mark Smith and Chris Withe's parody of the management team (Malcolm Musgrove and Fred Davies respectively) was a high spot, which even the Chairman's singing could not surpass.

The retained list saw Mark Blake, 'Tufty' Donaldson, John Brough, Jason Yates and Steve Mackenzie released, with injuries featuring strongly in the decisions. Dean Spink was chosen for the Third Division Select Eleven, while Michael Brown won the player of the year award. This was the season that the substitute goalkeeper was introduced to the Endsleigh League. Jimmy Mulvey was on duty for the opening 15 League and cup games, before the arrival of Tim Clarke from Altrincham, although he may not have made an appearance on the Park, he played his part nonetheless. It was truly a team effort.

AND FINALLY..........

Of course the story does not end there. Mark Hughes from Tranmere, Ray Woods permanently, and Ian Stevens from Bury, were added to the squad, before the 1994-95 pre-season tour of the West country. The season opened with a 4-0 victory at Rotherham and a 2-1 victory over Birmingham in the Coca Cola Cup first round first leg, and Mark Taylor became Town's first coloured skipper.

Hopefully this book may be the prelude to the production of a complete 'Who's Who', for the fiftieth League season - and provide the opportunity to update any errors that come to light. That is, as Joe Maloney would say, 'God willing'!

CHAPTER 16 - MANAGERS 1950 - 1994

SAMMY CROOKS: May 22 1950 - June 21 1954
Crooks faced up to the unenviable task of establishing the fledgling club in the Football League, by plumping for experience. He brought in several players with proven records, particularly ex team-mates from Derby County. It would in the long run have left the club with little chance of selling players for profit. Something he appeared to have recognised with his final two acquisitions, Russell Crossley and Joe Maloney, who were two of the youngest players he ever signed and both proved excellent long term assets. It was a pity Sammy was not a little younger when he was appointed, as even at 42 he still had enough ability to consider returning to action as player-manager.

WALTER ROWLEY: June 21 1954 - June 27 1957
A true gentlemen, who was almost at retiring age before taking on the job - Walter gave youth its head. He knew he had no money to spend, and set about discovering local talent. Norman Hobson, Ron Manders and 'Curly' Edgley all came through under Mr Rowley. He also used his own vast experience to make sure there was a steady, but noticeable improvement, in the club's League standing. Arguably he laid the ground rules for keeping Shrewsbury Town both successful and solvent. He remained in the area after his retirement and was always willing to discuss the game, even into his nineties.

HARRY POTTS: July 1957 - February 25 1958
Recommended by Walter Rowley, on his retirement, and easily Shrewsbury's most successful manager, albeit not with the club. His time at Shrewsbury was short and he did not enjoy the best of luck. Injuries and illness depleted his squad as Town struggled to keep in the top half of the division. At the time of his departure Town had 38 points from 33 games and were 14th in the Third Division table.

JOHNNIE SPUHLER: Feb.27 1958 - May 14 1958
The fourth consecutive North-Easterner arrived well recommended by both previous incumbents, but had a sorry time. Just seven points from twenty-six condemned Town to Division Four and saw a bitter manager sacked. Save for a three match unbeaten run in March it was an unhappy stewardship, short and at a difficult time.

GEORGE ARTHUR ROWLEY:
June 5 1958 - July 3 1968
A big man in every way, Arthur had one major advantage, no other Town manager has been able to match. He had a regular source of goals, himself. Having said that he had a good eye for a player, something with which Tommy Seymour and his Scottish scout Bill Dennis helped with, but something he proved at other clubs he could also do on his own. He had a forthright manner and does not suffer fools gladly, something which is not surprising given his proven ability to make the right decision. Being a forward, his natural inclination was to attack and in League and Cup, in each of

his first three seasons, Town hit a hundred goals. Given the substitute rule, which would have enabled him to come on and turn a game, he may well have extended his career. Whilst the shape he would have hit a modern football into, does not bear thinking.

He established Shrewsbury as a Cup force, and his goalscoring record speaks for itself. Arguably the biggest personality to play for Shrewsbury, well in a positive sense anyway. Truly a big man.

HARRY GREGG: July 22 1968 - October 11 1972
Arthur Rowley was obviously a hard act to follow. One man who would be unconcerned by following anybody would be Harry Gregg. A giant in the game, a hero at Munich, and intensely proud. His commitment to everything he does is total and he expects everyone else to do likewise. Sadly that desire, that will to win, saw his sides run into trouble on disciplinary grounds. If he could have tempered his fear of losing he may have been a more successful manager. However, if it came to having a man on your side it is certain Harry would be that man. He once agreed to play Sunday League football for the Author's team, but the chairman - diplomatically - suggested it may be inappropriate. Currently he has a hotel in Ireland these days and it is certain only the best will be good enough, so why not pay a visit (I hope I'm on commission!).

MAURICE EVANS: Oct. 12 1972 - Dec. 3 1973
A good coach, an excellent judge of a player, it is eminently possible that Maurice Evans is too nice a man to be a football manager. However, he did not have the best of starts, Harry Gregg having resigned over the sales of Wood and Groves. It took Evans almost a month to be put in full charge and less than three, to see Jim Holton, John Moore, Jimmy McLaughlin and George Andrews all leave. He responded by buying Graham Turner and was forced to use 28 players. Some of the players he had nurtured, began to break through, such as Sammy Irvine and Jake King, but these were traumatic times. It is little wonder that he has been reluctant to be a manager on several occasions since, and also little wonder that he remains in the game and is held in such high esteem.

ALAN DURBAN: Dec. 4 1974 - Feb. 12 1978
After an illustrious career, Alan was obviously keen to break into management, and it was no surprise when Shrewsbury Town allowed him to realise that ambition. His appointment of Richie Barker was a shrewd move, as was using the rest of the season to re-organise, in order to be ready for a promotion push. An impressive unbeaten April showed the groundwork had been done, and the signing of two goalscorers, 'Chic' Bates and Ray Haywood, gave Town a potential, unavailable to them since Alf Wood's departure. Alan would once more prove the benefit of a player-manager at this level and but for a flu epidemic may have realised a second promotion. It was no surprise when he moved to a bigger club.

RICHIE BARKER: Feb. 23 1978 - Nov. 19 1979
The Author's consideration as the best Shrewsbury manager. After losing Irvine, Hornsby, Bates and Roberts - amongst others - from a useful squad, Richie proved organisation is a wonderful asset. It was ironic that he would lose his first and last games in charge, both to Swindon, as he lost only five other League games. Making the best out of what is available was moved into an art-form, and hard-work and honesty were watchwords. He has gone on to prove, he is an ideal number two, something at which most Shrewsbury managers prove to be adept. It may not have been a beautiful game, but it certainly had beautiful results. One sad note, Shrewsbury are the only team with which he had worked in management, that he did not take to Wembley.

GRAHAM TURNER: Nov. 20 1978 - July 18 1984
The promotion from within continued, with Graham Turner hardly having time to learn the coach's job, before moving to manager. What he did learn was invaluable and he gave the promotion aspirations a timely boost. The Cup run added to the glamour and the verbal volley on 'Match of the Day' increased his stature. His ability to lead, by example on the field, proved to be a major asset and his commonsense approach won many friends. One often wonders, if he surprised himself with the ease with which he adapted, particularly to the media. Although one senses a slightly more battle-hardened approach after recent skirmishes. Another who fitted the no nonsense hard-work approach which Town fans expect, and coupled it with success.

CHIC BATES - July 23 1984 - November 1987
Another who had been schooled in the Shrewsbury way of doing things. Bates continued the Turner miracle of keeping Town in Division Two. Nearly everyone in the country was convinced Salop would be relegated every season, (almost like Coventry), but the team kept creeping up the table. Chic changed the emphasis slightly, most notably asking Gary Stevens to return to scoring goals, not stop them. Like Graham, he had a genuine love for the club, which sadly would be slightly tarnished. His team continued to do the Town proud until they drew Sheffield Wednesday in the League Cup. The loss of Nigel Pearson for money and David Linighan injured was just too much of a blow. The board's insistence on accepting a cheque for a player with a suspect knee was understandable, but surely Wednesday would have waited a short while. As it was the sale and his dismissal were both completed with somewhat indecent haste. Just look at his record since.

KEN BROWN - December 1 - December 8 1987
A genial man, still traumatised by his dismissal at Norwich, Ken was neither ready, or felt able to commit himself to Shrewsbury.

IAN McNEIL - December 9 1987 - January 5 1990
Arguably the most colourful reign of any Town manager. Ian had been used, since leaving Wigan, to a bigger stage. He had a good eye for a player and without doubt brought some of the most skilful players to ever grace the Meadow, to the club. Sadly, although they at times graced the pitch, they all too often disgraced themselves. The manager's unswerving supporter of his players, which the Author knows of first-hand, just added to their irresponsibility. His transfer dealings have been maligned in certain quarters, but if the fees realised by McNally, Linighan, McGinlay and Steele, did not balance the books then not all the blame is the manager's. The initial escape from relegation was almost a fairy-tale. It is ironic, that the desire to purchase John Cornforth would appear to be the final straw. Ian has often claimed he might have been the final piece of the jigsaw, the one thing we do know is, we will never know.

ASA HARTFORD: January 6 1990-January 16 1991
A model professional, hard working, and a respected coach, he probably needed to convince himself, after Stockport, that management is not his bag. The training he enjoys, the boardroom, the pressroom and other ancillary bits and pieces are major drawbacks. Having faced up to the traumas of the hole-in-the-heart saga, he is entitled to believe he knows a bit about life, and over 660 games means he knows something about football. Long may he enjoy coaching the principles of both.

JOHN BOND: January 17 1991 - May 11 1993
Shares the same belief as Pele, that football is a beautiful game. Some of the things he tried to teach would have been difficult for internationals, never mind the lower divisions. Has an abrasive style of management, which is often pilloried, but look at the number of players he has signed more than once. Bond was never an obvious Shrewsbury Town manager, and having managed a team which had no money, and seeing Kelly Brown and Heathcote sold, out of a useful looking squad, earned and deserved much sympathy. His restructuring of the bonus scheme was calculated to have made a substantial saving and helped the club turn that corner. His recruiting of Fred Davies and Malcolm Musgrove did much to turn around the playing fortunes.

FRED DAVIES: May 12 1993 -
Typical 'back to basics' Shrewsbury Town manager. From a terrible start, he led Town to the Championship, in his first ever League management season. Needs to consolidate, before pushing to regain true Second Division status, but will give you an honest answer to an honest question. Also give you very short shrift for any underhand dealings. Favours playing with two wingers and this has led to an almost paranoidal search for a left-winger to give correct balance. The departure of Mickey Brown was a body-blow, but signs are beginning to look promising again.

AUTHOR'S SUMMARY
I like to think most of our former managers were still friends even after they departed. I trust they will remain so, and hope my character assassinations are perceived to be fair, because they are what I believe.

Who's Who

NAME	Born	From	To	Other Clubs	F.League		F.A.Cup		Lge. Cup		Welsh C.	
					A.	G.	A.	G.	A.	G.	A.	G.
AMBLER Roy	Wakefield 2/12/37	Leeds 1/59	Wrexham 5/61	York, Southampton	29	8						
ANDREWS George	Dudley 23/4/42	Southport 11/69	Walsall 1/73	Cardiff	123/1	49	7/1	7	4			
ARNOTT John H.	Sydenham 6/9/32	West Ham 8/55	Bournemouth 7/56	West Ham, Gillingham	30	6	4	1				
ASHWORTH Fred	Oldham 26/1/28	Blackburn 11/51	Tonbridge 7/53		56	1	7					
ASKEW Billy	Lumley 2/10/59	Loan-Newcastle 1/91		Middlesbrough, Hull	5		1					
ATKINS Arthur W.	Tokyo 21/2/25 (1988)	Birmingham 6/54			16		1					
ATKINS Ian	Birmingham 16/1/57	App. 1/75	Sunderland 8/82	Ever.Ips.B'ham.Colch.	273/6	58	23	3	13	3	27	12
AYTON Jimmy	Barrhd.15/10/23(1988)	Leicester 6/51	Bedford 7/52		25	1	1					
BAKER T. George	Maerdy 6/4/36	Plymouth 6/60			52	5	5		8			
BANNISTER James H.	Chesterfield 26/1/42	Chesterfield 6/52	Northampton 7/58	Aldershot	238	6	9					
BARHAM Mark F.	Folkestone 12/7/62	Brighton 9/92	Woking	Nor.Hudd.Mid'b.W.Brom	7/1	1						
BARKER Robert C.	Kinglassie 1/12/27	West Brom. 8/50			25	1						
BARTON Michael G.	Gainsborough 23/9/73	Youth Team 7/90			1							
BATES Mark	Walsall 25/4/65	Walsall 7/84			7/1							
BATES Philip (Chic)	West Brom.28/11/49	Stourbridge 5/74	Swindon 1/78 (12/80)	Bristol R.	274/20	64	24	9	18	3	26/1	10
BEEL William J.L.	Leominster 23/8/45	App. 7/63	Birmingham 1/65		3				1			
BELL Douglas K.	Paisley 5/9/59	Hibernian 12/87	Birmingham 10/89	Loan Hull 3/89	47/2	6	3		4		1	
BENNETT David A.	Manchester 11/7/59	Loan Swindon 11/91		Man.C.Cov.Shef.Wed	2	2						
BEVAN Paul P.	Shrewsbury 20/10/52	App.10/70	Swansea 8/73	Crewe A.	66/5	1	0/1		1			
BEYNON Edwin R.	Abercwmmai 17/11/24	Wrexham 10/51	Wellington 7/55		91	6	8					
BIGGINS Stephen J.	Walsall 20/6/54	Hednesford 12/77	Oxford 7/82	Derby,Wolv,P.Vale.Exe	140/6	41	13	3	9	3	14	9
BIRCH Trevor N.	Ormskirk 16/2/58	Liverpool 3/79	Chester 7/80		23/2	4			2		4	
BIRKETT Wilfred	Warrington 26/6/22	Southport 7/52	Southport 7/53		20		6					
BLAKE Mark C.	Portsmouth 19/12/67	Southampton 3/90	Fulham 9/94	Loan Colchester	142	4	9		14			
BLAKE Noel L.G.	Jamaica 12/1/62	Loan A.Villa 3/82		(5 League clubs)	6							
BOARDMAN George	Glasgow 14/8/43	Queen's Park 6/63	Barnsley 6/69		172/4	50	23	7	10	4		
BOOKER Kenneth	Sheffield 3/3/18	Chesterfield 7/52			9							
BOSWELL Alan H.	Walsall 8/8/43	Walsall 8/60	Wolves 9/68	Bolton, P.Vale	222		23		11			
BOWERS Ian(Danny)	Stoke 16/1/55	Loan Stoke 3/78		Crewe	6							
BRADLEY James	Greenock 21/3/27	Third Lanark 7/52			1							
BRADLEY Peter K.	Donnington 18/3/55	App. 7/73			3				1			
BREMNER Kevin J.	Banff 7/10/57	Loan Dundee 3/92		(8 League Clubs)	7	2						
BRENNAN Harold	Derby 17/11/30	Gresley Rovers 12/53	Buxton 7/55		19	3	1	1				
BRIDGWOOD Gerald	Stoke 17/10/44	Stoke 2/69			113/4	7	9		6			
BROADBENT Peter F	Dover 15/5/33	Wolves 1/65	A.Villa 10/66	Brentford, Stock C.	69	7	9	3	6	1		
BRODIE Eric	Blairgowrie 8/11/40	Dundee U. 6/63	Chest. 5/68	Tranmere	181/4	24	20	4	10	1		
BROOKS Chris	Huthswaite 6/6/72	Loan Luton 2/93			1							
BROUGH John	Heanor 18/1/73	Notts County 5/92	Telford 7/94	Hereford	7/9	1	1		1/1			
BROWN Alan	Easington 22/5/59	Sunderland 8/82	Doncaster 3/84	Loan Newcastle	65	15	4	2	6	3	3	1
BROWN A.(Sandy)	Grangemouth 24/3/39	Everton 5/71	Southport 7/72		21		3		2			
BROWN John M.	London 1934	Queen's Park 5/53			5	3						
BROWN Michael A.	Birmingham 8/2/68	App. 2/86 (12/92)	Bolton 8/91 (P.N.E.)		231/18	17	13	1	23/1	3	2/1	3
BROWN Robert	Glasgow 9/8/24	Southend 7/50	Barnsley 7/53	Rotherham	104	41	8	4				
BULLIONS James L.	Stirling 12/3/24	Leeds 9/50		Derby	131	2	3					
BURTON Michael J.	Birmingham 5/11/69	Shef. Wed. 3/91		Birmingham	3/3							
BUTLER David J.	Wednesbury 30/3/53	W.Brom 6/73	Workington 3/74		5/5		1		1			
BUTLER J.(Jackie)	Dawley 16/10/20	Dawley 8/50	Wellington		58	8	5	2				
CALLOWAY L.J.	Birmingham 17/6/45	York 12/72	San Jose Earth.	Roch.B'burn,Sou.Port	77/5	3	3		1		4	
CANDLIN Maurice H	Jarrow 11/11/21	Northampton 7/53			69	2	4					
CARR Clifford P.	Hackney 19/6/64	Stoke 8/91	Mansfield 10/91	Fulham	1	1			0/1	1		
CASH Stuart P.	Tipton 5/9/65	Loan Nott.For. 9/91		Roth,Brent,Wyc.C'Field	8	1			2			
CHAPMAN R.D.	Wednesday 18/8/46	Notts.Co.7/78	Tulsa Rough. 5/80	Nottingham Forest	36/1	6	8	3			2	
CLAPHAM Graham	Lincoln 23/9/47	Newcastle 8/67	Chester 1/72		74/16	5	5/1	1	3/1			
CLARK Howard W.	Coventry 19/9/68	Coventry 12/91	Hereford 7/93	Loan at Darlington	51/5		2					
CLARKE Frank J.	Willenhall 15/7/42	St.Giles Will.11/61	Q.P.R. 2/68	Ipswich, Carlisle	188	77	20	9	10	3		
CLARKE Wayne	Wolverhampton 28/2/61	Loan Man.City 10/90, signed from Walsall 8/93		Wolv.Bir.Ever.Leic.Stoke	34/1	17	2		2/1			
CLEMENTS Kenneth	Manchester 9/4/55	Limerick 10/90		Man.C.,Oldham,Bury	19/1		6					
CLOWES John A.	Alton(Staffs) 5/11/29	Stoke 6/52	Wellington 8/54	Back to Stoke	11	2						
COCKRANE Alan	Belfast 16/3/56	App. 3/74	Telford Utd. 12/74		3						1	1
COLLIER David	Colwyn Bay 2/10/57	App. 10/75	Crewe Alex. 8/77		20	4	1		1		3	
COLLINS Albert D.	Chesterfield 15/4/23	Bournemouth 8/51	Accrington St.7/52	Chest,H'fax.Carl,Barrow	9	2	1					
COLLINS Kevin	Birmingham 21/7/64	Boldmere St.M.1/84			1						1	
COMERFORD P.	Ches.-l-Street 30/11/25	Bedford 6/52			7							
COOKE William H.	Whittington 7/3/19	Luton 7/53	Watford 7/54	Bournemouth 4/38	4							

NAME	Born	From	To	Other Clubs	F.League		F.A.Cup		Lge. Cup		Welsh C.	
					A.	G.	A.	G.	A.	G.	A.	G.
COOPER Mark D.	Watford 5/4/67	Loan Spurs 9/87	Gillingham 10/87	Camb. Ley.O. Barnet	6	2						
COPP Leonard J.H.	Aberystwth 7/10/40	Leeds 7/58			2	1	1		2	2		
CORBETT Anthony	Wolverhampt. 28/4/40	Wolverhampton 7/60	Sankeys 7/62		8				1			
CORNFIELD Allen.H.	Dudley 19/12/40	Lower Gornal 11/59	Lower Gornal 7/62		9				2			
CORNFORTH John M.	Whitley Bay 7/10/67	Loan Sun'land 11/89		Donc. Linc. Swansea	3							
COUGHLIN Russell J.	Swansea 15/2/60	Loan Balckpool 9/90		(5 League Clubs)	4/1				1			
COYNE Brian	Glasgow 13/12/59	Glas.Celtic 6/79	Motherwell 2/81		1						5	1
CROFT Brian G.A.	Chester 27/9/67	Loan Q.P.R. 12/93		Chester, Cambridge	4							
CROSS Stephen C.	Wolverhamt. 22/12/59	App. 12/77	Derby 6/86	Bristol Rovers	240/22	33	14/1	3	15/2	3	27/3	13
CROSSLEY Russell	Hebden Bridge 25/6/27	Liverpool 7/54	Kettering 11/59		173		11					
CRUSE Peter L.	Camden 10/1/51	Loan Luton 2/74			2							
CRUTCHLEY W.Ronald	Walsall 20/6/1922	Walsall 9/50	Wellington 7/55		146	1	4					
CURRAN John	Glasgow 22/6/24	East Fife 8/56	Watford 6/57		24		1					
DALE Eric	Manchester 6/7/24	From M.League 49			1							
DALY Gerald A.	Dublin 30/4/54	Birmingham 10/85	Stoke 3/87	(5 League Clubs)	55	8	2		7		1	
DAWES Derek M.	Dawley 23/6/44	App. 6/62	Wellington 2/64		9							
DEPEAR E. Roland	Spalding 10/12/23	Newport Co. 7/50	Bangor 7/52		74	5	1					
DICKINSON Ronald A.	Coventry 29/6/30	Nuneaton B. 5/53	Coventry 6/54		11		1					
DODD William D.	C-le-St. 25/8/33(1982)	Derby 8/50	Southport 6/57		28	1						
DOLBY Peter	Derby 18/5/40	Heanor 2/60			303/21	21	31/1	4	15	4		
DONALDSON O'Neill	Birmingham 24/11/69	Hinckley T. 11/91	Doncaster 7/94	Mansfield, Shef.Wed.	15/13	4						
DONOWA B. Louie	Ipswich 24/9/64	Loan Bir'ham.1/94		Nor.Stoke,Ips.B.City	4							
DOUGLAS Patrick G.	Baschurch 7/9/51	App/ 7/69			12/1	1						
DUFFEY Chris. P.	Kirkby 8/1/52	Bury 5/75	Rochdale 11/75	Bolton, Crewe.A.	4/4	1			0/2	1		
DUNGWORTH John H.	Rotherham 30/3/55	Aldershot 11.79	Mansfield 8/82	(6 League Clubs)	81/5	17	3/3		2		13	8
DUNNE Thomas	Dublin 19/3/27 (1988)	Exeter 8/56	Southport 7/57	Leicester	3		1					
DURBAN W. Alan	Port Talbot 7/7/41	Derby C. 9/73		Cardiff	150/6	32	10/1	2	6/1	1	12	6
EDGLEY Brian K.	Shewsbury 26/8/37	Juniors 2/56	Cardiff 7/60	Brentford, Barnsley	113	12	5	1				
EDWARDS Dean S.	Wolverhamt. 25/2/62	App. 2/80	Telford	Wolvs.Exe.Torq.North.	7/6	1					4/3	4
EDWARDS Paul	Liverpool 22/2/65	Crewe Alex. 8/92			84		6		8			
EGGLESTONE Patrick	Penrith 17/3/27	Halifax 8/50	Wrexham 2/53	Bradford City	109		1					
EVANS Jason S.	Cambridge 22.1.74	Youth Trainee	Newton		0/1							
EVANS Paul S.	Oswestry 1/9/74	Youth Trainee 7/91			15/4		1/1		5/1	1		
FELLOWS Geoffrey A.	West Brom. 26/7/44	Aston Villa 6/65			277/4	3	24		12			
FINLEY Alan J.	Liverpool 10/12/67	Marine 6/88	Stockport 8/90	Rochdale	60/3	2	2		3		1	
FISHER Frederick	Het.-le-Hole 28/11/24	Reading 7/52	Leyton O. 7/54		64	10	8	2				
FISHER Peter M.	Edinburgh 17/2/20	Northampton 8/50	Wrexham 10/51		39							
FOSTER Karl A.	Birmingham 15/9/65	App. 9/83	Aston Villa 4/84		1/1						0/3	1
FRANKLIN Paul L.	Hainault 5/10/63	Loan Watford 10/86		Swindon, Reading	6							
FRENCH Graham E.	Wolverhampton 6/4/45	App. 11/62	Swindon 8/63	W'fd,L'ton,Read.Southp.	27	1	5		4	1		
GALLEN Joseph	Hammersmith 2/9/72	Watford 6/93			4/2	1	0/1	1				
GARBETT W. Edward	Dawley 14/9/45	App/ 9/67	Barrow 7/69	Stockport Co.	7/4	2	0/2					
GEDDIS David	Carlisle 12/3/58	Birmingham 2/87	Swindon 10/88	(6 League clubs)	36/3	11	1		1			
GIBSON Charles	Dumbarton 12/6/61	St.Anthony's 3/81	Dumbarton 7/82		2/4						1	
GIBSON Michael J.	Derby 15/7/39	Nuneaton B. 3/60	Bristol City 4/63	Gillingham	76		12		10			
GOODALL David G.	Madeley 18/5/43	Juniors 5/61	Welington 7/63		1							
GORIN Edward R.	Cardiff 2/2/24	Scusnthorpe 1/51	Lovell's Ath. 2/52	Cardiff	18	3						
GORMAN Paul A.	Dublin 6/8/63	Carlisle 11/89	Carlisle 12/91	Arsenal, B'ham. C.	58/6	1	4		5			
GREEN Richard E.	Wolverham. 22/11/67	Youth Trainee 7/86	Swindon 10/90	Gillingham	120/5	5	5		11	1	3	
GREEN Ronald R.	Birmingham 3/10/56	Walsall 6/84 (Loan Wim.,Bromsgrove) To: Brist.R.2/85		Scunthorpe	36				2		2	
GREGORY Anthony T.	Dawley 10/3/1947	App. 3/65	Telford 7/76		286/7		19		10/1		5	
GREGSON John	Skelmersdale 17/5/39	Chester 3/63	Mansfield 11/64	B'pool,Lincs.Camb.U.	56	6	1		2			
GRIFFIN Colin R.	Dudley Jan. 8/56	Derby 1/76			402/4	7	30		24		37	1
GRIFFIN Frank A.	Pendlebury 28/3/28	St.Augustines 3/50	West Brom. 4/51	Northampton	37	5						
GRIFFITHS Carl B.	Welshpool 16/7/71	Youth Trainee 9/88	Man. City 10/93		110/34	54	6	2	7/4	3	2	1
GROVES Alan J.	Southp.24/10/48(1978)	Chester 2/71	Bournemouth 10/72	South'pt,Oldham,B'Pool	76	11	3		3	1		
GUNN Bryn C.	Kettering 21/8/58	Loan Nott.For.11/85		Wal.,Man'fd,Peter'.Chest.	9							
HACKETT Gary S.	Stourbridge 11/10/62	Bromsgrove 7/83	Aberden 7/87	Stoke,W.Brm,Peter,Chest	142/8	17	6	1	15	2	11/1	4
HALPIN John T.	Manchester 5/6/27	Bury 8/51	Hereford 7/53		42		6					
HARKIN Terence	Derry 14/9/41	Southport 3/69	Finn Harps 7/71		79	30	4		1			
HARLEY Albert G.	Chest. 17/4/40(1994)	Lache FC 8/56	Swansea 9/64	Crewe,Stock.C.Chest.	220	14	16	1	13	2		
HARMON Darren J.	Northampton 30/1/73	Notts. Co. 2/92	Northamtpon 10/92		1/5	2						
HARPER Kenneth	Farnworth 27/4/24	Rochdale 8/50			1							

NAME	Born	From	To	Other Clubs	F.League A.	F.League G.	F.A.Cup A.	F.A.Cup G.	Lge. Cup A.	Lge. Cup G.	Welsh C. A.	Welsh C. G.
HARRIS A.T.(Razzer)	Berrington 20/12/45	App. 7/63	Bradford P.A. 7/68		54/1	4	4		2			
HARTFORD R. Asa	Clydebank 24/10/50	Oldham 8/89		(7 League Clubs)	22/3		1		3			
HAWKINS Dennis R.	Swansea 22/10/47	Leeds 10/68	Newport 5/72	Chester, Workington	50/8	9	4		2			
HAYES Stephen C.	Smethwick 28/1/52	Warley B. 2/74	Torquay 7/80		69/3		4		3/1		12	
HAYLOCK Paul	Lowestoft 24/3/63	Colchester 9/92		N'wich,Gill,Maid,Barnet	16/2	1	1					
HAYWOOD Raymond J.	Dudley 12/1/49	Stourbridge 5/74	Northampton 3/77		75/12	27	6	1	6		7/2	6
HEATHCOTE Michael	Kelloe 10/9/65	Sunderland 7/90	Cambridge 9/91	Halifax, York	43/1	6	5		6			
HEMSLEY Edward J.O.	Stoke 1/9/43	Juniors 7/61	Sheffield U. 8/68	Doncaster	234/1	21	25		12	1		
HENRY Anthony	Hough-le-Sp.26/11/57	Stoke 8/91	Mazda (Japan) 5/92	Man.C,Bolton,Oldham	39/1	7			4			
HILL James	Wishaw 19/8/31	Millwall 7/57			8							
HINES Derek J.	Moira 8/2/31	Leicester 11/61			16	5	2	3	1			
HOBSON Norman	Shrewsbury 22/8/33	Oswestry 10/54	Sankeys 1/62		212	5	10		2	1		
HOCKADAY David	Billingham 9/11/57	Hull 8/93		B'pool,Swindon,Stoke	30/2		3		4			
HODGES David	Ross-on-Wye 17/1/70	Trial 8/92		Mansfield, Torquay	1				1			
HOLTON James A.	Lesmaghow 11/4/51 (1993)	West Brom. 6/71	Manchest.U. 1/73	S'land,Cov,Shef.W.	67	4	6		3			
HOPE Eric	Oakengates 2/12/27	Man.City 8/50	Wrexham 10/51		27	3						
HOPKINS Robert A.	Birmingham 25/10/61	Birmingham 6/91	Hong Kong 5/92	A.Villa,Man.City,W.Brom,Col.	18/9	3			2/2			
HORNSBY Brian G.	Gt.Shelford 10/9/54	Arsenal 6/76	Sheff.Wed 3/78	Chest,Carlisle,Chestfd.	75	16	8	1	2		9	4
HUDSON John	Blaydon 5/10/21	Chesterfield 9/53	Buxton 7/55		48	20	1					
HUGHES Darren J.	Prescot 6/10/65	Everton 6/85	Brighton 9/86	Port Vale	34/3	1	1		5/1		1	
HUGHES Kenneth D.	Barmouth 9/1/66	Crystal P. 7/86	Wrexham 7/92		74		7		3		2	
HUGHES Terence P.	Llanidloes 10/3/53	App. 3/71			67/5	22	5				3	1
HUMPHREYS Alan	Chester 18/10/39	Lache 8/56	Leeds 2/60	Mansfield, Chest'fd.	32		1					
HUMPHRIES David W.	Wolverhampt. 10/8/39	Juniors 3/60	Wellington 8/61		3		1		1			
IRELAND Geoffrey J.C.	Paddington 1/12/35	Tottenham H.6/59	Folkestone 7/60		38	3	1					
IRVINE Alan J.	Broxburn 29/11/62	Dundee U. 2/88	Mazda, Japan 5/89	Liverpool	32/5	6	1		2			
IRVINE Samuel	Glasgow 7/1/56	App. 1/74	Stoke 6/78		198/9	18	13	1	8/1		15/1	5
JACKSON Arnold	Manchester 10/11/25	Joined M.League 49	Stockport 6/54		144	39	8	3				
JENKINS David J.	Bristol 2/9/46	Hereford 8/74	Workington 10/75	Ars.Tott,B'ford.Newpt.	2	1						
JOHNSON Paul	Stoke 25/5/59	Stoke 5/81	York 7/87		178/2	3	8/1		15		19/2	2
JOHNSTON Leslie H.	Glasgow 16/8/20	Stoke 7/53			16	6	1					
JONES Alan H.	Wrexham 22/9/49	App. 5/67			3							
JONES Bernard	Coventry 10/4/34	Cardiff 7/57			43	15	1					
JONES Michael Henry	Dawley 1940	App. 7/59	Wellington 2/62		22	1	1		3			
KASULE Victor P.A.	Glasgow 28/5/65	Meadow B.Th. 1/88	Hamilton Acc. 10/89		28/12	4	0/2		1/3			
KEARNEY Michael J.	Glasgow 18/2/53	Petershill 12/72	Chester 3/77	Reading	143/6	41	9	2	8		8/2	2
KEAY John P.	Glasgow 14/6/60	Celtic 7/77	Wrexham 9/82		152/3	20	15	1	7		17/1	2
KEERY Stanley	Derby 9/9/31	Blackburn 8/52	Newcastle 11/52		15	2						
KELLY Anthony G.	Prescot 1/1/64	West Brom. 1/89	Bolton 8/91	(6 League clubs)	100/1	15	7	1	8	1		
KEMP Stephen D.	Shrewsbury 2/5/55	App. 7/73			7/1							
KENNING Michael J.	Birmingham 18/8/40	Aston Villa 5/61	Charlton 11/62	N'wich,Wolvs,Watford	62	17	5	3	5			
KERR Andrew A.	West Bromwich 7/4/66	Youth Trainee 4/84	Cardiff 8/86	Wycombe W.	9/1		1/1				6	
KERR Archibald	Motherwell 30/8/35	Motherwell 1/57	Motherwell 7/57		13							
KING John (Jake)	Glasgow 29/1/55	App. 1/73	Wrexham 8/82	Cardiff	304/2	20	26	1	14		29	2
KINNAIRD Paul	Glasgow 11/11/66	Partick Thistle 2/93	St.Johnstone 3/93		4	1						
LARKIN Anthony G.	Wrexham 12/1/56	Wrexham 7/78	Carlisle 7/81	Hereford	54/1		5		2		8/1	2
LAWRENCE Leslie O.	Wolverham. 18/5/57	Stourbridge 2/75	Telford	(7 League clubs)	10/4	2	0/1				3/2	1
LEACH Albert	Bolton 10/7/31	From Amateur 8/51			2							
LEE Gordon E.	Hednesford 13/7/34	Aston Villa 7/66	Port Vale 5/68		2							
LEONARD Carleton C.	Oswestry 9/75	Juniors 9/75	Hereford 6/83	Cardiff	224/3	1	17	1	12		28	
LEONARD Gary A.	Newcastle 28/11/65	West Brom. 7/85	Bury 7/88	Hereford, Stockp.C.	48/18	1	1		8/2	1	4	2
LEWIS Norman	Shifnal 28/5/27	Oakengates T. 8/50	Hereford 7/53	Newport	62		7					
LEWORTHY David J.	Portsmouth 22/10/62	Loan Oxford 10/87		Portmth,Tott,Reading	6	3						
LINDSAY James Y.	Hamilton 12/7/49	Hereford 8/77		W.Ham,Watford,Colch	80/6		5	1	5/1		10	1
LINIGHAN David	Hartlepool 9/1/65	Derby 12/86	Ipswich 6/88	Hartlepool U.	65	1	3		5		2	
LOSKA Anthony S.P.	Chesterton 11/2/50	App. 3/68	Port Vale 7/71	Chester, Halifax	12		1		3			
LOUCHNANE J. Brian	Manchester 16/6/30	Leeds U. 7/53	Bournemouth 7/56		42	7						
LOUGHNANE Peter B.	Bournemouth 18/3/58	Manchester U. 2/77			24/7	4	0/1				5	4
LOYDEN Edward	Liverpool 22/12/45	Chester 5/68	Barnsley 12/68	Blackpool, Tranmere	11/1	2			1			
LYNCH Thomas M.	Limerick 10/10/64	Sunderland 1.90			164/10	10	12		12			
LYNE Neil G.F.	Leicester 4/4/70	L.Not.For.3/91 Sign.7/91	Cambridge 1/93	Walsall,C'field,Here.	77/3	17	3	2	6	2		
McALINDEN John	Carlisle 25/12/30	Celtic 5/57			12	3						
McBRIDE John	Kilsyth 31/12/23	Reading 12/52			78		1					
McCUE Alexander B.	Greenock 25/11/27	Grimsby 7/51			91	27	4	2				

NAME	Born	From	To	Other Clubs	F.League		F.A.Cup		Lge. Cup		Welsh C.	
					A.	G.	A.	G.	A.	G.	A.	G.
McCULLOCH Adam B.	Crossford 4/6/20	Northampton 1/52	Aldershot 2/53		46	17	7					
McGINLAY John	Inverness 8/4/64	Elgin City 2/89	Bury 7/90	Millwall, Bolton	58/2	27	1	2	4			
McGREGOR Alex. G.P.	Glasgow 12/11/50	Hibernian 1/75	Aldershot 9/76		46/3	7	2		2	1	7	1
McGUIRE Bernard P.	Liverpool 23/11/32	From Amateur 7/53	Winsford 7/54		2							
MacKENZIE Stephen	Romford 23/11/61	Sheff.Wed. 12/91		C.Pal.Man.C,W.Brom,Charl	19/5	1			2/1	1		
McKEOWN Gary J.	Oxford 19/10/70	Loan Arsenal 3/92			8	1						
MacLAREN Ross	Edinburgh 14/4/62	Glasgow Rang. 8/80	Derby 7/85	Swindon	158/3	18	7/1	1	11	3	16	2
McLAUGHLIN James C.	Derry 22/12/40	Birm.7/60·Peter 9/67	Swan. 5/63 & 11/72		283/14	77	25	14	18	9		
McLAUGHLIN J.M.L.	Clarkston 12/4/36	Loan T.Lanark 9/63			5							
McNAB Alexander D.	Birmingham 6/4/32	signed 12/54	Rugby 7/59		4							
McNALLY Bernard A.	Shrewsbury 17/2/63	App.2/81	West Brom. 7/89		278/4	23	13		22	3	16/1	9
MAGUIRE Paul B.	Glasgow 21/8/56	Kilbrnie Lades. 8/76	Stoke 9/80	Port Vale	143/8	35	18	12	8	1	16	9
MALONEY Joseph J.	Liverpool 26/1/34	Liverpool 7/54	Port Vale 7/61	Crewe Alex.	237	1	12					
MANDERS Ronald E.	Shrew.13/11/31(1980)	Juniors 12/54	Wellington 7/58		6							
MANN Arthur F.	Burntisland 23/1/48	Notts.Co. 6/79	Mansfield 10/79	Man.City, Blackpool	8	1			4			
MANNING John J.	Liverpool 11/12/40	Tranmere R. 10/66	Norwich 9/67	Bolton,Walsl,Crewe,Barns.	39	18	3	3	1	2		
MARLOWE Richard R.	Edinburgh 10/8/60	Derby 12/73	Brighton 7/74	Aldershot	31	4	2	1			4	3
MARSDEN Eric	Bolsover 3/1/30	Southend 3/53	Bath City 7/54		11							
MATTHIAS Terence	Wrexham 10/11/49	App. 5/67	Australia 6/74		96/3		3		3		2	
MAYLE Robert J.	Llandysul 18/12/38	Sentinel Jnrs.7/57	Walsall 7/59		8							
MELROSE James M.	Glasgow 7/10/58	Leeds 2/88		(5 League clubs)	27/22	3	0/1		3/1	2	1	
MEREDITH Trevor G.	Stottesdon 25/12/36	Burnley 4/64			229/6	41	23	7	12	1		
MIDDLETON Harold	Birmingham 18/3/37	Portsmouth 2/62	Mansfield 11/64	Wolves,Scun,Walsall	85	36	3	3	4	2		
MILLER J. Paul	Wolver.9/12/40(1963)	St.Nic.Boys Club 7/59			77		2		3			
MOIR Ian	Aberdeen 30/6/43	Wrexham 3/72	Wrexham 7/73	Man.U.B'pool,Chester	22/3	2	3					
MOIR Richard J.	Glasgow 22/10/45	Cumnock Jun. 3/69	Halifax 7/74		159/6	27	9	5	4		2	
MOORE John	Liverpool 9/9/45	Stoke 8/68	Swansea 1/73		144	1	11		4			
MOORE John	Consett 1/10/66	F.C.Utrecht 7/90	Crewe 1/91	(7 League clubs)	7/1	1			4	1		
MOORE Kevin	Loughb'urgh 20/10/57	App. 10/75			15/3	1					4/1	1
MORRALL Terence S.	Smethwick 24/11/38	Aston Villa 5/61	Wrexham 7/63	Southport	31		2		2			
MORRIS Geoffrey	Birmingham 8/2/49	Walsall 1/73	Port Vale 8/75		71/4	9	4		3	1	1	1
MORRIS Kevin G.	M.Wenlock 22/9/53	App. 7/71			9							
MOYES David W.	Glasgow 25/4/63	Bristol C. 10/87	Dunfermline 8/90	Camb. Preston	91/5	11	3	1	4		2	1
MULHEARN Ken.J.	Liverpool 16/10/45	Manchester C. 3/71	Crewe 8/80	Stockport	370		22		19		21	
MYCOCK John	Manchester 11/2/36	Congleton T. 12/58			6	1	1					
NARBETT J.V.	Birmingham 21/11/68	App. 9/86	Hereford 10/88	Luton	20/6	3	1		4		1/1	
NARDIELLO Gerardo	Warley 5/5/66	App. 5/84	Torquay 7/86	Cardiff	32/6	11	1/1		1		6/2	4
NAUGHTON W.B.S.	Catrine 20/3/62	Walsall 8/89	Walsall 1/91	Preston	43/6	4			5	2		
NIXON Jonathan C.	Ilkeston 20/1/48	Peterborough 8/77	Barnsley 3/88	Notts.C. Halifax	21/2	3	3	1	2		2	
NIXON William J.	Ballynaminch 28/9/41	Norwich 3/62	Ards 7/65		17	1	1					
O'DONNELL William	Clydebank 8/8/24	Northampton 6/51			130	45	6	2				
O'LOUGHLIN Nigel	Denbigh 19/1/54	Rhyl 8/72	Rochdale 8/76		23/10	7	1		1/1		2/2	
O'TOOLE C.Patrick	Dublin 1/2/65	Leicester 3/91	Cobh Ramblers 7/93		26/20	1	2/1					
OGRIZOVIC Steven	Mansfield 12/9/57	Liverpool 8/82	Coventry 8/84		84		5		7		2	
OLIVER Ralph	Tredager 30/3/34	Hereford 8/55	Hereford 7/58		7		1					
ORMSBY Brendon T.C.	Birmingham 1/10/60	Loan Leeds 1/90		Aston V.Donc.R.Scarb.	1							
OSBOURNE C. Gary J.	Wolver'ton 22/10/69	Youth Trainee 7/88	Telford		3/4						0/2	
OWEN Derek W.	Shrewsbury 11/3/38	Coton Rov. 1/57	Kidderminster 7/58		13	3	1					
PALIN Leigh G.	Worcester 12/9/65	Loan A. Villa 12/84		Brad.C.Stoke,Hull,Roch	2							
PARKIN Maurice	Sheffield 8/9/49	Leeds 7/68			4/1				1			
PARKIN Timothy J.	Penrith 31/12/57	Loan Port.V. 9/91		B.Burn,Bris.R.Swind.Darl.	5				1/1		·	
PARR John	Derby 21/11/20	Derby Co. 7/53			112		4					
PARRISH Sean	Wrexham 14/3/72	Touth Trainee 7/90	Telford 7/93	Doncaster	1/2				1			
PASKIN W. John	Capetown 1/2/62	Loan Wolves 2/92		WBA,Stock,Birm,Wrex	1							
PATTERSON Gary	Newcastle 27/11/72	Notts.C. 5/93	Wycombe 12/94		35/4	1	3		3			
PEARSON Nigel	Nottingham 21/8/63	Heanor 11/81	Sheff.Wed. 10/87	Middlesbrough	153	5	6		19		8	1
PERKS Stephen J.	M.Wenlock 19/4/63	App. 4/81			243		7		24		18	
PETTS Paul A.	Hackney 27/9/61	Bristol R. 8/80			138/11	16	7/2		11/1		13	
PHILIPS John T.S.	Shrewsbury 7/7/51	App. 11/68	A.Villa 10/69	Chel,Crewe,Bri'ton,Charl.	51		2		3			
PIGGOTT Gary D.	Warley 1/4/67	West Brom. 3/91			3/1							
PITTMAN Stephen	N.Carolina 18/7/67	E.Fife 3/89			31/1	2	1		3			
PLEAT David J.	Nottingham 15/1/45	Luton 7/67	Exeter 7/68	Nott.F. Peterbor.	10/2	1						
POTTER Harold	Tyldesley 20/5/23	Winsford U. 7/49	Rochdale 6/52		67		1					
POUTNEY David H.	Baschurch 12/10/39	Myddle 9/57	A.Villa 10/63 · 2/68	Chester 6/70	229/4	11	19		17	2		
PRAGG Michael K.	Shrewsbury 8/10/41	Juniors 5/59			5	1	1					

NAME	Born	From	To	Other Clubs	F.League A.	F.League G.	F.A.Cup A.	F.A.Cup G.	Lge. Cup A.	Lge. Cup G.	Welsh C. A.	Welsh C. G.
PRATLEY Richard G.	Banbury 12/1/63	Derby Co. 7/83		Scunthorpe	44/2	1	1		3	1	0/1	
PRICE Derek.E.	Wellington 14/2/32	Donnington 2/53	Aldershot 7/58		125	28	8	1				
PRICE John G.	Aberystwth 22/11/36	Walsall 7/58		Liverpool	9							
PRIEST Philip	Warley 9/9/66	Chelsea 7/87		Blackpool, Brentford	54/6	3	2/1		2/1		1	
PURDIE Jonathan	Corby 22/2/67	Brentford 6/89	Cheltenham 3/90	Wolves,Camb,Oxford	9/3	1			2/1			
QUINTON Walter	Anston 13/12/17	Trial Southend 10/52	Turned down Extension	R'ham,Birm,Brentford	3							
RAY John D.	Wolverhampt. 7/11/46	Amateur 7/64	Telford 7/66		7							
REAGAN C. Martin	York 12/5/24	Middlesborough 8/51	Portsmouth 1/53	Norwich,Hull,York	58	9	6	2				
REES Anthony A.	Merthyr Tydfil 1/8/64	Loan Birmingham 3/86		Peter,Barns,Grim,W.Brom	1/1							
REGAN M. John	Worcester 18/6/44	Birmingham 10/64	Brentford 3/66	Crewe A.Donc.	21	6	5	3	2			
ROBERTS David A.	Birmingham 21/12/46	Aston Villa 3/68	Swansea 5/74		224/6	20	11/1		8	1	2	
ROBERTS Harold	Liverpool 12/1/20	Birmingham 6/51	Scunthorpe 7/53	Chesterfield	70	16	2	2				
ROBERTS Ian P.	Glasgow 28/9/55	App. 9/72	Crewe 7/76		93/2	1	6		2		3	
ROBERTS Lee J.	Market Dray. 23/7/57	App. 1/75	Exeter 9/77		9/6	1			1		3	1
ROBERTS Michael J.	Birmingham 21/5/60	Apprentice			0/1						3	1
ROBINSON Colin R.	Birmingham 15/5/60	Mile Oak Rov. 11/82	Birmingham 1/88	Hereford	176/18	41	5/2	2	19	8	16/1	2
ROBINSON David W.	Manchester 25/11/21	Man.United 8/49			10	1						
RODGERS Arnold W.	Rotherham 5/12/23	Bristol City 6/56	Chippenham T. 2/57	Huddersfield	13	3	1					
ROSS Robert H.	Edinburgh 18/5/42	Hearts 6/63	Brentford 3/66	Cambridge United	99	29	13	3	4	1		
ROUGVIE Douglas	Ballingry 24/5/56	Brighton 8/88	Fulham 2/89	Chelsea	20/1	3	1				1	
ROWLEY G. Arthur	Wolverhampt. 21/4/26	Leicester 6/58		Fulham,West Brom.A.	236	152	19	11	12	4		
RUSSELL Raymond J.	Walsall 9/3/30	Burton Albion 5/54	Crewe Alex. 3/60		168	55	9	6				
RUTHERFORD Mark R.	Birmingham 23/3/72	Loan Shelborne 2/94			7/7							
RYAN Darren T.	Oswestry 3/7/72	Youth Trainee 10/90	Chester 7/92	Stockport,Rochdale	3/1							
SANKEY Martin A.	Telford 4/5/64	App. 2/82	Telford 7/84		0/5				1/2		2	
SCOTT S. Robin	Shrewsbury 31/3/46	Juniors 4/64	Rugby 7/65		18	2						
SEABURY Kevin	Shrewsbury 24/11/73	Youth Trainee 11/91			0/1							
SHAW Gary R.	Birmingham 21/1/61	Klagenfurt(Aust)9/90		Aston V.B'pool,Walsall	20/2	5	5/1	5	1			
SHIELDS James	Glasgow 28/11/31	Hibernian 5/56	Cowdenbeath 7/57		24	6						
SIMPSON Alexander	Glasgow 24/11/24	Southampton 7/55			100	4	6					
SKEECH H. Gordon	Earlsdon 15/5/34	Runcorn 11/54	Runcorn 7/63		223	2	20	1	11			
SMALE T. Harold	Swansea 16/7/28	Derby Co. 7/50	Aldershot 8/52		14	1	1					
SMITH Kenneth	South Shields 21/5/32	Blackpool 10/57	Gateshead 11/58	Sund.Darling,Car.H'fax	44	20	1	1				
SMITH Mark A.	Bellshill 16/12/64	Nott.For. 8/91		Stoke,Reading,Mansf'd	54/7	2	3/1	1	5			
SMITH Neil	Warley 10/2/70	Youth Trainee 7/88	Redditch U. 7/89	Lincoln	0/1						2	
SMITH Nigel P.	Leeds 21/12/69	Trial Bury 8/92		Burnley	2							
SMITH Terrance P.	Cheltenham 10/6/51	Loan Stoke 2/73			2							
SPINK Dean P.	Birmingham 22/1/67	Aston Villa 3/90		Scar. Bury.	137/22	31	12/1	2	14/2			
STAMPS J.D.(Jackie)	Maltby 2/12/18 (1991)	Derby 12/53		Mansfield,N.Brighton	22	4						
STARKEY Malcolm J.	Bulwell 25/1/36	Blackpool 6/59	Chester 4/63		121	34	12	5	7	1		
STEELE Timothy W.	Coventry 1/2/67	App. 12/85	Wolves 2/89	Stoke,Brad.C.Hereford	41/20	5			3/1	1	2/1	
STEPHENSON G.R.	Derby 19/11/42	Derby 6/64	Rochdale 7/65		3							
STEVENS Gary M.	Birmingham 30/8/54	Cardiff 9/82	Brentford 7/86	Hereford	144/6	30	6	1	9	2	15	5
STEWART George	Chirnside 18/10/20	Q.P.R. 1/53		Brentford	10	2						
STOBART Barry H.	Doncaster 6/6/38	Aston Villa 10/67		Wolves,Man.City	34/2	9	6/1					
SUMMERFIELD Kevin	Walsall 7/1/59	Plymouth 10/90		(5 League clubs)	126/18	21	10/1	1	13	7		
TARBUCK Alan D.	Liverpool 10/10/45	Preston 3/73	Rochdale 7/76	Crewe,Chester	107/17	17	3		6		11	1
TAYLOR Brian J.	Walsall 24/3/37	Rotherham 8/63	Port Vale 8/65	Walsall,Birm,Barnsley	73	8	6		4			
TAYLOR R. Mark	Walsall 22/2/66	Sheff.Wed. 2/91		Walsall	131	11	8		9			
TESTER Paul L.	Stroud 10/3/59	Cheltenham T. 7/83	Hereford 8/88		86/12	12	1/3		7/3	1	17	8
THOM Lewis M.	Stornaway 10/4/44	Dundee U. 9/65	Lincoln 5/67	Bradford P.A.	48/1	5	2		1			
THOMAS Michael R.	Mochdre 7/7/54	Wichita 8/88	Leeds 6/89	(8 League clubs)	40	1	1		1		1	
THOMPSON Joseph P.	Seaham. 15/11/27	Luton 7/51			7		1					
TONG David A.	Blackpool 21/9/55	Blackpool 9/78	Cardiff 8/82	Roch,Bris.C.Gill,Camb.U	156/4	8	16	1	8		15	2
TOOZE Robert W.	Bristol 19/12/46	Bristol City 3/69		Gillingham	73		5		1			
TREHERNE Cyril A.	Wellington 12/3/28	Amateur 11/50	Wellington 8/51		4	1						
TUCKER Kenneth J.	Merthyr 15/7/35	Cardiff 2/58	Northampton 3/60		46	8						
TURNER Alan	Hull 5/7/43	Coventry 7/66	Bradford P.A. 5/67		14/2	3	2	2	1			
TURNER Graham J.	Elles.Port 5/10/47	Chester 1/73		Wrexham	342/13	22	27	1	17	2	32	3
TURNER Kenneth	Barnsley 22/4/41	Huddersfield 7/63	York 8/66		64	1	3		4			
TURNER Robert P.	Durham 18/9/66	Loan Notts.C. 3/93		(8 League clubs)	9							
TYRER Arthur S.	Manchester 25/2/31	Leeds 6/55	Aldershot 6/56		24	3	3					
WAKEMAN Alan D.	Walsall 20/11/20	Blox.Strollers 2/53		Donc. Aston Villa	6							
WALKER Michael S.G.	Colwyn Bay 28/11/45	Reading 6/64	York 6/66	Watf'd,Charlton,Colch	7							

NAME	Born	From	To	Other Clubs	F.League		F.A.Cup		Lge. Cup		Welsh C.	
					A.	G.	A.	G.	A.	G.	A.	G.
WALKER ROGER W.	Shrewsbury 17/2/44	Juniors 5/60			1							
WALKER Ronald	Swansea 24/2/33	Amateur 11/55			1							
WALL Peter	Westbury 13/9/44	App. 9/62	Wrexham 11/65	Liv.Palace,Leyton.O	18		4					
WALLACE Joseph B.	Glas.25/12/33(1994)	RAOC Donn. 3/54	Southport 10/62		337	3	21		11			
WALLER David H.	Urmston 20/12/63	Crewe 7/86	Chesterfield 3/87		11	3	1	1	4/1	2	2	2
WALSH Alan	Darlington 9/12/56	Besiktas(Turkey)1/92	Southampton 2/92	(6 League clubs)	2							
WALTERS George	Wolverhampt.21/6/35	Jenks + Cattell 2/57	Newport Co. 9/63		246	3	19	1	13			
WALTERS Robert	Glasgow 9/3/44	Winsford 12/62	Sankey's 7/64		1							
WALTON David	Ashington 10/4/73	Sheffield U. 11/93			27	5	3	1				
WARDLE Robert I.	Halifax 5/3/55	Bristol C. 7/74	Liverpool 8/82	Wrexham 9/83	131		16		4		15	
WASSALL Kim D.	Wolverhampt. 9/6/57	Finland 11/89		N'ton,Hull,Swan,Wolves	0/2		0/1					
WATTS Julian D.	Sheffield 17/3/71	Loan Shef.Wed.12/92		Rotherham	9							
WEBB James K.	Warrington 6/7/38	Lymm Rovers 4/56			2	1						
WEIGH Raymond E.	Flint 23/6/28	Stockport 6/54	Aldershot 7/57	Bournemouth	107	44						
WEIR William H.	Bailleston 11/4/68	Bailleston Jun. 3/90	Bailleston Jun. 8/91		4/13	1	0/2					
WHEATLEY H. Joseph	Eastham 9/5/20	Port Vale			7							
WHITAKER Colin	Leeds 14/6/32	Bradford P.A. 6/56	Q.P.R. 2/61	Shef.W,Roch,Old,Barrow	152	59	9	1	1			
WILLIAMS Brian	Salford 5/11/55	Bristol City 7/87		Bury,QPR,Swin,Bris.R.	62/3	1	2	1	6			
WILLIAMS Derek O.	Chirk 3/9/49	Oswestry 10/69	Oswestry 7/70		1							
WILLIAMS Lee	Birmingham 3/2/73	Loan Aston V. 11/92		Peterborough	2/1		1/1	1				
WILLIAMS Mark	Bangor 10/12/73	App. 7/92	Newtown 7/93		0/2							
WILLIAMS Mark S.	Cheshire 28/9/70	Newtown 3/92			63/5	2	5		5/1			
WILLIAMS Robert R.	Liverpool 25/10/27	Wrexham 10/51			5							
WILLIAMS Wayne	Telford 17/11/63	App. 11/81	Northampton 1/89	Walsall	212/9	7	8/1		24	4	17/1	
WIMBLETON Paul P.	Havant 13/11/64	Bristol C. 1/90	Exeter 9/91	Ports.Cardiff,Maidst.	25/9	1	1/1		1			
WITHE Christopher	Liverpool 25/11/62	Mansfield 8/93		(5 League clubs)	23/3		1		4/1			
WOOD Alfred E.H.	Macclesfield 25/10/45	Man.City 6/66	Millwall 6/72	Hull,M'bro,Walsall	257/1	65	15	4	11	5		
WOODS Raymond G.	Birkenhead 7/6/65	Coventry 3/94		Tranmere,Wigan	7/2	1						
WORSLEY Graeme	Liverpool 4/1/69	Bootle 3/89		Bury	83/22	4	8		7			
WRIGHT M. Howard	Winsford 22/10/40	App. 3/64	Crewe 9/66		0/1							
WRIGHT Patrick D.J.	Oldbury 17/11/40	Birmingham C. 9/62	Derby 10/67	Rotherham,Southend	201	3	21		12			

OTHER PLAYERS (No Football League appearances)

NAME	Born	From	To	Other Clubs	F.League		F.A.Cup		Lge. Cup		Welsh C.	
					A.	G.	A.	G.	A.	G.	A.	G.
CRANE Andrew D.	Ipswich 1/3/67	Ipswich T. 6/87	Hereford 7/88								2	
HODGETTS Andrew	West Brom. 25/3/70	Trainee 7/86	Stourbridge 5/88								1	
HOYLE Philip	Shrewsbury 23/4/49	Juniors									1	
KELLY Mark D.	Blackpool 27/10/66	Blackpool 12/85	Cardiff 6/87	Fulham							2	
KING Steven											1	
MALCOLM Paul A.	Gateshead 11/12/64	Rochdale 7/85	Barnsley 6/86	Doncaster					1		1	
MEREDITH Neil	Telford 30/12/67	Yts Trainee									1	
NEIL Michael	Kilmarnock 8/1/54	Kilbirnie Lades. 2/79	Stranraer 6/80								1	
O'CONNOR Andrew	Stoke 1/11/65	W.B.A.									2/1	1

The following made appearances in Shropshire Senior Cup matches only:

ARCH David, BROOKMAN Nick, COOK Timothy, FEE Gregory, GOODWIN Robert, JONES Glynn,
JONES Trevor, McDONNELL Matthew, MACEY John, MELLORS Duane, MULCAHY David, PIKE Richard, STEELE James, YATES Jason.

KEY:
The above tables are generally self explanatory. The second column shows the place and date (or year) of birth. Similarly the third and fourth columns shows the Club the player came from (to Shrewsbury) and was transferred to (from Shrewsbury), with dates (or month and year). Where a player has been transferred to and or from Shrewsbury more than once, then the details appear in brackets within the appropriate column. The fifth column lists (often in abbreviated form) the player's other Football League clubs (where known). The appearance ('A.') columns show the number of appearances made in that competition, followed by substitute appearances (where applicable). The number of goals scored in that competition are shown in the 'G.' columns.

THINGS YOU STILL DON'T KNOW ABOUT SHREWSBURY TOWN F.C.

1. Commentator Alan Parry had an unsuccessful trial while Arthur Rowley was manager.

2. The quickest goal Town ever conceded was scored in eight seconds, by Keith East for Bournemouth at Dean Court on 31 August 1968.

3. Town's lucky Blue and Yellow stripes, which won promotion in 1979, were Tim Yates' Racing Colours.

4. Current Chairman Ray Bailey is an England International Clay Pigeon shot.

5. The Pigeon Box press box started life behind the Station goal.

6. Paul Petts and his dad, John, are the only father and son England Youth Internationals.

7. From Richie Barker's 2nd game in charge until the 2nd home game in Division Two, Town were unbeaten at home. A run of 31 games.

8. Town have played League Football on 104 different grounds (plus Highbury and Goodison Park in the F.A. Cup).

9. All the other five sides in the bottom six of Division Three North, at the end of Town's first season are no longer in the League.

10. The most penalties converted by a Town player in the League is 21, by Ian Atkins.

STATISTICAL NOTES

The seasonal statistical pages that follow have been designed for easy reference, and are generally self explanatory, however the following notes are added to avoid confusion:

Left hand (first) column: Provides the match numbers of the particular competition (e.g. Football League, Friendly, etc.), or the round number in a Cup Competition (E = extra, PR = preliminary round, Q = qualifying round, R = round proper -e.g. 1R = 1st round proper, Rr = round replay - e.g. 2Rr = 2nd round replay, 2R2r = 2nd round 2nd replay, R1 = round 1st leg, R2 = round 2nd leg - e.g. 1R2 = 1st round 2nd leg, SF = Semi-final, F = Final).
Second column: Provides the date (Months abbreviated)
Third column: Provides the opposition ('Home' matches in upper case - capital letters)
Fifth column: Is the final score. Sixth column: The half-time score. Seventh column: The attendance (where known).
Eighth column: The goalscorers. O.G. indicates a goal scored by an opposition player.

The numbers used in the charts refer to the normally accepted position for that period (numbered shirts did not appear until the 1939-40 season), e.g. 1 = goalkeeper, 2 = right-back .... 10 = inside-left, 11 = left-winger. Substitutes are included, i.e. 12 and/or 14. Where used, 12 replaced the asterisk suffixed player (e.g. 4*), and 14 replaced the 'hash' suffixed player (e.g. 6#).
Where 'additional player(s)' are listed, their position/shirt number is shown followed by the match number(s) (or cup round) played in, e.g. 4/8 = position number 4 played in match number 8.
A blank in any column (including 'missing' goalscorers) indicates that that specific detail is unknown.

SEASON 1886/87

Friendlies

No	Date	Opposition	Res.	Goalscorers
1	18 Sep	Wellington	1-1	A.Davies
2	25	Crosswells Brewery	2-7	A.Davies(2)
3	2 Oct	Chirk	1-6	Morris
4	16	WELLINGTON T.	5-2	O.G., Watkins(3), A.Davies
5	23	Birmingham Excelcior	0-3	
6	30	STAFFORD ROAD	2-1	
7	11 Nov	Grammer Schools	3-6	
8	20	Druids	1-0	A.Davies
9	7 Dec	Oswestry	1-4	
10	14	OLD SALOPIANS	7-0	
11	17	Shrewsbury School	1-2	
12	25	St. George's	1-1	O.G.
13	29 Jan	CROSSWELLS BREWERY	1-1	Bowdler
14	5 Feb	St. George's	1-2	
15	12	Wellington T.	3-0	Pearson
16	19	Grammer Schools	2-0	Brazier
17	26	BIRMINGHAM EXCELCIOR	9-1	Bowdler, O.G., Watkins, Steadman
18	5 Mar	St. George's	0-1	
19	12	OSWESTRY	3-1	Bowdler(2), Watkins
20	19	IRONBRIDGE	2-1	Brazier, Stanford
21	26	CHIRK	1-3	A.Davies
22	3 Apr	Ironbridge	1-0	Edwards
23	8	DRUIDS	6-0	
24	16	Oswestry	0-7	

Welsh Senior Cup

No	Date	Opposition	Res.	Goalscorers
1R	6 Nov	Wem White Stars	10-0	
2R	18 Dec	NEWTOWN	0-1	

Birmingham Senior Cup

No	Date	Opposition	Res.	Goalscorers
1R	9 Oct	STAFFORD RANGERS	6-1	Pearson,A.Davs(2),Wtkns(2),Frnce
2R	13 Nov	Wellington T.	3-1	A.Davies, Watkins
3R	4 Dec	DARLASTON ALL SAINTS	2-2	France, A.Davies
3Rr	27	Darlaston All Saints	0-1	

SEASON 1887/88

Friendlies

No	Date	Opposition	Res.	Goalscorers
1	17 Sep	GREAT BRIDGE UNITY	4-4	France,Rhodes,Steadman,Morris
2	24	CHIRK	2-4	Pearson, Brazier
3	6 Oct	CHESTER COLLEGE	3-1	Edwards, Morris, G.Jones
4	8	NEWPORT	2-3	Watkins(2)
5	22	Aston Unity	1-2	Watkins
6	26 Nov	Shrewsbury Schools	1-0	A.Davies
7	3 Dec	Aston Villa Res.	2-0	Rowlands, Gosson
8	10	CHIRK	2-5	Morris(2)
9	17	OSWESTRY	1-1	O.G.
10	24	BUILTH	2-3	A.Davies, Rhodes
11	26	ASTON VILLA	1-0	Pearson
12	31	Stafford Road	1-2	
13	28 Jan	MARKET DRAYTON	7-1	Edwrds(2),Pearsn(2),Brazr(2),Gssn
14	18 Feb	Wellington T.	1-4	
15	25	Newport	2-1	Brazier, Pearson
16	30 Mar	WREXHAM OLYMPIC	3-2	Brazier, Edwards, Hancox
17	31	West Bromwich Albion Res.	2-1	

F.A. Cup

No	Date	Opposition	Res.	Goalscorers
1R	15 Oct	Macclesfield	3-1	Pearson(3)
2R	5 Nov	Chirk	2-10	Watkins, Morris

Welsh Senior Cup

No	Date	Opposition	Res.	Goalscorers
1R	29 Oct	OSWESTRY	0-2	

Birmingham Senior Cup

No	Date	Opposition	Res.	Goalscorers
1R	1 Oct	Stoke	0-2	

Shropshire Mayor's Charity Cup

No	Date	Opposition	Res.	Goalscorers
1R		Wellington T.		
1Rr		Wellington T.	w/o	scratched
SF	14 Apr	St. George's	1-2	Pearson

SEASON 1888/89

Friendlies

No	Date	Opposition	Res.	Goalscorers
1	15 Sep	LUDLOW	3-1	Bowdler, A.Davies, Brazier
2	22	IRONBRIDGE	2-2	Bowdler(2)
3	29	Newport	2-3	
4	20 Oct	NANTWICH	3-2	Ritchie(2)
5	17 Nov	Wellington T.	7-1	A.Davies(2), Ellis
6	1 Dec	Wrexham	2-2	Bowdler, Hancox
7	22	CREWE STEAM SHEDS	3-1	Ritchie, Edwards
8	29	ST. GEORGE'S	0-1	
9	5 Jan	SHIFNAL	7-1	Edwrds(2),Hncx,Prsn,A.Davs,Rtche
10	2 Feb	CHIRK	3-0	Ritchie, Gosson, Edwards
11	9	Wellington St. George's	2-3	
12	16	Shifnal	4-1	
13	19	Shrewsbury Schools	5-1	A.Davies(2), Pearson(2), Edwards
14	23	NEWPORT	7-1	Rtche,Hncx,Edwrds,Gssn,Prsn,A.Davs(2)
15	8 Mar	Shrewsbury Schools	6-2	Gosson(3),Edwards,Wlliams,Pearsn
16	16	WELLINGTON T.	1-5	
17	23	Chester St. Oswald's	0-1	
18	14 Apr	Wrexham	1-1	Gosson

F.A. Cup

No	Date	Opposition	Res.	Goalscorers
1Q	6 Oct	St. George's	1-1	Pearson
1Qr	13	ST. GEORGE'S	2-1	
2Q	27	Burton Wanderers	0-4	

Birmingham Senior Cup

No	Date	Opposition	Res.	Goalscorers
1Q		Bye		
2Q	5 Nov	ASBURY	9-0	Pearsn,Rtche(3),Gssn,Edwrds,Hncx
3Q	24	Aston Shakespeare	2-2	Ritchie, Gosson
3Qr	15 Dec	ASTON SHAKESPEARE	4-1	Pearson(2), Ritchie, Edwards
1R	24	WOLVERHAMPTON W.	0-10	

Shropshire Mayor's Charity Cup

No	Date	Opposition	Res.	Goalscorers
1R	26 Jan	Wem T.	6-1	Edwards
SF	30 Mar	OSWESTRY	1-0	A.Davies
F	27 Apr	ST. GEORGE'S	1-2	

SEASON 1889/90

Friendlies

No	Date	Opposition	Res.	Goalscorers
1	14 Sep	NEWPORT T.	2-2	Rowlands, Murphy
2	21	SHIFNAL	11-1	A.Davs(4),A.Ells(2),Rwlnds(2),Prsn,Mphy
3	28	Ludlow	1-4	
4	6 Oct	Grammer School	3-3	Bills, O.G., Jagger
5	16 Nov	NEWTOWN	5-0	A.Davies(2),Pearsn,Mrphy,Rowlnds
6	30	Chirk	0-10	
7	7 Dec	Ludlow	2-0	A.Davies, Murphy
8	14	St. George's	1-2	Murphy
9	21	Wrexham	1-5	
10	26	BURTON ALMA		
11	28	Chester St. Oswald's	0-4	
12	4 Jan	Chirk	0-1	
13	18	DRUIDS	3-0	Phasey
14	25	SHREWSBURY VICTORIA	4-1	Pearson(2), Gosson, O.G.
15	1 Feb	STAFFORD RANGERS	3-0	Gosson, Holloway, Phasey
16	15	CHIRK	0-2	
17	22	WELLINGTON T.	18-0	*
18	8 Mar	WELSHPOOL	11-0	
19	22	CHESTER ST. OSWALD'S	4-0	A.Davies(3), Pearson
20	29	WREXHAM	4-1	Bowdler, Phasey(2)
21	12 Apr	CHIRK	3-3	Holloway, Rowlands, Pearson

* Bowdler(8), Phasey(3), Rowlands(2), Gosson(3), Aston, Murphy

F.A. Cup

No	Date	Opposition	Res.	Goalscorers
Q1	5 Oct	NANTWICH	3-2	Pearson, Rowlands, A.Davies
Q2	26	Chester St. Oswald's	1-6	Murphy

Welsh Senior Cup

No	Date	Opposition	Res.	Goalscorers
1R	19 Oct	ABERDARE	11-0	*
2R		Bye		
3R	11 Jan	Newtown	0-4	

* Rowlands(4), A.Davies(2), Morris(2), Gosson, Steadman, A.Ellis

Birmingham Senior Cup

No	Date	Opposition	Res.	Goalscorers
1R	12 Oct	NEWPORT T.	3-0	A.Davies(2), Gosson
2R		Bye		
3R	23 Nov	Oldbury T.	0-4	

Shropshire Senior Cup

No	Date	Opposition	Res.	Goalscorers
1R	9 Nov	Wellington T.	3-1	
SF	1 Mar	Ironbridge	1-4	Aston

Shropshire Mayor's Charity Cup

No	Date	Opposition	Res.	Goalscorers
	5 Apr	ST. GEORGE'S	4-0	Phasey(2), J.Davies, Gosson
	19	IRONBRIDGE	4-1	Gosson(2), Pearson, A.Davies
	3 May	NEWPORT	5-1	Bowdlr,Gossn,Pearsn,A.Davs,Phsy

SEASON 1890/91

Shropshire & District League

No	Date	Opposition	Res.	Goalscorers
1	13 Sep	Wellington T.	1-2	
2	20	NEWPORT	5-0	A.Davies(2),Phasey,Hollowy,A.Ellis
3	18 Oct	OSWESTRY	9-0	A.Ells(2),Phsy(2),A.Davs,Brdly,Hllwy(2)
4	15 Nov	ST. GEORGE'S	3-2	A.Davies, Gosson
5	6 Dec	Whitchurch	3-2	
6	26	LUDLOW	7-2	A.Ellis(4), Gosson, Green(2)
7	17 Jan	St. George's	2-3	
8	24	WELLINGTON T.	2-2	A.Ellis(2)
9	7 Feb	Newport	0-1	
10	14	Oswestry	3-0	
11	28	Ludlow	1-0	A.Ellis
12	11 Apr	Ironbridge	0-4	
13	18	IRONBRIDGE	2-0	A.Davies
14	25	WHITCHURCH	4-1	A.Ellis(2), A.Davies, Green

```
P  W  D  L  F  A  Pts
14 9  1  4  42 21 19    (Pos. Runners Up)
```

Welsh Senior Cup

No	Date	Opposition	Res.	Goalscorers
1R		Bye		
2R	29 Nov	BUILTH	4-1	Holloway, Pearson, O.G., A.Ellis
3R	3 Jan	OSWESTRY	6-0	A.Ellis, Gosson(4), O.G.
SF	31	Mold T.	5-0	Gosson, A.Davies, Green, A.Ellis
F	30 Mar	Wrexham	5-2	Holloway,A.Ellis,Green,A.Davies(2)

Shropshire Mayor's Charity Cup

No	Date	Opposition	Res.	Goalscorers
1R	14 Mar	NEWPORT	2-1	Green
SF	2 May	Ironbridge	0-5	

SEASON 1891/92

Shropshire & District League

No	Date	Opposition	Res.	Goalscorers
1	26 Sep	Newport	4-5	
2	3 Oct	Wolverhampton W.Res.	0-5	
3	14 Nov	Nantwich	1-7	
4	21	WHITCHURCH	7-1	Holloway, A.Ellis(5)
5	5 Dec	St. George's	3-7	
6	12	WELLINGTON T.	4-1	
7	26	WOLVERHAMPTON W.RES.	1-5	A.Ellis
8	2 Jan	IRONBRIDGE	3-2	
9	16	Whitchurch	2-2	
10	23	NEWPORT	8-0	Hllwy,Jnes,Gssn(2),Davs,Blss(2),A.Ells
11	30	NANTWICH	2-0	Holloway, Bostock
12	6 Feb	Ironbridge	2-2	
13	13	Stafford R.	1-2	
14	5 Mar	ST. GEORGE'S	4-4	Gosson(2), A.Ellis(2)
15	12	Wellington T.	3-3	
16	19	STAFFORD R.	3-2	

```
P  W  D  L  F  A  Pts
16 6  4  6  48 48 16    (Pos. 6th)
```

Welsh Senior Cup

No	Date	Opposition	Res.	Goalscorers
1R	31 Oct	St. George's		
2R	28 Nov	CARDIFF	7-0	A.Ellis(4), G.Ellis, Green(2)
3R	19 Dec	NEWTOWN	5-1	
SF	20 Feb	Westminster Rvrs.	4-0	A.Ellis(2), Holloway, Bostock
SFr	14 Mar	Westminster Rvrs.	1-3	Bostock

SEASON 1892-93

Shropshire & District League

No	Date	Opposition	Res.	Goalscorers
1	24 Sep	HEREFORD	4-2	
2	8 Oct	NEWTOWN	2-1	Holloway, Edwards
3	15	NEWPORT	2-0	
4	22	Whitchurch	7-3	
5	29	Wellington T.	4-4	
6	12 Nov	Ironbridge	3-3	O.G.
7	26	Newport	3-3	
8	10 Dec	St. George's	6-6	
9	21 Jan	Hereford	2-2	
10	28	STAFFORD RANGERS	2-1	A.Ellis
11	4 Feb	ST. GEORGE'S *	9-0	Edwards(2), A.Ellis(2)
12	25	IRONBRIDGE	1-1	A.Ellis
13	4 Mar	WELLINGTON T.	3-2	E.Bowdler, R.C.Jones, A.Ellis
14	11	WHITCHURCH	3-2	Stinchcombe(2), Rowlands
15	18	Stafford Rangers	0-1	
16	1 Apr	Newtown	1-3	
17	22	ST. GEORGE'S	2-3	

P W D L F A Pts
16 7 6 3 45 37 20   (Pos. 4th)

Shropshire Mayor's Charity Cup

No	Date	Opposition	Res.	Goalscorers
1R	25 Mar	OSWESTRY U.	3-0	R.C.Jones, A.Ellis
SF	15 Apr	Wrockwardine Wood	w/o	
F	29	WELLINGTON T.	2-1	R.C.Jones

* St. Georges fielded reserve side, result did not count.

SEASON 1893-94

Shropshire & District League

No	Date	Opposition	Res.	Goalscorers
1	2 Sep	Newtown	0-9	
2	9	OSWESTRY U.	6-0	Bliss(2),R.C.Jones(3),Stinchcombe
3	16	WELLINGTON T.	4-2	
4	23	Newport	4-1	
5	30	MARKET DRAYTON	8-3	R.C.Jones, E.H.Bowdler(3)
6	21 Oct	Oswestry U.	3-2	Bliss, W.Hobin, R.C.Jones
7	4 Nov	Hereford U.	1-2	E.H.Bowdler
8	25	WHITCHURCH	7-3	JCH.Bwdlr(3),W.Bliss(2),RC.Jnes,Lter
9	2 Dec	Ironbridge	2-1	
10	23	ST. GEORGE'S	1-2	J.C.H.Bowdler
11	30	NEWPORT	1-1	Luter
12	13 Jan	Whitchurch	2-3	
13	10 Mar	Market Drayton	3-2	Hobin, E.H.Bowdler, R.C.Jones
14	31	NEWTOWN	3-0	
15	14 Apr	Wellington T.	1-1	Holloway
16	16	St. George's	0-5	
17	19	IRONBRIDGE	4-1	
18	26	HEREFORD	11-1	

P W D L F A Pts
17 11 2 4 60 37 24   (Pos. 3rd)

F.A. Amateur Cup

No	Date	Opposition	Res.	Goalscorers
1R	3 Feb	BEESTON (NOTTS)	5-2	W.Blss,Hobn,JCH.Bwdlr(2),RC.Jnse
2R	17	Old St. Stephens	2-2	O.G., J.C.H.Bowdler
2Rr	24	OLD ST. STEPHENS	4-0	
3R	3 Mar	Bishop Auckland	1-3	W.Bliss

Welsh Senior Cup

No	Date	Opposition	Res.	Goalscorers
1R	28 Oct	WELLINGTON ST. GRGE'S	6-1	W.Bliss(4), J.C.H.Bowdler, Barratt
2R		WELLINGTON T.	w/o	
3R	9 Dec	Ironbridge	4-1	E.H.Bowdler
4R	20 Jan	Oswestry U.	0-2	

Birmingham Senior Cup

No	Date	Opposition	Res.	Goalscorers
1R	7 Oct	Old Hill Wanderers	0-3	

Shropshire Mayor's Charity Cup

No	Date	Opposition	Res.	Goalscorers
1R	10 Feb	Oswestry U.	3-2	EH.Bowdler,JCH.Bowdler,W.Bliss
SF	7 Apr	St. George's	2-3	JCH.Bowdler,W.Bliss (played at Irobridge)

Wednesbury Charity Cup

No	Date	Opposition	Res.	Goalscorers
1R	11 Nov	MADELEY T.	7-0	RC.Jnes(2),EH.Bwdlr(2),Lutr,Brdley
2R	1 Jan	Wellington St. George's	0-1	

SEASON 1894/95

Shropshire & District League

No	Date	Opposition	Res.	Goalscorers
1	8 Sep	NEWTOWN	4-3	W.Bliss,Gwilliam,Rogers,EH.Bowdlr
2	15	WROCKWARDINE WD.	4-1	Barratt, W.Bliss(2), R.C.Jones
3	22	Wellington T.	6-0	RC.Jnes,Gwlliam,EH.Bwdlr,A.Ellis(2),Wllms
4	29	Whitchurch	1-1	A.Ellis
5	6 Oct	IRONBRIDGE	4-1	
6	20	HEREFORD	12-1	EH.Bowdler(3),RC.Jones(4),A.Ellis(4),G.Ellis
7	10 Nov	NEWPORT	6-0	Horly,Rgrs,Gwlliam,EH.Bwdlr(2),RC.Jnes
8	24	Wrockwardine Wd.	0-2	
9	1 Dec	Ironbridge	2-4	
10	5 Jan	Newport	1-4	
11	19	Oswestry Utd.	0-2	
12	16 Mar	Newtown	2-2	
13	28	HEREFORD	1-0	
14	6 Apr	ST. GEORGE'S	2-1	Garrett, Watkins
15	13	Hereford	0-2	
16	20	OSWESTRY UTD.	1-1	A.Ellis
17	25	WHITCHURCH	6-2	R.C.Jones(4), W.H.Ellis(2)
18	29	WELLINGTON T.	2-2	A.E.Jones, L.Salt

P W D L F A Pts
17 8 4 5 42 28 20   (Pos. 3rd)

F.A. Amateur Cup

No	Date	Opposition	Res.	Goalscorers
1R	2 Feb	Leek T.	3-3	J.C.H.Bowdler(3)
1Rr	9	LEEK T.	2-0	R.C.Jones, J.C.H.Bowdler
2R	16	Crewe Alex.	0-2	

Welsh Senior Cup

No	Date	Opposition	Res.	Goalscorers
1R	27 Oct	MOLD ALYN STARS	21	*
2R	17 Nov	Druids	0-4	

* O.G., E.H.Bowdler(3), A.Ellis(7), Horley(3), R.C.Jones(2), Rogers, Morris(2), G.Ellis

Shropshire Mayor's Charity Cup

No	Date	Opposition	Res.	Goalscorers
1R	23 Feb	NEWPORT	4-0	Garrett, Rogers
S/F	9 Mar	Oswestry Utd.	3-2	Morris, R.C.Jones
F	30	St. George's	0-1	

SEASON 1895/96

Birmingham League

No	Date	Opposition	Res.	Goalscorers
1	7 Sep	Wolverhampton W. Res.	0-14	
2	14	REDDITCH T.	2-3	R.C.Jones, A.F.Ellis(pen)
3	21	Hereford Thistle	1-6	R.C.Jones
4	28	WOLVERHAMPTON W. RES.	2-2	Rogers(2)
5	5 Oct	ASTON VILLA RES.	2-3	Rogers, Gwilliam
6	12	WORCESTER ROVERS	1-1	Rogers
7	19	Stourbridge	2-2	
8	26	Aston Villa Res.	1-4	Ball
9	9 Nov	BERWICK RANGERS	0-1	
10	23	STOURBRIDGE	0-1	
11	30	Redditch T.	1-2	Garrett
12	7 Dec	W.B.A. RES.	5-2	Heath, L.Benbow(2), Tracey(2)
13	16	Brierley Hill All.	1-3	
14	21	KIDDERMINSTER HARR.	4-1	Gwilliam(2), Tracey, Garrett
15	25	Small Heath Res.	0-13	
16	26	BRIERLEY HILL ALL.	1-0	Bradeley
17	28	W.B.A. Res.	1-7	Bradley
18	4 Jan	Berwick Rangers	2-4	L.Benbow, Tracey
19	11	STAFFORD R.	1-0	Heath
20	25	OLDBURY TOWN	3-3	L.Salt(2), Gwilliam
21	8 Feb	SMALL HEATH RES.	1-1	A.F.Ellis
22	7 Mar	Stafford R.	0-1	
23	28	Worcester Rovers	0-9	
24	28	SINGERS (COVENTRY)	3-0	Gwilliam(2), L.Salt
25	3 Apr	Oldbury Town	1-5	L.Benbow
26	4	Kidderminster Harr.	0-3	
27	7	Singers (Coventry)	3-1	Gwilliam, Hobin
28	11	HEREFORD THISTLE	4-0	A.F.Ellis(2), O.G., L.Benbow
29	18	Halesowen	2-5	Garrett, O.G.
30	25	HALESOWEN	2-1	Gwilliam, L.Salt

P W D L F A Pts
30 8 5 17 46 98 21   (Pos. 12th)

F.A. Amateur Cup

No	Date	Opposition	Res.	Goalscorers
1R	1 Feb	Casuals	4-2	Garrett, Gwilliam, R.C.Jones(2)
2R	15	OLD BRIGHTONIANS	6-2	L.Salt(2),Garrett(2),Tracey,Gwlliam
3R	29	Marlow	2-1	L.Salt, Gwilliam
S/F	21 Mar	Royal Artillary	0-2	

SEASON 1896/97

Birmingham League

No	Date	Opposition	Res.	Goalscorers
1	5 Sep	KIDDERMINSTER H.	1-3	Benbow
2	12	WOLVERHAMPTON W. RES.	2-2	Bliss, Benbow
3	19	Worcester Rovers	2-5	Benbow, Gwilliam
4	26	HEREFORD THISTLE	1-5	Benbow
5	3 Oct	Wolverhampton W. Res.	1-2	Gwilliam
6	10	Berwick Rangers	1-6	Salt
7	17	WEST BROMWICH A. RES.	3-1	Ireland, Gwilliam, E.H.Bowdler
8	24	OLDBURY T.	1-1	Gwilliam
9	31	HEREFORD TOWN	3-1	Gwilliam(2), Garrett
10	14 Nov	SMALL HEATH RES.	3-1	E.H.Bowdler, Tracey, Bliss
11	21	REDDITCH	8-3	Bnbw,Trcy(2),Blss(2),Gwlliam(2),Brdley
12	28	Singers (Coventry)	1-3	Gwilliam
13	5 Dec	BERWICK RANGERS	6-1	OG,Benbow(2),Bliss(2),EH.Bowdler
14	19	Oldbury T.	2-3	Gwilliam(2)
15	26	BRIERLEY HILL ALL.	3-1	Benbow, Ireland, Bliss
16	28	STOURBRIDGE	2-0	Benbow, Tracey
17	2 Jan	Kidderminster H.	1-5	E.H.Bowdler
18	9	Hereford Town	0-3	
19	23	Small Heath Res.	0-5	
20	30	ASTON VILLA RES.	2-1	Salt, Gwilliam
21	6 Feb	Halesowen	1-3	Bliss
22	27	West Bromwich A. Res	1-2	Benbow
23	13 Mar	Stourbridge	2-2	Gwilliam, Bliss
24	20	SINGERS (COVENTRY)	0-1	
25	3 Apr	WORCESTER ROVERS	2-1	Benbow(2)
26	10	Hereford Thistle	0-1	
27	16	Aston Villa Res.	0-1	
28	17	Brierley Hill All.	0-3	
29	20	Redditch	3-1	
30	24	HALESOWEN	6-0	Benbow(6)

```
P   W   D   L   F   A   Pts
30  11  3   16  58  67  25    (Pos. 12th)
```

SEASON 1897/98

Birmingham League

No	Date	Opposition	Res.	Goalscorers
1	11 Sep	Eastville Rovers	0-1	
2	18	Hereford Thistle	4-1	Tracey, White(2), Bliss
3	25	WOLVERHAMPTON W. RES.	0-0	
4	2 Oct	BRISTOL ST. GEORGE'S	0-0	
5	9	Kidderminster Harr.	0-1	
6	16	Wolverhampton W. Res.	0-4	
7	23	Hereford Town	0-2	
8	30	SINGERS (COVENTRY)	4-1	Baker, Gwilliam, Graves, White
9	13 Nov	Singers (Coventry)	0-4	
10	20	Aston Villa Res.	1-6	Fessey
11	27	HALESOWEN	5-3	White(2),Gwlliam,JCH.Bwdlr,HE.Bwdlr
12	4 Dec	STOURBRIDGE	3-0	Gwilliam, White, H.E.Bowdler
13	11	West Bromwich A. Res.	1-5	O.G.
14	18	Berwick Rangers	3-4	Hatton, W.H.Ellis
15	27	HEREFORD THISTLE	3-1	White(2), H.E.Bowdler
16	28	WEST BROMWICH A. RES.	3-2	White(2,1pen), Fessey
17	1 Jan	Small Heath Res.	0-4	
18	15	ASTON VILLA RES.	0-3	
19	5 Feb	EASTVILLE ROVERS	0-2	
20	12	KIDDERMINSTER HARR.	4-2	Bliss, Tracey, A.F.Ellis, Fessey
21	5 Mar	Worcester Rovers	0-3	
22	12	SMALL HEATH RES.	1-2	Rogers
23	19	Halesowen	0-3	
24	26	Stourbridge	0-0	
25	2 Apr	BRIERLEY HILL ALL.	3-2	Bliss, Ireland(2)
26	9	Bristol St. George's	0-3	
27	12	BERWICK RANGERS	3-0	Bliss, A.F.Ellis(2)
28	16	Brierley Hill All.	2-3	Tracey, Hobin
29	23	WORCESTER ROVERS	1-2	Bliss
30	30	HEREFORD TOWN	3-1	Gwilliam, W.H.Ellis(2)

```
P   W   D   L   F   A   Pts
30  10  3   17  44  65  23    (Pos. 11th)
```

Shropshire Mayor's Charity Cup

No	Date	Opposition	Res.	Goalscorers
1R	22 Jan	St. George's	2-2	Bliss, Hatton
1Rr		St. George's		Scratched
S/F		NEWPORT	5-2	
F		Ironbridge	0-1	(played at Wellington)

SEASON 1898/99

Birmingham League

No	Date	Opposition	Res.	Goalscorers
1	3 Sep	Small Heath Res.	2-2	Lewis, Gwilliam
2	10	BRIERLEY HILL ALL.	2-2	Tracey, Lewis
3	17	Kidderminster Harr.	1-1	Rogers
4	24	WOLVERHAMPTON W. RES.	1-2	Lewis
5	15 Oct	Berwick Rangers	4-3	Lewis, Gwilliam(3)
6	22	BRISTOL EASTVILLE RVRS.	2-4	Tracey(2)
7	29	ASTON VILLA RES.	0-2	
8	5 Nov	COVENTRY C.	3-2	Coyne(2), Lewis
9	12	Stourbridge	1-3	Tracey
10	19	DUDLEY T.	4-0	
11	26	Halesowen T.	1-5	Gwilliam
12	3 Dec	HEREFORD TOWN	2-0	H.E.Bowdler, Lewis
13	10	WORCESTER R.	6-1	Bliss, O.G. Lewis(3), Coyne
14	17	Bristol St. George's	4-6	Bliss(2), Tracey, Gwilliam
15	24	WEST BROMWICH A. RES.	1-3	H.E.Bowdler
16	26	WELLINGTON T.	3-1	Tracey, Lewis, H.E.Bowdler
17	27	Hereford Thistle	1-3	
18	31	SMALL HEATH RES.	2-2	H.E.Bowdler, W.H.Ellis(pen)
19	7 Jan	Brierley Hill All.	0-3	
20	21	Wolverhampton W. Res.	1-4	Lewis
21	28	HEREFORD THISTLE	4-0	Bliss, Lewis(2), A.F.Ellis
22	11 Feb	BERWICK RANGERS	2-1	Tracey(2)
23	18	Bristol Eastville Rvrs.	1-9	Gwilliam
24	25	Aston Villa Res.	2-8	Tracey, Bliss
25	4 Mar	Coventry C.	1-3	
26	18	Dudley T.	1-4	Lewis
27	25	HALESOWEN T.	1-1	Tracey
28	31	Wellington T.	0-3	
29	1 Apr	Hereford Town	2-3	
30	3	STOURBRIDGE	1-1	A.F.Ellis
31	4	KIDDERMINSTER HARR.	3-2	Tracey, Gwilliam
32	8	Worcester R.	2-4	Gwilliam, Tracey
33	15	BRISTOL ST. GEORGE'S	3-0	Gwilliam, Lewis(2)
34	22	West Bromwich A. Res.	1-2	Lewis

P   W D L   F   A   Pts
34 10 6 18 65 90 26   (Pos. 13th)

F.A. Cup

No	Date	Opposition	Res.	Goalscorers
Q1	1 Oct	Stourbridge	1-2	Coyne

SEASON 1899/1900

Birmingham League

No	Date	Opposition	Res.	Goalscorers
1	2 Sep	DUDLEY T.	1-2	Taylor
2	9	Coventry C.	0-1	
3	16	SMALL HEATH RES.	1-2	Coyne
4	23	West Bromwich A. Res.	2-5	Taylor(2)
5	7 Oct	Halesowen T.	2-3	Taylor, Cotterill
6	21	Brierley Hill All.	1-4	Taylor
7	28	BRISTOL ROVERS	1-0	Cotterill
8	4 Nov	Hereford Town	2-2	Cotterill, Tracey
9	11	WALSALL RES.	4-2	France, Cotterill(2), Ireland
10	2 Dec	Kidderminster Harr.	1-5	
11	9	Wolverhampton W. Res.	1-11	
12	16	WORCESTER ROVERS *	8-3	Coyne(2),Cotterill(3),Lewis,Grve(2)
13	23	Stourbridge	4-2	Coyne, O.G., Parish, Cotterill
14	25	Aston Villa Res.	2-3	Lewis
15	26	WELLINGTON T.	1-0	
16	30	Dudley T.	1-5	Coyne
17	1 Jan	W. St. George's *	2-0	Taylor
18	6	COVENTRY C.	2-0	
19	13	Small Heath Res.	0-1	
20	20	WEST BROMWICH A. RES.	2-1	Taylor, Coyne
21	27	HEREFORD TOWN	2-0	Coyne, Lewis
22	17 Feb	Berwick Rangers	0-3	
23	24	BRIERLEY HILL ALL.	3-2	Taylor, Coyne, Cotterill
24	3 Mar	Bristol Rovers	0-0	
25	10	HALESOWEN T.	0-0	
26	17	Walsall Res.	0-4	
27	24	ASTON VILLA RES.	0-1	
28	7 Apr	KIDDERMINSTER HARR.	0-2	
29	13	Wellington T.	1-5	
30	14	WOLVERHAMPTON W. RES.	1-2	Tracey
31	17	BERWICK RANGERS	3-2	
32	28	STOURBRIDGE	2-3	Tracey

* These clubs withdrew from the League this season, all results expunged, only included for
interest value.

P   W D L   F   A   Pts
30 9 3 18 40 73 21   (Pos. 14th)

F.A. Cup

No	Date	Opposition	Res.	Goalscorers
Q1		Bye		
Q2	14 Oct	WELLINGTON T.	1-2	Tracey

Shropshire Mayor's Charity Cup

No	Date	Opposition	Res.	Goalscorers
1R	6 Nov	Druids	2-3	Taylor(2) (played at Ruabon)

SEASON 1900/01

Birmingham League

No	Date	Opposition	Res.	Goalscorers
1	1 Sep	Berwick Rangers	0-4	
2	8	HALESOWEN	1-2	France
3	15	STAFFORD R.	1-3	Mason
4	22	Stourbridge	0-5	
5	29	DUDLEY T.	2-1	Smart, Steadman
6	6 Oct	Wolverhampton W. Res.	0-2	
7	13	ASTON VILLA RES.	0-2	
8	20	Druids	0-4	
9	27	HEREFORD T.	0-1	
10	17 Nov	Brierley Hill All.	1-4	Steadman
11	24	COVENTRY C.	3-2	Steadman, Moonie, Coyne
12	1 Dec	Stoke Res.	1-8	Coyne
13	8	WEST BROMWICH A. RES.	1-3	Graves
14	15	Small Heath Res.	1-2	Steadman
15	22	KIDDERMINSTER HARR.	4-0	Steadman(2), Mason, Morris(pen)
16	24	Ironbridge	1-8	Steadman
17	26	WELLINGTON T.	1-1	Ireland
18	29	BERWICK RANGERS	1-5	Mason
19	5 Jan	Halesowen	0-3	
20	12	Stafford R.	1-3	Rogers
21	19	STOURBRIDGE	2-1	Steadman, Morris(pen)
22	9 Feb	WOLVERHAMPTON W. RES.	0-2	
23	16	Aston Villa Res.	0-1	
24	23	DRUIDS	1-0	Coyne
25	2 Mar	Hereford T.	0-3	
26	9	IRONBRIDGE	3-1	Graves(2), O.G.
27	23	BRIERLEY HILL ALL.	1-1	Coyne
28	30	Coventry C.	1-5	O.G.
29	5 Apr	Wellington T.	0-4	
30	6	STOKE RES.	1-0	Coyne
31	10	Dudley T.	0-2	
32	13	West Bromwich A. Res.	0-6	
33	20	SMALL HEATH RES.	1-1	France
34	27	Kidderminster Harr.	0-6	

```
P  W  D  L  F  A  Pts
34 7  3  24 29 96 17   (Pos. 18th)
```

F.A. Cup

No	Date	Opposition	Res.	Goalscorers
Q3*	3 Nov	WALSALL*	1-1	Steadman
Q3r		Walsall	0-1	

Shropshire Mayor's Charity Cup

No	Date	Opposition	Res.	Goalscorers
1R		WEM	w/o	
S/F	8 Apr	WELLINGTON T.	1-1	Steadman
S/Fr	24	Wellington T.	0-2	

SEASON 1901/02

Birmingham League

No	Date	Opposition	Res.	Goalscorers
1	7 Sep	STOKE RES.	0-0	
2	14	Ironbridge	0-5	
3	21	BERWICK RANGERS	2-0	Steadman(2)
4	28	Small Heath Res.	0-4	
5	12 Oct	Dudley T.	2-3	Gwilliam, Wynne
6	24	HALESOWEN	4-1	Gwilliam(2), Roberts, Slater
7	26	Stafford R.	3-4	Roberts(2), O.G.
8	2 Nov	WOLVERHAMPTON W RES*	1-3	Slater
9	9	West Bromwich A. Res.	0-6	
10	22	ASTON VILLA RES.	1-5	Roberts
11	29	Hereford	0-3	
12	14 Dec	Kidderminster Harr.	1-1	Slater
13	21	BRIERLEY HILL ALL.	3-2	J.Morris, Slater, Roberts
14	26	CREWE ALEXANDRA	2-1	Gwilliam(2)
151	28	Coventry C.	3-3	Wynne, Rhodden, Roberts
16	4 Jan	Stoke Res.	2-3	Steadman, J.Morris
17	11	IRONBRIDGE	3-0	J.Morris(pen), Rhodden, Steadman
18	18	Berwick Rangers	0-3	
19	25	SMALL HEATH RES.	2-1	J.Morris, Rhodden
20	1 Feb	Halesowen	2-5	Wynne, Wharton
21	8	DUDLEY T.	4-2	Wharton(2), Rhoden, Wynne
22	15	Stourbridge	2-5	Wharton, Roberts
23	22	STAFFORD R.	3-1	Wharton, Roberts, Slater
24	1 Mar	Wolverhampton W. Res.	0-3	
25	8	WEST BROMWICH A. RES.	2-1	Wharton, Rhodden
26	10	Druids	1-3	Wharton
27	15	WOLVERHAMPTON W. RES.	1-4	J.Morris
28	22	Aston Villa Res.	1-1	J.Morris
29	27	Crewe Alexandra	2-0	Wharton, Rhodden
30	29	HEREFORD	3-1	Wharton, Rhodden, Garnett
31	31	STOURBRIDGE	2-6	Wharton, Rhodden
32	5 Apr	DRUIDS	1-0	Rhodden
33	12	KIDDERMINSTER HARR.	0-2	
34	19	Brierley Hill All.	3-1	Wharton, J.Morris(pen), Roberts
35	26	COVENTRY C.	2-0	Rhodden, Wharton

* Match mistakenly stopped after 77 mins, result not counted.

```
P  W  D  L  F  A  Pts
34 14 4  16 57 80 32   (Pos. 11th)
```

F.A. Cup

No	Date	Opposition	Res.	Goalscorers
Q1	5 Oct	OSWESTRY U.	1-1	Roberts
Q1r	10	Oswestry U.	0-2	

Walsall Senior Cup

No	Date	Opposition	Res.	Goalscorers
1R	19 Oct	DRUIDS	2-2	Gwilliam, W.Nightingale
1Rr		Druids		scratched

Shropshire Mayor's Charity Cup

No	Date	Opposition	Res.	Goalscorers
S/F	10 Apr	WELLINGTON T.	1-0	Slater
F	30	WREXHAM	4-1	J.Morris, Roberts(2), Rhodden

SEASON 1902/03

Birmingham League

No	Date	Opposition	Res.	Goalscorers
1	6 Sep	Kidderminster Harr.	4-2	Wharton,Rhodden,Slater,S.Roberts
2	13	BRIERLEY HILL ALL.	2-3	Wharton(2)
3	20	Crewe Alexandra	1-4	Rhodden
4	27	STOKE RES.	0-0	
5	11 Oct	WORCESTER	3-0	Rhodden, R.Morris, Roberts
6	18	Small Heath Res.	2-2	Jones, Rhodden
7	25	WEST BROMWICH A. RES.	0-1	
8	1 Nov	Halesowen	2-0	R.Morris, Wharton
9	8	DUDLEY T.	7-0	Whrtn(3),R.Mrrs(pen),OG,Rhddn,Wynne
10	15	Ironbridge *	1-2	Rhodden
11	22	STAFFORD R.	2-0	Roberts, Wharton
12	29	Wolverhampton W. Res.	1-3	Wharton
13	6 Dec	IRONBRIDGE	4-0	Rhodden, Jones, Roberts, O.G.
14	13	DRUIDS	1-0	Rhodden
15	20	Aston Villa Res.	0-0	
16	26	WELLINGTON T.	5-1	R.Morris, Wynne(2), Wharton(2)
17	27	COVENTRY C.	0-0	
18	3 Jan	KIDDERMINSTER HARR.	3-3	Jones, Rhodden, Roberts
19	10	Brierley Hill All.	3-2	Rhodden(2), Jones
20	17	CREWE ALEXANDRA	0-0	
21	24	Stoke Res.	1-0	Wynne
22	7 Feb	Worcester	0-2	
23	14	SMALL HEATH RES.	2-1	Slater, Wharton
24	21	West Bromwich A. Res	0-4	
25	28	HALESOWEN	2-2	Rhodden, Roberts
26	7 Mar	Dudley T.	2-0	R.Morris, Wynne
27	14	STOURBRIDGE **	1-0	Wharton
28	21	Stafford R.	0-0	
29	28	WOLVERHAMPTON W. RES.	4-1	Wharton,Roberts,Rhodden,Slater
30	30	STOURBRIDGE	1-1	Slater
31	4 Apr	Ironbridge	2-3	Slater(2)
32	10	Wellington T.	2-1	Roberts, Wharton
33	11	Druids	0-0	
34	18	ASTON VILLA RES.	1-2	Rhodden
35	25	Coventry C.	2-3	Roberts, Wharton
36	27	STOURBRIDGE	1-2	Rhodden

* Abandoned after 75 mins due to bad light.

** Abandoned after 30 mins due to waterlogged pitch.

P W D L F A Pts
34 13 11 10 60 44 37   (Pos. 6th)

F.A. Cup

No	Date	Opposition	Res.	Goalscorers
Q1	4 Oct	WELLINGTON T.	1-2	Jones

SEASON 1903/04

Birmingham League

No	Date	Opposition	Res.	Goalscorers
1	5 Sep	WEST BROMWICH A. RES.	3-2	Wharton(2), Wynne
2	12	Small Heath Res.	2-2	Roberts, Jones
3	19	CREWE ALEXANDRA	2-1	Roberts(2)
4	26	Worcester	4-2	Wynne, Roberts(2), Wharton
5	10 Oct	Stourbridge	0-4	
6	24	Stoke Res.	1-1	Wynne
7	7 Nov	STAFFORD R.	1-3	Wharton
8	21	WOLVERHAMPTON W. RES.	0-1	
9	5 Dec	COVENTRY C.	0-2	
10	19	KIDDERMINSTER HARR.	2-1	Williams(2)
11	26	WELLINGTON T.	5-1	Whrtn,Rhddn,Jnes(2),R.Mrrs(pen)
12	28	DUDLEY T.	5-0	Jones(2),Roberts,Wharton,Rhodden
13	2 Jan	West Bromwich A. Res.	0-3	
14	9	SMALL HEATH RES.	3-0	Roberts(2), Wynne
151	16	Crewe Alexandra	3-0	Jones, Rhodden, Wynne
16	23	WORCESTER	4-0	R.Mrrs(pen),Rhddn,Rbrts,Wlliams
17	6 Feb	STOURBRIDGE	2-2	Slater, Jones
18	13	Halesowen	1-2	Roberts
19	20	STOKE RES.	2-1	R.Morris, Wynne
20	27	ASTON VILLA RES.	1-2	Wynne
21	29	Brierley Hill All.	0-0	
22	5 Mar	Stafford R.	0-2	
23	12	WALSALL	3-0	M.Morris, Rhodden, Wharton
24	26	DRUIDS	1-0	Wynne
25	1 Apr	Wellington T.	0-2	
26	2	Coventry C.	1-2	Wharton
27	5	Dudley T.	0-3	
28	9	BRIERLEY HILL ALL.	1-0	Wharton
29	13	Druids	0-3	
30	16	Kidderminster Harr.	0-2	
31	18	Walsall	1-1	Roberts
32	23	Aston Villa Res.	1-0	Wynne
33	25	Wolverhampton W. Res.	1-1	Chapman
34	30	HALESOWEN	1-2	Richards

P W D L F A Pts
34 14 6 14 51 48 34   (Pos. 10th)

F.A. Cup

No	Date	Opposition	Res.	Goalscorers
Q1		Bye		
Q2	17 Oct	WELLINGTON	4-3	Jones(3), R.Morris
Q3	31	Stourbridge	2-1	Tracey, Rhodden
Q4	14 Nov	OSWESTRY U.	1-0	Wynne
Q5	28	WALSALL	1-0	Rhodden
IR	12 Dec	Stockton	1-2	Wharton

IR = Intermediate Round, the round immediately preceding the First Round Proper.

Shropshire Mayor's Charity Cup

No	Date	Opposition	Res.	Goalscorers
1R	19 Mar	Welshpool	4-0	Wharton, Lee, Rhodden, Wynne
S/F	21 Apr	WREXHAM	1-1	Rhodden
S/Fr	26	Wrexham	0-2	

SEASON 1904/05

Birmingham League

No	Date	Opposition	Res.	Goalscorers
1	3 Sep	Worcester Rvrs.	1-3	Boden
2	17	Kidderminster Harr.	0-4	
3	24	CREWE ALEXANDRA	0-0	
4	1 Oct	Stoke Res.	1-2	Manning
5	8	SMALL HEATH RES.	1-0	Manning
6	15	West Bromwich A. Res.	0-1	
7	22	HALESOWEN	1-1	Wynne
8	5 Nov	DUDLEY T.	2-1	Manning, Taylor
9	12	BURSLEM PORT VALE RES.	2-0	Davies(2)
10	19	Stafford R.	0-2	
11	26	WOLVERHAMPTON W. RES.	0-1	
12	3 Dec	Aston Villa Res.	1-6	Davies
13	10	WALSALL	6-2	Davies(3),Coopr,Nwbound,Rchards
14	17	Coventry C.	0-4	
15	24	BRIERLEY HILL ALL.	1-1	Davies
16	26	WELLINGTON T.	2-3	Reed(2)
17	31	WORCESTER RVRS.	2-1	Breeze(2)
18	14 Jan	KIDDERMINSTER HARR.	0-1	
19	21	Crewe Alexandra	1-3	Davies
20	28	STOKE RES.	1-0	Davies
21	11 Feb	WEST BROMWICH A. RES.	4-0	Davies(2), A.Morris(2)
22	18	Halesowen	2-0	Roberts(2)
23	25	Stourbridge	1-2	Roberts
24	4 Mar	Dudley T.	1-4	Roberts
25	11	Burslem Port Vale Res.	1-3	Davies
26	18	STAFFORD R.	2-3	Tracey(2)
27	25	Wolverhampton W. Res.	0-2	
28	1 Apr	ASTON VILLA RES.	2-2	A.Morris, Williams
29	8	Walsall	0-3	
30	15	COVENTRY C.	3-1	Wynne, Randle, Newbound
31	21	Wellington T.	0-1	
32	22	Brierley Hill All.	0-3	
33	24	STOURBRIDGE	2-0	A.Morris, W.Davies
34	29	Small Heath Res.	2-3	Newbound, Breeze

```
P  W  D  L  F  A  Pts
34 10 4  20 42 63 24   (Pos. 16th)
```

SEASON 1905/06

Birmingham League

No	Date	Opposition	Res.	Goalscorers
1	2 Sep	WEST BROMWICH A. RES.	2-1	Freeman, Pickering
2	9	Birmingham C. Res.	2-6	Freeman, G.Jones
3	16	KIDDERMINSTER HARR.	0-2	
4	23	Stourbridge	1-3	Freeman
5	30	BURSLEM PORT VALE	2-0	Pickering(2)
6	7 Oct	Wrexham	0-5	
7	14	DUDLEY T.	3-2	Pickering(2), Freeman
8	21	Coventry C. Res.	1-5	R.Morris
9	28	Walsall	3-2	Pickering(2), Blackburn
10	4 Nov	ASTON VILLA RES.	1-7	Pickering
11	11	Stafford R.	3-2	Freeman, Blackburn, Pickering
12	18	WOLVERHAMPTON W. RES.	2-0	A.Morris, W.Davies
13	25	Brierley Hill All.	1-2	Freeman
14	2 Dec	STOKE C. RES.	1-1	W.Davies
151	9	Dudley T.	1-2	Freeman
16	16	CREWE ALEXANDRA	2-1	Pickering, Hoare(pen)
17	26	WELLINGTON T.	4-0	G.Jones, Freeman(3)
18	30	West Bromwich A. Res.	1-8	G.Jones
19	13 Jan	BIRMINGHAM C. RES.	4-1	Pickering(2), Freeman, Peters
20	20	Kidderminster Harr.	0-1	
21	27	STOURBRIDGE	3-3	Hamer(2), R.Morris
22	3 Feb	Burslem Port Vale	1-6	R.Morris
23	10	WREXHAM	2-3	Bowen, Clements
24	24	COVENTRY C. RES.	1-0	G.Jones(pen)
25	3 Mar	WALSALL	2-0	Bowen, Pickering
26	10	Aston Villa Res.	0-10	
27	17	STAFFORD R.	1-1	Bowen
28	24	Wolverhampton W. Res.	0-2	
29	31	BRIERLEY HILL ALL.	1-0	Clements
30	7 Apr	Stoke C. Res.	0-2	
31	13	Wellington T.	4-1	Pickering, Riddell(3)
32	14	WORCESTER C.	3-0	Riddell, Clements, Pickering
33	17	Worcester C.	4-2	
34	21	Crewe Alexandra	1-3	Clements

```
P  W  D  L  F  A  Pts
34 15 3  16 57 84 33   (Pos. 10th)
```

Welsh Senior Cup

No	Date	Opposition	Res.	Goalscorers
3R	6 Jan	Whitchurch T.	1-1	Pickering
3Rr	11	WHITCHURCH T.	0-0	(played again at Whitchurch)
3R2r	17	Whitchurch T.	0-1	

Shropshire Mayor's Charity Cup

No	Date	Opposition	Res.	Goalscorers
1R	8 Feb	WHITCHURCH T.	2-1	Randles, W.Jones
S/F	8 Mar	OSWESTRY UTD.	1-0	Home
F	28 Apr	St. George's Victoria	1-2	Pickering (played at Wellington)

SEASON 1906/07

Birmingham League

No	Date	Opposition	Res.	Goalscorers
1	1 Sep	Birmingham C. Res.	4-7	Riddell(4)
2	8	HALESOWEN	2-2	Scarratt, A.Morris
3	15	Kidderminster Harr.	0-3	
4	29	WOLVERHAMPTON W. RES.	1-3	Riddell
5	6 Oct	Burslem Port Vale	2-3	Riddell, A.Morris
6	13	STOURBRIDGE	6-0	Evans, Scarratt(2), Riddell(3,1pen)
7	20	WALSALL	3-1	Riddell(2,1pen), Evans
8	27	ASTON VILLA RES.	4-3	A.Morris, Colley(3)
9	3 Nov	Walsall	0-2	
10	10	STAFFORD R.	3-1	Evans, Colley, A.Morris
11	17	Coventry C. Res.	1-5	Evans
12	24	WORCESTER C.	1-2	Colley
13	1 Dec	Stoke C. Res.	0-2	
14	8	BRIERLEY HILL ALL.	1-2	Slynn
15	15	Crewe Alexandra	0-4	
16	22	WEST BROMWICH A. RES.	2-2	Scarratt, Price
17	26	CREWE ALEXANDRA	6-2	Scrrtt(2),R.Mrrs,Prce,Clmnts,Evns
18	29	BIRMINGHAM C. RES.	1-0	Price
19	5 Jan	Halesowen	3-3	Evans(2), A.Morris
20	12	Dudley T.	2-5	R.Morris, O.G.
21	19	KIDDERMINSTER HARR.	1-1	Scarratt
22	26	WREXHAM	2-2	A.Morris, Evans
23	2 Feb	Wolverhampton W. Res.	1-3	A.Morris
24	9	BURSLEM PORT VALE	2-6	Scarratt(2,1pen)
25	16	Stourbridge	1-6	Colley
26	23	DUDLEY T.	3-2	W.Jones, P.Evans(2)
27	2 Mar	Aston Villa Res.	1-4	Simpson
28	16	Stafford R.	0-5	
29	23	COVENTRY C. RES.	1-2	G.Evans
30	29	Wrexham	4-5	Scarratt(2), G.Evans(2)
31	30	Worcester C.	1-6	Scarratt
32	6 Apr	STOKE C. RES.	1-2	Scarratt
33	13	Brierley Hill All.	1-3	Scarratt
34	27	West Bromwich A. Res.	0-7	

```
P  W  D  L  F   A   Pts
34 7  5  22 61  106 19   (Pos. 18th - bottom)
```

SEASON 1907/08

Birmingham League

No	Date	Opposition	Res.	Goalscorers
1	7 Sep	BRIERLEY HILL ALL.	4-1	Paddock(2), Riddell, Scarratt
2	14	Stoke C. Res.	1-3	Paddock
3	21	BIRMINGHAM C. RES.	3-2	J.Jones(2), Paddock
4	28	West Bromwich A. Res.	4-3	Scarratt,Riddell,W.Jones,J.Jones
5	5 Oct	CREWE ALEXANDRA	2-2	Riddell(2)
6	12	Coventry C.	1-3	Scarratt
7	19	STAFFORD R.	1-5	Scarratt
8	26	Wrexham	1-1	Scarratt
9	2 Nov	STOURBRIDGE	2-1	Riddell, J.Jones(pen)
10	9	Dudley T.	0-1	
11	16	Aston Villa Res.	1-2	Riddell
12	23	WALSALL	5-3	Riddell(2), Scarratt, J.Jones(2)
13	30	Burton Utd.	1-3	Paddock
14	7 Dec	WOLVERHAMPTON W. RES.	5-4	Scarratt, J.Jones, Bowen(3)
15	14	Kidderminster Harr.	2-1	J.Jones, Paddock
16	21	WORCESTER C.	2-0	Scarratt(2)
17	26	HALESOWEN T.	1-0	Scarratt
18	28	Crewe Alexandra	0-6	
19	4 Jan	Brierley Hill All.	2-2	G.Jones, J.Jones
20	11	STOKE C. RES.	2-1	J.Jones, Scarratt
21	18	Birmingham C. Res.	6-3	J.Jones(3), Riddell, G.Jones(2)
22	25	WEST BROMWICH A. RES.	1-0	Paddock
23	1 Feb	Halesowen T.	0-2	
24	8	COVENTRY C.	4-1	J.Jones,G.Jones,Randle,Paddock
25	15	Stafford R.	1-1	G.Jones
26	22	WREXHAM	3-2	Randle, Colley, Scarratt
27	29	Stourbridge	2-3	Randle(2)
28	7 Mar	DUDLEY T.	4-2	J.Jones(4)
29	14	ASTON VILLA RES.	1-1	J.Jones
30	21	Walsall	0-0	
31	28	BURTON UTD.	0-2	
32	4 Apr	Wolverhampton W. Res.	2-2	
33	11	KIDDERMINSTER HARR.	2-0	Randle(2)
34	18	Worcester C.	1-2	G.Jones

```
P  W  D  L  F  A  Pts
34 16 7  11 67 65 39   (Pos. 5th)
```

Shropshire Mayor's Charity Cup

No	Date	Opposition	Res.	Goalscorers
1R	14 Nov	IRONBRIDGE	7-0	Price(2),Riddell(3),J.Jones,Colley
S/F	30 Jan	CHIRK	2-2	Colley, J.Jones
S/Fr	19 Mar	Chirk	0-0	
S/F2r	2 Apr	CHIRK	5-1	Scarratt(2),Paddock,J.Jnes,G.Jnes
F	28	Whitchurch	3-1	Scarratt,J.Jones(2) (played at Wellington)

SEASON 1908/09

Birmingham League

No	Date	Opposition	Res.	Goalscorers
1	5 Sep	Worcester C.	0-1	
2	12	DUDLEY T.	1-3	J.Jones
3	26	BIRMINGHAM C. RES.	4-0	Colley, J.Jones, Morris, Owen
4	10 Oct	WREXHAM	1-2	Paddock(pen)
5	12	Halesowen	1-0	Owen
6	17	WALSALL	2-1	Scarratt, Owen
7	24	Stourbridge	1-1	Randle
8	31	STAFFORD R.	2-2	Paddock(2)
9	7 Nov	Wolverhampton W. Res.	2-2	J.Jones(2)
10	14	BURTON U.	1-1	Owen
11	21	Aston Villa Res.	2-2	J.Jones, Owen
12	28	STOKE	3-1	Scarratt, H.Jones(pen), Owen
13	12 Dec	KIDDERMINSTER HARR.	5-1	J.Jnes,H.Jnes(p),F.W.Jnes,Mrris,Owen
14	19	Brierley Hill All.	1-2	F.W.Jones
15	24	Crewe Alexandra	1-4	Scarratt
16	26	WELLINGTON T.	1-1	J.Jones
17	28	West Bromwich A. Res.	2-1	Paddock, Price
18	2 Jan	WORCESTER C.	4-1	J.Jones,Price,Scarratt,Paddock
19	9	Dudley T.	2-2	F.W.Jones, J.Jones
20	23	WEST BROMWICH A. RES.	2-1	Scarratt, W.Jones(pen)
21	30	Birmingham C. Res.	1-0	J.Jones
22	6 Feb	HALESOWEN	2-1	O.G., J.Jones
23	20	Walsall	1-1	Owen
24	27	STOURBRIDGE	1-1	Scarratt
25	13 Mar	WOLVERHAMPTON W. RES.	0-1	
26	15	Wrexham	1-2	W.Jones(pen)
27	20	Burton U.	2-2	J.Jones(2)
28	27	ASTON VILLA RES.	1-2	Scarratt
29	3 Apr	Stoke	2-1	J.Jones, Owen
30	9	Wellington T.	1-1	F.W.Jones
31	10	CREWE ALEXANDRA	0-0	
32	13	Stafford R.	0-3	
33	17	Kidderminster Harr.	0-3	
34	24	BRIERLEY HILL ALL.	1-1	Morris

P W D L F A Pts
34 11 13 10 51 48 35   (Pos. 6th)

F.A. Cup

No	Date	Opposition	Res.	Goalscorers
PQR	19 Sep	WITTON ALBION	4-1	Bull, Owen, J.Jones, Paddock
Q1	3 Oct	Nantwich	1-2	J.Jones(pen)

SEASON 1909/10

Birmingham League

No	Date	Opposition	Res.	Goalscorers
1	4 Sep	STOURBRIDGE	0-1	
2	11	Worcester C.	2-2	F.W.Jones, Home(pen)
3	23	STOKE C. RES.	1-0	Slater
4	9 Oct	Dudley T.	0-4	
5	23	Stafford R.	0-2	
6	30	BRIERLEY HILL ALL.	2-1	Watton, Myatt
7	13 Nov	CREWE ALEXANDRA	1-4	F.W.Jones
8	27	WOLVERHAMPTON W. RES.	4-1	Owen(2), F.W.Jones(2)
9	11 Dec	Walsall	0-4	
10	13	ASTON VILLA RES. *	1-2	F.W.Jones
11	27	WELLINGTON T.	0-0	
12	28	Wrexham	1-2	Green
13	1 Jan	Kidderminster Harr.	1-2	Scarratt
14	8	Stourbridge	1-5	Slater
15	22	WORCESTER C.	3-2	Myatt, Scarratt, Owen(pen)
16	27	KIDDERMINSTER HARR.	1-0	Holmes
17	29	Stoke C. Res.	0-2	
18	12 Feb	HALESOWEN	4-1	James(2), Scarratt, Holmes
19	19	DUDLEY T.	3-2	Holmes, Tarplin, Homes(pen)
20	24	BIRMINGHAM C. RES.	0-2	
21	26	Birmingham C. Res.	1-1	Holmes
22	5 Mar	STAFFORD R.	2-0	Tarplin(2)
23	10	ASTON VILLA RES.	0-1	
24	12	Brieley Hill All.	0-1	
25	17	WREXHAM	3-1	Tarplin(2), Slater
26	25	Wellington T.	2-2	Scarratt(2)
27	26	Crewe Alexandra	0-4	
28	29	WEST BROMWICH A. Res.	4-2	Dobson(2), Paddock, Scarratt
29	2 Apr	BURTON U.	3-1	Myatt, Scarratt, Tarplin
30	7	Burton U.	3-1	F.W.Jones, Dobson, Tarplin
31	9	Wolverhampton W. Res.	0-3	
32	14	Halesowen	2-3	Dobson(2)
33	16	West Bromwich A. RES.	1-1	Tarplin
34	23	WALSALL	2-0	Tarplin, Dobson
35	30	Aston Villa Res.	1-5	Dobson

* Abandoned after 78 mins, due to heavy snow on pitch.

P W D L F A Pts
34 13 5 16 48 63 31   (Pos. 11th)

F.A. Cup

No	Date	Opposition	Res.	Goalscorers
PQR	13 Sep	WELLINGTON T.	3-0	Myatt, Owen, F.W.Jones
1Q	2 Oct	DRUIDS	2-1	Morris, Sambrook
2Q	16	Connah's Quay	2-1	Lloyd, Slater
3Q	6 Nov	Tranmere R.	2-0	Owen, W.Jones
4Q	20	King's Lynn	1-0	F.W.Jones
5Q	4 Dec	Clapton	1-1	Paddock
5Qr	9	CLAPTON	4-1	Grady, Owen, F.W.Jones, Myatt
1R	15 Jan	Portsmouth	0-3	

Shrewsbury line-up 1910:

(Back): Morris, H.A.Jones, Home, H.Jones, Scarratt, A.Davies, J.Davies, F.Davies.
(Middle): Price, Grady, F.Jones, W.Jones, Myatt, Lines, Crane(Sec.), Adams(Trainer).
(Front): Paddock, Tarplin, Dobson, Hemmings, Holmes

SEASON 1910/11

Birmingham League

No	Date	Opposition	Res.	Goalscorers
1	3 Sep	West Bromwich A. Res.	1-3	Dilly
2	10	WOLVES RES.	1-2	Scarratt
3	17	Stafford R.	0-2	
4	24	HALESOWEN	2-1	Freeman, Dobson
5	1 Oct	Dudley T.	2-2	Smith, Freeman
6	8	CREWE ALEXANDRA	5-1	Freeman(3), F.W.Jones, Tarplin
7	15	Stoke C.	0-3	
8	22	WEDNESBURY OLD ATH.	5-3	F.W.Jones, Freeman(3), Tarplin
9	29	Stourbridge	4-2	Freeman(2), F.W.Jones, Dilly
10	5 Nov	BRIERLEY HILL	3-2	Freeman, Tarplin, F.W.Jones
11	12	Walsall	1-1	Freeman
12	26	Kidderminster	1-0	Freeman
13	10 Dec	Wrexham	1-2	F.W.Jones
14	17	BIRMINGHAM C. RES. *	3-1	Dilly, Price, Freeman
15	24	ASTON VILLA RES.	1-0	Freeman
16	26	WELLINGTON T.	3-2	Scarratt, Tarplin(2)
17	27	STAFFORD R.	2-2	Dilly, Tarplin
18	31	WEST BROWMICH A. RES.	2-3	Freeman, Scarratt
19	7 Jan	Wolves Res.	0-6	
20	14	BIRMINGHAM C. RES.	4-3	Dilly, Riddell, Freeman, Tarplin
21	28	Halesowen	0-2	
22	4 Feb	DUDLEY T.	3-0	Tarplin, Freeman(2)
23	11	Crewe Alexandra	3-2	Riddell(2), Dilly
24	18	STOKE C.	0-1	
25	25	Wednesbury Old Ath.	0-2	
26	4 Mar	STOURBRIDGE	3-2	Dilly(2), Freeman
27	11	Brierley Hill	1-1	Dilly
28	18	WALSALL	0-1	
29	23	WORCESTER C.	2-1	Dilly, Riddell
30	25	KIDDERMINSTER	2-0	Dilly, Rumsey
31	8 Apr	Worcester C.	0-3	
32	14	Wellington T.	0-4	
33	15	WREXHAM	1-3	O.G.
34	22	Birmingham C. Res.	4-6	Riddell,Rumsey,Freeman,Scarratt
35	29	Aston Villa Res.	4-6	Scarratt, Tarplin, Freeman(2)

```
P  W  D  L  F  A  Pts
34 14 4  16 61 74 32    (Pos. 11th)
```

* Aban. after 70 mins, due to waterlogged pitch.

F.A. Cup

No	Date	Opposition	Res.	Goalscorers
4Q	19 Nov	MERTHYR T.	1-0	Tarplin
5Q	5 Dec	Gainsborough T.	0-4	

SEASON 1911/12

Birmingham League

No	Date	Opposition	Res.	Goalscorers
1	2 Sep	WREXHAM	2-1	W.Jones, Slater
2	9	WEST BROMWICH A. RES.	0-0	
3	16	West Bromwich A. Res.	0-5	
4	23	Worcester C.	0-2	
5	7 Oct	Brierley Hill All.	1-4	Hemmings(pen)
6	21	Birmingham C. Res.	2-4	Rumsey, Morris
7	28	Darlaston	2-3	Bridge, Rumsey
8	4 Nov	WALSALL	0-3	
9	11	Aston Villa Res.	2-9	Morris, Williams
10	18	WILLENHALL SWIFTS	1-2	Scarratt
11	25	Wolves Res.	0-3	
12	2 Dec	STOKE C. RES.	0-1	
13	9	Stourbridge	0-1	
14	23	Wrexham	1-2	Foxall
15	26	WELLINGTON T.	1-2	Wakelam
16	30	WEDNESBURY OLD ATH.	2-1	Wakelam, Morris
17	6 Jan	DUDLEY T.	0-3	
18	13	STAFFORD R.	2-1	Corfield, Morris
19	27	WORCESTER C.	3-2	Bridge, Williams(2)
20	3 Feb	Stafford R.	0-1	
21	10	BRIERLEY HILL ALL.	2-1	Williams(2)
22	17	KIDDERMINSTER HARR.	4-0	Scarratt, Williams, Foxall(2)
23	24	BIRMINGHAM C. RES.	3-2	Williams(3,1pen)
24	2 Mar	DARLASTON	1-2	Williams
25	9	Walsall	0-1	
26	16	ASTON VILLA RES.	3-3	O.G., Williams(2,1pen)
27	23	Willenhall Swifts	1-2	Scarratt
28	27	Kidderminster Harr.	0-4	
29	30	WOLVES RES.	3-1	Moore, Williams(pen), Lloyd
30	5 Apr	Wellington T.	2-2	Lloyd, Williams
31	6	Stoke C. Res.	0-1	
32	13	STOURBRIDGE	5-0	Lloyd(2), Scarratt, Williams, O.G.
33	22	Wednesbury Old Ath.	0-3	
34	29	Dudley T.	1-4	

```
P  W  D  L  F  A  Pts
34 9  3  22 44 76 21    (Pos. 17th)
```

F.A. Cup

No	Date	Opposition	Res.	Goalscorers
1Q	30 Sep	Chester	1-6	Corfield

(Back): Adams (Trainer), Higley (Chairman), W.Jones, Scarratt, Norris, Morgan, Hemmings, Rumsey.
(Middle): F.Jones, Slater, Gorman, Foxall, Ince (Treasurer). (Front): Bridge, Tremlett, Davies, Peplow.

SEASON 1912/13

Birmingham League

No	Date	Opposition	Res.	Goalscorers
1	7 Sep	Wednesbury Old Ath.	1-3	Hoskins(pen)
2	14	STOKE C. RES.	4-0	Hoskins(2), Stone, Slater
3	21	KIDDERMINSTER HARR.	0-3	
4	28	Coventry C. Res.	1-1	Williams
5	5 Oct	WALSALL	4-0	Williams(3,2pens), G.Jones
6	19	WOLVERHAMPTON RES.	4-1	Hoskins, G.Jones(2), Williams
7	26	Aston Villa Res.	1-3	Hoskins
8	2 Nov	DARLASTON	6-1	Williams(3), Hoskins, Moore, Lloyd
9	9	Worcester C.	0-2	
10	16	COVENTRY C. RES.	0-1	
11	23	Stourbridge	1-1	Slater
12	7 Dec	Wrexham	2-3	Morgan, Hoskins
13	21	Birmingham C. Res.	2-5	Hoskins, Harvey
14	25	WELLINGTON T.	1-3	
15	28	WEDNESBURY OLD ATH.	3-1	
16	30	Willenhall Swifts	0-1	
17	4 Jan	Stoke C. Res.	1-1	Moore
18	11	WEST BROMWICH A. RES.	3-1	Harvey(2), G.Jones
19	18	Kidderminster Harr.	0-1	
20	25	BRIERLEY HILL	3-2	Moore, Bowen, G.Jones
21	1 Feb	West Bromwich A. Res.	1-0	H.Boxley
22	8	Walsall	0-1	
23	15	WILLENHALL SWIFTS	2-0	G.Jones, Slater
24	22	Wolverhampton Res.	0-1	
25	1 Mar	ASTON VILLA RES.	2-0	Williams, G.Jones
26	8	Darlaston	0-3	
27	15	WORCESTER C.	2-1	Bowen, Williams
28	21	Wellington T.	0-0	
29	22	Brierley Hill	0-2	
30	29	STOURBRIDGE	2-1	Harvey, Hoskins
31	12 Apr	WREXHAM	1-3	G.Jones
32	19	Dudley T.	3-1	Hoskins, G.Jones(2)
33	26	BIRMINGHAM C. RES.	3-3	Rogers, H.Boxley, G.Jones
34	28	DUDLEY T.	6-0	H.Boxley(2),Hrvey(2),Rgers,Bwen

P W D L F A Pts
34 14 5 15 59 50 33 (Pos. 10th)

F.A. Cup

No	Date	Opposition	Res.	Goalscorers
4Q	30 Nov	Northwich Victoria	2-1	Williams, G.Jones
5Q	14 Dec	LONDON CALEDONIANS	2-2	Williams(2,1pen)
5Qr	19	London Caledonians	0-1	

SEASON 1913/14

Birmingham League

No	Date	Opposition	Res.	Goalscorers
1	6 Sep	WEST BROMWICH A. RES.	2-1	Parsonage, Bowser
2	13	Stoke C. Res.	2-1	Bould, Parsonage
3	20	WORCESTER C.	1-0	G.Jones
4	27	Birmingham C. Res.	0-2	
5	4 Oct	Brierley Hill	2-2	Parsonage, F.Boxley(pen)
6	11	DARLASTON	6-1	Parsonage
7	18	Willenhall Swifts	0-2	
8	25	WOLVERHAMPTON W. RES.	2-1	G.Jones, Rogers
9	31	Aston Villa Res.	0-1	
10	8 Nov	WREXHAM	2-1	Parsonage(2)
11	15	Kidderminster Harr.	1-1	Parsonage
12	22	WALSALL	6-0	Parsonage, Bould(4), H.Boxley
13	6 Dec	STOURBRIDGE	1-1	Bowen
14	13	Dudley T.	0-2	
15	20	WEDNESBURY OLD ATH.	3-1	Pott, Parsonage, Edwards
16	26	WELLINGTON T.	4-2	Edwards(2), Parsonage, Rogers
17	27	West Bromwich A. Res.	0-6	
18	3 Jan	STOKE C. RES.	0-1	
19	10	COVENTRY C. RES.	5-1	Weate, Harris, Parsonage(3)
20	17	Worcester C.	1-5	Parsonage
21	24	BIRMINGHAM C. RES.	3-1	Weate(2), Parsonage
22	31	Coventry C.	2-1	Weate, Parsonage(pen)
23	7 Feb	BRIERLEY HILL	5-0	Joyce,Bowen,Rogers,Bowser,Pace
24	14	Darlaston	4-2	Weate(3), Parsonage
25	21	WILLENHALL SWIFTS	3-2	Weate(2), Parsonage
26	28	Wolverhampton W. Res.	2-1	Bishop, Weate
27	7 Mar	ASTON VILLA RES.	2-3	Weate, W.Jones
28	14	Wrexham	1-0	Pace
29	21	KIDDERMINSTER HARR.	4-0	Pace(2,1pen), O.G., Bowser
30	28	Walsall	1-1	Joyce
31	10 Apr	Wellington T.	1-1	Parsonage
32	11	Stourbridge	4-1	G.Jones(2), Joyce, Parsonage
33	18	DUDLEY T.	5-3	Parsonage(2), Weate(3)
34	25	Wednesbury Old Ath.	1-0	Weate

P W D L F A Pts
34 21 5 8 76 48 47 (Pos. 2nd)

F.A. Cup

No	Date	Opposition	Res.	Goalscorers
4Q	29 Nov	Stoke	0-2	

(Back): Adams (Trainer), Crump, Boxley, Bott, H.Jones (Chairman).
(Middle): W.Jones, Moore, Slater.
(Front): Stones, Rogers, Williams, Hoskins, G.Jones.

SEASON 1914/15

Birmingham League

No	Date	Opposition	Res.	Goalscorers
1	5 Sep	Walsall	0-0	
2	12	COVENTRY C. RES.	1-1	Haycock
3	19	WILLENHALL SW.	2-0	Haycock, Bowser
4	26	Kidderminster H.	0-5	
5	3 Oct	BRIERLEY HILL	0-1	
6	17	DARLASTON	1-0	Parsonage
7	24	Aston V. Res.	2-2	Haycock, Westwood
8	31	WOLVES RES.	7-1	Hycock(2),Hghes(2),Prsnge(2),Wstwood
9	7 Nov	Stoke C. Res.	0-3	
10	14	WORCESTER C.	4-0	Hughes, Parsonage(2), Westwood
11	28	STOURBRIDGE	3-2	Haycock, Westwood, Hughes
12	12 Dec	DUDLEY T. *	1-4	Haycock
13	26	WELLINGTON T.	4-1	Bowser, Westwood(3)
14	15 Jan	Coventry C. Res.	1-2	Hughes
15	23	Willenhall Sw.	2-2	Hughes(2)
16	30	WREXHAM	2-1	Parsonage, Weate
17	6 Feb	Brierley Hill	1-1	Rogers
18	13	KIDDERMINSTER H.	0-1	
19	20	Darlaston	2-1	Hughes, Rogers
20	27	ASTON V. RES.	4-2	Hughes(2), Haycock, Westwood
21	6 Mar	Wolves Res.	2-3	Parsonage, Hughes
22	13	STOKE C. RES.	2-2	Parsonage, Westwood
23	17	Birmingham C. Res.	1-5	Hughes
24	20	Worcester C.	4-0	Parsonage(2), Haycock(2)
25	24	Wrexham	0-4	
26	26	Wellington T.	0-2	
27	27	Stourbridge	0-3	
28	29	WEST BROMWICH A. RES.	3-6	Parsonage, Hughes, Haycock
29	31	Wednesbury Ath.	0-4	
30	10 Apr	WEDNESBURY ATH.	7-0	Hughes, Parsonage(3), Rogers(3)
31	11	Dudley T.	2-1	Hughes, Parsonage
32	19	WALSALL RES.	1-3	Hughes
33	24	BIRMINGHAM C. RES.	2-4	Westwood, Rogers(pen)
34	27	West Bromwich A. Res.	1-2	Parsonage

* Abandoned 2 mins. from time due to crowd invasion of pitch.

```
P  W  D  L  F  A  Pts
34 12 6  16 62 69 30    (Pos. 12th)
```

F.A. Cup

No	Date	Opposition	Res.	Goalscorers
4Q	21 Nov	WORCESTER C.	1-0	Boxley(pen)
5Q	5 Dec	WALSALL	2-1	Hughes, Rogers
6Q	19	Nottingham Forest	1-6	Hughes

SEASON 1919/20

Birmingham League

No	Date	Opposition	Res.	Goalscorers
1	30 Aug	Walsall	2-1	Watts(2)
2	6 Sep	WALSALL	4-1	Watts(2), Cookson, Parker
3	13	WORCESTER C.	4-2	Izon, Parker(3)
4	20	Worcester C.	1-3	Cookson
5	27	STOKE C. RES.	2-0	Phillips, Watts
6	4 Oct	Stoke C. Res.	2-1	Parker, Watts
7	11	COVENTRY C. RES.	3-2	Watts, Parker, O.G.
8	18	Coventry C. Res.	2-7	Parker, Izon
9	25	BIRMINGHAM C. RES.	2-1	Parker, Watts
10	1 Nov	Birmingham C. Res.	1-0	Parker
11	15	WOLVERHAMPTON W. RES.	3-2	Izon(2), Parker
12	29	Wrexham	0-6	
13	20 Dec	Wednesbury Old Ath.	2-5	Parker(2)
14	26	WELLINGTON T.	2-5	Izon, Barker
15	27	WEDNESBURY OLD ATH.	1-3	Pearce
16	3 Jan	West Bromwich A. Res.	2-2	Pearce, Phillips
17	10	Wolverhampton W. Res.	1-4	Pearce
18	17	WEST BROMWICH A. RES.	2-0	E.F.Roberts, W.Morris
19	24	STOURBRIDGE	5-0	Pearce, D.A.Robers(2), Reece(2)
20	31	Stourbridge	1-4	D.A.Roberts
21	7 Feb	Kidderminster	0-1	
22	14	KIDDERMINSTER	3-1	Watts(2), A.Morris
23	21	DARLASTON	4-2	A.Morris, Watts, Pearce(2)
24	28	Darlaston	0-4	
25	6 Mar	HEDNESFORD	2-2	D.Roberts, Bowser(pen)
26	13	Hednesford	0-7	
27	20	Brierley Hill	1-4	Watts
28	27	BRIERLEY HILL	1-0	W.Jones
29	2 Apr	Wellington T.	0-5	
30	3	WILLENHALL	2-4	W.Morris, A.Morris
31	10	Willenhall	1-5	Rowson
32	17	Nuneaton	1-4	D.Roberts
33	24	NUNEATON	0-1	
34	1 May	WREXHAM	2-6	W.Jones(pen), Stephenson

```
P  W  D  L  F  A  Pts
34 14 2  18 59 95 30    (Pos. 14th)
```

F.A. Cup

No	Date	Opposition	Res.	Goalscorers
4Q	22 Nov	HEDNESFORD	0-8	

SEASON 1920/21

Birmingham League

No	Date	Opposition	Res.	Goalscorers
1	28 Aug	Birmingham C. Res.	0-2	
2	4 Sep	BIRMINGHAM C. RES.	1-2	T.Griffiths
3	6	Wednesbury Old Ath.	0-0	
4	11	Coventry C. Res.	1-2	Lamb
5	18	COVENTRY C. RES.	1-0	C.Thomas
6	2 Oct	WEDNESBURY OLD ATH.	5-2	Thmas,Rbrts,Nghtngle,Lamb,Osbrne
7	16	BRIERLEY HILL ALL.	2-3	Lamb, Roberts
8	6 Nov	WALSALL RES.	4-1	Lamb,Wall(pen),Nightingale,Parker
9	13	Walsall Res.	0-2	
10	20	KIDDERMINSTER	1-0	Nightingale
11	27	NUNEATON	7-1	Fnney(2),Thmas(2),Prker,Rberts(2)
12	18 Dec	Worcester C.	0-6	
13	27	WELLINGTON T.	1-3	Nightingale
14	1 Jan	WORCESTER C.	5-0	Thomas(2), Parker(2), Nightingale
15	8	Brierley Hill All.	1-1	Parker
16	15	Stourbridge	2-2	Thomas, Nightingale
17	22	STOURBRIDGE	1-0	T.Griffiths
18	29	DARLASTON *	1-1	Parker
19	5 Feb	Darlaston	2-1	Williams, Nightingale
20	12	Wrexham	3-2	Nightingale, Brueton, Williams
21	19	WREXHAM	0-1	
22	26	West Bromwich A. Res.	1-1	Walpole
23	4 Mar	WEST BROMWICH A. RES.	2-1	Parker, Williams
24	12	Nuneaton	0-5	
25	19	Kidderminster	4-1	Roberts(2), Brueton, Parker
26	26	Willenhall Swifts	5-3	Thmas(2),Cnninghm,Cook(p),Nghtngle
27	28	Wellington T.	1-2	Parker
28	2 Apr	WILLENHALL SWIFTS	0-1	
29	9	Wolves Res.	1-0	Wolpole
30	11	DARLASTON	1-0	Roberts
31	16	WOLVES RES.	1-0	Parker(pen)
32	23	STOKE C. RES.	5-2	Parker(3), Williams(2)
33	25	Hednesford	2-3	Parker(pen), Williams
34	30	Stoke C. Res.	2-3	Parker, T.Griffiths
35	7 May	HEDNESFORD	7-2	Williams(2), Roberts(4), Parker

* Match abandoned when Darlaston players left the pitch,
after accusations of 2nd referee being biased in favour of Shrewsbury.

```
P  W  D  L   F  A  Pts
34 17 4  13  69 55 38    (Pos. 6th)
```

F.A. Cup

No	Date	Opposition	Res.	Goalscorers
PQR	25 Sep	St. George's	2-1	Pearce, Thomas
1Q	9 Oct	WALSALL	1-0	Lamb
2Q	23	Hednesford	2-3	Osbourne, Nightingale

SEASON 1921/22

Birmingham League

No	Date	Opposition	Res.	Goalscorers
1	27 Aug	BILSTON	4-2	Taylor, Parker(2), D.Roberts
2	3 Sep	Hednesford	3-1	Taylor(2), Belfield
3	17	Worcester C.	2-2	Roberts(2)
4	24	STOURBRIDGE	4-0	Roberts(3), Morris
5	1 Oct	Nuneaton	2-2	Parker, Roberts
6	8	Kidderminster	0-2	
7	15	COVENTRY C. RES.	2-1	Parker(pen), O.G.
8	29	WILLENHALL	2-2	Taylor, Roberts
9	5 Nov	Cannock T.	0-2	
10	12	BURTON ALL SAINTS	0-2	
11	26	Brierley Hill All.	2-2	Parker(2)
12	3 Dec	KIDDERMINSTER	4-1	Parker, Pearce, Roberts(2)
13	10	Redditch	3-1	Parker(2), Roberts
14	17	Tamworth Castle	0-0	
15	24	CANNOCK T.	3-0	Bowen, Cunningham, H.Taylor
16	26	WELLINGTON T.	1-3	H.Taylor
17	31	Wednesbury Old Ath.	3-3	H.Taylor(2), Franks
18	7 Jan	Bilston	2-5	Parker, Plews
19	14	HEDNESFORD	1-1	Parker
20	21	Stafford R.	4-4	Pearce(4,1pen)
21	28	WORCESTER C.	1-3	Pearce
22	4 Feb	Stourbridge	3-2	Pearce(2), H.Taylor
23	11	NUNEATON	2-3	Paker, H.Taylor
24	18	Coventry C. Res.	2-2	Pearce, Rogers
25	25	Darlaston	0-0	
26	4 Mar	Willenhall	1-1	Parker
27	18	STAFFORD R.	3-2	H.Taylor, J.Taylor(2)
28	25	Burton All Saints	1-1	H.Taylor
29	8 Apr	BRIERLEY HILL ALL.	5-1	H.Taylor(2), J.Taylor(2), Parker
30	14	Wellington T.	0-3	
31	17	DARLASTON	4-0	H.Taylor(2), Parker, Rogers
32	22	REDDITCH	1-0	Parker
33	29	TAMWORTH CASTLE	3-0	Parker(3)
34	6 May	WEDNESBURY OLD ATH.	3-0	Crabtree, H.Taylor, D.Roberts

```
P  W  D  L   F  A  Pts
34 14 12 8   71 54 40    (Pos. 5th)
```

F.A. Cup

No	Date	Opposition	Res.	Goalscorers
4Q	19 Nov	WALSALL	0-1	

Welsh Senior Cup

No	Date	Opposition	Res.	Goalscorers
3R	19 Jan	WREXHAM	1-3	H.Taylor

Walsall Senior Cup

No	Date	Opposition	Res.	Goalscorers
1R	3 Oct	ST. GEORGE'S	2-0	Roberts, J.Taylor
2R	22	OAKENGATES T.	4-0	Roberts(2), Parker(2)
3R	1 Jan	WELLINGTON T. RES.	0-0	
3Rr	16 Mar	WELLINGTON T. RES.	4-0	Williams(2), A.Morris(2)
S/F	26 Apr	Stafford Rangers	1-2	Williams

Walsall Challenge Cup

No	Date	Opposition	Res.	Goalscorers
S/F	20 Apr	Bilston	1-4	

SEASON 1922/23

Birmingham League

No	Date	Opposition	Res.	Goalscorers
1	26 Aug	Cradley Heath	3-1	Elvidge(3)
2	2 Sep	TAMWORTH CASTLE	4-0	Crutchley(2), Taylor(2)
3	16	BRIERLEY HILL A.	4-0	Elvidge(2), Taylor, Crutchley(pen)
4	30	WORCESTER C.	1-2	Taylor
5	14 Oct	STAFFORD R.	2-1	Rogers, Bowyer
6	28	WEDNESBURY O.A.	4-1	Elvidge(3,1pen), Crutchley
7	11 Nov	BURTON ALL SAINTS	2-0	Elvidge(2)
8	18	Nuneaton	0-2	
9	25	HEDNESFORD	8-1	Williams(5), Crutchley(2), Gibson
10	2 Dec	Cannock T.	3-2	Gibson, Elvidge(2)
11	16	REDDITCH	2-0	Williams, J.Evans
12	23	CRADLEY HEATH	4-0	J.Evans, Elvidge(2), Williams
13	26	WELLINGTON T.	1-0	Bowyer
14	30	Tamworth Castle	3-1	Williams(2), J.Evans
15	6 Jan	Stourbridge	1-0	Hatton
16	20	Brierley Hill A.	4-0	Gibson, J.Evans(2), Elvidge
17	27	KIDDERMINSTER	2-1	J.Evans, Gibson
18	3 Feb	Worcester C.	2-3	Hatton, J.Evans
19	10	BILSTON	5-4	Elvidge(2),Bowyer,Taylor,J.Evans
20	17	Stafford R.	1-1	Taylor
21	24	WILLENHALL	3-3	Elvidge, Whatmore, Taylor
22	3 Mar	Wednesbury O.A.	3-2	Elvidge, J.Evans, Whatmore
23	10	Darlaston	1-2	Elvidge
24	17	Burton All Saint	0-0	
25	24	NUNEATON	3-0	Taylor, Lovibond, Whatmore
26	30	Wellington T.	1-2	Gibson
27	31	Hednesford	1-1	Taylor
28	2 Apr	DARLASTON	2-1	Bowyer, Whatmore
29	7	CANNOCK T.	4-1	Elvidge,Whatmore,J.Evans,Gibson
30	16	Willenhall	0-1	
31	18	Kidderminster	2-1	Gibson, J.Evans
32	21	Redditch	2-1	J.Evans, Williams
33	28	Bilston	2-1	Elvidge, R.Jones
34	5 May	STOURBRIDGE	2-5	Whatmore, Gibson

```
P  W  D  L  F  A  Pts
34 23 4  7  82 41 50    (Pos. Champions)
```

F.A. Cup

No	Date	Opposition	Res.	Goalscorers
EQPR	9 Sep	Chirk	2-1	Bowyer, R.Jones
PRQ	23	WORCESTER C.	3-2	Crutchley(pen), Elvidge(2)
1Q	7 Oct	Bilston U.	4-1	R.Jones(2), Elvidge(2)
2Q	21	Stafford R.	3-2	Crutchley(pen),Bowyer,Merrington
3Q	4 Nov	St. George's	1-2	Merrington

Welsh Senior Cup

No	Date	Opposition	Res.	Goalscorers
3R	20 Nov	Oakengates T.	3-1	Bowyer, Gibson, Williams
4R	9 Dec	Ogwen Valley	5-0	Williams(2),J.Evans,Hatton(2pens)
5R	18 Jan	Oswestry T.	1-3	J.Evans

SEASON 1923/24

Birmingham League

No	Date	Opposition	Res.	Goalscorers
1	25 Aug	WORCESTER C.	2-2	Edwards(pen), Elvidge
2	1 Sep	Burton T.	0-4	
3	8	NUNEATON	1-0	Edwards(pen)
4	10	WEDNESBURY	7-1	Lovibnd,Rhdes(2),Elvdge(2),Vaughn,Jnes
5	15	Nuneaton	4-2	Elvdge,Hawkes,Rhdes,Edwrds(pen)
6	29	Cradley Heath	0-3	
7	13 Oct	Kidderminster	2-0	Jones, Vaughn
8	27	Redditch	1-6	Rhodes
9	10 Nov	Darlaston	2-0	Elvidge(2)
10	24	Bilston	1-4	Vaughn
11	1 Dec	OAKENGATES T.	5-0	Elvdge,Edwrds(p),Cashmre,Jnes(2)
12	8	STAFFORD R.	4-0	Cashmore(2), Elvidge, Hatton
13	15	Brierley Hill	3-1	Elvidge(3)
14	22	Worcester C.	2-2	Walters, Elvidge
15	26	WELLINGTON T.	0-1	
16	29	BURTON T.	3-2	Elvidge(2), Walters
17	5 Jan	Hednesford T.	2-3	Cashmore, Rhodes
18	12	STOURBRIDGE	1-0	Cashmore
19	26	Wednesbury	2-1	Cashmore, Walters
20	2 Feb	CRADLEY HEATH	3-0	Walters, Rhodes(2)
21	16	KIDDERMINSTER	3-0	Walters(3)
22	23	Stourbridge	0-1	
23	29	REDDITCH	6-1	Walters(3), Cashmore(2), Vaughn
24	8 Mar	Cannock T.	0-1	
25	15	DARLASTON	3-0	Cashmore(2), Elvidge
26	22	Willenhall	1-3	Crutchley
27	29	BILSTON	3-1	Elvidge, Cashmore, Vaughn
28	5 Apr	Oakengates T.	1-2	Hatton
29	12	Stafford R.	1-1	Elvidge
30	18	Wellington T.	1-0	Cashmore
31	19	BRIERLEY HILL	3-0	Vaughn, Rhodes, Walters
32	21	HEDNESFORD T.	3-0	Lovibond, Cashmore(2)
33	28	CANNOCK T.	3-0	Vaughn(2), Cashmore(2)
34	3 May	WILLENHALL	6-1	Elvidge(2),Cashmore(2),OG.Harvey

```
P  W  D  L  F  A  Pts
34 21 3  10 79 43 45    (Pos. 2nd)
```

F.A. Cup

No	Date	Opposition	Res.	Goalscorers
PQR	22 Sep	DARLASTON	3-1	Cull, Lovibond, Edwards(pen)
1Q	6 Oct	WORCESTER C.	2-1	Vaughn, O.G.
2Q	20	WILLENHALL	2-0	Vaughn(2)
3Q	3 Nov	BLOXWICH STR.	3-1	Sheldon(pen), Vaughn(2)
4Q	17	Hinckley	1-3	Rhodes

Welsh Senior Cup

No	Date	Opposition	Res.	Goalscorers
3R	14 Feb	CARDIFF C.	0-0	
3Rr	27	Cardiff C.	0-3	

1922/23 Season:
(Back) Harley, Lewis, Sheldon, Gamble, Crutchley, Causer, Challis   (2nd Row) Officials including - Powell, Wood, Blent, Corfield, Vicars (3rd Row) Weston, Bowyer, Evans, Gascoigne, Halton, Elvidge, J.Williams, Whatmore, H.Jones   (Front) Edwards, R.Jones, Gibson, Taylor.

SEASON 1924/25

Birmingham League

No	Date	Opposition	Res.	Goalscorers
1	30 Aug	Redditch	5-3	Elvidge(2),Crutchley,Rhodes,White
2	1 Sep	Stourbridge	1-3	Winsper
3	13	STAFFORD R.	4-2	Cull, Crutchley, O.G., White
4	27	BURTON T.	2-0	Cashmore, Elvidge
5	11 Oct	OAKENGATES T.	6-0	Crtchly(2),Cshmre(2),Elvdge,Rhdess
6	18	Bilston U.	0-2	
7	1 Nov	Willenhall	1-1	White
8	8	HEDNESFORD T.	8-1	Cashmre(3),Elvdge(2),Whte(2),Wnsper
9	15	Cannock T.	0-1	
10	29	Worcester C.	1-1	Elvidge
11	6 Dec	KIDDERMINSTER	1-1	Rhodes
12	13	Brierley Hill	1-2	Cashmore
13	20	Oswestry T.	0-2	
14	26	WELLINGTON T.	3-1	Cashmore, Elvidge, Edwards(pen)
15	27	ST. GEORGE'S	0-2	
16	29	Cradley Heath	0-4	
17	17 Jan	Stafford R.	1-2	Cull
18	24	STOURBRIDGE	0-4	
19	31	Burton T.	0-2	
20	7 Feb	Oakengates T.	2-1	Hatton(pen), Cashmore
21	14	Darlaston	2-2	Crutchley, Rhodes
22	21	BILSTON U.	4-1	White, Elvidge(2), Cull
23	7 Mar	WILLENHALL	2-1	Lea, Edwards
24	14	Hednesford T.	4-1	Edwards,Sambrook,Elvidge,White
25	21	CANNOCK T.	7-0	Edwards, Elvidge(6)
26	3 Apr	Wellington T.	0-3	
27	4	WORCESTER C.	0-0	
28	11	Kidderminster	0-2	
29	13	CRADLEY HEATH	1-0	Williams
30	18	BRIERLEY HILL	6-0	Elvidge(3), Williams(2), Cull
31	20	DARLASTON	7-0	Elvidge(3), Cunningham, White(3)
32	25	OSWESTRY T.	1-0	White
33	27	REDDITCH	5-0	Higgs(2), Williams(2), White
34	2 May	St. George's	0-1	

P W D L F A Pts
34 16 5 13 75 46 37   (Pos. 9th)

F.A. Cup

No	Date	Opposition	Res.	Goalscorers
EPQR	6 Sep	CHIRK	8-0	Crtchley,Elvdge(3),Whte(2),Lea,Cull
PQR	20	STAFFORD R.	1-1	Cull
PRQr	24	Stafford R.	2-1	Cashmore(2)
1Q	4 Oct	Willenhall	1-2	White

Welsh Senior Cup

No	Date	Opposition	Res.	Goalscorers
3R	22 Jan	RHOS	3-2	Cashmore, Crutchley, Rhodes
4R	12 Feb	Rhyl	2-0	Cashmore, Elvidge
5R	9 Mar	Merthyr T.	1-3	Edwards

SEASON 1925/26

Birmingham League

No	Date	Opposition	Res.	Goalscorers
1	29 Aug	STOURBRIDGE	2-0	Evans(pen), Crutchley
2	31	St. George's	1-3	White
3	5 Sep	BURTON T.	2-2	Evans, White
4	12	Hednesford T.	3-2	Evans(pen), Savage, Jackson
5	26	Kidderminster	3-0	Jackson, Brown, Savage
6	10 Oct	Bilston U.	0-1	
7	7 Nov	OSWESTRY T.	0-1	
8	14	Cannock T.	3-4	Evans(2), Higgs
9	21	REDDITCH	5-2	Savage(2), Evans(3,1pen)
10	28	WILLENHALL	3-0	Jackson, Evans(2,1pen)
11	5 Dec	Stafford R.	1-6	Evans
12	12	Cradley Heath	2-3	Savage, Baxter
13	19	DARLASTON *	1-0	O.G.
14	26	WELLINGTON T.	1-0	Savage
15	2 Jan	Stourbridge	0-3	
16	9	OAKENGATES T.	2-3	Oldacre, Baxter
17	16	Burton T.	2-4	Evans, Savage
18	23	HEDNESFORD T.	6-1	Savage(3),Evans,Oldacre,Jackson
19	30	Oakengates T.	5-0	Jackson, Oldacre(2), Savage(2)
20	6 Feb	KIDDERMINSTER	3-2	Savage, Evans(2)
21	13	Worcester C.	1-0	Oldacre
22	20	BILSTON U.	3-1	Evans, Jackson, Oldacre
23	27	Willenhall	0-3	
24	11 Mar	WORCESTER C.	2-0	Evans, Savage
25	13	Brierley Hill	0-1	
26	20	Oswestry T.	4-4	Elvidge, Oldacre(2), Savage
27	27	CANNOCK T.	3-1	Winsper, Savage, Brown
28	2 Apr	Wellington T.	1-1	Evans
29	3	Redditch	3-5	White(2), Oldacre
30	5	ST. GEORGE'S	6-0	Oldacre(3), White, Evans(2,1pen)
31	10	STAFFORD R.	2-1	Savage, Oldacre(pen)
32	17	Darlaston	0-2	
33	24	CRADLEY HEATH	2-2	Oldacre(2pens)
34	26	BRIERLEY HILL	3-1	Evans, Oldacre(2)
35	1 May	DARLASTON	2-0	Evans, Winsper

* Abandoned after 74 mins due to bad light.

P W D L F A Pts
34 17 4 13 76 59 38   (Pos. 5th)

F.A. Cup

No	Date	Opposition	Res.	Goalscorers
PQR	19 Sep	OSWESTRY T.	3-2	Jackson(2), Savage
1Q	3 Oct	STOURBRIDGE	3-1	Jackson, Evans(pen), Savage
2Q	17	Stafford R.	1-1	Evans
2Qr	22	STAFFORD R.	6-0	White, Evans, Jackson(2)
3Q	31	Wellington	1-5	O.G.

SEASON 1926/27

Birmingham League

No	Date	Opposition	Res.	Goalscorers
1	4 Sep	OSWESTRY T.	7-1	Baxter(3), Savage, Brown, Reid(2)
2	11	BILSTON U.	4-2	Savage, O.G., Reid, Rhodes
3	25	WILLENHALL T.	1-2	Brown
4	9 Oct	KIDDERMINSTER	2-2	Reid(2)
5	23	CANNOCK T.	4-0	Jackson(3,1pen), Brown
6	30	OAKENGATES T.	2-2	Jackson, Savage
7	13 Nov	STOURBRIDGE	3-8	Jackson, Reid, O.G.
8	20	Cradley Heath	2-3	Reid, Rotton
9	27	HEDNESFORD T.	7-0	Rottn,Savge(2),Rhdes(2),Brwn,Reid
10	4 Dec	Burton T.	0-2	
11	11	WORCESTER C.	4-1	Rotton(2), Winsper, Reid
12	18	Stafford R.	1-2	Rotton
13	26	WELLINGTON T.	2-1	Savage, Rotton
14	28	Redditch	1-6	Rhodes
15	1 Jan	STAFFORD R.	2-1	Reid, Rhodes(pen)
16	8	Willenhall T.	2-5	Jackson, Rotton
17	15	Darlaston	4-1	Goodrick,Reid,Rhodes(pen),Rotton
18	29	Worcester C.	1-5	T.Jeavons
19	5 Feb	BRIERLEY HILL	3-4	Brown, G.Jones, Savage
20	12	Bilston U.	0-4	
21	19	REDDITCH	3-0	Reid, Baxter(2)
22	26	Kidderminster	0-2	
23	5 Mar	Oswestry T.	3-2	O.G., G.Jones, Reid
24	12	Cannock T.	1-4	Rowley
25	19	Oakengates T.	1-0	Reid
26	26	DARLASTON	6-0	Bxter(3),JW.Jeavns,Svage,Rhdes
27	2 Apr	Stourbridge	1-1	Reid
28	9	CRADLEY HEATH	0-3	
29	15	Wellington T.	1-3	Rowley
30	16	Hednesford T.	1-1	Reid
31	18	ST. GEORGE'S	0-4	
32	30	St. George's	1-2	Rhodes
33	2 May	BURTON T.	2-1	Savage, Rowley
34	7	Brierley Hill	1-4	Rowley

```
P  W  D  L  F  A  Pts
34 13 4  17 73 79 30   (Pos. 13th)
```

F.A. Cup

No	Date	Opposition	Res.	Goalscorers
PQR	18 Sep	Worcester C.	2-0	Baxter(2)
1Q	2 Oct	CRADLEY HEATH	1-1	Reid
1Qr	7	Cradley Heath	0-6	

Welsh Senior Cup

No	Date	Opposition	Res.	Goalscorers
1R	10 Mar	WALSALL	1-3	Reid

SEASON 1927/28

Birmingham League

No	Date	Opposition	Res.	Goalscorers
1	27 Aug	ST. GEORGE'S	3-1	Rowley(3)
2	9 Sep	STAFFORD R.	4-4	Rowley(2), Castle(2)
3	24	Bilston U.	3-4	Rowley(2), Rice
4	8 Oct	Hednesford	6-1	Castle(2), Rowley(2), Rice(2)
5	22	Worcester C.	1-0	Rowley
6	29	OAKENGATES T.	4-3	Rowley(2), Nightingale, Morgan
7	12 Nov	Redditch	3-2	Rowley, Rice, Castle
8	19	DARLASTON	10-0	*
9	26	Cradley Heath	2-5	Castle, Rice
10	3 Dec	CANNOCK T.	7-2	Rice(3), O.G., Castle, Rowley(2)
11	10	Oswestry T.	5-3	Rice(2), Goodrick, Nightingale(2)
12	17	STOURBRIDGE	6-0	Castle,Rowley(2),Rice(2),Morgan
13	26	WELLINGTON T.	1-3	Rice
14	31	Kidderminster	5-5	Castle, Rowley(3), Roberts
15	7 Jan	KIDDERMINSTER	2-1	Morgan, Castle
16	14	Stourbridge	0-2	
17	21	OSWESTRY T.	6-1	Cstle,Nghtingle,Rice(2),Mrgan,Rwley
18	4 Feb	CRADLEY HEATH	5-1	Rice, Castle(4)
19	11	Darlaston	3-2	Rowley, Nightingale, Rice
20	25	Willenhall	2-3	Rice(2)
21	3 Mar	Oakengates T.	2-2	Rowley, Castle
22	10	WORCESTER C.	1-0	Morgan
23	17	Brierley Hill	1-4	Castle
24	24	HEDNESFORD	8-0	Castle(2),Rice(2),Rowley(3),Arch(p)
25	31	Burton T.	2-4	Nightingale, Castle
26	6 Apr	Wellington T.	1-2	Rowley
27	7	BILSTON U.	7-0	Rwley(3),Cstle,Nghtingle,Shldn(p),Rberts
28	9	BURTON T.	2-1	Nightingale, Morgan
29	14	Stafford R.	0-3	
30	16	Cannock T.	4-4	Rowley(2), Wood, Morgan
31	21	WILLENHALL	5-1	Wood(2),Rowley,Mrgan,Nghtingale
32	28	St. George's	1-6	Rice
33	3 May	REDDITCH	4-1	Castle(3), Rice
34	5	BRIERLEY HILL	3-0	Castle(2), Rice

* Castle(2), Rice, Nightingale, Rowley(2), Scorer, Winsper, Morgan(2)

```
P  W  D  L  F   A  Pts
34 20 4  10 119 71 44   (Pos. 4th)
```

F.A. Cup

No	Date	Opposition	Res.	Goalscorers
EQPR	3 Sep	OAKENGATES T	2-0	Castle, Morgan
PQR	17	WOLVERHAMPTON AMAT.	6-1	Cstle,Rwley,Wnsper,OG.,Rwley,Screr
Q1	1 Oct	CRADLEY HEATH	1-0	Morgan
Q2	15	OSWESTRY T.	3-4	Castle(2), Nightingale

SEASON 1928/29

Birmingham League

No	Date	Opposition	Res.	Goalscorers
1	25 Aug	Walsall Res.	0-1	
2	1 Sep	STOURBRIDGE	6-2	Rice(2), Wood(2), Castle, Morgan
3	8	Stafford R.	1-8	Castle
4	22	OAKENGATES T.	6-0	Shakeshaft(3), Wood, O.G., Castle
5	6 Oct	WORCESTER C.	3-3	Wood(2), Morgan
6	20	OSWESTRY T.	1-2	Morgan
7	27	Kidderminster	2-4	Rice, Wood
8	3 Nov	BRIERLEY HILL	2-2	Goodrick, Wood
9	10	Hednesford	3-2	Rotton, Wood(2)
10	17	ST. GEORGE'S	11-2	Rice(5),Rotton(3),Morgan,Wood(2)
11	24	St. George's	3-1	Rotton, Wood(2)
12	1 Dec	Hereford U.	3-1	Wood, O.G., Rotton
13	8	Bilston U.	0-4	
14	15	WILLENHALL	6-2	Rotton(5), Wood
15	22	Willenhall	1-3	Fraser
16	26	WELLINGTON T.	2-1	Rotton, Wood
17	29	BILSTON U.	8-1	Tranter(3), Rotton(5)
18	5 Jan	HEREFORD U.	3-0	Rotton(2), Morgan
19	12	Oakengates T.	2-1	Rotton, Wood
20	26	KIDDERMINSTER	4-1	Rotton(2), Wood, Morgan
21	2 Feb	HEDNESFORD	4-0	Wood(2), Rotton, Morgan
22	9	Brierley Hill	2-2	Swash, Rotton
23	16	WALSALL RES.	1-0	Rotton
24	23	Oswestry T.	4-6	Rice(2), Rotton, Tranter
25	2 Mar	CRADLEY HEATH	4-1	Rotton(pen), Rice(2), Morgan
26	9	Worcester C.	0-2	
27	23	Cradley Heath	1-2	Rice
28	29	Wellington T.	0-5	
29	30	Redditch	3-1	Rotton(3),
30	1 Apr	REDDITCH	3-0	Rotton, Swash, Rice
31	6	STAFFORD R.	2-0	Rotton, O.G.
32	13	Stourbridge	4-3	Swash(2), Rotton, Riley
33	27	BURTON T.	2-3	Morgan, Rotton(pen)
34	4 May	Burton T.	0-3	

```
P  W  D  L  F  A  Pts
34 19 3  12 97 69 41   (Pos. 5th)
```

F.A. Cup

No	Date	Opposition	Res.	Goalscorers
PRQ	15 Sep	Leamington	1-1	Rice
PRQ	20	LEAMINGTON	2-4	Fraser, Morgan

Welsh Cup

No	Date	Opposition	Res.	Goalscorers
3R	19 Jan	DRUIDS	6-0	O.G., Rotton(2), Wood(3)
4R	14 Feb	LLANDUDNO	2-1	Bryan, Rice
5R	7 Mar	BANGOR C.	1-1	Rice
5Rr	13	Bangor C.	1-3	Scorer

SEASON 1929/30

Birmingham League

No	Date	Opposition	Res.	Goalscorers
1	14 Sep	STAFFORD R.	0-0	
2	28	WILLENHALL	3-3	Bancroft, Gummery(pen), Taylor
3	12 Oct	HEREFORD U.	3-0	Tranter(2), Taylor
4	19	Kettering U.	0-2	
5	26	Bilston U.	0-1	
6	2 Nov	Worcester C.	3-8	Tranter, Griffiths, Gummery(pen)
7	9	WALSALL RES.	2-1	Mound, Taylor
8	16	Cradley Heath	0-2	
9	23	OSWESTRY T.	3-1	Taylor(pen), Imbrey, Mound
10	30	Brierley Hill	1-2	Taylor(pen)
11	7 Dec	HEDNESFORD	3-2	Mound, O.G., Lees,
12	14	St. George's	3-3	Tranter, Mound(2)
13	21	Kidderminster	2-0	Gummery, Fraser
14	26	WELLINGTON T.	3-1	Mound(2), Lees
15	28	KIDDERMINSTER	3-0	Lees, Taylor(pen), Mound
16	4 Jan	ST. GEORGE'S	9-0	Mound(4), Lees(3), Fraser, Taylor
17	11	Hednesford	3-2	Mound, Taylor, Swash
18	18	BRIERLEY HILL	0-3	
19	25	Oswestry T.	3-1	Mound, Roberts(2)
20	1 Feb	CRADLEY HEATH	6-1	Rberts(2),Gmmery(2,1pen),Mound(2)
21	8	Walsall Res.	3-2	Roberts, Imbrey, Scorer
22	15	Worcester C.	2-1	Roberts, Lees
23	22	KETTERING	0-1	
24	8 Mar	Hereford U.	3-2	Mound(2), Roberts
25	15	STOURBRIDGE	8-2	Mound(4),Taylor(2),Imbry,Gmmery
26	22	WILLENHALL	0-1	
27	29	OAKENGATES T.	0-1	
28	5 Apr	Stafford R.	1-0	Roberts
29	18	Wellington T.	1-1	Tranter
30	19	BURTON T.	3-1	Traner(2), Roberts
31	21	BILSTON U.	3-1	Roberts, O.G., Taylor
32	26	Burton T.	1-4	Lees
33	28	Stourbridge	2-5	Griffiths(2)
34	3 May	Oakengates T.	1-0	Tranter

```
P  W  D  L  F  A  Pts
34 19 4  11 78 55 42   (Pos. 4th)
```

F.A. Cup

No	Date	Opposition	Res.	Goalscorers
EPRQ	7 Sep	CANNOCK T.	12-0	Bancrft(5),Lees(3),Frser(2),Grmmry(2)
PRQ	21	BLOXWICH STROLLERS	5-2	Lees(3), Fraser, Bancroft
1Q	5 Oct	WELLINGTON T.	0-1	

Welsh Senior Cup

No	Date	Opposition	Res.	Goalscorers
3R	8 Feb	HOLT UNITED	12-1	*
4R	22	OSWESTRY T.	3-2	Imbrey, Taylor, Mound

* Price(4), Baddeley(3), Swash, Griffiths(2), Davies, Bryan

SEASON 1930/31

Birmingham League

No	Date	Opposition	Res.	Goalscorers
1	30 Aug	WORCESTER C.	1-0	Mound
2	13 Sep	STAFFORD R. RES.	2-1	Griffiths(2)
3	20	Worcester C.	1-6	Mound
4	11 Oct	CRADLEY HEATH	3-1	Mound, Roberts, Vaughn
5	18	Kettering T.	3-3	Buckingham(2), Mound
6	25	HEREFORD U.	0-0	
7	1 Nov	Burton T.	1-1	Mound
8	15	Kidderminster	2-2	Buckingham, Taylor
9	22	OAKENGATES T.	4-2	Mound(2), O.G., Buckingham
10	6 Dec	Brierley Hill	1-4	Buckingham
11	13	WEST BROMWICH A. 'A'	2-5	Roberts, Mound
12	20	Bilston	1-0	F.Taylor
13	26	Wellington T.	2-3	Imbrey, Mound
14	27	BILSTON	5-2	Mound(3), F.Taylor, Tranter
15	3 Jan	West Bromwich A. 'A'	3-0	F.Taylor, Vaughn, Fryer(pen)
16	10	BRIERLEY HILL	3-1	F.Taylor(2), Mound
17	17	Stafford R. Res.	0-5	
18	24	ST. GEORGE'S	8-1	F.Tylor(5),Rberts,Mound,Bckingham
19	7 Feb	WALSALL RES.	3-1	F.Taylor(2,1pen), Vaughn
20	14	Cradley Heath	1-3	F.Taylor(pen)
21	21	KETTERING T.	6-0	Buckingham(4), Fryer(pen), Mound
22	28	Hereford U.	0-4	
23	7 Mar	BURTON T.	3-1	F.Taylor(2), Tranter
24	14	Hednesford T.	2-5	F.Taylor(2)
25	21	KIDDERMINSTER	3-2	F.Taylor, Buckingham(2)
26	28	Oakengates T.	1-4	Roberts
27	3 Apr	Wellington T.	1-3	Mound
28	6	STOURBRIDGE	8-2	Buckingham(4),Mound(2),Tranter(2)
29	7	Stourbridge	1-2	Buckingham
30	21	HEDNESFORD T.	0-1	
31	23	Walsall Res.	3-4	
32	25	Oswestry T.	0-6	
33	30	OSWESTRY T.	0-0	
34	2 May	St. George's	2-4	Groves(pen), Vaughn

P W D L F A Pts
34 14 5 15 76 79 33   (Pos. 9th)

F.A. Cup

No	Date	Opposition	Res.	Goalscorers
EPQR	6 Sep	St. Georges	0-4	

Welsh Senior Cup

No	Date	Opposition	Res.	Goalscorers
3R	22 Jan	GWERSYLLT	10-2	Bckingham(6),Tylor(2),Rberts,Trnter
4R	31	WELSHPOOL T.	11-2	Tylor(6),Trnter(2),Vaughn,Rberts,OG
5R	26 Feb	NEWPORT C.	5-2	Bckingham,Mound,Rberts(2),Vaughn
6R	19 Mar	LOVELLS ATH.	0-0	
6Rr	26	Lovells Ath.	1-0	Taylor
S/F	13 Apr	CARDIFF C.	1-0	Roberts
F	27	Wrexham	0-7	

SEASON 1931/32

Birmingham League

No	Date	Opposition	Res.	Goalscorers
1	29 Aug	Oswestry T.	0-3	
2	26 Sep	COLWYN BAY	2-3	Sambrook, Chambers
3	10 Oct	BILSTON U.	2-0	Sambrook, C.Millington
4	17	Hednesford U.	2-2	Chambers(2)
5	24	KIDDERMINSTER	1-0	Chambers
6	31	Stafford R.	0-7	
7	7 Nov	OAKENGATES T.	3-0	Blakemore, Fryer, Williams
8	14	WALSALL RES.	2-1	Williams(2)
9	21	Hereford U.	3-3	Fryer, Blakemore, Sambrook
10	28	RHYL ATHLETIC	2-4	Fryer, Sambrook
11	5 Dec	Burton T.	0-9	
12	12	CRADLEY HEATH	4-2	Sambrook,Smith,J.Grffiths,Wlliams
13	19	Stourbridge	0-2	
14	26	WELLINGTON T.	1-1	Williams
15	2 Jan	WORCESTER C.	1-3	F.Williams
16	9	Worcester C.	2-10	J.Williams, Smith
17	16	OSWESTRY T.	1-0	Rotton
18	23	Bilston U.	1-1	Wassall
19	30	HEDNESFORD U.	3-1	Rotton(2), Blunt
20	6 Feb	Colwyn Bay	1-2	Wassall
21	13	STAFFORD R.	2-1	J.Williams, Rotton
22	27	BREIRLEY HILL	0-1	
23	12 Mar	WREXHAM RES.	1-1	Fryer(pen)
24	19	Oakengates T.	1-4	Williams
25	25	Wellington T.	2-1	Rotton(2)
26	26	Walsall Res.	4-3	Smbrook,Rtton,F.Wlliams,Brookes
27	28	STOURBRIDGE	8-1	Rtton(4),J.Wlliams,F.Wlliams,Brooke(2)
28	2 Apr	HEREFORD U.	7-2	*
29	9	Rhyl Athletic	1-4	Sambrook
30	16	BURTON T.	2-2	Rotton(2)
31	18	Brierley Hill	2-2	Sambrook, Rotton
32	23	Cradley Heath	1-4	Sambrook
33	30	Wrexham Res.	2-2	Rotton, J.Williams
34	7 May	Kidderminster	0-2	

* Brookes(2), Doody, Sambrook(2), J.Williams, Rotton

P W D L F A Pts
34 13 7 14 64 81 33   (Pos. 10th)

F.A. Cup

No	Date	Opposition	Res.	Goalscorers
EPQR	5 Sep	BOURNVILLE	6-1	Fryr(p),OG,Wlliams,Smbrook,Smth,Blakemre
1PQ	19	WALSALL LMS	4-1	Sambrook(3), Chambers
1Q	3 Oct	OAKENGATES T.	1-2	Sambrook

Welsh Senior Cup

No	Date	Opposition	Res.	Goalscorers
5R	19 Feb	COLWYN BAY	5-1	J.Wlliams,F.Wlliams,Wssall,Rtton,Smth
6R	5 Mar	Wrexham	2-4	Rotton, Butler

SEASON 1932/33

Birmingham League

No	Date	Opposition	Res.	Goalscorers
1	27 Aug	Bangor C.	1-2	J.Williams
2	29	OAKENGATES T.	3-1	Sambrook, Harrison, Taylor
3	5 Sep	Oakengates T.	3-1	Taylor, Cull, O.G.
4	10	HEREFORD U.	0-1	
5	24	WORCESTER C.	3-1	J.Williams, Sambrook, Taylor
6	8 Oct	BRIERLEY HILL	3-3	Taylor(2), Sambrook
7	22	Hereford U.	1-2	Taylor
8	5 Nov	Stafford U.	4-1	Burgess, Sambrook, Williams, Fryer
9	12	OSWESTRY T.	2-5	Sambrook, Taylor
10	19	Hednesford T.	0-2	
11	26	WREXHAM RES.	2-2	Cull, Sambrook
12	3 Dec	Cradley Heath	1-3	Blackmore
13	10	WALSALL RES.	2-0	Sambrook, Cull
14	17	Stourbridge	3-3	Taylor(2), Fryer(pen)
15	24	RHYL ATH.	2-0	Taylor, Cull
16	26	WELLINGTON T.	4-1	Taylor(3), Williams
17	31	BANGOR C.	6-1	Fryer(p), Taylor(3), Wlliams, Sambrook
18	14 Jan	KIDDERMINSTER	5-2	Taylor(5)
19	21	Worcester C.	0-1	
20	28	COLWYN BAY	1-0	Cull
21	4 Feb	Brierley Hill	3-3	Taylor, Sambrook, Cull
22	11	Burton T.	1-6	Taylor
23	4 Mar	STAFFORD R.	1-0	Taylor
24	11	Oswestry T.	1-2	Williams
25	18	HEDNESFORD T.	3-2	Taylor, Sambrook(2)
26	25	Wrexham Res.	0-3	
27	1 Apr	CRADLEY HEATH	2-1	O.G., Taylor
28	8	Walsall Res.	3-4	Taylor, Sambrook, Williams
29	14	Wellington T.	2-1	Price, Burgess
30	15	STOURBRIDGE	3-3	Price, Taylor(2)
31	17	Colwyn Bay	0-0	
32	22	Rhyl Ath.	0-2	
33	24	BURTON T.	4-0	Williams, Price, Taylor, Sambrook
34	29	Kidderminster	1-3	Williams

```
P  W  D  L  F  A  Pts
34 15 6  13 70 62 36    (Pos. 8th)
```

F.A. Cup

No	Date	Opposition	Res.	Goalscorers
PQR	17 Sep	Nuneaton	3-1	O.G., Burgess, Taylor
1Q	1 Oct	KIDDERMINSTER	5-1	Smbrook, Fryer(p), Taylor(2), Wlliams
2Q	15	Whitchurch	3-3	Taylor, Sambrook, Cull
2Qr	20	WHITCHURCH	1-0	Williams
3Q	29	Hereford U.	1-3	Williams

Welsh Senior Cup

No	Date	Opposition	Res.	Goalscorers
4R	1 Dec	Llanidloes	3-0	Cull, Williams(2)
5R	7 Jan	MACHYNLLETH	3-1	Williams(2), Sambrook
6R	18	Bangor C.	3-3	Cull(2), Taylor
6Rr	26	BANGOR C.	0-1	

SEASON 1933/34

Birmingham League

No	Date	Opposition	Res.	Goalscorers
1	26 Aug	Oakengates T.	3-3	Taylor, Lawley, Wardell
2	2 Sep	BRIERLEY HILL	3-2	Taylor(3)
3	9	Stourbridge	2-1	Marson, Price
4	23	WREXHAM RES.	3-3	Taylor(2), Lawley(pen)
5	25	Brierley Hill	2-1	Taylor(2)
6	7 Oct	Hereford U.	1-2	Lawley(pen)
7	21	Worcester C.	2-1	Taylor, Driscoll
8	4 Nov	STAFFORD R.	7-2	Taylor(3), Lawley(2), Driscoll, Wrdell
9	18	BANGOR C.	5-2	Gittens, Taylor(2), Mound, Wardell
10	25	Rhyl	0-1	
11	2 Dec	CANNOCK	3-1	Driscoll(2), Gittens
12	9	Oswestry T.	8-3	Taylor(6), Driscoll, Wardell
13	16	PORT VALE RES.	6-3	Taylor(4), Marson, Wardell
14	23	Cradley Heath	3-1	Mound, Taylor(2)
15	26	WELLINGTON T.	3-3	Taylor, Marson, Lawley
16	30	BURTON ALBION.	2-0	Lawley, Taylor
17	6 Jan	OAKENGATES T.	6-1	Lwley(p), Mrson(2), Tylor, Mound, Wrdell
18	13	Nuneaton T.	0-3	
19	20	Hednesford T.	1-4	Wardell
20	27	Colwyn Bay	3-1	Wardell(2), Taylor
21	3 Feb	Wrexham Res.	1-4	Wardell
22	10	HEDNESFORD T.	0-0	
23	17	HEREFORD U.	2-2	Anderson, Taylor
24	3 Mar	WORCESTER C.	0-3	
25	8	COLWYN BAY	6-1	Taylor(6)
26	17	Stafford R.	0-5	
27	21	Burton Albion	0-2	
28	24	KIDDERMINSTER H.	2-1	Taylor(2)
29	30	Wellington T.	0-4	
30	31	Bangor C.	1-3	Wardell
31	2 Apr	STOURBRIDGE	2-1	Taylor, Driscoll
32	7	RHYL	0-2	
33	14	Cannock	0-0	
34	16	NUNEATON T.	3-1	Morris, Taylor(2)
35	21	OSWESTRY T.	1-3	Driscoll
36	25	Kidderminster H.	0-1	
37	28	Port Vale Res.	2-3	Taylor, Morris
38	5 May	CRADLEY HEATH	6-3	Taylor(3), Driscoll, O.G., Edwards

```
P  W  D  L  F  A  Pts
38 18 6  14 89 77 42    (Pos. 10th)
```

F.A. Cup

No	Date	Opposition	Res.	Goalscorers
EPRQ	16 Sep	OSWESTRY T.	1-0	Wardell
1Q	30	HEREFORD U.	3-1	Lawley, Taylor, Wardell
2Q	14 Pct	Wellington T.	2-2	Lawley(pen), Mound
2Qr	19	WELLINGTON T.	4-1	Gittens, Wardell, Taylor(2)
3Q	28	BRIERLEY HILL	2-1	Gittens(2)
4Q	11 Nov	Gainsborough Trinity	0-0	
4Qr	16	GAINSBOROUGH TRINITY	1-3	Wardell

(Back) 'Money' Jones, Roscamp, Bates, Plant, Bennett, Holmes, Powell, Wassall.
(Front) Lloyd, Bird, Quayle, Driscoll, McCorkindale, 'Sacker' Mound.

1934

(Back) Ramsey, Edwards, Bates, Williams, Parkinson, Powell, Darrall, Holmes, Lucas,
(Front) Clarke, Jeavons, Hewitson, Matthews, Wyness, Hopley.

1935-36 Season

SEASON 1934/35

Birmingham League

No	Date	Opposition	Res.	Goalscorers
1	25 Aug	BURTON AL.	1-1	Bird
2	27	OSWESTRY T.	4-1	Corkindale,Driscoll,Quayle(2,1pen)
3	3 Sep	RHYL	2-1	Corkindale, Quayle
4	8	BANGOR C.	7-0	Driscoll(5,1pen), Bird(2)
5	22	Rhyl	2-1	Corkindale, Driscoll
6	4 Oct	Oswestry T.	1-3	Meaney
7	6	CANNOCK	9-1	Rscamp(4),Llyd(2),Driscll(2),Crkindale
8	10	Colwyn Bay	1-0	O.G.
9	20	Oakengates	3-1	Quayle(2), Corkindale
10	10 Nov	HEDNESFORD T.	2-2	Lloyd, Corkindale
11	17	Worcester C.	1-3	Ridby(pen)
12	24	STAFFORD R.	3-2	Roscamp(3)
13	1 Dec	Stourbridge	2-2	Rigby, Lloyd
14	8	Brierley Hill	4-1	Shakeshaft, Rigby(2), Corkindale
15	15	COLWYN BAY	8-0	Rscamp(4),Hopley(2),Crkindale,OG
16	26	WELLINGTON T.	1-2	Holmes
17	5 Jan	Burton Al.	1-3	Bird
18	12	HEREFORD U.	4-0	Quayle(3), Hopley
19	19	Bangor C.	1-3	Quayle
20	26	CRADLEY HEATH	5-2	Bates(pen),OG,Lloyd,Hopley,Quayle
21	9 Feb	WREXHAM RES.	2-0	Quayle, Roscamp
22	2 Mar	OAKENGATES	3-0	O.G., Quayle(2)
23	9	STOURBRIDGE	1-0	Jones
24	16	KIDDERMINSTER H.	1-0	Bates(pen)
25	23	Hednesford T.	1-2	Clarke
26	30	WORCESTER C.	2-0	Hopley, Roscamp
27	6 Apr	Stafford R.	2-1	Rigby, Jones
28	10	Kidderminster H.	1-0	Clarke
29	13	Nuneaton Boro.	0-0	
30	15	Wrexham Res.	1-4	W.Jones
31	19	Wellington T.	2-1	B.Jones, Lloyd
32	20	BRIERLEY HILL	0-0	
33	23	Cradley Heath	1-0	College
34	27	Cannock	1-4	W.Jones
35	29	NUNEATON BORO.	0-1	
36	4 May	Hereford U.	1-1	B.Jones

```
P  W  D  L  F   A   Pts
36 21 6  9  81  43  48   (Pos. 4th)
```

F.A. Cup

No	Date	Opposition	Res.	Goalscorers
1Q	1 Sep	CANNOCK	2-2	Bird, College
1Qr	6	CANNOCK	5-2	Driscoll(2), Lloyd, Bird(2)
2Q	15	Brierley Hill	2-2	Corkindale, Driscoll
2Qr	20	BRIERLEY HILL	3-1	Quayle(2), Lloyd
3Q	29	STAFFORD R.	1-0	Corkindale
4Q	13 Oct	DUDLEY T.	1-1	Roscamp
4Qr	17	Dudley T.	1-1	Corkindale
4Q2r	22	Dudley T.	1-1	Corkindale
4Q3r	25	Dudley T.	3-1	Quayle(2), Driscoll
5Q	27	BIRMINGHAM TRAMS	1-4	Bird

Welsh Cup

No	Date	Opposition	Res.	Goalscorers
4R	22 Dec	KIDDERMINSTER H.	2-0	Roscamp(2)
5R	2 Feb	Llanidloes	3-1	Roscamp(2), Lloyd
6R	21	TROEDYRHIW	5-3	Rigby, Quayle(3), Roscamp
7R	21 Mar	NEW BRIGHTON	0-0	
7Rr	28	NEW BRIGHTON	4-4	Lloyd, Roscamp, College, Rigby
7R2r	4 Apr	NEW BRIGHTON	2-0	Sambrook, G.Hopley
S/F	25	TRANMERE R.	0-3	

SEASON 1935/36

Birmingham League

No	Date	Opposition	Res.	Goalscorers
1	31 Aug	Hereford U.	2-0	Hewitson(2)
2	2 Sep	COLWYN BAY	6-1	Hpley,Wynss,Hewitsn(2,1pen),Shrp,Clrke
3	9	Oswestry T.	0-1	
4	14	CANNOCK	10-1	Hwitsn(6,1pen),Mtthews,Wyns(2),Hpley
5	16	OSWESTRY T.	4-2	Ramsay, Lloyd, Hewitson(2)
6	23	Colwyn Bay	2-1	Hopley, Hewitson
7	28	RHYL	5-1	Wassall, Hewitson(3), Clarke
8	12 Oct	CARDIFF RES.	1-4	O.G.
9	26	BANGOR C.	4-2	Hewitson(3), Hopley
10	2 Nov	Cannock	6-1	Wyness, Hewitson(4,1pen), Sharp
11	9	Kidderminster	2-3	Hewitson(3), Hopley
12	16	HEDNESFORD	6-0	Wyness, Hewitson(4,1pen), Sharp
13	23	Oakengates	2-1	Hewitson(2)
14	30	CRADLEY HEATH	10-1	Shrp(2),Wynss(4,1pen),Wheelr(2),OG,Hpley
15	7 Dec	STOURBRIDGE	4-1	Hewitson(3,1pen), Wyness
16	14	Worcester C.	1-4	Wassall
17	21	Nuneaton T. *	0-0	
18	26	WELLINGTON T.	3-2	Hewitson(3)
19	28	WREXHAM RES.	2-1	Wyness, Ramsay
20	4 Jan	Dudley T.	2-1	Hewitson(2)
21	11	STAFFORD R.	7-1	Hewitson(4), Hopley, Jeavons(2)
22	18	HEREFORD U.	0-1	
23	25	BRIERLEY HILL	9-2	Jeavns(3),Shrp,Hewitsn(3,1p),Wheelr,Hple
24	8 Feb	Stafford R.	1-0	Wyness
25	15	NUNEATON T.	3-2	Lucas, Hewitson(2)
26	22	Stourbridge *	1-2	Hewitson
27	29	Bangor C.	3-2	Sharp, Jeavons, Hewitson
28	14 Mar	Brierley Hill	2-11	Wyness, Clark
29	21	Hednesford	2-5	Wyness(2,1pen)
30	26	DUDLEY T.	6-0	Wyness, Hewitson(4), Roberts
31	28	OAKENGATES	3-0	Hewitson, Lucas, Wyness
32	2 Apr	KIDDERMINSTER	6-2	Wynss,Jeavns,Hewitsn(2),Shrp,Lcas
33	4	Cradley Heath	1-1	Clarke
34	10	Wellington T.	1-2	Sharp
35	11	Stourbridge	1-4	Hopley
36	14	Nuneaton T.	2-1	Hopley, Hewitson
37	18	WORCESTER C.	1-2	Lucas
38	23	Wrexham Res.	0-5	
39	27	Cardiff Res.	2-0	Hewitson, Clarke
40	2 May	Rhyl	2-1	Hewitson(2)

* Abandonded matches.

```
P  W  D  L  F    A   Pts
38 26 1  11 124  70  53   (Pos. 3rd)
```

F.A. Cup

No	Date	Opposition	Res.	Goalscorers
EPQ1	7 Sep	BOLDMERE ST. MICHAELS	3-0	Hewitson(2), Matthews
EPQ2	21	Oakengates	3-1	Wyness(2), Hewitson
1Q	5 Oct	Worcester C.	2-2	Hewitson, Sambrook
1Qr	10	WORCESTER C.	1-0	Sharp
2Q	19	Kidderminster	2-2	Hewitson(2)
2Qr	24	KIDDERMINSTER	1-2	Hewitson

Welsh Cup

No	Date	Opposition	Res.	Goalscorers
6R	6 Feb	NEW BRIGHTON	8-1	Wynss(2),Hewtsn(2),Hpley(2),Jeavns,Shrp(p)
7R	7 Mar	Aberdare	1-3	Wyness
7Rr	6 Apr	ABERDARE *	4-1	Hewitson(p),Jeavns,Sharp,Wyness
SF	22	Crewe Alex.	0-0	
SFr	24	Crewe Alex.	0-4	

* After a Shrewsbury protest, Welsh F.A. decided Aberdare's ground did not comply to th
rules. Match ordered to be replayed.

SEASON 1936/37

Birmingham League

No	Date	Opposition	Res.	Goalscorers
1	29 Aug	HEREFORD U.	3-0	Hopley, Brown(2)
2	31	Oswestry T.	4-1	Breeze(pen),Liggins,Brown,Hopley
3	5 Sep	Bangor	2-1	Liggins, Hopley
4	12	Kidderminster	1-4	Liggins
5	14	OSWESTRY T.	3-1	Harkin, Martin, Breeze(pen)
6	26	NUNEATON T.	8-0	Liggns(2),Harkin(2),Brown,Baker(3)
7	10 Oct	HEDNESFORD T.	5-0	Breeze(p),Brwn,Harkn,Short,Liggns
8	17	Cannock	0-1	
9	24	WREXHAM RES.	2-4	Fletcher, Breeze(pen)
10	31	Brierley Hill All.	3-1	Liggins(2), Harkin
11	7 Nov	STAFFORD R.	5-0	Jones(2), Liggins, Baker(2)
12	14	Worcester C.	1-1	Jones
13	28	Oakengates T.	1-0	Harkin
14	5 Dec	BRISTOL R. RES.	2-2	Wilson, Harkin
15	12	Colwyn Bay	3-0	Harkin(2), Wilson
16	19	Cardiff C. Res.	2-3	Baker, Wilson
17	26	WELLINGTON T.	2-2	Liggins, O.G.
18	2 Jan	Hereford U.	0-3	
19	9	KIDDERMINSTER	3-0	Breeze(2), Wilson
20	16	BANGOR	11-1	Brze(6,1p),Brwn,Bakr(2),Wlliams,Hpley
21	23	DUDLEY T.	4-2	Hopley, Breeze, Wilson, Baker
22	30	Nuneaton T.	9-5	Hopley(2),Wlliams(4),Harkn,Bakr(2)
23	9 Dec	Bristol R. Res.	0-5	
24	13 Feb	Hednesford T.	4-1	Brown(2), Baker(2)
25	27	Wrexham Res. **	1-3	Williams
26	6 Mar	BRIERLEY HILL ALL.	8-2	Bakr(3),Brze(p),Wlliams(2),Young,Hpley
27	10	Wrexham Res.	4-2	Hopley, Wilson, Williams(2)
28	20	WORCESTER C.	2-0	Baker, Williams
29	26	Wellington T.	2-3	Williams, Young
30	27	CRADLEY HEATH	5-1	Hopley(2), Baker, Brown, Williams
31	30	STOURBRIDGE	5-0	Brown(2), Williams(2), Hopley
32	3 Apr	OAKENGATES T.	12-2	Shrt,Hply(3),Wlliams(4),Bakr(2),Wssll,Young
33	10	CARDIFF C. RES.	3-1	Brown(2), Breeze(pen)
34	17	COLWYN BAY	10-3	Williams(6),Brwn,Breeze(p),Bakr(2)
35	19	Stourbridge	0-5	
36	21	Stafford R.	1-2	Williams
37	26	Cradley Heath	2-5	Baker, Williams
38	1 May	Dudley T.	1-1	Wilson

* Match did not count as Cannock resigned from the League.
** Abandonded after 38 mins due to snow and high winds.

P W D L F   A Pts
36 23 4 9 133 64 50   (Pos. 2nd)

F.A. Cup

No	Date	Opposition	Res.	Goalscorers
EPQ	19 Sep	BRIERLEY HILL ALLIANCE	5-1	Brown, Baker(2), Liggins(2)
1Q	3 Oct	WELLINGTON T.	2-2	Liggins, Brown
1Qr	9	Wellington T.	2-3	Liggins, Baker

Welsh Senior Cup

No	Date	Opposition	Res.	Goalscorers
6R	20 Feb	KIDDERMINSTER	1-2	Wilson

SEASON 1937/38

Midland Counties League

No	Date	Opposition	Res.	Goalscorers
1	28 Aug	NOTT'M FOREST RES.	2-1	Almond, Williams
2	30	Rotherham Res.	0-1	
3	6 Sep	ROTHERHAM RES.	11-0	Hoply(2),Wlliams(4),Rberts,Wilsn(3),Brze(p)
4	11	Nott'm Forest Res.	0-0	
5	20	DENABY UTD.	6-0	Brze(p),OG,Hoply,Williams,Rberts,Race
6	6 Oct	Scarborough T.	0-1	
7	9	Burton	0-1	
8	27	Gainsborough Tr.	2-1	Race, Wilson
9	30	MANSFIELD T. RES.	3-1	Roberts, Breeze(pen), O.G.
10	6 Nov	Notts C. Res.	3-1	Wilson, Williams(2)
11	9	SCARBOROUGH T.	3-0	Wilson, Williams, Nicholls
12	13	BARNSLEY RES.	1-1	Breeze(pen)
13	27	HULL C. RES.	1-0	Williams
14	4 Dec	Lincoln C. Res.	0-2	
15	11	PETERBOROUGH U. *	0-0	
16	18	DONCASTER R. RES.	2-2	Brown, Roberts
17	25	BRADFORD P.A. RES.	2-2	Williams(2)
18	27	NOTTS C. RES.	7-0	Williams(3),Almnd,Rberts,Brwn(2)
19	28	Scunthorpe U. Res.	1-2	Williams
20	1 Jan	GRIMSBY T. RES.	2-1	Roberts, Williams
21	8	Newark T.	3-1	Williams(2), Race
22	22	Gainsborough Tr.	4-1	Davies, Roberts(2), Race
23	29	Frickley Colliery	1-0	Almond
24	5 Feb	BOSTON	3-0	Almond(2), Williams
25	14	Denaby Utd.	9-1	Race(2),Dvies,Wllms(2),Brwn(2),Almnd,Hrkn
26	26	BRADFORD C. RES.	2-1	Williams, Davies
27	5 Mar	Barnsley Res.	2-2	Williams, Almond
28	12	SCUNTHORPE U.	5-1	Williams(3), Brown(2)
29	19	Grimsby T. Res.	0-4	
30	24	LINCOLN C. RES.	4-1	Williams(2), Hopley, Nicholls
31	26	NEWARK T.	3-2	Williams(3)
32	28	BURTON	2-1	Breeze(pen), Williams
33	9 Apr	FRICKLEY COLLIERY	2-1	Williams(2)
34	11	Doncaster R. Res.	1-1	Hopley
35	13	Bradford P.A. Res.	4-1	Brown, Wilson, Baker, Breeze(pen)
36	15	Peterborough U.	1-1	Brown
37	16	Mansfield T. Res.	3-2	Williams(2), O.G.
38	19	Boston	1-4	Hopley
39	21	Grantham	0-1	
40	23	GRANTHAM	6-2	Williams(2),Race,Hopley(2),Brze(p)
41	30	Bradford C. Res.	2-2	Baker, Wilson
42	2 May	PETERBOROUGH U.	5-1	Breeze(pen),Williams(2),Race,Brow

* Abandoned after 61 mins. due to heavy snow.

P W D L F   A Pts
42 25 9 8 111 50 59   (Pos. Champions)

F.A. Cup

No	Date	Opposition	Res.	Goalscorers
EPQR	4 Sep	EVESHAM T.	10-2	Rbrts(2),Wlliams(2),Hply(3),Wlsn(3)
1Q	18	Hereford U.	2-1	Brown, Williams
2Q	2 Oct	SHIRLEY TOWN	5-2	Roberts, Race, William(2), Harkin
3Q	16	Stourbridge	0-0	
3Qr	21	STOURBRIDGE	2-3	Almond, Brown

Welsh Cup

No	Date	Opposition	Res.	Goalscorers
3R	19 Nov	Oswestry T.	1-1	Williams
3Rr	25	OSWESTRY T.	6-3	Roberts, Williams(4), Brown
4R	9 Dec	MACCLESFIELD T.	7-0	Hopley(2), Roberts(3), Williams(2)
5R		Bye		
6R	9 Feb	Wrexham	3-1	Williams(3)
7R	9 Mar	Chester	0-0	
7Rr	2 Apr	CHESTER	2-1	Brown, Wiliams
S/F	26	NEWPORT C.	3-2	Breeze(pen), Brown, Davies
F	4 May	SWANSEA T.	2-2	Williams, Race
Fr	19 Sep	SWANSEA T.	2-1	Brown, Roberts

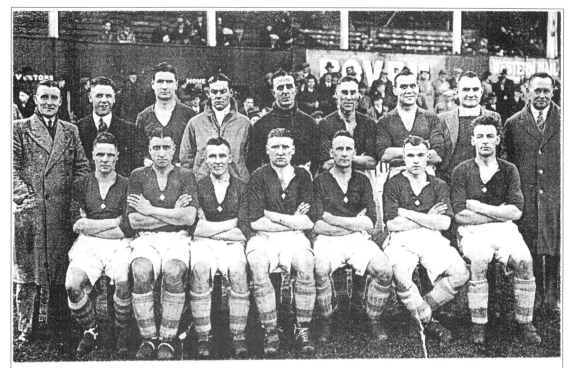

1936-37 Season. Back: Boustead (Manager), Brown, Bulling, Morgan, Burrows, Wassall, Breeze, Powell, Edwards (Director). Front: Baker, Short, Harkin, Wilson, Jones, Hopley, Seymour.

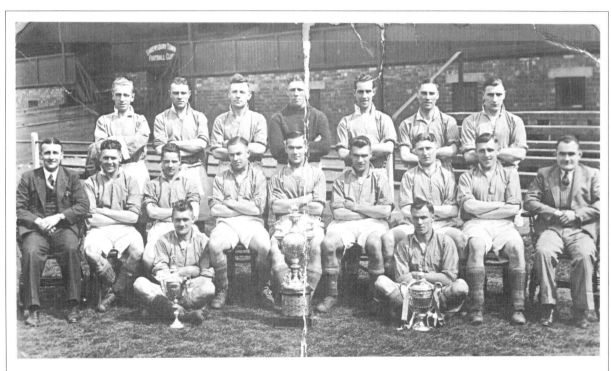

1937/8 Squad and Officials include: Breeze, Miller, Smith, Seymour, Halston, Wassall, Wilson, Almond, Brown, Race, Harkin, Nicholls, Hopley, Williams, Boustead, Powell, Robert.

SEASON 1938/39

Midland Counties League

No	Date	Opposition	Res.	Goalscorers
1	27 Aug	GRANTHAM T.	5-0	Nicholls, Williams(2), Almond(2)
2	29	BRADFORD P.A. RES.	3-2	Bartley(3)
3	3 Sep	Grantham T.	3-3	Wilson(3)
4	5	GRIMSBY T. RES.	3-0	Bartley, Roberts, Breeze
5	10	PETERBROUGH U.	3-0	Bartley(2), Nicholls
6	12	DONCASTER RES.	4-2	Almond(2), Dodd, Brown
7	17	Scunthorpe U.	1-3	Dodd
8	22	Hull C. Res.	2-3	Roberts, Williams
9	24	FRICKLEY COLLIERY	3-0	Lewis, Almond, Brown
10	29	Newark T.	2-4	Williams(2)
11	1 Oct	Nottm Forest Res.	7-0	Bartley(2), Williams(5)
12	6	HULL C. RES.	6-1	Bartley(2), Williams(3), O.G.
13	8	GAINSBORO' TRNTY	5-1	Williams(3), Bartley, Lewis
14	15	LINCOLN C. RES.	8-0	Lwis(3),Hrkin,Brwn(2),Almnd,Brtley
15	31	Rotherham U. Res.	0-1	
16	5 Nov	Lincoln C. Res.	3-0	Williams(2), Almond
17	19	Barnsley Res.	2-1	Almond, Williams
18	26	NOTTM FOREST RES.	2-4	Breeze(2pens)
19	3 Dec	Bradford C. Res.	4-3	Brown,Williams,Breeze(p),Bartley
20	10	BARNSLEY RES.	1-2	Brown
21	24	Scarborough	2-2	Brown, Williams
22	26	BURTON TOWN	1-1	Williams
23	27	Burton Town	2-1	Salmon, Williams
24	31	SCUNTHORPE U.	4-2	Lewis, Williams, Almond(2)
25	21 Jan	Mansfield T. Res.	4-0	Williams, Dodd, Salmon, Baker
26	28	NOTTS C. RES.	3-2	Dodd, Williams(2)
27	2 Feb	Notts C. Res.	4-1	Dodd(2), Almond(2)
28	4	Frickley Colliery	0-3	
29	18	Gainsboro' Trnty	0-3	
30	25	NEWARK T.	7-0	Wlliams(2),Dodd,Brwn(2),Bker,Brze(p)
31	18 Mar	BOSTON U.	3-2	Williams(2), Almond
32	25	Grimsby T. Res.	1-2	Lewis
33	1 Apr	MANSFIELD T. RES.	2-1	Williams(2)
34	7	Peterborough U.	1-1	Dodd
35	8	Denaby U.	1-1	Lello
36	10	DENABY U.	9-1	Bartley(4), Salmon(2), Brown(3)
37	17	Doncaster Res.	2-4	Dodd, Baker
38	22	SCARBOROUGH	4-1	Brown, Almond, Dodd(2)
39	24	BRADFORD C. RES.	3-1	Dodd(3)
40	29	Bradford P.A. Res.	0-2	
41	1 May	ROTHERHAM U. RES.	2-3	Powwell(2)
42	6	Boston U.	3-2	Powell(2), Dalton

```
P  W  D  L  F   A  Pts
42 25 5 12 125 66 55   (Pos. 3rd)
```

F.A. Cup

No	Date	Opposition	Res.	Goalscorers
4Q	12 Nov	WELLINGTON T.	0-1	

Welsh Cup

No	Date	Opposition	Res.	Goalscorers
5R	18 Jan	South Liverpool	1-2	Williams

SEASON 1939/40

Midland League

No	Date	Opposition	Res.	Goalscorers
1	26 Aug	MANSFIELD T.	3-1	Dalton, Arthur, Nicholls
2	28	Scunthorpe U.	2-4	Noralee, Arthur
3	2 Sep	PETERBOROUGH U.	2-4	Williams(2)

```
P W D L F A Pts
3 1 0 2 7 9 2   (Pos. 14th)
```

War Time Friendlies

No	Date	Opposition	Res.	Goalscorers
1	16 Sep	PORT VALE	3-0	Moralee, J.Butler, O.G.
2	23	COVENTRY C.	0-6	
3	30	BRIMINGHAM C.	1-1	Price
4	7 Oct	WELLINGTON T.	4-2	Wassall, Price, Rogers(2)
5	14	NOTTM FOREST	4-3	O.G., Lello, Baldry, Nicholls
6	21	WEST BROM. ALBION	0-5	
7	28	PRESTON N.E.	1-1	Nicholls
8	4 Nov	CARDIFF C.	6-4	Powell(2),Kelly(2),Dalton,Hncock(p)
9	11	BIRMINGHAM C.	1-3	Nicholls
10	18	COVENTRY C.	2-2	Hancock(2,1pen)
11	25	NOTTM FOREST	4-7	Hancock(p),Wharton,Kelly,Wassall
12	2 Dec	WEST BROM. ALBION	1-3	Wharton
13	9	CARDIFF C.	3-1	Nicholls, Wassall, Hancock
14	16	Crewe Alexandra	1-3	Kelly
15	25	WREXHAM	0-3	
16	26	Wrexham	1-3	Kelly
17	2 Mar	COVENTRY C.	2-1	Swinnerton, Kelly
18	16	HEREFORD U.	1-1	J.Butler
19	23	BLACKPOOL	5-0	Armstrong(4,1pen), Rogers
20	25	CREWE ALEXANDRA	1-1	Powell
21	6 Apr	MANCHESTER UNITED	2-2	Powell, Armstrong

Welsh Senior Cup

No	Date	Opposition	Res.	Goalscorers
4R	13 Jan	Chester *	2-4	Kelly(2)

* This, apart from Shropshire Senior Cup tie's, was the last competitive match that Shrewsbury were to take part in for the next six years.

SEASON 1945/46
Midland League

No.	Date	Opposition	Res.	H.T.	Att.	Goalscorers
1	25 Aug	BARNSLEY RES.	3-0	0-0		Lane, Soo(pen), Richardson
2	1 Sep	Peterborough U.	5-0	1-0		Butler, Bailey, Maund, Richardson(2)
3	8	NOTTS FOREST RES.	5-2	3-1		Nicholls, Richardson(3), Soo
4	15	Grantham T.	1-1	0-1		Jones
5	22	LINCOLN C. RES.	6-0	1-0		Richardson(3), Butler, Soo, Bailey
6	29	GRANTHAM T.	3-0	0-0		Lane(2), Richardson
7	6 Oct	Lincoln C. Res.	3-2	1-1		Richardson, Butler, Maund
8	13	GAINSBOROUGH TR.	6-1	4-1		Lane, Bailey(2), Richardson, Maund, Butler
9	27	Frickley Colliery	4-4	0-2		Bailey, Richardson(3)
10	10 Nov	NOTTS C. RES.	7-0	3-0		Richardson(7,1pen)
11	1 Dec	MANSFIELD T. RES.	5-1	1-1		Soo(2pens), Lane, Butler, S.Hughes
12	25	Rotherham U.	1-1	1-1		Maund
13	26	ROTHERHAM U.	6-1	3-1		Richardson(4), Lane(2)
14	29	Mansfield T. Res.	6-1	1-0		Richardson(3), Butler, Hancocks(2)
15	5 Jan	GRIMSBY T. RES.	4-2	1-0		Richardson(3), White
16	12	Ransomes & Marles	0-0	0-0		
17	19	SCUNTHORPE U.	0-0	0-0		
18	2 Feb	BOSTON U.	8-0	1-0		Hancock(3,1pen), Maund(2), Bailey, Richardson(2)
19	9	Notts C. Res.	3-1	2-0		White, Richardson, Lane
20	16	Boston U.	3-4	2-2		White, Lane, Richardson
21	23	OLLERTON COLLIERY	9-3	5-3		Butler(2), Richrdson(2), Bailey(3), Maund(p), Wheatley
22	2 Mar	Scunthorpe U.	3-2	2-1		O.G., Hancocks, White
23	9	Bradford P.A. Res.	3-3	1-2		Lane(2), White
24	16	BRADFORD P.A. RES.	2-0	2-0		White, Richardson
25	23	Ollerton Colliery	5-1	1-0		Richardson(2), Bailey, White, Lane
26	25	Denaby U.	1-2	0-1		Richardson
27	30	PETERBOROUGH U.	3-0	2-0		Maund, Bailey, Richardson
28	3 Apr	Barnsley Res.	1-5	0-2		Knight
29	6	Gainsborough Tr.	4-2	2-1		Richardson(2), Bailey, Butler
30	3 May	Notts Forest Res.	1-0	0-0		Richardson
31	6	Grimsby T. Res.	2-0	1-0		Soo, Lane
32	20	DENABY U.	6-0	3-0		Butler(3), Richardson(2), Maund
33	22	FRICKLEY COLLIERY	7-2	5-0		Richardson(4), Lane(3)
34	27	RANSOMES & MARLES	0-1	0-1		
35	29	DONCASTER R. RES.	4-1	1-1		Richardson(2), Lane, Soo
36	2 Jun	Doncaster R. Res.	3-0	1-0		Butler, Richardson, Hagan

Player appearances (shirt numbers)

No.	Sambrook T.	Tabbener	Birch	Soo F.	Hughes S.	Nicholls H.	Maund J.H.	Lane H.	Richardson	Bailey	Rogers	Streten B.	Wheatley J.	Butler J.	Sykes W.	Lawrence	Franklin S.T.	Smith L.	Downing	Breeze E.C.	Aldred W.R.	Hancock J.	Patterson G.D.	White F.	Sibley E.S.	Brown	Wands A.M.D.	Eccleston	Coop J.Y.	Knight
1	1	2	3	4	5	6	7	8	9	10	11																			
2		2	3		5	6	7	8	9	10		1	4	11																
3			3	4	5	6	7	8	9	10		1		11	2															
4				4	5	6	7	8	9	10		1		11	2	3														
5			3	4	5	6	7	8	9	10		1		11		2														
6					5	6	7	8	9	10		1	4	11	2		3													
7					5	6	7	8	9	10		1	4	11	2		3													
8					5	6	7	8	9	10		1	4	11	2		3													
9					5	6	7	4	9	10		1		11	2		3	8												
10					5	6	7	8	9	10		1	4	11	2		3													
11				10	5	6	7	8	9			1		11	2		3		4											
12					5	6	7	8	9	10		1	4		2					3				11						
13					5	6		8	9	10		1	4		2		3					7		11						
14					5	6		8	9	10		1	4	11	2						3	7								
15						6	7	8	9	10		1	4		2						3		5	11						
16					5	6	7	8	9	10		1	4	11	2						3									
17					5	6	7	8	9	10		1	4	11	2						3									
18					5	6		8	9	10		1	4	11	2		3					7								
19					5	6		8	9	10		1	4		2				7		3			11						
20					5	6	7	8	9	10		1	4		2						3			11						
21					5	6	7	8	9	10		1	4	11	2						3									
22					5	6		8	9	10		1	4		2						3	7		11						
23					5	6		8	9	10		1	4		2						3	7		11						
24					5			8	9	10		1	4		2						3	7		11		6				
25					5	6	7	8	9	10		1	4		2						3			11						
26					5	6		8	9	10		1	4	11	2						3	7								
27					5	6	7	8	9	10		1	4		2		3							11						
28					5	6		8	9			1	4	11	2						3	7								10
29					5	6		8	9	10		1	4	11	2						3	7								
30					5	6		8	9	10		1	4	11	2						3	7								
31				10	5	6	7	8	9			1	4		2						3								11	
32					5		7	8	9	10		1	4	11	2						3						6			
33					5		7	8	9	10		1	4	11	2						3						6			
34				4	5	6	7	8	9	10		1		11	2						3									
35				6	5			8	9	10		1	4		2						3			11	7					
36				6	5		7	8	9			1	4	11	2						3									

Owen = 3/29,30,32,36   Hewitt = 1/31   Hagan J. = 10/36

F.A. Cup

	Date	Opposition	Res.	H.T.	Att.	Goalscorers
4Q	3 Nov	BOURNVILLE	6-2	5-2		Butler(3), Jones(2), Bailey
1P	17	WALSALL	5-0	2-0		Maund(3,1pen), Bailey, Nicholls(pen)
1P2	24	Walsall	1-4	0-1		Nicholls
2P	8 Dec	WREXHAM	0-1	0-0	8000	
2P2	15	Wrexham	1-1	1-1	11566	Jones

F.A. Cup player appearances (shirt numbers)

	Hughes S.	Nicholls H.	Maund	Lane H.	Richardson	Bailey	Streten B.	Wheatley J.	Butler J.	Sykes W.	Franklin S.T.	Smith L.	Aldred W.R.	White F.
4Q	5	6	7	8	9	10	1	4	11	2	3		4	
1P	5	6	7	8	9	10	1	4	11	2	3	8		
1P2	5	6	7	8	9	10	1	4	11	2	3	8		
2P	5	6		8	9	10	1	4	11	2				11
2P2	5	6	11	8	9	10	1	4		2		8		11

Additional Player: Jones = 9/1,2,3   7/5

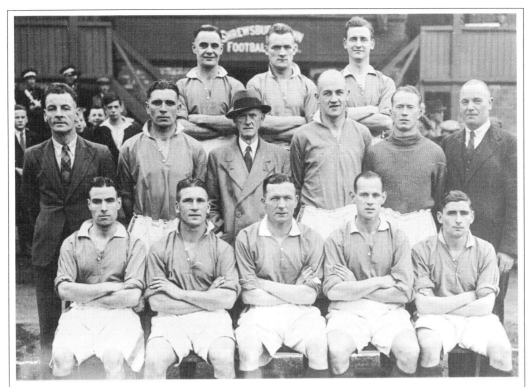

Back: Sykes, Nichols, Wheatley, Middle: Seymour, Franklin, Knighton (Manager), Hughes, Stretton, Fullwood.
Front: Maund, Lane, Richardson, Bailey, Butler

1945-46 Season

1947/48 Team who beat Wellington 1-0, 4th Qualifying Round F.A. Cup:
Back: Hayes, Wheatley, Hapgood, Rowley, Laking, Hughes Seymour, Prince.
Front: Mulraney, Argue, Davie, Sheen, Butler

SEASON 1946/47
Midland League

No.	Date	Opposition	Res.	H.T.	Att.	Goalscorers	Streten B.	Sykes W.	Owen	Wheatley J.	Hughes S.	Rogers A.	Hughes A.	Lello C.	Maxwell J.	Pringle A.	Butler J.	Aldred W.R.	Hatfield T.F.	Black W.	Girtham R.W.	Phillips R.R.	Comley	Gennoe	Lovatt	Rowley H.	Morris	Dowen	Meaney J.	Scott	Roberts D.	Curran F.	Paget	Smith C.	Dudley
1	31 Aug	BRADFORD C. RES.	6-3	1-1		Maxwell(3), Pringle, Lello, Butler	1	2	3	4	5	6	7	8	9	10	11																		
2	2 Sep	BOSTON U.	4-1	1-0		Lello(2), Maxwell, Butler	1	2	3	4	5	6	7	8	9	10	11																		
3	7	SCUNTHORPE U.	3-1	2-1		Maxwell, Butler(2)	1	2		4	5	6	7	8	9	10	11	3																	
4	14	Peterborough U.	2-3	2-0		A.Hughes, Maxwell	1	2		4	5	6	7	8	9	10	11	3																	
5	18	Bradford C. Res.	6-0	2-0		Maxwell, A.Hughes(2), Butler(2), Lello	1	2		4	5	6	7	8	9	10	11	3																	
6	21	ROTHERHAM U.	4-1	2-0		Butler(3), Hughes	1	2		4	5	6	7	8	9	10	11	3																	
7	26	HULL C. RES.	3-2	1-1		Pringle, Butler(2)	1	2		4	5	6	7	8	9	10	11	3																	
8	28	Rotherham U.	0-3	0-1			1	2		4	5	6	7	8	9	10	11	3																	
9	5 Oct	Scarborough U.	1-0	0-0		O.G.	1	2		4	5	6	7	8	9	10	11	3																	
10	12	GRANTHAM T.	3-1	2-1		Maxwell(2), Lello	1	2		4		6	7	8	9	10	11	3	5																
11	19	Barnsley Res.	1-2	1-1		Black	1	2		4		6	7		9	10	11	3	5	8															
12	26	GAINSBOROUGH TR.	3-2	1-1		Butler(pen), Maxwell, Phillips	1	2		4			7		10	6	11	3	5	8		9													
13	2 Nov	Frickley Colliery	3-1	1-1		Girdham, Phillips, Butler		2		4					10	6	11	3	5	8	7	9	1												
14	9	NOTTS FOREST RES.	0-4	0-1			1	2		4	5			10		6	11	3		8	7	9													
15	23	DONCASTER R. RES.	2-2	0-1		Butler(pen), Phillips	1	2		4			7	10		6	11	3	5	8		9													
16	30	Notts Forest Res.	3-3	2-1		Lello, Butler(2,1pen)	1	2		4				10		6	11		5	8	7	9		3											
17	7 Dec	DENABY U.	8-1	5-0		Butler(3,1pen), Lello, Black, Phillips(3,1pen)	1	2		4	5			10		6	11	3		8	7	9													
18	14	Doncaster R. Res.	2-0	2-0		A.Hughes, Lello	1	2		4			7	10		6	11	3	5	8		9													
19	26	BRADFORD P.A. RES.	7-3	2-2		O.G., Phillips(3), Butler, Black, Lello		2		4				10		6	11	3	5	8	7	9			1										
20	28	Denaby U.	3-2	2-2		Phillips, A.Hughes, Butler		2		4	5			10		6	11	3		8	7	9			1										
21	4 Jan	BARNSLEY RES.	3-3	1-1		O.G., Butler, Lello		2		4	5		7	10		6	11	3		8		9				1									
22	11	Mansfield T. Res.	4-1	3-0		Phillips(3), Butler		2		4				10		6	11	3	5	8	7	9				1									
23	25	Lincoln C. Res.	2-3	2-2		Lello, Phillips		2		4				10		6	11	3	5	8		9				1									
24	1 Feb	SCARBOROUGH U.	2-1	1-1		Butler(pen), Lello		2		4				10		6	11	3	5	8	7	9				1									
25	22	PETERBOROUGH U.	5-0	2-0		Phillips(2), Pringle, Lello(2)		2		4				10		6	11	3	5	8	7	9				1									
26	15 Mar	Grantham T.	5-2	3-1		Girham, Lello(2), Phillips, Butler		2		4				10		6	11	3	5	8	7	9				1									
27	22	Boston U.	3-6	2-1		Butler, Lello, Phillips		2		4	5	6		10		3	11			8	7	9				1									
28	29	Scunthorpe U.	2-6	2-5		Phillips, Lello		2		4	5			10		6	11	3		8	7	9				1									
29	4 Apr	MANSFIELD T. RES.	1-1	0-1		Butler		2		4				10		6	11	3	5	8	7	9					1								
30	5	RANSOMES & MARLES	1-0	1-0		Lello		2		4				9		6	11		5	8	7					1		3	10						
31	12	Grimsby T. Res.	0-4	0-3				2		4	5			10		6	11	3		8	7	9				1									
32	14	Hull C. Res.	0-1	0-0				2		4	5			8		3	11			7		9				1									
33	19	FRICKLEY COLLIERY	2-0	1-0		Lello, Butler		2		4	5			10		6	11		5	8	7	9				1		3	10						
34	26	LINCOLN C. RES.	2-1	1-1		Butler, Lello		2		4	5		7	10		6	11			8	7					1		3		9					
35	30	Gainsborough Tr.	0-1	0-1						4	5			10		6		2	5	8	7	9				1		3						
36	3 May	NOTTS C. RES.	5-1	3-1		Black(2), Phillips(2), Lello		2		4	5			10		6	11	3	5	7		9				1				9	8				
37	10	GRIMSBY T. RES.	0-2	0-1				2		4	5			8		6	11	3	5	7						1				9	8				
38	17	Notts C. Res.	1-5	1-4		Curran				4	5		7	8		6	11	3	5							1						9	10		
39	24	Ollerton Colliery	4-1	2-1		Black, Butler(3,pen)				4	5		7			6	11	3	5	8		9				1						9	10		
40	26	OLLERTON COLLIERY	5-0	3-0		Curran(2), Butler, Lello, Black		2		4	5		7	10		6	11	3		8		9										9		1	
41	28	Bradford P.A. Res.	2-3	1-2		Butler(2,1pen)		2		4	5		7	10		6	11	3		8	7	9				1						9	4		
42	31	Ransomes & Marles	4-0	2-0		Lello(2), Curran, Black		2		4	5			10		6	11	2		8	7	9				1	1	3				9			7

Rogers J. = 4/35

F.A. Cup

No.	Date	Opposition	Res.	H.T.	Att.	Goalscorers	Streten B.	Sykes W.	Owen	Wheatley J.	Hughes S.	Rogers A.	Hughes A.	Lello C.	Maxwell J.	Pringle A.	Butler J.	Aldred W.R.	Hatfield T.F.	Black W.	Girtham R.W.	Phillips R.R.
40	16 Nov	Brush Sports	1-5	1-1		Phillips	1	2		4		6	7	8	10		11	3	5	8		9

Welsh Cup

No.	Date	Opposition	Res.	H.T.	Att.	Goalscorers	Streten B.	Sykes W.	Owen	Wheatley J.	Hughes S.	Rogers A.	Hughes A.	Lello C.	Maxwell J.	Pringle A.	Butler J.	Aldred W.R.	Hatfield T.F.	Black W.	Girtham R.W.	Phillips R.R.
4R	21 Dec	Bala Town	1-1	1-1		Butler(pen)		2		4		6	7	10			11	3	5	8		9
4Rr	2 Jan	BALA TOWN	9-1	4-0		Lello(3), Phillips(3), Butler, A.Hughes(2)		2		4		6	7	8			11	3	5		7	9
5R	18	OSWESTRY T.	8-2	5-0		Phillips(3), A.Hughes, Butler(2), Lello(2)		2		4	5	6	7	10				3	5	8		9
6R	24 Apr	NEWPORT C.	0-0	0-0	7000			2		4	5	6		10			11	3		8	7	9
6Rr	5 May	NEWPORT C.	0-1	0-1				2		4	5	6		10			11	3		8	7	9

SEASON 1947/48
Midland League

Appearance/position columns (left to right across the chart):
Rowley · Laking G. · Hapgood E. · Wheatley J. · Hughes S. · Pringle A. · Hughes A. · Black W. · Davie J. · Sheen J. · Butler J. · Aldred W.R. · Lello C. · Reed A.H. · Mulraney A. · Rogers A. · Argue J. · Phillips R.R. · Smith C. · Day J.N. · Sykes W. · Hatfield T.F. · Curran F. · Rogers J. · McKendrick J. · Howarth J. · Blanchard C.

No.	Date	Opposition	Res.	H.T.	Att.	Goalscorers
1	23 Aug	BRADFORD P.A. RES.	3-1	2-0		Davie, A.Hughes, Butler
2	25	DENABY U.	0-1	0-0		
3	30	Scarborough T.	2-1	1-0		Lello, Sheen
4	1 Sep	Lincoln C. Res.	2-0	1-0		Argue, Davie
5	6	SCARBOROUGH T.	2-1	0-0		Mulraney, Davie
6	11	Grantham T.	2-0	0-0		Davie(2)
7	13	SCUNTHORPE U.	1-1	0-1		Butler
8	20	Notts. C. Res.	4-0	2-0		Sheen(2), Davie(2)
9	27	PETERBOROUGH U.	2-1	0-0		Davie, Sheen
10	4 Oct	Rotherham Res.	4-3	2-2		Phillips(2), Butler(2,1pen)
11	11	Mansfield T. Res.	2-1	2-0		Argue, Mulraney
12	18	Ransomes & Marles	0-1	0-0		
13	25	BRADFORD C. RES.	3-0	0-0		Argue, Sheen, Davie
14	1 Nov	DONCASTER R. RES.	2-1	1-0		Davie, Mulraney
15	8	Bradford P.A. Res.	2-2	0-2		Butler(pen), Davie
16	22	FRICKLEY COLLIERY	7-2	3-1		Argue(3), Mulraney(2), Sheen, Davie
17	6 Dec	HULL C. RES.	3-1	0-0		Davie(2), Argue
18	26	YORK C. RES.	3-3	1-1		A.Rogers, Davie, S.Hughes
19	27	GRANTHAM T.	2-1	2-1		Butler, Phillips
20	1 Jan	Denaby U.	0-3	0-2		
21	3	BOSTON U.	4-0	3-0		Phillips(2), Butler, Mulraney
22	10	Bradford C. Res.	2-2	1-1		Butler(pen), Davie
23	17	Nottingham Forest Res.	3-0	1-0		A.Hughes, Butler, Davie
24	24	Gainsborough Tr.	3-5	2-4		Phillips, Sheen, Davie
25	31	NOTTINGHAM FOREST RES.	2-1	1-0		Butler(2)
26	14 Feb	RANSOMES & MARLES	3-2	2-0		Davie, Sheen, Phillips
27	21	LINCOLN C. RES.	1-0	1-0		Mulraney
28	28	OLLERTON COLLIERY	8-0	3-0		Davie(4), Sheen(4)
29	6 Mar	York C. Res.	1-2	0-1		Butler(pen)
30	13	ROTHERHAM RES.	4-1	3-0		Davie(2), Sheen, Butler(pen)
31	20	Doncaster R. Res.	1-1	1-1		Sheen
32	22	GRIMSBY T. RES.	2-0	1-0		Butler, Davie
33	29	MANSFIELD T. RES.	2-1	1-0		Curran(2)
34	3 Apr	Scunthorpe U.	0-2	0-2		
35	5	Hull C. Res.	0-1	0-1		
36	10	Peterborough U.	0-3	0-2		
37	12	Boston U.	3-0	2-0		Sheen, Butler(pen)
38	17	GAINSBOROUGH TR.	3-0	2-0		A.Hughes, Curran, Butler(pen)
39	19	Frickley Colliery	3-1	1-0		Curran, Phillips, Butler(pen)
40	24	NOTTS. C. RES.	2-1	1-1		Sheen(2)
41	26	Grimsby T. Res.	2-1	1-1		Phillips, Argue
42	27	Ollerton Colliery	4-2	1-2		Sheen(2), Phillips(2)

F.A. Cup

No.	Date	Opposition	Res.	H.T.	Att.	Goalscorers
4Q	15 Nov	Wellington T.	1-0	0-0	10500	Sheen
1P	29	Gt. Yarmouth T.	4-1	3-0	4160	Davie(2), Mulraney(2)
2P	13 Dec	Stockport C.	1-1	0-0	17800	Davie (AET)
2Pr	20	STOCKPORT C.	2-2	0-1	13489	Sheen, Argue (AET) (Aband. 22 mins, due to fog)
2P2r	22	Stockport C.*	2-3	0-1	12812	Phillips, Butler (AET)* At Maine Road, Manchester

Welsh Cup

No.	Date	Opposition	Res.	H.T.	Att.	Goalscorers
5R	5 Feb	TROEDRHIW	6-3	3-0	5000	Sheen(3), Phillips(2), Mulraney
6R		Bye				
7R	25	Bangor C.	2-1	0-1		Butler(2)
SF	8 Apr	Barry T.*	3-1	1-1		Butler(pen), Curran, Wheatley * At Merthyr Tydfil
F	22	Lovells Ath.**	0-3	0-0	12000	** At Racecourse Ground, Wrexham

SEASON 1948/49
Midland League

No.	Date	Opposition	Res.	H.T.	Att.	Goalscorers
1	21 Aug	YORK C. RES.	4-4	0-4		Jones(2), Sheen(2)
2	23	Denaby U.	0-3	0-3		
3	28	ROTHERHAM RES.	3-2	1-1		Jones, Sheen(2)
4	4 Sep	Scunthorpe U.	0-3	0-1		
5	6	FRICKLEY COLLIERY	4-2	2-1		Sheen(3), Phillips
6	11	SCARBOROUGH	5-0	2-0		Davie(2), Sheen, Phillips(2)
7	13	Gainsborough Tr.	2-5	2-5		Davie(2)
8	18	Notts C. Res.	2-1	1-1		Chapman, Sheen(pen)
9	25	BRADFOR P.A. RES.	2-0	0-0		Pringle, Davie
10	2 Oct	Lincoln C. Res.	0-3	0-1		
11	9	NOTTINGHAM FOREST RES.	0-3	0-1		
12	16	GAINSBOROUGH TR.	2-0	1-0		Phillips, Sheen
13	23	Rotherham Res.	0-1	0-1		
14	6 Nov	Hull C. Res.	1-3	1-1		Sheen
15	20	DENABY U.	2-1	1-1		Davie(2)
16	27	Ransomes & Marles	3-1	1-2		A.Hughes, V.Hughes, Davie
17	4 Dec	Boston U.	2-3	0-1		Butler(2)
18	18	HULL C. RES.	6-0	2-0		V.Hughes(2), Butler(4)
19	25	Bradford C. Res.	1-3	1-1		Scott
20	26	NOTTS C. RES.	2-2	1-1		V.Hughes, Butler
21	1 Jan	Grantham T.	1-2	0-1		S.Hughes
22	8	GRANTHAM T.	3-3	3-2		Scott, Johnson, Allchurch
23	15	Peterborough U.	1-3	0-1		Scott
24	22	GOOLE T.	2-1	0-0		Phillips(2)
25	29	Bradford P.A. Res.	0-0	0-0		
26	5 Feb	BOSTON U.	4-1	2-0		Butler(2,1pen), Phillips(2)
27	12	DONCASTER R. RES.	2-0	2-0		Phillips(2)
28	26	Nottingham Forest Res.	0-3	0-0		
29	5 Mar	BRADFORD C.RES.*	1-1	1-1		Phillips
30	12	Doncaster R. Res.	1-0	0-0		Johnson
31	19	LINCOLN C. RES.	2-2	2-2		Butler, O.G.
32	23	Frickley Colliery	1-1	1-1		Johnson
33	26	PETERBOROUGH U.	4-1	2-0		Holland, Butler(3)
34	2 Apr	Grimsby T. Res.	1-2	1-0		Butler
35	4	Goole T.	1-2	1-0		Johnson
36	9	GRIMSBY T. RES.	1-2	0-1		Phillips
37	15	Mansfield T. Res.	0-3	0-2		
38	18	MANSFIELD T. RES.	1-1	0-0		Sykes
39	23	SCUNTHORPE U.	5-1	1-0		Butler(3), Phillips, Holland
40	25	BRADFORD C. RES.	1-0	0-0		Phillips
41	29	RANSOMES & MARLES	5-0	4-0		Butler, Phillips(4)
42	1 May	York C. Res.	1-1	1-1		O.G.
43	7	Scarborough	4-2	1-1		Butler(3), J.Rogers

Richards = 4/43

* Abandoned after 45 minutes due to snowstorm

F.A. Cup

No.	Date	Opposition	Res.	H.T.
4Q	13 Nov	Witton Albion	0-4	0-2

Additional Player: Cullis = 9

Welsh Cup

No.	Date	Opposition	Res.	H.T.
5R	20 Jan	Lovells Athletic	0-1	0-0

* At Somerton Park, Newport County.

Appearances grid (shirt numbers)

No.	Day J.N.	Laking G.	Robinson V.	Wheatley J.	Hughes S.	Kirby D.	Johnson J.W.	McCall J.	Jones C.W.	Sheen J.	Butler J.	Rowley H.	Pringle A.	Hughes A.	Davie J.	Phillips R.	Chapman R.	Aldred W.R.	Reed A.H.	Rogers A.	Sykes	Allchurch	Hughes V.	Hassall J.K.	Scott G.	Holland K.	Howarth J.	Hatfield T.F.	Treherne C.	Lewis H.
1	1	2	3	4	5	6	7	8	9	10	11																			
2		2	3	4	5	6	7	8	9	10	11																			
3		2	3	4		6	7		9	10	11														8			5		
4		2	3	4	5	6	7		9				8																	
5		2	3	4	5	6				10		1		7	8	9	11													
6		2	3	4	5	6				10		1		7	8	9	11													
7				4	5							1		7	8	9	11													
8				4	5					10		1	6	7	8	9	11	3												
9		2		4	5			10				1	6	7	8	9	11	3												
10	1	2		4	5		7						6			9	11	3		10										
11	1			4	5						11					9	11	3												
12				4	5						11	1			10	9	11	3	6	8										
13				4	5		7			10					8	9	11	3	6		2									
14	1	2		4	5		7			10	10				8	9	11	3	6		2									
15				4	5					10	11	1			9			3				8								
16				4	5						11	1	6	7				3	6		2	8	10							
17				4	5					8	11	1	6	7				3			2		10							
18				4	5					8	11					9		3			2	8	10	1						
19		2		4	5		7				11							3					10	1	9					
20		2		4	5		7				11					9		3			2	8	10	1	9					
21		2		4	5		7				11				9		11	3							9					
22		2		4	5			10			11	1		7				3			2	8	10		9					
23				4	5			10			11	1	6					3			2	8			9					
24				4	5		7	10			11	1	6					3			2	8								
25				4	5			10			11	1						3			2								8	
26				4	5			10			11	1	6	7		9		3			2	8			8					
27				4	5			10			11	1	6	7		9		3			2									
28				4	5			10			11	1						3			2	8								
29				4	5		7	8			11	1				9		3			2	8				9	8			
30				4	5		7	8			11	1				9		3			2					6	8			
31				4	5		7	8			11	1	6			9		3		4	2	8				10				
32					5		7	10			11	1				9		3			2									
33				4	5		7	8			11	1				9		3			2					10				
34				4	5		7	8			11	1				9		3			2					10				
35				4	5		7	8			11	1	6			9		3	8		2					10				
36				4	5		7	8			11	1	6	7		9		3			2					10				
37				4	5		9	8			11	1	6	7					8							10				3
38				4	5			8			11	1	6				11	2	2		9					10				3
39				4	5			8			11	1	6			9		3			2				9	10				
40				4	5						11	1	6			9		3			2		10			8				
41				4	5			8			11	1	6			9		3			2					10				
42			6	4	5			8			11	1				7		2	2			10				9				3
43				4	5			8			11	1				7		2	2	6		10				9				3

SEASON 1949/50
Midland League

No.	Date	Opposition	Res.	H.T.	Att.	Goalscorers	Rowley H.	Potter H.	Bonell A.	Wheatley J.	Harper K.	Robinson D.	Griffin F.	Hood R.	Robertson W.L.	Vaughn N.G.	Chapman R.	Kernick D.	Roberts W.E.	McCall J.	Lewis N.	Butler J.	Veacock J.	Herrick R.	Jackson A.	Cuishaw H.	Foulkes W.	Scrimshaw S.	Rowley E.	Dale E.	Treherne C.A.	Herrick G.
1	20 Aug	RANSOMES & MARLES	3-0	2-0		Griffin, Bonell(pen), Robertson	1	2	3	4	5	6	7	8	9	10	11															
2	22	Denaby U.	3-2	3-1		Chapman, Vaughn, Kernick	1	2	3	4	5	6	7	8		10	11	9														
3	27	Scunthorpe U.	1-1	0-0		Harper	1	2	3	4	5	6	7	8	9	10	11															
4	29	MANSFIELD T. RES.	3-2	1-0		Hood(2), Vaughn	1	2	3	4	5	6	7	8	9	10	11															
5	3 Sep	SCARBOROUGH U.	3-1	2-0		Hood(2), Robertson		2	3	4	5	6	7	9	8	10	11		1													
6	7	Frickley Colliery	2-4	0-3		Chapman, Hood		2	3	4	5	6	7	9	8	10	11		1													
7	10	DONCASTER R. RES.	1-1	1-0		Butler		2		4	5	6		8			7		1	10	3	11	9									
8	17	Scarborough U.	1-2	1-1		Chapman	1	2		4	5	6		8			7			10	3	11	9									
9	19	Hull C. Res.	0-0	0-0			1	2		4	5	6		8		10	7				3	11	9									
10	24	FRICKLEY COLLIERY	3-0	0-0		Veacock, Chapman, R.Herrick	1	2		4	5	6	7	8			11				3		9	10								
11	29	Boston	1-3	1-2		Griffin	1	2			5	6	7	8		10	11	4			3		9									
12	1 Oct	Gainsborough Tr.	1-4	0-1		Veacock	1	2	3	4	5	6	7	8		10	11						9									
13	8	Mansfield T. Res.	1-2	1-1		Veacock	1	2	3	4	5	6	7	8		10	11						9									
14	15	BRADFORD P.A. RES.	4-0	1-0		Jackson, Veacock(2), Butler	1		2	4	5	6				10				8	3	11	7		9							
15	22	HALIFAX T.	1-1	1-1		Jackson	1		2	4	5	6				10				8	3	11	7		9							
16	29	YORK C.	6-2	2-0		Griffin(2), Butler(2,1pen), Jackson, O.G.	1		2	4	5		7			10				8	3	11			9	6						
17	5 Nov	Peterborough U.	0-1	0-1			1		2	4	5					10				8	3	11	7		9	6						
18	19	GRANTHAM T.	4-0	2-0		Butler(3,1pen), Jackson			2	4		6	7	8		10					3	11			9		1	5				
19	26	Ransomes & Marles	4-1	2-0		Jackson, Lewis, Hood, Butler			2	4		6	7	8		10					3	11			9		1	5				
20	3 Dec	Lincoln C. Res.	1-1	1-1		Butler			2	4		6	7	8		10					3	11			9		1	5				
21	10	HULL C. RES.	4-1	3-0		Griffin, Hood, Jackson, Robinson			2	4		6	7	8		10					3	11			9		1	5				
22	17	Notts C. Res.	1-5	0-3		Wheatley			2	4		6	7	8		10					3	11			9		1	5				
23	26	WORKSOP TOWN	2-0	1-0		Butler, Jackson			2	4		6	7	8		10					3	11			9		1	5				
24	27	DENABY U.	3-3	2-1		Vaughn, Butler(2pens)			2	4		6	7	8		10					3	11			9		1	5				
25	31	NOTTS C. RES.	4-2	2-2		Griffin, Jackson(2), Butler			2	4		6	7	8		10					3	11			9		1	5				
26	2 Jan	Halifax T.	1-3	0-2		Jackson			2	4		6	7			10				8	3	11			9		1	5				
27	7	BRADFORD C. RES.	2-0	1-0		Griffin, Butler(pen)		2			5	6	7			10				8	3	11			9	4	1					
28	14	Nottingham Forest Res.	1-4	0-1		Butler(pen)		2		4	5	6	7	8		10					3	11			9		1					
29	21	NOTTINGHAM FOREST RES.	2-2	0-1		Jackson, Butler(pen)		2			5	6	7	8		10		4			3	11			9		1					
30	28	Doncaster R. Res.	2-2	2-1		Butler(2)		2		4	5		7	8				6		10	3	11			9		1					
31	4 Feb	GOOLE T.	6-1	4-0		Jackson(3), McCall(2), Griffin		2		4	5		7	8				6		10	3	11			9		1					
32	18	Goole T.	0-4	0-1				2		4	5		7	8				6		10	3	11			9		1					
33	25	LINCOLN C. RES.	2-1	0-1		McCall, Griffin		2	3	4		6	7	8						10		11			9		1	5				
34	4 Mar	GRIMSBY T. RES.	2-6	2-3		Butler(pen), Hood		2	3	4		6	7	8						10		11			9		1	5				
35	8	Bradford P.A. Res.	0-4	0-1				2	3	4		6	7	8						10		11			9		1	5				
36	18	Rotherham U. Res.	0-1	0-0				2	3	4	5	6	7	8						10		11			9		1					
37	25	Grimsby T. Res.	2-6	1-2		Jackson, Butler(pen), Griffin		2	3	4	5	6	7	8						10		11			9		1					
38	1 Apr	GAINSBOROUGH TR.	2-2	2-1		Butler, Kernick		2	3	4	5	6		8				7		10		11			9				1			
39	7	Worksop Town	2-0	0-0		Hood, Lewis	1	2		4	5	6		8						10	3	11			9					7		
40	8	Bradford C. Res.	2-3	0-1		Hood, Lewis	1	2		4	5	6		8						10	3	11			9					7		
41	13	Grantham T.	1-1	1-0		Treherne		2	3	4	5		7									11	8		10			6	1		9	
42	15	Scunthorpe U.	1-4	0-2		Jackson		2	3	4	5		7					10				11	8		9	6			1			
43	22	ROTHERHAM U. RES.	3-1	2-0		Hood, Dale, Butler	1	2	3		5	6		8						10		11			9					7		4
44	24	BOSTON	0-0	0-0			1	2	3		5	6	7							10		11	8		9							4
45	29	PETERBOROUGH U.	5-0	4-0		G.Herrick(3), Butler, Robinson	1	2	3		5	6		8						10		11			9					7		4
46	4 May	York C.	3-2	2-2		Butler(2), Harper	1	2	3		5	6								8		11		10	9					7		4

F.A. Cup

No.	Date	Opposition	Res.	H.T.	Att.	Goalscorers	Rowley H.	Potter H.	Bonell A.	Wheatley J.	Harper K.	Robinson D.	Griffin F.	Hood R.	Robertson W.L.	Vaughn N.G.	Chapman R.	Kernick D.	Roberts W.E.	McCall J.	Lewis N.	Butler J.	Veacock J.	Herrick R.	Jackson A.	Cuishaw H.	Foulkes W.	Scrimshaw S.	Rowley E.	Dale E.	Treherne C.A.	Herrick G.
40	12 Nov	Bromsgrove Rovers	2-5	2-1	5000	Jackson(2)	1	2		4	5		7			10				8	3	11			9	6						

- Harry Chapman (back row, left) 1949-50 squad -

1950-51: Back - Seymour (Trainer), Potter, Bullions, Egglestone, Depear, Lewis, Crutchley.
Front - Griffin, Jackson, Treherne, Brown, Butler

SEASON 1950/51
Division 3 (North)

No.	Date	Opposition	Res.	H.T.	Att.	Goalscorers
1	19 Aug	Scunthorpe	0-0	0-0	11847	
2	21	WREXHAM	2-1	1-1	16070	Jackson, Griffin
3	26	LINCOLN	1-2	0-2	11019	Jackson
4	30	Wrexham	0-1	0-1	15879	
5	2 Sep	Darlington	1-2	1-1	7666	Smale
6	5	Rochdale	0-5	0-2	8863	
7	9	STOCKPORT	0-3	0-1	16005	
8	11	ROCHDALE	0-2	0-0	8017	
9	16	Halifax	1-3	0-1	7532	Depear
10	23	HARTLEPOOLS	1-0	1-0	9255	Brown
11	30	Gateshead	0-3	0-2	9374	
12	7 Oct	ACCRINGTON S.	0-1	0-1	10000	
13	14	Carlisle	2-2	1-0	11000	Treharne, Griffin
14	21	TRANMERE	1-2	0-0	11077	Butler
15	28	Southport	2-1	2-1	7567	Brown, Jackson
16	4 Nov	OLDHAM	2-2	2-1	11500	Brown(2)
17	11	Bradford P.A.	4-2	1-2	10807	Brown(3), Hope
18	18	YORK	1-0	0-0	8567	Butler
19	25	GATESHEAD	1-0	1-0	9709	Hope
20	2 Dec	ROTHERHAM	1-2	1-1	10307	Griffin
21	16	SCUNTHORPE	3-1	1-0	6620	Griffin, Bullions, Brown
22	23	Lincoln	0-5	0-4	6634	
23	25	Chester	1-3	0-1	5544	Jackson
24	26	CHESTER	1-0	1-0	10857	Jackson
25	30	DARLINGTON	2-2	2-1	4408	Hope, Brown
26	13 Jan	Stockport	0-2	0-0	10500	
27	20	HALIFAX	2-0	1-0	8360	Brown, Butler
28	27	BRADFORD CITY	2-0	2-0	7578	Brown, Butler
29	3 Feb	Harlepools	0-1	0-0	7011	
30	10	New Brighton	0-0	0-0	3827	
31	24	Accrington S.	0-2	0-1	3417	
32	3 Mar	CARLISLE	0-3	0-1	10000	
33	10	Tranmere	1-0	1-0	10489	Brown
34	17	Southport	1-5	0-3	7201	Crutchley
35	23	Crewe	2-1	1-0	7842	Barker, Griffin
36	24	Oldham	1-2	1-0	13079	Jackson
37	26	CREWE	0-1	0-1	10637	
38	31	BRADFORD P.A.	1-0	0-0	7598	Jackson
39	7 Apr	York	0-2	0-2	5510	
40	14	BARROW	1-0	0-0	7575	Gorin
41	19	Barrow	0-0	0-0	5012	
42	21	Rotherham U.	0-2	0-2	15906	
43	25	Bradford C.	0-1	0-1	9247	
44	28	MANSFIELD T.	1-1	0-3	10172	Brown
45	30	Mansfield T.	0-4	0-3	7590	
46	5 May	NEW BRIGHTON	4-2	2-1	7320	Brown, Gorin(2), O.G.

Player appearances (shirt numbers)

No.	Eggelstone	Fisher	Lewis	Wheatley	Depear	Robinson	Griffin	Hope	Jackson	Brown	Barker	Butler	Smale	Harper	Dodd	Potter	Bullions	Crutchley	Treharne	Gorin	Dale
1	1	2	3	4	5	6	7	8	9	10	11										
2	1	2	3	4	5	6	7	8	9	10	11										
3	1	2	3	4	5	6	7	8	9	10	11										
4	1	2	3	4	5	6	7	8	9	10	11										
5	1	2	3	4	5	6	7	8		10	11		9								
6	1	2	3	4	5	6	7	8		10	11		9								
7	1	2	3	4	5	6	7	8		10	11		9								
8	1	2	3		5	6	7			10	11		9	4	8						
9	1	2	3		5	6	7			10	11		9	4	8						
10	1	3			5		7	8	9	10	11			4		2		6			
11	1	3			5		7	8	9	10	11			4		2		6			
12	1	3			5		7	8	9	10	11			4		2		6			
13	1	3			5		7	8		10		11				2	4	6	9		
14	1	3			5		7	8	9	10		11				2	4	6			
15	1	3			5		7	8	9	10		11				2	4	6			
16	1	3			5		7	8	9	10		11				2	4	6			
17	1	3			5		7	9	8	10		11				2	4	6			
18	1	3			5		7	9	8	10		11				2	4	6			
19	1	3			5		7	9	8	10		11				2	4	6			
20	1	3			5		7	9	8	10		11				2	4	6			
21	1	3			5		7	9	8	10		11				2	4	6			
22	1	3			5		7	9	8	10		11				2	4	6			
23	1	3			5		7	9	8	10		11				2	4	6			
24	1	3			5		7	9	8			11	2		10		4	6			
25	1	3			5		7	9	8	10		11				2	4	6			
26	1	3			5		7	9	8	10		11				2	4	6			
27	1	3			5		7	9	8	10		11				2	4	6			
28	1	3			5		7	9	8	10		11				2	4	6			
29	1	3			5		7	9	8	10	11					2	4	6			
30	1	3			5		7	9	8	10	11					2	4	6			
31	1	3			5		7	9	8	10	11					2	4	6			
32	1	3			5		7	8	9	10	11					2	4	6			
33	1	3			5		7	8	9	10	11					2	4	6			
34	1	3			5		7	8	9	10	11					2	4	6			
35	1	3			5		7	8	9	10	11					2	4	6			
36	1	3			5		7		9	10	11				8	2	4	6			
37	1	3			5		7		9	10	11				8	2	4	6			
38	1	3			5		7		9	10	11				8	2	4	6			
39	1	3			5		7	8	9	10	11					2	4	6			
40	1	3			5		7	8		10	11					2	4	6		9	
41	1	3			5		7	8	9	10	11					2	4	6			
42	1	3			5			8	9	10	11				7	2	4	6			
43	1	3			5		7	8	9	10	11					2	4	6			
44	1	3			5			8	9	10	11				7	2	4	6			
45	1	3			5			8	9	10	11				7	2	4	6			
46	1	3			5			8		10	11				7	2	4	6		9	

FINAL LEAGUE TABLE

	P	W	D	L	F	A	Pts
1 Rotherham	46	31	9	6	103	41	71
2 Mansfield	46	26	12	8	78	48	64
3 Carlisle	46	25	12	9	79	50	62
4 Tranmere	46	24	11	11	83	62	59
5 Lincoln	46	25	8	13	89	58	58
6 Bradford PA	46	23	8	15	90	72	54
7 Bradford City	46	21	10	15	90	63	52
8 Gateshead	46	21	8	17	84	62	50
9 Crewe	46	19	10	17	61	60	48
10 Stockport	46	20	8	18	63	63	48
11 Rochdale	46	17	11	18	69	62	45
12 Scunthorpe	46	13	18	15	58	57	44
13 Chester	46	17	9	20	62	64	43
14 Wrexham	46	15	12	19	55	71	42
15 Oldham	46	16	8	22	73	73	40
16 Hartlepools	46	16	7	23	64	66	39
17 York	46	12	15	19	66	77	39
18 Darlington	46	13	13	20	59	77	39
19 Barrow	46	16	6	24	51	76	38
20 Shrewsbury	46	15	7	24	43	74	37
21 Southport	46	13	10	23	56	72	36
22 Halifax	46	11	12	23	50	69	34
23 Accrington	46	11	10	25	42	101	32
24 New Brighton	46	11	8	27	40	90	30

F.A.Cup - Withdrew from competition

Herefordshire Senior Cup Final

Date	Opposition	Res.	H.T.	Att.	Goalscorers	Eggelstone	Fisher	Depear	Jackson	Brown	Barker	Smale	Dodd	Bullions	Crutchley	Gorin
10 May	Hereford U.	3:1	2:1	4535	Gorin, Brown, Jackson	1	3	5	8	10	11	2	7	4	6	9

SEASON 1951/52
Division 3 (South)

No.	Date	Opposition	Res.	H.T.	Att.	Goalscorers	Egglestone P.	Thompson J.P.	Fisher P.M.	Bullions J.L.	Depear E.R.	Crutchley R.	Reagan C.M.	Ayton J.	Gorin E.R.	Brown R.	Roberts H.	Jackson A.	Potter H.	Lewis N.	Collins A.D.	Ashworth F.	Beynon E.R.	Williams R.R.	Smale T.H.	Leach A.	Dodd W.D.	Halpin J.T.	McCulloch A.A.	Butler J.	Hope E.
1	18 Aug	WATFORD	2-3	1-2	12616	Roberts, Brown	1	2	3	4	5	6	7	8	9	10	11														
2	22	Reading	2-6	0-2	17228	Brown, Depear(pen)	1	2	3	4	5	6	7		9	10	11	8													
3	25	Bristol Rovers	3-3	1-1	20685	Brown(3)	1	2	3	4	5	6	7	8		10	11	9													
4	27	READING	2-1	1-0	12749	Roberts, Brown	1	2	3	4	5	6	7	8		10	11	9													
5	1 Sep	PLYMOUTH	1-3	1-1	12720	Jackson	1	2	3	4	5	6	7	8		10	11	9													
6	3	WALSALL	1-2	1-2	10414	Jackson	1	2	3	4	5	6		8		10	11	9			7										
7	8	Norwich	2-3	1-1	25332	Brown(2)	1			4	5	6		8		10	11	9	2	3	7										
8	13	Walsall	4-0	2-0	9938	Collins(2), Brown, Bullions	1			4	5	6		8		10	11	9	2	3	7										
9	15	EXETER	2-1	1-0	10402	Brown(2)	1			4	5	6		8		10	11	9	2	3	7										
10	22	Colchester	2-2	2-2	10314	Roberts(2)	1			4	5	6		8		10	11	9	2	3	7										
11	24	LEYTON ORIENT	3-0	0-0	9537	Ayton, Jackson(2)	1			4	5	6		8		10	11	9	2	3	7										
12	29	CRYSTAL PALACE	2-1	1-0	12493	Jackson, Brown	1			4	5	6				10	11	9	2	3	7		8								
13	6 Oct	SOUTHEND	0-1	0-0	11636		1			4	5	6		8		10	11		2	3	7									9	
14	13	Bournemouth & B.A.	0-2	0-1	12801		1			4	5	6		8		10	11	9	2	3	7										
15	20	MILLWALL	0-1	0-1	10441		1			4	5	6		8		10	11	9	2	3											
16	27	Brighton	0-1	0-0	16157		1			4	5	6	7	8		10	11	9	2	3											
17	3 Nov	GILLINGHAM	2-2	1-1	8267	Depear, Reagan	1			4	5	6	7	8		10	11	9	2	3											
18	10	Torquay	2-3	2-2	7124	Jackson, O.G.	1			4	5	6	7	8		10	11	9	2	3											
19	17	IPSWICH	0-2	0-1	8048		1			4	5	6	7	8		10	11	9	2	3											
20	1 Dec	PORT VALE	2-0	0-0	8690	Roberts, Reagan	1	3		4	5	6	7	8		9	11					2		10							
21	8	Northampton	0-6	0-3	13694		1			4	5	6	7	8		9	11				3	2		10							
22	22	BRISTOL ROVERS	2-1	1-0	7408	Reagan(pen), Jackson	1			4	5	6	7			10	11	9	2			3	8								
23	25	Newport	1-3	0-1	10000	Jackson	1			4	5	6	7			10	11	9	2			3	8								
24	26	NEWPORT	1-4	0-1	11172	Depear	1			4	5	6	7	8			11	9	2			3		10							
25	29	Plymouth	1-6	1-2	16840	Brown	1			4	5	6		8		10	11	7	3				9		2						
26	5 Jan	NORWICH	0-2	0-1	8464					4	5	6	9	8		10	11	7	3						2	1					
27	12	Watford	1-4	0-2	7501	Reagan				4	5	6	9	8		10	11	7	3						2	1					
28	19	Exeter	2-4	1-2	7980	Depear, Brown	1			4	9	6		7		10	11	8	3		5				2						
29	24	SWINDON	0-1	0-1	4025		1			4		6		7		10	11	8	3		5				2						
30	26	COLCHESTER	1-0	1-0	8464	Beynon	1			4		6		7			11	8	3		5		10					2	9		
31	2 Feb	ALDERSHOT	5-1	2-0	8969	Roberts(3), Beynon, McCulloch	1			4		6		7			11	8	3		5		10					2	9		
32	9	Crystal Palace	1-1	0-0	13541	McCulloch	1			4		6		7			11	8	3		5		10					2	9		
33	16	Southend	2-2	0-2	7552	Beynon(2)	1			4		6		7			11	8	3		5		10					2	9		
34	23	Aldershot	1-1	0-0	6998	McCulloch	1			4		6		7			11	8	3		5		10					2	9		
35	1 Mar	BOURNEMOUTH & B.A.	2-0	1-0	10705	Roberts, McCulloch	1			4		6		7			11	8	3		5		10					2	9		
36	8	Millwall	0-0	0-0	23291		1			4		6		7			11	8	3		5		10					2	9		
37	15	BRIGHTON	1-1	1-1	11500	Jackson	1			4				7			11	8	3		5		10					2	9	6	
38	22	Gillingham	0-0	0-0	10577		1			4				7			11	8	3		5		10					2	9	6	
39	29	TORQUAY	1-1	0-0	6701	Jackson	1			4				7	8		11	10	3		5							2	9	6	
40	5 Apr	Ipswich	0-1	0-0	10227		1			4				7			11	8	3		5							2	9	6	
41	12	BRISTOL CITY	2-0	1-0	11119	McCulloch(2)	1			4				7			11	8	3				10	5				2	9	6	
42	14	Leyton Orient	1-4	0-3	7000	Jackson	1			4				7			11	8	3		5		10					2	9	6	
43	19	Port Vale	0-1	0-0	14500		1			4							11	8	3		5		10				7	2	9	6	
44	22	Bristol City	0-3	0-2	7791		1			4				7				8	3		5							2	9	6	
45	26	NORTHAMPTON	3-1	2-0	9494	Brown, Jackson, McCulloch	1			4				7		10	11	8	3		5							2	9	6	
46	30	Swindon	2-1	1-0	4772	Jackson, McCulloch	1			4			7	8			11	10	3		5							2	9	6	

F.A. Cup

No.	Date	Opposition	Res.	H.T.	Att.	Goalscorers	Egglestone P.	Thompson J.P.	Fisher P.M.	Bullions J.L.	Depear E.R.	Crutchley R.	Reagan C.M.	Ayton J.	Gorin E.R.	Brown R.	Roberts H.	Jackson A.	Potter H.	Lewis N.	Collins A.D.	Ashworth F.	Beynon E.R.	Williams R.R.	Smale T.H.	Leach A.	Dodd W.D.	Halpin J.T.	McCulloch A.A.	Butler J.	Hope E.
1R	24 Nov	Leytonstone	0-2	0-0	6721		1	3		4	5	6	11	8		10		9	2		7										

FINAL LEAGUE TABLE

	P	W	D	L	F	A	Pts.
Plymouth Arg.	46	29	8	9	107	53	66
Reading	46	29	3	14	112	60	61
Norwich C.	46	26	9	11	89	50	61
Millwall	46	23	12	11	74	53	58
Brighton	46	24	10	12	87	63	58
Newport Co.	46	21	12	13	77	76	54
Bristol R.	46	20	12	14	89	53	52
Northampton	46	22	5	19	93	74	49
Southend U.	46	19	10	17	75	66	48
Colchester U.	46	17	12	17	56	77	46
Torquay U.	46	17	10	19	86	98	44
Aldershot	46	18	8	20	78	89	44
Port Vale	46	14	15	17	50	66	43
Bournemouth	46	16	10	20	69	75	42
Bristol C.	46	15	12	19	58	69	42
Swindon T.	46	14	14	18	51	68	42
Ipswich T.	46	16	9	21	63	74	41
Leyton O.	46	16	9	21	55	68	41
C. Palace	46	15	9	22	61	80	39
Shrewsbury T.	46	13	10	23	62	86	36
Watford	46	13	10	23	57	81	36
Gillingham	46	11	13	22	71	81	35
Exeter C.	46	13	9	24	65	86	35
Walsall	46	13	5	28	55	94	31

Back: Fisher, Depear, Bullions, Egglestone, Crutchley, Seymour (Trainer).
Front: Thompson, Collins, Ayton, Crooks (Manager), Jackson, Brown, Roberts.

Season 1951-52

Back: Crooks (Manager), Beynon, Halpin, Birkett, Seymour (Trainer) Lewis, Butler, Bannister.
Front: Fisher, Jackson, McCulloch, Ashworth, Brown, Regan.

Season 1952-53

SEASON 1952/53
Division 3 (South)

No.	Date		Opposition	Res.	H.T.	Att.	Halpin J.T.	Butler J.	Bullions J.L.	Ashworth F.	Crutchley W.R.	Reagan C.M.	Jackson A.	McCulloch A.	Beynon E.R.	Roberts H.	Booker K.	Comerford P.	Fisher F.	Keery S.	Quinton W.	Birkett W.	Lewis N.	Brown R.	Bannister J.H.	Clowes J.A.	Marsden E.	Stewart G.	Bradley J.	Wakeman A.	McBride J.	Dodd W.D.	Egglestone P.	Goalscorers
1	23 Aug		Bristol Rovers	1-2	1-0	23885	1	2	3	4	5	6	7	8	9	10	11																	Roberts
2	28		BRIGHTON	0-0	0-0	12662	1	2	3	4	6	7	8	9	10	11	5																	
3	30		EXETER	1-3	0-0	10797	1	2	3	4	6	7	8	9	10	11	5																	Reagan(pen)
4	3 Sep		Brighton	1-3	0-0	16730	1	2	3		6	7	8	9	10	11	5	4																McCulloch
5	6		Coventry	0-0	0-0	17233	1	2	3		5	11	8	9	10			4	7															
6	11		WATFORD	3-1	2-1	9314	1	2	3		5	11	8	9	10			4	7	6														Fisher, Reagan, Keery
7	13		NORWICH	1-8	1-4	11890	1	2	3		5	11	10	9			5	6	7	8														Fisher
8	18		Watford	1-1	1-1	12962	1	2	3	4	5	11	10	9			5	4	7	8														Jackson
9	20		Colchester	0-1	0-0	7779	1	2	3	4	6	11	10	9			5		7	8														
10	24		Ipswich	1-2	1-2	7000	1	3	4	5	6	11	9						7	8														Keery
11	27		ALDERSHOT	2-1	1-1	7741	1	3	4	5	6	11	9		10				7	8					2									Fisher, Reagan
12	2 Oct		Q.P.RANGERS	0-3	0-1	5988	1	3	4	5	6	11	9		10				7	8					2									
13	4		Swindon	2-2	2-1	8143	1	3	4		6	11	9		10				7	8					2									Reagan, Butler
14	11		Newport	2-4	0-0	9321	1	2	3		6	11	8	9	10				7															Jackson, Butler(pen)
15	18		CRYSTAL PALACE	1-1	1-0	8221	2	6	4	5		11	8	9					7	3	3			10										Jackson
16	25		Bristol City	2-3	1-2	19146	1	2	6	5		11	10	9	4				7	8	3													Jackson, McCulloch
17	1 Nov		TORQUAY	2-1	1-1	7263	1	2	6	5		11	10	9	4				7	8	3													McCulloch, Fisher
18	8		Northampton	1-3	0-3	13990	2	6		5		11	10	9	4				7	8		1	3											Reagan
19	15		LEYTON ORIENT	2-0	1-0	6527	2	6		5		11	8	9	4				7			1	3	10											Jackson, Brown
20	29		READING	1-1	1-0	6286	2	6	4		6		11	9	8				7			1	3	10											Brown
21	13 Dec		SOUTHEND	7-1	1-0	6095	2	6		5		7	10	9	8	11						1	3	10	2										Ashworth, Jackson(2), McCulloch(2), Roberts, Butler(pen)
22	20		BRISTOL ROVERS	0-1	0-0	8810	2	6		5		7	10	9	8	11						1	3												
23	26		Millwall	1-4	0-1	17000	1	2	6		6	11	8	9		11			7				3	10		2									Roberts
24	27		MILLWALL	2-4	1-4	11752	1	2	6		5	11	8	9	4	11			7				3	10		2									Butler(pen), Jackson
25	3 Jan		Exeter	2-2	1-1	9318	1	2	6		6	11	8	9	4	11			7				3	10		2									McCulloch, Fisher
26	15		Walsall	4-4	2-2	3330	2		4		6		9		4	11	5		7				3	10			8								McCulloch(3), Roberts(pen)
27	17		COVENTRY	1-0	0-0	12261				5	6		8	9	4	11			7				3	10			8								Fisher
28	24		Norwich	1-2	1-1	15264			6	5	6		8	9	4	11			7				3	10			8								McCulloch
29	5 Feb		WALSALL	1-0	0-0	3653			6	5	6		8	9	4	11			7				3	10											Brown
30	7		COLCHESTER	3-0	0-0	7624			5	5	6		8	9	4	11			7				3	10	2		8								Roberts(2, 1pen), Fisher
31	14		Aldershot	2-4	2-3	3622		6	5	5			9	9	4	11			7				3	10			8								Brown(2)
32	21		SWINDON	2-1	1-1	8556		6		5	6		8	9	4	11			7				3	10	2										Brown, Jackson
33	28		NEWPORT	1-1	1-0	8528		6		5	6		8	9	4	11		6	7				3	10	2										Brown
34	7 Mar		Crystal Palace	2-1	1-1	13215	3	6	5		6		8	9	4	11			7				3	10	2		9								Jackson, Brown
35	14		BRISTOL CITY	0-1	0-0	11093	3	6	5		6		8	9	4	11			7				3	10	2		9								
36	21		Torquay	0-4	0-4	6237	3	6	5		6		8	9	4	11			7				3	10	2		9								
37	28		NORTHAMPTON	2-4	1-1	7329		6	4	5	6		8	9	4	11			7				3	11	2		9			10					Stewart, Jackson
38	3 Apr		Gillingham	2-4	1-2	12070		6	5	5	6		9		4	11			7				3	10	2		9			8					Brown, Jackson
39	4		Leyton Orient	0-0	0-0	10259		6	5	5	6		9		4	11			7				3	10	2					8					
40	6		GILLINGHAM	3-1	1-0	8324		6	5	5			9		4	11			7				3	10	2		9			8					Brown, Clowes, O.G.
41	11		IPSWICH	2-2	0-1	8294		6	5	5			9		4	11			7				3	10	2		9			8					Brown, Roberts
42	15		Bournemouth	0-2	0-1	7620		6	5	5			9		4	11			7				3	10	2		9			8					
43	18		Reading	3-5	2-3	9226	3	6	4	5			10		4				7				3				9			8					Clowes, Stewart, Bannister(pen)
44	20		Q.P.Rangers	0-1	0-1	7153	3	4			6		8						7			1		11	2		9			10					Bannister(pen)
45	20		BOURNEMOUTH	1-0	0-0	7411	3	4			6		8				5		7			1		11	2		9	1		10					
46	2 May		Southend	2-2	2-2	3000	3	6		5	6		8				5		7					11	2		9	1		10					Brown, Jackson

F.A.Cup

Rnd	Date		Opposition	Res.	H.T.	Att.	Halpin J.T.	Butler J.	Bullions J.L.	Ashworth F.	Crutchley W.R.	Reagan C.M.	Jackson A.	McCulloch A.	Beynon E.R.	Roberts H.	Booker K.	Comerford P.	Fisher F.	Keery S.	Quinton W.	Birkett W.	Lewis N.	Brown R.	Bannister J.H.	Clowes J.A.	Marsden E.	Stewart G.	Bradley J.	Wakeman A.	McBride J.	Dodd W.D.	Egglestone P.	Goalscorers
1R	22 Nov		Q.P.Rangers	2-2	0-2	11475	2	6		5		11	8	9	4				7			1	3	10										Brown, Butler(pen)
1Rr	27		Q.P.RANGERS	2-2	1-2	7000	2	6		5		11	8	9	4				7			1	3	10										Jackson, Reagan
1R2r	1 Dec		Q.P.Rangers*	4-1	3-0	3799	2	6		5		11	8	9	4				7			1	3	10										Brown, Jackson, Butler(pen), Fisher
2R	6		CHESTERFIELD	0-0	0-0	13371	2	6		5		11	8	9	4				7			1	3	10										
2Rr	10		Chesterfield	4-2	2-2	7900	2	6		5		11	8	9	4				7			1	3	10										Brown(2), Fisher, Reagan
3R	10 Jan		FINCHLEY	2-0	2-0	16277	2		4	5	6		8	9					7				3	11										Roberts(2, 1pen)
4R	31		SOUTHAMPTON	1-4	0-0	17249	2			5	6		7	10	4	11			9				3	8										Jackson

* Played at Villa Park

FINAL LEAGUE TABLE

		P	W	D	L	F	A	Pts
1	Bristol Rovers	46	26	12	8	92	46	64
2	Millwall	46	24	14	8	82	44	62
3	Northampton	46	26	10	10	109	70	62
4	Norwich	26	25	10	11	99	55	60
5	Bristol City	46	22	15	9	95	61	59
6	Coventry	46	19	12	15	77	62	50
7	Brighton	46	19	12	15	81	75	50
8	Southend	46	18	13	15	69	74	49
9	Bournemouth	46	19	9	18	74	69	47
10	Watford	46	15	17	14	62	63	47
11	Reading	46	19	8	19	69	64	46
12	Torquay	46	18	9	19	87	88	45
13	Crystal Palace	46	15	13	18	66	82	43
14	Leyton Orient	46	16	10	20	68	73	42
15	Newport	46	16	10	20	70	82	42
16	Ipswich	46	13	15	18	60	69	41
17	Exeter	46	13	14	19	61	71	40
18	Swindon	46	14	12	20	64	79	40
19	Aldershot	46	12	15	19	61	77	39
20	Gillingham	46	12	15	19	55	74	39
21	QPR	46	12	15	19	61	82	39
22	Colchester	46	12	14	20	59	76	38
23	Shrewsbury	46	12	12	22	68	91	36
24	Walsall	46	7	10	29	56	118	24

SEASON 1953/54
Division 3 (South)

Match log

No.	Date	Opposition	Res.	H.T.	Att.	Goalscorers
1	22 Aug	WATFORD	6-4	4-2	11989	Bannister(pen), Jackson(3), Johnston, Fisher
2	24	CRYSTAL PALACE	1-1	0-0	11845	Johnston
3	29	Exeter	1-0	1-0	10123	McCue
4	2 Sep	Crystal Palace	2-3	0-3	11877	Johnston(2)
5	5	NEWPORT	2-1	1-1	11540	McCue, Johnston
6	7	ALDERSHOT	0-2	0-2	11299	
7	12	Norwich	0-1	0-0	21772	
8	16	Aldershot	0-1	0-1	5900	
9	19	Q.P.RANGERS	1-1	1-1	10153	Brown
10	21	WALSALL	4-1	1-0	7614	Hudson(2), Brown(2)
11	26	Southampton	2-4	1-2	17228	Bannister(pen), Johnston
12	1 Oct	Walsall	0-0	0-0	8031	
13	3	COLCHESTER	3-1	1-0	9915	Fisher, Beynon, Bannister(pen)
14	10	SOUTHEND	2-1	1-0	9660	Beynon, McCue
15	17	Reading	1-1	1-1	14764	Hudson
16	24	LEYTON ORIENT	3-3	3-1	9873	Hudson(3)
17	31	Millwall	1-3	0-1	15699	Jackson
18	7 Nov	IPSWICH	1-1	1-1	10227	Price
19	14	Bournemouth	1-2	1-1	8582	Hudson
20	28	Gillingham	0-2	0-1	10307	
21	5 Dec	NORTHAMPTON	2-4	1-3	7825	Brennan, McCue
22	12	Torquay	0-2	0-1	6086	
23	19	Watford	1-3	0-2	10914	Hudson
24	25	Swindon	1-2	0-1	6611	Hudson
25	26	SWINDON	1-0	0-0	11500	Candlin
26	2 Jan	EXETER	1-1	0-0	7676	McCue
27	9	COVENTRY	1-1	1-0	6710	Stamps
28	16	Newport	1-2	1-2	10011	Loughnane
29	23	NORWICH	4-0	3-0	7694	Stamps(2), McCue(2)
30	30	BRISTOL CITY	4-3	4-1	6816	Hudson(2), Brennan, O.G.
31	6 Feb	Q.P.Rangers	0-0	0-0	7851	
32	13	SOUTHAMPTON	3-2	2-2	10161	McCue, Stamps, Brennan
33	20	Colchester	1-3	0-1	7845	Hudson
34	27	Southend	0-3	0-1	7700	
35	6 Mar	READING	0-3	0-2	8711	
36	13	Coventry	1-2	0-2	7906	Dodd
37	20	GILLINGHAM	0-0	0-0	7137	
38	27	Ipswich	0-0	0-0	13429	
39	3 Apr	BOURNEMOUTH	1-1	0-1	6995	McCue(pen)
40	10	Northampton	0-1	0-0	8288	
41	16	Brighton	3-2	2-2	28143	Jackson, McCue(2)
42	17	TORQUAY	2-1	1-1	8932	McCue, Price
43	19	BRIGHTON	3-1	1-0	11702	Hudson(2), McCue
44	24	Leyton Orient	0-2	0-1	9052	
45	29	Bristol City	1-3	0-2	12797	Jackson
46	1 May	MILLWALL	3-1	2-0	6940	Hudson, McCue(2,1pen)

Player appearances (shirt numbers)

Players: McBride J. · Bannister J. · Parr J. · Bullions J.L. · Candlin M.H. · Crutchley R. · Fisher F. · Jackson A. · Marsden E. · Johnson L.H. · Loughnane · McCue A. · Beynon E.R. · Clowes J.A. · Brown J.M. · Dickenson R. · Price D.E. · Butler J. · Hudson J. · Cooke H.W. · Wakeman A. · Brennan H. · Stamps J.D. · Dodd W.D. · McGuire B.

No.	McBride	Bannister	Parr	Bullions	Candlin	Crutchley	Fisher	Jackson	Marsden	Johnson	Loughnane	McCue	Beynon	Clowes	Brown	Dickenson	Price	Butler	Hudson	Cooke	Wakeman	Brennan	Stamps	Dodd	McGuire
1	1	2	3	4	5	6	7	8	9	10	11														
2	1	2	3	4	5	6	7	8	9	10	11														
3	1	2	3	4	5	6	7	8	9	10		11													
4	1	2	3	4	5	6	7	8	9	10		11													
5	1	2	3	4	5	6	7		9	10		11	8												
6	1	2	3	4	5	6	7		9			11	8	10											
7	1	2	3	4	5	6	7	8		10		11			9										
8	1	2	3	4	5	6	7	8		10		11			9										
9	1	2	3	4	5	6	7	8		10		11			9										
10	1	2	3	4	5	6	7			10		11			8				9						
11	1	2	3	4	5	6	7			10		11			8				9						
12	1	2	3	4	5	6	7			10		11			8				9						
13	1	2	3	4	5	6	7					10	8						11	9					
14	1	2	3	4	5	6	7					10	8						11	9					
15	1	2	3	4	5	6	7			10		11	8						9						
16	1	2	3	4	5	6	7			10		11	8						9						
17	1	2	3	4	5	6	7	8		10		11							9						
18	1	2	3	4	5	6		8		10		11					7		9						
19	1	2	3	4		6		8		10		11				5	7		9						
20	1	2	3	4		6		8				11				5	7		9			10			
21	1	2	3	4	5	6		8				11					7		9			10			
22	1	2	3	4	5	6	7	8				11							9			10			
23	1	2	3	4	5	6		8			7	11							9			10			
24	1	2	3	4	5	6	7	8				11							9			10			
25	1	2	3	4	5	6	7	8				11							9			10			
26	1	2	3	4		6		8				11				5	7		9			10			
27	1	2	3	4		6		8				11				5	7		9				10		
28	1	2	3	4		6		8			11					5	7		9				10		
29	1	2	3	4		6						11				5	7		9			8	10		
30	1	2	3	4		6						11				5	7		9			8	10		
31	1	2	3	4		6						11				5	7		9			8	10		
32	1	2	3	4		6						11				5	7		9			10	8		
33		2	3	4		6						11				5	7		9		1	8	10		
34	1	2	3	4		6						11				5	7		9			8	10		
35	1	2	3		5	6		8				11					7		9				10	4	
36	1	2	3		5			8				11					7		9				10	4	6
37	1	2	3	4	5	6		8				11					7		9				10		
38	1	2	3	4	5	6		8			11								9				10		7
39	1	2	3	4	5	6		8			11	10							9						7
40	1	2	3	4	5	6		8				11					7		9				10		
41	1	2	3	4	5	6		8				11					7		9				10		
42	1	2	3	4	5	6		8				11					7		9				10		
43	1	2	3	4	5	6		8				11					7		9			10			
44	1	2	3	4	5	6		8				11					7		9				10		
45	1	2	3	4	5	6		8				11					7		9				10		
46	1	2	3	4	5	6						11					7		9				10	8	8

FINAL LEAGUE TABLE

	P	W	D	L	F	A	Pts.
Ipswich T.	46	27	10	9	82	51	64
Brighton	46	26	9	11	86	61	61
Bristol C.	46	25	6	15	88	66	56
Watford	46	21	10	15	85	69	52
Northampton	46	20	11	15	82	55	51
Southampton	46	22	7	17	76	63	51
Norwich C.	46	20	11	15	73	66	51
Reading	46	20	9	17	86	73	49
Exeter C.	46	20	8	18	68	58	48
Gillingham	46	19	10	17	61	66	48
Leyton O.	46	18	11	17	79	73	47
Millwall	46	19	9	18	74	77	47
Torquay U.	46	17	12	17	81	88	46
Coventry C.	46	18	10	18	61	56	46
Newport Co.	46	19	6	21	61	81	44
Southend U.	46	18	7	21	69	71	43
Aldershot	46	17	9	20	74	86	43
Q.P.R.	46	16	10	20	60	68	42
Bournemouth	46	16	8	22	67	70	40
Swindon T.	46	15	10	21	67	70	40
Shrewsbury T.	46	14	12	20	65	76	40
C. Palace	46	14	12	20	60	86	40
Colchester U.	46	10	10	26	50	78	30
Walsall	46	9	8	29	40	87	26

F.A. Cup

	Date	Opposition	Res.	H.T.	Att.
1R	21 Nov	Q.P.R.	0-2	0-0	13097

F.A. Cup line-up (shirt numbers): McBride 1, Bannister 2, Parr 3, Bullions 4, Dickenson 5, Crutchley 6, Price 7, Beynon 8, Hudson 9, McCue 10, Butler 11.

Back: Johnston, Candlin, Brocklehurst, Clowes, Cook, Loughnane, Middle: Butler (Asst.Trainer), Davie, Parr, McBride, Marsden, McGuire, Seymour (Trainer), Front: Fisher, Beynon, Bannister, Crooks (Secretary/Manager), Price, McCue, Keeting, Crutchley.

Season 1953-54

(Back): Parr, Candlin, Beynon, Crossley, Maloney, Bannister,
(Front): Price, O'Donnell, Hudson, Weigh, Loughnane.

Season 1954-55

SEASON 1954/55
Division 3 (South)

No.	Date	Opposition	Res.	H.T.	Att.	Goalscorers
1	21 Aug	Southend	1-4	1-3	10133	Price
2	26	Brentford	2-2	1-2	12743	Russell, Loughnane
3	28	READING	2-3	2-3	10279	Price, Loughnane
4	30	BRENTFORD	2-2	0-1	8352	Loughnane, McCue(pen)
5	4 Sep	Gillingham	3-3	0-3	11166	Price, McCue, Maldney
6	6	Brighton	0-0	0-0	14322	
7	8	LEYTON ORIENT	0-2	0-2	9298	
8	11	BRIGHTON	3-0	2-0	6418	Price(2), Loughnane
9	18	Millwall	0-2	0-1	16477	
10	22	Torquay	0-2	0-1	6472	
11	25	SOUTHAMPTON	3-1	1-0	8294	Weigh(2), Price
12	27	TORQUAY	3-2	2-0	6676	Russell, McCue, Price
13	2 Oct	Coventry	0-3	0-2	15313	
14	9	Swindon	1-2	0-2	8963	Loughnane
15	16	CRYSTAL PALACE	1-1	1-0	7322	Weigh
16	23	Northampton	1-3	1-2	8468	Weigh
17	30	NORWICH	2-1	2-0	8323	O'Donnell, Hudson
18	6 Nov	Bournemouth	1-3	0-2	9528	Hudson
19	13	Q.P.RANGERS	1-0	0-0	7372	Hudson
20	27	EXETER	1-1	0-0	5734	O'Donnell
21	4 Dec	Colchester	4-2	2-1	5168	Price(2), Hudson, O'Donnell
22	11	BRISTOL CITY	0-2	0-1	8121	
23	18	SOUTHEND	2-3	1-2	5870	O'Donnell(2)
24	25	Walsall	0-4	0-2	17054	
25	27	WALSALL	2-2	1-0	18179	O'Donnell(2)
26	1 Jan	Reading	2-1	2-0	6711	O'Donnell, Hudson
27	8	Aldershot	0-2	0-1	4340	
28	22	Leyton Orient	0-5	0-2	13031	
29	29	ALDERSHOT	1-0	0-0	5864	Weigh
30	5 Feb	MILLWALL	3-2	1-0	7331	Weigh(2), Price
31	12	Southampton	1-2	0-0	12224	Weigh
32	19	COVENTRY	1-0	0-0	6303	Candlin
33	5 Mar	Crystal Palace	2-2	2-1	7348	McCue, Weigh
34	12	NORTHAMPTON	4-0	1-0	7676	Weigh, McCue, Russell, O'Donnell
35	19	Norwich	0-2	0-0	10700	
36	2 Apr	Q.P.Rangers	0-2	0-1	8461	
37	9	NEWPORT	3-0	1-0	8652	McCue(pen), O'Donnell(2)
38	11	Bristol City	1-4	0-2	26208	Russell
39	16	Exeter	0-1	0-0	4944	
40	18	WATFORD	2-1	2-0	6804	Price, Weigh
41	23	COLCHESTER	2-0	2-0	6765	Price, McCue
42	25	BOURNEMOUTH	3-0	1-0	6952	Weigh(2), O.G.
43	28	Newport	1-1	0-1	6762	Weigh
44	30	Watford	1-2	1-2	7787	Russell
45	2 May	GILLINGHAM	1-1	0-1	7237	O'Donnell
46	6	SWINDON	7-0	3-0	6000	Weigh(4), O'Donnell, McCue(2)

Player appearances (shirt numbers)

No.	Crossley R.	Bannister J.	Dodd W.D.	Beynon E.R.	Candlin M.H.	Maloney J.L.	Price D.E.	O'Donnell W.	Hudson J.	McCue A.B.	Loughnane B.	Russell R.J.	Parr J.	Weigh R.E.	Wallace J.C.	Atkins A.W.	Manders R.E.	Brennan H.	McBride J.	McNab A.D.	Skeech H.G.
1	1	2	3	4	5	6	7	8	9	10	11										
2	1	2	3	4	5	6	7	8	9	10	11										
3	1	2	3		5	6	7	8		10	11	9									
4	1	2	3		5	6	7	8		10	11	9									
5	1	2		2	5	6	7	8	9	10	11										
6	1	2	3	4	5	6	7	8	9	10	11										
7	1	2	3	4	5	6	7	8	9	10	11										
8	1	2	3	4	5	6	7	8	8	10	11										
9	1	2	3	4	5	6	7	8	9	10	11										
10	1	2	3	4	5	6	7	8	9	10	11										
11	1	2	3	6	5	3	7	8		10	11			9	4						
12	1	2	3	6	5	3	7	8		10	11			9	4						
13	1	3	6		5	3	7	8	9	10	11		3	9							
14	1	2	6			3	7	10			11		3	9	6						
15	1	2	8			3	7	8					3	10	6						
16	1	2	9		4	3	7	8		11			3	10	6						
17	1	2		6	4	3	7	8	9	10			3	11		5		10			
18	1	2		6	4	3	7	9	9			8	3	11			5	10			
19	1	2		6	4	3	7	9	9	11		8	3			5		10			
20	1	2		6	4	3	7	8	9				3	11		5		10			
21	1	2		6	4	3	7	8	9				3	11		5		10			
22	1	2		6	4	3	7	8	9				3	11		5		10			
23	1	2		6	4	3	7	8	9				3	11		5		10			
24	1	2		6	4	3	7	8	9			10	3	11	4	5					
25	1	2		4		6	7	8	9	11		10	3	9		5		10			1
26	1	2		4		6	7	8	9	11		10	3	9		5					
27		2		4		6	7	8	10	11		10	3	9		5			1		
28		2		4		6	7	8	10	11		9	3	9					1		
29		2		6		5	7	8	9	11	11	10	3			5			1	4	
30		2		10	6		7	8		11		9	3	11	4				1		
31		2		6	6		7	8		11		10	3	9	4				1		
32		2			6		7	8		11		10	3	9	4				1		
33		2			6		7	8		11		10	3	9	4				1	6	
34		2			6		7	8		11		10	3	9	4				1		
35		2			6		7	8		11		10	3	9	4				1		
36		2			6		7	8		11		10	3	9	4				1		
37		2			6		7	8		11		10	3	9	4				1		
38		2			6		7	8		11		10	3	9	4				1		
39		2			6		7	8	7	11		10	3	9	4				1		
40		2			6		7	8		11		10	3	9	4				1		
41		2			6		7	8		11		10	3	9	4				1		
42		2			6		7	8		11		10	3	9	4				1		
43		2			6		7	8		11		10	3	9	4				1		
44		2			6		7	8			11	10	3	9	4				1		3
45		2			6		7	8		11	11	10		9	4				1		3
46		2			6			8		11	11	10		9	4				1		3

F.A. Cup

			Res.	H.T.	Att.	Goalscorers	Crossley R.	Bannister J.	Beynon E.R.	Maloney J.L.	Price D.E.	O'Donnell W.	McCue A.B.	Parr J.	Weigh R.E.	Atkins A.W.	Brennan H.	McNab A.D.
1R	20 Nov	Walsall	2-5	0-1	18311	Brennan, O'Donnell	1	2	4	6	7	8	11	3	5	5	10	10

FINAL LEAGUE TABLE

	P	W	D	L	F	A	Pts.
Bristol C.	46	30	10	6	101	47	70
Leyton O.	46	26	9	11	89	47	61
Southampton	46	24	11	11	75	51	59
Gillingham	46	20	15	11	77	66	55
Millwall	46	20	11	15	72	68	51
Brighton	46	20	10	16	76	63	50
Watford	46	18	14	14	71	62	50
Torquay U.	46	18	12	16	82	82	48
Coventry C.	46	18	11	17	67	59	47
Southend U.	46	17	12	17	83	80	46
Brentford	46	16	14	16	82	82	46
Norwich C.	46	18	10	18	60	60	46
Northampton	46	19	8	19	73	81	46
Aldershot	46	16	13	17	75	71	45
Q.P.R.	46	15	14	17	69	75	44
Shrewsbury T.	46	16	10	20	70	78	42
Bournemouth	46	12	18	16	57	65	42
Reading	46	13	15	18	65	73	41
Newport Co.	46	11	16	19	60	73	38
C. Palace	46	11	16	19	52	80	38
Swindon T.	46	11	15	20	46	64	37
Exeter C.	46	11	15	20	47	73	37
Walsall	46	10	14	22	75	86	34
Colchester U.	46	9	13	24	53	91	31

SEASON 1955/56
Division 3 (South)

No.	Date		Opposition	Res.	H.T.	Att.	Goalscorers
1	20 Aug		NEWPORT	5-0	3-0	9987	O'Donnell(2), Weigh(2), O.G.
2	24		Norwich	1-3	1-0	12694	Weigh
3	27		Swindon	1-2	1-2	6671	Price
4	29		NORWICH	6-0	1-0	9152	O'Donnell, Russell(3), Weigh, Price
5	3 Sep		Q.P.RANGERS	1-1	0-1	11223	Price
6	7		Torquay	0-5	0-3	6421	
7	10		Northampton	0-1	0-1	13144	
8	12		TORQUAY	1-2	1-1	8406	O'Donnell
9	17		ALDERSHOT	3-3	1-0	7590	Weigh(2), Russell
10	21		Ipswich	1-2	0-0	12627	McCue
11	24		Crystal Palace	1-0	0-0	13899	Russell
12	26		SOUTHAMPTON	2-0	2-0	6693	Weigh(2)
13	1 Oct		BRIGHTON	2-1	1-0	9393	Price, Arnott
14	8		GILLINGHAM	3-1	3-0	9732	Price, Weigh(2)
15	15		Millwall	2-1	1-0	9154	Price, Simpson
16	22		READING	3-0	1-0	9289	Price, Arnott, Russell
17	29		Watford	4-3	1-0	7714	O'Donnell(2), Price(2)
18	5 Nov		BRENTFORD	1-1	0-0	10551	Arnott
19	12		Coventry	1-2	0-1	16252	McCue(pen)
20	26		Exeter	0-3	0-2	7140	
21	3 Dec		LEYTON ORIENT	1-4	0-1	10282	O'Donnell
22	17		Newport	2-1	1-0	5287	Arnott, O'Donnell
23	24		SWINDON	1-1	1-0	8000	Tyrer
24	26		WALSALL	2-1	1-1	11861	Tyrer(2)
25	27		Walsall	0-1	0-1	17486	
26	31		Q.P.Rangers	1-1	1-0	7779	Simpson
27	7 Jan		Southampton	1-1	1-1	10218	O'Donnell
28	14		NORTHAMPTON	1-1	1-1	7914	McCue
29	21		Aldershot	0-2	0-0	4876	
30	28		Colchester	0-2	0-1	5679	
31	11 Feb		Brighton	2-3	1-1	11509	O'Donnell(2)
32	18		Gillingham	1-3	1-1	4071	Price
33	25		MILLWALL	3-1	1-1	6596	Arnott, O'Donnell(2)
34	3 Mar		Reading	1-0	1-0	5599	O'Donnell
35	10		WATFORD	0-0	0-0	8238	
36	17		Brentford	1-1	1-0	9156	Arnott
37	24		COVENTRY	3-0	2-0	8232	O'Donnell(2), McCue
38	30		Bournemouth	0-2	0-1	8206	
39	31		Southend	0-1	0-1	8173	
40	2 Apr		BOURNEMOUTH	1-1	0-0	9802	Wallace
41	7		EXETER	2-0	2-0	6676	Weigh, Loughnane
42	14		Leyton Orient	2-5	1-4	13212	O'Donnell, O.G.
43	21		COLCHESTER	2-1	0-1	6967	Simpson
44	23		SOUTHEND	1-0	0-0	6560	Webb
45	28		IPSWICH	1-1	0-0	7308	O.G.
46	30		CRYSTAL PALACE	2-0	0-0	6277	O'Donnell(2)

F.A. Cup

	Date		Opposition	Res.	H.T.	Att.	Goalscorers
1R	19 Nov		Gillingham	1-1	0-0	11347	Russell
1Rr	24		GILLINGHAM	4-1	1-0	8872	McCue(2,1pen), Arnott, Price
2R	10 Dec		TORQUAY U.	0-0	0-0	11490	
2Rr	14		Torquay U.	1-5	0-4	6917	O'Donnell

FINAL LEAGUE TABLE

	P	W	D	L	F	A	Pts.
Leyton O.	46	29	8	9	106	49	66
Brighton	46	29	7	10	112	50	65
Ipswich T.	46	25	14	7	106	60	64
Southend U.	46	21	11	14	88	80	53
Torquay U.	46	20	12	14	86	63	52
Brentford	46	19	14	13	69	66	52
Norwich C.	46	19	13	14	86	82	51
Coventry C.	46	20	9	17	73	60	49
Bournemouth	46	19	10	17	63	51	48
Gillingham	46	19	9	18	69	71	47
Northampton	46	20	7	19	67	71	47
Colchester U.	46	18	11	17	76	81	46
Shrewsbury T.	46	17	12	17	69	66	46
Southampton	46	18	8	20	91	81	44
Aldershot	46	12	16	18	70	90	40
Exeter City	46	15	10	21	58	77	40
Reading	46	15	9	22	70	79	39
Q.P.R.	46	14	11	21	64	86	39
Newport Co.	46	15	9	22	58	79	39
Walsall	46	15	8	23	68	84	38
Watford	46	13	11	22	52	85	37
Millwall	46	15	6	25	83	100	36
C. Palace	46	12	12	22	54	83	36
Swindon T.	46	8	14	24	34	78	30

Player Appearances (shirt numbers)

No.	McBride J.	Bannister J.H.	Skeech H.G.	Wallace J.B.	Maloney J.J.	Simpson A.	Price D.E.	O'Donnell W.	Weigh R.E.	Russell R.J.	McCue A.B.	Parr J.	Crossley R.	Tyrer A.S.	Loughnane B.	Arnott J.H.	Hobson N.	Edgley B.K.	Walker Ron	Oliver R.J.	Webb J.K.
1	1	2	3	4	5	6	7	8	9	10	11										
2	1	2	3	4	5	6	7	8	9	10	11										
3	1	2	3	4	5	6	7	8	9	10	11										
4	1	2		4	5	6	7	8	9	10	11	3									
5	1	2		4	5	6	7	8	9	10		3		11							
6	1	2		4	5	6	7	9		10	10	3		11							
7	1	2		4	5	6	7	8	9	10		3		11							
8	1	2		4	5	6	7	8	9	10	10	3		11							
9	1	2		4	5	6	7	8	9	10		3		11							
10	1	2		4	5	6	7	9		10		3		11							
11	1	2		4	5	6	7	8	9	10		3		11							
12		2		4	5	6	7	9	9	10	10	3	1								
13		2		4	5	6	7	9	9	11		3	1			8					
14		2		4	5	6	7	9	9	10		3	1			8					
15		2		4	5	6	7	9	9	10		3	1			8					
16		2		4	5	6	7	9	9	10		3	1			8					
17		2		4	5	6	7	9	9	10		3	1			8					
18		2		4	5	6	7	9	9	10		3	1		7	8					
19		2		4	5	6	7	9	9	10	10		1			8	3				
20		2		4	5	6	7	9	9		10		1	11		8	3				
21		2		4	5	6		10		11		3	1	11		8			9		
22		2		4	5	6		10	9	11			1	9	7	8	3				
23		2		4	5	6	3	10	9	11			1	9	7	8	3				
24		2		4	5	6		10	9	11			1	9	7	8	3				
25		2		4	5	6		10		11			1	9	7	8	3				
26		2		4	5	6		10	9	11		3	1		7	8					
27		2		4	5	6		10	9	11	11	3	1		7	8	3				
28		2		4	5	6		10	9	10	11	3	1		7	8	3				
29		2		4	5	6		10	9	10	11		1	9	7	8	3				
30		2	3	4	5	6		10	9	10	11	3	1		7		3	11			
31		2	3	4	5	6		10	9	10	11	3	1		7			11			
32		2		4	5	6	7	8	9	10		3	1					11			
33		2		4	5	6	7	10	9	10		3	1			8	3	11			
34		2		4	5	6		10	9	10		3	1	11		8			9		
35		2	3	4	5	6		10	9	10		3	1	11		8					
36		2	3	4	5	6		10	9	10		3	1	11		8	3	11		6	
37		2		4	5	6	7	10	9	10	7	3	1	7		8	3	11			
38		2		4	5	6	7	10	9	10	7	3	1			8	3	11			
39		2		4	5	6	7	10	9		7		1			8	3	11			8
40		2		4	5	6	7	10	9	11	7		1		7	8	3	11			6
41		2		4	5			8	9	10			1	11	7		3			6	
42		2		4	5	6		8	9	10	10		1		7		3	11			
43		2		4	5	6		8	9	10	10		1		7		3	11			
44		2		4	5	6		8	11	10			1		7	7	3	11			9
45		2		4	5	6		8	11	10			1	11	7	7	3	11		10	9
46		2		4	5	6		8	9	10			1	11	7	7	3	11		10	9

F.A. Cup Appearances

	McBride J.	Bannister J.H.	Skeech H.G.	Wallace J.B.	Maloney J.J.	Simpson A.	Price D.E.	O'Donnell W.	Weigh R.E.	Russell R.J.	McCue A.B.	Parr J.	Crossley R.	Tyrer A.S.	Loughnane B.	Arnott J.H.	Hobson N.	Edgley B.K.	Walker Ron	Oliver R.J.	Webb J.K.
1R		2		4	5	6	7	9	9	10	10	3	1	11		8					
1Rr		2	3	4	5	6	7	9	9	10	11	3	1			8					
2R		2	3	4	5	6	7	9	9	10	10		1			8					
2Rr		2		4	5	6	7	9	9	10	10		1	11		8					9

SHREWSBURY TOWN F.C.

BACK ROW (l. to r.) T. G. Seymour, (Trainer), J. Wallace, J. Bannister,
R. Crossley, J. Parr, A. Simpson, J. Maloney.
FRONT (l. to r.) D. Price, W. O'Donnell, R. Weigh, R. J. Russell, A. Tyrer.

Season 1955-56

Back: Dunne, Bannister, Crossley, Hobson, Moloney, Wallace.
Front: Edgley, O'Donnell, Weigh, Shields, Whitaker.

Season 1956-57

SEASON 1956/57
Division 3 (South)

No.	Date	Opposition	Res.	H.T.	Att.	Goalscorers
1	18 Aug	Brighton	3-4	0:2	17890	Hobson, O'Donnell, Whitaker
2	20	MILLWALL	2-0	0:0	9523	Whitaker(pen), Rodgers
3	25	GILLINGHAM	1-0	1:0	8347	Weigh
4	27	Millwall	0-0	0:0	9823	
5	1 Sep	Swindon	2-1	2:1	9196	O'Donnell, Whitaker
6	5	Bournemouth	1-6	1:1	8083	Whitaker
7	8	BRENTFORD	3-2	1:1	8953	Shields, Whitaker, Wallace
8	10	BOURNEMOUTH	0-0	0:0	8098	
9	15	Aldershot	1-1	1:0	5705	O'Donnell
10	17	TORQUAY	1-1	1:0	8394	Rodgers
11	22	WATFORD	1-0	0:0	9352	O'Donnell
12	26	Torquay	1-1	1:1	6960	Whitaker
13	29	Colchester	0-6	0:3	9784	
14	6 Oct	READING	1-1	1:0	8365	Weigh
15	13	Plymouth	1-1	0:1	14953	O'Donnell
16	20	Q.P.RANGERS	0-0	0:0	8473	
17	27	Northampton	1-1	0:0	8951	O'Donnell
18	3 Nov	SOUTHEND	0-0	0:0	7978	
19	10	Crystal Palace	1-0	0:0	13700	Rodgers
20	24	Southampton	0-4	0:2	13197	
21	1 Dec	COVENTRY	5-0	3:0	7997	Russell, Whitaker(2), Weigh, Bannister
22	15	BRIGHTON	4-0	1:0	6061	O'Donnell, Whitaker(2), Weigh
23	22	Gillingham	1-1	1:1	5051	O'Donnell
24	25	Walsall	1-1	1:1	12716	Russell
25	29	SWINDON	7-3	4:0	8229	Weigh, O.G., Russell(2), Whitaker(2), Price
26	12 Jan	Brentford	1-3	1:2	8952	Owen
27	19	ALDERSHOT	2-2	1:2	7128	Russell, O.G.
28	26	Ipswich	1-5	0:4	15101	Owen
29	2 Feb	Watford	3-2	2:1	8220	O'Donnell, Shields, Whitaker
30	9	COLCHESTER	1-3	0:2	11151	O'Donnell
31	16	Reading	2-2	1:2	9777	Shields(2)
32	23	PLYMOUTH	3-1	1:0	5447	Weigh(2), Shields
33	2 Mar	Q.P.Rangers	1-2	1:2	9938	Shields
34	9	NORWICH	4-5	4:2	7206	Weigh, Russell(2), Whitaker(pen)
35	16	Southend	2-1	1:1	7462	Weigh(2)
36	23	CRYSTAL PALACE	1-1	1:1	6674	Whitaker
37	28	Ipswich	1-1	0:1	3789	O'Donnell
38	30	Exeter	1-5	1:3	5500	Whitaker
39	6 Apr	SOUTHAMPTON	0-0	0:0	6590	
40	13	Coventry	3-3	1:2	8299	Whitaker, Weigh, Simpson
41	19	Newport	0-2	0:0	7783	
42	20	NORTHAMPTON	2-0	0:0	7214	Whitaker(pen), Weigh
43	22	NEWPORT	2-0	1:0	7580	O'Donnell, Weigh
44	27	EXETER	1-2	1:0	5729	Weigh
45	29	WALSALL	3-2	0:2	6369	Russell, O'Donnell, O.G.
46	1 May	Norwich	0-3	0:0	7620	

F.A. Cup

| 1R | 17 Nov | Weymouth | 0-1 | 0-0 | 7000 | |

FINAL LEAGUE TABLE

	P	W	D	L	F	A	Pts.
Ipswich T.	46	25	9	12	101	54	59
Torquay U.	46	24	11	11	89	64	59
Colchester U.	46	22	14	10	84	56	58
Southampton	46	22	10	14	76	52	54
Bournemouth	46	19	14	13	88	62	52
Brighton	46	19	14	13	86	65	52
Southend U.	46	18	12	16	73	65	48
Brentford	46	16	16	14	78	76	48
Shrewsbury T.	46	15	18	13	72	79	48
Q.P.R.	46	18	11	17	61	60	47
Watford	46	18	10	18	72	75	46
Newport Co.	46	16	13	17	65	62	45
Reading	46	18	9	19	80	81	45
Northampton	46	18	9	19	66	73	45
Walsall	46	16	12	18	80	74	44
Coventry C.	46	16	12	18	74	84	44
Millwall	46	16	12	18	64	84	44
Plymouth Arg.	46	16	11	19	68	73	43
Aldershot	46	15	12	19	79	92	42
C. Palace	46	11	18	17	62	75	40
Exeter C.	46	12	13	21	51	79	37
Gillingham	46	12	13	21	54	85	37
Swindon T.	46	15	6	25	66	96	36
Norwich C.	46	8	15	23	61	94	31

SEASON 1957/58
Division 3 (South)

No.	Date	Opposition	Res.	H.T.	Att.	Goalscorers
1	24 Aug	PLYMOUTH	2-0	0-0	10092	Whitaker, Jones
2	26	PORT VALE	1-0	1-0	9869	Russell
3	31	Reading	2-2	1-0	11268	Whitaker, McAlinden
4	2 Sep	Port Vale	0-0	0-0	15538	
5	7	NORTHAMPTON	3-1	2-0	9542	Jones(2), Owen
6	9	NORWICH	0-0	0-0	8728	
7	14	Watford	0-3	0-1	9259	
8	18	Norwich	0-2	0-1	17465	
9	21	CRYSTAL PALACE	0-0	0-0	7607	
10	23	BOURNEMOUTH	0-4	0-2	5115	
11	28	Torquay	2-0	0-0	6757	McAlinden, Russell
12	2 Oct	Bournemouth	1-3	0-1	7714	McAlinden
13	5	BRENTFORD	0-2	0-0	7057	
14	12	NEWPORT	1-1	0-0	6408	O'Donnell
15	19	Southampton	2-2	1-1	13989	Jones(2)
16	26	BRIGHTON	2-0	0-0	8056	Smith, Jones
17	2 Nov	Southend	1-5	1-1	10887	Pountney
18	9	Q.P.RANGERS	2-1	1-0	6514	Jones, Smith
19	23	GILLINGHAM	2-1	1-0	6125	Russell, Smith
20	30	Millwall	3-1	2-1	12424	Jones, Russell, Price
21	7 Dec	SWINDON	1-3	1-1	7140	Jones
22	14	Aldershot	1-0	0-0	3692	Russell
23	21	Plymouth	2-2	0-1	13638	Smith, Price
24	25	Walsall	1-0	1-0	9808	Smith
25	26	WALSALL	2-0	2-0	12168	Smith, Russell
26	28	READING	0-2	0-1	9175	
27	4 Jan	COLCHESTER	0-0	0-0	5600	
28	11	Northampton	0-2	0-1	8391	
29	18	WATFORD	1-1	0-0	5418	Russell
30	1 Feb	Crystal Palace	0-3	0-3	11739	
31	8	TORQUAY	3-0	2-0	5282	Jones, Smith, Tucker
32	15	Brentford	0-2	0-1	12850	
33	22	Newport	0-2	0-1	6268	
34	1 Mar	SOUTHAMPTON	1-3	1-1	6710	Jones
35	8	Brighton	1-2	1-1	11134	Russell
36	15	SOUTHEND	1-1	1-0	5527	Smith
37	22	Gillingham	3-1	1-1	5300	Smith(2), Price
38	29	ALDERSHOT	5-1	2-0	5317	Russell(2), Smith(3)
39	7 Apr	COVENTRY	1-3	1-0	8685	Russell
40	8	Coventry	0-5	0-2	12489	
41	12	MILLWALL	0-1	0-0	4581	
42	16	Exeter	1-2	1-0	3500	Smith
43	19	Swindon	0-1	0-1	11728	
44	21	Colchester	0-3	0-2	7092	
45	26	EXETER	1-0	0-0	3338	Tucker
46	28	Q.P.Rangers	0-3	0-1	6193	

Players: Crossley R., Bannister J., Hobson N., Wallace J.B., Maloney J.J., Simpson A., Owen D.W., Jones B., McAlinden J., Russell R.J., Whitaker C., Walters G., Harley A.G., Mayle R.J., Hill J., Price D.E., O'Donnell W., Pountney D.H., Skeech H.G., Smith K., Edgley B.K., Tucker K.J., Oliver R.J.

FINAL LEAGUE TABLE

	P	W	D	L	F	A	Pts.
Brighton	46	24	12	10	88	64	60
Brentford	46	24	10	12	82	56	58
Plymouth Arg.	46	25	8	13	67	48	58
Swindon T.	46	21	15	10	79	50	57
Reading	46	21	13	12	79	51	55
Southampton	46	22	10	14	112	72	54
Southend U.	46	21	12	13	90	58	54
Norwich C.	46	19	15	12	75	70	53
Bournemouth	46	21	9	16	81	74	51
Q.P.R.	46	18	14	14	64	65	50
Newport Co.	46	18	14	14	73	67	48
Colchester U.	46	17	13	16	77	79	47
Northampton	46	19	6	21	87	79	44
C. Palace	46	15	13	18	70	72	43
Port Vale	46	16	10	20	67	58	42
Watford	46	13	16	17	59	77	42
Shrewsbury T.	46	15	10	21	49	71	40
Aldershot	46	12	16	18	59	89	40
Coventry C.	46	13	13	20	61	81	39
Walsall	46	14	9	23	61	75	37
Torquay U.	46	11	13	22	49	74	35
Gillingham	46	13	9	24	52	81	35
Millwall	46	11	9	26	63	91	31
Exeter C.	46	11	9	26	57	99	31

F.A. Cup

1R	16 Nov	Port Vale	1-2	1-1	17600	Smith

1957-58 Season
(Back): Whitaker, McAlindon, Wallace, Bannister, Simpson, Walters, Russell. Middle: Butler, Maloney, Humphreys, Ludlam, Crossley, Hobson, Seymour. Front: Rees, Harley, Potts, Rimmer, O'Donnell, Price.

1958/59 Season: (Back) Butler, Wallace, Maloney, Hobson, Crossley, Oliver, Walters, Seymour.
(Front) Tucker, K.Smith, Russell, Rowley, Whitaker.

SEASON 1958/59
Division 4

No	Date	Opposition	Res	H.T.	Att	Goalscorers
1	23 Aug	Hartlepools U.	2-0	0-0	7344	Smith(2)
2	25	Gateshead	2-1	1-1	7976	Rowley(2)
3	30	COVENTRY C.	4-1	2-0	9622	Smith, Tucker, Rowley, Russell
4	1 Sep	GATESHEAD	1-1	1-0	9552	Rowley
5	6	Exeter C.	0-1	0-0	8442	
6	8	ALDERSHOT	3-1	2-0	7442	Smith, Rowley(2)
7	13	GILLINGHAM	3-2	0-1	8782	Tucker, Smith(2)
8	17	Aldershot	0-0	0-0	5388	
9	20	Carlisle U.	0-0	0-0	10548	
10	22	Millwall	0-0	0-0	11633	
11	27	BARROW	1-2	1-1	9622	Rowley
12	29	MILLWALL	1-2	0-0	6338	Rowley
13	4 Oct	Oldham A.	1-3	0-0	6114	Whitaker
14	9	Walsall	3-2	0-0	14612	Russell, Rowley(2)
15	11	Torquay U.	4-1	2-1	5869	Whitaker, Russell(2), Rowley
16	18	CREWE A.	2-2	0-1	11228	Rowley, Jones
17	25	Northampton T.	3-3	1-2	10000	Jones(2), Whitaker
18	1 Nov	WORKINGTON	1-1	1-1	7581	Pountney
19	8	York City	0-2	0-1	7725	
20	22	Port Vale	0-2	0-1	12058	
21	29	CRYSTAL PALACE	2-1	1-0	4135	Russell, Skeech(pen)
22	13 Dec	WATFORD	4-2	2-1	4422	Rowley(2), Mycock, Whitaker
23	20	HARTLEPOOLS U.	3-0	1-0	4659	Edgley, Rowley, Russell
24	25	Southport	1-0	0-0	1858	Russell
25	26	SOUTHPORT	6-2	3-1	10597	Whitaker(4), Edgley, Russell
26	1 Jan	Darlington	1-2	0-1	5406	Russell
27	3	Coventry C.	2-3	1-2	18485	Russell, Rowley
28	10	BRADFORD P.A.	0-1	0-1	5175	
29	24	Chester	5-3	0-2	8170	Rowley(2), Whitaker, Russell(2)
30	31	Gillingham	1-2	0-0	5819	Tucker
31	7 Feb	CARLISLE U.	4-1	0-0	5259	Wallace, Rowley, Russell(2)
32	14	Barrow	4-3	2-1	2761	Rowley(3), Tucker
33	21	OLDHAM A.	0-0	0-0	6152	
34	28	TORQUAY U.	5-0	0-0	5676	Whitaker(2), Rowley(2), Edgley
35	7 Mar	Crewe A.	4-2	3-0	7905	Rowley(2), Jones, O.G.
36	14	NORTHAMPTON T.	4-0	2-0	7227	Rowley(3), Whitaker
37	21	Workington	1-1	1-2	3373	Rowley
38	28	YORK CITY	2-2	0-1	9833	Rowley, Whitaker
39	30	DARLINGTON	1-0	1-0	8560	Russell
40	7 Apr	Bradford P.A.	1-3	0-1	7262	Tucker
41	11	PORT VALE	4-3	1-0	10619	Russell(3), Edgley
42	18	Crystal Palace	3-4	0-3	9207	Rowley(pen), Edgley, Russell
43	20	WALSALL	2-0	0-0	10878	Whitaker, Russell
44	25	CHESTER	3-0	0-0	7260	Russell, Rowley(2)
45	28	Watford *	5-2	4-1	5337	Rwley, Russll, Whtker, OG(2) (* Aband. after 78 mins)
46	30	EXETER C.	3-0	2-0	15318	Rowley(3,1pen)
47	7 May	Watford	4-1	2-0	5573	Rowley, Tucker, Russell, Whitaker

Player columns: Crossley R., Hobson N., Skeech H.G., Wallace J., Maloney J., Walters G., Tuckers K.H., Smith K., Russell R.J., Rowley A., Whitaker C., Humphreys A., Edgley B.K., Harley A.G., Pountney D., Jones B., Jones M.H., Mycock J., Ambler R., Price J.G.

F.A.Cup

Rd	Date	Opposition	Res	H.T.	Att	Goalscorers
1R	15 Nov	Newport I.O.W.	0-0	0-0	5600	
1Rr	20	NEWPORT I.O.W.	5-0	2-0	4899	Russell(2), Edgley, Walters, Whitaker
2R	6 Dec	Crystal Palace	2-2	1-2	16207	Russell(2)
2Rr	11	CRYSTAL PALACE	2-2	0-1	5428	Rowley, Skeech(pen)
2R2r	15	Crystal Palace *	1-4	1-2	8082	Russell (* Played at Molineux)

Additional Players: Copp = 7/1R   Oliver = 4/2R2r

FINAL LEAGUE TABLE

		P	W	D	L	F	A	Pts
1	Port Vale	46	26	12	8	110	58	64
2	Coventry	46	24	12	10	84	47	60
3	York	46	21	18	7	73	52	60
4	Shrewsbury	46	21	16	9	101	63	58
5	Exeter	46	23	11	12	87	61	57
6	Walsall	46	21	10	15	95	64	52
7	Crystal Palace	46	20	12	14	90	71	52
8	Northampton	46	21	9	16	85	78	51
9	Millwall	46	20	11	15	76	69	51
10	Carlisle	46	19	12	15	62	65	50
11	Gillingham	46	20	9	17	82	77	49
12	Torquay	46	16	12	18	78	77	44
13	Chester	46	16	12	18	72	84	44
14	Bradford PA	46	18	7	21	75	77	43
15	Watford	46	16	10	20	81	79	42
16	Darlington	46	13	16	17	66	68	42
17	Workington	46	12	17	17	63	78	41
18	Crewe	46	15	10	21	70	82	40
19	Hartlepools	46	15	10	21	74	88	40
20	Gateshead	46	16	8	22	56	85	40
21	Oldham	46	16	4	26	59	84	36
22	Aldershot	46	14	7	25	63	97	35
23	Barrow	46	9	10	27	51	104	28
24	Southport	46	7	12	27	41	86	26

SEASON 1959/60
Division 3

No.	Date	Opposition	Res.	H.T.	Att.	Goalscorers	Humphreys A.	Hobson N.	Skeech H.G.	Wallace J.	Maloney J.	Walters G.	Ireland G.J.C.	Russell R.J.	Edgley B.K.	Rowley A.	Whitaker C.	Price J.G.	Starkey M.J.	Pountney D.	Crossley R.	Harley A.G.	Ambler R.	Miller J.P.	Tucker K.J.	Cornfield A.	Jones M.H.
1	22 Aug	BOURNEMOUTH	0-0	0-0	9452		1	2	3	4	5	6	7	8	9	10	11										
2	24	Accrington St.	2-2	1-1	7321	Russell(2)	1	2	3	4	5	6	7	8	9	10	11										
3	29	Port Vale	3-0	1-0	18761	Whitaker, Rowley, Russell	1	2	3	4	5	6	7	8	9	10	11										
4	31	ACCRINGTON ST.	5-0	3-0	9670	Rowley(3,1pen), Whitaker, Edgley	1	2	3	4	5	6	7	8	9	10	11										
5	5 Sep	NORWICH	1-3	1-1	14494	Edgley	1	2	3	4	5	6	7	8	9	10	11										
6	9	Reading	3-2	2-2	12924	Starkey(2), Whitaker	1	2		4	5	6	7		9	10	11	3	8								
7	12	Brentford	1-2	0-1	12551	Walters	1	2		4	5	6	7		9	10	11	3	8								
8	14	READING	3-2	3-0	8888	Rowley, Edgley, Starkey	1	2		4	5	6	7		9	10	11	3	8								
9	19	COLCHESTER	4-1	1-0	9068	Whitaker(3), Starkey	1	2		4	5	6	7		9	10	11	3	8								
10	23	Southampton	3-6	2-3	19172	Starkey(2), Rowley	1	2	3	4	5		7		9	10	11		8			6					
11	26	Southend	1-2	1-2	10555	Starkey	1	2	3	4	5		7		9	10	11		8			6					
12	28	SOUTHAMPTON	1-1	0-0	8470	Rowley	1	2	3	4	5		7		9	10	11		8			6					
13	3 Oct	MANSFIELD	6-3	1-3	8722	Rowley(3,1pen), Starkey, Ireland, O.G.	1	2	3	4	5		7		9	10	11		8			6					
14	5	Halifax	2-1	1-0	4864	Edgley, Whitaker	1	2	3	4	5		7		9	10	11		8			6					
15	10	NEWPORT	6-2	1-1	9162	Rowley(3), Starkey(2), Ireland	1	2	3	4	5		7		9	10	11		8			6					
16	17	Chesterfield	2-2	1-1	5944	Edgley, Whitaker	1	2	3	4	5				9	10	11		8			6			7		
17	24	SWINDON	3-0	0-1	8522	Rowley(2), Starkey	1	2	3	4	5		7		9	10	11		8			6					
18	31	Tranmere	3-3	0-1	9004	Whitaker(2), Ireland	1	2	3	4	5		7		9	10	11		8			6					
19	7 Nov	COVENTRY	3-2	1-0	9922	Rowley(2), Starkey	1	2	3	4	5		7		9	10	11		8			6					
20	21	Q.P.RANGERS	1-1	1-1	10084	Pountney	1	2	3	4		6	7		9	10	11		8	5							
21	28	Grimsby	1-2	1-1	10958	Edgley	1	2	3	4		6	7		9	10	11		8	5							
22	12 Dec	YORK CITY	4-0	2-0	7686	Whitaker(2), Starkey, Rowley	1	2	3	4		6	7		9	10	11		8	5							
23	19	Bournemouth	2-2	0-2	6852	Rowley(2)	1	2	3	4		6	7		9	10	11		8	5							
24	26	BURY	0-2	0-1	14614		1	2	3	4		6	7		9	10	11		8	5							
25	28	Bury	1-2	1-2	16310	Whitaker	1	2	3	4		6	7		9	10	11		8	5							
26	2 Jan	PORT VALE	2-1	1-1	9754	Whitaker, Rowley	1	2	3	4		6	7		9	10	8			5						11	
27	23	BRENTFORD	1-1	0-1	6997	Rowley	1	2	3	4		6	7		9	10	11		8	5							
28	30	WREXHAM	3-2	1-1	10124	Starkey, Walters, Rowley	1	2	3	4		6	7		9	10	11		8	5							
29	6 Feb	Colchester	2-3	1-0	7144	Starkey, Rowley	1	2	3	4		6	7		9	10	11		8	5							
30	13	SOUTHEND	1-3	1-3	6263	Starkey	1	2	3	5		6	7		9	10	11		8	4							
31	20	Mansfield	0-1	0-0	6579		1	2	3	5		6	7		9	10	11		8	4							
32	27	Newport	3-1	0-0	4278	Rowley, Whitaker, O.G.	1	2	3	5		6	7		9	10	11		8	4							
33	5 Mar	CHESTERFIELD	2-4	1-2	7191	Starkey, Rowley	1	2	3	5		6	7		9	10	11		8	4							
34	12	Swindon	2-4	2-1	7595	Ambler(2)		2	3	5		6				10	11		8	4			9	1		7	
35	16	Bradford City	3-2	2-1	7299	Rowley(2,1pen), Ambler		2	3	5		6	7			10	11		8	4			9	1			
36	19	GRIMSBY	5-2	0-1	6107	Harley, Edgley, Ambler, Rowley, Whitaker		2	3	5			7			10	11		8	4		6	9	1			
37	26	Coventry	1-1	0-1	12945	Rowley		2	3	5						10	11		8	4		6	9	1			7
38	30	Norwich	1-1	0-0	29031	Harley		2	3	5			7			10	11		8	4		6	9	1			
39	2 Apr	BRADFORD CITY	3-0	1-0	7227	Whitaker, Rowley, Ambler		2	3	5			7			10	11		8	4		6	9	1			
40	9	Q.P.Rangers	1-1	1-2	6743	Ambler		2	3	5			7			10	11		8	4		6	9	1			
41	16	TRANMERE	0-0	0-0	8915			2	3	5			7			10	11		8	4		6	9	1			
42	18	BARNSLEY	2-2	2-2	8500	Starkey, Ireland		2	3	5		6	7				11		8	10		4	9	1			
43	19	Barnsley	0-0	0-0	5271			2	3	5		6	7				11		8	10		4	9	1			
44	23	Wrexham	1-1	1-1	7678	Whitaker		2	3	5		6	7		10		11		8			4	9	1			
45	25	HALIFAX	2-2	2-0	7514	Starkey, Rowley(pen)		2	3	5		6	7			10	11		8			4	9	1			
46	30	York	1-0	1-0	4801	Whitaker		2	3	5		6	7			10	11		8			4	9	1			

F.A. Cup

1R	14 Nov	Peterborough U.		3-4	16341	Starkey(2), Rowley

1	2	3	4	5	6	7	8	9	10	11

Floodlight Opener

25 Nov	STOKE		5-0	2-0	5448	Cornfield, Rowley(pen), Whitaker(2), Ireland

1	2	3	4	5	6	7	8	9	10	11

FINAL LEAGUE TABLE

		P	W	D	L	F	A	Pts
1	Southampton	46	26	9	11	106	75	61
2	Norwich	46	24	11	11	82	54	59
3	Shrewsbury	46	18	16	12	97	75	52
4	Coventry	46	21	10	15	78	63	52
5	Grimsby	46	18	16	12	87	70	52
6	Brentford	46	21	9	16	78	61	51
7	Bury	46	21	9	16	64	51	51
8	QPR	46	18	13	15	73	54	49
9	Colchester	46	18	11	17	83	74	47
10	Bournemouth	46	17	13	16	72	72	47
11	Reading	46	18	10	18	84	77	46
12	Southend	46	19	8	19	76	74	46
13	Newport	46	20	6	20	80	79	46
14	Port Vale	46	19	8	19	80	79	46
15	Halifax	46	18	10	18	70	72	46
16	Swindon	46	19	8	19	69	78	46
17	Barnsley	46	15	14	17	65	66	44
18	Chesterfield	46	18	7	21	71	84	43
19	Bradford City	46	15	12	19	66	74	42
20	Tranmere	46	14	13	19	72	75	41
21	York	46	13	12	21	57	73	38
22	Mansfield	46	15	6	25	81	112	36
23	Wrexham	46	14	8	24	68	101	36
24	Accrington	46	11	5	30	57	123	27

Left to right; (back row) J. Wallace, N. Hobson, D. Pountney, A. Humphreys (now with Leeds United), G. Skeech, A. Harley; (front row) J. Ireland, B. Edgley, A. Rowley (Captain), M. Starkey, C. Whitaker.

SEASON 1960/61
Division 3

No.	Date	Opposition	Res	H.T.	Att	Miller J.P.	Hobson N.	Corbett A.	Harley A.G.	Wallace J.B.	Walters J.J.	Baker T.G.	Starkey M.J.	McLaughlin J.	Rowley A.	Whitaker C.	Pountney D.H.	Skeech H.G.	Ambler R.	Gibson M.J.	Jones M.H.	Pragg M.K.	Copp L.J.H.	Cornfield A.H.	Humphries D.W.	Dolby P.	Walker Roger	Hemsley E.J.O.	Morrall T.S.	Goalscorers
1	20 Aug	Torquay U.	0-2	0-1	10000	1	2	3	4	5	6	7	8		10	11			9											Rowley
2	24	PORT VALE	1-1	1-0	9022	1	2		4	5	6	7	8		10	11		3	9											Rowley
3	27	SWINDON T.	1-1	0-1	7330	1	2		4	5	6	7	8		10	11		3	9											Whitaker
4	29	Port Vale	1-4	1-2	9212	1	2		4	5	6	7	8		10	11		3	9											Starkey
5	3 Sep	Brentford	0-4	0-2	8900		2		4	5	6	7	8		10	11		3	9	1										
6	7	BURY	2-1	1-1	7760	1	2		4	5	6	7	8	11	10			3	9											Rowley(pen), O.G.
7	10	WATFORD	2-2	2-1	6437	1	2		4	5	6	7	8	11	10			3	9											Rowley(2,1pen)
8	17	Tranmere R.	2-4	0-0	8792	1	2		4	5	6	7	8	11	10			3	9											McLaughlin, Rowley
9	21	SOUTHEND U.	2-2	0-1	6959	1	2		6	4				11	10	8	5	3	9		7									Rowley(pen), McLaughlin
10	24	HALIFAX T.	1-1	1-0	7205	1	2		6	4				11	10	8	5	3	9		7									Whitaker
11	26	Southend U.	1-1	0-1	6972	1	2		6	4				11	10	8	5	3	9		7									Rowley
12	1 Oct	BARNSLEY	1-2	0-1	5547	1	2		6	4		7		11	10	8	5	3	9											Rowley
13	3	Walsall	2-3	2-1	12141	1			6	4	2		8	11	10		5	3	9			7								McLaughlin, Harley
14	8	Colchester U.	1-1	1-1	4191	1			6	4	2		8	11	10		5	3	9			7								McLaughlin
15	15	GRIMSBY T.	2-1	1-1	7184				6	4	2	7		9	10		5	3		1			8	11						Rowley, McLaughlin
16	22	Hull C.	1-3	0-2	9095				6	4	2	7		9	10		5	3		1			8	11						Copp
17	29	READING	6-1	1-1	6931		7		6	4	2	9	8	11	10		5	3		1										Hobson(2), Rowley(2), McLaughlin, Starkey
18	12 Nov	BRISTOL CITY	4-2	4-1	7998		7		6	4	2	9	8	11	10		5	3		1										Starkey(2), Hobson, Rowley(pen)
19	19	Q.P.Rangers	1-1	1-1	7680		7		6	4	2	9	8	11	10		5	3		1										McLaughlin
20	3 Dec	Bournemouth & B.A.	2-2	1-1	4978		7		6	4	2	9	8	11	10			3		1					5					Rowley, Walters
21	17	TORQUAY U.	2-1	1-1	6773		7		6	4	2	9	8	10			5	3		1				11						Starkey(2)
22	26	Chesterfield	3-2	1-1	5781		7		6	4	2	9	8	11	10		5	3		1										Rowley(2), Hobson
23	27	CHESTERFIELD	4-2	2-2	12223		7		6	4	2	9	8	11	10		5	3		1										Starkey(2), McLaughlin(2)
24	31	Swindon T.	2-2	2-1	9670		7		6	4	2	9	8	11	10		5	3		1										Starkey, McLaughlin
25	2 Jan	Bury	1-3	1-1	11568		7		6	4	2	9	8	11	10		5	3		1										McLaughlin
26	14	BRENTFORD	3-0	2-0	6397				6	4	2	9	8	11		7	5	3		1						10				Whitaker(2), Dolby
27	21	Watford	1-3	1-2	10001				6	4	2	9	8	11	10		5	3		1	7									McLaughlin
28	28	Coventry C.	2-3	0-2	9595				6	4	2	9		11	10		8	3		1	7				5					Rowley, McLaughlin
29	4 Feb	TRANMERE R.	1-2	0-1	9300				4	5	2	9	8	11	10		6	3		1	7									O.G.
30	11	Halifax T.	1-1	0-1	2981					4	2	9		11	10		6	3		1	7				5	8				Dolby
31	25	BOURNEMOUTH & B.A.	2-1	1-0	5946			2	6	4		9		11	10		5	3		1	7					8				Jones, Rowley
32	4 Mar	Grimsby T.	2-0	0-0	9145			2	6	4		9		11	10		5	3		1	7					8				Rowley(2)
33	8	NOTTS C.	4-0	2-0	8330			2	6	4		9		11	10		5	3		1	7					8				Rowley(2,1pen), McLaughlin, Dolby
34	11	HULL CITY	0-0	0-0	8698			2	6	4		9		11	10		5	3		1	7					8				
35	18	Reading	1-2	1-1	5066	1			6	4	2	9	8	11	10		5	3			7									McLaughlin
36	25	COVENTRY C.	2-1	0-0	8562				6	4	2	9	8	11	10		5	3		1				7						Rowley, McLaughlin
37	1 Apr	Bristol City	0-0	0-0	8659				6	4	2	9	8	11	10		5	3		1				7						
38	3	Newport C.	1-1	0-0	2892				6	4	2	9		11	10		5	3	8	1	7									Ambler
39	4	NEWPORT C. *	2-0	2-0	5892				6	4	2	9	8	11	10		5	3		1	7									Rowley, Starkey (* Aband. 45 mins due to fog)
40	8	Q.P.RANGERS	4-1	0-0	8401				6	4	2	9	8	11			5	3	10	1	7									McLaughlin, Baker, Ambler, Starkey
41	12	BRADFORD C.	2-0	0-0	6517				6	4	2	9	8	11	10		5	3		1	7									McLaughlin, Baker
42	15	Notts County	1-2	0-2	7107				6	4	2	9		11	10		5	3	8	1	7									Rowley
43	17	NEWPORT C.	5-0	3-0	5877				6	5	2	9	8	11	10		4	3		1							7			Rowley(3,1pen), McLaughlin, Baker
44	22	COLCHESTER U.	2-2	1-1	6891				6	5	2	9	8	11	10		4	3		1	7									McLaughlin, Baker
45	26	WALSALL	1-2	1-1	18917				6	4	2	9	8	11	10		5	3		1	7									Rowley
46	29	Bradford C.	1-1	0-1	4187	1			6	5	2	9	7	11	10		8	3										4		Rowley
47	3 May	Barnsley	2-4	0-3	3291	1			6		2	9	7		10		8	3						11				4	5	Baker, Pountney

F.A. Cup

	Date	Opponent	Score	HT	Att	Scorers
1R	5 Nov	NEWPORT C.	4-1	3-0	11396	McLaughlin(3), Rowley
2R	26	Swindon T.	1-0	0-0	11910	Rowley
3R	7 Jan	Aldershot	1-1	1-0	10045	Starkey
3Rr	11	ALDERSHOT	2-2	1-1	12334	Starkey, McLaughlin
3R2r	16	Aldershot*	0-2	0-0	8622	

* Played at Villa Park

League Cup

	Date	Opponent	Score	HT	Att	Scorers
2R	12 Oct	Swindon T.	1-1	0-1	10840	Copp
2Rr	24	SWINDON T.	2-2	1-1	5343	Copp, Rowley(pen)
2R2r	26	Swindon T.	2-0	0-0	6975	McLaughlin, Hobson
3R	16 Nov	BRADFORD C.	2-1	1-1	8363	Rowley, McLaughlin
4R	14 Dec	NORWICH C.	1-0	1-0	7427	McLaughlin
5R	15 Feb	EVERTON	2-1	1-1	15399	Dolby(2)
SF1L	21 Mar	Rotherham U.	2-3	1-2	13397	McLaughlin(2)
SF2L	29	ROTHERHAM U.	1-1	1-0	16722	Starkey

FINAL LEAGUE TABLE

		P	W	D	L	F	A	Pts
1	Bury	46	30	8	8	108	45	68
2	Walsall	46	28	6	12	98	60	62
3	QPR	46	25	10	11	93	60	60
4	Watford	46	20	12	14	85	72	52
5	Notts County	46	21	9	16	82	77	51
6	Grimsby	46	20	10	16	77	69	50
7	Port Vale	46	17	15	14	96	79	49
8	Barnsley	46	21	7	18	83	80	49
9	Halifax	46	16	17	13	71	78	49
10	Shrewsbury	46	15	16	15	83	75	46
11	Hull	46	17	12	17	73	73	46
12	Torquay	46	14	17	15	75	83	45
13	Newport	46	17	11	18	81	90	45
14	Bristol City	46	17	10	19	70	68	44
15	Coventry	46	16	12	18	80	83	44
16	Swindon	46	14	15	17	62	55	43
17	Brentford	46	13	17	16	56	70	43
18	Reading	46	14	12	20	72	83	40
19	Bournemouth	46	15	10	21	58	76	40
20	Southend	46	14	11	21	60	76	39
21	Tranmere	46	15	8	23	79	115	38
22	Bradford City	46	11	14	21	65	87	36
23	Colchester	46	11	11	24	68	101	33
24	Chesterfield	46	10	12	24	67	87	32

SHREWSBURY 1961 Left to right (back row): Wallace, Harley, Skeech, Gibson, Walters, Pountney, Whitaker (now Q.P.R.). (Front): T. Seymour (trainer), Jones, Starkey, Baker, Cornfield, McLaughlin.

SEASON 1961/62

Division 3

No.	Date	Opposition	Res.	H.T.	Att.	Goalscorers	Gibson M.J.	Walters G.	Skeech H.G.	Pountney D.H.	Wallace J.B.	Harley A.G.	Kenning M.J.	Starkey M.J.	Baker T.G.	Rowley G.A.	Cornfield A.H.	McLaughlin J.	Dolby P.	Goodall D.G.	Miller J.P.	Jones M.H.	French G.E.	Hemsley R.J.O.	Pragg M.K.	Hines D.J.	Morrall T.S.	Clarke F.J.	Middleton H.	Nixon W.J.	Corbett A.	Dawes D.M.
1	19 Aug	PORT VALE	4-2	2-2	8632	Rowley(3), Kenning	1	2	3	4	5	6	7	8	9	10	11															
2	23	Bournemouth	0-0	0-0	11040		1	2	3	4	5	6	7	8	9	10		11														
3	26	Bristol City	1-0	0-0	11727	Rowley	1	2	3	4	5	6	7	8	9	10		11														
4	30	BOURNEMOUTH	2-2	0-1	9559	Rowley, O.G.	1	2	3	4	5	6	7	8	9	10		11														
5	2 Sep	BRADFORD	4-1	1-1	6664	McLaughlin(2), Kenning, Rowley	1	2	3	4	5	6	7	8	9	10		11														
6	5	Watford	1-1	0-1	15558	Rowley	1	2	3	4	5	6	7	8	9	10		11														
7	9	Grimsby	1-2	1-2	7560	McLaughlin	1	2	3	4	5	6	7	8	9	10		11														
8	16	COVENTRY	1-1	0-0	7602	Rowley	1	2	3	4	5	6	7	9		10		11	8													
9	20	PETERBOROUGH	3-4	3-1	12547	McLaughlin(2), Dolby	1	2	3	4	5	6	7	9		10		11	8													
10	23	Brentford	0-4	0-3	7000		1	2	3		4	6	7	9	8	10		11		5												
11	25	Peterborough	3-0	1-0	17109	McLaughlin(3)		2	3	4	5	6	7	9		10		8			1	11										
12	30	READING	4-1	2-1	8529	McLaughlin, Starkey, Rowley, Kenning		2	3	4	5	6	7	9		10		8			1		11									
13	2 Oct	Southend	1-1	1-1	10287	McLaughlin		2	3	4	5	6	7	9	11			8	10		1											
14	7	CRYSTAL PALACE	1-5	1-2	7909	Rowley		2	3	4	5	6		9	7	10			8		1		11									
15	14	Portsmouth	1-3	0-2	16423	Starkey	1	2	3	6	5		7	9		10		8					11	4								
16	18	WATFORD	5-1	3-1	5711	Kenning(2), McLaughlin, Pragg, Rowley	1	2	3	5	4		7	9		10		11						6	8							
17	21	NORTHAMPTON	1-3	0-2	6872	Rowley	1	2	3	5	4	8	7	9		10		11						6								
18	25	SOUTHEND	1-1	0-0	5262	Rowley	1	2	3	5	4		7	9		10		11						6	8							
19	28	Hull City	1-3	1-2	6229	Starkey	1	2	3	5	4		7	10	9				8				11	6								
20	11 Nov	Swindon	2-1	1-0	7025	Rowley, McLaughlin	1	2	3	5	4	6	7	8		10		11								9						
21	18	TORQUAY	1-1	0-1	6675	Hines	1	2	3	5	4	6	7	8		10		11								9						
22	2 Dec	BARNSLEY	4-1	0-0	5635	Rowley(2), Hines, McLaughlin	1	2	3	5	4	6	7	8		10		11								9						
23	9	Q.P.Rangers	1-3	0-2	7433	Kenning	1	2	3	5	4	6	7	8		10							11			9						
24	16	Port Vale	1-4	0-3	8837	Kenning	1	2	3	5	4	6	7	8		10		11								9						
25	22	BRISTOL CITY	2-2	0-1	4408	Hines, Skeech	1	2	3	6	5	4	7	9		10		11								8						
26	26	Notts County	2-3	0-1	10197	McLaughlin(2)	1	2	3	6	5	4	7	9		10		11								8						
27	13 Jan	Bradford	1-1	0-1	7323	McLaughlin		2	3	6	5	4	7	9		10		11			1					8						
28	20	GRIMSBY	1-2	0-0	7576	McLaughlin	1	2	3	6	5	4	7	9		10		11								8						
29	3 Feb	Coventry	1-4	0-2	8262	McLaughlin		2	3	8		4	7	9		10		11			1			6			5					
30	7	Lincoln	2-1	1-0	5358	Hines, McLaughlin		2	3	10		4	7					11			1			6		8	5	9				
31	10	BRENTFORD	1-3	0-1	6037	Rowley(pen)		2	3	6		4	7			10		11			1					8	5		9			
32	17	Reading	0-3	0-0	7385			2	3	6	4	10	7					11			1					8	5		9			
33	24	Crystal Palace	1-2	0-2	12493	Middleton	1	2	3	6	5	4	7	10				11								8			9			
34	3 Mar	PORTSMOUTH	0-1	0-0	5636		1	2	3	6	5	4	7		8	10		11											9			
35	10	Northampton	1-3	1-0	8133	Middleton	1	2	3	6	5	4	7			10		11											9	8		
36	14	HALIFAX	0-0	0-0	4702		1	2	3		5	4	7			10		8					11	6					9			
37	17	HULL CITY	2-0	1-0	4722	Rowley(2,1pen)	1	2	3		5	4	7			10		11						6					9	8		
38	24	Halifax	2-1	1-1	3890	Harley, Kenning	1	2	3		5	4	7			10		11	6										9	8		
39	28	NOTTS COUNTY	3-0	1-0	3880	Kenning, McLaughlin, Rowley	1	2	3		5	4	7			10		11	6										9	8		
40	30	SWINDON	1-3	0-1	6330	McLaughlin	1	2	3		5	4	7			10		11	6										9	8		
41	7 Apr	Torquay	1-3	0-2	3107	Hemsley	1	2	3	8	5	4	7	10		9		11						6								
42	14	LINCOLN	0-0	0-0	4227			2			5	4	7	9		10		8			1		11	6							3	
43	16	Newport	2-3	2-2	2003	McLaughlin, Rowley		2	3		5	6	7	9		10		8			1		11	4								
44	21	Barnsley	1-1	0-0	3359	Rowley		2	3	6		4		9		10		7			1		11				5		8			
45	23	NEWPORT	4-1	0-0	6650	Kenning(2), Rowley, Starkey		2	3	6		4	7	9		10		8			1						5					11
46	28	Q.P.RANGERS	1-2	1-0	5823	Pountney		2	3	6		4	7	9		10		8			1						5					11

F.A. Cup

	Date	Opponent			Att	Scorers	1	2	3	5	4	6	7	9	10	11	8
1R	4 Nov	BANBURY S.	7-1	2-0	7750	Kenning(2), McLaughlin(2), Rowley(2), Starkey	1	2	3	5	4	6	7	9	10	11	8
2R	25	BRIERLEY HILL	3-0	0-0	9243	Hines(2), McLaughlin	1	2	3	5	4	6	7		10	11	8
3R	9 Jan	Southport	3-1	2-0	10810	Rowley, Hines, McLaughlin	1	2	3	6	5	4	7	9	10	11	8
4R	27	MIDDLESBOROUGH	2-2	0-2	14534	Rowley, Kenning	1	2	3	6	5	4	7	9	10	11	8
4Rr	31	Middlesborough	1-5	0-1	34751	Rowley(pen)	1	2	3	6	5	4	7	9	10	11	8

League Cup

	Date	Opponent			Att	Scorers	1	2	3	4	5	6	7	8	10	11	9
1R	11 Sep	Newport C.	0-0	0-0	7500		1	2	3	4	5	6	7	8	10	11	9
1Rr	28	NEWPORT C.	3-1	2-0	8313	Rowley, McLaughlin, Harley	1	2	3	4	5	6	7	8	10	11	
2R	9 Oct	BOURNEMOUTH	1-3	0-3	8468	French	1	2	3	4	5	7	9	8	10	11	6

Back: Harley, Dolby, Walters, Gibson, Skeech, Wallace.
Front: Kenning, Starkey, Rowley, Pountney, McLoughlin.

FINAL LEAGUE TABLE

		P	W	D	L	F	A	Pts
1	Portsmouth	46	27	11	8	87	47	65
2	Grimsby	46	28	6	12	80	56	62
3	Bournemouth	46	21	17	8	69	45	59
4	QPR	46	24	11	11	111	73	59
5	Peterborough	46	26	6	14	107	82	58
6	Bristol City	46	23	8	15	94	72	54
7	Reading	46	22	9	15	77	66	53
8	Northampton	46	20	11	15	85	57	51
9	Swindon	46	17	15	14	78	71	49
10	Hull	46	20	8	18	67	54	48
11	Bradford PA	46	20	7	19	80	78	47
12	Port Vale	46	17	11	18	65	58	45
13	Notts County	46	17	9	20	67	74	43
14	Coventry	46	16	11	19	64	71	43
15	Crystal Palace	46	14	14	18	83	80	42
16	Southend	46	13	16	17	57	69	42
17	Watford	46	14	13	19	63	74	41
18	Halifax	46	15	10	21	62	84	40
19	Shrewsbury	46	13	12	21	73	84	38
20	Barnsley	46	13	12	21	71	95	38
21	Torquay	46	15	6	25	76	100	36
22	Lincoln	46	9	17	20	57	87	35
23	Brentford	46	13	8	25	53	93	34
24	Newport	46	7	8	31	46	102	22

SEASON 1962/63
Division 3

No.	Date	Opposition	Res.	H.T.	Att.	Gibson M.J.	Harley A.G.	Skeech H.G.	Wallace J.B.	Morrall T.S.	Pountney D.H.	Kenning M.J.	Dawes D.M.	Starkey M.J.	Rowley A.G.	French G.E.	Walters G.	Middleton H.	McLaughlin J.	Nixon W.J.	Hines D.J.	Miller J.P.	Hemsley E.J.O.	Wright P.D.	Clarke F.J.	Dolby P.	Pragg M.K.	Gregson J.	Walters R.J.	Beel W.J.L.	Goalscorers
1	18 Aug	Reading	0-5	0-2	7591	1	2	3	4	5	6	7	8	9	10	11															
2	22	CRYSTAL PALACE	3-1	2-0	6827	1	4	3		5	6	7		9	10		2	8	11												Kenning, McLaughlin, Rowley(pen)
3	25	BRISTOL CITY	3-3	1-1	6097	1	4	3		5	6			9	10		2	7	11	8											Rowley(2), Middleton
4	29	Crystal Palace	2-2	2-1	15643	1	4	3		5	6	7		9	10		2	8	11												Middleton, Pountney
5	1 Sep	Watford	3-4	2-2	10279	1	4	3		5	6	7		9			2	8	11		10										Middleton(2), Kenning(pen)
6	3	Southend	1-3	0-1	14449		4	3		5	6	7		9	10		2	8	11			1									McLaughlin
7	7	BRADFORD P.A.	1-2	1-1	6507		6	3		5		7		9	10		2	8	11			1	4								Kenning
8	12	SOUTHEND	6-0	4-0	5422		8	3		5	6	7			10		2	9	11			1	4								Rowley(3), Pountney(2), Middleton
9	15	Coventry	0-0	0-0	14112		8	3		5	6	7			10		2	9	11			1	4								
10	17	Millwall	2-1	1-0	17301		8	3		5	6	7			10		2	9	11			1	4								Rowley, Kenning
11	22	BOURNEMOUTH	2-1	1-1	8593		8	3		5	6	7			10		2	9	11			1	4								Harley, Middleton
12	26	MILLWALL	3-3	2-2	8503		8	3		5	6	7			10		2	9	11			1	4								Middleton, Rowley, Hemsley
13	29	Notts County	5-1	2-1	10500		8	3		5	6	7			10		2	9	11			1	4								Rowley(3), Kenning(2)
14	3 Oct	COLCHESTER	1-2	0-1	8261		8	3		5	6	7			10		2	9	11			1	4								Rowley
15	6	Halifax	2-2	1-1	4423		8	3		5	6	7			10		2	9	11			1	4								Rowley, Harley
16	8	Colchester	2-3	0-0	6472		8	3		5	6	7			10		2	9	11			1	4								Harley, Pountney
17	13	BRISTOL ROVERS	7-2	4-1	6291		6			5				8	10	11	3		7			1	4	2	9						Clarke(3), McLaughlin(3), Rowley
18	20	Brighton	1-1	0-1	8220		8			5	6	7			10		3		11			1	4	2	9						McLaughlin
19	27	CARLISLE	1-1	1-1	5368		8			5	6	7					3		11	10		1	4	2	9						McLaughlin
20	10 Nov	PETERBOROUGH	5-4	3-4	7062		8			5	6				10	11	3		7			1	4	2	9						Clarke, Rowley(2), McLaughlin, Harley
21	17	Barnsley	0-1	0-0	7054		8			5	6		11		10		3		7			1	4	2	9						
22	1 Dec	Q.P.Rangers	0-0	0-0	10360		8			5	6				10		3		11		7	1	4	2	9						
23	8	HULL CITY	1-4	1-2	6976		8			5	6				10		3		11		7	1	4	2	9						Harley
24	15	READING	2-1	2-1	4163					5	6				10	11	3	8			7	1	4	2	9						Middleton, Rowley
25	22	Bristol City	1-3	0-0	6656					5	6				10		3	8	11		7	1	4	2	9						McLaughlin
26	26	WREXHAM	4-2	1-2	7680	1	8			5	6				10		3		11		7		4	2	9						Rowley(2), Harley, McLaughlin
27	23 Feb	HALIFAX	4-2	2-2	4320	1	4			5	6			8	10		3		11		7			2	9						McLaughlin, Clarke(2), Rowley(pen)
28	2 Mar	Bristol Rovers	0-2	0-1	7575	1	4			5	6			8	10	7	3		11					2	9						
29	9	BRIGHTON	2-1	0-1	3833	1	8	3		5	6				10		2		11	9	7		4								Hines, Harley
30	16	Carlisle	1-2	1-2	4825	1	4	3		5	6				10		2		11	8	7				9						Clarke
31	20	Wrexham	0-2	0-1	12867	1	8				6				10		3		11		7		4	2	9	5					
32	23	SWINDON	1-2	1-0	5817			3			6				10	11			7	8		1	4	2	9	5					Rowley
33	26	Bradford P.A.	1-2	1-2	6890	1	4	3			6				10	11			7	8				2	9	5					Nixon
34	2 Apr	Peterborough	3-2	2-1	8890	1	4	3			6				10	11		8	7					2		5	9				Middleton(2), French
35	6	BARNSLEY	1-3	0-1	4263	1	4	3			6		8		10	11			7					2	9	5					O.G.
36	12	Port Vale	0-0	0-0	11305		4	3			6		8		10	11			7			1		2	9	5					
37	13	Northampton	0-1	0-1	13350		4	3			6		8		10	11			7			1		2	9	5					
38	15	PORT VALE	2-1	1-1	6819		4	3							10	11		8	7			1	6	2	9	5					Rowley, Middleton
39	20	Q.P.RANGERS	0-3	0-2	3890		4	3					8		10	11	2		7			1	6		9				5		
40	24	NOTTS COUNTY	2-2	2-1	3891		4	3							10	11	2		8			1	6		9	5		7			McLaughlin, O.G.
41	27	Hull City	2-2	1-0	5607		4	3							10	11	2		8			1	6		9	5		7			McLaughlin, Gregson
42	1 May	NORTHAMPTON	1-0	0-0	6052		4	3			6				10	11	2		8			1				5	9	7			McLaughlin
43	4	Bournemouth	0-0	0-0	8573		4	3			6				10	11	2		8			1			9	5		7			
44	11	WATFORD	3-0	3-0	4067		4	3			6				10	11	2	8				1			9	5		7			Rowley(2), Clarke
45	14	Swindon	0-1	0-0	20471		4	3			6					11	2	8		10		1			9	5		7			
46	20	COVENTRY	2-1	1-0	4695		4	3			6		8			11	2			10					9	5		7		1	Clarke, Gregson

F.A. Cup

							8	5	6		10	11	3		7		1	4	2	9
1R	3 Nov	Chelmsford C.	6-2	4-1	8752	McLaughlin(4), Rowley, Clarke	8	5	6		10	11	3		7		1	4	2	9
2R	24	TORQUAY U.	2-1	0-1	8223	Middleton(2)	8	5	6		10	11	3		7		1	4	2	9
3R	21 Feb	SHEFFIELD W.	1-1	0-1	11428	Harley	4		6	8	10	7	3		11			2	9	5
3Rr	7 Mar	Sheffield W.	1-2	1-1	24207	Rowley	4	3	6		10	8		11	7			2	9	5

League Cup

							8		3	5	6	7	10	11	2	8	1	4	9
1R	5 Sep	MILLWALL	3-1	2-0	5986	Middleton(2), Rowley	8		3	5	6	7	10	11	2	8	1	4	9
2R	24	Barrow	1-3	1-2	4003	Pountney	8		3	5	6	7	10	11	2	9	10	1	4	3

(Back): Clarke, Harley, Hemsley, Beel, Starkey, Skeech, Dolby. (2nd Row): Seymour, Pountney, Dawes, Morrall, Gibson, Miller, Walters, W.Nixon, Middleton, Butler. (3rd Row): Goodall, Rimmer, Wallace, Kenning, Rowley, Hines, McLaughlin, Harris. (Front): French, Pragg, Wall, Gregory, Mitchell.

Final League Table

	P	W	D	L	F	A	Pts
1 Northampton	46	26	10	10	109	60	62
2 Swindon	46	22	14	10	87	56	58
3 Port Vale	46	23	8	15	72	58	54
4 Coventry	46	18	17	11	83	69	53
5 Bournemouth	46	18	16	12	63	46	52
6 Peterborough	46	20	11	15	93	75	51
7 Notts County	46	19	13	14	73	74	51
8 Southend	46	19	12	15	75	77	50
9 Wrexham	46	20	9	17	84	83	49
10 Hull	46	19	10	17	74	69	48
11 Crystal Palace	46	17	13	16	68	58	47
12 Colchester	46	18	11	17	73	93	47
13 QPR	46	17	11	18	85	76	45
14 Bristol City	46	16	13	17	100	92	45
15 Shrewsbury	46	16	12	18	83	81	44
16 Millwall	46	15	13	18	82	87	43
17 Watford	46	17	8	21	82	85	42
18 Barnsley	46	15	11	20	63	74	41
19 Bristol Rovers	46	15	11	20	70	88	41
20 Reading	46	16	8	22	74	78	40
21 Bradford PA	46	14	12	20	79	97	40
22 Brighton	46	12	12	22	58	84	36
23 Carlisle	46	13	9	24	61	89	35
24 Halifax	46	9	12	25	64	106	30

SEASON 1963/64
Division 3

No.	Date	Opposition	Res.	H.T.	Att.	Goalscorers	Boswell A.	Wright P.D.	Turner K.	Harley A.G.	Dolby D.	Pountney D.H.	Gregson J.	Ross R.H.	Clarke F.J.	Rowley A.G.	Taylor B.J.	Middleton H.	Boardman G.	McLaughlin John	Brodie E.	Nixon W.J.	Hemsley E.J.O.	Beel W.J.L.	Wall T.P.	Harris A.T.	Scott S.R.
1	24 Aug	PORT VALE	1-0	1-0	9710	Clarke	1	2	3	4	5	6	7	8	9	10	11										
2	26	Q.P.RANGERS	1-2	0-0	8051	Clarke	1	2	3	4	5	6	7	8	9	10	11										
3	31	Notts County	1-0	0-0	7788	Clarke	1	2	3	4	5	6	7	8	9	10	11										
4	7 Sep	CREWE	3-0	3-0	7950	Harley, Pountney, Taylor	1	2	3	4	5	6	7	8	9	10	11										
5	9	Q.P.Rangers	4-3	4-1	11090	Middleton(3), Harley	1	2	3	4	5	6	7			10	11	9	8								
6	14	Crystal Palace	0-3	0-1	14689		1	2	3	4	5	6	7			10	11	9	8								
7	18	BRISTOL CITY	2-0	0-0	7152	Rowley, Boardman	1	2	3	4	5	6	7			10	11	9	8	1							
8	21	WALSALL	2-1	2-1	8447	Boardman(2)		2	3	4	5	6	7	10				9	8	1	11						
9	28	Reading	0-2	0-1	5913			2	3	4	5	6	7	10				9	8	1	11						
10	1 Oct	Bristol City	2-2	2-0	9247	Clarke(2)	1	2	3	4	5	6	7	8	9	10	11										
11	5	LUTON	1-0	1-0	5887	Middleton	1	2	3	4	5	6	7	8	9		11	11		1	10						
12	7	Mansfield	1-3	1-1	10374	Turner(pen)	1	2	3	4	5	6	7	8	9		11	11		1		10					
13	12	OLDHAM	2-0	2-0	9504	Gregson, Hemsley	1	2	3	4	5		7	8	9		11	11		1	10		6				
14	16	MANSFIELD	2-0	1-0	8535	Clarke(2)	1	2	3	4	5	6	7	8	9			11			10						
15	19	Hull	2-4	1-3	7057	Clarke, Pountney	1	2	3	4	5	6	7	8	9			11			10						
16	22	Coventry	1-8	1-3	27294	Brodie		2	3	4	5		7	8	9	10		11			10		6	1			
17	26	BARNSLEY	3-1	1-1	6451	Middleton(2), Gregson	1	2	3	4	5		7	8	9		11	10		1			6				
18	30	COVENTRY	0-0	0-0	13669		1	2	3	4	5	6	7	8	9			11			10		4				
19	2 Nov	Millwall	2-2	1-1	8805	Middleton, Hemsley	1	2	3	4	5		7	8	9		11	11			10		6				
20	9	COLCHESTER	1-1	0-1	6413	Rowley	1	2	3	4	5		7	8	9	10	11	8					6				
21	23	SOUTHEND	2-2	0-2	5151	Rowley, Ross	1	2	3	4	5		7	8	9	10	11			1			6				
22	30	Peterborough	2-2	1-0	8010	Middleton(2)	1	2	3	4	5	6		8	9		11	7	10	1							
23	14 Dec	Port Vale	1-1	0-1	6856	Brodie	1	2	3	4	5		7	8	9	10	11				6						
24	21	NOTTS COUNTY	5-2	3-1	3738	Middleton(3), Ross(2)	1	2	3	4	5		7	8		10	11	9			6						
25	26	Wrexham	3-2	0-1	11954	Gregson, Middleton, Clarke	1	2	3	4	5		7	8	9	9	11	10	10		6						
26	28	WREXHAM	1-2	0-1	9199	Rowley	1	2		4	5		7	8	9	10	11				6				3		
27	4 Jan	Watford	1-2	0-1	9115	Taylor	1	2		4	5	6		7	8	10	11				9				3		
28	11	Crewe	2-3	0-2	5111	Dolby, Middleton	1	2		4	5	6	7	8	9	10	11	9							3		
29	18	CRYSTAL PALACE	1-1	1-1	4303	O.G.	1	2		4	5	6	7	8	9	10	11								3		
30	25	BOURNEMOUTH	5-2	3-1	4663	Middleton(3), Taylor, Dolby	1	2		4	5	6	7	8	9		11	10					3				
31	1 Feb	Walsall	1-1	0-0	6662	Clarke	1	2		4	5	6	7	8	9		11	10					3				
32	8	READING	2-1	2-1	5904	Harley, Middleton(pen)	1	2		4	5	6	7	8	9		11	10					3				
33	15	Luton	0-2	0-1	6282		1	2		4		6	7	8	9	5	11	10					3				
34	22	Oldham	4-2	2-2	8378	Boardman(2), Ross, Clarke	1	3		4		6	7	8	9	5	11		10				6				
35	29	BRISTOL ROVERS	0-1	0-1	6061		1	2		4		6	7	8	9	5	11		10				3				
36	7 Mar	Barnsley	1-2	0-1	3502	Clarke	1	2		4	5	6	7	8	9		11	10	10				3				
37	14	MILLWALL	0-1	0-1	3234		1	2		4	5			8			11	7	10		9		3			6	
38	21	Bristol Rovers	0-7	0-5	8902		1	2		4	5		7	8	9		11				10		6		3		
39	28	WATFORD	3-0	2-0	5173	Rowley(pen), Middleton, Clarke	1	2		4		6	7		9	10	11	8			6		3				
40	30	Brentford	1-0	1-0	10047	Ross	1	2		4		6	7	8	9	10	11	10			6		3				
41	31	BRENTFORD	1-1	1-0	5493	Taylor		2		4		6		8	9		11	10			6		3	1			7
42	4 Apr	Southend	1-7	0-4	4744	Wright	1	2		4			7	8	9		11	10			6		6				
43	11	PETERBOROUGH	0-0	0-0	4340		1	2			4		7	8	9	10	11				6		3				
44	18	Bournemouth	0-2	0-1	7710		1	2			5		7	8	9	10	11	11			6		8			5	
45	20	Colchester	0-1	0-1	3649		1	2			10		7	8	9		11				6		8			5	
46	25	HULL	5-1	1-0	3125	Middleton(2), Clarke(2), Gregson	1	2			8		7	9	9		11	10			6		6			5	7

F.A. Cup

								1	2	3	4	5		7	8	9		11	10	6
1R	16 Nov	Exeter C.	1-2	1-1	7322	Middleton														

League Cup

								1	2	3	4	5	6	7	8	9		11	10	
1R	4 Sep	BRISTOL R.	1-1	0-0	6950	Pountney														
1Rr	23	Bristol R.	2-6	0-2	8219	Harley, Boardman													9	8	1

Final League Table

		P	W	D	L	F	A	Pts
1	Coventry	46	22	16	8	98	61	60
2	Crystal Palace	46	23	14	9	73	51	60
3	Watford	46	23	12	11	79	59	58
4	Bournemouth	46	24	8	14	79	58	56
5	Bristol City	46	20	15	11	84	64	55
6	Reading	46	21	10	15	79	62	52
7	Mansfield	46	20	11	15	76	62	51
8	Hull	46	16	17	13	73	68	49
9	Oldham	46	20	8	18	73	70	48
10	Peterborough	46	18	11	17	75	70	47
11	Shrewsbury	46	18	11	17	73	80	47
12	Bristol Rovers	46	19	8	19	91	79	46
13	Port Vale	46	16	14	16	53	49	46
14	Southend	46	15	15	16	77	78	45
15	QPR	46	18	9	19	76	78	45
16	Brentford	46	15	14	17	87	80	44
17	Colchester	46	12	19	15	70	68	43
18	Luton	46	16	10	20	64	80	42
19	Walsall	46	13	14	19	59	76	40
20	Barnsley	46	12	15	19	68	94	39
21	Millwall	46	14	10	22	53	67	38
22	Crewe	46	11	12	23	50	77	34
23	Wrexham	46	13	6	27	75	107	32
24	Notts County	46	9	9	28	45	92	27

Players of 1963/64, including: Walters, Harris, Hemsley, Harley, Wall, Beel, Wright, Gregory, Dolby, Gregson, Nixon, Dawes, Boardman, Hines, Dawes, Scott, Turner, Pountney, Seymour, Clarke, Ross, Rimmer, Rowley, Pragg, Taylor, Brodie, Butler.

SEASON 1964/65
Division 3

No.	Date	Opposition	Res.	H.T.	Att.	Goalscorers	Boswell A.	Wright P.D.	Turner K.	Harley A.G.	Dolby P.	Brodie E.	Meredith T.	Ross R.H.	Middleton H.	Rowley G.A.	Taylor B.J.	Hemsley E.	Clarke F.J.	Boardman G.	Walker M.J.S.	Regan J.M.	Gregson J.	Harris A.T.	Wall T.P.	Broadbent P.	Scott S.R.	Stephenson G.R.	Gregory A.T.	Nixon W.J.
1	22 Aug	Southend	0-1	0-1	10879	Middleton	1	2	3	4	5	6	7	8	9	10	11													
2	26	Reading	1-3	1-1	8175	Meredith, Ross, Middleton	1	2	3	4	5	6	7	8	9	10	11													
3	29	BARNSLEY	3-3	2-1	5260	Clarke(2), Taylor, Brodie	1	2	3	4	5	6	7	8		10	11		9											
4	1 Sep	READING	4-0	1-0	5643	Meredith, Ross	1	2	3		5	6	7	8	10		11	4	9											
5	4	Scunthorpe	2-3	0-2	6695	Taylor	1	2	3		5	6	7	8	10		11	4	9											
6	8	EXETER	1-0	0-0	6557	Taylor	1	2	3		5	6	7	8	10		11	4	9											
7	11	WALSALL	3-1	2-1	8439	Ross(3,1pen)	1	2	3		5	6	7	8		10	11	4	9											
8	16	Exeter	1-0	0-0	7672	Ross	1	2	3		5	6	7	8		10	11	4	9											
9	19	Watford	2-2	1-2	7741	Ross, Clarke	1	2	3		5	6	7	8			11	4	9	10										
10	26	WORKINGTON	6-1	2-0	6014	Ross(2,1pen), Boardman(2), Clarke, Taylor	1	2	3		5	6	7	8			11	4	9	10										
11	3 Oct	Hull	2-1	0-0	6731	Meredith, O.G.	1	2	3		5	6	7	8	10		11	4	9											
12	5	Q.P.Rangers	1-2	0-2	5722	Ross	1	2	3		5	6	7	8			11	4	9	10										
13	10	BRISTOL ROVERS	2-1	0-0	7345	Boardman, Regan	1	2	3			6	7	8		5	11	4		10		9								
14	13	GILLINGHAM	2-0	0-0	8005	Boardman, Ross(pen)		2	3			6	7	8		5		4		10	1	9	11							
15	17	Brentford	0-2	0-1	11397			2	3			6	7	8		5		4		10	1	9	11							
16	21	Gillingham	0-5	0-3	7857		1	2	3			6	7	8		9	11	4		10				5						
17	24	COLCHESTER	3-0	2-0	4770	Brodie, Ross(pen), Boardman	1	2	3			6	7	8		5	11	4		10		9								
18	28	Bournemouth	1-2	1-0	8371	Clarke	1	2	3			6	7	8		5	11	4	9	10										
19	31	Port Vale	1-1	1-0	6362	Ross	1	2				6	7	8		5	11	4	9	10					3					
20	3 Nov	MANSFIELD	1-1	1-0	5463	Meredith	1	2	3		6		7	8		5	11	4	9	10										
21	7	CARLISLE	2-2	1-2	5416	Meredith, Clarke	1	2	3		5		7	8			11	4	9	10										6
22	28	Grimsby	2-2	2-1	7006	Meredith, Boardman	1	2	3		5	6	7	8			11	4		10		9								
23	12 Dec	SOUTHEND	1-3	1-0	4047	Regan	1	2	3		5	6	7	8			11	4		10		9								
24	18	Barnsley	2-6	1-4	2318	Rowley, Meredith	1	2	3		5	6	7	8		10		4				9					11			
25	26	OLDHAM	1-3	0-1	6305	Ross	1	2	3		5	6	7	8		10	11	4				9								
26	28	Oldham	3-1	1-1	10045	Regan(2), Boardman	1	2	3		5	6	7	8			11	4		10		9								
27	2 Jan	SCUNTHORPE	3-2	1-1	4707	Ross, Brodie, Taylor	1	2	3		5	6	7	8			11	4		10		9								
28	16	Walsall	1-1	0-0	8253	Regan	1	2			5	6	7	8			11	4		10		9			3					
29	23	WATFORD	2-2	2-1	6778	Regan, Meredith	1	2	3		5	6	7	8			11	4		10		9								
30	5 Feb	Workington	2-2	2-1	3975	Meredith, Hemsley	1	2	6		5		7	8			11	4		10		9			3					
31	13	HULL	0-4	0-1	7652		1	2			5	6	7	8			11	4		10		9			3					
32	23	Bristol Rovers	0-0	0-0	13143		1	2	3		5	6	7	8			11	4		10		9								
33	27	BRENTFORD	1-0	1-0	5564	Ross(pen)	1	2	3		5	6	7	8			11	4	9	10										
34	10 Mar	Luton	7-2	3-1	4914	Boardman(4), Scott(2), Ross	1	2				6	7	8				4		10		9		5	3		11			
35	13	PORT VALE	0-0	0-0	5546		1	2				6	7					4		10		9		5	3	8	11			
36	15	Peterborough	1-4	1-2	6701	Boardman	1	2			5		7	8				6		9				4	3	10	11			
37	19	Carlisle	1-2	0-1	10435	Brodie	1	2			5	6	7	8				4		9					3	10	11			
38	26	LUTON	0-2	0-1	4800		1	2			5	6	7	8				4		9					3	10	11			
39	3 Apr	Mansfield	0-1	0-0	8914		1	2	3		5	6	7	8				4		9						10	11			
40	7	PETERBOROUGH	1-1	1-0	5118	Boardman	1	2			5	6	7	10				4		9					3	8	11			
41	10	GRIMSBY	1-3	0-2	3868	Dolby	1	2			5		7	10				6		9				4	3	8		11		
42	12	Q.P.RANGERS	3-2	0-2	3415	Boardman(2), Broadbent	1	2			5	6		9			11	4		10					3	8	7			
43	17	Colchester	4-0	3-0	3415	Ross(2), Boardman, Broadbent	1	2			5	6		9			11	4		10					3	8	7			
44	19	BRISTOL CITY	1-5	1-1	5857	Boardman	1	2	3		5			9			11	4		10				6		8		7		
45	20	Bristol City	0-3	0-3	16423		1	2	3		5			9			11	4		10		8		6				7		
46	24	BOURNEMOUTH	1-2	0-2	3053	Rowley	1	2						9		5	11		4	10				6		8	7		3	

F.A.Cup

	Date	Opponent			Att	Scorers													
1R	14 Nov	Kings Lynn	1-0	1-0	4183	Regan	1	2	3		5		7	8	9	10	11	4	6
2R	5 Dec	Exeter C.	2-1	2-0	6528	Regan(2)	1	2	3		5	6	7	8	9	10	11	4	
3R	9 Jan	Manchester C.	1-1	1-0	16151	Ross	1	2			5	6	7	8	9	10	11	4	3
3Rr	13	MANCHESTER C.	3-1	0-1	16084	Dolby, Meredith, Ross	1	2			5	6	7	8	9	10	11	4	3
4R	30	Millwall	2-1	0-1	20611	Boardman, Meredith	1	2			5	6	7	8	9	10	11	4	3
5R	20 Feb	Leeds U.	0-2	0-1	47740		1	2			5	6	7	8	9	10	11	4	3 9

League Cup

	Date	Opponent			Att	Scorers												
1R	23 Sep	Stoke C.	1-1	1-1	13531	Hemsley	1	2	3	5	6	7	8	9	10	11	4
1Rr	24	STOKE C.	0-1	0-0	15304		1	2	3	5	6	7	8	9	10	11	4

FINAL LEAGUE TABLE

		P	W	D	L	F	A	Pts
1	Carlisle	46	25	10	11	76	53	60
2	Bristol City	46	24	11	11	92	55	59
3	Mansfield	46	24	11	11	95	61	59
4	Hull	46	23	12	11	91	57	58
5	Brentford	46	24	9	13	83	55	57
6	Bristol Rovers	46	20	15	11	82	58	55
7	Gillingham	46	23	9	14	70	50	55
8	Peterborough	46	22	7	17	85	74	51
9	Watford	46	17	16	13	71	64	50
10	Grimsby	46	16	17	13	68	67	49
11	Bournemouth	46	18	11	17	72	63	47
12	Southend	46	19	8	19	78	71	46
13	Reading	46	16	14	16	70	70	46
14	QPR	46	17	12	17	72	80	46
15	Workington	46	17	12	17	58	69	46
16	Shrewsbury	46	15	12	19	76	84	42
17	Exeter	46	12	17	17	51	52	41
18	Scunthorpe	46	14	12	20	65	72	40
19	Walsall	46	15	7	24	55	80	37
20	Oldham	46	13	10	23	61	83	36
21	Luton	46	11	11	24	51	94	33
22	Port Vale	46	9	14	23	41	76	32
23	Colchester	46	10	10	26	50	89	30
24	Barnsley	46	9	11	26	54	90	29

(BackRow): Harris, Wall, Dolby, Nixon, Walker, Boswell, (Apprentice), Middleton, Clarke, P.Wright.
(2nd Row): Seymour, Gregory, K.Turner, Dawes, B.Taylor, Ross, Brodie, Boardman, H.Wright, Harley, Gregson, Butler,
(Front): R.Scott, Meredith, Stephenson, Rimmer, Rowley, Pragg, plus apprentices.

SEASON 1965/66
Division 3

No.	Date	Opposition	Res.	H.T.	Att.	Goalscorers
1	21 Aug	YORK CITY	4-1	2-0	5226	Meredith(2), Clarke, Boardbent
2	24	Bristol Rovers	2-3	1-1	10371	Ross(2,1pen)
3	28	Oxford	1-0	1-0	9801	Meredith
4	3 Sep	SWANSEA	5-0	3-0	8309	Clarke(3), Broadbent, Meredith
5	11	Walsall	0-3	0-2	13603	
6	14	Brentford	0-4	0-1	10030	
7	17	WORKINGTON	1-1	1-1	6926	Boardman
8	25	Bournemouth	0-2	0-1	4585	
9	1 Oct	SOUTHEND	3-0	1-0	5334	Clarke, Boardman, Thom
10	6	BRENTFORD	0-0	0-0	4982	
11	9	OLDHAM	3-1	0-0	4756	Clarke(2), Boardman
12	16	Gillingham	1-0	0-0	9235	Clarke
13	22	MILLWALL	2-0	1-0	6096	Meredith(2,2pen)
14	30	Peterborough	1-4	0-3	8105	Harris
15	1 Nov	BRISTOL ROVERS	1-0	0-0	4997	Boardman
16	6	EXETER	4-0	1-0	4559	Meredith, Hemsley, Clarke, Boardman
17	20	HULL	2-2	1-0	5316	Thom, Boardman
18	11 Dec	Brighton	1-1	1-0	11192	Harris
19	27	SCUNTHORPE	1-4	1-1	7520	Hemsley
20	28	Scunthorpe	4-1	1-1	6054	Broadbent, Clarke, Boardman, Ross
21	1 Jan	Oldham	1-0	1-0	14099	Ross
22	8	READING	3-3	2-2	5686	Hemsley, Broadbent, Clarke
23	15	Millwall	2-4	1-3	11563	Boardman, O.G.
24	29	York City	2-2	1-1	4569	Ross, Brodie
25	5 Feb	OXFORD	4-0	3-0	5708	Meredith(2), Clarke(2)
26	19	Swansea	0-4	0-2	8686	
27	11 Mar	Workington	3-1	0-0	4071	Clarke(2), Meredith
28	14	Southend	0-2	0-2	5964	
29	19	BOURNEMOUTH	0-2	0-2	5333	
30	21	Mansfield	3-0	2-0	5753	Clarke, Brodie, Hemsley
31	24	WALSALL	1-2	1-0	8924	Hemsley
32	30	GILLINGHAM	2-1	0-1	4203	Brodie, Broadbent
33	2 Apr	Exeter	0-0	0-0	4515	
34	8	Watford	0-1	0-0	7290	
35	9	Q.P.RANGERS	0-0	0-0	4791	
36	11	WATFORD	0-0	0-0	4068	
37	16	Hull	1-2	1-0	24313	Clarke
38	22	MANSFIELD	2-1	1-1	3585	Wright, Clarke
39	26	Swindon	0-0	0-0	11190	
40	30	Q.P.Rangers	1-2	1-1	5713	Clarke
41	2 May	GRIMSBY	3-1	1-0	3012	Meredith, O.G., Thom
42	4	Grimsby	1-2	1-2	3195	Thom
43	6	BRIGHTON	3-1	1-1	2775	Brodie(2), Meredith(pen)
44	12	PETERBOROUGH	3-1	1-1	2892	Brodie, Clarke(2)
45	18	SWINDON	1-1	0-0	2719	Meredith
46	20	Reading	1-4	0-2	4860	M.H.Wright

Player appearances (shirt number; * = substitute)

No.	Walker M.S.J.	Wright P.D.	Fellows G.A.	Hemsley E.	Brodie E.	Broadbent P.	Meredith T.	Boardman G.	Clarke F.J.	Regan J.M.	Ross R.H.	Gregory A.T.	Turner K.	Scott S.R.	Harris A.T.	Boswell A.	Thom L.M.	Dolby P.	Ray J.D.	Matthias T.	Wright M.H.
1	1	2	3	4	5	6	7	8	9	10	11	12		11							
2	1	2	3	4	5	6	7	8	9	10*	11	12	3								
3	1	2	3	4	5	10	7	8	9		11			11							
4		2	3	4	5	10	7	8	9		11		12	12	6	1					
5		2	3	4	5	10	7	8	9				12		6	1					
6		2	3	4	5	10	7	8	9				12		6	1					
7		2	3	4	5	10	7	8	9		11				6	1	11				
8		2	3	4	5	10	7		9	8					6	1	11				
9		2	3	4	5	6	7	10	9	8						1	11				
10		2	3	4	5	6	7	10	9	8						1	11				
11		2		4	5	6	7	10	9	12						1	11				
12			3	4	5	6	7	10	9	8		2			4	1	11				
13			3	12	5	6	7	10	9	8		2			4	1	11				
14			3	12	5	6	7	10	9	8		2			4	1	11				
15			3	4	5	8	7	10	9	12	11	2			6	1					
16			3	4	5	8	7	10	9		11	2			6	1					
17			3	4	5	8	7	10	9		10	2			6	1	11				
18	2		3	4	5	8	7	10	9		11				6	1	11	12			
19	2		3	4	5	8	7	10	9		11				6	1	11*	12			
20	2		3	4	5	8	7	10	9		11				6	1					
21	2		3	4	5	8	7	10	9		11				6	1					
22	2		3	4	5	8	7	10	9		11	12			6	1					
23	2		3	4	5	8	7	10	9		11			12	6	1	12				
24	2		3*	4	6	8	7	10	9		10			12	5	1	11				
25	2		3	4	6	8	7	10	9		8	12			6	1	11*	5			
26	2		3	4		7*	7		9		8	10				1	11	5			
27	2		3	4	6	8	7	10	9						6	1	11	5			
28	2		3	4	6	8	7	10	9						6	1	11	5			
29	2		3*	4	6	8	7	10	9			12				1	11	5			
30	2	8		4	6	8	7		9			3		12	12	1		5			
31	3	3	12	4	6	10	7		9			3			6	1		5*			
32	1	2		4	6	10	7	12	8			3			5		11				
33	2	2	7	4	6	8		10	9		3	3		10	5	1	11*	5	4		
34	2	2	6	12	8	11	7	10	9		8	3		5	5	1	11	5	4		
35	2	2	6	4	8	8	7	10	9		8	3		5	5	1	11	5			
36	2	2	6	4	5	8	7	10	9			3				1	11	5			
37	2	2	3*	12	6	8	7	10	9			4			5	1	11	5			
38	8	8		4	5	10	7		9			2		12		1	11	5*	6		
39	3	3		4	5	10	7		9			2	12	8		1	11		6		
40	2	2		4	6	10	7		9			3		8*		1	11	5			
41	2	2		4	6	10	7		9		3	3	8	8	5	1	11	5	6	12	
42	2	2		4	6	10	7		9		3	3	8	8	5	1	11	5	6		
43	2	2		4	9	10	7		8		3	3	12	12	5	1	11	5	6		
44	2	2			6	10	7		9		3	3	8	8	5	1	11	5	4		
45	2	2			6	10	7		9		2	2	8	8	5	1	11	5	4		
46	12	12			6		7		9		2	2	3	8	5	1	11	5	4	6	10*

F.A.Cup

1R	13 Nov	TORQUAY U.	2-1	0-0	6896	Clarke, Broadbent	2	3	4	5	8	7	10	9		6	1	11
2R	4 Dec	PETERBOROUGH U.	3-2	1-1	8980	Meredith(2), Clarke	2	3	4	5	8	7	10	9		6	1	11
3R	22 Jan	Q.P.Rangers	0-0	0-0	15738		2	3	4	6	11	7	10	9	8	5	1	
3Rr	26	Q.P.RANGERS	1-0	0-0	14879	Meredith	2	3	4	6	8	7	10	9	11	5	1	
4R	12 Feb	CARLISLE U.	0-0	0-0	13967		2	3	4	6	8	7	10	9	11		1	5
4Rr	15	Carlisle U.	1-1	0-0	17841	Ross	2	3	4	6	8	7	10	9	11		1	5
4R2r	21	Carlisle U.*	4-3	0-1	18678	Brodie, Broadbent, Clarke, Boardman	2	3	4	6	8	7	10	9	11		1	5
5R	5 Mar	Chelsea	2-3	0-1	51144	Clarke, Broadbent	2	3	4	6	8	7	10	9	11		1	5

* Played at Preston

League Cup

1R	1 Sep	TORQUAY U.	3-0	2-0	4820	Boardman(2), Ross	2	3	4	5	10	7	8	9		11	6	1
2R	22	BRISTOL C.	1-0	1-0	7168	Clarke	2	3	4	5	11	7	10	9	8		6	1
3R	13 Oct	ROTHERHAM U.	2-5	1-2	8440	Meredith, Clarke	2	3	4	6	5	7	10	9	8		1	11

FINAL LEAGUE TABLE

	P	W	D	L	F	A	Pts
1 Hull	46	31	7	8	109	62	69
2 Millwall	46	27	11	8	76	43	65
3 QPR	46	24	9	13	95	65	57
4 Scunthorpe	46	21	11	14	80	67	53
5 Workington	46	19	14	13	67	57	52
6 Gillingham	46	22	8	16	62	54	52
7 Swindon	46	19	13	14	74	48	51
8 Reading	46	19	13	14	70	63	51
9 Walsall	46	20	10	16	77	64	50
10 Shrewsbury	46	19	11	16	73	64	49
11 Grimsby	46	17	13	16	68	62	47
12 Watford	46	17	13	16	55	51	47
13 Peterborough	46	17	12	17	80	66	46
14 Oxford	46	19	8	19	70	74	46
15 Brighton	46	16	11	19	67	65	43
16 Bristol Rovers	46	14	14	18	64	64	42
17 Swansea	46	15	11	20	81	96	41
18 Bournemouth	46	13	12	21	38	56	38
19 Mansfield	46	15	8	23	59	89	38
20 Oldham	46	13	11	22	55	81	37
21 Southend	46	16	4	26	54	83	36
22 Exeter	46	12	11	23	53	79	35
23 Brentford	46	10	12	24	48	69	32
24 York	46	9	9	28	53	106	27

(Back) Boswell, Fellows, Hensley, Thom, Brodie, Dolby, Harris. (Front) Meredith, Clarke, Broadbent, Ross, Wright Boardman.

SEASON 1966/67
Division 3

No.	Date	Opposition	Res.	H.T.	Att.	Goalscorers	Boswell A.	Wright P.D.	Fellows G.A.	Hemsley E.	Wood A.E.H.	Brodie E.	Meredith T.	Dolby P.	Clarke F.J.	Boardman G.	Broadbent P.	Gregory A.T.	Thom L.M.	Matthias T.	Turner A.	Harris A.T.	Manning J.T.	Lee G.
1	20 Aug	Q.P.Rangers	2-2	0-1	6343	Meredith(2,1pen)	1	2	3	4	5	6	7	8	9	10	11	12						
2	27	COLCHESTER	2-1	1-1	4819	Boardman, Wood	1	2	3	4	5	6	7	8	9	10	11			12				
3	3 Sep	Bristol Rovers	0-1	0-0	7145		1	2	3	4	5	6	7	8	9	10	11	12						
4	6	Watford	0-1	0-0	5474		1	2	3	4	5		7		9	10	11				8	12		
5	10	OXFORD	1-0	0-0	4286	Boardman	1	2	3*	4	5		7		9	10	11				8	12		
6	17	Oldham	1-4	0-3	14061	Meredith	1	2	3*	4	5		7	8	9	10	11		12			6		
7	21	TORQUAY	3-2	1-1	4272	Wright, Harris, Meredith	1	2	3	4	5		7	8	9	10		12	11			6		
8	24	SCUNTHORPE	4-3	1-1	3844	Hemsley(2), Meredith, Dolby	1	2	3	4	5		7	8	9	10		12	11			6		
9	26	WATFORD	1-1	1-1	4784	Meredith	1	2	3	4	5		7	8	9	10	11		12			6		
10	8 Oct	Swindon	2-2	0-1	8149	Clarke, Dolby	1*	2	3	4	5	6	7	8	9	10		12	11					
11	15	READING	1-0	1-0	3942	Dolby	1	2	3	4	5	6	7	8	9	10		12	11					
12	19	BOURNEMOUTH	4-1	2-0	5632	Clarke(3), Meredith	1	2	3	4	5	6	7	12	8*	10			11					
13	21	Doncaster	1-2	1-1	10558	Thom	1	2	3	4	5	6	7	12	8	10			11					
14	29	MANSFIELD	1-0	1-0	4925	Fellows	1	2	3	4	5	6	7		9	10		12	11					
15	2 Nov	BRISTOL ROVERS	3-4	0-2	5768	Manning(2), Meredith	1	2	3*	4	5		7		9	10		12	11			6	8	
16	5	Grimsby	1-1	0-1	5087	Manning	1	2	3	4	12		7	5	9	10			11				8	
17	12	WALSALL	1-2	0-1	7798	Manning	1	2	3	4	12		7	5	9	10			11				8	
18	16	Bournemouth	3-0	1-0	4351	Turner(2), Meredith	1	2		4	12	6	7	5	9	10		3			11		8	
19	19	Peterborough	2-0	1-0	7030	Clarke, Manning	1	2		4	12	6	7	5	9	10		3			11		8	
20	3 Dec	Brighton	1-2	1-1	10820	Hemsley	1	2		4	12	6	7	5	9	10		3			11		8	
21	10	DARLINGTON	3-0	1-0	4833	Meredith(2), Manning	1	2		4	5	6	7		9	10		3			11		8	12
22	17	Q.P.RANGERS	0-0	0-0	6520		1	2		4	5	6	7		9	12		3			11		8	
23	26	Swansea	2-5	2-1	7431	Clarke, O.G.	1	2		4	10	6			9			12			8			
24	27	SWANSEA	2-2	0-0	8667	Meredith, Manning	1			4	5	6	7		9	10		3		8	11			2
25	31	Colchester	1-3	0-2	4890	Dolby	1			4	5	6	7	6	9	10		3		8	11			2
26	14 Jan	Oxford	1-2	1-1	5391	Wood	1	2		4	5	6	7	11	9	10		2			7		8	12
27	21	OLDHAM	3-1	1-1	5038	Clarke(2), Manning	1	2	6	4*	12	6	7	5	9	10		3		12	7		8	
28	4 Feb	Scunthorpe	0-2	0-1	4467		1	2	3	4*	12	6	7	5	9	8			11				8	
29	11	WORKINGTON	3-1	1-1	3491	Clarke, Boardman, Turner	1	2	2	4	5	12	7	6	10	8		3		12	7	4	8	
30	18	Orient	2-2	1-2	5032	Brodie(2)	1	2		6	5	11	7	6	10	8		3				4	9	
31	25	SWINDON	3-1	2-0	5057	Clarke, Manning, Brodie	1	2	2	4	6	11	7	5	8	10		3				4	9	
32	4 Mar	Reading	0-2	0-1	6168		1	2	3	4	6	11	7	5	8	10							9	12
33	11	ORIENT	6-1	1-0	3159	Manning(3), Boardman(2), Clarke	1	2	3	4	12	11*	7	5	8	10						6	9	
34	18	DONCASTER	2-1	0-0	4875	Clarke, Manning	1	2	3	4	6	8	7	5	8	10						12	9	
35	25	Mansfield	1-0	0-0	10192	Meredith	1	2	3	4	6	11	7	5	8	10						12	9	
36	27	Middlesbrough	0-1	0-0	23452		1	2	3	4	6	11	7	5	8	10						12	9	
37	29	MIDDLESBROUGH	1-0	0-0	6407	Boardman	1	2	3	4	5	11		5	8	10	12				12	7	9*	
38	1 Apr	GRIMSBY	0-1	0-1	4035		1	2	3	4	6	11*	7	5	8*	10				12	7	9	9*	
39	8	Walsall	2-2	0-0	5705	Meredith, Brodie	1	2	3	4	6	8	7	5	8	10				12	11	3	9	
40	12	GILLINGHAM	3-1	3-1	3632	Manning(2), Clarke	1	2	3	4*	6	11	7	5	8	10						12	9	
41	15	PETERBOROUGH	1-1	0-1	3742	Manning	1	2	3	4	6	11	7	5	8	10						12	9	
42	22	Torquay	2-0	2-0	11125	Hemsley, Clarke	1	2	3	4	5	11	7	12	8	10					6	6	9	
43	26	Gillingham	1-1	1-1	4683	Manning	1	2	3	4	5	11	7	12	8	10						6	9	
44	29	BRIGHTON	0-0	0-0	4042		1	2	3*	4	5	11	7	12	8*	10						6	9	
45	6 May	Darlington	1-1	1-1	3546	Brodie	1	2	3*	4	5	6	7	12	8	10				12	12	11	9	
46	17	Workington	3-2	1-0	1175	Harris, Boardman, Brodie	1	2	2	4	5	6	7	12	8*	10					11	11	9	

F.A. Cup

	Date	Opponent			Att	Scorers	1	2	3	4		6	7	5	9	10	12	11	8
1R	26 Nov	HARTLEPOOLS U.	5-2	2-0	6515	Manning(2), Turner(2), Clarke	1	2	3	4		6	7	5	9	10	12	11	8
2R	7 Jan	WREXHAM	5-1	1-0	13430	Boardman(3), Meredith, Manning	1	2	3	4	5	6	7		9	10	3	11	8
3R	28	Ipswich T.	1-4	0-1	14853	Meredith	1	2	3	4	12	6	7	5	9	10		11	8

League Cup

	Date	Opponent			Att	Scorers	1	2	3	4	5	6	7*	8	9	10	11	12
1R	24 Aug	WREXHAM	6-1	5-1	7003	Broadbent, O.G., Brodie, Dolby(2), Clarke	1	2	3	4	5	6	7*	8	9	10	11	12
2R	14 Sep	BURNLEY	1-1	0-0	10320	Boardman	1	2	3	4	5	6	7		9	10	11	12
2Rr	29	Burnley	0-5	0-4	8880		1	2	3	4	5	6	7		9	10	11	12

Final League Table

		P	W	D	L	F	A	Pts
1	QPR	46	26	15	5	103	38	67
2	Middlesbrough	46	23	9	14	87	64	55
3	Watford	46	20	14	12	61	46	54
4	Reading	46	22	9	15	76	57	53
5	Bristol Rovers	46	20	13	13	76	67	53
6	Shrewsbury	46	20	12	14	77	62	52
7	Torquay	46	21	9	16	73	54	51
8	Swindon	46	20	10	16	81	59	50
9	Mansfield	46	20	9	17	84	79	49
10	Oldham	46	19	10	17	80	63	48
11	Gillingham	46	15	16	15	58	62	46
12	Walsall	46	18	10	18	65	72	46
13	Colchester	46	17	10	19	76	73	44
14	Leyton Orient	46	13	18	15	58	68	44
15	Peterborough	46	14	15	17	66	71	43
16	Oxford	46	15	13	18	61	66	43
17	Grimsby	46	17	9	20	61	68	43
18	Scunthorpe	46	17	8	21	58	73	42
19	Brighton	46	13	15	18	61	71	41
20	Bournemouth	46	12	17	17	39	57	41
21	Swansea	46	12	15	19	85	89	39
22	Darlington	46	13	11	22	47	81	37
23	Doncaster	46	12	8	26	58	117	32
24	Workington	46	12	7	27	55	89	31

(Back) Boswell, Wood, Brodie, Dolby, Lee, Wright, Gregory, Harris, Rowley.
(Front) Meredith, A.Turner, Broadbent, Clarke, Boardman, Thom, Fellows.

SEASON 1967/68
Division 3

No.	Date	Opposition	Res.	H.T.	Att.	Goalscorers	Boswell A.	Wright P.D.	Fellows G.A.	Hemsley E.	Wood A.E.H.	Dolby P.	Meredith T.	Boardman G.	Clarke F.J.	Manning J.T.	Pleat D.J.	Brodie E.	Gregory A.T.	Clapham G.L.	McLaughlin J.	Lee G.	Matthias T.	Stobart B.	Pountney D.H.	Garbett W.E.	Roberts D.A.
1	19 Aug	OXFORD	2-0	0-0	5030	Clarke, Hemsley	1	2	3	4	5	6	7	8	9	10	11	12									
2	26	Brighton	0-3	0-1	12834		1	2	3	4	5	6	7	8	9	10	12	11*									
3	2 Sep	STOCKPORT	0-0	0-0	5357		1	2	3	4	5	6	7	8	9	10	11	12									
4	6	READING	2-1	1-0	4975	Meredith(pen), Clarke	1	2	3	4	5	6	7	8	9	10	11*	12									
5	8	Tranmere	1-4	1-3	9369	Meredith	1	2	3	4	5	6	7	8	9	10	11	12									
6	16	ORIENT	2-2	1-1	4903	Clarke, Manning	1	2	3	4	5	6	7	8	9	10	11	12									
7	23	Northampton	2-2	1-0	8922	Boardman, Clarke	1	2	3	4	5	6	7	8	9	10	12				11*						
8	27	Reading	0-0	0-0	9698		1	2	3	4	5	6	7	8*	9			6	11	10	11*	12					
9	30	WALSALL	0-1	0-0	8475		1	2	3	4	5	6	7	8	9		11*	6	11	10		12					
10	4 Oct	Torquay	0-3	0-0	7039		1	2	3	4	5		7	8	9*			6			11		12				
11	7	Bournemouth	1-1	1-0	5434	Dolby	1	2	3	4	5	8	7		9			6			11		12				
12	14	COLCHESTER	4-0	1-0	4162	Clarke(2), Hemsley(2)	1	2	3	4	5	6		8	9		12	6	2	12	11			10*			
13	21	Peterborough	1-0	1-0	8310	Boardman	1	2	3	4	5	6	7	8	9		12		2	10	11						
14	25	TORQUAY	5-0	2-0	6346	Stobart, Boardman(2), McLaughlin, Hemsley	1	2	3	4	5	6	7	8	9				2	12	11			10			
15	28	MANSFIELD	2-1	1-1	5660	Clarke, Hemsley	1	2	3	4	5	6	7	8	9				2	10	11			12			
16	4 Nov	Watford	0-2	0-2	7039		1	2	3	4	5	6	7	8	9				2	12	11			10			
17	11	SOUTHPORT	3-2	1-1	6187	Boardman, Dolby, O.G.	1	2	3	4	5	6	7	8	9				2	12	11			10			
18	13	Stockport	2-4	2-3	7010	Clapham, Clarke	1	2	3	4	5	6	7	8	9				2	7	11			10			
19	17	Scunthorpe	0-0	0-0	3124		1		3	3	5	6	7	8	9			12	2	4	11			10			
20	25	OLDHAM	4-2	0-1	4772	Clarke, McLaughlin, Dolby(pen), Stobart	1		3	4	5	6	7	8	9			12	2	12	11*			10			
21	2 Dec	Bristol Rovers	1-4	1-1	7454	McLaughlin	1		3	4	5	6	7	8	9				2	2	11			10			
22	16	Oxford	2-2	1-0	6091	Brodie, Hemsley	1		3	4	5	6	7	8	9		12	10	2	7	11						
23	23	BRIGHTON	0-0	0-0	5142		1		3	4	5	6	7*	8	9		12	10	2		11			10			
24	26	GRIMSBY	3-2	2-1	7208	Clarke, McLaughlin, Hemsley	1		3	4	5	6		8	9		7	12	2	10	11			8			
25	30	Grimsby	1-0	0-0	3116	Brodie	1		3	4	5	6		8	9		7	4	2	7	11			10			
26	20 Jan	Orient	1-1	0-1	5506	McLaughlin	1		3	4	5	6			9		7	7	2	12	11			8			
27	3 Feb	NORTHAMPTON	2-0	1-0	5382	Brodie, Pleat	1		3	4	5	6			9		7	10	2	12	11			8			
28	10	Walsall	2-1	0-1	14166	Clarke, Brodie	1		3	4	5	6			9		7	10	2	12	11			8	10		
29	17	GILLINGHAM	1-2	1-0	7032	Clarke	1		3	4	5	10		7*	9		12		2		11				6		
30	24	BOURNEMOUTH	1-0	0-0	4853	Stobart	1		3		5	6		8	9			4	2		11			9	10		
31	2 Mar	Colchester	3-0	0-0	3877	Hemsley, Boardman, O.G.	1		3	4			7	8	9		7	4	2	10	11			9	10	12	
32	5	TRANMERE	1-1	0-0	7836	Boardman	1		3	4			7	8	9		7	4	2	7	11			9	10	12	
33	9	SWINDON	0-1	0-1	7810		1		3	4	5	6		8	9			12	2	12	11			9	10		
34	16	PETERBOROUGH	1-1	1-1	4549	Brodie	1		3	4	5	6	7	8	9		9	12	2	12	11			8	12		7
35	19	Swindon	0-0	0-0	14541		1		3	4	5	6	7		9		9	9	2	10	11			8		12	7
36	23	Mansfield	1-0	0-0	6701	Stobart	1		3	4	5	6	7		9		12	9	2	12	11			10	8		
37	30	WATFORD	3-1	1-0	6435	Stobart, Boardman, Clapham	1		3		5	5	7*	12	9		7	4	2	10	11			8	8	9*	
38	5 Apr	Southport	0-0	0-0	5532		1		3	4		5	7*	8	9		7	4	2		11			9	6	12	
39	12	Bury	0-2	0-1	13400		1		3	4		5	7	8	9		10	10	2		11			9	6	12	
40	13	SCUNTHORPE	4-0	2-0	5578	Stobart(2), Garbett, McLaughlin	1		3	4*	5	6	7	8			12	12	2	10	11			9	6	7	
41	15	BURY	1-0	1-0	13517	Stobart	1		3	4	5	6	7	8				9	2		11			10	6	7	
42	20	Oldham	0-0	0-0	6533		1		3	4		6	7	8					2	12	11			9*	12		
43	24	BARROW	1-0	1-0	10614	Brodie	1		3	4		6	7	8			9	9	2	10*	11				12	10*	
44	27	BRISTOL ROVERS	0-0	0-0	11401		1		3	4		6	7	8			9	9	2					12	12		
45	4 May	Barrow	0-3	0-2	5749		1		3	4	5	6	7	8			9	9	2	10*	11				10	12	
46	11	Gillingham	1-0	0-0	5157	McLaughlin	1		3	4	5	6	7	8					2	12	9			12	10	11	11

F.A. Cup

							1	3	4	5	6	7*	8	9		2	12	11		10	
1R	13 Dec	DARLINGTON	3-0	1-0	7394	Clarke(2), Boardman	1	3	4	5	6	7*	8	9		2	12	11		10	
2R	15 Jan	Tow Law T.	1-1	0-1	5100	Clarke	1	3	4	5	6		8	9		2	7	11		10	
2Rr	18	TOW LAW T.	6-2	3-0	14508	Brodie(3), McLaughlin, Dolby, Boardman	1	3	4	5	6		10	9*		12		11	8		12
3R	27	ARSENAL	1-1	0-1	18280	Dolby	1	3	4	5	6		10	9		7	12	11	8		
3Rr	30	Arsenal	0-2	0-1	41963		1	3	4	5	6			9		7	10*	11	8		12

League Cup

							1	2	3	4	5	6	7	8	9*	10	11	12
1R	22 Aug	Walsall	2-4	1-1	9834	Manning(2)	1	2	3	4	5	6	7	8	9*	10	11	12

Hemsley, Gregory, Clarke, Fellows, Boardman, Pleat, Clapham, Stobart, McLaughlin, Garbett, Harris, Dolby, Brodie, Meredith, Wood, Boswell.

FINAL LEAGUE TABLE

		P	W	D	L	F	A	Pts
1	Oxford	46	22	13	11	69	47	57
2	Bury	46	24	8	14	91	66	56
3	Shrewsbury	46	20	15	11	61	49	55
4	Torquay	46	21	11	14	60	56	53
5	Reading	46	21	9	16	70	60	51
6	Watford	46	21	8	17	74	50	50
7	Walsall	46	19	12	15	74	61	50
8	Barrow	46	21	8	17	65	54	50
9	Swindon	46	16	17	13	74	51	49
10	Brighton	46	16	16	14	57	55	48
11	Gillingham	46	18	12	16	59	63	48
12	Bournemouth	46	16	15	15	56	51	47
13	Stockport	46	19	9	18	70	75	47
14	Southport	46	17	12	17	65	65	46
15	Bristol Rovers	46	17	9	20	72	78	43
16	Oldham	46	18	7	21	60	65	43
17	Northampton	46	14	13	19	58	72	41
18	Leyton Orient	46	12	17	17	46	62	41
19	Tranmere	46	14	12	20	62	74	40
20	Mansfield	46	12	13	21	51	67	37
21	Grimsby	46	14	9	23	52	69	37
22	Colchester	46	9	15	22	50	87	33
23	Scunthorpe	46	10	12	24	56	87	32
24	Peterborough	46	20	10	16	79	67	31

SEASON 1968/69
Division 3

No.	Date	Opposition	Res.	H.T.	Att.	Goalscorers	Boswell A.	Gregory A.T.	Fellows G.A.	Hemsley E.	Wood A.E.H.	Dolby P.	Meredith T.	Garbett W.E.	Loyden E.	Boardman G.	McLaughlin J.	Clapham G.L.	Moore J.	Pountney D.H.	Stobart B.	Phillips J.J.S.	Parkin M.	Jones A.H.	Mathias T.	Roberts D.A.	Hawkins D.R.	Douglas P.G.	Bridgewood G.	Harkin T.	Tooze R.W.	Loska A.S.	Moir R.J.
1	10 Aug	WALSALL	0-1	0-1	7968		1	2	3	4	5	6	7	8	9	10*	11	12															
2	17	Watford	0-2	0-1	9574	Loyden(pen)	1	2	3	4	5	6	7		9	12	11	10		8*						9							
3	24	CREWE	1-1	0-0	7532	Dolby, McLaughlin	1	2	3		5	6	7		9	12	11	10	4	8													
4	27	Bristol Rovers	2-1	1-1	7820		1	2	3		5	6	7		9	12	11*	10*	4	8													
5	31	Bournemouth	0-2	0-2	7330		1	2	3		5	6	7		9	10	11	10*	4	8	12												
6	7 Sep	PLYMOUTH	1-0	0-0	6035	McLaughlin	1	2	3		5	6	7		9	10	11		4	8	12												
7	13	Hartlepool	0-0	0-0	5028			2	3				7		9	10	11		4	8		1											
8	16	Stockport	3-4	2-2	7171	Boardman, McLaughlin, Garbett		2	3				7		9	10	11		8	8	9*	1		5									
9	21	READING	3-3	1-2	5769	Boardman(3)		6	3				7	12	9	10	11	12	4	8	9	1	2	4	12								
10	28	Swindon	0-3	0-2	12283		3	3	10				7		8*	10	11	12	4	5		1	2	6	12								
11	5 Oct	BARNSLEY	0-0	0-0	4544		2	2	3				7		9*	10	11		4	5		1			6	8							
12	9	BRISTOL ROVERS	1-0	1-0	6209	Loyden		2	3		5		7		9		11	12	4	6		1			10	8							
13	12	Barrow	1-2	1-0	5407	Fellows		2	3		5	12	7		9		11		4	6		1			10	8	7						
14	19	ROTHERHAM	1-0	1-0	6658	Hawkins		2	3		5		7		9		11		4	6	12	1			10	8	7						
15	26	Torquay	0-2	0-2	8132		2*	2	3		5				12		11		4	6		1			10	8	7						
16	2 Nov	ORIENT	1-0	1-0	3601	Hawkins		2	3		5		7		9	12	11		4	6		1			10	8	7						
17	5	OLDHAM	0-1	0-1	3629			2	3		5	12	7		9		11		4	6	9	1			10	8	7						
18	8	Tranmere	1-3	0-3	7507	McLaughlin			3			5	7	9*	10	10	11*		6	9*	1		2	4		8							
19	23	Gillingham	1-4	1-1	5270	Hawkins		2	3*		5		7	12	9	10	11*	11	6	9	1			4		7	8	10					
20	30	MANSFIELD	1-1	1-1	2594	Stobart		2	3		5		7	12	9	9	8	6	9	1			4	4*		7	10					
21	4 Dec	BARROW	1-0	1-0	2211	Meredith		2	3		5	6	11			12	11	8	4	9	1					7	10					
22	21	Rotherham	0-1	0-0	7218			2	3		5	6	11			12	8	8	4	9	1				7	10					
23	26	Barnsley	0-1	0-1	11733			2	3		5	6	11			12	8	8	4	9	1				7	10					
24	8 Jan	LUTON	3-1	2-1	4729	Douglas, Meredith(pen), Wood		2	3		5	6	7			8	11*	12	4	4		1		11*			9	10				
25	18	TRANMERE	0-1	0-1	5780			2	3		5	6	7		9	8	11*	12	4		1			11*			9	10				
26	25	Oldham	2-2	1-1	3049	Wood, Dolby		2	3		5	6	7			8	11	10	4		1					9	9				
27	1 Feb	Brighton	0-3	0-1	11716			2	3		5	6	7			8	11	12	4		1					9	9				
28	1 Mar	Walsall	0-2	0-1	4773		2*	2	3		5	4	7			10	11	12	4		1					9	9	8			
29	5	Luton	1-2	0-1	14337	Harkin			3		5	6	7			8*	11	10	4	12	12	1		2		12	7	8	9			
30	8	WATFORD	1-1	1-1	6507	Hawkins		2	3		5	6				12	11	10	4	12	8	1		2		12	11	10	9			
31	12	BRIGHTON	1-2	0-1	2854	Wood		2	3		5	6	6				11	10	4	8	1		2		7	11	10	9			
32	14	Crewe	1-0	1-0	5179	Wood		2	3		5	6	12				11	10	4		1		2		7	8	10	9			
33	17	Southport	0-5	0-1	3050			2	3		5	6	11				11	10	4		1		2		7	8	10	9			
34	22	BOURNEMOUTH	1-0	0-0	3747	Harkin		2	3		5	6	11				11	10	4		1				7	8	6	9			
35	29	Plymouth	1-1	0-0	11010	Clapham		2	3		5	6	11				12	10	4		1				7	8	6	9		1	
36	5 Apr	SWINDON	1-1	0-1	7387	Wood		2	3		8*	6	11			11	12	10	4		1				7	8		9			
37	7	STOCKPORT	2-1	2-1	5212	Harkin, Wood		2	3		8	6	11*				12	10	4		1			7	7	10		9			
38	8	Northampton	4-3	1-3	5521	O.G., Wood, O.G., Dolby		2	3		8	6				11	10	4		1			7	7	11		9			
39	11	Reading	4-2	2-0	4769	Wood(2,1pen), McLaughlin, Harkin		2	3		8	6	11				11	10	4		1			7	8		9			
40	16	NORTHAMPTON	1-0	0-0	6770	Harkin		2	3		8	6	11				11	10	4		1			7	8	12	9			
41	19	HARTLEPOOL	1-1	0-0	7793	McLaughlin		2	3		8	6	11				11	10	4					7	8	12	9	1		
42	23	TORQUAY	1-0	0-0	6000	Meredith		2	3		8	6	12				11	10	4					7	10*	12	9	1		
43	28	Orient	0-4	0-2	6115			2	3		8*	6	11				11	10	4		1			7	12	9			
44	2 May	SOUTHPORT	5-1	3-1	5405	Harkin(3), Wood(2)		2	3		8	6	10				11	10	4		1			7	7	12	9			
45	6	GILLINGHAM	1-1	0-1	7837	Clapham		2	3		8	5	10				11	6	4		1			7*	12	9		3	
46	9	Mansfield	2-1	1-0	5716	Dolby, Hawkins		2	3		9	5	10			11	11	6	4		1			7	8	9		7	3	12

									2 3		5		7			10 11			12 6 9 1		4 8
1R	16 Nov	PORT VALE		1-1	1-0	5933	Wood		2 3		5		7			10 11			6 9 1		4 8
1Rr	18	Port Vale		1-3	0-3	8800	Wood		2 3		5		7			10 11	12		6* 8 1		4 9

								1		3 4 5 6 7			9 12 11 10		8	2
1R	14 Aug	Walsall		0-2	0-2	9168		1		3 4 5 6 7			9 12 11 10		8	2

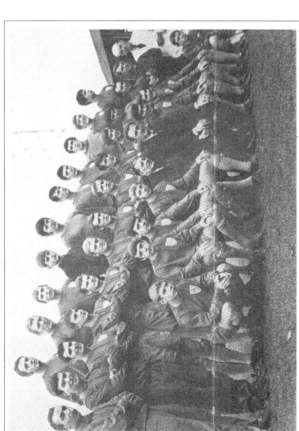

Back Row, *from left to right* : A. Jores, D. Pountney, P. Douglas, J. Phillips, J. Corrigan, P. Dolby, D. Roberts, E. Loyden, A. Wood, M. Parkin.

Middle Row, from left to right : J. Morgan (*Groundsman*), M. Evans (*Trainer Coach*), J. McLaughlin, A. Gregory, G. Fellows, J. Moore, T. Matthias, B. Stobart, G. Boardman, G. Clapham, P. Bevan, T. Meredith, M. Starkey (*Asst. Trainer Coach*), T. Seymour (*Physiotherapist*).

Front Row, from left to right : M. Dalby, J. Healey, T. Boucher, A. Loska, L. E. Rimmer (*Secretary*), H. Gregg (*Manager*), D. Hawkins, W. E. Garbett, P. Marandola, K. Howells.

FINAL LEAGUE TABLE

	P	W	D	L	F	A	Pts
1 Watford	46	27	10	9	74	34	64
2 Swindon	46	27	10	9	71	35	64
3 Luton	46	25	11	10	74	38	61
4 Bournemouth	46	21	9	16	60	45	51
5 Plymouth	46	17	15	14	53	49	49
6 Torquay	46	18	12	16	54	46	48
7 Tranmere	46	19	10	17	70	68	48
8 Southport	46	17	13	16	71	64	47
9 Stockport	46	16	14	16	67	68	46
10 Barnsley	46	16	14	16	58	63	46
11 Rotherham	46	16	13	17	56	50	45
12 Brighton	46	16	13	17	72	65	45
13 Walsall	46	14	16	16	50	49	44
14 Reading	46	15	13	18	67	66	43
15 Mansfield	46	16	11	19	58	62	43
16 Bristol Rovers	46	16	11	19	63	71	43
17 Shrewsbury	46	16	11	19	51	67	43
18 Orient	46	14	14	18	51	58	42
19 Barrow	46	17	8	21	56	75	42
20 Gillingham	46	13	15	18	54	63	41
21 Northampton	46	14	12	20	54	61	40
22 Hartlepool	46	10	19	17	40	70	39
23 Crewe	46	13	9	24	52	76	35
24 Oldham	46	13	9	24	50	83	35

SEASON 1969/70
Division 3

No.	Date	Opposition	Res.	H.T.	Att.	Goalscorers	Phillips J.J.S.	Fellows G.A.	Loska A.S.	Moore J.	Dolby P.	Clapham G.L.	Roberts D.A.	Meredith T.G.	Harkin T.	Hawkins D.R.	McLaughlin J.	Moir R.J.	Wood A.E.H.	Gregory A.T.	Bridgewood G	Pountney D.H.	Tooze R.W.	Andrews G.	Hughes T.P.	Williams D.O.	Matthias T.
1	9 Aug	Halifax	0-1	0-1	5926		1	2	3	4	5	6	7	8	9	10*	11	12									
2	16	ROTHERHAM	1-0	1-0	4627	Wood(pen)	1	2	3	4	5	6	7	8		10	11		9								
3	23	Tranmere	1-3	0-2	6613	Roberts	1	2	3	4	5	6	7	8	10		11		9		12						
4	27	DONCASTER	0-0	0-0	4912		1	2	3	4	5	6	7	8	10		11		9		12						
5	30	READING	0-0	0-0	3970		1	2	3	4	5	6	7	8		10	11		9	12							
6	6 Sep	Fulham	1-3	0-1	8990	Wood	1		3	4	5	6	7	8		10	12		9								
7	13	SOUTHPORT	1-2	0-1	3470	Wood	1	3	4	5		12	7*	6		10			9		8						
8	17	Bournemouth	3-3	1-0	6020	Roberts, Harkin, Pountney	1	3				6	7	11	10		12		9	2	8	4					
9	20	Luton	2-2	0-0	15396	Roberts(2)	1	3	4				7	11	9	10		12		2	8	6					
10	27	MANSFIELD	0-0	0-0	3801		1	3	4				7	11	9	10		12	5	2	8	6					
11	1 Oct	TORQUAY	1-0	0-0	4075	Hawkins	1	3	4				7	11	9	10		12	5	2	8	6*					
12	4	Rochdale	0-3	0-1	6492		1	3	4				7	11	9	10		12	5	2	8	6					
13	7	Rotherham	2-1	2-0	4981	Harkin, Moir	1	3	4				7	11	9	10		12	5	2	8	6*					
14	11	BRIGHTON	2-2	1-1	3921	Harkin, Wood	1	3	4				7		9	10		11	5	2	8	6					
15	18	Stockport	1-1	1-1	3273	Hawkins	1	3	4				8		9	10		11	5	2	7	6*					
16	25	BRADFORD C.	1-0	1-0	3938	Harkin	1	3	4				8		9	10		11	5	2	7	6					
17	1 Nov	Bristol Rovers	3-1	2-0	10025	Moir, Harkin(2)	1	3	4				7		9	8	11	12	5	2	10	6					
18	8	BARROW	1-1	0-1	4002	Harkin	1	3	4				7		9	8	11	6	5	2	10						
19	22	ORIENT	1-1	0-0	4538	Andrews	1	3	4				7		9		11	6	5	2	8		1	10			
20	26	BURY	3-3	2-3	4138	McLaughlin, Harkin, Andrews	1	3	4				7		9	12	11	6	5	2	8*		1	10			
21	29	Walsall	2-3	2-3	4530	Andrews(2)	1	3*	4				7		8	12	10	6	5	2			1	9			
22	13 Dec	Southport	2-0	1-0	2694	Harkin, Moir	3*	3	4				8	10	9	12	11	6	5	2			1				
23	20	FULHAM	1-1	0-0	3975	Bridgewood	3		3	4			8	12	9		10	6	5	2	11		1	10			
24	26	TRANMERE	2-0	1-0	6578	Andrews, McLaughlin	3	3	4				7			10	11	6	5	2	8		1	9			
25	27	Reading	1-3	1-3	8486	Hawkins	3	3	4				8			10	11	6	5	2	7	12	1	9			
26	10 Jan	LUTON	5-1	4-0	4406	Andrews, Moir(2), McLaughlin, Harkin	3	3	4						9	12	11	6*	5	2	7		1	10			
27	17	Mansfield	0-2	0-0	6280		3	3	4						9	12	11	6	5	2	7		1	10			
28	24	BARNSLEY	1-1	1-1	5360	Bridgewood	3	3	4				7		9	12	11	6	5	2	8		1	10			
29	31	ROCHDALE	1-0	0-0	4091	Harkin	3	3	4				7		9	12	11	6	5	2	8		1	10			
30	7 Feb	Brighton	0-1	0-1	15540		3	3	4				7		9	12	11	6	5	2			1	10			
31	14	HALIFAX	3-1	2-1	3874	McLaughlin, Moir, Andrews	3	3	4				7		9	12	11	6	5	2	8*		1	10			
32	21	Bradford C.	2-2	2-0	6806	Harkin, Andrews	3	3	4			8	7		9	12	11	6	5	2			1	10			
33	28	STOCKPORT	3-1	2-1	3879	Moir, Andrews, D.Roberts	3	3	4			8	7		9	12	11	6	5	2			1	10			
34	11 Mar	Gillingham	1-2	1-2	4534	Hawkins	3	3	4			8	7		9	10	11	6	5	2			1		12		
35	14	WALSALL	1-1	1-0	4640	Harkin	3	3		4		12	7		9		11	6	5	2			1	10			
36	17	Barnsley	1-1	0-0	7786	Andrews	3	3		4			7		9		11	6	5	2			1	10			
37	21	Plymouth	2-4	0-0	7037	Andrews, Harkin	3	3		4			7		9		11	6	5	2	8		1	10			
38	27	Barrow	0-2	0-0	3427		3	3		4	4		7		9		11	6	5	2	8*		1	10			
39	28	GILLINGHAM	2-2	1-0	3542	Moir, Wood	3	3		4			7		9	10	11	6	5	2	8		1				
40	30	BRISTOL ROVERS	0-0	0-0	6178		3	3		4			7			10	11	6	5	2	8		1	9			
41	4 Apr	Doncaster	1-2	0-0	3984		3	3		4			7		9	12	11	6	5	2			1	8			
42	7	Bury	2-2	0-0	2931	Wood, Andrews	3	3		4			7	10		12	11	6	5	2	12		1	9			
43	15	BOURNEMOUTH	2-0	1-0	3350	Moir, Harkin	3	3		4			7		9		11	6	5	2	8		1		10		
44	18	PLYMOUTH	3-0	3-0	3469	Andrews, Hughes, Harkin	3	3		4			7		8		11	6	5	2	12		1	9	10		
45	22	Torquay	0-3	0-1	3670		3		3	4			7				6	12	5	2	8			9	10	1	
46	25	Orient	0-1	0-0	13268		3		3	4			7	12			11	12	5	2	8		1	9	10		6

F.A. Cup

	Date	Opponent			Att	Scorers																
								3	4			7		9	10	11	6	5	2	8	12	1
1R	15 Nov	Yeovil T.	3-2	3-1	6495	O.G., Moir, McLaughlin		3	4			7	8	9	10	11	6	5	2	8	12	1
2R	6 Dec	MANSFIELD T.	1-2	0-1	5661	Moir		3	4	12	7	8	9	10	11	6	5	2			1

League Cup

	Date	Opponent			Att	Scorers	1	2	3	4	5	6	7	8	9	10	11	12
1R	13 Aug	WALSALL	1-0	0-0	6971	McLaughlin	1	2	3	4	5	6	7	8	9	10	11	12
2R	2 Sep	SOUTHEND U.	2-2	1-1	4969	Wood(pen), McLaughlin	1	2	3	4	5	6	7		9	10	11	12
2Rr	8	Southend U.	0-2	0-1	11026		1	6	3		5		7	11		10	12	4

FINAL LEAGUE TABLE

		P	W	D	L	F	A	Pts
1	Orient	46	25	12	9	67	36	62
2	Luton	46	23	14	9	77	43	60
3	Bristol Rovers	46	20	16	10	80	59	56
4	Fulham	46	20	15	11	81	55	55
5	Brighton	46	23	9	14	57	43	55
6	Mansfield	46	21	11	14	70	49	53
7	Barnsley	46	19	15	12	68	59	53
8	Reading	46	21	11	14	87	77	53
9	Rochdale	46	18	10	18	69	60	46
10	Bradford City	46	17	12	17	57	50	46
11	Doncaster	46	17	12	17	52	54	46
12	Walsall	46	17	12	17	54	67	46
13	Torquay	46	14	17	15	62	59	45
14	Rotherham	46	15	14	17	62	54	44
15	Shrewsbury	46	13	18	15	62	63	44
16	Tranmere	46	14	16	16	56	72	44
17	Plymouth	46	16	11	19	56	64	43
18	Halifax	46	14	15	17	47	63	43
19	Bury	46	15	11	20	75	80	41
20	Gillingham	46	13	13	20	52	64	39
21	Bournemouth	46	12	15	19	48	71	39
22	Southport	46	14	10	22	48	66	38
23	Barrow	46	8	14	24	46	81	30
24	Stockport	46	6	11	29	27	71	23

(Back) Evans, Pountney, Roberts, Harkin, Dolby, Tooze, Philips, Wood, Douglas, McLaughlin, Moore, Starkey.
(Middle) Matthias, Loska, Moir, Bridgwood, Tudor Owen, Gregg, Harley, Fellows, Gregory.
(Front) Apprentices including, Hughes, K.Morris, Bevan, Howells.

SEASON 1970/71
Division 3

No.	Date	Opposition	Res.	H.T.	Att.	Goalscorers	Tooze R.W.	Gregory A.T.	Fellows G.A.	Moore J.	Wood A.E.H.	McLaughlin J.	Roberts D.A.	Bridgewood G.	Andrews G.	Clapham G.L.	Harkin T.	Bevan P.P.	Hughes T.P.	Matthias T.	Moir R.J.	Meredith T.	Dolby P.	Groves A.	Mulhearn K.	Morris K.	Loska A.S.	Hawkins D.R.
1	15 Aug	ROTHERHAM	4-2	2-0	4684	Wood(3), Moore	1	2	3	4	5	11	7*	8	9		10				6	12						
2	22	Bristol Rovers	2-2	1-1	8994	McLaughlin, Andrews	1	2	3	4	5	11	7	8	9		10				6	12						
3	28	MANSFIELD	5-2	1-1	5836	Andrews, Moir(2), Wood(pen), McLaughlin	1	2	3	4	5	11	7*	8	9	12	10				6							
4	1 Sep	Swansea	0-5	0-4	7695		1	2	3	4	5	11		8	9		10				6	7						12
5	5	Bradford City	0-1	0-0	6348		1	2	3	4	5	11	7*	8	9		10				6							12
6	12	PORT VALE	7-3	2-1	5855	Andrews(2),Harkn(2,1pen),Hghes,Claphm,Wood(pen)	1	2	3	4	5				9	8	11		10		6	12						7
7	19	Bury	1-1	1-1	3605	Harkin	1	2	3	4	5		7		9	8	11		10		6	12						
8	23	Reading	1-2	1-0	8202	Wood(pen)	1	2	3	4	5		7	8	9	10	11				6							
9	25	TRANMERE	3-1	1-0	6623	Wood, Andrews, Bridgewood	1	2	3	4	5		7*	8	9	10	11				6							
10	30	PRESTON N.E.	0-1	0-1	8053		1	2	3	4	5		7	8	9	10	11			12	6*							
11	3 Oct	Halifax	0-2	0-2	3322		1	2	3*	4	5		7*	8	9	10	11	12			6							
12	10	FULHAM	0-1	0-1	6440		1	2	3	4	5		7	8	9	6	11	12	10									
13	17	Rotherham	1-1	0-0	7479	Andrews	1	2	3	4	5		7	8	9	3			10	12	6	11						
14	19	Wrexham	1-2	0-1	10092	Andrews	1	2	3	4	5		7	8	9	3			10	12	6	11						
15	24	CHESTERFIELD	1-1	0-0	4273	Hughes	1	2	3	4	5		7	8	9	3			10	6		11	12					
16	31	Gillingham	2-0	2-0	3918	Andrews(2)	1	2	3	4	5	8	7		9	3			10		6	11	12					
17	6 Nov	BARNSLEY	1-0	1-0	4490	Wood	1	2	3	4	5		7	8	9	3			10		6	11						
18	11	Plymouth	4-4	0-3	6966	Andrews(2), Moir, Hughes	1	2	3	4	5	12	7	8	9	3			10		6	11						
19	14	Walsall	1-0	0-0	4663	Moir	1	2	3	4	5		7	8	9	3			10		6	11						
20	27	DONCASTER	0-3	0-2	5215		1	2	3	4	5		7	8	9	3			10		6	11						
21	5 Dec	Rochdale	2-1	1-0	3217	Harkin, Andrews	1	2	12	4	5		7	8	9	3	10					11	6					
22	18	BRISTOL ROVERS	1-4	0-1	4546	Harkin	1	2	3	4	5		7	8*	9	3	10				6	11*	5					
23	26	Aston Villa	0-2	0-0	31186	Aband. 60 mins waterlogged pitch	1	2	3	4	5	10	7	8	9	6			12		6							
24	9 Jan	Preston N.E.	0-2	0-1	11961	Andrews	1	2	3	4	5	11	7*	8	9		10		12		6							
25	16	WREXHAM	1-0	0-0	6361	Harkin	1	2	3	4	5	11	7	8	9		10		12		6							
26	30	Doncaster	1-1	0-0	2416	Andrews	1	2		4	5	3	7	8	9		10				6	11	12					
27	6 Feb	ROCHDALE	0-2	0-2	3759		1	2	3	4	5	11	7*	8	9	3	10				6		6					
28	13	Brighton & H.A.	2-1	0-0	8241	Wood, Dolby	1	2	3	4	5	11*	7		9	6					8		10					
29	20	PLYMOUTH	1-1	1-0	3326	Wood	1	2	3	4	5		7		9	8					6		4	11				
30	26	GILLINGHAM	0-0	0-0	3428		1	2	3	4	5	10	7		9	6							4	11				
31	6 Mar	Chesterfield	0-2	0-1	6883		1	2	3	4	5	10*	7		9	6	8					3*	5	11				
32	10	READING	3-1	1-0	3065	Andrews, Hughes(2)	1	2	3	4	5		7		9		8		10		6	5	12	11				
33	13	WALSALL	1-1	0-1	4150	Groves	1	2	3	4	5	8	7		9	10	6		12	4			12	11				
34	17	Torquay *	1-0	0-1	2266		1	2	3		5	8	7	12	9	8	6		12	4			12	10				
35	20	Barnsley	1-2	0-1	4939	Andrews		2	3		5	8*	7	12	9	8	6		12	4				11				
36	24	BRIGHTON & H.A.	0-0	0-0	3089			2	3		5		7*	6	9	8			9	4			6	11				
37	27	BRADFORD C.	1-1	1-0	2816	Andrews		2	3		5	8*	7	6	9	8				4		8	6	11	1			
38	3 Apr	Mansfield	1-1	0-0	4289	Groves		2	3		5	8	7		9	8	6		10	4			12	11	1			
39	10	ASTON VILLA	2-1	0-0	13636	Groves, Roberts		2	3		5	10	7		9	10	3		12	4	8	3	4	11	1			
40	12	Port Vale	1-0	0-0	5655	Moir		2	3		5	10	7	12	9	4	6		4		8	3	12	10	1			
41	14	HALIFAX	2-2	1-1	5046	Groves(2)		2	3		5	10	7	12	9	4	8		4		8	3*	12	11	1			
42	17	Fulham	0-0	0-0	12702			2	3		5	9	7			4	4		4		8		12	11	1			
43	20	TORQUAY	1-0	0-0	4191	Wood		2	3		5	10	7			10	6	9	4		8		12	11	1			
44	23	BURY	2-0	0-0	3219	Roberts, Andrews	2	2	3		5	10	7	12	9	2	8		4		6	8	12	11	1			
45	28	SWANSEA	1-0	1-0	4578	Andrews	2	2	3		5	10	7	12	9	8	8		4		8*	4	12	11	1			
46	30	Tranmere	0-1	0-1	2847		2				5	10	7	12	9	8	8*		4		6		12	11	1		2	
47	6 May	Torquay	0-1	0-1	2706		2				5	10*	7	9	9	8	8		4		6		12	11	1	3	2	3

							1	2	4	5	7	8	9	3	12	10	6	11
1R	21 Nov	Minehead	2-1	1-1	3000	Moir, Andrews	1	2	4	5	6	7	8	9	3	10		11
2R	12 Dec	READING	2-2	1-1	5978	Andrews, Clapham(pen)	1	2	12	4	5	11	8	9	3	10		11 5
2Rr	21	Reading	0-1	0-0	8418		1	2	3	4	5	7		9	8	12	10	6

League Cup

							1	2	4	5	7	8	9	3	10	6	12
1R	19 Aug	Chester	1-2	1-1	5847	Wood	1	2	3	4	5	11	7	8	9	10	6	12

Final League Table

		P	W	D	L	F	A	Pts
1	Preston	46	22	17	7	63	39	61
2	Fulham	46	24	12	10	68	41	60
3	Halifax	46	22	12	12	74	55	56
4	Aston Villa	46	19	15	12	54	46	53
5	Chesterfield	46	17	17	12	66	38	51
6	Bristol Rovers	46	19	13	14	69	50	51
7	Mansfield	46	18	15	13	64	62	51
8	Rotherham	46	17	16	13	64	60	50
9	Wrexham	46	18	13	15	72	65	49
10	Torquay	46	19	11	16	54	57	49
11	Swansea	46	15	16	15	59	56	46
12	Barnsley	46	17	11	18	49	52	45
13	Shrewsbury	46	16	13	17	58	62	45
14	Brighton	46	14	16	16	50	47	44
15	Plymouth	46	12	19	15	63	63	43
16	Rochdale	46	14	15	17	61	68	43
17	Port Vale	46	15	12	19	52	59	42
18	Tranmere	46	10	22	14	45	55	42
19	Bradford City	46	13	14	19	49	62	40
20	Walsall	46	14	11	21	51	57	39
21	Reading	46	14	11	21	48	85	39
22	Bury	46	12	13	21	52	60	37
23	Doncaster	46	13	9	24	45	66	35
24	Gillingham	46	10	13	23	42	67	33

(Back) Moore, Gregory, Moir, Tooze, Fellows, Wood, Meredith,
(Front) Roberts, Bridgwood, Andrews, Harkin, McLaughlin.

SEASON 1971/72
Division 3

No.	Date	Opposition	Res.	H.T.	Att.	Goalscorers	Mulhearn K.	Gregory A.T.	Brown S.	Matthias T.	Holton J.	Bevan P.P.	Bridgewood G.	Roberts D.	Wood A.E.H.	McLaughlin M.	Groves A.	Andrews G.	Clapham G.L.	Dolby P.	Moir R.	Morris K.	Hughes T.P.	Fellows G.A.	Moore J.	Meredith T.G.	Tooze R.W.	Moir I.	Roberts I.
1	14 Aug	Bournemouth	1-3	0-2	11259	Wood	1	2	3	4	5	6	7	8	9	10	11							12					
2	21	TORQUAY	2-0	2-0	4341	Andrews, Groves	1	2	3	4	5		6	7	9	10	11	8								12			
3	28	Barnsley	3-1	2-0	4915	McLaughlin, Wood(2)	1	2	3	4	5		6	7	9	10	11	8								12			
4	1 Sep	WALSALL	4-1	2-0	6873	D.Roberts, Wood, Andrews(2)	1	2	3	4	5		6	7	9	10	11	8								12			
5	4	OLDHAM	2-4	0-1	6198	Groves, Wood	1	2	3	4	5		6	7	9	10	11	8								12			
6	11	Notts County	0-1	0-1	13328		1	2	3		5		6	7	9	10	11	8*	4		12								
7	18	PORT VALE	0-0	0-0	5443		1	2*	3		5		6	7	9	10	11	8		4	12								
8	25	Bradford City	1-2	0-0	4259	Wood	1		3		5		6	7	9	10*	11	8		4		2	12						
9	29	WREXHAM	2-1	1-1	5920	Moir, Andrews	1				5		6	7	9		11	8		4	10	2		3	12				
10	2 Oct	BLACKBURN	7-1	5-0	4519	Wood(5,1pen), Andrews(2)	1				5		6	7	9		11	8		4	10*	2		3	12				
11	9	York	1-1	1-1	5435	Andrews	1				5		6	7	9		11	8			10	2		3*	4				
12	15	BOURNEMOUTH	3-2	2-1	6181	Andrews, Wood, Holton	1				5		6	7	9		11*	8		4	10	2		3					
13	20	Chesterfield	0-0	0-0	8203		1				5		6	7	9		11	8		12	10	2		3	4				
14	23	ROTHERHAM	0-1	0-0	6295		1				5		6	7	9		11*	8	12		10	2		3	4				
15	30	Brighton	0-2	0-1	9778		1				5		6	7	9*		11	8			10	2		3	4				
16	5 Nov	SWANSEA	3-0	2-0	5417	Wood, Andrews(2)	1		2		4		6	7	9		11	8		5	10			3					
17	13	Bristol Rovers	1-3	1-2	8849	Wood(pen)	1		2		5		6	7	9		11	8		4	10*			3					
18	26	BOLTON	1-0	1-0	6605	Wood	1		2		5		6	7	9		11	8		4	10			3		12			
19	4 Dec	Plymouth	2-1	1-0	8717	Holton, Wood	1		2		5		6	7	9		11	8		4	10			3		12			
20	18	Oldham	4-1	1-1	6296	Wood(2,1pen), D.Roberts(2)	1		2		5		6	7	9		11	8		4	10			3		12			
21	27	TRANMERE	0-0	0-0	9359		1		2		5		6	7	9		11	8		4	10			3		12			
22	1 Jan	Port Vale	1-2	1-0	5056	Wood(pen)	1	12	2		5		6	7	9		11	8		4	10			3					
23	7	BARNSLEY	1-0	1-0	3344	Andrews	1	12	2*		5		6	7	9		11	8		4	10			3					
24	19	Aston Villa	0-3	0-2	27239		1	12*	2		5		6	7	9		11	8	4		10			3					
25	22	Wrexham	1-2	1-0	7043	Wood	1		2		5		6	7	9		11	8	4	12	10			3					
26	28	CHESTERFIELD	3-4	1-1	4198	Bridgewood, Groves, Moir	1		2		5		6*	7	9		11	8*		4	10			3					
27	5 Feb	Rochdale	0-0	0-0	3502			2			5	8	6	7	9		11	12		4	10			3			1		
28	12	Rotherham	1-2	0-2	6677	Moir		2			5	10*	6	7	9		11	8			4			3			1		
29	19	BRIGHTON	3-5	0-0	3866	Wood(pen), Bridgewood, Holton		2			5	12	6	7	9		11	8		4	10			3			1		
30	26	Swansea	0-1	0-1	5068		1	2			5	12	6	7	9		11	8		4	10			3					
31	4 Mar	BRISTOL ROVERS	2-2	0-1	3001	Wood, Andrews	1	2			5	12		7	9		11	8		4*	10			3					
32	10	YORK	2-1	2-1	3487	D.Roberts, Wood	1	2			5	12		7	9		11	8		4	10			3	6				
33	15	ASTON VILLA	1-1	1-0	16336	Moir	1	2				5		7	9	10	11	8			6			3*	4*			12	
34	18	Torquay	0-2	0-2	4073		1	2			5			7	9		11	8			10			3	4				
35	20	Mansfield	2-2	0-2	5961	Wood(2)	1		10		5	8			9	12	11							3	4			7	
36	25	NOTTS COUNTY	1-1	0-1	5211	Wood(pen)	1	2	3		5	12		7	9		11	8			10				4				
37	31	Blackburn	0-1	0-1	8998		1			4	5				9		11	8			10			3				7	
38	4 Apr	BRADFORD CITY	3-0	1-0	3757	D.Roberts(2), Andrews	1			4				7	9	10	11				6			3	8			7*	
39	8	ROCHDALE	2-1	2-1	2539	Wood, Andrews	1			4			6	7	9	10	11	8						3					
40	15	Bolton	0-2	0-1	5720		1			4		2	6	7	9	10	11	8						3					
41	19	MANSFIELD	4-2	2-0	2693	Wood(2), Andrews, Moir	1			4	5	2		7	9		11	8			10			3					
42	22	PLYMOUTH	1-2	1-0	3179	Andrews	1				5	10*		7	9		11	8						3	2				
43	25	Walsall	1-4	1-2	6697	Wood(pen)	1				5	12		7	9		11	8		4	10			3	2				
44	29	Halifax	0-0	0-0	2405		1				5	2		7	9		11	8		4	10			12					3
45	3 May	HALIFAX	3-0	1-0	2329	Wood(3,1pen)	1				5	2		7	9	6	11	10			8			12	4				3
46	10	Tranmere	4-0	0-0	3502	Wood(2), McLaughlin, Andrews	1				5	2		7	9	6	11	8			10			12	4				3

F.A. Cup

1R	20 Nov	Colchester U.	4-1 2-1	5573	Andrews(3), Wood	1	2	5	6 8 9	11 10	4 7	3		12
2R	11 Dec	GUILDFORD C.	2-1 2-1	7163	Wood, Moir	1	2	5	6 7 9	11 8	10	3 4		12
3R	15 Jan	Derby C.	0-2 0-0	33463		1	2	5	6 7 9	11 8	10	3 4		12

League Cup

1R	18 Aug	Port Vale	2-0 1-0	4638	Wood(2)	1	2 3	4 5	6 7 9	10 11 8			12
2R	7 Sep	Grimsby T.	1-2 0-2	13592	Wood	1	2 3	4 5	6 7 9	10 11 8			12

FINAL LEAGUE TABLE

		P	W	D	L	F	A	Pts
1	Aston Villa	46	32	6	8	85	32	70
2	Brighton	46	27	11	8	82	47	65
3	Bournemouth	46	23	16	7	73	37	62
4	Notts County	46	25	12	9	74	44	62
5	Rotherham	46	20	15	11	69	52	55
6	Bristol Rovers	46	21	12	13	75	56	54
7	Bolton	46	17	16	13	51	41	50
8	Plymouth	46	20	10	16	74	64	50
9	Walsall	46	15	18	13	62	57	48
10	Blackburn	46	19	9	18	54	57	47
11	Oldham	46	17	11	18	59	63	45
12	Shrewsbury	46	17	10	19	73	65	44
13	Chesterfield	46	18	8	20	57	57	44
14	Swansea	46	17	10	19	46	59	44
15	Port Vale	46	13	15	18	43	59	41
16	Wrexham	46	16	8	22	59	63	40
17	Halifax	46	13	12	21	48	61	38
18	Rochdale	46	12	13	21	57	83	37
19	York	46	12	12	22	57	66	36
20	Tranmere	46	10	16	20	50	71	36
21	Mansfield	46	8	20	18	41	63	36
22	Barnsley	46	9	18	19	32	64	36
23	Torquay	46	10	12	24	41	69	32
24	Bradford City	46	11	10	25	45	77	32

(Back) Mulhearn, Bevan, Roberts, Dolby, Holton, Harkin, Tooze. (2nd Row) Starkey (Sec.), McLaughlin, Brown, Morris, Groves, Andrews, Moir, Bridgwood, Gregory, Evans (Trainer/Coach), Gregg (Manager)

(3rd Row) Wood, Matthias, Clapham, Hughes, Hawkins, Fellows, Meredith. (Front) King, Knight, Jones, Adams, Kemp, Bradley.

SEASON 1972/73
Division 3

No.	Date	Opposition	Res.	H.T.	Att.	Goalscorers	Mulhearn K.	Bevan P.P.	Roberts I.	Moore J.	Holton J.	Bridgewood	Roberts D.	Moir R.	Andrews G.	McLaughlin	Groves A.	O'Loughlin N.	Fellows G.A.	Moir I.	Hughes T.P.	Dolby P.	Matthias T.	Tooze R.W.	Gregory A.T.	Calloway L.	Turner G.L.	Morris G.	Kearney M.J.	Smith T.P.	King J.	Tarbuck A.D.	Irvine S.	Kemp S.D.
1	12 Aug	NOTTS COUNTY	0-0	0-0	3775		1	2	3	4*	5	6	7	8	9	10	11	12																
2	19	Charlton	2-1	0-1	5312	R.Moir, O.G.	1	2	3	4*	5	6	7	8	9	10	11			12														
3	25	HALIFAX	0-0	0-0	3458		1	2	3*	4	5	6	7	8	9	10*	11*			12														
4	29	WATFORD	0-0	0-0	2919		1	2	3	4	5	6	7	8	9*	10*	11				10													
5	2 Sep	Oldham	1-2	1-1	4516	Hughes	1	2	3	4	5	7	8	6	9*	12	11				10													
6	9	BLACKBURN	2-0	0-0	2722	Hughes, Groves	1	2	3*	4	5	7	8	6	9	12	11				10													
7	16	Plymouth	0-3	0-1	5952		1	2	3*	4	5	7	8	6	9*	12	11				10													
8	19	Rotherham	0-2	0-0	5508		1	2	3	4	5	6	7	8	9	10	11	12																
9	23	SWANSEA	2-1	1-1	2415	Groves, R.Moir	1	2	3	4	5	8	7	6		12	11		3		9													
10	26	YORK	1-0	0-0	2362	Groves	1	2	3	6	5	8	7	8		10*	11				9													
11	30	Bournemouth	0-2	0-1	10833		1	2	3	6	5	8	7*				11		12	11	10													
12	6 Oct	Southend	0-2	0-1	7274		1	8	3*	4	5	6	7		9	9	11	10	12	11														
13	10	GRIMSBY	3-2	0-1	1763	Hughes(2), Roberts	1	2	3	4	5	6	7	8	9	10		10	12	11														
14	14	ROCHDALE	3-2	1-1	2502	Hughes, Bridgewood, O.G.	1	2	3	4	5	6	7	8		10			12	11	9	5												
15	21	Bristol Rovers	1-5	0-2	7336	R.Moir	1	2	3	6		4	7	8*		10			12	11	9	12												
16	23	Port Vale	1-1	1-1	5213	Dolby	1	2	3	4	5	7	7	8		10			3	11	9	6		1										
17	27	CHESTERFIELD	2-0	1-0	2694	Hughes, Holton	1	2		4	5	12	7*	8		10			3	11	9*	6		1										
18	4 Nov	York	1-2	0-0	2620	I.Moir	1	2		6	5	12	7	8		10			3	11	9*	6												
19	11	ROTHERHAM	1-1	1-1	2395	Hughes	1	2*		6	5	10	7	8					3	11	9	4												
20	25	Scunthorpe	0-1	0-1	2596		1	10*		4		6	7	8	9				3	11	10	5			12									
21	2 Dec	BRENTFORD	2-0	2-0	2079	Bridgwood, I.Moir	1	12		4	5	8	7	10	9				2	11		6			2									
22	16	Wrexham	0-0	0-0	4098		1	10	3	4	5	7	7	8					11		9	4			2	6								
23	22	TRANMERE	0-0	0-0	2320		1	10*	3	4	5	7	12	8					11		9	4			2	6								
24	26	Swansea	2-0	2-0	4460	Bevan, Hughes	1	2	3	6	5	7	12	8*	8*				11		9	4			2	6								
25	30	CHARLTON	0-0	0-0	3338		1	10		6	5	11	7		8					12		4			2	6	5							
26	19 Jan	OLDHAM	2-2	2-2	2949	Andrews, Hughes	1	2	3	4	5	12	7	8	10			12		11	9	4				6	5							
27	27	Blackburn	0-0	0-0	8279		1	8	3	4	5	12	7							10	9	4				4	5	11						
28	9 Feb	PLYMOUTH	1-1	0-0	2600	Dolby	1	2	3	4	5	8	7	8						10*	9	6	4		2	6	5	11						
29	13	Grimsby	2-3	1-3	11382	Kearney(2)	1	8	3			7	7	8						10*		8	4			6	5	11	12					
30	17	Notts County	0-1	0-1	8903		1	6	3			7	8								10	12	4			6	5	11	9					
31	23	WREXHAM	0-0	0-0	2490		1	2	3			7	8							12	9	4				6	5	11	9					
32	27	Halifax	1-0	0-0	1474	Hughes	1	2	3			7	7	8						12	10	10	4		12	6	6	11	9					
33	2 Mar	SOUTHEND	1-0	0-0	2542	Hughes	1	2	3			7	7	8						12	10	6	4			6	5	11	9		9			
34	6	WALSALL	1-1	1-1	3449	Roberts(pen)	1	2	3			7	7	8						12	10	6	4			6	5	11	9		9			
35	10	Rochdale	1-1	0-1	1993	Calloway	1	2	3			7	7	8						12	9	4				8	6	5	11		9	2		
36	16	BRISTOL ROVERS	4-2	2-1	3593	Kearney, Tarbuck, Roberts(pen), Morris	1	2	3			7	7	8						12	9	4			2	6	5	11	9		10			
37	21	Bolton	0-2	0-0	18472		1	8	3			12	7	8						10*	9	8	4			6	5	11	9		10			
38	24	Chesterfield	0-0	0-0	3730		1	6	3				7							9	12	4		2*	6	5	11	7		10		2*	
39	27	PORT VALE	2-3	2-3	4419	Kearney, Tarbuck	1	2	3			6	7	8						12	12	4			8	7	5	11	9		10			
40	30	SCUNTHORPE	4-2	2-0	2277	Tarbuck, Roberts(pen), Kearney, R.Moir	1	2					7	6						12	12	6	4			3	5	11	9		10			
41	7 Apr	Brentford	2-1	0-1	6760	Hughes, Morris	1	2					7	8				12		12	10	6	4			3	5	11	9		10			
42	13	BOLTON	0-2	0-2	6574		1	6					7	8						9*	9*	6			2	8	5	11	12		10			
43	20	Tranmere	0-1	0-0	5198		1	6	3				12	8						9	9	4			2	3	5	11	12		10			
44	21	Walsall	0-1	0-1	4020		1		3				7									8*	4		2	6	5	11	12		10	7	
45	24	BOURNEMOUTH	0-0	0-0	3457		1	12	3				7									8*	4		2	6	5*	11	9		10	8	
46	28	Watford	1-0	1-0	6026	Tarbuck	1		3				7										4		2	6	5	11	9		10	8	12

F.A. Cup

	Date	Opponent			Att	Scorers	1		4	5	6	7	8		3	11	9	10	2
1R	18 Nov	Spennymoor	1-1	0-0	1818	Dolby	1		4	5	6	7	8	12	3	11	9	10	2
1Rr	21	SPENNYMOOR	3-1	0-0	3922	Andrews(2), Moir	1		4	5	6	7	8	12	3	11	9*	10	2
2R	9 Dec	Bolton W.	0-3	0-3	8403		1	12	3	6	5	8	9		11	4	10	2

League Cup

	Date	Opponent			Att	Scorers	1	2	3	4	5	8	7	6	9	10	11	12
1R	16 Aug	Chester	3-4	2-0	3521	D.Roberts, McLaughlin, Groves	1	2	3	4	5	8	7	6	9	10	11	12

Hereford Senior Cup Final

	Date	Opponent			Att	Scorers	1	8*	3				7			9	11	2
1L	20 Apr	HEREFORD U.	1-1	1-0	2203	Morris	1	8*	3				7			9	11	2
2L	4 May	Hereford U.	0-2	0-2	4826		1	12	3				7			4	11	2

Additional Player: Bradley = 4/1

(Back) McLaughlin, Matthias, Bridgwood, Dolby, ?, ?, Bevan.
(2nd Row) Seymour, Fellows, Gregory, Tooze, Jones, Mulhearn, I.Moir, Evans.
(3rd Row) Roberts, Groves, Hughes, Gregg, Andrews, Moore, R.Moir. (Front) ?, King, Roberts, Kemp.

Final League Table

		P	W	D	L	F	A	Pts
1	Bolton	46	25	11	10	73	39	61
2	Notts County	46	23	11	12	67	47	57
3	Blackburn	46	20	15	11	57	47	55
4	Oldham	46	19	16	11	72	54	54
5	Bristol Rovers	46	20	13	13	77	56	53
6	Port Vale	46	21	11	14	56	69	53
7	Bournemouth	46	17	16	13	66	44	50
8	Plymouth	46	20	10	16	74	66	50
9	Grimsby	46	20	8	18	67	61	48
10	Tranmere	46	15	16	15	56	52	46
11	Charlton	46	17	11	18	69	67	45
12	Wrexham	46	14	17	15	55	54	45
13	Rochdale	46	14	17	15	48	54	45
14	Southend	46	17	10	19	61	54	44
15	Shrewsbury	46	15	14	17	46	54	44
16	Chesterfield	46	17	9	20	57	61	43
17	Walsall	46	18	7	21	56	66	43
18	York	46	13	15	18	42	46	41
19	Watford	46	12	17	17	43	48	41
20	Halifax	46	13	15	18	43	53	41
21	Rotherham	46	13	7	22	51	65	41
22	Brentford	46	15	7	24	51	69	37
23	Swansea	46	14	9	23	51	73	37
24	Scunthorpe	46	10	10	26	33	72	30

SEASON 1973/74
Division 3

No.	Date	Opposition	Res.	H.T.	Att.	Goalscorers	Mulhearn K.	Gregory A.T.	Roberts I.	Matthias T.	Turner G.L.	Calloway L.	Roberts D.	Moir R.J.	Kearney M.J.	Tarbuck A.D.	Morris G.	Irvine S.	King J.	Kemp S.D.	Dolby P.	Butler D.J.	Bradley P.K.	Hughes T.P.	Durban A.	Marlowe R.	Cochrane A.	Cruse P.	Roberts L.	O'Loughlin N.	Hayes S.
1	25 Aug	Port Vale	0-3	0-2	3717		1	2	3	4	5	6*	7	8	9	10	11	12													
2	1 Sep	WREXHAM	0-1	0-0	2666		1			5		3	7*		9	10	11	8	2		6	12									
3	8	Cambridge	1-2	1-1	4553	D.Roberts(pen)	1		12	4		3	7		9	10	11	8	2		6										
4	10	Tranmere	0-1	0-1	5404		1		12	4		3	7		9	10	11	8	2		6										
5	15	ROCHDALE	2-0	0-0	2516	Durban, Tarbuck	1		12	5		3	7	8*	9	10	11	8*	2	4					6						
6	18	BRISTOL ROVERS	0-2	0-2	3016		1		12	4		3	7		9	10	11	8	2	5					6						
7	22	Aldershot	2-2	1-1	4012	Durban, Kearney	1	12	3	4			7*		9	10	11	8	2	5					6						
8	29	GRIMSBY	1-1	0-1	2306	Kearney	1		3	4		11	7*		9	10		8	2	5	8				6						
9	2 Oct	Bristol Rovers	0-1	0-1	11459		1	2	3*	4		8			9*	10	11	9*		5					7						
10	6	Plymouth	2-2	0-0	7317	Morris, O.G.	1	2	3	4		8			9	10	11	7		5					6						
11	13	BOURNEMOUTH	1-1	1-0	2372	Kearney	1	2	3	4		8			9	10	11	7*		5					6						
12	20	Brighton	0-2	0-1	5308		1	2	3	4		8			9	12	11	7		5	10				6						
13	23	TRANMERE	1-3	0-2	2311	Tarbuck	1	2	3	4		8			9	10	11	7		5				9	6						
14	27	SOUTHEND	1-2	0-1	1815	I.Roberts	1	2	3	4		8			9*	10*	12	7		5				11	7						
15	3 Nov	Oldham	0-3	0-1	6746		1	2	3	4		8	10				12	9*		5	6			11	7						
16	10	SOUTHPORT	2-0	1-0	1742	Marlowe, Hughes	1	2	3	4	5	8				6*	11	12			6*	10		7		9					
17	13	Huddersfield	0-1	0-0	4154		1	2	3	4	5	8					11*	12			8	7		10		9					
18	17	YORK	0-2	0-0	1891		1	2	3	4	5	6						8*	12		6	7		11		9					
19	1 Dec	CHESTERFIELD	0-1	0-0	1397		1	2	3	4	5		7					8*			8*	12		12	6	9					
20	8	Walsall	0-2	0-1	3037		1	2	3	4	5	3				10	11	7			8*			7	6	9					
21	22	Grimsby	2-1	0-0	5244	Marlowe, Hughes	1	2	3	4	5	3				8	12	10			12			7	6*	9					
22	26	WATFORD	3-2	2-2	3875	Hughes, Durban(2)	1	2	3	4	5	3				10	11	7			12			8	6*	9					
23	29	CAMBRIDGE	2-0	1-0	3369	Tarbuck, Durban	1	2	3	4	5	3				10	11	7			12			8	6	9					
24	1 Jan	Wrexham	1-3	1-2	9572	Durban	1	2		5		3	12	4		10	11	7*						8*	6	9					
25	5	HALIFAX	0-2	0-1	2542		1	2		5		3	8			10	11	7			4			7	6	9					
26	12	Rochdale	2-3	1-1	1000	Tarbuck, Hughes	1	2		6		3	7			10*	11	11*			12	12		8	4	9					
27	19	PORT VALE	0-1	0-0	2771		1	2		4		3*	10		2	11				8	12	12		7	6	9					
28	27	Blackburn	0-2	0-1	10989		1	3		4		10				11		8	2			6*		7	7	10	9				
29	3 Feb	Charlton	3-3	2-0	7880	D.Roberts(2,1pen), Tarbuck	1	3		4	12	7	7	11	5	10	11		2		6*	12		8	6*	9					
30	10	ALDERSHOT	0-0	0-0	2795		1	3		4	12	7	6	5	10	11		2		10			8		9						
31	16	Bournemouth	0-1	0-1	8690		1					12	6	11	5	10		6*	2					8	8	9		8			
32	23	PLYMOUTH	0-0	0-0	1993		1				4	4	7	11	6	10		12	2			12			8*	9		8*			
33	1 Mar	Watford	0-1	0-1	5860		1			12	5	3	7	4	6	11		7	2					10	4	9					
34	8	Southend	0-2	0-1	5038		1			8	6	3	7		5	11			2					7	4	9			12		
35	16	BRIGHTON	1-0	1-0	2077	Calloway	1			4	6	3		8	5	11			2					11	7	9			12		
36	19	CHARLTON	3-3	2-1	1232	Kearney, Durban, Tarbuck	1			8	6	3		10	5	11		10*	2					7	4	9			12		
37	23	Southport	0-1	0-1	1091		1			8	6	3		7	5	11		10*	2					8	4	9			12		
38	26	Halifax	0-1	0-1	1346		1			8	6	3		8	5	11		4	2					7	4	9			10		
39	30	OLDHAM	0-2	0-2	2326		1			4	4	3		8	5	11	12	8	2					10	4	9			10*		
40	2 Apr	BLACKBURN	3-0	3-0	1392	Tarbuck, Marlowe, Moir	1	12			6	3		8	5	10	11	8	2					7	4*	9			12		
41	6	HUDDERSFIELD	3-0	1-0	1675	Durban(2), Morris	1		12	12	6	3	10	10	5	8	11	7*	2					7*	4	9				12	
42	13	York	1-0	0-0	7001	Moir	1				6	3	7	4	5	10		4	2						8	9				12	
43	15	Hereford	1-1	0-1	9005	Moir	1				6	3	8	4	5	10		4	2						4	9			10	12	
44	16	HEREFORD	1-1	0-0	5580	Marlowe	1				6	3	7	8	5	10		4	2						4	9			10*	12	
45	20	WALSALL	0-0	0-0	3182		1	12			6	3	7	8	5	10		4	2						4	9*			12	12	
46	27	Chesterfield	2-0	1-0	3637	Kearney, Morris	1	4	3	6	6	3	7	8	5	10	11		2						4	9				12	12

F.A. Cup

							1	2		6	12	5	3							11		8	7		10	4	9
1R	24 Nov	Wrexham	1-1	1-0	5668	Marlowe	1	2		6	12	5	3							11		8	7		10	4	9
1Rr	27	WREXHAM	0-1	0-1	1829		1	2	3	4	5			12							11			7		10	6	9

League Cup

							1	2	3	4	5*	6	7	8	9	10	11	12
1R	29 Aug	Walsall	1-6	1-2	4722	Morris	1	2	3	4	5*	6	7	8	9	10	11	12

Welsh Cup

3R	21 Nov	Portmadoc	2-0	0-0	235	Marlowe, Durban	1	8	11	4	5	3		7	10	11		2
4R	15 Dec	WELSHPOOL	5-0	1-0	929	Morris, Durban, Hughes(2), Marlowe	1	2		4	5	3	7			10	11	
5R	26 Feb	Newport C.	1-0	0-0	1232	Marlowe	1			6	3	7	11	5		10	12	9*	2
SF	13 Mar	CARDIFF C.	1-2	0-0	1193	Durban	1	8		6	3	7		10	5	11	12	4	2

Additional Players: Hoyle = 1/1, S.King = 6/1

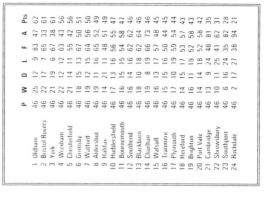

(Back) King, Bradley, Dolby, Kemp, O'Loughlin, Butler, Bridgwood. (2nd Row) Calloway, Hobson, Moir, M.J.Jones, Mulhearn, Bevan, Kearney, Turner, D.Roberts, Gregory. (3rd Row) Hobson, Morris, Matthias, Evans, Tarbuck, T.Hughes, Seymour. (Sitting) I.Roberts, Irvine.

Final League Table

		P	W	D	L	F	A	Pts
1	Oldham	46	25	12	9	83	47	62
2	Bristol Rovers	46	22	17	7	65	33	61
3	York	46	21	19	6	67	38	61
4	Wrexham	46	22	12	12	63	43	56
5	Chesterfield	46	21	14	11	55	42	56
6	Grimsby	46	18	15	13	67	50	51
7	Watford	46	19	12	15	64	56	50
8	Aldershot	46	19	11	16	65	52	49
9	Halifax	46	14	21	11	48	51	49
10	Huddersfield	46	17	13	16	56	55	47
11	Bournemouth	46	16	15	15	54	58	47
12	Southend	46	16	14	16	62	62	46
13	Blackburn	46	18	10	18	62	64	46
14	Charlton	46	19	8	19	66	73	46
15	Walsall	46	16	13	17	57	48	45
16	Tranmere	46	15	15	16	50	44	45
17	Plymouth	46	17	10	19	59	54	44
18	Hereford	46	14	15	17	53	57	43
19	Brighton	46	16	11	19	52	58	43
20	Port Vale	46	14	14	18	52	58	42
21	Cambridge	46	13	9	24	48	81	35
22	Shrewsbury	46	10	11	25	41	62	31
23	Southport	46	6	16	24	35	82	28
24	Rochdale	46	2	17	27	38	94	21

SEASON 1974/75
Division 4 (Promotion Season)

No.	Date	Opposition	Res.	H.T.	Att.	Goalscorers
1	17 Aug	ROCHDALE	1-1	1-1	3513	Kearney
2	24	Stockport	3-0	0-0	1906	Bates, Durban, Haywood
3	31	CREWE	0-1	0-1	3149	
4	7 Sep	Newport County	4-2	3-1	2754	Durban(3), Bates
5	14	SWANSEA	2-0	0-0	2880	Morris, Haywood
6	17	CHESTER	2-0	1-0	3637	Kearney(pen), Jenkins
7	21	Northampton	3-3	0-2	4001	Durban, Kearney, Morris
8	25	Southport	2-1	1-0	1747	Haywood, O.G.
9	28	SCUNTHORPE	5-0	3-0	3381	Haywood(2), Kearney(2,1pen), Tarbuck
10	1 Oct	Rotherham	0-0	0-0	6495	
11	5	HARTLEPOOL	0-1	0-0	4222	
12	12	Reading	2-1	1-1	8163	Irvine, Durban
13	15	Cambridge	2-0	1-0	2652	Durban, Haywood
14	19	BRENTFORD	1-0	1-0	4099	Kearney(pen)
15	23	Torquay	1-1	1-1	2576	Bates
16	26	Bradford C.	2-1	1-1	3982	Morris, Tarbuck
17	2 Nov	LINCOLN	0-4	0-2	4349	
18	5	TORQUAY	2-0	0-0	3283	Haywood, Morris
19	8	Doncaster	3-1	1-0	1673	Bates, Haywood(2)
20	16	WORKINGTON	2-0	1-0	3583	Bates, Irvine
21	30	BARNSLEY	3-1	1-1	3287	Tarbuck, Durban, Calloway
22	7 Dec	Mansfield	1-3	1-1	10036	Bates
23	21	EXETER	2-2	1-0	3097	O'Loughlin, Bates,
24	26	Swansea	4-1	3-0	3501	O'Loughlin, Haywood(2), Bates
25	28	CAMBRIDGE	1-0	1-0	4570	O'Loughlin
26	4 Jan	Chester	1-1	1-0	8019	Haywood
27	11	MANSFIELD	0-1	0-0	8913	
28	18	Barnsley	0-1	0-0	5201	
29	25	Darlington	2-1	2-1	1864	Tarbuck, Haywood
30	1 Feb	DONCASTER	7-4	2-0	3632	Haywood(3), Bates(2), McGregor(2)
31	8	Lincoln	0-3	0-2	8579	
32	15	DARLINGTON	2-0	1-0	3207	Bates, Tarbuck
33	22	Workington	2-0	2-0	1750	Haywood, Durban(pen)
34	28	Crewe	0-0	0-0	4156	
35	8 Mar	SOUTHPORT	1-0	0-0	3765	McGregor
36	15	Scunthorpe	0-1	0-1	1663	
37	17	Rochdale	0-0	0-0	1427	
38	22	NEWPORT	1-0	1-0	3465	Bates
39	29	Exeter	0-1	0-0	3240	
40	31	NORTHAMPTON	6-0	4-0	4315	Bates(2), O'Loughlin(2), Haywood, Durban(pen)
41	5 Apr	BRADFORD C.	3-2	2-2	3398	Haywood(2), Bates
42	8	ROTHERHAM	3-1	1-0	6538	O'Loughlin, Bates, McGregor
43	12	Hartlepool	1-1	1-1	2162	Durban
44	19	READING	2-0	1-0	5050	Haywood, O'Loughlin
45	22	STOCKPORT	0-0	0-0	5641	
46	26	Brentford	1-2	1-1	5810	Bates

Player appearances (shirt numbers; * = substitute)

No.	Mulhearn	King J.	Gregory A.T.	Durban A.	Kearney M.J.	Turner G.L.	Irvine S.	Bates P.D.	Hayward R.	Tarbuck A.D.	Morris G.	Calloway L.	Jenkins D.J.	O'Loughlin	Roberts I.	Cochrane A.	Dolby P.	McGregor A.	Hayes S.C.	Moore K.	Collier D.
1	1	2	3	4	5	6	7	8	9	10	11	12									
2	1	2	3	4*	5	6	7	8	9	10	11	12									
3	1	2	3	4	5	6	7	8	9	10*	11	12									
4	1	2	3	8	6	5	7	10	9	12	11	4									
5	1	2	3	4*	5	6	7	8	9	12	11	10									
6	1	2	3		5	6	7	10	9	12	11	8*	4								
7	1	2	3	4	5	6	7	10	9	12	11	8	8*								
8	1	2	3	4	5	6	7	10	9	8	11			12							
9	1	2	3	4	5	6	7	10	9	8	11*			12							
10	1	2	3	4	5	6	7	10	9	8	11			12							
11	1	2	3	4*	5	6	7	10	9	8	11			12							
12	1	2	3	4	5	6	7	10	9	8	11*	12									
13	1	2	3	4	5	6	7	10	9	8	11			12							
14	1	2	3*	4	5	6	7	10	9	8	11	2		12							
15	1	2		4	5	6	12	10	9	8	11	3			7*						
16	1	2		4	5	6	12	10	9	8	11	7			3*						
17	1	2*		4	5	6*	7	10	9	8	3			12							
18	1	2		4	5	6		10	9	8	11	3		8	12	7					
19	1	2		12	4	6		10	9	8	11	3			12	7					
20	1	2			7	4		10	9	8	11*	3				7					
21	1	2		4	7	6		10	9	8	11	3*			12						
22	1	2		4	5	6	7	10	9	8	11	3*		12	3*						
23	1	2		4	5	6*	7	11	9	8	12			10	3		6				
24	1	2		4	5		7	10	9	11	12	8*		8	3		5				
25	1	2		4*	6		7	10	9	8	12			11	3		5				
26	1	2		4	6	8	7	10	9		12			11*	3		5				
27	1	2		4	5	7		10	9	12	11	8		11*	3						
28	1	2		4	5	6	7	10	9	11	12			12	3						
29	1	2	3*	4	5	6	7	10	9	11				12	3			7			
30	1	2		4	5	6	7	10	9	8	11*				3			7			
31	1	2	3	4	12	6	7	10	9	8	11*			11				7*			
32	1	2	3	4		7	6	10	9	8	12			12				11			
33	1	2	3	4	12	6	7	10	9	8				12				11	5		
34	1	2	3	4		6	7	10	9	11				12				8			
35	1	2	3	4		6	7	10	9	11				12				8			
36	1	2	3*	4		6	7	10	9	11				12				8	12		
37	1	2		4		6	7	10	9	11				12				8	5		
38	1	2		4	12	6		10	9	11				3	3			8	5		
39	1	2		4	12	6		10	9					6	6			8	3		
40	1	2		4*	12	6		10	9	7	11*			11	6			8*	5		
41	1	2		4	12	6		10	9					11	3			8	5		
42	1	2		4	12	6		10	9	7				11	3			8	5		
43	1	2		4	12	6		10	9	11	11*			7	3			8	5		
44	1	2		4	12	6		10	9	12				11	3			8*	5		
45	1	2		4	12	4		10	9	12				11	3			8	5		
46	1	2	3*	4	7	6	7	10	9	7*				11	3			8	5	12	3

F.A.Cup

	Date	Opponent			Att	Scorer	1	2		4	5	6	7	10	9	8	11	3		12
1R	23 Nov	WIGAN A.	1-1	0-0	7650	Kearney	1	2		4	5	6	7	10	9*	8	11	3		12
1Rr	25	Wigan A.	1-2	1-0	11860	Haywood	1	2		4	5	6	7	10	9	8	11	3		12

League Cup

	Date	Opponent			Att	Scorer	1	2	3	4	6	5	7	8	9	10	11	12
1R	21 Aug	Hereford U.	1-1	0-0	7263	Durban	1	2	3	4	6	5	7	8	9	10	11*	12
1Rr	27	HEREFORD U.	0-1	0-1	5183		1	2	3	4	6	5	7	8	9	10	11	12

Welsh Cup

	Date	Opponent			Att	Scorer	1	2	3	4	6	12	8	10	9	11	3	7	5
4R	13 Dec	LLANIDLOES	9-0	5-0	1229	Haywd(2),Bates(2),Kearny,Drban(2),Cochrne,Trbuck	1	2		4	6	12	8	10	9	11	3	7	5
5R	11 Feb	BANGOR C.	1-1	0-0	1039	Haywood	1	2	3		6	4	7	10	9	7*	11	12	8
5Rr	19	Bangor C.	1-0	0-0	1345	Bates	1	2	3	4	6	7	10	9	11	12			8
SF	10 Mar	Wrexham	1-2	1-0	4014	Irvine	2	3*	4	5	6	7	10	9	11	12			8

Additional Players: R.Wardle = 1/4, I.Atkins = 5/2

Final League Table

		P	W	D	L	F	A	Pts
1	Mansfield	46	28	12	6	90	40	68
2	Shrewsbury	46	26	10	10	80	43	62
3	Rotherham	46	22	15	9	71	41	59
4	Chester	46	23	11	12	64	38	57
5	Lincoln	46	21	15	10	79	48	57
6	Cambridge	46	20	14	12	62	44	54
7	Reading	46	21	10	15	63	47	52
8	Brentford	46	18	13	15	53	45	49
9	Exeter	46	19	11	16	60	63	49
10	Bradford	46	17	13	16	56	51	47
11	Southport	46	15	17	14	56	56	47
12	Newport	46	19	9	18	68	75	47
13	Hartlepool	46	16	11	19	52	62	43
14	Torquay	46	14	14	18	46	61	42
15	Barnsley	46	15	11	20	62	65	41
16	Northampton	46	15	11	20	67	73	41
17	Doncaster	46	14	12	20	65	79	40
18	Crewe	46	11	18	17	34	47	40
19	Rochdale	46	13	13	20	59	75	39
20	Stockport	46	12	14	20	43	70	38
21	Darlington	46	13	10	23	54	67	36
22	Swansea	46	15	6	25	46	73	36
23	Workington	46	10	11	25	46	66	31
24	Scunthorpe	46	7	15	24	41	78	29

(Back) Durban, Gregory, Hayward, King, Mulhearn, Kearney, Roberts, Barker (Coach)
(Front) Irvine, Bates, Turner, Tarbuck, Morris, O'Loughlin.

SEASON 1975/76
Division 3

No.	Date	Opposition	Res.	H.T.	Att.	Mulhearn K.	King J.	Gregory A.T.	Durban A.	Turner G.L.	Kearney M.J.	O'Loughlin N.	MacGregor A.	Haywood R.	Bates P.D.	Tarbuck A.D.	Collier D.	Irvine S.	Duffey C.P.	Lawrence L.	Roberts I.	Atkins I.L.	Leonard C.	Griffin C.R.	Moore K.	Hayes S.C.	Dolby P.	Roberts L.	Goalscorers
1	16 Aug	Mansfield	2:1	1-0	6951	1	2	3	4	5	6	7	8	9	10	11				12									Bates, Haywood
2	23	PETERBOROUGH	3:1	1-0	4473	1		3	4	6	5		11*	9	8	10	2	7	12										O.G., Collier(pen), Durban
3	30	Grimsby	2:3	0-2	4709	1	2	3	4	5	6		8	9	11	10		7	12										Haywood(2)
4	6 Sep	SWINDON	3:0	0-0	4062	1		3	4	5	6		8	9	10	11	2	7		12									Collier(2pens), Haywood
5	13	Halifax	0:0	0-0	2501	1	2	3	4	5	6	7		9	10	11			12		8								
6	20	CRYSTAL PALACE	2:4	0-3	7480	1		3	4	5	6		8	9	10	11*	2				7						12		Collier(pen), Kearney
7	22	Walsall	0:2	0-2	4866	1		3	4	5	6		8	9	10		2		12		7	11							
8	27	Southend	3:1	1-0	2922	1		2	4	5	6		12	9	10	11		7*	8	8*	3								Durban(2), Duffey
9	4 Oct	BRIGHTON	1:2	0-2	4198	1	2		4	6	5			9	10	11	3	7	8*			12							Kearney
10	11	Chesterfield	1:2	1-0	4060	1			4	5	6			9	10	11	3	7	8*			12							Kearney
11	18	GILLINGHAM	1:0	1-0	3242	1			4	5	6			9	10	11	3	7	8			12							Durban
12	21	PORT VALE	1:0	0-0	4673	1			4	5	6	12	8	9	10	11	3	7											Irvine
13	25	Sheffield Wed.	1:1	0-1	12045	1			4	5	6		12	9	10	11*	3	7				8*							Tarbuck
14	1 Nov	CHESTER	2:0	0-0	4567	1			4	5	6			9	10	11	3	7				8							Kearney, Haywood
15	4	Millwall	0:0	0-0	7528	1		12	4	5	6			9	10	11	3	7				8							
16	8	Colchester	1:1	1-0	3088	1	8		4	5	6			9	10	11	3	7								12			Bates
17	15	ROTHERHAM	0:2	0-1	3775	1			4	5	6			9	10	11	3	7	12			8							
18	29	Cardiff	0:3	0-1	8002	1			4	5	6	8		9	10	11	3	7					12						
19	6 Dec	ALDERSHOT	5:3	3-1	3061	1	2		4	6	5		11	9	10	12		7			3*	8*							Kearney, Durban(2), Atkins, Bates
20	20	BURY	1:3	1-0	3735	1	2		4	6	5		11	9*	10	12		7			3*	8							McGregor
21	27	HEREFORD	2:1	2-0	9488	1	2	3	4	6	5		11*	9	10	12		7				8							Durban(2)
22	10 Jan	GRIMSBY	1:0	0-0	3344	1	2	3	4	6		7*	11	9	10	12						8		5	7*				McGregor
23	17	Crystal Palace	1:1	0-0	16531	1	2	3	4	5			11	9	10	12		7				8		6					Durban
24	24	HALIFAX	2:0	2-0	3398	1	2	3	4	6			11	9	10	12		7				8		5					Bates, Irvine
25	31	Port Vale	0:0	0-0	3835	1	2	3	4	6			11		10	12		7				8		5					
26	3 Feb	Preston N.E.	2:0	0-0	4995	1	2	3	4	6	9*		11		10	12	2*	7				8		5					Irvine, Durban
27	7	MILLWALL	1:0	0-0	4453	1	2	3	4	6	9		11		10	12		7				8		5					Bates
28	9	Wrexham	3:2	2-1	5356	1	2	3	4	6	9*		11*		10	12		7				8		5					Irvine, Kearney, Atkins(pen)
29	14	COLCHESTER	1:0	0-0	4486	1	2	3	4	6	9		11		10	12		7		12		8		5					Kearney
30	21	Rotherham	1:0	1-0	4947	1	2	3	4*	6		8	11		10	4		7		12				5	12				O.G.
31	24	WALSALL	1:1	1-0	9085	1	2	3	4	6	9		11		10	12		7	12			8		5					Bates
32	6 Mar	Chester	0:1	1-1	5916	1			4*	5	9		11		10	12		7				8	3	6					
33	13	Brighton	2:2	2-0	21423	1	2		4	6	8		11	9*	10	12		7		12	3			5					Haywood, O.G.
34	13	CHESTERFIELD	0:2	0-1	4967	1	2		4	6	8		11		10			7				12	3	5					
35	16	Gillingham	1:2	0-0	5139	1	2		4	6	8				10			7			11		3	5					Irvine
36	20	CARDIFF	3:1	0-0	7573	1	2		4	6	8		11		10	12		7	3	3*			3	5	12				Atkins(pen), Irvine, McGregor
37	27	Aldershot	1:1	1-1	3883	1	3		4	5	9				10			7	2			8	3*	6	12				Kearney
38	30	Bury	1:2	1-0	4626	1	2	10	9	6	8			9*	6	12		7		12		11		5	4			3*	Atkins
39	2 Apr	MANSFIELD	1:2	1-0	4580	1	2		4	6	8	12			10			7	8*	3		11		5					Bates
40	6	SOUTHEND	3:1	2-0	2493	1	2		4*	8	9				10			7		3	3	11		5	12				Turner, Kearney(2,1pen)
41	10	Swindon	0:3	0-1	5869	1	2			12	9	8	11		10	11		7					3	5	4*				
42	13	SHEFFIELD WED.	0:0	0-0	2968	1	2				9				10			7			8	8	3	5	6			12	
43	17	PRESTON N.E.	1:0	1-0	3547	1	2			4	9				10			7			8	8	3	5	6				King
44	19	Hereford	1:3	0-0	12314	1	2		12	6	9	7			10	11		4			6	8*	3	5	6	12			Kearney
45	21	WREXHAM	1:2	1-2	3097	1	2		4	8	9	11			10			7		10	6	12	3	5	6				Kearney
46	24	Peterborough	2:3	1-3	5023	1	2	4	4	10	9		11*		12	12		7	7	7	8	8	3	5	6			11*	Griffin, Kearney

F.A. Cup

	Date	Opponents	Score	HT	Att	Team (shirt nos.)	Scorers
1R	22 Nov	Rossendale	1-0	0-0	3450	1 4 6 5 8 9 10 11 2 7 12 3	Bates
2R	13 Dec	CHESTER	3-1	2-1	6061	1 2 4 6 5 11 9 10 12 7 3 8	Bates(2), Durban
3R	3 Jan	BRADFORD C.	1-2	0-0	6554	1 2 4 6 5 11 9 10 12 7 3 8	Kearney

League Cup

	Date	Opponents	Score	HT	Att	Team (shirt nos.)	Scorers
1R1	19 Aug	Walsall	0-0	0-0	5910	1 2 3 4 6 5 12 9 10 11 7	
1R2	26	WALSALL	2-1	0-1	5933	1 2 3 4 6 5 8* 9 10 11 7 12	Duffey(pen), McGregor
2R	10 Sep	Q.P.RANGERS	1-4	1-0	11250	1 3 4 6 5 8 9 10 11 2 7* 12	Bates

Welsh Cup

	Date	Opponents	Score	HT	Att	Team (shirt nos.)	Scorers
4R	14 Jan	Courtalds C.	5-0	2-0	1800	1 2 4 6 5 11 9 10 7 3 8 12	Tarbuck, Bates(2), Haywood, McGregor
5R	17 Feb	Worcester C.	2-2	1-1	2679	1 2 9 11 10 7* 3 8 6	Moore, Bates
5Rr	2 Mar	WORCESTER C.	3-0	2-0	2944	1 2 4* 6 9 11 12 10 7 8 3	Atkins(2), Durban
SF	23	Hereford U.	1-1	0-1	4748	1 2 4 6 9 10 11 7 8 3	Bates
SFr	8 Apr	HEREFORD U. *	5-6	0-0	2714	1 2 9 8 11* 10 4 3 7 12	Irvine (O'Loughlin, Collier, Irvine, Tarbuck, pens)

Additional Player: Wardle = 1/2

* 1-1 after extra time

(Back) Cochrane, I.Roberts, Hayes, Wardle, Dolby, Butler, Hickenbottom, Atkins, O'Loughlin, Tarbuck.
(2nd Row) Barker, Seymour, Irvine, Calloway, Hayward, Bates, Mulhearn, King, Turner, Kearney, Morris, Durban, Malam.
(3rd Row) Starkey, Woodhouse, Tudor Owen, Yates, Fry, Williams. (Front) Moore, Collier, L.Roberts.

FINAL LEAGUE TABLE

		P	W	D	L	F	A	Pts
1	Hereford	46	26	11	9	86	55	63
2	Cardiff	46	22	13	11	69	48	57
3	Millwall	46	20	16	10	54	43	56
4	Brighton	46	22	9	15	78	53	53
5	Crystal Palace	46	18	17	11	61	46	53
6	Wrexham	46	20	12	14	66	55	52
7	Walsall	46	18	14	14	74	61	50
8	Preston	46	19	10	17	62	57	48
9	Shrewsbury	46	19	10	17	61	59	48
10	Peterborough	46	15	18	13	63	63	48
11	Mansfield	46	16	15	15	58	52	47
12	Port Vale	46	15	16	15	55	54	46
13	Bury	46	16	16	14	51	46	44
14	Chesterfield	46	17	9	20	69	69	43
15	Gillingham	46	15	12	19	55	58	43
16	Rotherham	46	15	12	19	54	65	42
17	Chester	46	15	12	19	53	62	42
18	Grimsby	46	15	10	21	62	74	40
19	Swindon	46	16	8	22	62	75	40
20	Sheff Wed	46	12	16	18	48	59	40
21	Aldershot	46	13	13	20	59	75	39
22	Colchester	46	12	14	20	41	65	38
23	Southend	46	12	13	21	65	75	37
24	Halifax	46	11	13	22	41	61	35

SEASON 1976/77
Division 3

No.	Date	Opposition	Res.	H.T.	Att.	Goalscorers	Mulhearn K.	King J.	Leonard C.C.	Turner G.J.	Griffin C.R.	Atkins I.L.	Irvine S.	Hornsby B.G.	Kearney M.J.	Bates P.D.	Durban A.	Maguire P.B.	Haywood R.J.	Roberts L.	Lawrence L.	Moore K.	Loughnane P.	Hayes S.C.	Collier D.	Cross S.C.
1	21 Aug	Lincoln	1-1	1-1	6372	Hornsby	1	2	3	4	5	6	7	8	9	10	11*	12								
2	24	GILLINGHAM	4-2	2-0	3858	Kearney, Bates, Atkins(pen), Maguire	1	2	3	4	5	6	7	8	9	10	11*	12								
3	28	READING	2-0	0-0	4111	Bates, Kearney	1	2	3	6	5	4	7	8	9	10	12	11								
4	4 Sep	Wrexham	0-1	0-0	8646		1	2	3	4	5	6	7*	8	9	10	12	11								
5	11	Walsall	3-3	3-2	5320	Turner, Hornsby, Kearney	1	2	3	4	5	6	7	8	9	10	11*		12							
6	18	NORTHAMPTON	3-0	2-0	4191	Bates, Kearney, Atkins	1	2	3	6	5	4	7	8	9	10	11*	12								
7	25	Port Vale	2-1	0-0	4180	Turner, Hornsby	1	2	3	4	5	6	7	8	9	10	11*		12							
8	2 Oct	PORTSMOUTH	4-1	3-0	4782	Bates(2), Kearney, Atkins(pen)	1	2	3	4	5	6	7	8	9	10	11*	12								
9	9	Swindon	0-1	0-0	9017		1	2	3	4	5	6	7	8	9	10	11*	12								
10	16	CHESTERFIELD	3-0	1-0	4737	Kearney, Bates(2)	1	2	3	4	5	6	7	8	9	10	12	11								
11	23	Sheffield Wed.	1-0	1-0	17030	Hornsby	1	2	3	4	5	6	7	8	9	10	12	11								
12	26	Crystal Palace	1-2	1-1	15809	Kearney	1	2*	3	4	5	6	7	8	9	10	12	11								
13	30	OXFORD	1-0	1-0	4923	Maguire	1	2	3	4	5	6	7	8	9	10	12	11								
14	2 Nov	MANSFIELD	0-0	0-0	6161		1	2	3	4	5	6	7	8	9	10	12	11								
15	6	Rotherham	0-1	0-0	4761		1	2	3	4	5	6	7	8	9*	10	4	11								
16	13	GRIMSBY	2-1	2-1	4639	Turner, Bates	1	2	3	4*	5	6	7	8	9	10		11	12							
17	27	York	3-0	1-0	2514	Kearney, Bates, Turner	1	2	3	4	5	6	7	8	9	10		11	12	3						
18	4 Dec	BRIGHTON	1-0	1-0	9121	Hornsby	1	2	3	4	5	6	7	8	9	10		11	12							
19	17	Preston N.E.	1-2	0-0	7809	Hornsby	1	2	3	4	5	6	7	8	9*	10		11	12							
20	27	TRANMERE	2-2	1-1	8887	Griffin, O.G.	1	2	3	4	5	6*	7	8	9	10	11*		9*		12					
21	27	Chester	2-1	2-1	8155	Turner, Durban	1	2	3	4	5	6*	7	8	9	10	10*	11								
22	11 Jan	BURY	0-1	0-1	5339		1	2	3	4	5		7	8	9		10*	11	12	6						
23	22	LINCOLN	2-1	1-0	5074	Atkins(pen), Maguire	1	2	3	4	5	6	7	8	9	10	4	11*	11*		9	11				
24	29	Peterborough	1-2	1-0	5541	Kearney	1	2	3		5	6	2	8	9	10	7	11*	12		7	4				
25	1 Feb	ROTHERHAM	0-0	0-0	5509		1	2	3		5	6	2	8	9	10		11*	12		9	11				
26	5	Reading	0-0	0-0	5432		1	2	3	9	5	6	7	8	9	10	4	11								
27	12	WREXHAM	3-2	1-0	10487	Kearney(2), Hornsby	1	2	3	4	5	6	7*	8	9	10		11	12		9	12				
28	15	Gillingham	1-2	0-1	4798	Kearney	1	2	3	4	5	6	7	8	9	10	12	11				12				
29	19	WALSALL	1-2	0-1	6697	Bates	1	2	3	4	5	6	7	8	9	10	6*	11	12							
30	26	Northampton	3-5	1-2	5112	Griffin, L.Roberts, Moore	1	2	3	4	5	6	7	8	9*	10	4	12	12	6	9	11				
31	1 Mar	Oxford	2-4	1-4	3964	Maguire, Lawrence	1	12	3			6	2	8		10	7	11			9	4			12	
32	5	PORT VALE	1-1	1-1	4236	Hornsby	1	2	3	4	5*	6	2	8		10		11			7	9	12			
33	12	Portsmouth	0-2	0-0	9904		1	2	3	4	5	6	7	8		10		11			9	11	12			
34	15	Brighton	0-4	0-0	17404		1	2	3	9		6	7*	8		10	4	11			9	11	12			
35	19	SWINDON	2-2	2-1	2898	Turner, Leonard	1	7	3	4		6		8		10	5	11			9	12	7	5		
36	26	Chesterfield	1-1	1-0	3978	Loughnane	1	7	3	4	5	6		8		10	12	11					9		2	
37	2 Apr	SHEFFIELD WED.	1-1	0-1	3657	Turner	1	7	3	4	5	6		8		10		11			9			9	2	
38	8	Tranmere	1-2	0-1	3151	Turner	1	9	3	4	5	6		8		10	11	7			9		9	12	2*	
39	9	CHESTER	2-0	0-0	3362	Atkins, Bates	1	2	3	4	5	6	7	8	8	10		11			12			9		
40	12	Mansfield	0-1	0-0	9840		1	2	3	4	5	10	7*	8	9	10		11						6		12
41	16	CRYSTAL PALACE	1-1	0-1	4240	Atkins(pen)	1	2	3	7	5	10	6	8	9	10		11				12		6		4
42	19	PETERBOROUGH	2-1	1-1	2360	Turner, Bates	1	2	3	4	6	10	6	8	9	10		11				12		5		7
43	23	Grimsby	1-2	1-1	2430	O.G.	1	2	3	6	5		7	8	9	10	12	11			7	7		4*		9*
44	30	YORK	2-1	0-0	2352	Maguire, Lawrence	1	2	3	9	5	6	7	8	9	10		11			12	7		4*		
45	3 May	Bury	1-0	0-0	3287	Bates	1	2	3	4	5	6	7	8	9	10		11			10			12		
46	14	PRESTON N.E.	1-2	0-2	2849	Hornsby	1	2	3	4	5	6	7	8	10	10		11	12	12	9*					7

F.A. Cup

	Date	Opponent			Att	1	2	3	4	5	6	7	8	9	10	11	12		Scorers
1R	20 Nov	Doncaster R.	2-2	1-1	5231	1	2	3	4	5	6	7	8	9	10	11	12		Atkins, Maguire
1Rr	23	DONCASTER R.	4-3	2-2	6234	1	2	3	4	5	6	7	8	9	10	12	11		Maguire(3), Bates
2R	11 Dec	Bury	0-0	0-0	6854	1	2	3	4	5	6	7	8	9	10	12	11		
2Rr	21	BURY	2-1	0-0	7115	1	2	3	4	5	6	7	8	9	10	11	9*	12	Irvine, Turner
3R	8 Jan	Q.P.Rangers	1-2	0-0	18285	1	2	3	4	5	6	7	8	9	10	12	11*	12	Bates

League Cup

	Date	Opponent			Att	1	2	3	4	5	6	7	8	9	10	11	12	
1R1	16 Aug	WALSALL	0-1	0-0	5553	1	2	3	4	5	6			9	10	11*	8	12
1R2	18	Walsall	0-1	0-0	6748	1	2	3	4	5	6			9	10	7	11	8 12

Welsh Cup

	Date	Opponent			Att	1	2	3	4	5	6	7	8	9	10	11	12		Scorers
4R	18 Jan	CHESTER	3-3	1-2	1364	1	2	3	4	5	6	7	8	9	10	11	12		Lawrence, Hornsby, Turner
4Rr	25	Chester	2-1	0-1	1442	1	2	3	4	5	6	7	8	9	10	11	12		Irvine, Bates
5R	9 Feb	Pwllheli & D.	6-1	4-0	1200			3	4		6	7	8	9	10*	11		2	Irvine(2), Haywood(2), Kearney, Bates
SF	21 Mar	Wrexham	1-1	1-0	6357	1	4	3			6		8	10	9*	11	12	7 5 2	Loughnane
SFr	26 Apr	WREXHAM	4-1	3-0	3585	1	2	3	4	6	10		8	9		11	7	5	King, Maguire(2), Hornsby
F1	16 May	Cardiff C.	1-2	1-0	2907	1	2	3	4	5	6	7	8	9	12	11	10		Hornsby
F2	18	CARDIFF C.	3-0	1-0	3178	1	2	3	4	5	6	7*	8	10	11	9	12		Griffin, O.G., L.Roberts

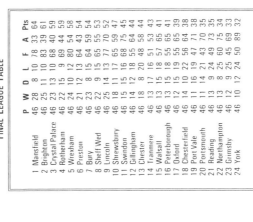

Final League Table

		P	W	D	L	F	A	Pts
1	Mansfield	46	28	8	10	78	33	64
2	Brighton	46	25	11	10	83	39	61
3	Crystal Palace	46	23	13	10	68	40	59
4	Rotherham	46	22	15	9	69	44	59
5	Wrexham	46	24	10	12	80	54	58
6	Preston	46	21	12	13	64	43	54
7	Bury	46	23	8	15	64	59	54
8	Sheff Wed	46	22	9	15	65	55	53
9	Lincoln	46	19	14	13	77	70	52
10	Shrewsbury	46	18	11	17	65	59	47
11	Swindon	46	15	15	16	68	75	45
12	Gillingham	46	16	12	18	55	64	44
13	Chester	46	18	8	20	48	58	44
14	Tranmere	46	13	17	16	51	53	43
15	Walsall	46	13	15	18	57	65	41
16	Peterborough	46	13	15	18	55	65	41
17	Oxford	46	12	15	19	55	64	39
18	Chesterfield	46	14	10	22	56	64	38
19	Port Vale	46	11	16	19	47	71	38
20	Portsmouth	46	11	13	22	43	70	35
21	Reading	46	13	9	24	49	73	35
22	Northampton	46	13	8	25	60	75	34
23	Grimsby	46	12	9	25	45	69	33
24	York	46	10	12	24	50	89	32

Additional Player: Wardle = 1/3

(Back) Malam, Collier, Griffin, Hayes, Mulhearn, Wardle, King, Atkins, Leonard, Barker
(Middle) Irvine, Hornsby, Kearney, Turner, Durban, Bates, Haywood, Maguire
(Front) Lawrence, Moore, Hewson, Hampson, Trench, Steele, Westray, Roberts, Hickenbottom.

SEASON 1977/78
Division 3

No.	Date	Opposition	Res.	H.T.	Att.	Goalscorers	Mulhearn K.	Hayes S.C.	Roberts L.	Turner G.L.	Griffin C.R.	Atkins I.L.	Nixon J.C.	Hornsby B.G.	Bates P.D.	Lindsay J.Y.	Maguire P.	Leonard C.C.	Irvine S.	Loughnane P.	Cross S.C.	Keay J.P.	Durban A.	King J.	Wardle R.I.	Biggins S.J.	Moore K.	Bowers I.
1	20 Aug	WREXHAM	2-1	1-1	5261	Turner, O.G.	1	2	3	4	5	6	7	8	9	10	11											
2	26	Lincoln	3-1	1-1	4714	Maguire, O.G., Irvine	1		3	4	6	5	7*	8	9	10	11		12									
3	3 Sep	EXETER	0-2	0-2	3302		1		3		5	6	7	8*	9	10	11					12	4					
4	7	Chesterfield	1-3	0-2	4060	Loughnane	1		3		5	6	7	8	9	10	11	2		12			4					
5	10	Sheffield Wed.	1-0	1-0	10234	Maguire	1		3		6	5	12	8	9	10	11	2					4					
6	13	CAMBRIDGE	3-3	2-1	2618	Hornsby(2), Irvine	1		3		5	6	12	8	9	10	11	2	7				4					
7	17	WALSALL	0-0	0-0	4635		1			5		6	12	8	10	9	11	2	7				4					
8	24	Bury	3-0	2-0	5430	Maguire, Atkins(pen), Hornsby	1				5	6	12	8	10	9	11	3	7				4	2				
9	27	ROTHERHAM	4-1	2-0	4191	Bates(2), Hornsby, Atkins(pen)	1				5	6	11	8	10	9		3	12				4	2				
10	30	Swindon	0-5	0-1	6809		1				5	6	11	8	10	9		3	12				4	2				
11	4 Oct	Plymouth	2-2	1-2	4661	Nixon, Atkins(pen)	1				5	6	11	8	10	9		3					4	2			12	
12	8	PORT VALE	3-0	2-0	3553	Bates(3)	1				5	6	11	8	10	9		3		12			4*	2				
13	15	Peterborough	1-2	0-1	5563	Durban	1				5	6	11	8	10	9		3		12			4*	2				
14	22	PORTSMOUTH	6-1	3-0	3726	Atkins(3,2pens), Hornsby, Irvine, Nixon	1				5	6	11	8*	10	9		3	7				4	2				
15	29	Gillingham	1-1	0-1	7938	Durban	1				5	6	11		10	9	12	3	7				4	2				
16	5 Nov	HEREFORD	3-0	2-0	6116	Irvine(3,1pen)	1				5	6	11	8	10	9	8	3	7	12			4	2				
17	12	Tranmere	0-2	0-0	4708		1				5	6	11	8	10	9	10*	3	7	12		8	4	2				
18	19	CARLISLE	0-3	0-2	3701		1				5	6		8	9	9	12	3	7			8	4	2				
19	3 Dec	Oxford	1-1	0-1	4551	Bates	1				5	6	11	8	10	9		3	7	12			4*	2				
20	6	GILLINGHAM	1-2	0-0	2907	Irvine	1			6	5	12	11	8	10	9		3	7				4*	2				
21	10	PRESTON N.E.	0-0	0-0	3764		1			4	5	4	11*	8*	10	6		3	7	10				2				
22	26	Chester	0-1	0-0	5701		1	12		4	5	4	12	8	10	11		3	7	9				2				
23	27	BRADFORD C.	4-0	2-0	3929	Bates(2), Irvine, Hornsby	1			4	3	6	8	4	10	9		2	7	11			6		1			
24	31	COLCHESTER	1-0	0-0	4336	Irvine	1			5	3	6	8	4	10	9		2	7	11	12							
25	2 Jan	Hereford	1-1	1-0	6392	Biggins	1	2		5	3	4		8		9	11	3					12		6	7		
26	14	Wrexham	0-0	0-0	13631		1	5		6			12				11	3	7				6	4	6	4		
27	21	LINCOLN	0-1	0-1	3385		1	5		6			12				11	3	7				4	2*	4	2*		
28	28	Exeter	1-1	0-1	3906	Hornsby	1			4	3			8		9	11	3	7		5	5		2				
29	31	CHESTERFIELD	1-1	1-0	2018	Turner	1			4	3	12	11			12	11	3	7	10	5	5		2				
30	11 Feb	Walsall	0-3	0-1	8341		1			4	3	6	6	8		10	11	3	7	10	5	5		2				
31	25	SWINDON	2-3	0-1	3117	Nixon, Maguire	1			4	12	9	11	8		10	12	3	7	9		6		2				
32	28	SHEFFIELD WED.	0-0	0-0	2901		1			4		9	11	8			12	3	7	9	10			2				
33	4 Mar	Port Vale	2-1	1-0	3499	Maguire, Atkins(pen)	1			4		6	8	8*		9	12	3	7	10		5		2				
34	7	Cambridge	0-2	0-1	5090		1			4		9				6	11	3	7	10		5				12	2	
35	11	PETERBOROUGH	0-0	0-0	2591		1			4		9				6	11	3	7	10		5				12	8	12
36	18	Portsmouth	0-2	0-1	8575		1			4		9				6	11	3	7	10		5				12	8	3
37	25	CHESTER	0-0	0-0	2592		1			4	5	8				9	11	3	7	10	5	5		2		4	8	3
38	27	Bradford C.	0-2	0-1	4341		1			4	5	9				12	11	3	7	10	5	5		2			12	3
39	1 Apr	Colchester	2-1	1-0	2910	Loughnane, Biggins	1			4	12	9					11	3	7	10		5		2		10*		3
40	4	Rotherham	0-0	0-0	4262		1				12					4	8	3	7	11		5		2		10		
41	8	TRANMERE	3-1	0-0	2364	Loughnane, Biggins(2)	1				12	9				6	8	3	7	11		4		2		10	12	3
42	15	Carlisle	0-1	0-0	4247		1				12	8				4	8	3	7	11		5		2		10		3
43	18	BURY	5-3	2-1	1727	Maguire(3), Irvine, Biggins	1			11	12	9				6	8	3	7			4		2		10	2	
44	22	OXFORD	1-0	1-0	2510	Biggins	1			11	12	9				6*	8	3	7			4		2		10	8	
45	25	PLYMOUTH	3-1	3-0	2308	Biggins, Atkins, Irvine	1			11	12	10				6*	11	3	7			4		2		9	12	
46	29	Preston N.E.	2-2	2-1	16078	Atkins, Keay	1			8	12	9				6	11	3	7			4		2		10	8	3

F.A. Cup

Rd	Date	Opponent	Score	HT	Att	Scorers
1R	26 Nov	Doncaster R.	1-0	0-0	5279	Nixon
2R	17 Dec	STOCKPORT C.	1-1	1-1	4482	Maguire
2Rr	19	Stockport C.	2-1	1-0	8370	Maguire, Lindsay
3R	7 Jan	Blackburn R.	1-2	1-1	12712	Hornsby

Line-up (shirt numbers):

Rd																
1R	1				5	12	11	8	10	6	9	3	7		4	2
2R	1			4	5		12	8	10	9	11	3	7		6	2
2Rr	1			4	5	12		8	10	9	11	3	7		6	2
3R	1			6	5	4	7	8	10	9	11*	3		12		2

League Cup

Rd	Date	Opponent	Score	HT	Att	Scorers
1R1	13 Aug	Oxford U.	0-3	0-1	3694	
1R2	16	OXFORD U.	2-2	0-1	2253	Bates, Turner

Line-up (shirt numbers):

Rd														
1R1	1	12		2		5	6	7	8	9	10*	11	3	4
1R2	1		3	4		5	6	7	8	9	12	11		10

Welsh Cup

Rd	Date	Opponent	Score	HT	Att	Scorers
4R	11 Jan	PORTMADOC	3-0	2-0	625	Loughnane, Hornsby, Maguire
5R	7 Feb	Bridgend T.	2-1	2-1	1000	Maguire(2)
SF	14 Mar	Bangor C.	2-4	0-1	2200	Turner, Loughnane

Line-up (shirt numbers):

Rd																	
4R	1	2		4		5		7	8	9	11		3	10*	12	6	
5R	1				3*	4		9	8		6	11	2	7	10	5	
SF	1	6		4	12	9				11		3	7	10		2	8

FINAL LEAGUE TABLE

		P	W	D	L	F	A	Pts
1	Wrexham	46	23	15	8	78	45	61
2	Cambridge	46	23	12	11	72	51	58
3	Preston	46	20	16	10	63	38	56
4	Peterborough	46	20	16	10	47	33	56
5	Chester	46	16	22	8	59	56	54
6	Walsall	46	18	17	11	61	50	53
7	Gillingham	46	15	20	11	67	60	50
8	Colchester	46	15	18	13	55	44	48
9	Chesterfield	46	17	14	15	58	49	48
10	Swindon	46	16	16	14	67	60	48
11	Shrewsbury	46	16	15	15	63	57	47
12	Tranmere	46	16	15	15	57	52	47
13	Carlisle	46	14	19	13	59	59	47
14	Sheff Wed	46	15	15	16	50	52	46
15	Bury	46	13	19	14	62	56	45
16	Lincoln	46	15	15	16	53	61	45
17	Exeter	46	15	14	17	49	59	44
18	Oxford	46	13	14	19	64	67	40
19	Plymouth	46	11	17	18	61	68	39
20	Rotherham	46	13	13	20	51	68	39
21	Port Vale	46	8	20	18	46	67	36
22	Bradford	46	12	10	24	56	86	34
23	Hereford	46	9	14	23	34	60	32
24	Portsmouth	46	7	17	22	31	75	31

(Back) Leonard, Hayes, Wardle, Mulhearn, Irvine, L.Roberts, K.Moore.
(2nd Row) J.Nixon, Hornsby, Atkins, Griffin, Maguire.
(Front) Bates, Turner, Durban, King, P.Loughnane.

SEASON 1978/79
Division 3 (Champions)

No.	Date	Opposition	Res.	H.T.	Att.	Goalscorers	Mulhearn	King J.	Leonard C.C.	Turner G.I.	Griffin C.R.	Hayes S.C.	Cross S.C.	Lindsay J.Y.	Atkins I.L.	Biggins S.I.	Maguire P.	Keay J.P.	Loughnane P.	Chapman S.	Tong D.I.	Larkin G.A.	Wardle R.I.	Birch T.N.	Roberts M.	Edwards D.	Jones T.
1	19 Aug	BRENTFORD	1-0	1-0	2346	Atkins(pen)	1	2	3	4	5	6	7*	8	9	10	11	12									
2	23	Oxford	1-0	0-0	3877	Turner	1	2	3	4	5	6		8	9	10	11	12	7								
3	26	SWINDON	0-0	0-0	2672		1	2	3	4	5	6		8	9	10	11	12	7								
4	2 Sep	Walsall	1-1	1-1	4269	Turner	1	2	3	4	5	6		8*	9	10	11		7	12							
5	9	BLACKPOOL	2-0	1-0	4179	Biggins, Maguire	1	2	3	4	5	6	12	8	9	10	11			7							
6	13	Exeter	1-0	0-0	3732	Maguire	1	2	3	4	5	6	12	8	9	10	11			7							
7	15	Colchester	0-1	0-0	2788		1	2	3*	4	5	6	12	7	8	10	11			9							
8	23	LINCOLN	2-0	1-0	2902	Turner, Atkins(pen)	1	2	3	4	5	6	12		9	10	11			7	8						
9	26	HULL	1-0	0-0	3777	Maguire	1	2		4	5	6		12	8	10	11			9	7	3					
10	29	Southend	1-0	0-0	6773	Atkins	1	2		4	5	6		9	8	10	11			7	12	3					
11	7 Oct	MANSFIELD	2-2	2-1	4388	Maguire(2)	1	2		4	5	6		12	9	10	11			7	8*	3					
12	14	Plymouth	1-1	0-0	9901	Atkins		2	3	4	5	6		8	9	10	11			7	12		1				
13	16	Tranmere	2-2	0-1	3087	Atkins(2,1pen)	1	2	3	4	5	6	12	9*	8*	10	11			7							
14	21	SHEFFIELD WED.	2-2	0-0	6294	Maguire, Tong	1	2*	3	4	5	6		8*	9	10	11			7	12						
15	28	Rotherham	2-1	2-0	4476	Turner, Biggins	1	2	3	4	5	6	12		9	10	11			7	8						
16	4 Nov	CARLISLE	0-0	0-0	4656			2	3	4	5	6	12		9	10	11			8	7		1				
17	10	WALSALL	1-1	1-0	7615	Tong		2	3	4	5	6			8	10	11			7	9	12	1				
18	18	Swindon	1-2	2-0	7317	Griffin		2	3	4	5	6		12	9	10	11			7	8		1				
19	6 Dec	Peterborough	2-0	2-0	3087	Griffin, Atkins		2	3	4	5	6		12	9	10	11			7	8		1				
20	9	GILLINGHAM	1-0	0-0	3924	Keay		2	3	4	5			8		10	11	6		7	9	12	1				
21	23	SWANSEA	3-0	2-0	8567	Atkins, Biggins, Maguire		2	3	4	5			12	8*	10	11	6		7	9		1				
22	26	Watford	2-2	1-2	20276	Chapman, Maguire		2	3	4	5			12	8	10	11	6		7	9		1				
23	9 Jan	COLCHESTER	2-0	1-0	2917	Chapman, Biggins		2	3	4	5			12	8	10	11	6		7	9		1				
24	30	CHESTER	1-0	0-0	6693	Biggins		2	3	4	5			12	8	10	11	6		7	9		1				
25	3 Feb	Hull	1-1	1-1	5129	Turner		2	3	4	5			12	8	10	11	6		7	9		1				
26	9	SOUTHEND	2-0	2-0	5749	Chapman, Atkins(pen)		2	3	4	5*		12	7	8	10	11	6			9		1				
27	24	PLYMOUTH	2-0	1-0	6087	Chapman, Maguire		2	3	4	5		12	7	8	10	11	6			9		1				
28	3 Mar	Sheffield Wed.	0-0	0-0	11284			2*	3	4	5				8	10	11	6		7	9		1				
29	7	Chesterfield	1-2	0-0	4324	Tong		2	3	4	5		12		8	10	11	6		7	9		1				
30	17	Carlisle	1-1	0-0	5075	Biggins		2	3	4	5		12	7	8	10	11	6			9*		1				
31	20	Blackpool	0-5	0-1	5330			2	3	4	5		12	7	8	10	11	6			9	2	1				
32	24	OXFORD	0-0	0-0	6791			2	3	4	5		12		8	10	11	6			9		1				
33	26	Brentford	3-2	2-1	7760	Cross, Keay, Biggins		2	3		5		4	11	8	10		6			9*		1	7			
34	31	Bury	0-3	0-0	3340			2	3		5		4	11	8	10		6			9		1	7			
35	7 Apr	PETERBOROUGH	2-0	0-0	5600	King, Cross(pen)	1	2	3		5		4	11	8	10		6			9	2		7	12		
36	10	Swansea	1-1	0-1	19556	Atkins	1	2	3		5		4	11	8	10		6			9	2		7	12		
37	14	WATFORD	1-1	1-1	13320	Birch	1	2	3		5		4	11	8	10		6			9			7	12		
38	16	Chester	0-0	0-0	6249		1	2	3		5			11	4	10	8	6			9			7			
39	21	CHESTERFIELD	1-1	1-0	6360	King	1	2			5			8	4	10	11	6			9	3		7			
40	24	TRANMERE	2-1	0-0	6013	Birch, Maguire	1	2	3		5			8	4	12	11	6			9	3		7	10		
41	28	Gillingham	0-2	0-0	14902		1	2	3		5			10	4	12	11*	6		8	9	3		7			
42	2 May	Lincoln	2-1	0-0	1677	King, Maguire	1	2	3		5			11	4	10	8	6			9	3		7			
43	5	BURY	1-0	0-0	6604		1	2	3		5		4	12		10	8	6			9	3		7			
44	7	Mansfield	2-2	0-1	6413	Biggins, Maguire	1	2	3		5	12	4	7	8	10	11	6			9	3			12		
45	10	ROTHERHAM	3-1	1-1	8450	King, Tong, Maguire	1	2	3		5		4	12	8	10	11	6			9	3		7			
46	17	EXETER	4-1	3-1	14441	King(2), Atkins(pen), Tong	1	2	3		5		4	7	8	10	11	6			9	3			12		

F.A. Cup

	Date	Opponent	Res	HT	Att	Scorers	Line-up (squad numbers)
1R	25 Nov	Mansfield T	2-0	1-0	4881	Biggins, Atkins	2 3 4 5 6 12 8 10 11 7 9 1
2R	16 Dec	Doncaster R.	3-0	1-0	3720	Chapman, Maguire(2)	2 3 4 5 12 8 10 11 6 7 9 3 1
3R	6 Jan	CAMBRIDGE U.	3-1	1-0	7416	Maguire, Turner, Chapman	2 3 4 5 12 8 10 11 6 7 9 3 1
4R	27	MANCHESTER C.	2-0	1-0	14215	Maguire, Chapman	2 3 4 5 12 8 10 11 6 7 9 3 1
5R	20 Feb	Aldershot	2-2	0-0	11895	Maguire, Tong	2 3 4 5 12 8 10 11 6 7 9 3 1
5Rr	26	ALDERSHOT	3-1	1-1	13720	Biggins(2), Leonard	2 3 4 5 12 8 10 11 6 7 9 1
6R	10 Mar	Wolverhampton Wanderers	1-1	0-0	40946	Atkins(pen)	3 4 5 2 12 8 10 11 6 7 9 1
6Rr	13	WOLVERHAMPTON W.	1-3	0-1	16279	Keay	3 4 5 2 12 8 10 11 6 7 9 1

League Cup

	Date	Opponent	Res	HT	Att	Scorers	Line-up (squad numbers)
1R1	14 Aug	STOCKPORT C.	1-0	1-0	2435	Biggins	1 2 3 4 5 6 7 8 10 9 11 12
1R2	16	Stockport C.	1-3	0-2	4025	Cross	1 2 3 4 5 6 7 8 9 10 11 12

Welsh Cup

	Date	Opponent	Res	HT	Att	Scorers	Line-up (squad numbers)
4R	9 Jan	RHYL	6-0	2-0	1513	Cross(2), Biggins, Lindsay, M.Roberts, Edwards	3 6 11 7 8 10* 5 9 2 1 4 12
5R	5 Mar	TON PENTRE	4-0	3-0	1308	Atkins, Cross, Loughnane, Larkin	1 2 5 9 8 6* 10 7 3 11 4 12
SF	4 Apr	WORCESTER C.	2-0	0-0	2616	Biggins, Cross	1 2 4 7 8 3 10 5 6 9 11 12
F1	21 May	Wrexham	1-1	1-1	6174	Biggins	2 5 4 11 8 10 6 9 3 1 7 12
F2	24	WREXHAM	1-0	0-0	8889	Maguire	2 5 4 7 8 10 11 6 9 3 1 12

FINAL LEAGUE TABLE

		P	W	D	L	F	A	Pts
1	Shrewsbury	46	21	19	6	61	41	61
2	Watford	46	24	12	10	83	52	60
3	Swansea	46	24	12	10	83	61	60
4	Gillingham	46	21	17	8	65	42	59
5	Swindon	46	25	7	14	74	52	57
6	Carlisle	46	15	22	9	53	42	52
7	Colchester	46	17	17	12	60	55	51
8	Hull	46	19	11	16	66	61	49
9	Exeter	46	17	15	14	61	56	49
10	Brentford	46	19	9	18	53	49	47
11	Oxford	46	14	18	14	44	50	46
12	Blackpool	46	18	9	19	61	59	45
13	Southend	46	15	15	16	51	49	45
14	Sheff Wed	46	13	19	14	53	53	45
15	Plymouth	46	15	14	17	67	68	44
16	Chester	46	14	16	16	57	61	44
17	Rotherham	46	17	10	19	49	55	44
18	Mansfield	46	12	19	15	51	52	43
19	Bury	46	11	20	15	59	65	42
20	Chesterfield	46	13	14	19	51	65	40
21	Peterborough	46	11	14	21	44	63	36
22	Walsall	46	10	12	24	56	71	32
23	Tranmere	46	6	16	24	45	78	28
24	Lincoln	46	7	11	28	41	88	25

(Back) Wardle, Lindsay, Mulhearn. (2nd Row) Leonard, P.Loughnane, Atkins, Griffin, Cross, Hayes, Larkin, Keay. (3rd Row) Turner (Player/Coach), King, Barker (Manager), Malam, Roberts, Maguire. (Front) I.Loughnane, Jones.

SEASON 1979/80
Division 2

No.	Date	Opposition	Res.	H.T.	Att.	Goalscorers	Mulhearn K.	King J.	Leonard C.C.	Turner G.L.	Griffin C.R.	Keay J.P.	Birch T.N.	Atkins I.L.	Tong D.J.	Biggins S.J.	Mann A.F.	Cross S.C.	Larkin G.A.	Edwards D.	Lindsay J.	Chapman S.	Wardle R.I.	Hayes S.C.	Maguire P.	Dungworth J.	Coyne B.	Neil M.
1	18 Aug	Swansea	0-2	0-0	17041	Griffin	1	2	3	4	5	6	7	8	9	10	11				12							
2	21	NOTTS COUNTY	1-1	0-0	7369	Tong(pen)	1	2	3	4	5	6	7	8	9	10*	11	12										
3	25	Bristol Rovers	1-2	0-2	5713	Turner	1	2	3	4	5	6	7	8	9		11	10			12							
4	1 Sep	CAMBRIDGE	0-1	1-0	5670	Turner	1	2		4	5	6		8	9	10	11		3		12							
5	8	Cardiff	0-1	0-0	8688		1	2	3		5	6	7	8	9		11	4*		12	10							
6	15	CHELSEA	3-0	0-0	9271	Biggins, Mann, Keay(pen)	1	2	3		5	6	7	8	9	10	11	12			4							
7	22	Charlton	1-2	0-0	5283	Birch	1		3		5	6	7	8	9	10*	11		2		4							
8	29	ORIENT	1-0	0-0	6176	Biggins	1	2	3		5	6		8	12	10	11			7		9						
9	6 Oct	LEICESTER	2-2	1-0	9045	Chapman, King	1	2	3		5	6		4	7	10		11		8	12	9						
10	9	Notts County	2-5	1-3	7251	Atkins, O.G.	1	2	3		5	6		8	4	10		11		7		9					12	
11	13	Newcastle	0-1	0-1	21513			2		4*	5	6		8	7	9		11				10*	1	3				
12	20	WREXHAM	3-1	2-1	11007	Biggins(3)				4*	5	6		7	11	10		12	3			9	1	2				
13	27	Birmingham	0-1	0-0	17869						5	6	11*	8	7			12	3			4	1	2	9	10		
14	3 Nov	SWANSEA	2-2	0-1	9815	Dungworth, Keay(pen)	1				5	6		4	8	12		11	3			7*		2	9	10		
15	10	Watford	1-0	0-0	8150	Keay(pen)	1				5	6		8	7	11			3		4			2	9	10	12	
16	17	Q.P.Rangers	1-2	0-1	12048	King	1	2			5	6		8	7	9			3		4	12			11	10		
17	24	Oldham	2-0	1-0	6332	Maguire(2)	1	2			5	6		8	7	11			3		9	12				10		
18	1 Dec	LUTON	1-2	1-2	8559	Keay	1	2			5	6		8	7	9			3		4	12			11	10		
19	8	Fulham	1-2	1-2	5337	Keay(pen)	1	2			5	6		8	7	12			3		4				11	10		
20	15	WEST HAM	3-0	0-0	8513	Maguire, Chapman, Atkins	1	2			5	6		8	7	12			3		4	9*			11	10		
21	21	Sunderland	1-2	0-1	21237	Maguire	1	2			5	6		8	7	12			3		4	9			11	10		
22	26	Preston N.E.	0-3	0-1	8875		1	2*			5	6		8	7	4		12	3			9*			11	10		
23	29	BRISTOL ROVERS	3-1	2-0	7097	Biggins, King, O.G.		2			5	6		8	7	9			3			12	1		11	10		
24	1 Jan	BURNLEY	2-0	1-0	10506	King, Maguire		2			5	6		8	7	9			3			12	1		11	10		
25	12	Cambridge	0-2	0-0	5179			2			5	6			8	9		7	12				1		11	10		
26	19	CARDIFF	1-2	0-0	6870	Dungworth		2			5	6			8	9		7		12			1		11	10		
27	2 Feb	Chelsea	4-2	3-1	18120	Dungworth(2), Keay(pen), Atkins		2			5	6		8	7	9							1		11	10	12	
28	9	CHARLTON	3-1	1-0	6988	Biggins, Dungworth, King		2			5	6		8	7	9							1		11	10	12	
29	16	Orient	1-0	0-0	4326	Biggins		2			5	6		8	7	9							1		11	10	12	
30	23	NEWCASTLE	3-1	2-0	10833	Maguire, King, Biggins		2			5	6		8	7	9					12		1		11	10		
31	1 Mar	Wrexham	1-0	1-0	12844	Maguire		2			5	6		8	7	9					12		1		11	10		
32	8	BIRMINGHAM	1-0	1-0	14801	Maguire		2			5	6		8	7	9					12		1		11	10		
33	15	Leicester	0-2	0-2	15391			2			5	6		8	7	9							1		11	10	12	
34	22	Watford	1-0	1-0	12833	Dungworth		2*			5	6	9	8	7			12					1		11	10		
35	29	Q.P.RANGERS	3-0	2-0	9050	Keay(pen), Turner, Biggins					5	6		8	7	9		2	12				1		11	10		
36	1 Apr	PRESTON N.E.	1-3	1-2	8643	Biggins		2			5	6		8	7	9		12					1		11	10		
37	5	Burnley	0-0	0-0	6258			2			5	6	10		7	9		12		8			1		11*			
38	8	SUNDERLAND	1-2	0-1	12346	Birch		2			5	6	10	8	7	9		11			12		1					
39	12	Luton	0-0	0-0	10739			2			5	6		8	7	9		11			12		1			10		
40	19	OLDHAM	0-1	0-1	6862			2			5	6		8	7	9		12					1		11	10		
41	26	West Ham	3-1	2-0	19765	Maguire, Keay(pen), Biggins		2			5	6		8	7	9		12					1		11	10		
42	3 May	FULHAM	5-2	2-0	6328	Biggins, Keay(pen), Dungworth, O.G., King		2			5	6		8	7	9		12					1		11	10		4

F.A.Cup

Rnd	Date	Opponent	FT	HT	Att.	Scorers	2	3	4	5*	6	8	7	9		12		1	11	10	
3R	5 Jan	Millwall	1-5	0-2	7026	Maguire	2	3	4	5	6	8	9	10		12		1	11	10	7

League Cup

Rnd	Date	Opponent	FT	HT	Att.	Scorers	2	3	4	5*	6	8	7	9		12		1	11	10	
1R1	11 Aug	Halifax T.	2-2	1-1	1904	Turner, Maguire	2	3	4	5	6	8	9	10	11	12		1	11	10	7
1R2	14	HALIFAX T.	1-0	0-0	4820	Atkins	2	3	4	5	6	8	9	10	11	12		1	11	10	7
2R1	29	Chesterfield	0-3	0-1	5119		2	3		5	6	8	9	10	3			1	11	10	
2R2	5 Sep	CHESTERFIELD	0-0	0-0	4270		2	3		5	6	8	9	10	4	12		1	11	10	4

Welsh Cup

Rnd	Date	Opponent	FT	HT	Att.	Scorers	2	3	4	5*	6	8	7	9		12		1	11	10	
4R	8 Jan	OSWESTRY T.	2-2	1-0	1392	Cross, Maguire	2	3		12	8	6		9	6		4	1	5	11	10	7
4Rr	23	Oswestry T.	6-1	4-0	2124	Biggins(3), Coyne, Tong, Maguire	2	3	4	6	8		7	9*	12		5	1	11	10
5R	26 Feb	NANTLLE VALE	4-1	2-1	1386	Atkins, Dungworth, King, Edwards	2		4	5	6	8			3	12	1	11	10
SF	25 Mar	Swansea C.	2-2	1-2	10021	Atkins, Dungworth		3*	5	6	9	8	7		2	12	1	11	10	4
SFr	15 Apr	SWANSEA C. *	6-5	1-0	6698	Turner,Dungworth (Keay,Dngwrth,Atkins,Mguire,)	2	3	4	6	8	8	9	7	5	1	11	10	12
F1	6 May	Newport C.	1-2	1-1	9950	O.G.	2	3	4	5	6	8	7	9	12	1	11	10
F2	12	NEWPORT C.	0-3	0-2	8993		2	3*	4	5	6	8	7	9	12	1	11	10	4

* Score 2-2 after extra time.

Staffordshire Senior Cup

Rnd	Date	Opponent	FT	HT	Att.	Scorers	4	10	8	9	3	5
2R	19 Nov	Tamworth	1-2		208	Edwards	4	10	8	9	3	5

Additional Players: Perks = 1, Jones = 2, Mark Adams = 6, Roberts = 7, Perry = 11, Andrew Owen = 12

(Back) Malam (asst. coach), Keay, Mann, Maguire, Atkins, Wardle, Griffin, Mulhearn, Hayes, Birch, Neil, Jones, Turner (P/Manager)
(Front) Adams, Leonard, Larkin, Tong, Biggins, King, Cross, Lindsay, Roberts, Croft, Edwards, McNally.

FINAL LEAGUE TABLE

		P	W	D	L	F	A	Pts
1	Leicester	42	21	13	8	58	38	55
2	Sunderland	42	21	12	9	69	42	54
3	Birmingham	42	21	11	10	58	38	53
4	Chelsea	42	23	7	12	66	52	53
5	QPR	42	18	13	11	75	53	49
6	Luton	42	16	17	9	66	45	49
7	West Ham	42	20	7	15	54	43	47
8	Cambridge	42	14	16	12	61	53	44
9	Newcastle	42	15	14	13	53	49	44
10	Preston	42	12	19	11	56	52	43
11	Oldham	42	16	11	15	49	53	43
12	Swansea	42	17	9	16	48	53	43
13	Shrewsbury	42	18	5	19	60	53	41
14	Orient	42	12	17	13	48	54	41
15	Cardiff	42	12	16	14	41	48	40
16	Wrexham	42	16	6	20	40	49	38
17	Notts County	42	11	15	16	51	52	37
18	Watford	42	12	13	17	39	46	37
19	Bristol Rovers	42	11	13	18	50	64	35
20	Fulham	42	7	15	24	42	74	29
21	Burnley	42	6	15	21	39	73	27
22	Charlton	42	6	10	26	39	78	22

No.	Date	Opposition	Res.	H.T.	Att.	Goalscorers	Wardle R.I.	King J.	Leonard C.C.	Turner G.L.	Griffin C.R.	Keay J.P.	Tong D.J.	Atkins I.L.	Biggins S.J.	Dungworth	Petts P.A.	Lindsay J.Y.	Cross S.C.	Edwards D.	Larkin G.A.	MacLaren R.	Bates P.D.	McNally B.A.	Coyne B.	Jones G.
1	16 Aug	GRIMSBY	1-1	1-1	4998	King	1	2	3	4	5	6	7	8	9	10	11	12								
2	19	Swansea	1-2	0-0	12731	King	1	2	3	4	5	6	7	8	9	10	11	12								
3	23	CHELSEA	2-2	1-2	6672	Atkins, Biggins	1	2	3	4	5	6	7	8*	9	10	11	12								
4	30	Blackburn	0-2	0-1	8465		1	2	3*	4	5	6	7	8	9	10	11	12								
5	6 Sep	WATFORD	2-1	1-1	5500	Dungworth(2)	1	2	3	4	5	6	7	8*		10	11		12	9						
6	13	West Ham	0-3	0-1	22339		1	2	3	4	5	6	7	8		9	11	12		10						
7	20	CAMBRIDGE	2-1	1-0	4465	King, Dungworth	1	2		4	5	6	7	12	9*	10	11				3					
8	27	Preston N.E.	0-0	0-0	6309		1	2		4	5	6	7	12	9	10	11	8*			3					
9	4 Oct	Oldham	0-0	0-0	6093		1	2		4	5	6	7	8		10	11			9*	3					
10	7	BOLTON	1-2	0-0	5077	Turner	1	2	3	4	5	6	7	8		10	12		11	9	3					
11	11	ORIENT	1-2	1-1	4300	Keay(pen)	1	2	3	4	5	6	7	8	9	10	11		12							
12	18	Luton	1-1	0-0	8014	Turner	1	2	3	4	5		7	8	9	10	11	12			6*					
13	22	Newcastle	0-1	0-0	11973		1	2	3	4	5		7	8	9	10	11	12						12		
14	25	CARDIFF	2-0	0-0	4466	Keay(pen), Biggins	1	2	3	4	5	6	7	8	9	10	11	12								
15	1 Nov	Derby	1-1	1-0	15784	Keay(pen)	1	2	3	12	5	6	7	8	9	10	4*		11							
16	8	BRISTOL ROVERS	3-1	1-1	4446	Atkins, Biggins, Cross	1	2	3		5	6	7	8	9	10	4		11			12				
17	11	SWANSEA	0-0	0-0	5863		1	2	3*		5	6	7	8	9	10	4		11			12				
18	15	Grimsby	0-1	0-0	8737		1	2		12	5	6	7	8	9	10	4		11		3					
19	22	NOTTS COUNTY	1-1	0-0	5352	Biggins	1	2			5	6	7	8	9		4	10	11	12	3					
20	29	Q.P.Rangers	0-0	0-0	7982		1	2		4	5	6	7	8	9			10	11	12	3					
21	6 Dec	BRISTOL CITY	4-0	1-0	4435	Biggins, Tong, Atkins, Edwards	1	2		4	5	6	7*	8	9	10			11	12	3					
22	13	Orient	0-1	0-0	4801		1	2		4*	5	6	7	8	9	10			11		3					
23	19	LUTON	0-1	0-1	4521		1	2		4*	5*	6	7	8		10			11		3		9			
24	26	Sheffield Wed.	1-1	3-0	22863	Atkins	1	2	3	4	5	6	7	8		10			11				9			
25	27	WREXHAM	1-2	1-2	8320	Keay(pen)	1	2	3	4	5	6	7	8*	12	10			11				9		12	
26	10 Jan	Notts County	0-0	0-0	7139		1	2	3	4	5	6	7	8		12			11			12	9			
27	17	BLACKBURN	1-1	1-0	5212	Bates	1	2	3	4*	5	6	7	8	12	10			11			12	9			
28	31	Chelsea	0-3	0-2	14673		1	2	3	4	5	6	7	8	12	10			11*				9			
29	7 Feb	WEST HAM	0-2	0-1	9201		1	2	3	4	5	6	7*	8		10			11			10	9			
30	14	Watford	0-1	0-1	11034		1	2	3	4	5	6	7	8		10	11	8	11		12	4*	9			
31	21	PRESTON N.E.	3-0	3-0	4660	Keay(pen), Turner, Biggins	1	2	3	4	5	6	7	8	10	9					12		12	11*		
32	28	Cambridge	1-3	0-1	4007	Bates	1	2	3	4	5	6	7	8	10		11						12			
33	7 Mar	OLDHAM	2-2	0-0	4196	Keay(pen), King	1	2	3*	4	5	6	7	8	10	12			11				9			
34	14	Bolton	2-0	1-0	7900	Dungworth, O.G.	1	2	3	4	5		7	8*	10	9			11		5		12			
35	21	NEWCASTLE	1-0	0-0	4975	Turner	1	2	3	4	5	6	7	8	10	9			11		6		12			
36	28	Cardiff	2-2	2-1	5201	Atkins, Keay(pen)	1	2	3	4	5	6	7	8	10	9			11				12			
37	4 Apr	DERBY	1-0	1-0	6668	King	1	2	3	4	5	6	7	8	10	9			11*				12	11*		
38	11	Bristol Rovers	1-1	1-1	4151	Biggins	1	2	3	4	5	6	7	8	10	9			11				12			
39	18	Wrexham	2-1	1-0	8416	Biggins, Atkins	1	2	3	4	5	6	7	8	10	9			11				12			
40	21	SHEFFIELD WED.	2-0	1-0	8118	Biggins, O.G.	1	2	3	4	5	6	7	8	10	9			11				12			
41	25	Bristol City	1-1	0-1	5698	Cross	1	2	3	4	5	6	7	8	10*	9*			11				12			
42	2 May	Q.P.RANGERS	3-3	1-2	5714	Dungworth, Keay(pen), King	1	2	3	4	5	6	7	8*	10	9			11			12	10			

F.A. Cup

Rd	Date	Opponent	FT	HT	Att	Scorers												
3R	3 Jan	Huddersfield	3-0	1-0	14713	O.G., Cross, Bates	1	2	3	4	5	6	7	8	10*	11	12	9
4R	24	IPSWICH T.	0-0	0-0	18000		1	2	3	4	5	6	7	8	10	11	12	9
4Rr	27	Ipswich T.	0-3	0-1	27543		1	2	3	4	5	6	7	8	9*	11	12	10

League Cup

Rd	Date	Opponent	FT	HT	Att	Scorers												
1R		Bye																
2R1	26 Aug	NORWICH C.	1-1	0-1	5536	Biggins	1	2	3	4	5	6	7	8	9	10	11	12
2R2	3 Sep	Norwich C.	0-2	0-0	9185		1	2	3	4	5	6	7	8	9*	10	11	12

Welsh Cup

Rd	Date	Opponent	FT	HT	Att	Scorers												
3R	18 Nov	LLANIDLOES	5-0	3-0	1714	Edwards(2), Cross(2), Keay(pen)	1	2	3	4	5	6	7	8	9	10	11	12
4R	13 Jan	ABERCYNON ATH.	6-1	3-0	2778	Biggins(3), Larkin, Cross, Dungworth			3	4*	5	6	7	8	9	10	11	12
5R	17 Feb	HEREFORD U.	2-2	0-2	2350	Dungworth, McNally	2	3	4	5	6	7	8	9	10	11	12	
5Rr	4 Mar	Hereford U.	0-5	0-1	3003			3		5	6	7	8	9*	10	11	2	12

(Back) Adams, Coyne, Wardle, Jones, Leonard
(Middle) Jones, Keay, McLaren, Edwards, Griffin, Atkins, Biggins, Larkin, Hawkins
(Front) Dungworth, Cross, King, Turner, Tong, Petts, Bates.

Final League Table

		P	W	D	L	F	A	Pts
1	West Ham	42	28	10	4	79	29	66
2	Notts County	42	18	17	7	49	38	53
3	Swansea	42	18	14	10	64	44	50
4	Blackburn	42	16	18	8	42	29	50
5	Luton	42	18	12	12	61	46	48
6	Derby	42	15	15	12	57	52	45
7	Grimsby	42	15	15	12	44	42	45
8	QPR	42	15	13	14	56	46	43
9	Watford	42	16	11	15	50	45	43
10	Shef Wed	42	17	8	17	53	51	42
11	Newcastle	42	14	14	14	30	45	42
12	Chelsea	42	14	12	16	46	41	40
13	Cambridge	42	17	6	17	53	65	40
14	Shrewsbury	42	11	17	14	46	47	39
15	Oldham	42	12	15	15	39	48	39
16	Wrexham	42	12	14	16	43	45	38
17	Orient	42	13	12	17	52	56	38
18	Bolton	42	14	10	18	61	66	38
19	Cardiff	42	12	13	17	44	60	36
20	Preston	42	11	14	17	41	62	36
21	Bristol City	42	7	16	19	29	51	30
22	Bristol Rovers	42	5	13	24	34	65	23

SEASON 1981/82
Division 2

No.	Date	Opposition	Res.	H.T.	Att.	Goalscorers	Wardle R.I.	Leonard C.C.	Johnson P.	Petts P.A.	Griffin C.R.	Keay J.P.	Tong D.	McNally B.A.	Atkins I.L.	Bates P.D.	Cross S.C.	Dungworth J.	MacLaren R.	Biggins S.J.	Gibson C.	Edwards D.	King J.	Turner G.L.	Blake N.L.	Perks S.
1	29 Aug	Barnsley	0-4	0-2	13344		1	2	3	4	5	6	7*	8	9	10	11	12								
2	1 Sep	BLACKBURN	1-2	1-0	4220	Atkins	1	2	3	4	5	6	7	8	9	10	11	11	12							
3	5	DERBY	4-1	1-0	4373	Atkins(2), Bates, Tong	1	2	3	4	5	6	7	8	9	11										
4	12	Oldham	1-1	1-0	3994	Bates	1	2	3	4	5	12	7	8	9*	11			6							
5	19	CHELSEA	1-0	0-0	5616	Biggins	1	2	3	4	5		7	8	9	11			6	10*	12					
6	23	Newcastle	0-2	0-1	13846		1	2	3	4	5		7	8	9	11			6	10						
7	26	Crystal Palace	1-0	0-0	9803	Bates	1	2	3	4	5		7	8	9	11			6	10*						
8	3 Oct	ROTHERHAM	2-1	1-1	4646	O.G., McNally	1	2	3	4*	5		7*	8	9	11			6	10						
9	10	CHARLTON	1-1	1-0	4336	Bates	1	2	3	4	5	5	7	8	9	11			6	10						
10	17	Norwich	1-2	1-1	11979	Petts	1	2	3	4		5	7	8	9*	11			6	10						
11	24	Cardiff	1-1	0-0	4357	Atkins	1	2	3	4		5	7	8*	9	11	10		6			12				
12	31	WATFORD	0-2	0-2	5672		1	2*	4	4		5	7	8*	9	11	10		6	10		12				
13	7 Nov	Cambridge	0-2	0-1	3815		1	2*	3	4	3	6	7	12	9	11	10	8	12				2	12		
14	14	BOLTON	2-0	1-0	4062	O.G., Atkins(pen)	1	12	3		5	6	7		9	11	4	8	2							
15	21	Q.P.RANGERS	2-1	1-1	4675	Atkins(2,1pen)	1	12	3	12	5	6	7*		9	11	4	8	2	10*			2	12		
16	25	Blackburn	0-0	0-0	6892		1		3	12	5	6	7	8	9	11	4	8	2							
17	28	Orient	0-2	0-2	3327		1		3	12	5	6	7	8	9	11	4	8	2		10					
18	5 Dec	LUTON	2-2	2-1	5259	Dungworth, Atkins	1	12	3	4	5	6	7	10	9	11	4	8*	2							
19	30 Jan	Chelsea	1-3	0-1	11446	Atkins	1		3	4	5*	6	7	10	9	11	4	8	2							
20	2 Feb	BARNSLEY	0-2	0-0	4382		1	12	3	12	5	6	7	10	9	11	4	8*	2	8						
21	6	OLDHAM	2-1	1-1	4970	Cross, Biggins	1		3		5	6	7	10	9	11	4		2	8						
22	16	Rotherham	0-3	0-1	7497		1	12	3		5	6	7*	10*	9	11	4			10			2	10		
23	20	NEWCASTLE	0-0	0-0	4636		1	2	3		5		12	8	9	11	4	12			10					
24	27	Charlton	0-1	0-1	4575		1	2	3	12	5		7	8*	9	11	4	12			10					
25	2 Mar	Sheffield Wed.	0-0	0-0	13254		1	2	3*		5		7	10	9	12	4	8		10				11		
26	10	Derby	1-1	0-1	7518	Atkins	1	2	3		5*	7	7	12	9	11	4	10	6					8		
27	13	CARDIFF	1-1	1-0	4089	Dungworth	1	2	3		5			8	9	11	4	10	6					12		
28	16	WREXHAM	1-1	1-0	4741	Dungworth	1	2	3		5			12	9	11	4	10	6	7				8		
29	20	Watford	1-3	0-1	11780	Dungworth	1	2	3			12		8	9	11	4	10	6	7				8		
30	27	CAMBRIDGE	1-0	1-0	3159	Atkins	1	2	3			8		8	9	11	4*	10	6	7					5	
31	30	LEICESTER	1-1	1-1	5340	Atkins(pen)	1	2	3					12	9		4	10	6	7*	12			11*	5	
32	3 Apr	Bolton	1-1	0-1	5883	Atkins(pen)	1	2	3*	12				8	9		4	10	6	7	12			11	5	
33	10	SHEFFIELD WED.	0-1	0-0	8103		1	2	3				8	8	9	11	4	10	6	7*	12				5	
34	12	Wrexham	0-1	0-0	6506		1		3	7	2		12	12	9	11	4*	10	6		8				5	
35	17	Q.P.Rangers	1-2	0-0	11148	Dungworth	1	2	3	9	5		12	8	9	11	4	10	6	7*			2			
36	20	NORWICH	0-2	0-2	3590		1	12	3	7	2		9	8	9	11	4	10	6		8		2		5	
37	24	ORIENT	2-0	0-0	2898	Atkins(2)	1	2	3	12	5	6	7	8	9	11	10		2					4		
38	27	Grimsby	1-5	1-1	7051	Johnson	1	2	3	12	5	6	7	8	9	11	10		2					4		
39	30	Luton	1-4	0-1	14563	Atkins	1	3*	3	12	5	6	7	8	9	11	10		2					4		
40	4 May	CRYSTAL PALACE	1-0	0-0	3159	Atkins	1	2	3	12	5	6	7	8	9	11	10		2					4		
41	8	GRIMSBY	2-0	1-0	4036	Cross(2)	1	2	3	12	5	6	7	8	9	11	10		6					4		
42	15	Leicester	0-0	0-0	11368		1	2	3	12	5	6	7	8	9	11	10		2					4		

F.A. Cup

3R	5 Jan	PORT VALE	1-0	0-0	7230	Bates	1	3	12	5	6	7	10*	9	11	4	8	2
4R	23	BURNLEY	1-0	0-0	7674	Bates	1	3	12	5	6	7	10	8	11*	4*	9	2
5R	13 Feb	IPSWICH T.	2-1	2-0	13965	Cross, King	1	3		5	6	7	8	9	11	4	12	10*
6R	6 Mar	Leicester C.	2-5	2-2	29117	Bates, Keay	1	3		5	6	7	8	9	11	4	12	10	2*

League Cup

1R		Bye																	
2R1	6 Oct	WEST BROMWICH A.	3-3	0-3	9291	Atkins(pen), Biggins, McLaren	1	2	3	6	4		8	7	11	9	12	5	10
2R2	28	West Bromwich A.	1-2	0-2	12598	Atkins	1	2	3	4		5	7	8	9	11	12	6	10

Welsh Cup

3R	1 Dec	OSWESTRY T.	4-1	1-0	684	Dungworth, Cross, McLaren, Atkins	1	3	12	4	5	6	7	10	9		11	8	2
4R	13 Jan	Caernarfon T.	8-1	4-0	850	Keay, Dungworth, Atkins(5), Cross	1	3	12	5	6	7	10	9		11	4	8	2
5R	24 Feb	Bangor C.	1-2	1-2	2403	Tong	3	12		5		6	4			8	2	11	9	10	7	1

FINAL LEAGUE TABLE

		P	W	D	L	F	A	Pts
1	Luton	42	25	13	4	86	46	88
2	Watford	42	23	11	8	76	42	80
3	Norwich	42	22	5	15	64	50	71
4	Sheff Wed	42	20	10	12	55	51	70
5	QPR	42	21	6	15	65	43	69
6	Barnsley	42	19	10	13	59	41	67
7	Rotherham	42	20	7	15	66	54	67
8	Leicester	42	18	12	12	56	48	66
9	Newcastle	42	18	8	16	52	50	62
10	Blackburn	42	16	11	15	47	43	59
11	Oldham	42	15	14	13	50	51	59
12	Chelsea	42	15	12	15	60	60	57
13	Charlton	42	13	12	17	50	65	51
14	Cambridge	42	13	9	20	48	53	48
15	Crystal Palace	42	13	9	20	34	45	48
16	Derby	42	12	12	18	53	68	48
17	Grimsby	42	11	13	18	53	65	46
18	Shrewsbury	42	11	3	18	37	57	46
19	Bolton	42	13	7	22	39	61	46
20	Cardiff	42	12	8	22	45	61	44
21	Wrexham	42	11	11	20	40	56	44
22	Orient	42	10	9	23	39	61	39

(Back) Turner, King, MacLaren, Dungworth, Wardle, Petts, Griffin, Atkins, Hawkins.
(Front) Biggins, Leonard, McNally, Tong, Cross, Bates, Johnson, Keay.

SEASON 1982/83
Division 2

No.	Date	Opposition	Res.	H.T.	Att.	Goalscorers	Ogrizovic S.	Williams W.	Johnson P.	Turner G.L.	Pearson N.	Griffin C.R.	Petts P.A.	MacLaren R.	Brown Alan	Cross S.C.	Bates P.D.	Sankey M.A.	Stevens G.M.	Leonard C.C.	McNally B.	Robinson C.	Foster K.A.	Nardiello G.	Perks S.
1	28 Aug	Oldham	0-1	0-1	3731		1	2	3	4*	5	6	7	8	9	10	11	12							
2	4 Sep	FULHAM	0-1	0-0	3525		1	2	3		5	6	4	8	9	7	11	12	10						
3	7	Crystal Palace	1-2	0-1	6578	Petts	1	2	3		5	6	4	8	9	7	11	12	10						
4	11	Grimsby	0-2	0-0	7599		1	2	3	12	5	6	4	8	9	7	11		10						
5	18	NEWCASTLE	2-1	1-1	7907	Bates, Brown	1	2	3		5	6	4*	8	9*	7	11	12	10						
6	25	Burnley	2-1	1-1	6436	MacLaren(pen), Bates	1	2	3		5	6	4	8	9*	7	11	12	10						
7	28	CAMBRIDGE	2-1	1-1	2974	Stevens, Cross	1	2	3	5		6	4	8		7	11	12	10	9					
8	2 Oct	LEICESTER	0-2	0-1	5223		1	2	3	9*		6	4	8		7	11		10	5*					
9	9	MIDDLESBROUGH	2-2	1-0	3620	Stevens, Petts	1	2	3		5	6	4	8	9	7	11	12	10*						
10	16	Q.P.Rangers	0-4	0-3	9275		1	2	3		5	6	4	8	9	7	11	12	10*						
11	23	ROTHERHAM	2-0	0-0	3926	Johnson, Petts	1	2	3		5	6	4	8	9	7	11	12			10				
12	30	Barnsley	2-2	2-2	11150	MacLaren, Brown	1	2	3		5	6	4	8	9*	7	11	12			10*				
13	6 Nov	Bolton	4-1	1-0	4879	Petts(2), Williams, Cross	1	2			5	6	4	8	9*	7	11	12		3	10				
14	13	SHEFFIELD WED.	1-0	0-0	8033	Brown	1	2			5	6	4*	8	9	7	11	12		3	10*				
15	20	Chelsea	2-1	0-0	8690	McNally, Cross	1	2		12	5	6	4	8		7	11		9	3	10				
16	27	CHARLTON	0-0	0-0	4477		1	2		12	5	6	4	8	9	7	11			3	10				
17	4 Dec	Carlisle	3-2	2-2	4226	Bates(2), Brown	1	2			5	6	4*	8	9	7	11		12	3	10				
18	11	BLACKBURN	0-0	0-0	4833		1	2		8	5	6	4		9	7	11		12	3	10				
19	18	Leeds	1-1	0-1	8741	MacLaren(pen)	1	2		12	5	6	4	8	9	7	11			3*	10				
20	27	WOLVES	0-2	0-1	13336		1	2			5	6	4	8	9	7	11		12	3*	10				
21	29	Derby	3-2	2-0	13068	Cross, Stevens, Brown	1	2			5	6	4	8	9*	7	11		12	3	10				
22	1 Jan	CHELSEA	2-0	0-0	7545	Stevens, Brown	1	2	3		5	6	4*	8	9	7	12		11		10				
23	3	Fulham	1-2	0-0	7786	Cross	1	2	3		5	6	4*		9	7	12		11	8	10*				
24	15	OLDHAM	0-0	0-0	4630		1	2	3		5	6	4	8	9	7	12		11		10				
25	22	Newcastle	0-4	0-1	19352		1	2	3		5	6	12	8	9	7	4		11		10				
26	5 Feb	CRYSTAL PALACE	1-1	1-1	3716	Brown	1	2*	3		5	6	4*	8	9	7	12		11		10				
27	22	Leicester	2-3	1-1	6155	Williams, Robinson	1	2	3	4	5			8	9	7	10		11	6		12			
28	26	Q.P.RANGERS	0-0	0-0	4397		1	2	3		5		4	8	9	7	10		11	6		12			
29	5 Mar	Rotherham	3-0	1-0	4810	Williams, Bates, Brown	1	2	3		5	4*		8	9	7	6*	12	11			10			
30	8	Middlesbrough	1-2	1-1	7406	MacLaren	1	2	3		5	4		8	9	7	6	12	11			10			
31	12	BARNSLEY	3-1	0-1	4024	MacLaren(pen), Robinson, Pearson	1	2	3		5	4		8	9	7	11		6		12	10			
32	19	BOLTON	1-0	1-0	4163	Brown	1	2	3		5	4		8	9	7	11		6			10			
33	26	Sheffield Wed.	0-0	0-0	14320		1	2	3		5	4		8	9	7	11		6			10			
34	2 Apr	DERBY	1-1	0-1	7194	Robinson	1	2	3	12	5	4		8	9	7	11		6			10			
35	4	Wolves	2-2	1-2	17509	Bates(2)	1	2	3	4	5			8	9	7	11		6		10	12			
36	8	GRIMSBY	0-0	0-0	4446		1	2	3		5	4		8	9		11		6		7	10			
37	16	Cambridge	0-0	0-0	3615		1	2	3		5	4*		8	9		11		6		7	10			
38	23	CARLISLE	2-1	0-0	3220	Williams, Bates	1	2	3		5	4		8	9*		11		6		7	10			
39	29	Charlton	1-0	0-0	4838	Brown	1	2	3		5	4		8	9	10	11		6		7				
40	3 May	BURNLEY	1-2	0-0	3573	Bates	1	2	3		5	4*		8	9	10	11		6		7				
41	7	LEEDS	0-0	0-0	6052		1	2	3		5	4*		8	9		11		6		7	10	12		
42	14	Blackburn	0-1	0-1	3797		1	2	3		5	4*		8	9		11		6		7		10	12	

F.A.Cup

	Date	Opponent		HT	Att	Scorers	1	2	3		5	6	4		9	7	12	11	8	10
3R	8 Jan	ROTHERHAM U.	2-1	0-0	6027	Brown(2)	1	12	3		5	6	7		8	9	2	4	11	10
4R	30	Everton	1-2	0-1	35188	Cross	1		3		5	6	7		8	9	2	4	11	10

League Cup

	Date	Opponent		HT	Att	Scorers	1	2	3		5	6	4		9	7	12	11	8	10
1R1	31 Aug	Wrexham	0-1	0-1	3218		1	2	3		5	6	7		9	11	8	10	4	
1R2	14 Sep	WREXHAM	2-0	0-0	2850	Brown, Cross	1	2	3	12	5	4	6		11	8	9	7	10	
2R1	5 Oct	BIRMINGHAM C.	1-1	1-1	5003	Cross	1	2	3	9	5		4	8		7	11	12	10	6
2R2	26	Birmingham C.	1-4	1-1	7861	Brown	1	2	3		4	6	7	5	10	11	8	12		9

Welsh Cup

	Date	Opponent		HT	Att	Scorers	2	3	4	6	5		9	12	11	8	10	7	1
3R	14 Dec	Rhyl	1-1	1-0	1800	Brown(pen)	2	3	4	6	5		8		10	7			1
3Rr	20	RHYL	3-0	1-0	513	McNally, Stevens, Johnson	2	6	4	5			7	9	3	10	11		1
4R	18 Jan	Swansea C.	1-2	0-2	4511	Stevens	2	3		4	5		7	6	11	9	8	10	12	1

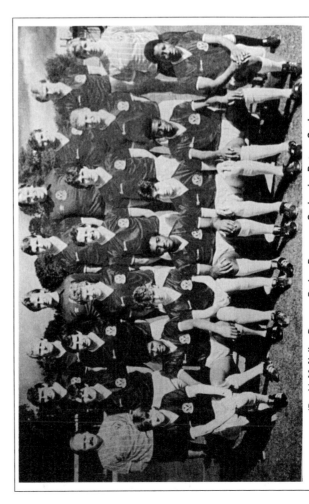

(Back) McNally, Brown, Perks, Pearson, Ogrizovic, Bates, Sankey
(Middle) Jones (Trainer), Williams, Griffin, Petts, Johnson, MacLaren, Cross, Turner (Man.)
(Front) Edge, Kerr, Pike, Foster, Nardiello, Buchanan, Myers.

FINAL LEAGUE TABLE

		P	W	D	L	F	A	Pts
1	QPR	42	26	7	9	77	36	85
2	Wolves	42	20	15	7	68	44	75
3	Leicester	42	20	10	12	72	44	70
4	Fulham	42	20	9	13	64	47	69
5	Newcastle	42	18	13	11	75	53	67
6	Sheff Wed	42	16	15	11	60	47	63
7	Oldham	42	14	19	9	64	47	61
8	Leeds	42	13	21	8	51	46	60
9	Shrewsbury	42	15	14	13	48	48	59
10	Barnsley	42	14	15	13	57	55	57
11	Blackburn	42	15	12	15	58	58	57
12	Cambridge	42	13	12	17	42	60	51
13	Derby	42	13	10	19	49	58	49
14	Carlisle	42	12	12	18	68	70	48
15	Crystal Palace	42	12	12	18	43	52	48
16	Middlesbrough	42	11	15	16	46	67	48
17	Charlton	42	13	9	20	63	86	48
18	Chelsea	42	11	14	17	51	61	47
19	Grimsby	42	12	11	19	45	70	47
20	Rotherham	42	10	15	17	45	68	45
21	Burnley	42	12	8	22	56	66	44
22	Bolton	42	11	11	20	42	61	44

SEASON 1983/84
Division 2

No.	Date	Opposition	Res.	H.T.	Att.	Ogrizovic S.	Williams W.	Cross S.C.	MacLaren R.	Pearson N.G.	Griffin C.R.	McNally B.A.	Petts P.A.	Brown Alan	Robinson C.R.	Hackett G.S.	Stevens G.M.	Bates P.D.	Johnson P.	Turner G.L.	Collins K.	Nardiello G.	Tester P.L.	Perks S.	Kerr A.	Foster K.	O'Connor A.	Goalscorers
1	27 Aug	Grimsby	1-1	0-0	5177	1	2	3	4	5	6	7	8	9	10	11*	12											McNally
2	29	Newcastle	1-0	1-0	9123	1	2	3	4	5	6	7	8	9	10	11*	12											Brown
3	3 Sep	CRYSTAL PALACE	1-1	0-0	3849	1	2	3	4	5	6	7	8*	9	10	11	12											MacLaren
4	6	CARDIFF	1-0	1-0	4405	1	2	3	4	5	6	7		9	10	11	12	8										Bates
5	10	Carlisle	0-1	0-0	3164	1	2	3	4	5	6	7		9	10	11	12	8										
6	17	BARNSLEY	3-2	2-1	3867	1	2	3	4	5	6	7	8	9*	10	11	12											McNally, Petts(2)
7	24	Portsmouth	1-4	1-1	11909	1	2	3	4	5	6	7	8	9*	10	11			12									Cross
8	1 Oct	LEEDS	5-1	0-1	6289	1	2	3	4	5	6	7	8	9	10	11			12									Robinson, Brown, Petts(3)
9	8	OLDHAM	2-0	0-0	4087	1		2	4	5	6	7	8	9	10	11	9		3				12					Robinson, MacLaren
10	16	Blackburn	1-1	0-1	5777	1		2	4	5	6		8	9	10	11	6	7	3				12					MacLaren
11	22	FULHAM	0-0	0-0	4767	1	2	3	4	5			8	9	10	11*		12										
12	29	Middlesbrough	0-4	0-0	6362	1	2	3	4	5		7	8	9	10	11	6	12										
13	5 Nov	MANCHESTER CITY	1-3	0-0	9471	1	2	3	4	5	6*	7	8	9	12	10												Cross
14	12	Huddersfield	0-1	0-1	8798	1	2	3	4	5		7*	8	9	10	11	6	11		12								
15	19	Brighton	2-2	0-1	9746	1	2	3	4	5		7	8	9	10	11	6	11		12								MacLaren(pen), Petts
16	26	CHARLTON	1-1	0-0	3141	1	2	3	4	5		7	8	9	10*	11	6	11										McNally
17	3 Dec	Sheffield Wed.	1-1	0-0	17703	1	2	3	4	5		7	8	9	10	11	6	12										Robinson
18	10	CAMBRIDGE	1-0	0-0	2457	1	2	3	4	5		7	8	9	10	11*	6	12										Petts
19	17	Derby	0-1	0-1	11265	1	2	3	4	5		7	8	9	10	11*	6											
20	26	CHELSEA	2-4	1-0	7526	1	2	3	4	5*		7	8	10	12	11	9											Brown, MacLaren
21	27	Swansea	2-0	0-0	7706	1	2	3	4			7	8	10	12	11	9			5								Hackett, Stevens
22	31	Crystal Palace	1-1	0-1	5275	1	2	3	4			7	8	10	12	11	9			5								Robinson
23	2 Jan	PORTSMOUTH	2-0	1-0	4907	1	2		4			7*	8	10	12	11	9			3								Hackett, Brown
24	14	GRIMSBY	1-2	1-1	3343	1	2	3	4			7*	8	10	12	11	9	12										Hackett
25	4 Feb	Leeds	0-3	0-2	10628	1	2	3	4			7	8	10	6	11	9											
26	11	CARLISLE	0-0	0-0	3439	1	2	3	4			7	8	10*	12	11*	9											
27	25	Fulham	0-3	0-0	5149	1	2	3	4			7	8	9	12	11	9											
28	28	MIDDLESBROUGH	1-0	0-0	3043	1	2	10	4			7	8	9	12	11*	5		3	4								Brown
29	3 Mar	Manchester City	0-1	0-0	20083	1	2	10	4			7	8	9	12	11	5		3									
30	10	HUDDERSFIELD	1-0	0-0	3627	1	2	10*	4			7	8	10	6	11	5		3									Petts
31	13	Barnsley	0-3	0-1	5576	1	2	10*	4			7	8			11	5		3									
32	17	Cardiff	0-2	0-1	3870	1	2	12	4	5		7	8	9	12	11	9		3		3							
33	24	NEWCASTLE	2-2	1-0	8313	1	2	11	4		6	7	6				9	8	3	5		10	11					Cross(2)
34	30	BLACKBURN	1-0	1-0	3352	1	2	11	4		6	7	6				9	8	3	5		10	12					Cross
35	7 Apr	Oldham	1-0	0-0	3428	1	2	11	4	4*	6	7	6				9	8	3	5		10*	12					Bates
36	14	BRIGHTON	2-1	1-0	3332	1	2	11	4		6	7	6		12		9	8	3	5		10	12					Nardiello(2)
37	21	Chelsea	0-3	0-2	17295	1	2	11	4		6	7	6		12		9	8	3	5		10	11					
38	24	SWANSEA	2-0	1-0	3060	1	2	9	4			7	6		12		5	8	3	5		10	11					Cross(2)
39	28	Charlton	4-2	0-0	3786	1	2	9	4			7	6		12		5		3			10	11					Cross(2), Nardiello, McNally
40	5 May	SHEFFIELD WED.	2-1	0-0	7885	1	2	9	4		6	7*	6		12	12	5	8	3	8		10*	11					MacLaren, Nardiello
41	7	Cambridge	0-1	0-1	2208	1	2	9	4	4*	6	7	6		8		5*		3			10	11					
42	12	DERBY	3-0	1-0	5562	1	2	9	4		6	7	6		12	8	5		3			10*	11					Nardiello, Bates(pen), MacLaren(pen)

F.A.Cup

	Date	Opponent	Res	HT	Att	Scorers	Line-up (1–12)
3R	7 Jan	OLDHAM A.	3-0	1-0	4650	Stevens, MacLaren(pen), Robinson	1 2 3 4 5 6 7 8 10* 12 11 9 7
4R	28	IPSWICH T.	2-0	0-0	11110	Hackett, Robinson	1 2 3 4 5 6 7 8 10* 12 11 9
5R	18 Feb	Everton	0-3	0-1	27106		1 2 3 4 5 6 7 8 10* 11 9 12

League Cup

	Date	Opponent	Res	HT	Att	Scorers	Line-up (1–12)
1R		Bye					
2R1	4 Oct	SHEFFIELD UNITED	2-1	0-1	4382	Stevens, Brown	1 2 3 4 5 6 7 8 9 10* 11 5
2R2	25	Sheffield United	2-2	0-1	9399	Hackett, Bates	1 2 4 5 7 8 9 10 11* 6 3 12
3R	8 Nov	Walsall	1-2	0-1	7952	Williams	1 2 3 4 5 7 8 9 10 11 6 8 12

Welsh Cup

	Date	Opponent	Res	HT	Att	Scorers	Line-up
3R	30 Nov	Connah's Quay Nomads	1-0	1-0	600	Pearson	
4R	31 Jan	COLWYN BAY	5-2	3-1	489	O'Conner, Collins, Robinson, Nardiello, Foster	
5R	8 Feb	Kidderminster	1-1	1-0	893	Tester	
5Rr	20	KIDDERMINSTER	1-0	1-0	567	Cross	
SF1	20 Mar	SWANSEA C.	2-0	0-0	950	Bates, Tester	
SF2	3 Apr	Swansea C	0-1	0-1	2659		
F1	18 May	WREXHAM	2-1	1-1	2607	Robinson, Cross	
F2	25	Wrexham	0-0	0-0	3148		

Additional Player: R.Goodwin = 3/1

Final League Table

	Team	P	W	D	L	F	A	Pts
1	Chelsea	42	25	13	4	90	40	89
2	Sheff Wed	42	26	10	6	72	34	88
3	Newcastle	42	24	8	10	85	53	80
4	Man City	42	20	10	12	66	48	70
5	Grimsby	42	19	13	10	60	47	70
6	Blackburn	42	17	16	9	57	46	67
7	Carlisle	42	16	16	10	48	41	64
8	Shrewsbury	42	17	10	15	49	53	61
9	Brighton	42	17	9	16	69	60	60
10	Leeds	42	16	12	14	55	56	60
11	Fulham	42	15	12	15	60	53	57
12	Huddersfield	42	14	15	13	56	49	57
13	Charlton	42	16	9	17	53	64	57
14	Barnsley	42	15	7	20	57	53	52
15	Cardiff	42	15	6	21	53	66	51
16	Portsmouth	42	14	7	21	53	61	49
17	Middlesbrough	42	14	7	21	73	64	49
18	Crystal Palace	42	12	11	19	41	47	47
19	Oldham	42	13	8	21	42	52	47
20	Derby	42	11	9	22	36	73	42
21	Swansea	42	7	8	27	36	85	29
22	Cambridge	42	4	12	26	28	77	24

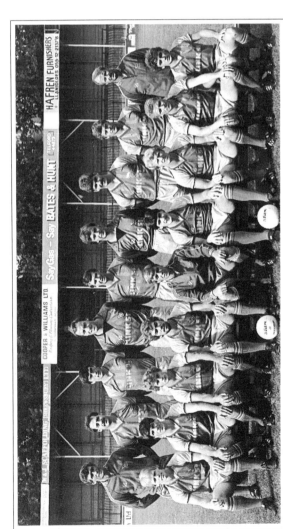

Back: Bates, Johnson, Stevens, Ogrizovic, Griffin, Perks, Pearson, Petts (Manager).
Front: Tester, W. Williams, Hackett, Robinson, Turner, MacLaren, Brown, Cross, McNally.

SEASON 1984/85
Division 2

No.	Date	Opposition	Res.	H.T.	Att.	Goalscorers	Green R.R.	Williams W.	Johnson P.	MacLaren R.	Griffin C.R.	Cross S.C.	McNally B.A.	Bates C.	Stevens G.M.	Robinson C.R.	Hackett G.S.	Nardiello G.	Bates M.	Tester P.L.	Petts P.A.	Perks S.J.	Palin L.A.P.	Kerr A.A.
1	25 Aug	Fulham	2-1	0-1	4898	Stevens, Hackett	1	2	3	4	5	6	7	8	9	10	11							12
2	1 Sep	CRYSTAL PALACE	4-1	3-0	3414	Robinson, Stevens, Cross, Hackett	1	2	3*	4	5	6	7	8	9	10	11							12
3	4	Carlisle	0-2	0-0	3321		1	2	3	4	5	6	7*	8	9	10	11		12					
4	8	Huddersfield	5-1	3-1	4980	Stevens(3), Robinson, Hackett	1	2	3	4	5	6	7	8	9	10	11		12					
5	15	WIMBLEDON	1-2	0-1	4094	Robinson	1	2	3	4	5	6	7	8	9	10	11	12						
6	18	OLDHAM	3-0	3-0	3646	Cross, Robinson, Stevens	1	2	3	4	5	6	7	8	9	10	11				12			
7	22	Portsmouth	0-3	0-0	12703		1	2	3	4	5	6	7	8*	9	10	11	9*			12			
8	29	NOTTS COUNTY	4-2	2-0	3504	Stevens(3), Griffin	1	2	3	4	5	6	7	8	9	10	11				8			
9	6 Oct	Blackburn	1-3	1-0	6226	Petts	1	2	3	4	5	6	7	12	9	10	11*				8			
10	13	MANCHESTER CITY	1-0	0-0	8563	Stevens	1	2	3	4	5	6	7	12	9	10	11				8			
11	20	Charlton	1-1	0-1	3744	Johnson	1	2	3	4	5	6	7	12	9	10	11				8			
12	27	BRIGHTON	0-0	0-0	4524		1	2	3	4	5	6	7	9		10	11				8			
13	3 Nov	Birmingham	0-0	0-0	9807		1	2	5	4	3	8	7		10	10*	11	12			6			
14	6	Crystal Palace	2-2	1-2	4002	Stevens, Robinson	1	2*	5	4	3	6	7	12	9	10	11				8			
15	10	OXFORD UNITED	2-2	0-2	6451	MacLaren(pen), Stevens	1		3	4	5	6	7*	12	9	10	11*				8			
16	17	Barnsley	1-3	0-2	6257	Robinson	1		3	4	5	6	7		9	10	11	12			8			
17	24	SHEFFIELD UNITED	3-3	2-2	4190	Cross, Stevens, Petts	1		3	4	5	6	7		9	10	11		12		8			
18	1 Dec	Grimsby	1-2	1-1	6146	Robinson	1		3	4	5	6	7		9	10					8			12
19	8	LEEDS	2-3	2-2	6358	Bates, Cross	1		3	4	5	6	7	11	9	10	12		2		8*			
20	14	Middlesbrough	1-1	1-0	4040	Stevens		2	3	4	5	6	7	11		10	12	9*	2		8*	1	8	
21	26	WOLVES	2-1	1-0	9183	Robinson, McNally			3	4	5	6	7	11	9	10			2			1	9*	
22	29	CARLISLE	4-2	1-1	3649	Tester, MacLaren, Stevens(2)			3	4	5	6	7	8	9	10		12		11	2	1		
23	1 Jan	Cardiff	0-0	0-0	4609				3	4	5	6	7	8	9	10				11	2	1		
24	26	FULHAM	3-1	1-1	3172	Cross, O.G., Robinson			3	4	5	6	7	8	9	10			2	11		1		
25	2 Feb	Notts County	3-1	2-1	4421	MacLaren(pen), Stevens, Robinson			3*	4	5	6	7		9	10	8			11	2	1		12
26	23	BIRMINGHAM	1-0	1-0	7177	Tester		12	3	4	5	6	7		9	10	8			11	2	1		
27	2 Mar	Brighton	0-1	0-0	8519				3	4		6	7		9	10	8			11	2	1		
28	9	CHARLTON	1-1	0-0	3236	MacLaren(pen)		12	3	4	5	6	7		9	10	8			11	2	1		
29	12	HUDDERSFIELD	5-1	3-0	3291	Tester(2), Robinson(2), MacLaren		12	3	4	5	6	7		9	10	8			11	2	1		
30	16	Manchester City	0-4	0-3	20828			12	3	4	5	6	7		9	10	8			11	2*	1		
31	23	BLACKBURN	3-0	0-0	4979	McNally, Stevens, Hackett		2	3	4	5	6	7		9	10	8			11	12	1		12
32	27	Wimbledon	1-4	0-2	2337	Robinson		2	3	4	5	6	7		9	10	8*			11	12	1		
33	30	PORTSMOUTH	0-0	0-0	4140			2	3*	4	5	6	7		9	10	8			11	6	1		
34	6 Apr	Wolverhampton	1-0	1-0	7258	O.G.		2	3	4	5	6	7		9	10	8			11	6	1		12
35	9	CARDIFF	0-0	0-0	3929			2	3*	4	5	6	7		9	10	8			11	12	1		
36	13	Oldham	1-0	0-0	3028	Nardiello		2		4	5	6	7		9	10	8	12		11		1		
37	20	BARNSLEY	2-0	2-0	3171	Hackett, O.G.		2	12	4	5	6	7			10	8	9		11	3	1		
38	24	Oxford United	0-1	0-1	12433			2		4		6	7		9	10	8	12		11	3	1		
39	27	Sheffield United	1-0	0-0	7809	Stevens		2		4	5	6	7		9	10	8			11	3	1		
40	4 May	GRIMSBY	4-1	2-1	2823	Tester, MacLaren(pen), Robinson, Stevens		2	12	4	5	6	7		9	10	8			11	3	1		
41	6	Leeds	0-1	0-0	12423			2	12	4	5	6	7		9	10	8			11	3	1		
42	11	MIDDLESBROUGH	0-2	0-2	5348			2	12	4	5	6	7		9	10	8			11	3	1		

F.A. Cup

			3	4	5	6	7	8	10	9*	12	11	2	1
3R	5 Jan	OXFORD UNITED	0:2	0-1	7906									

League Cup

						1	2	3	4	5	6	7	8	10	9*	12	11	2	1
1R		Bye																	
2R1	25 Sep	BOLTON W.	2:2	2-0	3720	MacLaren(2)	1	2	3	4	5	6	7	8	10	11	9*	12	2	1
2R2	9 Oct	Bolton W.	1:2	0-1	5445	Williams	1	2	3	4	5	6	7	12	9	10	11	8	2	1

Welsh Cup

																					5
3R	27 Nov	Bethesda Athletic	3-1	1-1	454	Hackett, McNally, Stevens				6	4			8	9		11	10		2	1	
4R	22 Jan	CARDIFF A.F.C.	6-0	3-0	586	Tester, Robinson, McNally(2), Cross, Nardiello	12		3	4	5	6	7			10	8	9	11	2	1	
5R	20 Feb	Rhyl	7-1	2-0	757	Tester(3), Hackett(2), Robinson, Stevens	1	5	3	4		6	7	9		10	8		12	11	2	5
SF1	2 Apr	Swansea C.	2-2	0-1	2074	Johnson, Nardiello		2	3	4		6		9		7	10	12	11	8	1	
SF2	16	SWANSEA C.	2-1	1-1	1491	Robinson, Nardiello		2			5	6	7		4	10	8	9	11	3	1	
F1	14 May	BANGOR C.	3-1	3-0	1507	Tester(2), Hackett		2	3	4	5	6			9	10	8	12	11	7	1	
F2	19	Bangor C.	2-0	0-0	1627	MacLaren, Stevens		2	3	4	5	6			9	10	7	12	11	8*	1	

Additional Players: K.Collins = 3/1, J.Dale 12/1, Richard Green 12/5

Back: Bates, W.Williams, Bates, Pearson, Kerr, Perks, Stevens, Green, Griffin, Petts, Cross, Nardiello, Mann,
Middle: Kelly, Sankey, Robinson, Johnson, MacLaren, McNally, Hackett, Tester, Steele, (Front - apprentices)

FINAL LEAGUE TABLE

		P	W	D	L	F	A	Pts
1	Oxford	42	25	9	8	84	36	84
2	Birmingham	42	25	7	10	59	33	82
3	Man City	42	21	11	10	66	40	74
4	Portsmouth	42	20	14	8	69	50	74
5	Blackburn	42	21	10	11	66	41	73
6	Brighton	42	20	12	10	58	34	72
7	Leeds	42	19	12	11	66	43	69
8	Shrewsbury	42	18	11	13	66	53	65
9	Fulham	42	19	8	15	68	64	65
10	Grimsby	42	18	8	16	72	64	62
11	Barnsley	42	14	16	12	42	42	58
12	Wimbledon	42	16	10	16	71	75	58
13	Huddersfield	42	15	10	17	52	64	55
14	Oldham Ath	42	15	8	19	49	67	53
15	Crystal Palace	42	12	12	18	46	65	48
16	Carlisle	42	13	8	21	50	67	47
17	Charlton	42	11	12	19	51	63	45
18	Sheffield Utd	42	10	14	18	54	66	44
19	Middlesborough	42	10	10	22	41	57	40
20	Notts Co	42	10	7	25	45	73	37
21	Cardiff	42	9	8	25	47	79	35
22	Wolves	42	8	9	25	37	79	33

SEASON 1985/86
Division 2

No.	Date	Opposition	Res.	H.T.	Att.	Goalscorers	Perks S.J.	Williams W.	Johnson P.	Cross S.C.	Pearson N.	Griffin C.	Hackett G.	Hughes D.	Stevens G.	Robinson C.	Tester P.	Nardiello G.	McNally B.	Kerr A.A.	Bates C.	Leonard G.	Daly G.A.	Gunn B.C.	Brown M.	Steele T.	Rees A.A.	Malcolm P.
1	18 Aug	CRYSTAL PALACE	0-2	0-2	4295		1	2	3	4	5	6	7	8	9*	10	11	12										
2	20	Oldham	3-4	1-1	3092	McNally(2,1pen)), Robinson	1	2	3*	4	5	6		12	9	10	11		7									
3	24	Blackburn	1-1	0-0	6071	Nardiello	1	2		4	5		8		6	10	11	9	7	3	12							
4	27	MILLWALL	1-1	0-0	3008	Tester	1	2		4	5		8			10	11	9	7	3	12							
5	31	Sheffield United	1-1	1-1	11241	Nardiello	1	2		4		5	8*		6	10	11	9	7	3	12							
6	3 Sep	PORTSMOUTH	1-1	1-1	3719	Robinson	1	2		4		5	8	3	6	10	11	9	7		12							
7	7	LEEDS	1-3	0-1	4168	Cross	1	2		4		5	8		6	10	11	9*	7	3	12							
8	14	Barnsley	0-2	0-1	4516		1	2		4	5	6	8	3		10	11	9	7			12						
9	21	SUNDERLAND	1-2	1-1	3919	Robinson	1	2		4	5	6	8	3	9	10	11		7									
10	28	Carlisle	2-0	1-0	2559	Stevens, Robinson	1	2		4	5	6	8	3	9	10			7	12								
11	5 Oct	Fulham	1-2	0-0	3412	Pearson	1	2		4	5	6	8	3	9	10	11		7	12								
12	12	HUDDERSFIELD	3-0	3-0	3986	Cross, Daly, Nardiello	1	2		4	5	6	8		6	10		9	7			12	11*					
13	19	Norwich	1-3	1-2	12500	O.G.	1			4	5	6	8		6	10		9	7	2			11					
14	26	HULL	0-0	0-0	3587		1	2*		4	5	6	8	3	9	10		12	7									
15	2 Nov	Charlton	1-4	1-2	3233	Stevens	1			4	5	6	8	12	5	10		9	7	2	3	11						
16	9	BRIGHTON	2-1	2-1	2942	Robinson, O.G.	1			4		6	8		5	10		9	7	2		12	11	3				
17	16	Wimbledon	1-2	1-1	2584	Daly	1			4	5	6	8			10		9	7	2		12	11	3				
18	23	BRADFORD	2-0	1-0	2148	Cross, Nardiello	1			4	5	6	8	3		10		9				7	11	2	12			
19	30	Middlesbrough	1-3	1-2	4506	Cross	1			4	5	6	8	3	9	10			7			12	11	2				
20	7 Dec	OLDHAM	2-0	1-0	2702	Hackett, Robinson	1			4	5	6	8	3	6	10			7			12	11	2				
21	15	Crystal Palace	1-0	0-0	8253	Hackett	1			4	5	6	8		9	10		12				7	11	2				
22	20	BLACKBURN	2-0	2-0	3147	Daly, Cross	1			4	5	6	8		9	10			12			7	11	2				
23	26	STOKE CITY	1-0	1-0	9595	O.G.	1			4	5	6	8*		9	10			12			7	11	2				
24	28	Portsmouth	0-4	0-1	12302		1			4	5	6	8		9	10			12			7	11	2				
25	1 Jan	Grimsby	1-3	1-1	4750	Cross	1	2		4	5	6	8			10		12				7	11					
26	11	BARNSLEY	3-0	2-0	2756	Nardiello, McNally(2)	1	2	3	4	5	6	8		6	10		9*	12			7	11					
27	18	SHEFFIELD UNITED	3-1	1-0	4261	Hackett, Robinson(2)	1	2	3	4	5		8*		6	10		9	7			12	11					
28	1 Feb	Millwall	0-2	0-0	4487		1	2	3	4	5*	6	8		6	10		9	7			12	11					
29	8	NORWICH	0-3	0-2	5157		1	2	3	4	5	6	8		6	10		9*	7			12	11					
30	1 Mar	CARLISLE	0-0	0-0	2364		1	2	3	4	4	6	8		5	10		9*	7			12	11					
31	4	Hull	3-4	1-2	6253	McNally, Leonard, Cross	1	2		9		6	8	12	6	10			7			4	11					
32	8	FULHAM	2-1	2-0	2563	Hackett, Stevens	1	2	3	4	5	6	8	2	6	10			7			4	11			12		
33	15	Huddersfield	0-1	0-0	4511		1	7	3	9*	5		8*	2	9	10			7			4	11			12		
34	22	Leeds	1-1	0-0	9641	Stevens	1	7	3	4	5	6	8		9	10					12	4	11					
35	29	GRIMSBY	0-2	0-0	3097		1	2*	3	4	5*	6	8		9	10		7	7			4					12	
36	31	Stoke	2-2	2-1	8998	McNally(pen), O.G.	1	2	3	4	5	6	8		9	10		7	7		12	4					4*	
37	5 Apr	CHARLTON	2-1	2-0	3380	Williams, Hackett	1	2	3	4	5	6	8		9	10		7	7		12		4				12	
38	12	Brighton	2-0	0-0	7210	Daly, Robinson	1	2	3	4	5	6	8		9	10		7	7				11					
39	19	WIMBLEDON	1-1	0-1	3948	Hackett	1	2	3	4	5	6	8		9	10		7	7			11	11					
40	26	Bradford C.	1-3	0-3	4663	Cross	1	2	3	4*	5	6	8	3	9	10		7	7			12	11					
41	29	Sunderland	0-2	0-0	15507		1	2	3			6	8	11*		10		12	7			12	11					
42	3 May	MIDDLESBROUGH	2-1	1-0	6695	Robinson, Hughes	1	2	3	5		6	8	12		10	9*	9*	7			4	11					

F.A. Cup

								1	2	4	5	6	8	3	10		9	7	12	11
3R	4 Jan	CHELSEA	0-1	0-0	8100															1

League Cup

								1	2	4	5	6	8	3	10	11*	9	7	12	11
1R		Bye																		
2R1	24 Sep	HUDDERSFIELD T.	2-3	2-2	2251	O.G., Stevens			2	4	5	6	8	3	9	10	11*	7	12	
2R2	8 Oct	Huddersfield T.	2-0	1-0	4966	Hackett, Robinson		1	2	4	5	6	8	3	9	10	12	7	11	
3R	29	EVERTON	1-4	0-1	10246	Robinson		1	2	4	5	6	8	3	9	10	12	7	2	11

Welsh Cup

							9	5	8	3	10	12	7*	2	4	11	6
3R	20 Nov	Kidderminster	1-3	1-2	439	Robinson	9	5	8	3	10	12	7*	2	4	11	6	1

Final League Table

		P	W	D	L	F	A	Pts
1	Norwich	42	25	9	8	84	39	84
2	Charlton	42	22	11	9	78	45	77
3	Wimbledon	42	21	13	8	58	37	76
4	Portsmouth	42	22	7	13	69	41	73
5	Crystal Palace	42	19	9	14	57	52	66
6	Hull	42	17	13	12	65	55	64
7	Sheffield United	42	17	11	14	64	63	62
8	Oldham	42	17	9	16	62	61	60
9	Millwall	42	17	8	17	64	65	59
10	Stoke	42	14	15	13	48	50	57
11	Brighton	42	16	8	18	64	64	56
12	Barnsley	42	14	14	14	47	50	56
13	Bradford	42	16	6	20	51	63	54
14	Leeds	42	15	8	19	56	72	53
15	Grimsby	42	14	10	18	58	62	52
16	Huddersfield	42	14	10	18	51	67	52
17	Shrewsbury	42	14	9	19	52	64	51
18	Sunderland	42	13	11	18	47	61	50
19	Blackburn	42	12	13	17	53	62	49
20	Carlisle	42	13	7	22	47	71	46
21	Middlesborough	42	12	9	21	44	53	45
22	Fulham	42	10	6	26	45	69	36

Back Row: Williams, Kerr, Perks, Malcolm, Stevens, Cross.
Middle Row: Mann (Physio), Pearson, Robinson, Tester, Nardiello, Hughes, Leonard, Bates (Player/Manager), Front Row: Petts, Johnson, Griffin, McNally, Hackett.

SEASON 1986/87
Division 2 (Centenary Season)

No.	Date	Opposition	Res.	H.T.	Att.	Perks S.J.	Williams W.	Johnson P.	Leonard G.	Pearson N.	Griffin C.	Narbet J.	Hackett G.	Waller D.	Robinson C.	Daly G.A.	Hughes D.	McNally B.	Brown M.	Green R.E.	Tester P.L.	Franklin P.	Linighan D.	Geddis D.	Hughes K.	Steele T.	Kelly M.	Goalscorers
1	23 Aug	Sheffield United	1-1	0-0	8865	1	2	3	4	5	6	7*	8	9	10	11	12											Waller
2	30	BLACKBURN R.	0-1	0-0	3186	1	2	3*		5	6		8	9	10	11	4	7	12									
3	6 Sep	Ipswich T.	0-1	0-1	9399	1	2	3	12	5	6*		8	9	10	11	4	7										
4	13	BARNSLEY	1-0	0-0	2435	1	2	3		5			8	9	10	11	4*	7	12	6								Waller
5	16	BRIGHTON	1-0	0-0	2684	1	2	3	12	5			8	9	10	11	4	7		6								Robinson
6	20	Reading	1-3	0-2	5233	1	2	3		5			8	9	10	11	4	7	12	6								Waller
7	27	BRADFORD C.	0-1	0-0	3215	1	2	3	12	5			8	9*	10	11	4	7		6								
8	4 Oct	GRIMSBY T.	4-1	2-1	2491	1	2	3	12	5*			8	9	10	4		7		6	11							Tester(2), Daly, McNally
9	11	Millwall	0-4	0-3	3123	1	2	3	12	5			8	9	10	4		7		6	11							
10	18	DERBY C.	0-1	0-0	5714	1	2	3		5		12	8	9	10	4		7		6	11	6						
11	21	Huddersfield	1-2	0-1	4097	1	2	3	4	5			8	9	10			7	9		11	6						Robinson
12	25	Crytal Palace	3-2	1-0	4856	1	2	3	4	5			12	12	10	4*		7	9		11	6						McNally(pen), Pearson, Robinson
13	1 Nov	Leeds United	0-1	0-0	14966	1	2	3	4	5			8	12	10	4		7	9	12	11	6						
14	8	PLYMOUTH AR.	1-1	0-1	3821	1	2	3	4	5			8*		10	12		7	9		12	6						McNally(pen)
15	15	PORTSMOUTH	1-0	1-0	3827	1	2	3	4	5			8		10	11		7	9		12	6						Hackett
16	22	Sunderland	1-1	1-0	12374	1	2	3	4	5			8	12	10	11		7	9	6	12	6						M.Brown
17	29	HULL CITY	3-0	1-0	2869	1	2	3	4	5				12	10	11		7	9	6	12							Tester, Daly, Robinson
18	6 Dec	Oldham A.	0-3	0-1	5419	1	2	3	4	5			8		10	11		7	9	6	8		12					
19	13	BIRMINGHAM C.	1-0	1-0	4797	1	2	3	4	5			8		10	11		7*	9	6	8		6					Tester
20	21	Brighton	0-3	0-2	8220	1	2	3	4*	5			8		10	11		7	9	6	8		6					
21	26	W.B.A.	1-0	0-0	9261	1	2	3	4	5			8		10	11		7	9	6	8		6					Daly
22	29	Portsmouth	0-3	0-0	15006	1	2	3	4	5			10		12	11		7	9	6	8*		6					
23	1 Jan	Stoke C.	0-1	0-1	19382	1	2	3	4*	5			8	9	12	11		7		12			6					
24	3	IPSWICH T.	2-1	1-1	4783	1	2	3	4	5			8		10*	11		8	9	4	12		6					Pearson, McNally(pen)
25	24	SHEFFIELD UNITED	1-0	0-0	3832	1	2	3	4	5			8	12	10	11		7	9		12		6					McNally(pen)
26	7 Feb	Blackburn R.	1-2	0-1	5598	1	2	3	4	5			8		4	11		7*	9				6					Daly(pen)
27	14	HUDDERSFIELD	1-2	0-1	3285	1	2	3		5			12		10	11		7		8	8		6	9				Geddis
28	21	Bradford C.	0-0	0-0	8616			3	7	5			8		10	2		7		4	12		6	9				
29	28	READING	0-0	0-0	3445			3	2	5			8		10	2		7		4	12		6	9				
30	3 Mar	Barnsley	1-2	1-0	4718	1		3	7	5			8		10	4		7	10	4	12		6	9				Pearson
31	14	Derby C.	1-3	0-3	14393	1		3	4	5			8		12	11		7*	10	4	8		6	9				Hackett
32	21	MILLWALL	1-2	0-2	2799	1	2	4	2	5			8		12	11		7*	10*		12	3	6	9				Geddis
33	24	CRYSTAL PALACE	0-0	0-0	2555	1	2	3	4	5			8*		4	11		7		6	11	3	6	9		12		
34	28	Grimsby T.	1-0	0-0	3437	1	2	3	4	5			8*		10	11		7			11*		3	9		12		Robinson
35	4 Apr	Plymouth Ar.	2-3	2-1	8905	1	2*	3	4*	5			8		10	11		7	9	3	11		6		1			Brown, Robinson
36	14	LEEDS UNITED	0-2	0-1	4186	1	2	3	4	5			8		10	11		7			11*		6	9	1	12		
37	18	STOKE C.	4-1	3-0	6777	1	2*	3	4	5			8		10	11		7	9	3	11*		6*		1	12		Robinson, Geddis, Tester, O.G.
38	20	w.b.a.	2-1	1-1	7307	1	2	3	12	5			8		10	11		7			11		6	9*	1	4		Robinson, Geddis
39	25	SUNDERLAND	0-1	0-0	5431	1	2	3	12	5	3		8*		10	11		7	9*		11		6	9		4		
40	2 May	Hull City	0-3	0-2	5114	1	2	3	12	5			8		10	11		7			11		6	9		4		
41	5	OLDHAM ATH.	2-0	2-0	4651	1	2	3	12	5			8		10	11		7			11		6	9	4	4		Steele, Geddis
42	9	Birmingham C.	2-0	0-0	7724	1	2	3	12	5			8		10	11		7			11		6	9	4	4		Hackett, Robinson

F.A. Cup

	Date	Opponent		HT	Att	Scorers															
3R	31 Jan	HULL C.	1-2	0-2	4130	Waller	1	2	3	4#	12	8	9	10	11	5	14	7		6	

League Cup

	Date	Opponent		HT	Att	Scorers	1	2	3	4#	5	6	7*	8#	9	10	11	12		14			5 14	6
1R1	26 Aug	CREWE ALEXANDRA	0-0	0-0	1819		1	2	3	4	5	6		8	9	10	11	12		14				
1R2	2 Sep	Crewe Alexandra	4-0	0-0	1703	Waller, Robinson(3)	1	2	3	14	5	6		8	9	10	11	4	7	12				
2R1	23	STOKE C.	2-1	0-1	5343		1	2*	3		5			8	9	10	11	4	7	14	6	12		
2R2	8 Oct	Stoke C.	0-0	0-0	6468	Robinson, Waller	1	2	3	12	5		8*	9	10	4		7	14	6	11			
3R	28	HULL C.	1-0	0-0	3077	Williams	1	2	3	4	5		8*	12	10	14		7	9	6	11			
4R	18 Nov	CARDIFF C.	1-0	0-0	4673	McNally	1	2	3	4	5		8	14	10#	11		7	9	6	12			
QF	27 Jan	Southampton	0-1	0-0	12940		1	2	3	4	5		8		10	11		7	9	14	12	6		

Welsh Cup

	Date	Opponent		HT	Att	Scorers	12	3	4		9	10		7	10	6*	8		1	11
3R	2 Dec	CEFN ALBION	10-0	6-0	472	McNally(4,1pen),O.G.,Brown(2),Waller(2),Leonard	12	3	4		9	10		7	10	6*	8		1	
4R	10 Feb	NEWPORT C.	0-1	0-1	634		1*	2	3	4		8	9	10		5	11		12	7

Additional Players: N.Meredith = 2/1, P.Bates = 5/1

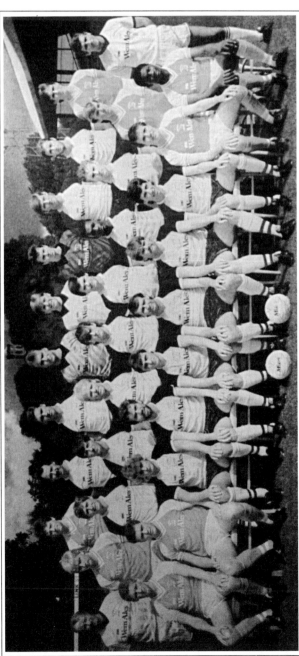

(Back) Neil Smith, Johnson, Pearson, Perks, Webb, K.Hughes, Green, D.Hughes, Narbett
(Middle) Mann, Mulcahy, Daly, W.Williams, Tester, M.Kelly, G.Leonard, Brown, N.Meredith, Orbell, Bates
(Front) Hodgetts, Carmichael, Hackett, Robinson, McNally, Griffin, Waller, Steele, Mellors, Osbourne.

Final League Table

		P	W	D	L	F	A	Pts
1	Derby Co	42	25	9	8	64	38	84
2	Portsmouth	42	23	9	10	53	28	78
3	Oldham	42	22	9	11	65	44	75
4	Leeds	42	19	11	12	58	44	68
5	Ipswich	42	17	13	12	59	43	64
6	Crystal Palace	42	19	5	18	51	53	62
7	Plymouth	42	16	13	13	62	57	61
8	Stoke	42	16	10	16	63	53	58
9	Sheffield Utd	42	15	13	14	50	49	58
10	Bradford	42	15	10	17	62	62	55
11	Barnsley	42	14	13	15	49	52	55
12	Blackburn	42	15	10	17	45	55	55
13	Reading	42	14	11	17	52	59	53
14	Hull	42	13	14	15	41	55	53
15	West Brom	42	13	12	17	51	49	51
16	Millwall	42	14	9	19	39	45	51
17	Huddersfield	42	13	12	17	54	61	51
18	Shrewsbury	42	15	6	21	41	53	51
19	Birmingham	42	11	17	14	47	59	50
20	Sunderland	42	12	12	18	49	59	48
21	Grimsby	42	10	14	18	39	59	44
22	Brighton	42	9	12	21	37	54	39

SEASON 1987/88
Division 2

No.	Date	Opposition	Res.	H.T.	Att.	Goalscorers	Perks S.J.	Williams W.	Williams B.	McNally B.A.	Pearson N.G.	Linighan D.	Steele T.W.	Narbett J.B.	Geddis D.	Robinson C.R.	Tester P.L.	Leonard G.A.	Brown M.A.	Green R.E.	Griffin C.R.	Cooper M.D.	Leworthy D.J.	Moyes D.W.	Smith N.	Hughes K.D.	Priest P.	Bell D.	Crane A.D.	Kasule V.P.	Melrose J.	Pratley R.G.	Irvine A.J.	Osbourne G.
1	15 Aug	Leicester C.	1-0	0-0	8469	Geddis	1	2	3	4	5	6	7	8	9#	10	11	12		14															
2	22	IPSWICH T.	0-0	0-0	3610		1	2	3	8	5	6	7	4		10	11	12	9	14															
3	29	Huddersfield	0-0	0-0	4478		1	2	3	8	5	6	7	4		10	11	7	9	12	14														
4	1 Sep	READING	0-1	0-1	3223		1	2	3	8	5	6	7	4		10#	11	12	9	14	14														
5	5	w.b.a.	1-2	0-0	8560	Narbett	1	2	3	8	5	6	7	4		10	11	12	9	14														
6	12	MANCHESTER CITY	0-0	0-0	6280		1	2	3	8	5	6	7	4		10	11	12				9												
7	15	Hull City	1-1	0-0	7939	Steele	1	2	3	8	5	6	7	4		10	11	12				9#												
8	19	Birmingham C.	0-0	0-0	7183		1	2	3	8	5	6	7	4		10	11	12				9#												
9	26	BRADFORD C.	2-2	0-0	4247	Cooper(2)	1	2	3	8#	5	6	7	4		12	11*	14				9												
10	29	Swindon T.	1-1	0-0	8261	Steele(pen)	1	2	3	8	5	6	7	4		12	11	14				9												
11	3 Oct	CRYSTAL PALACE	2-0	1-0	3999	Linighan, Steele	1	2	3	8	5	6	7	4		12	11*	14				9												
12	17	Millwall	1-4	1-2	5202	Leworthy	1	2	3	8	5			4		12	11	14*		5	6		10											
13	20	Bournemouth	0-2	0-2	5587		1	2	3	8				4		12	11*	14		5	6		10											
14	24	OLDHAM	2-3	2-0	3337	W.Williams, Leworthy	1	2#	3	8		6	7#	4		12	11	4		5	6		10											
15	31	Middlesbrough	0-4	0-1	10183		1	2*	3	8#		6	7			7	11	11*		14			10	5										
16	3 Nov	ASTON VILLA	1-2	1-1	7089	Leworthy	1	2	3	8		6	7	4		10	11	11	14	2			9*	5										
17	7	Leeds U.	1-2	0-1	13760	Narbett	1	2	3	8		6	7	4		10	11	12		2#			9*	5	14									
18	14	BLACKBURN R.	1-2	0-0	3164	Brown	1	2*	3	8		6	7	4		10	11#	12	14				9	5	14									
19	17	SHEFFIELD UNITED	2-0	0-0	2555	Brown, Narbett			3	8		6	7	12	1	10	11	8	9	2	14			5	14	1	12							
20	21	Barnsley	1-2	0-2	5364	Brown			3	8		6	7	14	1	10	11	4	9*	2				5		1	14							
21	28	STOKE C.	0-3	0-3	5158		1		3	8		6		11*		10#	12	4		2				5	14		4#							
22	5 Dec	Plymouth	0-2	0-0	7603		1		3	8		6		14		10*	12	4		2				5			7							
23	12	HULL CITY	2-2	1-2	2588	McNally(pen), Tester	1		3	8		6	7	14		10	11*	11*	9	2				5			11#							
24	18	Ipswich T.	0-2	0-0	9930		1		3	8		6	7	14		10	11#	12	9	2				5			4#							
25	26	Bradford C.	1-1	0-0	12474	Green	1		3	8		6	7	14		10	11*	12	9	2				5			4							
26	28	BIRMINGHAM C.	0-0	0-0	6397		1	14	3	8		6	7			10	11	12	9	2				5			4#	12						
27	1 Jan	HUDDERSFIELD	3-1	1-0	5448	Brown, Bell, Robinson	1	14	3#	8		6	7*			10	12	9	9	2				5			4	11						
28	2	Manchester City	3-1	2-0	21455	Moyes(2), Bell	1	12	3	8		6	7			10#	12	9	9	2				5			4	11						
29	16	LEICESTER C.	0-0	0-0	5025		1	12	3	8		6	7	14		10#	11*	9	9	2				5			4*	11	14					
30	23	Reading	0-1	0-0	5170		1	12	3	8		6	7	14	14	10*	7	9	9	2				5			4*	11						
31	6 Feb	W.B.A.	0-1	0-0	6360		1	2	3	8		6		14	10			12	12	2				5			4	11						
32	13	Sheffield United	1-0	1-0	8227	Priest	1	2	3	8		6		14	10		14	11	11	2							4	7#		7		5		
33	20	SWINDON T.	2-1	2-1	5649	McNally(pen), Kasule	1	11#	3	8		6			10					2							4*			7	9*	5	12	
34	27	Crystal Palace	2-1	1-1	8210	O.G., Irvine	1	11	3	8		6		2			14		10	2#							4*	14	14	7	9	5	12	
35	5 Mar	MILLWALL	0-0	0-0	5408		1	14	3	8		6							11								4*			7	9	5	10*	
36	19	MIDDLESBROUGH	0-1	0-0	5603		1	2		8		6			9		12		10	3							4	4	14	7	9	5		
37	26	Oldham	2-2	1-0	5379	Kasule, Priest	1	2	3	8		6			9		11*	3	10	3	14						4	11*		7*	9	5		
38	2 Apr	LEEDS U.	1-0	0-0	7369	Kasule	1	2	3	8		6		14	10			5	10	3	14			5			4	7#	14	11*	14	5		
39	4	Blackburn R.	2-2	0-2	13741	Green, W.Williams	1	2	3	8		6		14	9			5	10	12				5			4	14	14	7*	12	7		
40	8	BOURNEMOUTH	2-1	1-0	7106	Melrose, Geddis	1	14	3	8		6			9			5	10	12				5			4	14	14	7	11*			
41	23	Aston Villa	0-1	0-1	18396		1	12	3	8		6		14	9			11	11	2							4*	11*	14	7	10#	5	14	
42	30	BARNSLEY	1-1	0-0	4712	Geddis	1	14	3	8		6			9					2							4	11		7*	10#	5		
43	2 May	Stoke C.	1-1	1-0	7452	Brown	1		3	8		6			9				10	2							4*	11		7	12	5		
44	7	PLYMOUTH	2-1	1-0	4510	Geddis(2)	1	3	3	8		6		14	9				10*	2							4#	11		7	12	5	10#	

F.A.Cup

							1	12	3	8	6	7*	10	14	9	2		5		4#	11	
3R	9 Jan	BRISTOL R.	2:1	1-0	6554	Moyes, B.Williams	1	12	3	8	6	7*	10	14	9	2		5		4#	11	
4R	30	Plymouth A.	0-1	0-1	12749		1	7	3	8	6		10	14	9#	2	10	5		4*	11	12

League Cup

							1	2	3	8		6	4	10	11	7	9	5		12
1R1	25 Aug	Crewe Alexandra	3-3	1-1	1200	Tester, Leonard, W.Williams	1	2	3	8		6	4	10	11	7	9	5		12
1R2	8 Sep	CREWE ALEXANDRA	4-1	1-0	2824	Robinson(2), Brown, Steele(pen)	1	2	3		5	6	7	10	11	8	9	12		14
2R1	22	SHEFFIELD WED.	1-1	1-1	4364	McNally	1	2	3	8	5	6	7	10	11	12	9	14		
2R2	6 Oct	Sheffield Wed.	1-2	0-1	8572	McNally(pen)	1	2	3	8	5	6	7	10	11	4	9	14	12	

Welsh Cup

							1				6	7	14	10	11#	4	9	5	2	8*	3
3R	1 Dec	Llanfairpwll	1-0	0-0	675	Moyes	1				6	7	14	10	11#	4	9	5	2	8*	3	12
4R	13 Jan	Caernarfon T.	1-3	0-1	742	Leonard(pen)	1	2			7		11	8		5		4*	1	3		12

Additional Players: Mulcahy = 6/2, Hodgetts = 9/2, Griffiths = 10/2, Orbell = 14/2

(Back) Priest, Leonard, Hughes, Linighan, Perks, Green, Steele (2nd Row) Mann (Youth coach/physio), Pearson, Crane, Tester, Brown, Williams, Geddis, Griffin (P/Coach) (3rd Row) McLean, Robinson, Williams, Bates (P/Manager), Narbett, McNally, Hodgetts (Front) Griffiths, Mulcahy, Webb, Smith, Orbell, Osbourne.

FINAL LEAGUE TABLE

		P	W	D	L	F	A	Pts
1	Millwall	44	25	7	12	72	52	82
2	Aston Villa	44	22	12	10	68	41	78
3	Middlesbrough	44	22	12	10	63	36	78
4	Bradford City	44	22	11	11	74	54	78
5	Blackburn Rovers	44	21	14	9	68	52	77
6	Crystal Palace	44	22	9	13	86	59	75
7	Leeds United	44	19	12	13	61	51	69
8	Ipswich Town	44	19	9	16	61	52	66
9	Manchester City	44	19	8	17	80	60	65
10	Oldham Athletic	44	18	11	15	72	64	65
11	Stoke City	44	17	11	16	50	57	62
12	Swindon Town	44	16	11	17	73	60	59
13	Leicester City	44	16	11	17	62	61	59
14	Barnsley	44	15	12	17	61	62	57
15	Hull City	44	14	15	15	54	60	57
16	Plymouth Argyle	44	16	8	20	45	67	56
17	Bournemouth	44	13	10	21	56	68	49
18	Shrewsbury T.	44	13	16	17	42	54	49
19	Birmingham City	44	11	15	18	62	70	48
20	West Brom. A.	44	12	11	21	50	69	47
21	Sheffield United	44	13	7	24	45	74	46
22	Reading	44	10	12	22	54	70	42
23	Huddersfield T.	44	6	10	28	41	100	28

SEASON 1988/89
Division 2 (Relegated)

No.	Date	Opposition	Res.	H.T.	Att.	Goalscorers	Perks S.J.	Williams W.	Williams B.	Priest P.	Green Richard	Finley A.	Kasule V.P.	McNally B.A.	Irvine A.J.	Thomas M.R.	Brown M.A.	Melrose J.	Griffin C.R.	Rougvie D.	Geddis D.	Bell D.	Steele T.W.	Moyes D.W.	Green Ron	Griffiths C.	Pratley R.G.	Osbourne G.	Hughes K.D.	Smith N.	Kelly A.G.	McGinlay J.	Pittman S.	Worsley G.
1	27 Aug	PORTSMOUTH	1-2	1-1	5333	McNally(pen)	1	2	3	4*	5	6	7	8	9	10#	11	12	14															
2	3 Sep	Bradford C.	0-1	0-1	9765	Geddis	1	2	3	7*	5	6	12#	8	10	11		9			14													
3	10	W.B.A.	1-1	0-0	5851	Geddis	1	2	3	7*	5	6		8	10#	11					9													
4	17	Crystal Palace	1-1	1-0	7006	Rougvie	1	2	3		5	6	7*	8	10*		11			4	12		14											
5	20	IPSWICH T.	1-5	1-3	4225	Rougvie	1	2	3		5	6	11	8*	10	10#				5	4	4*	14	12										
6	24	SUNDERLAND	0-0	0-0	4195		1	2	3		3	6	7		9#	7	10			4	4	8	12											
7	1 Oct	Oxford United	1-4	1-2	4385	Moyes		2*		7*	3	6	7#	8*	10	11	11			4*	9	7	14	4	1	14								
8	4	Stoke C.	0-0	0-0	8075			2			3	6				11	12	9		4	9	7	14	4	1	10*								
9	8	HULL C.	1-3	0-2	3287	Green		2*			3	6		8	14	11	12			4	9	7	8	4#	1	10								
10	15	WALSALL	0-0	0-0	5026				3	8	2	6				11	7*	14		5	9	4	12	4	1									
11	21	Bournemouth	1-0	0-0	5449	Irvine			3	8	2	6			10	11	7	14		5	9	4	5	5	1	14								
12	25	Plymouth	0-0	0-0	6298					8	2	6			10*	11#	7#	12		12		4#	5	5	1	14								
13	29	LEICESTER C.	3-0	1-0	5178	Finley, Irvine(2)			14		2	6	12		10	11#	7#	9		3			5	5	1	8								
14	5 Nov	Brighton	1-3	0-0	7365	Green					2	6	14		10	11	7#			3			5	5	1	12								
15	11	OLDHAM	0-0	0-0	4701					4*	2	6			10	11	12	9*	14	3		8	5	5	1	9								
16	19	WATFORD	1-1	1-0	4621	Steele				4#	2	6			10	11	9	9*	14	3		8	7	5	1	12	12							
17	22	Blackburn R.	1-0	1-0	6898	Irvine				4*	2				10		9#		14	3		8	7	5	1	12	12							
18	26	Chelsea	0-2	0-2	11595					4*	2		9		10	11			12	3		8	7#	5	1	14	12							
19	3 Dec	SWINDON T.	0-1	0-1	3525				4	4*	2		9*			11	7	10#		3		8	5	5	1	14	6							
20	10	Leeds United	3-2	2-0	19967	Rougie, Griffiths(2)			4	4*	2				10	11#	7*			3		8	14	5	1	9	7							
21	17	Manchester City	2-2	2-0	19613	Griffiths(2)			3	4#	2				10	11				12		8	14	5	1	9	6							
22	26	BIRMINGHAM C.	0-0	0-0	7347				3	4*	2				10	11				3		8#	14	5	1	9	6							
23	31	BARNSLEY	2-3	1-1	4401	Bell(pen), Irvine		14	4	4	2*	6	12		10	11	7			3		8		5	1	9	7							
24	2 Jan	w.b.a.	0-4	0-0	18411			3	4	4	2		14									8		5	1	9#			1					
25	14	BLACKBURN R.	1-1	1-0	3879	Kasule			3	4	2	6	8				7						14	6	1	9	5		1	14				
26	21	Portsmouth	0-2	0-1	8449				3	4	2	6	8				7							6	1	9	6		1				
27	4 Feb	STOKE C.	1-2	1-0	6646	Priest	1		3	4*	2#	2	8		14		7					11	14	5		9	6		1				
28	11	Hull C.	0-3	0-2	11472		1		3	4*	2	2	8#				7	9				11	12	5		14	6		1				
29	25	Walsall	1-1	1-1	5871	Green	1		3	4	2	6				11	7	9*								9	9*						
30	28	PLYMOUTH	2-0	1-0	2978	Kelly, McGinlay	1		3	14	2	6	14	12	10	11	7					4	10	5		10	5			14	8	12	
31	3 Mar	Oldham	0-3	0-1	6014		1		3	14	2				9#	11#	7					4		5		10	5			14	9*	3	
32	11	BRIGHTON	1-1	0-1	4029	Kelly	1		3	2	12	6	12	8	10	11	7					4		5		10	5			8	9*	3	
33	15	Leicester C.	1-1	1-1	7750	B.Williams	1		3	2	14	6		8	10	11	7					4	12	5		14	5			4	9#	3*	
34	18	Ipswich T.	0-2	0-0	10913		1		3		12	6		8	10#	11*	7					4*	12	5		14	5			4	9#	3*	
35	25	BRADFORD C.	1-3	0-1	4575	Kelly(pen)	1			14	12			8	10#	11	7	10					6	5		9*	5			4	9	12	
36	27	Birmingham C.	2-1	0-1	4960	Thomas, Kelly	1			12	2		14	8	10	11	7	10					6	6		9	5			4	9#	3	
37	1 Apr	CRYSTAL PALACE	2-1	2-1	4160	Kelly, McGinlay	1				2	6	14	8	10	11#	7*	10					12	6		14	5			4*	9#	3	
38	4	MANCHESTER CITY	0-1	0-0	8271		1				2	6		8	10	11#	7	10#					12	6			5			4	9	3	
39	8	Barnsley	0-1	0-1	5252		1			11	2	6		8			7	14									5		1	4	9*	3	
40	11	BOURNEMOUTH	1-0	0-0	2457	Melrose	1			10	2	6	12	8		7	7	9					12			10	5			4	14	3	2
41	15	OXFORD UNITED	2-2	0-1	3583	McGinlay, Melrose	1			10#	2	6*	11*	8	9#	7	7	9								10	5			4	14	3	2
42	22	Sunderland	1-2	0-1	9427	McGinlay	1		12	10#	2	6	14	8		7	7	9			7		12			10	5			4	10	3*	2
43	29	CHELSEA	1-1	0-0	5588	McGinlay	1			7*	14	14		8	9	7	7	9*				7*	6			5	5			4	10	3*	2
44	1 May	Swindon T.	0-1	0-1	8698		1				12	14		8	10#	7	7						6			9*	5			4	9*	3	2
45	6	Watford	0-0	0-0	10052		1				9	14		8	7	7	7						6			12	5			4	10	3*	2
46	13	LEEDS UNITED	3-3	2-2	4693	McNally, Griffiths(2)	1			2	2	12		8		11	7						6			9	5			4	10	3	14

N.B. Match no.2, Kasule came on but was then withdrawn

F.A. Cup

						4	12		6	14		10	11	11	7		3	8*		2	9#	5	1
3R	7 Jan	COLCHESTER U.	0-3	0-1	3982																		

League Cup

							1	2	3	4	5	6	7*	8	10		11	9		14	12
1R1	20 Aug	WALSALL	2-2	1-0	4579	Melrose, Brown															
1R2	6 Sep	Walsall	0-3	0-0	5552		1	2	3	4	5	6	14	8	10	11#	7	12*		9	

Welsh Cup

								2	6*		8#		11	14	10		3	4	9	5	1	7	12
3R	15 Nov	CAERNARFON T.	2-0	1-0	413	Griffiths, Brown																	
4R		Newport C.																					

Expelled due to Ron Green being ineligible, which Town strongly deny and have not again entered the competition to date

FINAL LEAGUE TABLE

		P	W	D	L	F	A	Pts
1	Chelsea	46	29	12	5	96	50	99
2	Manchester C.	46	23	13	10	77	53	82
3	Crystal Palace	46	23	12	11	71	49	81
4	Watford	46	22	12	12	74	48	78
5	Blackburn R.	46	22	11	13	74	59	77
6	Swindon T.	46	20	16	10	68	53	76
7	Barnsley	46	20	14	12	66	58	74
8	Ipswich T.	46	22	7	17	71	61	73
9	W.B.A.	46	18	18	10	65	41	72
10	Leeds U.	46	17	16	13	59	50	67
11	Sunderland	46	16	15	15	60	60	63
12	Bournemouth	46	18	8	20	53	62	62
13	Stoke C.	46	15	14	17	57	72	59
14	Bradford C.	46	13	17	16	52	59	56
15	Leicester C.	46	13	16	17	56	63	55
16	Oldham Ath.	46	11	21	14	75	72	54
17	Oxford U.	46	11	21	14	62	70	54
18	Plymouth Arg.	46	14	12	20	55	66	54
19	Brighton & HA	46	14	9	23	57	66	51
20	Portsmouth	46	13	12	21	53	62	51
21	Hull C.	46	11	14	21	52	68	47
22	Shrewsbury	46	8	18	20	40	67	42
23	Birmingham C.	46	8	11	27	31	76	35
24	Walsall	46	9	16	25	31	80	31

SHREWSBURY TOWN 1988-89. *Back row (left to right):* Richard Pratley, Alan Finley, Ken Hughes, Steve Perks, Richard Green, Dougie Bell.
Centre row: Paul Tester, David Geddis, Neil Smith, David Moyes, Alan Irvine, Wayne Williams, Phil Priest.
Front row: Colin Griffin (Coach), Bernard McNally, Jim Melrose, Victor Kasule, Ian McNeill (Manager), Brian Williams, Mickey Brown, Les Helm (Physiotherapist).
Sitting: Micky Thomas, Tim Steele, Jon Narbett, Garry Osbourne.

SEASON 1989/90
Division 3

No.	Date	Opposition	Res	H.T.	Att.	Goalscorers	Perks S.J.	Green R.E.	Pittman S.	Kelly A.G.	Pratley R.G.	Moyes D.W.	Brown M.A.	Bell D.	Melrose J.	Griffiths C.	Naughton W.	Kasule V.P.	Hartford A.	McGinlay J.	Purdie J.	Finley A.	Priest P.	Worsley G.	Gorman P.A.	Cornforth I.	Wassall K.D.	Lynch T.	Wimbleton	Ormsby B.I.C.	Weir W.	Spink D.P.	Blake M.C.	Parrish S.	Bywater P.
1	19 Aug	Reading	3-3	2-1	3909	Bell, Griffiths, Kelly	1	2	3	4	5	6	7	8	9#	10*	11	12																	
2	26	LEYTON ORIENT	4-2	1-1	3299	Moyes, McGinley(2), Pratley	1	2	3	4	5	6	7	8	9*		11	12		10	14														
3	2 Sep	Blackpool	1-0	1-0	4109	Bell	1	2	3	4	5	6	7	8			11	9		10		12	14												
4	9	BIRMINGHAM C.	2-0	1-0	4714	Naughton(pen), McGinley	1	2	3	4	5	6	7	8			11	9#		10		12	14												
5	16	Northampton T.	1-2	1-1	3131	Pittman	1	2	3	4	5	6	7	8			11	9#	12	10															
6	23	BURY	3-1	2-1	3525	Bell, McGinley, Griffiths	1	2	3	4	5	6	7	8		12	11			10*	9			14											
7	26	Bristol City	1-2	0-1	9188	Purdie	1	2	3	4		6	7	8		12	11			10*	9		14												
8	30	CREWE ALEXANDRA	0-0	0-0	5118		1	2	3#	4		6	7	8			11			10*	9														
9	7 Oct	MANSFIELD T.	0-1	0-0	3148		1	2	3	4		6	7	8			11		12	10*	9			14											
10	14	Wigan Athletic	0-0	0-0	2279		1	2	3	4		6	7	8			11			10#	9														
11	17	Walsall	2-0	0-0	4266	Moyes, Pittman	1	2	3*	4		6	7				11		8	10	9	5		14											
12	21	BRENTFORD	1-0	0-0	3073	Moyes	1	2#	3#	4		6	7				11		8	10	9	5		14											
13	28	Huddersfield T.	1-1	1-1	6001	Moyes	1	2	3	4		6	7*				11#		8	10	9	5		14											
14	31	TRANMERE R.	3-1	1-1	4927	McGinley(2), Finley	1	2	3	4		6	7			14	11		8	10	9	5													
15	4 Nov	Preston N.E.	1-2	0-1	5418	Naughton	1	2	3#	4		6	7*				11		8	10	9	5		14											
16	11	BRISTOL ROVERS	2-3	1-1	4746	McGinley, Griffiths	1	2	3	4		6	7*			12	11#		8	10		5				9	14								
17	25	Rotherham U.	2-4	2-2	5694	Brown, Griffiths	1	2	3	4		6	7			12	11			10		5			8#	9	14								
18	2 Dec	CHESTER C.	2-0	2-0	2905	McGinley, O.G.	1	2	3	4#		6	7				11			10		5			8	9									
19	16	BOLTON WANDERERS	3-3	0-2	3443	Gorman, McGinley, Moyes	1	2	3	4		6	7			12	11			10*		5			8	9									
20	26	Notts County	0-4	0-1	7819		1	2	3	4		6	7				11			10		5			8	9									
21	30	Fulham	1-2	1-1	3622	McGinley	1	2	3	4		6	7			14	11			10		5	9#		8										
22	1 Jan	SWANSEA C.	1-1	1-0	3515	McGinley	1	2	3	4		6	7			9*	11			10		5	14		8										
23	13	Leyton Orient	0-1	0-1	3715		1	2	3	4		6	7				11			10		5			8				4#						
24	20	READING	1-1	1-0	3504	McGinley	1	2		4		6	7			9	11		14	10				12	8			3		5					
25	27	Birmingham C.	1-0	1-0	7461	McGinley	1	2		4		6	7			9*	11			10		5		14	8			3#							
26	3 Feb	Bury	0-0	0-0	2677		1	2		4		6	7				11		9#	10		5		14	8			3							
27	13	BLACKPOOL	1-1	1-0	2300	Kelly	1	2		4		6	7				11			10*		5		14	8#			3							
28	17	Chester C.	0-1	0-1	2500		1	2		4		6	7				11			10		5		14	8			3							
29	24	ROTHERHAM U.	1-1	0-2	3282	Naughton	1	2		4		6	7			9	11		14	10		5			12			3							
30	2 Mar	Cardiff C.	1-0	0-0	2751	O.G.	1	2		4		6	7*			9*	11			10		5			12			3							
31	6	Crewe Alexandra	1-1	1-1	4318	McGinley	1	2		4		6					11		9#	10		5		12				3			7				
32	10	BRISTOL CITY	0-1	0-0	4785		1	2		4		6					11			10		5			14			3	8#		7				
33	13	CARDIFF C.	0-0	0-0	2318		1	2		4		6					11*		9#	10		5			14			3	8#						
34	17	Mansfield T.	1-2	1-1	2230	Spink	1	2		4		6					11			10		5		14				3	8			9			
35	20	WIGAN ATHLETIC	1-3	0-2	2297	Kelly	1	2		4		6					11			10		5		14				3	8		12	9			
36	24	WALSALL	2-0	2-0	3225	Moyes, Kelly	1	2		4		6					11			10				14				3	8		12	9	5		
37	31	Brentford	1-1	0-0	5387	Kelly	1	2		4		6					11			10*		14						3	8		7*	9	5		
38	3 Apr	NORTHAMPTON T.	2-0	1-0	2314	McGinley, Moyes	1	2		4		6					11			10				14				3	8		7	9	5		
39	7	HUDDERSFIELD T.	3-3	1-1	2867	McGinley(3,1 pen)	1	2		4		6					11			10		14						3	8			9*	5#		
40	9	Tranmere R.	1-3	1-2	7812	Moyes	1	2#		4		6					11#			10				14				3	8			9	5		
41	14	Swansea C.	1-0	0-0	3386	McGinley	1			4		6					11#			10				2				3	8		12	9	5		
42	17	NOTTS COUNTY	2-2	1-0	3536	Spink(2)	1			4		6					11#			10				2				3	8		12	9	5		
43	21	Bolton Wanderers	1-0	1-0	5665	McGinley	1			4		6					11#			10				2				3#	8		14	9	5		
44	24	FULHAM	2-0	2-0	2831	Spink, McGinley	1			4		6					11#			10*				2				3#	8		14	9	5		
45	28	Bristol Rovers	0-1	0-1	7903		1			4		6					11			10				2					8*		14	9	5	12	
46	5 May	PRESTON N.E.	2-0	0-0	5319	McGinley, Spink	1			4		6				14	11			10				2					8*		7	9	5	12	

F.A.Cup

Rd	Date	Opponent	Res	HT	Att	Scorers	Line-up / subs
1R	18 Nov	CHESTERFIELD	2-3	1-2	3842	McGinley(2pens)	1 2 3 4 5 6 7 8 14 11# 11 12 10 14 5 9* 12

League Cup

Rd	Date	Opponent	Res	HT	Att	Scorers	Line-up / subs
1R1	22 Aug	NOTTS C.	3-0	1-0	2848	Melrose, Green Pratley	1 2 3* 4 5 6 7 8 9# 11 12 10 14
1R2	29	Notts C.	1-3	0-1	2559	Naughton(pen)	1 2 3 4 5 6 7 8 9# 11 12 10
2R1	19 Sep	SWINDON T.	0-3	0-3	3518		1 2 3 4* 5 6 7 8 12 11 10 9* 14
2R2	3 Oct	Swindon T.	1-3	0-0	5544	Naughton(pen)	1 2 4 6 7 8 12 11 3 10 9* 5 14

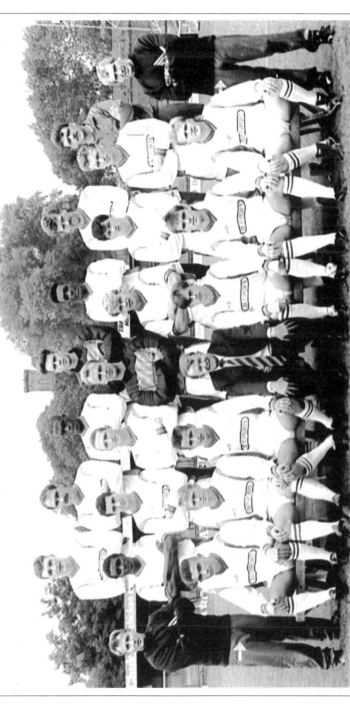

(Back) Finley, Pratley, McLean, Hughes, Brown, Bell, B.Williams.
(Middle) Hartford (Player/Coach), Kasule, Worsley, Green, Perks, Pittman, Kelly, Moyes, Helm (Physio).
(Front) Roberts, Priest, Griffiths, McNeil (Manager), Melrose, Purdie, McGinlay.

Final League Table

		P	W	D	L	F	A	Pts
1	Bristol R.	46	26	15	5	71	35	93
2	Bristol C.	46	27	10	9	76	40	91
3	Notts.Co.	46	25	12	9	73	53	87
4	Tranmere R.	46	23	11	12	86	49	80
5	Bury	46	21	11	14	70	49	74
6	Bolton W.	46	18	15	13	59	48	69
7	Birmingham C.	46	18	12	16	60	59	66
8	Huddersfield T.	46	17	14	15	61	62	65
9	Rotherham U.	46	17	13	16	71	62	64
10	Reading	46	15	19	12	57	53	64
11	Shrewsbury T.	46	16	15	15	59	54	63
12	Crewe Alex	46	15	17	14	56	53	62
13	Brentford	46	18	7	21	66	66	61
14	Leyton Orient	46	16	10	20	52	56	58
15	Mansfield T.	46	16	7	23	50	65	55
16	Chester C.	46	13	15	18	43	55	54
17	Swansea C.	46	14	12	20	45	63	54
18	Wigan Ath.	46	13	14	19	48	64	53
19	Preston NE	46	14	10	22	65	79	52
20	Fulham	46	12	15	19	55	66	51
21	Cardiff C.	46	12	14	20	51	70	50
22	Northampton T.	46	11	14	21	51	68	47
23	Blackpool	46	10	16	20	49	73	46
24	Walsall	46	9	14	23	40	72	41

SEASON 1990/91
Division 3

No.	Date	Opposition	Res.	H.T.	Att.	Goalscorers	Perks S.J.	Worsley G.	Lynch T.	Kelly A.G.	Heathcote M.	Blake M.C.	Griffiths C.	Wimbleton P.	Spink D.P.	Brown M.A.	Gorman P.	Moore J.	Naughton W.	Hartford R.	Weir W.	Coughlin R.J.	Shaw G.R.	Summerfield	Parrish S.	Hughes K.D.	Clarke W.	Clements K.	Ryan D.	Askew W.	Taylor M.	Lyne N.G.F.	Burton M.G.	O'Toole C.P.
1	25 Aug	BOLTON W.	0-1	0-0	4608	Naughton, O.G.	1	2	3	4	5	6	7*	8	9	10	11	12	14															
2	1 Sep	Rotherham U.	2-2	0-1	4817	Spink, Moore	1	2	3	4	5	6		12	9	10	11	7	14	8*	14													
3	8	FULHAM	2-2	1-0	2929	Spink, Moore	1	2	3	4	5	6	14	8	9*	10	3	7		8	14	12												
4	14	Tranmere R.	1-1	0-1	7105	Weir	1	12	3	4*	5	6	11	8	9	10#	3	7			14													
5	18	Southend U.	1-2	1-2	5100	O.G.	1	2	3	4	5	6	11	8	9	10	3	7																
6	22	GRIMSBY T.	1-2	2-0	2904	Lynch	1	2	3	4	5	6	11	14	9*	10	3	7																
7	29	Stoke C.	3-1	2-1	12672	Spink, O.G., Worsley	1	2	3	4	5	6	11	12	9	10*	3	7				8												
8	2 Oct	BURY	1-1	1-0	3258	Shaw	1	2	3	4	5*	6	11#		9	10	3	7			14	8#	7											
9	6	MANSFIELD T.	0-3	0-1	2587		1	2	3	4	5	6			9*	10	3	7			14	8	12											
10	13	Leyton Orient	2-3	1-3	4394	Spink, Summerfield	1	2	3	4	5#	6			9	10	3	7					7	8										
11	20	Chester C.	2-3	0-1	1431	Shaw, Clarke(pen).		2	3	4	5	6		11	12	7	3			11#			7	8		1	9							
12	23	SWANSEA C.	1-2	1-0	2589	Summerfield		2	3	4	5	6		11	12	14	3			11#	12		9	8		1	10							
13	27	BIRMINGHAM C.	4-1	2-0	6050	Clarke(3), Wimbleton		2	3	4	5	6		11	12	7	3			11#			9*	8		1	10							
14	3 Nov	Bournemouth	2-3	2-2	5561	Lynch, Summerfield		2	3	4	5	6		11	12	7	3			11	14		9*	8		1	10							
15	9	CREWE ALEXANDRA	1-0	0-0	4461	Clarke		2	3	4	5	6		12	12	7	3		14				9*	8		1	10	14						
16	24	Cambridge U.	1-3	0-2	3632	Clarke		2	3	4	5	6		12	12	7	3		14				9*	8		1	10							
17	1 Dec	Preston N.E.	3-4	0-2	4515	Summerfield, Blake, Kelly		2	3	4	5	6		12	9	7	3						9*	14		1	10	5#						
18	15	WIGAN ATHLETIC	0-0	0-0	2227			2	3	4	6	6			9	7*	2						10	8*		1	10#	5						
19	22	Bradford C.	4-2	1-2	5722	Blake, Shaw(3)		2	3	4	6	6		12	9	7	8		14	4			10			1		5						
20	29	EXETER C.	2-2	1-0	3179	Heathcote, Spink		2	3	4	14	6		12	9	7	14		14	4#			10	8		1		5						
21	1 Jan	Brentford	0-3	0-1	7064			2	3	4	5	6		12	9	7	2						10	8#		1		5						
22	12	ROTHERHAM U.	0-0	0-0	2800			5	3	4	6	2			12	10	2		14	4#			10			1		5	14					8
23	19	Bolton W.	0-1	0-1	6164			14	3	4	6	2	12	12	9	7			4*				10			1			14	8				6
24	2 Feb	SOUTHEND U.	0-1	0-1	4377			14		4	6	2	12	9	9*	7							10			1		5	8	8	11			6
25	5	Grimsby T.	0-1	0-0	5683			14	3	4#	6	2	12		9	7							10*			1		5	8	8	11			6
26	19	HUDDERSFIELD T.	0-0	0-0	2821				3	4	5	2		8	9	7			14		12		10	8#		1		5	8	8	11			6#
27	22	Crewe Alexandra	2-1	0-0	3940	O.G., Taylor		4			5	2		8	9	7	3		4*				2#			1		6	12		11			6
28	2 Mar	PRESTON N.E.	0-1	0-1	2989	Lyne		4*			5	2		8	9	7	3						8*	12		1		6	14	11#	11#	10		9*
29	9	Wigan Athletic	2-2	1-1	2269	Brown, Summerfield		11			5	2		12	12	7#	3						8*	9		1		6	14	10		11		9
30	12	Bury	1-2	0-1	2417	Kelly		11			5	2		9	12	7	3						8*	9		1		6	14	10#	10#	11		9
31	16	STOKE C.	2-0	0-0	6210	Lyne(2)			3	4	5	2		14	8	7							12			1		6	14	10		11		9
32	19	LEYTON ORIENT	3-0	0-0	2236	O.G., Spink, Taylor			3	4	5	2		12	8	7	3						12			1		6	14	10		11		9
33	23	Mansfield T.	1-2	0-1	2524	Lyne			3	4	5	2		12	8	7	3				12		10*	2#		1		6	14	10		11		9
34	26	TRANMERE R.	0-1	0-0	3949				3		5	2		4	8	7	3						8	7		1		6	6#	11#		11	9*	9
35	30	Huddersfield T.	1-2	1-2	5684	Lyne				4	5	2		9	14	7	3						12	12		1		6	6#	10		11	9	
36	2 Apr	BRADFORD C.	1-0	0-0	3090	Heathcote				4	5	2			8	7	3						8*	9		1		6	14	10		11	14	
37	6	Exeter C. *	0-0	0-0	3277	* (Abandoned at half time – waterlogged pitch)				4	5	2			12	3	3						8*	9		1		6	14	10#		11	14	
38	9	Fulham	0-4	0-0	3415					4	5	2			12	7	3						12	9		1		6	14	10		11	14	
39	13	BRENTFORD	1-1	0-0	2841	Spink			14	4	5	2		12	8	7	3						9*		9	1		6	10	10		11	6#	
40	18	CAMBRIDGE U.	1-2	0-1	2571	Heathcote			6	4	5	2	9#	12	8	7	3						8	9		1			14	10		11	6	
41	20	CHESTER C.	1-0	1-0	2952	Heathcote			6	4	5	2	9#	12	8	7	3							9		1			14	10		11	9#	
42	23	Reading	2-1	2-1	2422	Griffiths(2)			6	4	5	2	9#		14	7	3				12		7			1			14	10		11	8	
43	27	Swansea C.	1-0	0-0	3152	O.G.		3	6	4	5	2	9#		9*	3#	3						7			1			14	10		11	8	
44	30	Exeter C.	0-3	0-1	2763			3	6	4	5	2	9#		14		3#						7	10		1			14	10		11	8	
45	4 May	Birmingham C.	1-0	1-0	6256	Griffiths			6	4	5	2	9		14	7	3						10	10		1						11	14	8
46	7	READING	5-1	4-1	2425	Kelly(3), Lyne, Griffiths		12	6#	4	5	2	9		14	7	3						7			1			8#			11	4*	8
47	11	BOURNEMOUTH	3-1	0-0	5016	Heathcote(2), Lyne		12	6	4	5	2	9		14	7	3*						10	10		1			8#			11	8	

F.A. Cup

		Opponent	Score	HT	Att	Scorers	Team (shirt numbers)
1R	17 Nov	Bradford C.	0-0	0-0	6629	Shaw(2)	3 4 11 6 12 9 7 5 10 8* 1 2 14
1Rr	21	BRADFORD C.	2-1	0-1	3708	Spink	3 4 11* 6 14 9 7 5 10 8 1 2 12
2R	11 Dec	CHORLEY	1-0	1-0	3380		2 3 4 6 11 9 7# 8* 10 12 1 5 14
3R	5 Jan	WATFORD	4-1	1-0	5327	Brown, Kelly(pen), Shaw(2)	2 3 4 11 6 12 9 7 10 8 1 5 14
4R	26	WIMBLEDON	1-0	1-0	9269	Shaw	12 3 4 11 6 9 7 10 2 1 5 14 8
5R	27 Feb	ARSENAL	0-1	0-0	12356		11 3 4 5 2 9 7 12 8* 1 6 14 10

League Cup

		Opponent	Score	HT	Att	Scorers	Team (shirt numbers)
1R1	28 Aug	Gillingham	0-1	0-0	2613		1 2 3 4 5 6 8 9 10 12 7 14 11
1R2	4 Sep	GILLINGHAM	2-0	2-0	2193	Moore, Kelly	1 2 3 4 5 6 12 9 10 7 11 8 14
2R1	25	IPSWICH T.	1-1	1-1	2764	Griffiths	1 2 12 4 5 6 14 9 10 3 7 8
2R2	9 Oct	Ipswich T.	0-3	0-2	7306		1 2 6 4 5 14 12 10 9* 3 7 8 11

Final League Table

		P	W	D	L	F	A	Pts
1	Cambridge U.	46	25	11	10	75	45	86
2	Southend U.	46	26	7	13	67	51	85
3	Grimsby T.	46	24	11	11	66	34	83
4	Bolton W.	46	24	11	11	64	50	83
5	Tranmere R.	46	23	9	14	64	46	78
6	Brentford	46	21	13	12	59	47	76
7	Bury	46	20	13	13	67	56	73
8	Bradford C.	46	20	10	16	62	54	70
9	Bournemouth	46	19	13	14	58	58	70
10	Wigan Ath.	46	20	9	17	71	54	69
11	Huddersfield T.	46	18	13	15	57	51	67
12	Birmingham C.	46	16	17	13	45	49	65
13	Leyton Orient	46	18	10	18	55	58	64
14	Stock C.	46	16	12	18	55	59	60
15	Reading	46	17	8	21	53	66	59
16	Exeter C.	46	16	9	21	58	52	57
17	Preston NE	46	15	11	20	54	67	56
18	Shrewsbury T.	46	14	10	22	61	68	52
19	Chester C.	46	14	9	23	46	58	51
20	Swansea C.	46	13	9	24	49	72	48
21	Fulham	46	10	16	20	41	56	46
22	Crewe Alex.	46	11	11	24	62	80	44
23	Rotherham U.	46	10	12	24	50	87	42
24	Mansfield T.	46	8	14	24	42	63	38

(Back) Gorman, Moore, Green, Perks, Hughes, Pratley, Worsley, Blake. (Middle) Spink, Naughton, Kelly, Heathcote, Lynch, Copeland, Brown. (Front) B.Williams, Weir, Wimbleton, Hartford, Parris, Griffiths, Bond.

SEASON 1991/92
Division 3

No.	Date	Opposition	Res.	H.T.	Att.	Goalscorers
1	18 Aug	WIGAN ATHLETIC	1-0	0-0	3834	Carr
2	24	Bury	0-0	0-0	2373	
3	31	EXETER CITY	6-1	3-1	2912	Hopkins, Henry(2, 1pen), Summerfield, Lynch, Lyne
4	4 Sep	Stoke City	0-1	0-0	10182	
5		BRENTFORD	1-0	0-0	3193	Lyne
6	14	Torquay U.	2-1	1-1	2811	Summerfield, Henry(pen)
7	17	Bournemouth	0-1	0-0	5500	
8	21	SWANSEA C.	0-0	0-0	3427	
9	28	Bradford C.	0-3	0-0	5234	
10	5 Oct	BIRMINGHAM C.	1-1	0-1	7035	Henry
11	12	West Bromwich A.	0-2	0-1	12547	
12	19	Darlington	3-3	2-0	2188	Griffiths(2), Henry
13	26	READING	1-2	0-0	2398	Griffiths
14	2 Nov	PETERBOROUGH U.	2-0	0-0	1866	Griffiths, Cash
15	5	Hull City	0-4	0-3	5025	
16	23	HARTLEPOOL U.	1-4	0-3	2368	Donaldson
17	26	Stockport C.	4-1	2-0	3650	Bennett(2), Summerfield, Lyne
18	30	BOLTON W.	1-3	1-1	3937	Smith
19	14 Dec	Chester C.	4-1	1-1	1016	MacKenzie, O.G., Griffiths(2)
20	21	BURY	1-1	0-0	2573	Worsley
21	26	Exeter City	0-1	0-0	3857	
22	28	Wigan Athletic	1-1	1-1	2276	Summerfield
23	1 Jan	STOKE CITY	1-0	1-0	8557	Summerfield
24	11	PRESTON N.E.	2-0	0-0	3154	Griffiths, Hopkins
25	18	Fulham	1-0	0-0	3440	Lyne
26	25	HUDDERSFIELD T.	1-1	1-0	3688	Lyne
27		Leyton Orient	0-2	0-1	3197	
28	1 Feb	DARLINGTON	0-2	0-1	2675	
29	8	Reading	1-2	0-1	3303	Spink
30	11	Bolton W.	0-1	0-1	5276	
31	15	CHESTER C.	2-2	1-2	2807	Summerfield, M.Taylor
32	22	Preston N.E.	2-2	0-0	3342	Harmon(2)
33	29	LEYTON ORIENT	0-1	0-1	2873	
34	3 Mar	FULHAM	0-0	0-0	2137	
35	7	Huddersfield T.	1-2	1-1	4674	Summerfield
36	10	HULL CITY	2-3	0-2	1956	Griffiths, Lyne
37	14	Peterborough U.	0-1	0-0	7377	
38	20	STOCKPORT C.	0-1	0-1	3186	
39	28	Hartlepool U.	2-4	1-2	2515	Lynch, Bremner
40	31	TORQUAY U.	2-2	2-0	2172	McKeown, Lyne
41	4 Apr	BOURNEMOUTH	0-2	0-1	5561	
42		Bournemouth	1-2	1-0	2586	Lyne
43	17	Swansea C.	2-1	0-1	3429	M.Taylor, Hopkins
44	21	BRADFORD C.	3-2	2-0	2707	Bremner, Henry(2)
45	25	Birmingham C.	0-1	0-1	19868	
46	2 May	WEST BROMWICH A.	1-3	0-3	7442	Donaldson

Player appearances (shirt numbers by match)

No.	Hughes K.D.	Gorman P.A.	Lynch T.	Henry A.	Heathcote M.	Blake M.C.	Smith M.A.	Summerfield K.	Spink D.P.	Carr C.P.	Lyne N.G.F.	Hopkins R.A.	Griffiths C.B.	O'Toole C.P.	Cash S.P.	Taylor M.R.	Parkin T.J.	Worsley G.	Perks S.J.	Ryan D.T.	Donaldson O.M.	Bennett D.A.	Evans P.S.	MacKenzie S.	Clark H.W.	Walsh A.	Paskin W.J.	Harmon D.J.	McKeown G.	Williams M.S.	Bremner K.J.	Barton M.	Williams M.
1	1	2	3	4	5	6	7#	8	9	10	11	12	14																				
2	1	2	3	4	5	6	7	8	9#	12	11	10	14																				
3	1	2	3	4	5*	6	7#	8	9		11	10	14	12																			
4	1	2	3	4	5	6	7#	8	9*		11	10	14	12	14																		
5	1	2	3	4	5	6	7*	8	14		11#	10	9	12	14																		
6	1	2	5	4	5	6	7	8	9		11#	12				10																	
7	1	2	14	4	5	5	7	8	9		11	12				6*																	
8	1	2	14	4	5	5	7	8	9		11	12				6	7																
9	1	2	9	4#	5	5	7	8	14		11	12				6	10																
10	1	2	11.	4		6	7*	8	14		9	12	12		14	3#	5																
11	1	2	11.	4		6	7*	8	14		9	12			14	3#	5																
12		14	3	4		6	7*	8			9	12	11		14	10	5																
13		14	3	4		6	7*	8			9	5	11	12	7	10#			2														
14		14	3	4		6	14	8	12		9	5	11*		7	10#			2	10													
15		2#	3*	4		6			12		9	5	11		7				14														
16		2	5	4		6	7*		12		9			14	7				3#		10	11											
17		2		4		6	11#		12		9#			10		6*	5		1		12	7*	14										
18		2	3	4		6	7*		5		9#		10	11		10	5		1		14												
19			3	4		6	7#		5		9	11							2		14			10									
20			3	4		6	12		5		9#	14	11		7			12	2		14			10	7								
21			3	4		6			5		9#	11	11			7		12	1		14			10	10	2							
22			3	4		6	7#		5		14		12			11*		2	1		9				2								
23			3*	4		6			5		11	14	9#					2	1		7				10	12							
24			3	4		6	14		5		11#	7#	9					2	1	9*	7*			10	10	12							
25			12	4		6			5		11	12						2	1	14	9*			10	10				14				
26			12	4		6			5		10	7	12	11*		6		2	1	9*	9*			10*	2								
27			12	4		6			5		10	9	12	10				2	1	14				10	2								
28		1	3	4		6	7#	8#	5		11	9#	9#	11		10*	1	2	1		14			3	12	7							
29		1	3	4*		6	7	8	5		11*	7		14		10		2	1		12			3	3	4#							
30		1				6		8	5		11	7#	9			10		2	1	14	12				3	3							
31		1	3*	4*		6	7	8	5		11	7*	9	4		10		2	1	14	7				2	3	9						
32		1	3	4		6		8	5			14	12	12		10		2	1	9*	7*				2	2		14					
33		1	3	4*		6#		8	5			7#	11	11				2	1	12	9				2	2		10	4*				
34		1	3	4			14	8	5		11	12	10			6		1	1	14	9*				2	2		14					
35		1	3	4				8	5		10	9	12	11*				7	1		14				2	3	6	14	6	6			
36		1	3*	4			7#	8	5		10	12	9	11			11	7#	1		14				2	3	6	14	6	6			
37		1	3				7#	8	5		10		9	12		11			1		14				2	3	6	14	6	6			
38		1	3				7	8	5		10	7*	9	12		11			1		12				2	3	6		6	6			
39		1	3					8	5		11	14		14		7	2		1		9			11	2	2#			6	5	9		
40		1	3					8	5		11	14		12		2	2		1		12			10	2				6		9		
41		1	3#			6#		8	5		11	10		12		7#	2	7	1		9		14		4	2	2#			4*	9		
42			3			6	14	8	5		11	10		12		7#	2	7	1		9				4	2					9		
43		1	3*			6	14	8	5		11	10		12		7	2	7	1		4*				4	2		14		14	9		
44		1	8			6	12	8	5		11	10	3	12		7*	2	7	1		9*				4	2#					9		
45		1	14			6		8	5		11	10*	12			7*	2	7	1						4	2#					9		
46		1	3			6			5		11		8	7*			2	7*	1		9		10	9	4	2#			9	14		1	12

F.A. Cup

	Date	Opponent	Score	HT	Att	Scorers																			
							2	5		6	7	8	12		9	11	11		10		4	1		14
1R	16 Nov	Hartlepool U.	2-3	1-1	2864	Lyne, Smith																		

League Cup

	Date	Opponent	Score	HT	Att	Scorers	1	2	3	4	5	6	7	8	9	11	10	12						
1R1	20 Aug	PLYMOUTH A.	1-1	1-0	2152	Summerfield	1	2	3	4	5	6	7	8	9	11	10	12						
1R2	27	Plymouth A.	2-2	0-1	3580	Summerfield, Carr	1	2	3	4	5	6*	7	8	9	11	10#	14						
2R1	24 Sep	Wolves	1-6	1-4	12229	Summerfield	1	2	14	4	5	6	7	8	9*	11	12				3	6	10	
2R2	8 Oct	WOLVES	3-1	1-1	5784	Summerfield, Lyne(2)			5	4	6	7	8	11#	9	12				3	10	14	2*	1

(Back) Blake, Spink, Worsley, Heathcote, Perks, Kelly, ? Hughes, Lyne, Summerfield, Gorman, Lynch
(Front) Wimbleton, Brown, Ryan, O'Toole, Harrish, Griffiths, Hopkins.

FINAL LEAGUE TABLE

		P	W	D	L	F	A	Pts
1	Brentford	46	25	7	14	81	55	82
2	Birmingham C.	46	23	12	11	69	52	81
3	Huddersfield T.	46	22	12	12	59	38	78
4	Stoke C.	46	21	14	11	69	49	77
5	Stockport Co.	46	22	10	14	75	51	76
6	Peterborough U.	46	20	14	12	65	58	74
7	W.B.A.	46	19	14	13	64	49	71
8	Bournemouth	46	20	11	15	52	48	71
9	Fulham	46	19	13	14	57	53	70
10	Leyton Orient	46	18	11	17	62	52	65
11	Hartlepool U.	46	18	11	17	57	57	65
12	Reading	46	16	13	17	59	62	61
13	Bolton W.	46	14	17	15	57	56	59
14	Hull C.	46	16	11	19	54	54	59
15	Wigan Ath.	46	15	14	17	58	64	59
16	Bradford C.	46	13	19	14	62	61	58
17	Preston NE	46	15	12	19	61	72	57
18	Chester C.	46	14	14	18	56	59	56
19	Swansea C.	46	14	14	18	55	65	56
20	Exeter C.	46	14	11	21	57	80	53
21	Bury	46	13	12	21	55	74	51
22	Shrewsbry T.	46	12	11	23	53	68	47
23	Torquay U.	46	13	8	25	42	68	47
24	Darlington	46	10	7	29	56	90	37

SEASON 1992/93
Division 3 (Reconstituted, previously Div. 4)

No.	Date	Opposition	Res.	H.T.	Att.	Goalscorers	Edwards P.	Worsley G.	Clark H.W.	Evans P.S.	Spink D.P.	Blake M.C.	Taylor M.R.	Summerfield K.	Brough J.R.	Hodges D.	Lyne N.G.F.	Griffiths C.B.	Williams M.S.	Smith N.P.	O'Toole C.P.	Lynch T.	Smith M.A.	Barham M.F.	Haylock P.	Harmon D.J.	Williams M.	Seabury K.	Williams L.	Watts J.	Brown M.A.	Evans J.S.	MacKenzie S.	Kinnaird P.	Brooks C.	Piggott G.	Turner R.P.
1	15 Aug	York C.	0-2	0-1	2414		1	2	3	4	5	6	7#	8	9*	10	11	12	14																			
2	22	DONCASTER R.	2-1	1-1	1867	Summerfield, Griffiths	1	2		14	5	3	6	8	9*		11	10	4	7	12																	
3	29	Scunthorpe U.	1-1	0-1	3438	Taylor	1	2		14	5	6	4	8	12		11#	10	9	7*		3	12															
4	1 Sep	Colchester U.	2-0	1-0	3230	Griffiths, Brough	1	2			5	6	4	8*	7		11	10	9			3	12															
5	5	ROCHDALE	1-2	0-1	2547	Haylock	1	2	3	8	5	6	4	8*	7		11*	10#	9					12	14													
6	12	Wrexham	0-2	0-0	4265		1	2	3		5	6	4		12		11	10	9					7	2	14												
7	19	SCARBOROUGH	2-0	1-0	1527	Griffiths, Lyne	1	12	8		5	6	4#				11	10			12	3	9	7	2	14												
8	15	BURY	2-0	2-0	2307	Griffiths(2,1pen)	1	12	8		5	6	4				11#	10	12			3	9*	7	2	14												
9	26	Lincoln C.	1-0	0-0	2746	Barham	1	14	8#		5	6	4					10				3	9	7*	2*													
10	3 Oct	Barnet	2-2	2-0	2913	Griffiths, Summerfield	1	12	8#		5	6	4	11	12		14	10				3	9	7	2#													
11	10	DARLINGTON	1-2	0-1	2829	Griffiths	1		8		5	6	4	11			14	10	14			3	9	7	2													
12	17	Chesterfield	4-2	1-2	3207	Taylor, Griffiths(2), Lyne	1		8		14	6	4	11			9	10	14			3	12	7	2													
13	24	CARDIFF C.	3-2	2-1	4161	Griffiths(3)	1	12	8		12	6	4	11			9	10	14			3	7*		2													
14	31	Northampton T.	0-0	0-0	2731		1	12	8	7*	5	6	4	11			9	10	14			3			2													
15	3 Nov	HALIFAX T.	1-0	1-0	2704	O'Toole	1		8		5	6	4		7*		9	10	12		11	3			2			14										
16	21	WALSALL	0-3	0-3	4353		1	12	8		5	6	4#	11			9	10			14	3	9		2				7*					11#				
17	12 Dec	GILLINGHAM	2-1	1-0	2442	Griffiths(2,1pen)	1	2	8		5	6	4	12			11	10*	14			3*			2				7									
18	20	Torquay U.	0-1	0-1	1960		1	2	8				4#	5	12		11	10*	6		9	3							14	7								
19	26	Hereford U.	1-1	0-0	3287	Worsley	1	2	2				8	4			9#	10	5			6	11							3	7							
20	28	CREWE ALEXANDRA	4-1	0-1	4789	Taylor, Brown, Lyne, Griffiths	1	2	12		14		4	8	12		9	10	5		14	3	11						6	7								
21	2 Jan	WREXHAM	0-1	0-0	6179		1	2	8		12		4				9	10	5			3	11						6	7								
22	16	LINCOLN C.	3-2	2-1	2509	Spink, Summerfield, Taylor	1		12		9#	6	4	8				10*					11		2*					5	7	14						
23	26	SCUNTHORPE U.	2-1	0-1	2190	Lynch, Griffiths	1	12				6	4	8	14			10	5			9	11		2					3	7		14					
24	29	Doncaster R.	1-0	1-0	2227	Summerfield	1	12				6	4	8				10	5			9	11#		2					3	7		14					
25	6 Feb	YORK C.	1-1	0-1	3532	Taylor	1	7	8			6*	4					10	5*		14	9	11		2			14		3	7		12					
26	13	Rochdale	0-2	0-1	2446		1	12				6	4	8				10	5			9	5		2*					3				7				
27	20	COLCHESTER U.	4-3	1-0	2653	Griffiths(2), M.Smith, O.G.	1	2	12		6	6	4#	8	14			10	5		14	3	11											7				
28	27	Darlington	2-0	1-0	1422	Griffiths(2)	1	2	9		6		4	8	9*			10	5		14	3	11											7	12			
29	6 Mar	BARNET	1-0	1-0	4518	Kinnaird	1		2		6	6	4	8				10	5			3	11		14								12	7		9		
30	9	Carlisle U.	0-1	0-0	4022		1		2			6	4	8				10	5			3	11#		14						7		9*					
31	20	Halifax T.	1-1	0-1	3872	Blake	1		2			6	4	8#	12			10	5		14	3	11								7		12			9*	
32	27	Walsall	1-1	0-0	5573	Griffiths	1		2			6*	4	8				10	5		14	3	11								7		8#			12	
33	30	Bury	0-0	0-0	2976		1	12			6		4	8				10	5		14	3	11								7						
34	3 Apr	CARLISLE U.	2-3	1-1	3100	M.S.Williams, Summerfield	1	9	2		6		4#	8	14			10	5		14	3	11								7#		12			12	
35	6	Gillingham	2-0	1-0	3086		1	2	12		6		4	8				10	5		14	3	11								7					9*	
36	10	HEREFORD U.	1-1	1-1	3604	Griffiths	1	2	6				4	8				10	5		12	3	11								7#						9
37	12	Crewe Alexandra	2-2	0-1	4215	Griffiths(2)	1	12	2		6		4	8	14			10	5			3	11#								7		12				9
38	17	TORQUAY U.	0-1	0-1	3082		1	6	2				4	8	14			10	5			3	11					12			7					9*	9*
39	20	Scarborough	2-1	1-1	1325	Summerfield, Griffiths	1	7	2			6	4	8	14			10	5		12	3	11									14				12	9
40	24	CHESTERFIELD	2-2	2-1	3473	Worsley, Griffiths(pen)	1	7	2			6	4	8	14			10	5		12	3	11														9#
41	1 May	Cardiff C.	1-2	1-1	17253	Summerfield	1	7#	2	12	12	6	4	8				10				3	11					14			5		14				9
42	8	NORTHAMPTON T.	2-3	2-0	6612	Lynch, Griffiths	1	14	2	12	12	6	8#	8#				10				3	11					7			5		7				9

F.A.Cup

1R	14 Nov	MANSFIELD T.	3-1	2-1	3353	Summerfield, Lyne, L.Williams	1	3			5	6	4	11		9	10		8			2	14	12	7
2R	5 Dec	Burnley	1-1	0-0	10038	Griffiths	1	2	8		5	6	4	11		10		12	3	9		7	14		
2Rr	15	BURNLEY	1-2	0-0	5671	Griffiths	1	2	8		5	4	7		11	10*		12	3	9#		6	14		

League Cup

1R1	18 Aug	WIGAN ATH.	1-2	0-1	1337	Griffiths	1	2		4	5	6	7	8	9	10*	11	12	14	3
1R2	25	Wigan Ath.	1-0	1-0	1380	N.Smith	1	2		12	5	6	4	8	14	11#	10	9	7*	3

(Back) Bond (Manager), Summerfield, Donaldson, Lynch, Lyne, Edwards, McKenzie, Spink, Clark, Blake, Brough, Pratley (Youth Coach)
(Front) Davies (Asst. Manager), Williams, Smith, Griffiths, Taylor, O'Toole, Harmon, Worsley, Musgrove (Physio/Coach).

FINAL LEAGUE TABLE

		P	W	D	L	F	A	Pts
1	Cardiff C.	42	25	8	9	77	47	83
2	Wrexham	42	23	11	8	75	52	80
3	Barnet	42	23	10	9	66	48	79
4	York C.	42	21	12	9	72	45	75
5	Walsall	42	22	7	13	76	61	73
6	Crewe Alex.	42	21	7	14	75	56	70
7	Bury	42	18	9	15	63	55	63
8	Lincoln C.	42	18	9	15	57	53	63
9	Shrewsbury T.	42	17	11	14	57	52	62
10	Colchester U.	42	18	5	19	67	76	59
11	Rochdale	42	16	10	16	70	70	58
12	Chesterfield	42	15	11	16	59	63	56
13	Scarborough	42	15	9	18	66	71	54
14	Scunthorpe U.	42	14	12	16	57	54	54
15	Darlington	42	12	14	16	48	53	50
16	Doncaster R.	42	11	14	17	42	57	47
17	Hereford U.	42	10	15	17	64	60	45
18	Carlisle U.	42	11	11	20	51	65	44
19	Torquay U.	42	12	7	23	45	67	43
20	Northampton T.	42	11	8	23	48	74	41
21	Gillingham	42	9	13	20	48	64	40
22	Halifax T.	42	9	9	24	45	68	36

No.	Date	Opposition	Res.	H.T.	Att.	Goalscorers	Edwards P.	Hockaday D.	Lynch T.	Evans P.S.	Spink D.P.	Blake M.C.	Patterson G.	Clarke W.	Summerfield K.	Griffiths C.B.	MacKenzie S.	Brown M.A.	Withe C.	Mulvey J.R.	Taylor M.R.	Williams M.S.	Donaldson O.M.	Gallen J.M.	Clarke T.	Seabury K.	Smith M.A.	Walton D.L.	Brough J.R.	Croft B.G.A.	Donowa B.L.	Rutherford M.R.	Woods R.G.
1	14 Aug	Mansfield T.	0-1	0-0	2983		1	2	3	4	5	6	7*	8	9	10	11#	12	14	G													
2	21	WALSALL	1-2	0-0	3681	Brown	1	2	3	4	5	6	11	8	9	10		7	12	G													
3	28	Preston N.E.	1-6	0-5	4941	Brown	1	2		10*	9#	6	11	8	5			7	3	G	4		14										
4	31	Colchester U.	3-3	1-3	2723	Lynch, Summerfield, Spink	1	2	3	11#	12	6	14	8	10			7		G	4	5	9*										
5	4 Sep	BURY	1-0	1-0	2669	Donaldson	1	2	3#	11	14	6	14					7		G	4	5	9*										
6	11	Darlington	2-0	2-0	1702	Clarke(2)	1	2		11	14	6		8	10			7		G	4	5	9*										
7	18	GILLINGHAM	2-2	1-1	2811	Griffiths, Blake	1		3	11	5	6	12	8	10	14		7		G	4*	5											
8	25	Scarborough	3-1	2-1	1137	Griffiths(3)	1	2#	3	11	5	6	4	8	10	9		7		G	8	5											
9	2 Oct	TORQUAY U.	3-2	0-1	2725	O.G., Spink, Summerfield	1		9*	10	9*	6	11	12	4			7		G	2	5											
10	9	CARLISLE U.	1-0	0-1	3254	Griffiths	1	14		10	12	6	4	8	11	9		7		G	2#	5											
11	16	Chester C.	0-1	0-1	3052		1	14	12	2	8*	6	11#		11	9		7		G		5											
12	23	DONCASTER R.	0-1	0-1	2675		1	2#	3	10	9	6	12	8	11*			7			4	5	14		G	14							
13	30	Wycombe W.	1-1	0-1	5064	Brown	1	2	5	12	10	6	11	8#	8			7			4	5	9		G								
14	2 Nov	CREWE ALEXANDRA	2-2	1-1	5585	Donaldson, Spink	1	2	5	12	9	6	11	8	8			7			4	5	10#	14	G								
15	6	Northampton T.	3-0	1-0	2650	Spink(2), Lynch	1	2	5	12	9	6	11	8#	8			7			4	5		14	G		14						
16	20	SCUNTHORPE U.	0-0	0-0	2436		1	2	3		9	6	11	8#	8		8	7			4	5		14	G		10						
17	27	Wigan Athletic	5-2	1-0	1498	Clarke(2,1pen), Spink(3)	1	2	3	12	9		11	8	14			7	12		4	5		12	G		14						
18	11 Dec	Walsall	1-0	1-0	4979	Spink	1	2	12		9		10	8	14			7	3		4	5			G		12			11#	11		
19	17	MANSFIELD T.	2-2	0-1	3392	Walton, Clarke	1	2	12		9		10	8	14			7			4	5#			G			6		11	11		
20	27	Hereford U.	1-0	1-0	4333	Clarke	1	2	12		9		11	8#	14			7			4	5			G					10			
21	1 Jan	Chesterfield	2-1	1-1	3614	Spink(2)	1	2	12		9		10	8#				7			4	5			G			6		11*			
22	3	COLCHESTER	2-1	0-1	4245	Walton, Spink	1	2	12		9		10#	8*				7			4	5			G		11*	6					
23	15	CHESTER C.	3-0	2-0	5365	Clarke(2,1pen), Williams	1		2		9		10	8	14			7			4	5#		14	G		11#	6			11		
24	29	WYCOMBE W.	1-0	0-0	5967	Spink	1		2		9		10	8				7			4	5	12		G		12	6			11		
25	5 Feb	Doncaster R.	0-0	0-0	2047		1		2		9		10	8	14			7			4	5	14	8*	G			6			11		
26	12	ROCHDALE	1-1	1-0	4882	O.G.	1	2	2		9	6	10	8#				7#			4	5		8#	G		14	6	14		11*		
27	19	PRESTON N.E.	1-0	0-0	5391	Lynch	1	2	2		9	12	10	8	12			7			4	5		8*	G			6			11		
28	26	Bury	3-2	0-2	3443	Clarke(pen), Spink, Brown	1	2	2		9		10	8	12			7			4	5			G			6				14	11#
29	1 Mar	LINCOLN C.	1-2	0-0	4706	Walton	1	2	2*		9		10	8*	12			7			4	5	8*	14	G			6				11	11
30	5	DARLINGTON	1-1	0-1	4011	Taylor	1	2	2*		9		10	8	7#			7			4	5			G			6				11	11
31	12	Gillingham	2-0	0-0	3038	Walton, Spink	1	2			9		10	8	12			7			4	5		14	G			6				11	11
32	19	SCARBOROUGH	2-0	1-0	3901	Gallen, Spink	1	2			9			8	10			7			4	5		8*	G		14	6				11	11
33	26	Torquay U.	0-0	0-0	4085		1	2	3		9		10	8	12			7			4	5		8#	G		14	6	14			11	14
34	2 Apr	HEREFORD U.	2-0	0-0	5310	Spink, Lynch	1	2	3		9		10	8*	12			7			4	5		8*	G		8#	6				14	11#
35	4	Lincoln C.	1-0	0-0	2823	Brown	1	2	3		9		10	8*	12			7			4	5		8*	G		8*	6				14	11
36	9	CHESTERFIELD	0-0	0-0	4846		1	2	3		9		10	8	12			7			4	5			G			6				14	11#
37	12	Rochdale	2-1	0-0	2408	Spink, Walton	1	2	3		9		10	12	8			7			4	5			G			6				11	14
38	19	Crewe Alexandra	0-0	0-0	5251		1	2	3		9		10	12	8			7			4	5			G			6				11#	11#
39	23	NORTHAMPTON T.	2-1	1-1	6512	Woods, Clarke	1	2	3		9		10	8				7			4*	5			G			6				14	11#
40	30	Scunthorpe U.	4-1	0-2	4587	Patterson, Brown, Clarke, Taylor	1	2	3		9		10*	8*	12			7			4	5			G			6				14	11
41	3 May	Carlisle U.	1-2	0-0	8007	Brown	1	2	3		9		10	8	12			7			4	5			G			6				14	11#
42	7	WIGAN ATHLETIC	0-0	0-0	7686		1	2	3*		9		10	8	12			7			4	5			G			6				14	11#

F.A.Cup

			Result	HT	Att	Scorers	1	2	3	9	11	8		7	14		12	G	5	4*	6
1R	13 Nov	DONCASTER R.	1-1	0-0	3408	Gallen	1	2	3	9	11	8		7	14			G	5	4*	6
1Rr	1 Dec	Doncaster R.	2-1	0-0	3524	Spink, Walton	1	2	3	12	9	11	8		7		G	14	5	4*	6
2R	4	PRESTON N.E.	0-1	0-1	5018		1	2	3	9	11	8		7	14		G	12	5	4*	6

League Cup

			Result	HT	Att	Scorers	1	2	3	11	6	5	14	8	9	10		7	12	G	4*
1R1	17 Aug	SCUNTHORPE U.	1-0	1-0	1936	P.S.Evans	1	2	3	11	6	5	14	8	9	10		7	12	G	4*
1R2	24	Scunthorpe U.	1-1	1-0	2320	Griffiths	1	2	3	11	9	6	14	8	5	10*		7		G	4
2R1	22 Sep	Southampton	0-1	0-1	5038		1		3	4	9	6	8	11*	10	12		7	14	G	5
2R2	5 Oct	SOUTHAMPTON	2-0	1-0	5247	Summerfield, Brown	1	14	3	8	9	6	4	11	10	12		7		G	2	5
3R	26	Blackburn R.	0-0	0-0	10603		1	2	14	6	12	10		9*	8		7		G	4	5
3Rr	9 Nov	BLACKBURN R.	3-4	1-1	7330	Summerfield(2), Mackenzie(pen)	1	2	6	9	12	8	11	7	3		G	10*	4	5	14

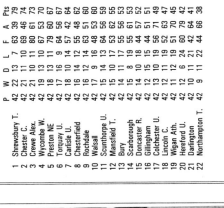

FINAL LEAGUE TABLE

		P	W	D	L	F	A	Pts
1	Shrewsbury T.	42	22	13	7	63	39	79
2	Chester C.	42	21	11	10	69	46	74
3	Crewe Alex.	42	21	10	11	80	61	73
4	Wycombe W.	42	19	13	10	67	53	70
5	Preston NE	42	18	13	11	79	60	67
6	Torquay U.	42	17	16	9	64	56	67
7	Carlisle U.	42	18	10	14	57	42	64
8	Chesterfield	42	16	14	12	55	48	62
9	Rochdale	42	16	12	14	63	51	60
10	Walsall	42	17	9	16	48	53	60
11	Scunthorpe U.	42	15	14	13	64	56	59
12	Mansfield T.	42	15	10	17	53	62	55
13	Bury	42	14	11	17	55	56	53
14	Scarborough	42	15	8	19	55	61	53
15	Doncaster R.	42	14	10	18	44	57	52
16	Gillingham	42	12	15	15	44	51	51
17	Colchester U.	42	13	10	19	56	71	49
18	Lincoln C.	42	12	11	19	52	63	47
19	Wigan Ath.	42	11	12	19	51	70	45
20	Hereford U.	42	12	6	24	60	79	42
21	Darlington	42	10	11	21	42	64	41
22	Northampton T.	42	9	11	22	44	66	38

(Back) Davies, Edwards, W.Clarke, Patterson, Summerfield, T.Clarke, Walton, Williams, Taylor, Woods, Musgrove
(Front) Brown, Spink, Lynch, Rutherford, Hockaday.

TEAMS FOR ALL SEASONS

1950's

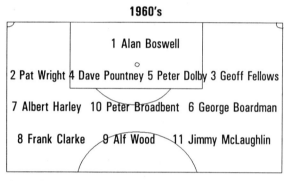

1 Russell Crossley
2 Jimmy Bannister   3 Gordon Skeech
4 Joe Wallace   5 Joe Maloney   6 Ron Crutchley
8 Arnold Jackson   10 Arthur Rowley
7 Frank Griffin   9 Bobby Brown   11 Colin Whitaker

1960's

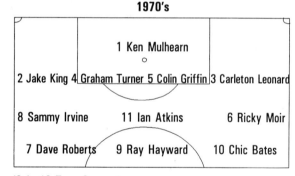

1 Alan Boswell
2 Pat Wright 4 Dave Pountney 5 Peter Dolby 3 Geoff Fellows
7 Albert Harley 10 Peter Broadbent 6 George Boardman
8 Frank Clarke   9 Alf Wood   11 Jimmy McLaughlin

(Sub: 12 Ted Hemsley)

1970's

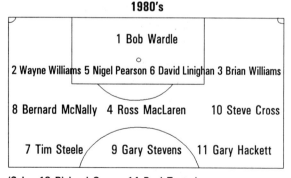

1 Ken Mulhearn
2 Jake King 4 Graham Turner 5 Colin Griffin 3 Carleton Leonard
8 Sammy Irvine   11 Ian Atkins   6 Ricky Moir
7 Dave Roberts   9 Ray Hayward   10 Chic Bates

(Sub: 12 Tony Gregory)

1980's

1 Bob Wardle
2 Wayne Williams 5 Nigel Pearson 6 David Linighan 3 Brian Williams
8 Bernard McNally   4 Ross MacLaren   10 Steve Cross
7 Tim Steele   9 Gary Stevens   11 Gary Hackett

(Subs: 12 Richard Green 14 Paul Tester)

1990's (excluding current players)

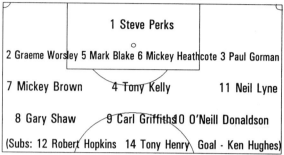

1 Steve Perks
2 Graeme Worsley 5 Mark Blake 6 Mickey Heathcote 3 Paul Gorman
7 Mickey Brown   4 Tony Kelly   11 Neil Lyne
8 Gary Shaw   9 Carl Griffiths 10 O'Neill Donaldson

(Subs: 12 Robert Hopkins 14 Tony Henry Goal - Ken Hughes)

LOAN(LY) TEAM

1 John McLaughlin
2 Cliff Carr 4 Julian Watts 5 Noel Blake 3 Stuart Cash
7 Mark Barham 8 Dave Bennett 6 Gary McKeown 11 Mark Rutherford
9 Mark Cooper   10 David Leworthy

(Subs: 12 Billy Askew 14 Darren Currie)

SOUL BROTHERS:

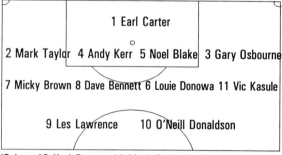

1 Earl Carter
2 Mark Taylor 4 Andy Kerr 5 Noel Blake 3 Gary Osbourne
7 Micky Brown 8 Dave Bennett 6 Louie Donowa 11 Vic Kasule
9 Les Lawrence   10 O'Neill Donaldson

(Subs: 12 Karl Foster 14 Mark Rutherford)

ONE HIT WONDERS

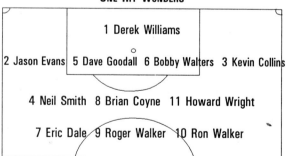

1 Derek Williams
2 Jason Evans 5 Dave Goodall 6 Bobby Walters 3 Kevin Collins
4 Neil Smith 8 Brian Coyne 11 Howard Wright
7 Eric Dale 9 Roger Walker 10 Ron Walker

(Subs: 12 Mike Roberts 14 Ken Harper Goal - Mike Barton)

And finally.... **BLOOD BROTHERS** (They played for Town and their brothers also made League appearances):
1 Eric Skeech (Gordon), 2 Ken Crutchley (Ron), 3 Alf Pountney (Dave), 4 Les Harley (Albert), 5 Colin Hemsley (Ted), 6 William Butler (Jackie), 7 Ian Loughnane (Peter), 8 Lloyd Irvine (Sammy), 9 Graham Scott (Robin), 10 Tony Mayle (Bobby), 11 Eric Price (Derek)

ADVANCED SUBSCRIBERS

Shrewsbury Town F.C. · Presentation Copy

John Treleven
G.T. Allman
A.N. Other
Raymond Shaw, Sutton-in-Ashfield
Harry Kay, Yorkshire
For David and Marion
David Keats, Thornton Heath
M.J. Cripps
Graham Spackman
L.A. Zammit
Moira & Frederick Furness
Fred Lee, Plymouth Argyle
Geoffrey Wright
David Jowett
Dave McPherson, Colchester
W.D. Phillips
Jonathan Hall
Steve Emms
Mark Tyler, Rayleigh, Essex
Richard Wells
Stephen Kieran Byrne
J. Ringrose
Jonny Stokkeland, Kvinesdal, Norway
Keith Coburn
Robert M. Smith
Göran Schönhult, Trelleborg, Sweden
Malc Hartley Wyke, Bradford
Peter Pickup, Pudsey
Trond Isaksen, Norway
Stephen Carr
David Earnshaw, Belper, Derbyshire
Philip H. Whitehead
Alan Davies
Chris Sheila Mary Hooker
Bob Lilliman
Willy Østby, Norway
Brian Tabner
Christer Svensson, Sweden
Chris Owen, remembering Barry
Arran Matthews, Tylers Green

Derek Hyde
Gordon Small, Preston
Memories of Eric Allen
David Lumb
Property of Alan Nicholas
John Rawnsley
Orjan Hansson, Sweden
Peter Baxter
Eric George Allen
Mr. L. Burgess
Mike Jones
Kevin Davies
Shropshire County Libraries
Doreen Roberts
Alan Boswell, Hadnall
Tim & Fliss Sumner
Robert Edwards, (9) Welshampton
Paul Overs, Stafford
Mark Seddon, Welshpool, Powys
Peter Francis, Snailbeach
Shelia Downes, Wentnor, Shropshire
Kenneth Davies, Kingsway Crescent
Simon Asquith, Rowton, Shropshire
Graham Pearse, Bayston Hill
David Gavin Taylor, Copthorne
Mathew Mead, Much Wenlock
Susan Davies, Sutton Farm
Christopher Breakwell, Sutton Park
Morris Family, Stottesdon
Mr. Graham Hughes
Mr. Peter Badger
Vivienne Dodd, Bucknell
Mervyn Traylor, Bucknell
Molly Watkins, Bucknell
Ian Robinson, Shrewsbury
Howard Archer, Shrewsbury
Susan Archer, Shrewsbury
Ben Pattison, Shrewsbury
John Graham George Lloyd
A True Salopian

John Matthias, Shrewsbury
Jon Matthias, Shrewsbury
David Matthias, Shrewsbury
Duncan Ellson, Ford, Shrewsbury
Grant Ellson, Ford, Shrewsbury
Vince & Steve Burmingham
Gareth Hopkins, Welshpool
John Coombs, Broxbourne, Hertfordshire
Wyn Rees, Kerry, Powys
Charles Ralphs, Ellesmere
Jill Lucas, Bayston Hill
Peter Smethurst
Kevin Bright, Shrewsbury
Gary Bright, Shrewsbury
John Andrew Grove, Shawbury
George Warren, Wem, Shropshire
Philip Mead, Much Wenlock
Richard Griffiths, Herne Bay
R. Ellis, 9, Mereside
Ian Jones
Paul Masters, Sedgley
Peter Masters, Kingswinford
Helen Masters, Kingswinford
Vickey Lewis
John Hotchkiss, Meole Brace
David Evanson, Wem
Ashley Mitchell
Stephen David Bennett
Stuart Roberts, Nalgo Club
Chris Smith
Pat Wright
Matthew Ashton
Ruth Williams
Jason Jones
Mark Jones
Greg Jones
Pat Wright
Tom Jones
Louise Jones
Beacon Radio/WABC

A SELECTION OF TITLES

From
'YORE PUBLICATIONS'
12 The Furrows, Harefield,
Middx. UB9 6AT

(Free lists issued 3 times per year. For your first list please send a S.A.E.)

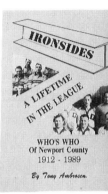

DONNY - The Official History of Doncaster Rovers *(Tony Bluff and Barry Watson)*
Written by two supporters of the Club, with the full statistics (from 1879) incl. line-ups (from 1901). The book is well illustrated, with the full written history of the Club. Hardback with dustjacket and 240 pages. Price £14-95 plus £1-80 postage.

COLCHESTER UNITED - The Official History of the 'U's' *(Hal Mason)*
With football involvement from the 1920's, the Author - a former journalist and Colchester programme editor - is well qualified to relate this complete history of the Club since its formation in 1937 (including complete statistics and lineups from this season). Large Hardback with dustjacket, 240 pages, priced £14-95 plus £2-70 postage.

AMBER IN THE BLOOD - History of Newport County: *(Tony Ambrosen).* The full written story of football in Newport from the pre-County days up to and including the recently formed Newport AFC club. The text is well illustrated, and a comprehensive statistical section provides all the results, attendances, goalscorers, etc. from 1912 to 1993 - the various Leagues and principal Cup competitions; additionally seasonal total players' appearances are included. A hardback book, containing 176 large pages is exceptional value at only £13-95 plus £2-60 postage.

KILLIE - The Official History (125 Years of Kilmarnock F.C.) *(David Ross).* A very detailed history of Scotland's oldest professional Club. The statistics section (including line-ups) cover the period 1873 to 1994, and over 200 illustrations, incl.a team group for most seasons. A large hardback of 256 pages, priced £15-95 plus £3-50 postage.

REJECTED F.C. VOLUME 1 (Reprint) *(By Dave Twydell)* The revised edition of this popular book - now in hardback - this volume provides the comprehensive histories of: Aberdare Athletic, Ashington, Bootle, Bradford (Park Avenue), Burton (Swifts, Wanderers and United), Gateshead/South Shields, Glossop, Loughborough, Nelson, Stalybridge Celtic and Workington. The 288 well illustrated pages also contain the basic statistical details of each club. Price £12-95 plus £1-30 postage. (Also *Rejected F.C. of Scotland:* Volume 1 covers Edinburgh and The South (Edinburgh City, Leith Athletic, St.Bernards, Armadale, Broxburn United, Bathgate, Peebles Rovers, Mid-Annandale, Nithsdale Wanderers and Solway Star - 288 pages). Volume 2 covers Glasgow and District (Abercorn, Arthurlie, Beith, Cambuslang, Clydebank, Cowlairs, Johnstone, Linthouse, Northern, Third Lanark, and Thistle - 240 pages). Each £12-95 plus £1-30 postage.

FOOTBALL LEAGUE - GROUNDS FOR A CHANGE (By Dave Twydell). A 424 page, A5 sized, Hardback book. A comprehensive study of all the Grounds on which the current English Football League clubs previously played. Every Club that has moved Grounds is included, with a 'Potted' history of each, plus 250 illustrations. Plenty of 'reading' material, as well as an interesting reference book. £13-95 Plus £1-70 Postage.

THROUGH THE TURNSTILES *(by Brian Tabner)* This incredible book which provides the average attendance of every English Football League club, for every season from 1888/89 to 1991/92. Well illustrated, and also relates the development of the game (angled towards attendances). Also details of the best supported 'away' teams, season ticket sales over the years, etc. A large format hardback and 208 packed pages. An excellent read at £13-95 plus £1-70 Postage.

COVENTRY CITY FOOTBALLERS (The Complete Who's Who)
By Martin & Paul O'Connor. One of the most detailed books of its type. Every Football (and Southern) League player has been included - around 700. Seasonal appearances of every player, brief personal details, 'pen pictures', together with very detailed information on the movements of the players to other clubs. Plus: around 100 photo's of the Club's most memorable men, and information on the principal players from the very early days. A hardback book with 224 large pages. £13-95 plus £2-60 postage.

HISTORY OF THE LANCASHIRE FOOTBALL ASSOCIATION 1878-1928. A rare historical and fascinating hardback reprint (first published in 1928). Contains the history of the formative days of Lancashire football. Sections within the 288 pages include the early histories of about 20 Clubs (Manchester Utd., Wigan Borough, Rochdale, etc.), Lancashire Cup competitions, Biographies, etc. For those interested in the development of the game, this is a 'must'. Price £12-95 Plus £1-30 Postage.

THE CODE WAR *(Graham Williams)* A fascinating look back on football's history - from the earliest days up to the First World War. 'Football' is covered in the broadest sense, for the book delves into the splits over the period to and from Rugby Union and Rugby League, as well as Football (Soccer). Potted histories of many of the Clubs are included, as is a comprehensive index. 192 page hardback, £10-95 plus £1-20 postage.